THE MAD BATHROOM COMPANION

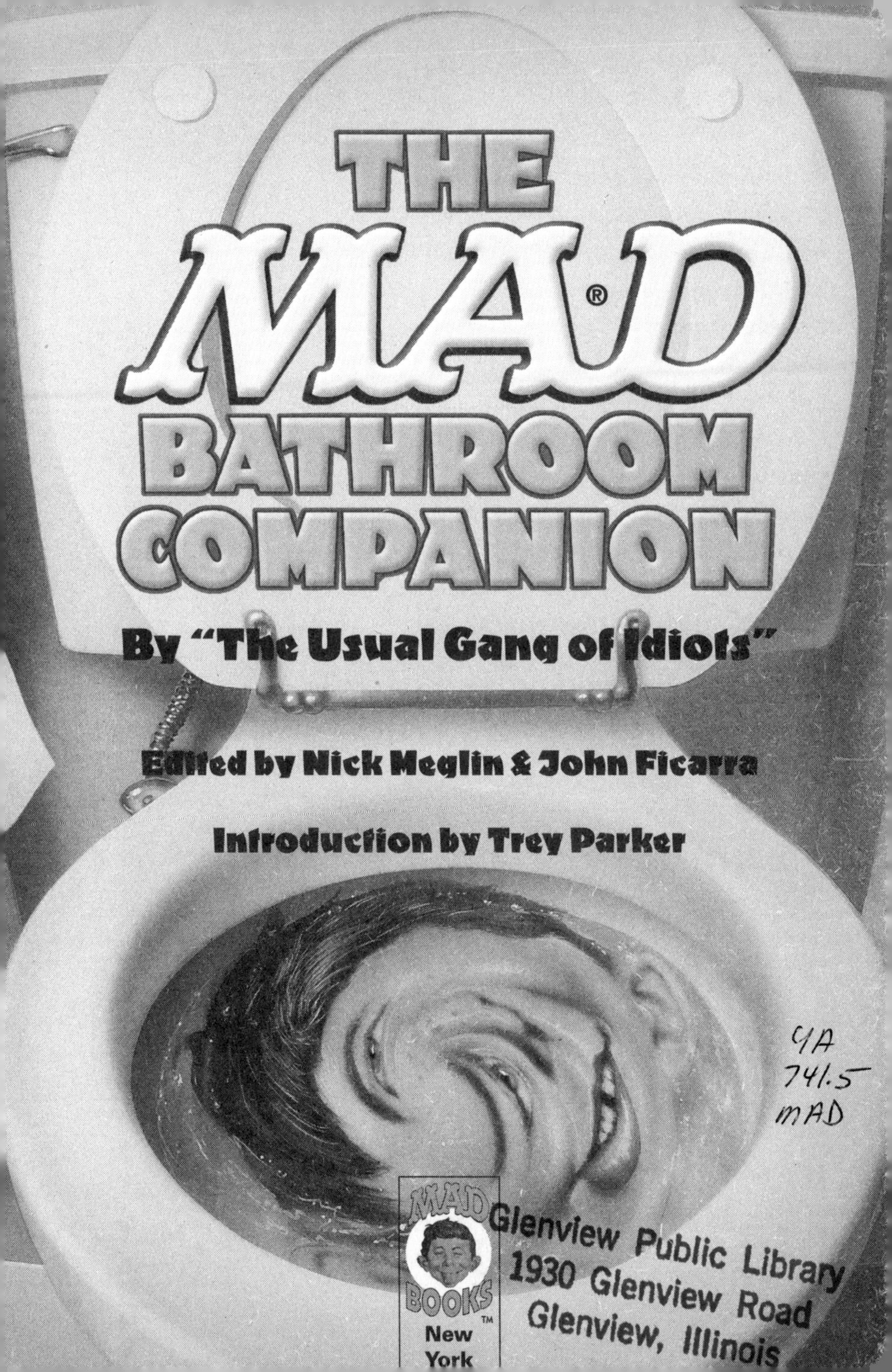

THE MAD® BATHROOM COMPANION

By "The Usual Gang of Idiots"

Edited by Nick Meglin & John Ficarra

Introduction by Trey Parker

MAD BOOKS™
New York

MAD BOOKS

Compilation and new material (introduction) © 2000 by E.C. Publications, Inc. All Rights Reserved.

MAD, Boy's Head device, and all related indicia are trademarks of E.C. Publications, Inc.

Mr. Hankey character is used with permission of Comedy Central.

Published by MAD Books. An imprint of E.C. Publications, Inc., 1700 Broadway, New York, NY 10019.
A division of Warner Bros. — A Time Warner Entertainment Company.

ISBN 1-56389-684-2

Printed in Canada

First edition
10 9 8 7 6 5 4 3 2 1

Visit *MAD* online at www.madmag.com

Though Alfred E. Neuman wasn't the first to say "A fool and his money are soon parted," here's your chance to prove the old adage right—subscribe to *MAD*! Simply call 1-800-4-MADMAG and mention code 9MBC7. Operators are standing by (the water cooler).

CONTENTS

"Quick Recoveries for Embarrassing Situations" written and illustrated by Al Jaffee (*MAD* #278)
"The Lighter Side of . . . " written and illustrated by Dave Berg (*MAD* #267)
"The Stupefying Suicide Situation" written and illustrated by Duck Edwing (*MAD* #278)
"Dangerous Sports for the Very Daring and the Super Stupid"
written and illustrated by Paul Peter Porges (*MAD* #278)
"*MAD's* Instant Guide to Zodiac Types" by Frank Jacobs, illustrated by Harry North (*MAD* #278)
"Tell-Tale Comic Strip Balloons (The Sequel)"
by Duck Edwing, illustrated by Bob Clarke (*MAD* #279)
"A *MAD* Look at Real-Life Government 'Logic'"
by Mike Snider, illustrated by Harry North (*MAD* #279)
"One Evening at a Masquerade Party" written and illustrated by Don Martin (*MAD* #158)
"New Cigarette Warning Labels You May Have Missed"
idea by Anne Gaines, written by Charlie Kadau & Joe Raiola, photographed by Irving Schild (*MAD* #280)
"*MAD*'s Post-Nuclear Publications" by Barry Liebmann, illustrated by Bob Clarke (*MAD* #280)
"A *MAD* Look at Garage ale" written and illustrated by Sergio Aragonés (*MAD* #281)
"The Disastrous Desert Drama" written and illustrated by Duck Edwing (*MAD* #278)
"Spy vs Spy" written and illustrated by Antonio Prohias (*MAD* #267)
"Drama on Page 134" written and illustrated by John Caldwell (*MAD* #280)
"A Beginners Guide to Cartoon Sound Effects"
by Duck Edwing, illustrated by Paul Coker (*MAD* #282)
"A *MAD* Look at Staying Cool" written and illustrated by Sergio Aragonés (*MAD* #282)
"The Manhattan Monster Monkeyshine" written and illustrated by Duck Edwing (*MAD* #281)
"Same Words . . . Different Circumstances!"
idea by Christopher Allen, written by J. Prete, illustrated by Paul Coker (*MAD* #283)
"A *MAD* Look at Fat" written and illustrated by Sergio Aragonés (*MAD* #283)
"We're Looking for People Who Are Looking for a Course on How to Write Children's Books."
by Dick DeBartolo (*MAD* #282)
"The Lighter Side of . . . " written and illustrated by Dave Berg (*MAD* #275)
"The Terrible Toilet Trauma" written and illustrated by Duck Edwing (*MAD* #282)
"'Don't Be Fooled'" by Frank Jacobs, illustrated by Gerry Gersten (*MAD* #285)
"Other McD.L.T. Type Ideas We'd Like to See from McDonald's"
by Mike Snider, illustrated by Al Jaffee (*MAD* #283)
"The Pesky Pecker Puzzler" written and illustrated by Duck Edwing (*MAD* #283)
"Toys 'R' U" by Charlie Kadau & Joe Raiola, illustrated by George Woodbridge (*MAD* #285)
"It's Safe to Go to the Bathroom When . . . "
written and illustrated by Paul Peter Porges (*MAD* #286)
"Hand-Me-Down" written and illustrated by Sergio Aragonés (*MAD* #286)
"More 'You'd Be Rich If You Had a Nickel . . !'"
by Charlie Kadau, illustrated by Paul Coker (*MAD* #286)
"Duck Edwing Contemplates Suicide" written and illustrated by Duck Edwing (*MAD* #286)
"One Evening in Spain" written and illustrated by Don Martin (*MAD* #161)
"A *MAD* Look at Female Bodybuilders" written and illustrated by Sergio Aragonés (*MAD* #287)
"It's Never a Good Sign When . . . " written by J. Prete, illustrated by Al Jaffee (*MAD* #287)
"Scientific Advances That Unimprove Our Lives!"
written by Tom Koch, illustrated by George Woodbridge (*MAD* #288)
"The Exquisite Execution Experiment" written and illustrated by Duck Edwing (*MAD* #283)
"The Rookstone Catalog of Really Useful Tools, Nifty Gadgets, Hi-Tech Thingamajigs and Crafty Geegaws" written and illustrated by Al Jaffee (*MAD* # 289)
"A *MAD* Look at Driver's Ed" written and illustrated by Sergio Aragonés (*MAD* #289)
"Ten College Athletes" by Frank Jacobs, illustrated by Jack Davis (*MAD* #290)
"Why You Are Sure to Win the Next Magazine Publishers' Sweepstakes"
by Tom Koch, illustrated by John Caldwell (*MAD* #291)
"The Unnerving Undertaker's Undertaking" written and illustrated by Duck Edwing (*MAD* #287)
"*MAD's* Big Ego Busters" by Stan Hart, illustrated by Al Jaffee (*MAD* #291)
"The *MAD* Week" by Charlie Kadau, illustrated by Paul Coker (*MAD* #292)
"*MAD* Asks: Which Is the Lesser of Two Evils???"
by Mike Snider, illustrated by Paul Coker (*MAD* #293)
"The Diabolical Dungeon Deception" written and illustrated by Duck Edwing (*MAD* #288)
"*MAD* Curses!!!" by Joy Chonoles, illustrated by Greg Theakston (*MAD* #298)
"A *MAD* Look at Self-Defense" written and illustrated by Sergio Aragonés (*MAD* #288)

"The Haunting Hunting Hullabaloo" written and illustrated by Duck Edwing (*MAD* #289)
"Do You REALLY Need to Know . . . "
idea by Mary Pat Lindl, written by J. Prete, illustrated by Al Jaffee (*MAD* #294)
"The *MAD* 'Don't' Book (Chapters 2-5)"
by Charlie Kadau & Joe Raiola, illustrated by Paul Coker (*MAD* #294)
"The Dreaded Dental Debacle" written and illustrated by Duck Edwing (*MAD* #290)
"The Art of Breaking Bad News Gently" by Tom Koch (*MAD* #294)
"Get a Life!!!!!!!!" by Charlie Kadau, illustrated by Jack Davis (*MAD* #294)
"'When I Was Your Age . . .' Stories Today's Kids Will Be Telling Their Grandchildren"
by Mike Snider, illustrated by George Woodbridge (*MAD* #295)
"Some Truly Joyous Things You Could Do If You Won the Lottery"
by Tom Koch, illustrated by Paul Coker (*MAD* #295)
"More Quick Recoveries for Embarrassing Situations"
written and illustrated by Al Jaffee (*MAD* #296)
"Drama on Page 218" written and illustrated by John Caldwell (*MAD* #294)
"2 Hour School of Dentistry" by Charlie Kadau & Joe Raiola, illustrated by Tom Bunk (*MAD* #296)
"12 Sure Signs That You've Realized Adulthood" by Tom Koch, illustrated by Rick Tulka (*MAD* #297)
"A *MAD* Guide to Devolution" by Hy Bender (*MAD* #297)
"The Lusty Ledge Legend" written and illustrated by Duck Edwing (*MAD* #291)
"A *MAD* Look at Boxing" written and illustrated by Sergio Aragonés (*MAD* #297)
"Really Difficult Is . . . " by Frank Jacobs, illustrated by Paul Coker (*MAD* #298)
"When TV Sports Advertisers Decide to 'Sponsor' More than Just Kickoffs & Home Runs"
by Mike Snider, illustrated by Jack Davis (*MAD* #297)
"Really Appropriate Brand Name Sound Effects"
by Russ Cooper, illustrated by John Pound (*MAD* #298)
"The Extraordinary Eulogy Entrapment" written and illustrated by Duck Edwing (*MAD* #293)
"Babar's Final Adventure" by Frank Jacobs, illustrated by Bob Clarke (*MAD* #302)
"*MAD*'s Handy Clues, Hints and Tipoffs That You're Really, Unquestionably, Without a Doubt . . . Stipud!" by Dan Birtcher, illustrated by Sergio Aragonés (*MAD* #298)
"The Hymn of the Battered Republic"
by Frank Jacobs, illustrated by George Woodbridge (*MAD* #301)
"Small Scale Examples of How History Repeats Itself!"
by Dan Birtcher, illustrated by Tom Bunk (*MAD* #302)
"Advertising Characters & Corporate Mascots That Better Reflect the Miserable Companies They Work For" by Charlie Kadau, illustrated by George Woodbridge (*MAD* #302)
"A *MAD* Look at How Far We've Come" by Tom Koch, illustrated by Paul Coker (*MAD* #302)
"A *MAD* Guide to How Simple Things Work, Part II"
written and illustrated by Al Jaffee (*MAD* #303)
"Give It Up!" by J. Prete, illustrated by Paul Coker (*MAD* #303)
"*MAD's* By-the-Numbers Guide to Predicting TV Tabloid and 'Info-tainment' Stories"
by Mike Snider, illustrated by Rick Tulka (*MAD* #303)
"America . . . Land of Opportunity" by Mike Snider, illustrated by George Woodbridge (*MAD* #304)
"More Same Words . . . Different Circumstances!" by J. Prete, illustrated by Rick Tulka (*MAD* #304)
"A *MAD* Guide to Sports Phrases On and Off the Playing Field"
by Mike Snider, illustrated by Jack Davis (*MAD* #305)
"Unofficial Yo-Yo Tricks Every Kid Knows" by Dan Birtcher, illustrated by Paul Coker (*MAD* #297)
"America's Traditional Songs as They Sound to Five-Year-Olds"
by Tom Koch, illustrated by Paul Coker (*MAD* #305)
"Why We Get the Holiday Blahs" by Barry Liebmann, illustrated by George Woodbridge (*MAD* #305)
"The Astounding Aeronautic Adventure" written and illustrated by Duck Edwing (*MAD* #293)
"Making Games More Dangerous" written and illustrated by Tom Cheney (*MAD* #306)
"Only When You're Sure No One Is Watching . . . "
by Mike Snider, illustrated by Paul Coker (*MAD* #306)
"Salesmen's Claims and Come-Ons That Should Set You Running"
by Dick DeBartolo, illustrated by Tom Bunk (*MAD* #306)
"Cause or Coincidence??" by Dan Birtcher, illustrated by George Woodbridge (*MAD* #306)
"Will You Make a Good Flight Attendant?"
by Frank Jacobs, illustrated by George Woodbridge (*MAD* #303)
"Once Upon a Time . . . " by Tom Koch, illustrated by Sergio Aragonés (*MAD* #306)
"I Sent a Letter Through the Mail . . . " by Frank Jacobs (*MAD* #306)

Introduction

I was thrilled when *MAD* Magazine, one of the most important magazines of the twentieth century, asked me to write the introduction to their Bathroom Companion. It seems like more and more that when people think of poo, they think of me.

I started reading *MAD* when I was eight years old. I was an impressionable child, with a mind that was pure like morning snow. I had dreams of growing up to be an astronaut or a scientist. Reading *MAD* changed all that, however, and now I make cartoons with anal probes and Barbra Streisand monsters.

What I learned from *MAD*, is that anything that becomes too "cool" or too popular in our culture must be destroyed. Usually while everyone was singing something's praises, *MAD* was knocking it down. When I was a kid and everyone loved *Star Wars*, they made fun of *Star Wars*. When everyone started liking Jordache jeans, they made fun of that too. Anything that become cool in the country's eye was an open target for *MAD* Magazine, and that's what made it so great then—and what still makes it so great today. Why, I even opened a *MAD* Magazine last year and saw that they were making fun of *South Park*. But this, of course, was not great; it was juvenile, thoughtless, mindless crap, and if the *MAD* people ever do it again I will kick all their asses.

But enough about *MAD*, and enough about me. It is time to focus on your task at hand.

This book was meant to be used as a companion to pooping, and if you are using this book as it was intended, you are now seated on the toilet, as you have been countless other times. But did you know that right now, as you are pooping, an estimated *2.3 million* people around the world are pooping too? That's right, from Japan to Germany, Israel to Canada, people of all races and ethnicities are doing *exactly* what you're doing right now. Isn't that beautiful? Pooping is the common bond that unites us all; it is what makes us one.

Even more wonderful than the fact that people all around the world poop, is the fact that nobody can go without pooping. No matter how rich somebody is, or how famous or how sexy or beautiful, everyone has to put in time on the porcelain. Even Jennifer Lopez poops. Think about that. Go on, visualize Jennifer Lopez pooping for one second. That's it... Good.

What still puzzles me, though, is that if pooping is such a world-uniting, culture-crossing, and wonderful thing, why is it still so shrouded in silence and embarrassment? Why don't people talk more freely about their various bathroom habits and pleasures?

For example, most women do not realize that men often like to pretend they are giving birth when they poop. That's right. The truth is, we men are somewhat jealous that we can't have babies, and our potty time is the only time for us to fantasize. Men will try to deny it, but the fact remains that almost all men, at some point in their lives, have sat on the toilet doing breathing exercises, and waiting for the joyous moment to arrive so they can shout, *"It's a girl!"* and then name her something cute before flushing her away forever.

And most men would be surprised to know that women usually like to play a game called Bombs Away in the bathroom. They fill the toilet bowl with small cardboard ships that they have spent hours beforehand creating. Then, instead of sitting on the toilet, they stand on the rim, and the fun begins as they see how many Japanese D-42s they can sink.

Pooping is not about nastiness or vulgarity; pooping is about fun. Toilet time is precious time, not only for birthing fantasies and war games, but also for reading fine books like this one, or for reflecting on memories past, or even...for pondering our own reality and deep metaphysical inner self. And so, as you dive deeper into this eloquent collection, and continue with your toilet time, do not ask yourself what the nutritionist would ask: "What am I pooping?" Ask yourself the question the Zen Buddhist would ask: "What is it that is pooping?"

Howdy Ho!

—Trey Parker

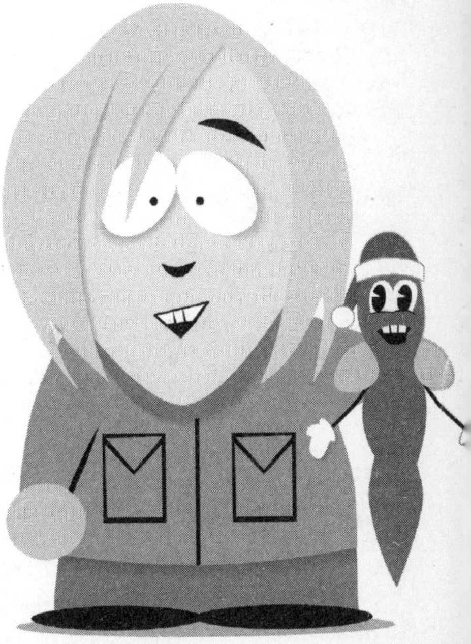

ILLUSTRATION BY GREY BLACKWELL

DON MARTIN DEPT.

ONE FAIRLY NICE DAY DOWNTOWN

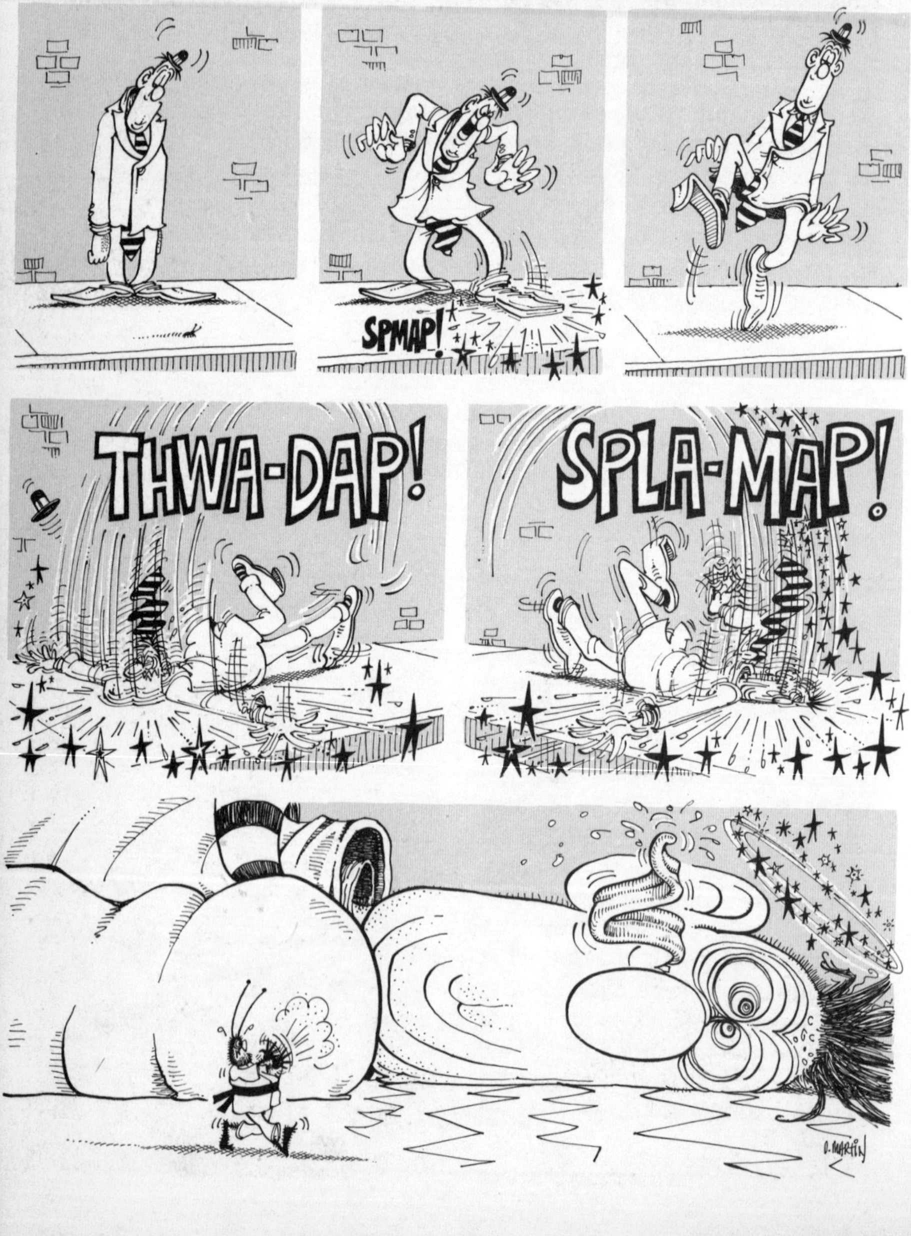
SPMAP!
THWA-DAP!
SPLA-MAP!
D. MARTIN

JOKE AND DAGGER DEPT.

CLICK
SPY VS SPY
BOOM

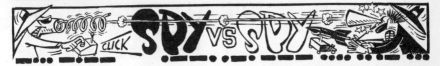

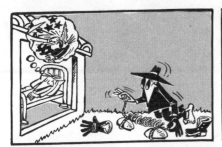

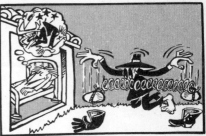

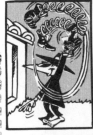

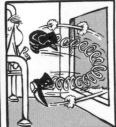

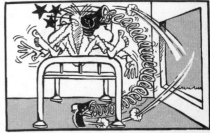

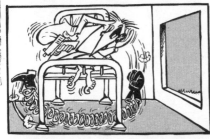

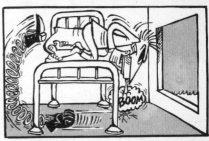

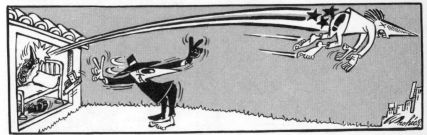

POLITE SWITCH DEPT.

MAD'S 14 GOOD B

ARTIST: PAUL COKER

RULE # 1

Be helpful despite one's own problems

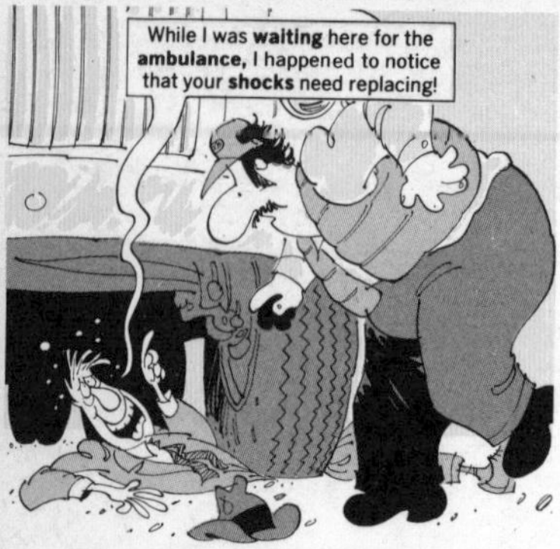
While I was waiting here for the ambulance, I happened to notice that your shocks need replacing!

RULE # 3

Show regard for the possessions of others.

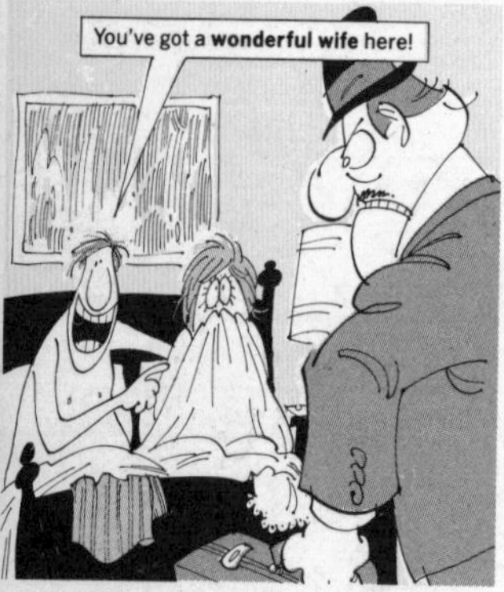
You've got a wonderful wife here!

RULE # 4

Bolster the spirits of the ailing.

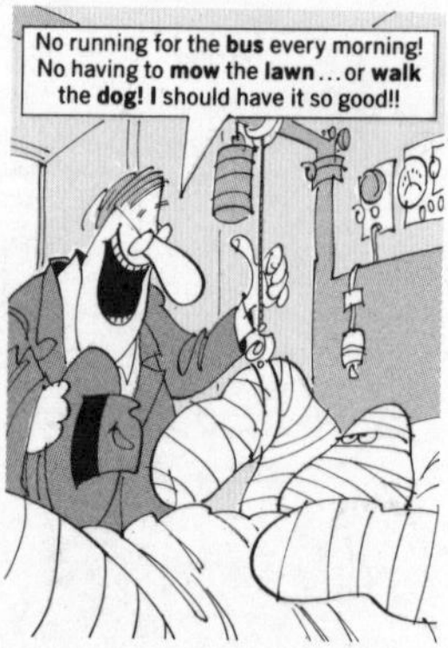
No running for the bus every morning! No having to mow the lawn . . . or walk the dog! I should have it so good!!

RULE # 5

Give comfort to those facing hardship.

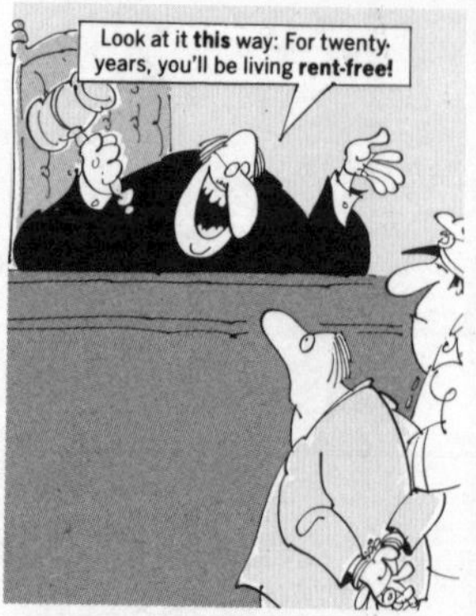
Look at it this way: For twenty-years, you'll be living rent-free!

RULE # 9

Be sensitive to the sad and downhearted.

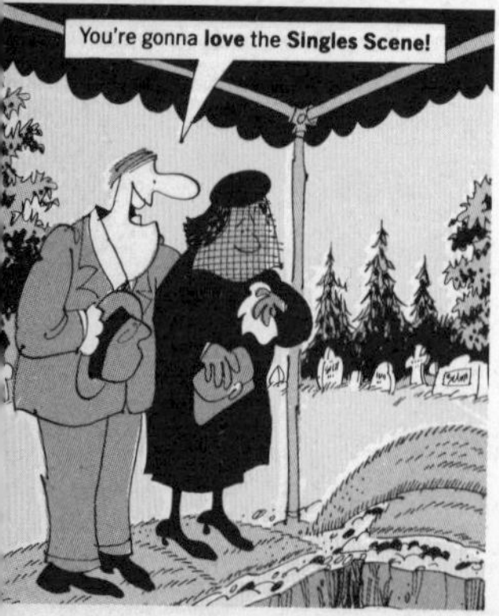
You're gonna love the Singles Scene!

RULE # 10

Give helpful advice to the troubled.

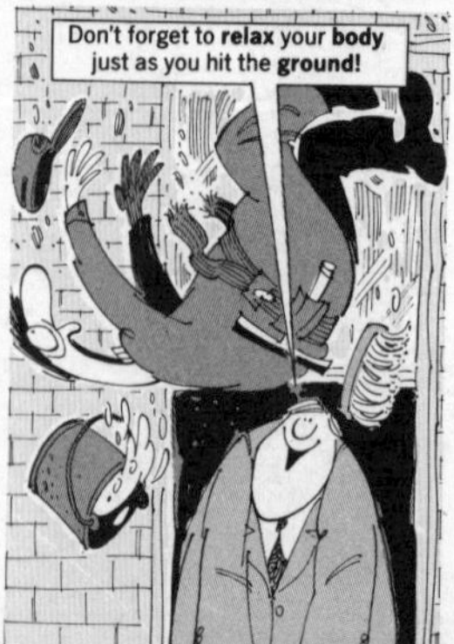
Don't forget to relax your body just as you hit the ground!

RULE # 11

Be tolerant of the mistakes of others.

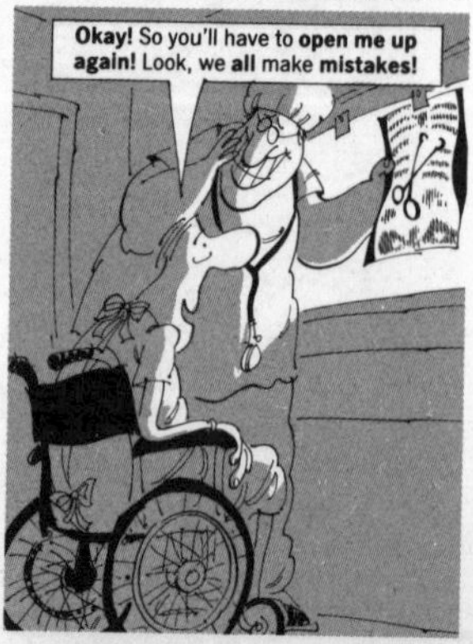
Okay! So you'll have to open me up again! Look, we all make mistakes!

RULES OF EHAVIOR

WRITER: FRANK JACOBS

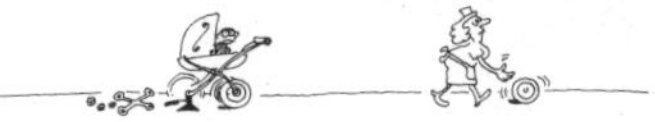

RULE # 2

Always help others to help themselves.

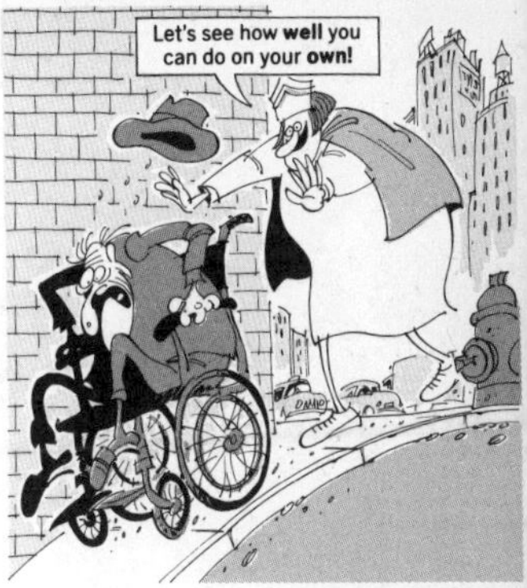
Let's see how **well** you can do on your **own**!

RULE # 6

Maintain a positive outlook in times of crisis.

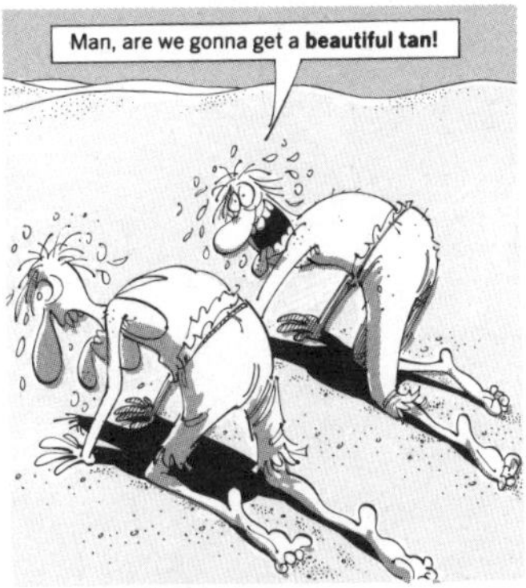
Man, are we gonna get a **beautiful tan**!

RULE # 7

Be gracious in victory . . .

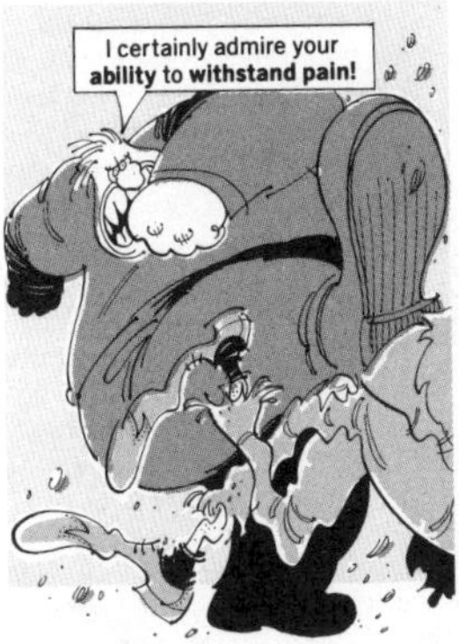
I certainly admire your **ability** to **withstand pain**!

RULE # 8

. . . and also in defeat.

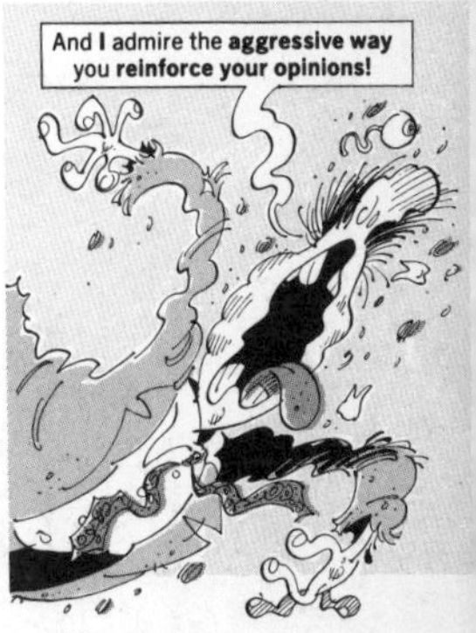
And **I** admire the **aggressive way** you **reinforce your opinions**!

RULE # 12

Be courteous in times of stress.

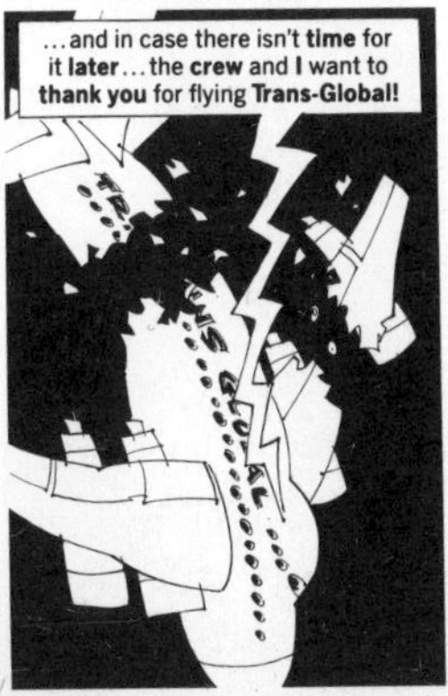
. . . and in case there isn't **time** for it **later** . . . the **crew** and **I** want to **thank you** for flying **Trans-Global**!

RULE # 13

Display good manners on all occasions.

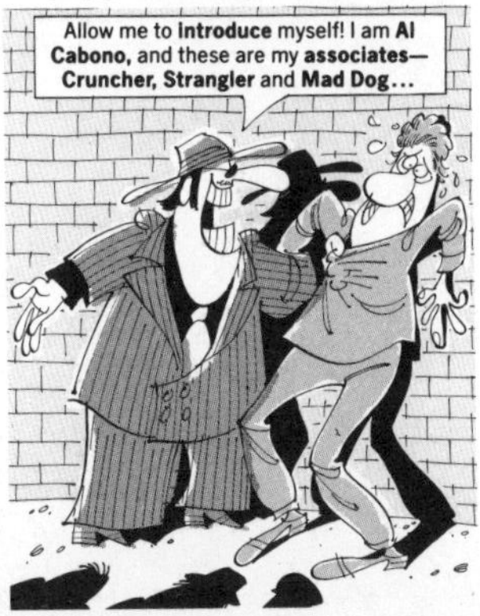
Allow me to **introduce** myself! I am **Al Cabono**, and these are my **associates— Cruncher, Strangler** and **Mad Dog** . . .

RULE # 14

Show compassion for the less fortunate

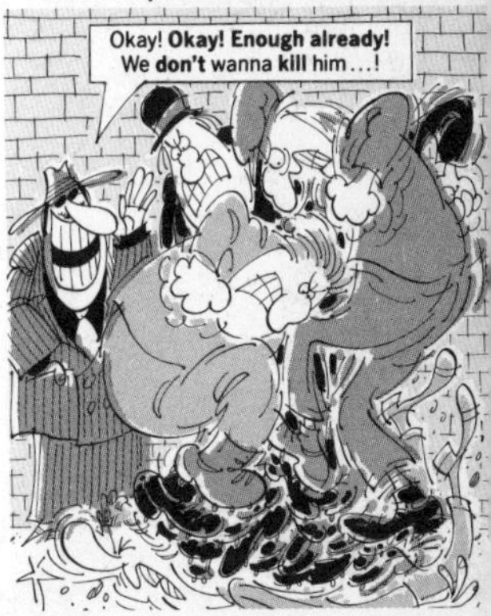
Okay! **Okay! Enough already!** We **don't** wanna **kill** him . . . !

WIDE WORLD OF SNORTS DEPT.

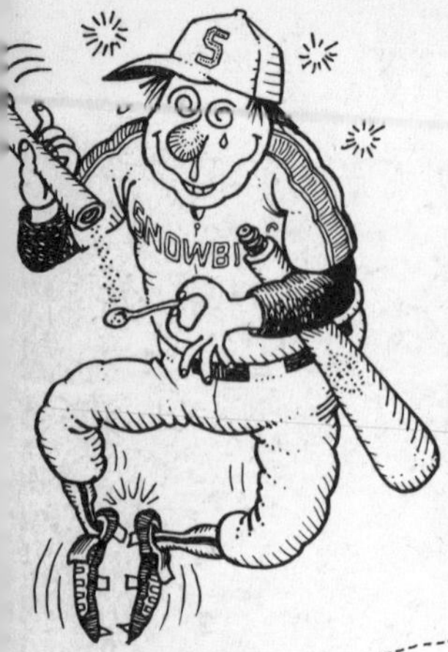
SNOWBIRDS
S

What with the recent drug scandals rocking the baseball world, it's time to revise that grand old song, "Take Me Out to the Ball Game." So sing along, sports fans, as Mad presents...

ZONK ME OUT AT THE BALL GAME

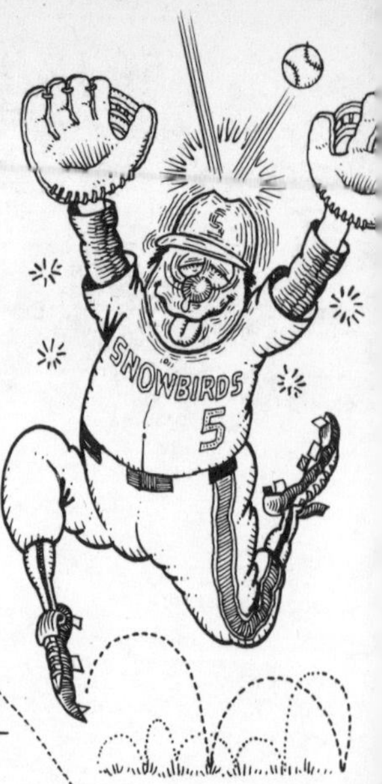
S
SNOWBIRDS
5

ARTIST: AL JAFFEE WRITER: FRANK JACOBS

IDEA BY: JOHN AMBROSIO

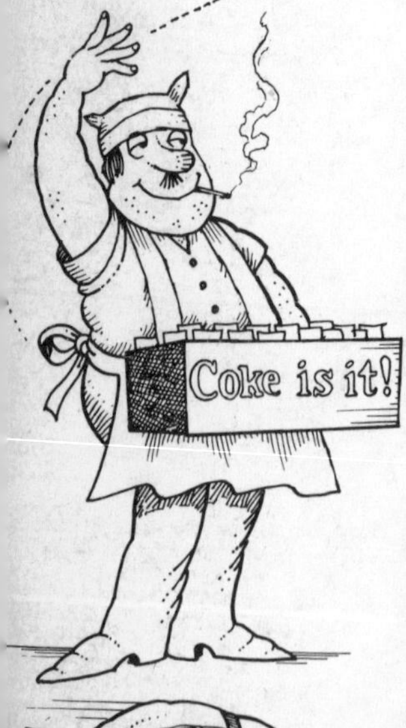
Coke is it!

Zonk me out at the ball-game—
Zonk me out with co-caine!
I've got a gram in my catch-er's mitt—
Grab... a... straw and we'll all take a hit!
So let's toot, toot, toot in the club-house—
If you're... not high, that's a shame!
For it's one, two, three snorts—
Get stoned!
It's a new... ball... game!

Zonk me out at the ball-game—
Zonk me out of my skull!
I've got a dealer who treats... me nice—
Highs... cost... high, but it's sure worth the price!
So let's toot, toot, toot in the bull-pen—
Hell, win... or lose, it's the same!
For it's one, two, three snorts—
You're hooked!
It's a new... ball... game!

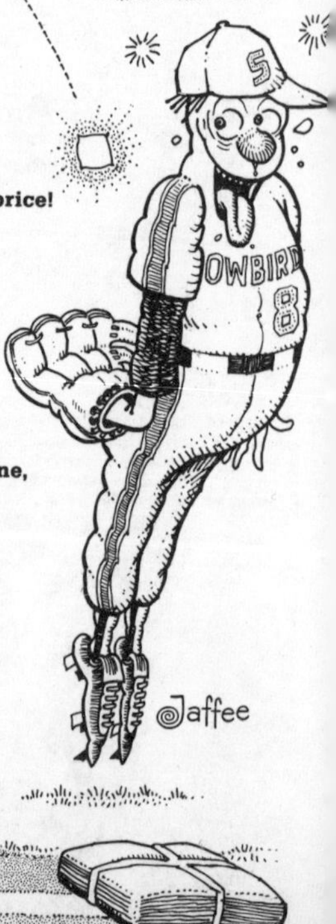
S
OWBIRD
8
Jaffee

Zonk me out at the ball-game—
Zonk me till we get caught!
I'll tell the league that my nose... is clean,
Help... them... clean up the whole rotten scene,
'Cause I'll rat, rat, rat on my team-mates!
Who cares... if they get the blame!
For it's one, two, three snorts—
Sell out!
It's a new... ball... game!

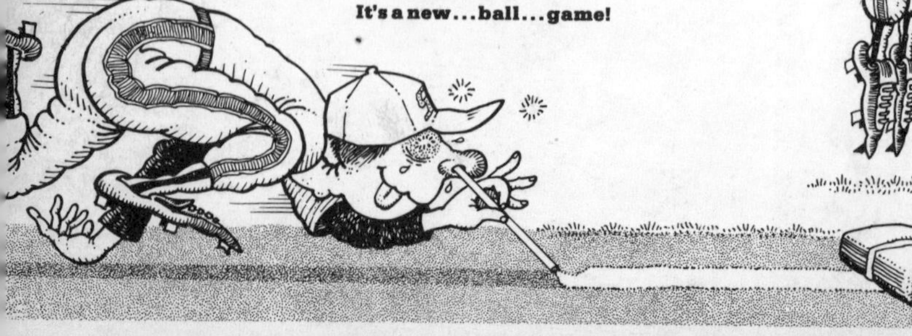
S

A PERFECT 10 COUNT DEPT.

DRAMA ON PAGE 15

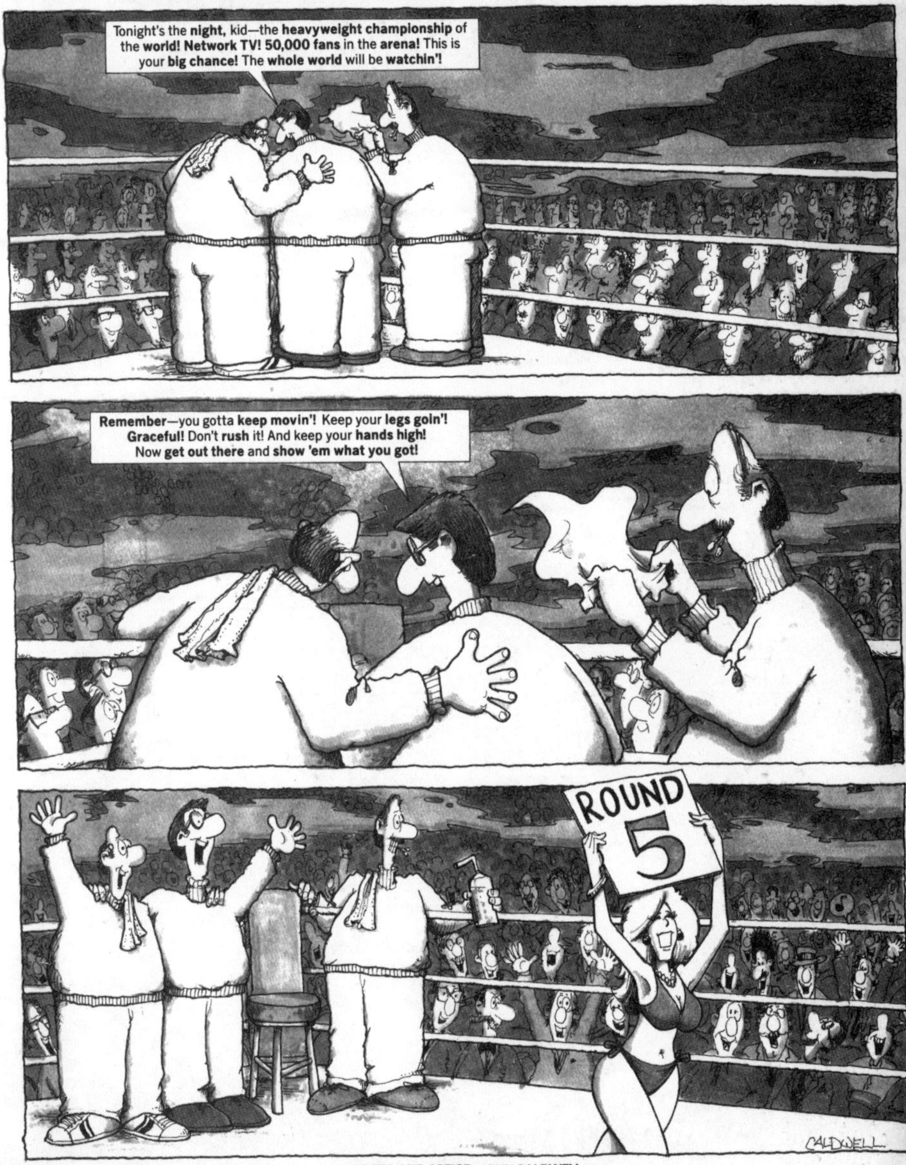
Tonight's the night, kid—the heavyweight championship of the world! Network TV! 50,000 fans in the arena! This is your big chance! The whole world will be watchin'!
Remember—you gotta keep movin'! Keep your legs goin'! Graceful! Don't rush it! And keep your hands high! Now get out there and show 'em what you got!
ROUND
5
CALDWELL

WRITER AND ARTIST: JOHN CALDWELL

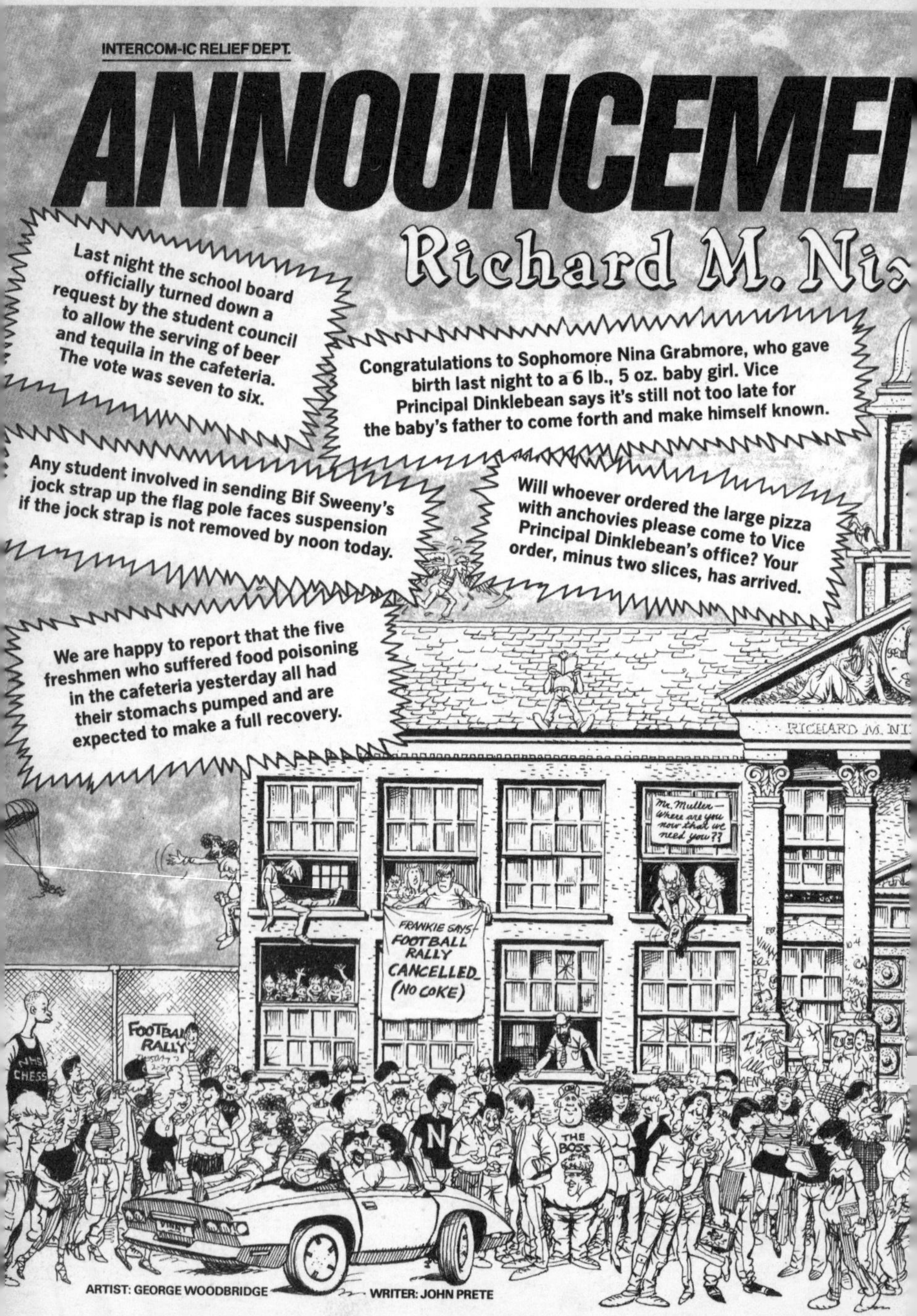
INTERCOM-IC RELIEF DEPT.
ANNOUNCEME
Richard M. Ni
Last night the school board officially turned down a request by the student council to allow the serving of beer and tequila in the cafeteria. The vote was seven to six.
Congratulations to Sophomore Nina Grabmore, who gave birth last night to a 6 lb., 5 oz. baby girl. Vice Principal Dinklebean says it's still not too late for the baby's father to come forth and make himself known.
Any student involved in sending Bif Sweeny's jock strap up the flag pole faces suspension if the jock strap is not removed by noon today.
Will whoever ordered the large pizza with anchovies please come to Vice Principal Dinklebean's office? Your order, minus two slices, has arrived.
We are happy to report that the five freshmen who suffered food poisoning in the cafeteria yesterday all had their stomachs pumped and are expected to make a full recovery.
RICHARD M. NI
Mr. Muller— Where are you now that we need you??
FRANKIE SAYS— FOOTBALL RALLY CANCELLED (NO COKE)
RALLY
CHESS
N
THE BOSS
ARTIST: GEORGE WOODBRIDGE
WRITER: JOHN PRETE

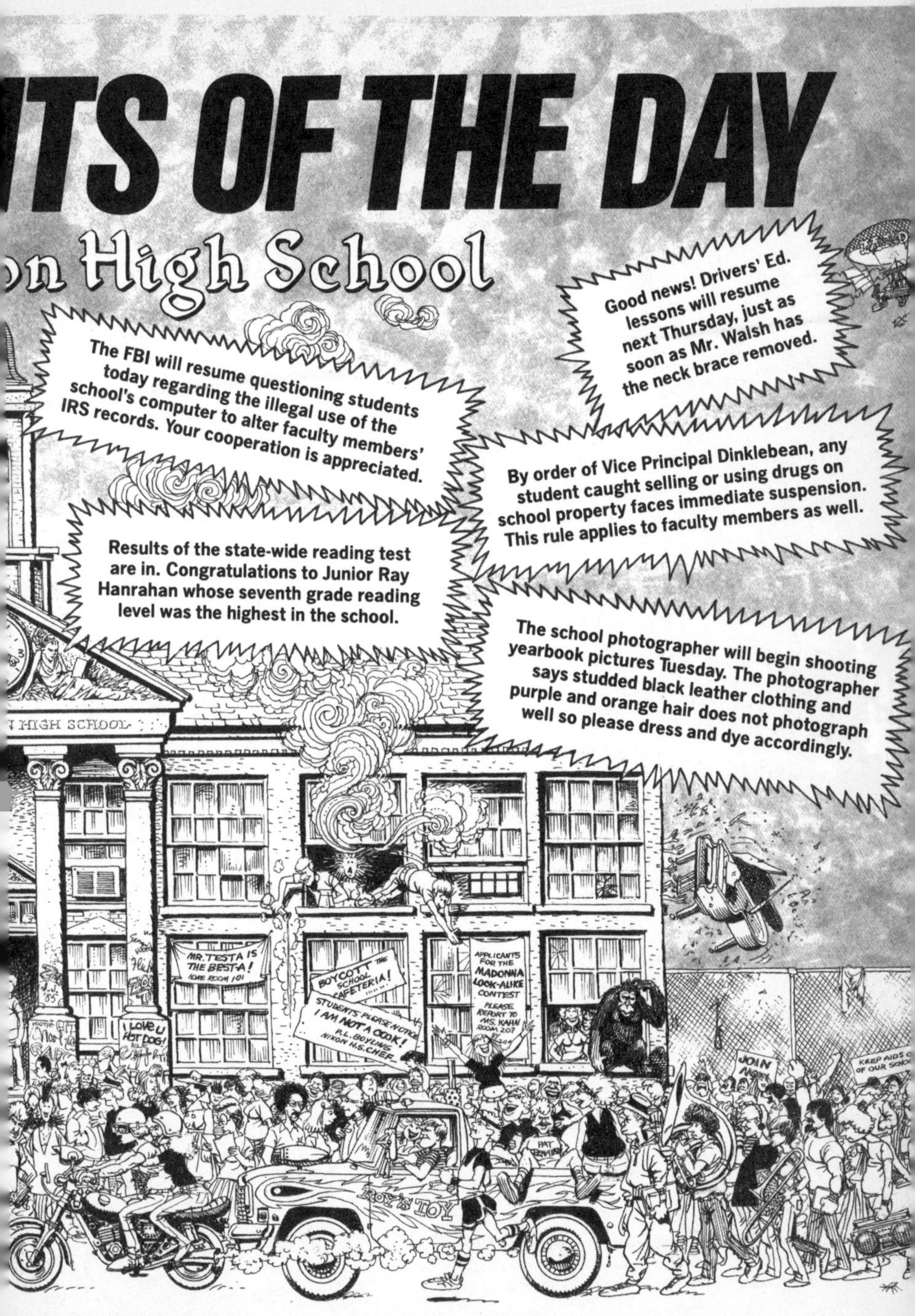

TS OF THE DAY
on High School
The FBI will resume questioning students today regarding the illegal use of the school's computer to alter faculty members' IRS records. Your cooperation is appreciated.
Good news! Drivers' Ed. lessons will resume next Thursday, just as soon as Mr. Walsh has the neck brace removed.
By order of Vice Principal Dinklebean, any student caught selling or using drugs on school property faces immediate suspension. This rule applies to faculty members as well.
Results of the state-wide reading test are in. Congratulations to Junior Ray Hanrahan whose seventh grade reading level was the highest in the school.
The school photographer will begin shooting yearbook pictures Tuesday. The photographer says studded black leather clothing and purple and orange hair does not photograph well so please dress and dye accordingly.
N HIGH SCHOOL
MR. TESTA IS THE BEST-A! HOME ROOM 101
BOYCOTT THE SCHOOL CAFETERIA!
STUDENTS PLEASE NOTICE I AM NOT A COOK!
APPLICANTS FOR THE MADONNA LOOK-ALIKE CONTEST PLEASE REPORT TO MS. KAHN ROOM 207
I LOVE U HOT DOG!
ROY'S TOY

UTILIZE-CAPADES DEPT.

Everything in this article serves a dual purpose, except this intro, which serves no purpose at all! If

MAD'S DUA CLOT ACCES

ARTIST: AL JAFFEE

Q-TIP HAT PIN

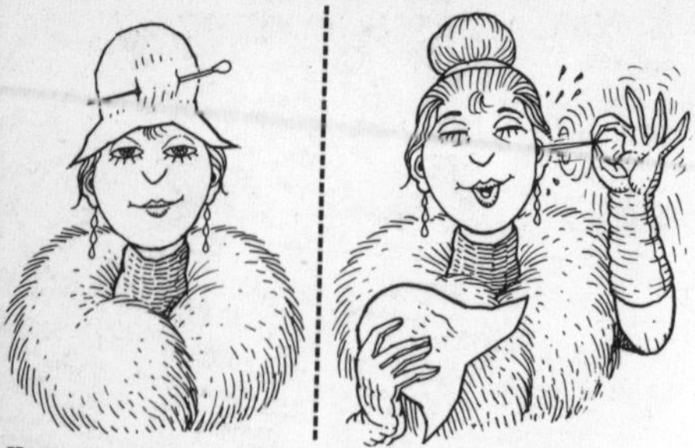

Keep your hat on and your ears clean! Stainless steel hat pin is the perfect addition to any wardrobe. Head of pin is covered with hand-spun cotton to safely clean your ears, cassette heads or navel!

SHOELACE DENTAL FLOSS

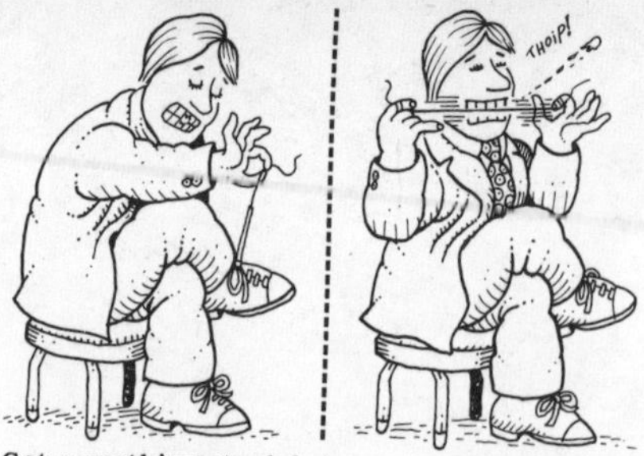
THOIP!

Got something stuck between your teeth? Just pull out one of the strands of dental floss entwined in your shoe laces and get rid of the disgusting food particle! Approved by the American Dental Association!

CAR DOOR LOCK-LIFTER EARRINGS

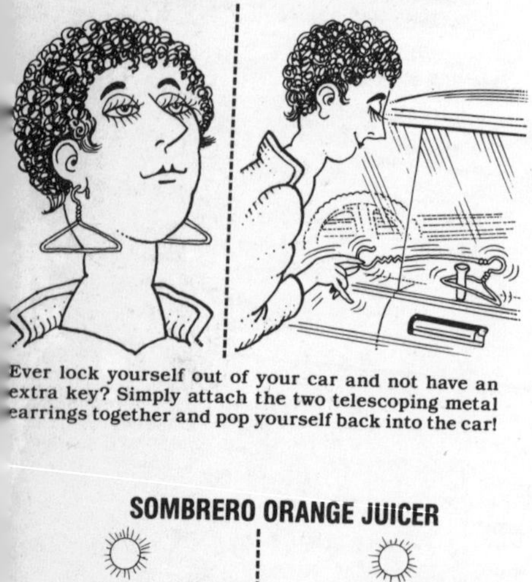

Ever lock yourself out of your car and not have an extra key? Simply attach the two telescoping metal earrings together and pop yourself back into the car!

SOMBRERO ORANGE JUICER

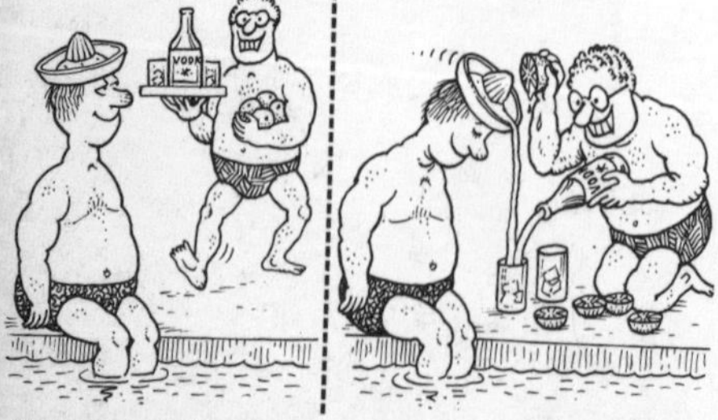

Hats off to this invention! What better way to keep the sun out of your eyes and vitamin "C" in your body! Just squeeze oranges on hardened steel top to make as many screwdrivers as needed on hot days!

TOUPEE TEA COZY

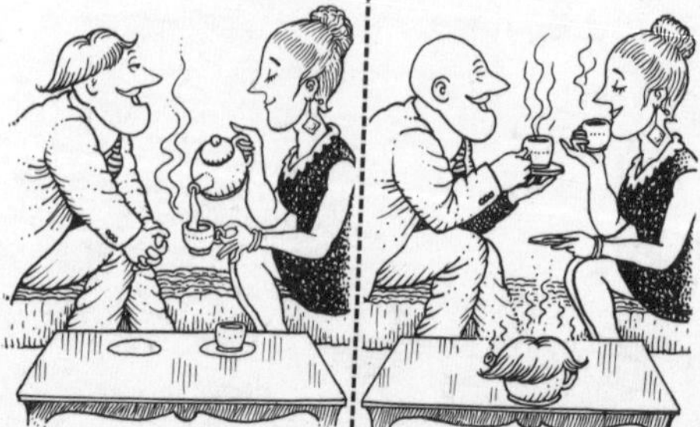

Hot tea all day! This grooming accessory will keep your teapot steaming! Uniquely designed from human hair, fits most standard tea pots. Available in blonde, brunette, and silver blue for older folks.

NAPKIN TIES

Tie stained? No problem! Just rip off another sheet and you're ready for a night on the town or that big meeting. Also handy if you run out of toilet paper!

PEARL NECKLACE BIRTH CONTROL PILLS

Don't leave home without them! Convenient! Practical! Great for those mornings when you left the house in a rush! Also available: Diaphragm earmuffs.

you don't understand what this article is about just from the title, then you probably don't need ...

L PURPOSE
HING
SORIES

WRITER: MARK A. DRESSLER

SUBWAY TOKEN CUFFLINKS

A must for any city dweller! With these decorative cufflinks you can get mugged and still take a subway home! Also available: matching token tie clip!

CORN-ON-THE-COB FALSE FINGERNAIL SPEARS

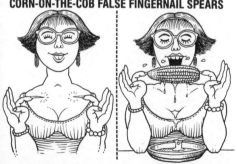

Enjoy corn-on-the-cob without all the fuss and mess! Index fingernails have sharpened elongated tip to spear corn for carefree eating. Also great for cocktail parties when there aren't any toothpicks left!

UNDERWIRE BRA ANTENNA

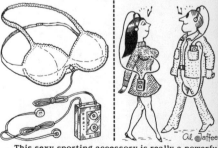

This sexy sporting accessory is really a powerful FM Antenna! Simply plug your Walkman into this specialized piece of underwear and you're all set! The bigger the cup size, the better the reception! Men—get the all-new Underwire Athletic Supporter!

SERGIO ARAGONES DEPT.

A MAD LOOK AT PRO

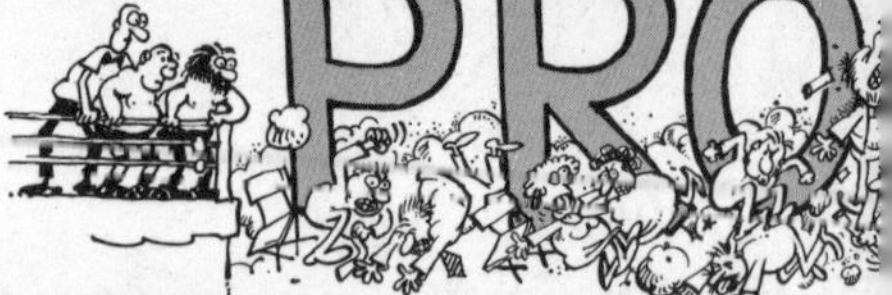

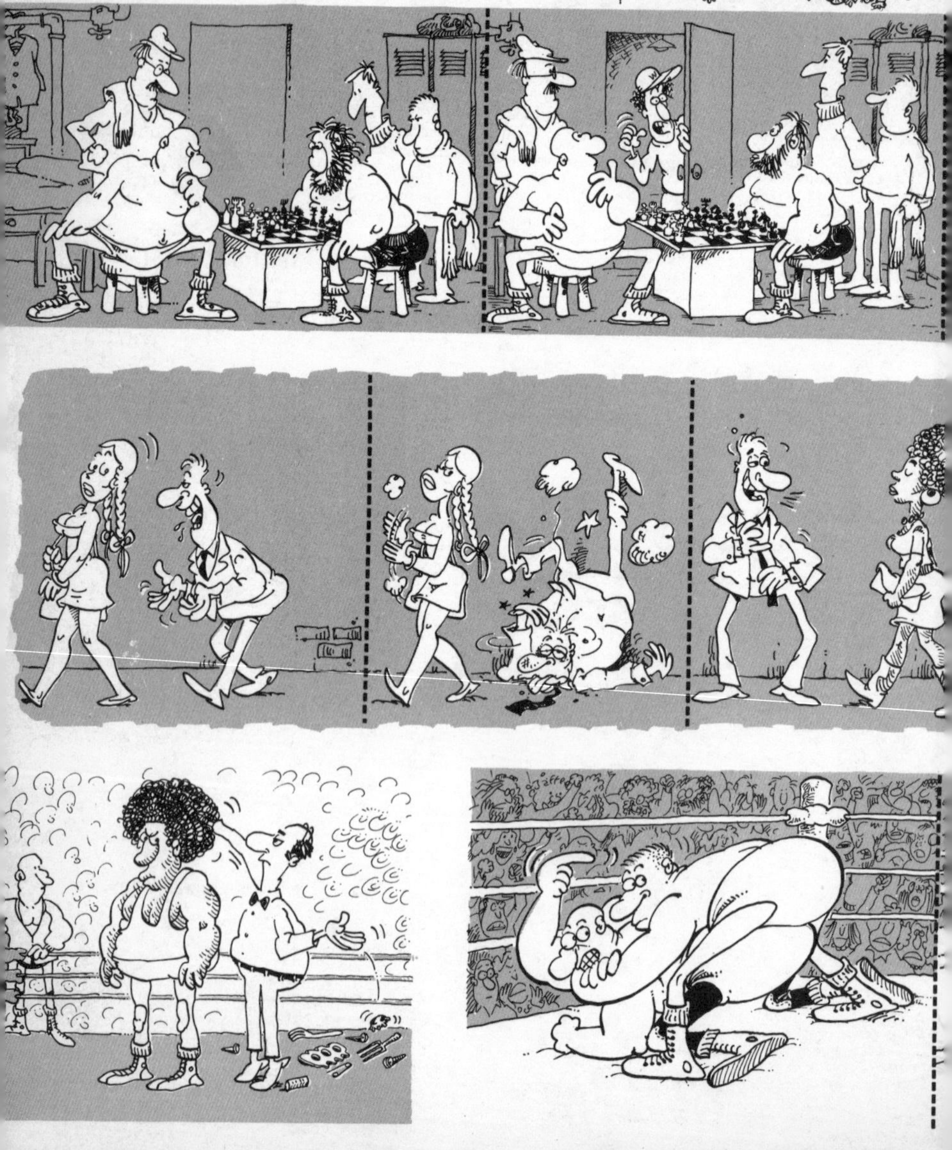

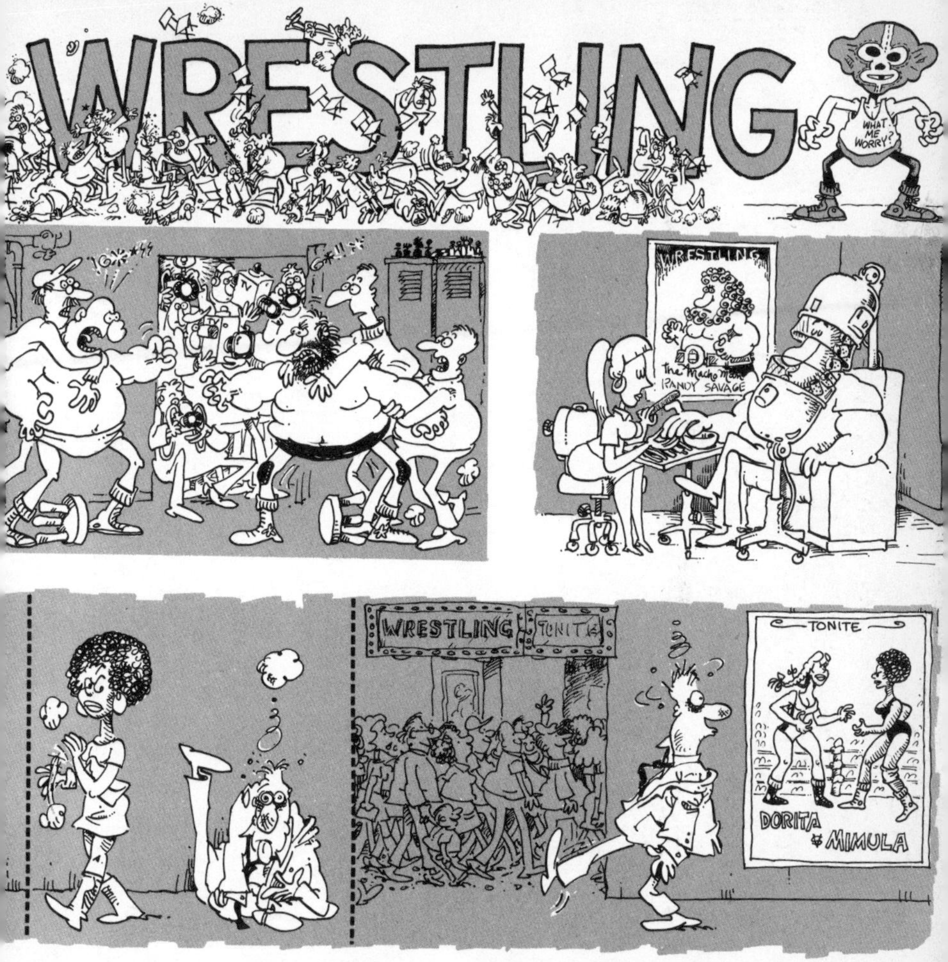
WRESTLING
WHAT ME WORRY?
TV
WRESTLING
The Macho Man
RANDY SAVAGE
WRESTLING
TONITE
TONITE
DORITA
vs MIMULA

WRITER AND ARTIST: SERGIO ARAGONES

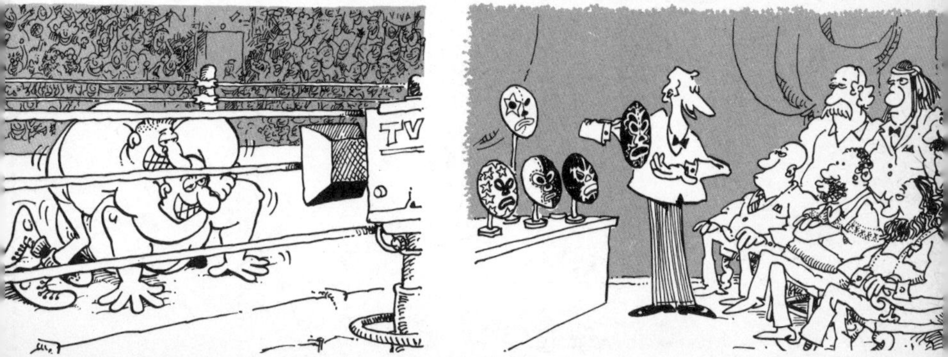
VIVA
TV

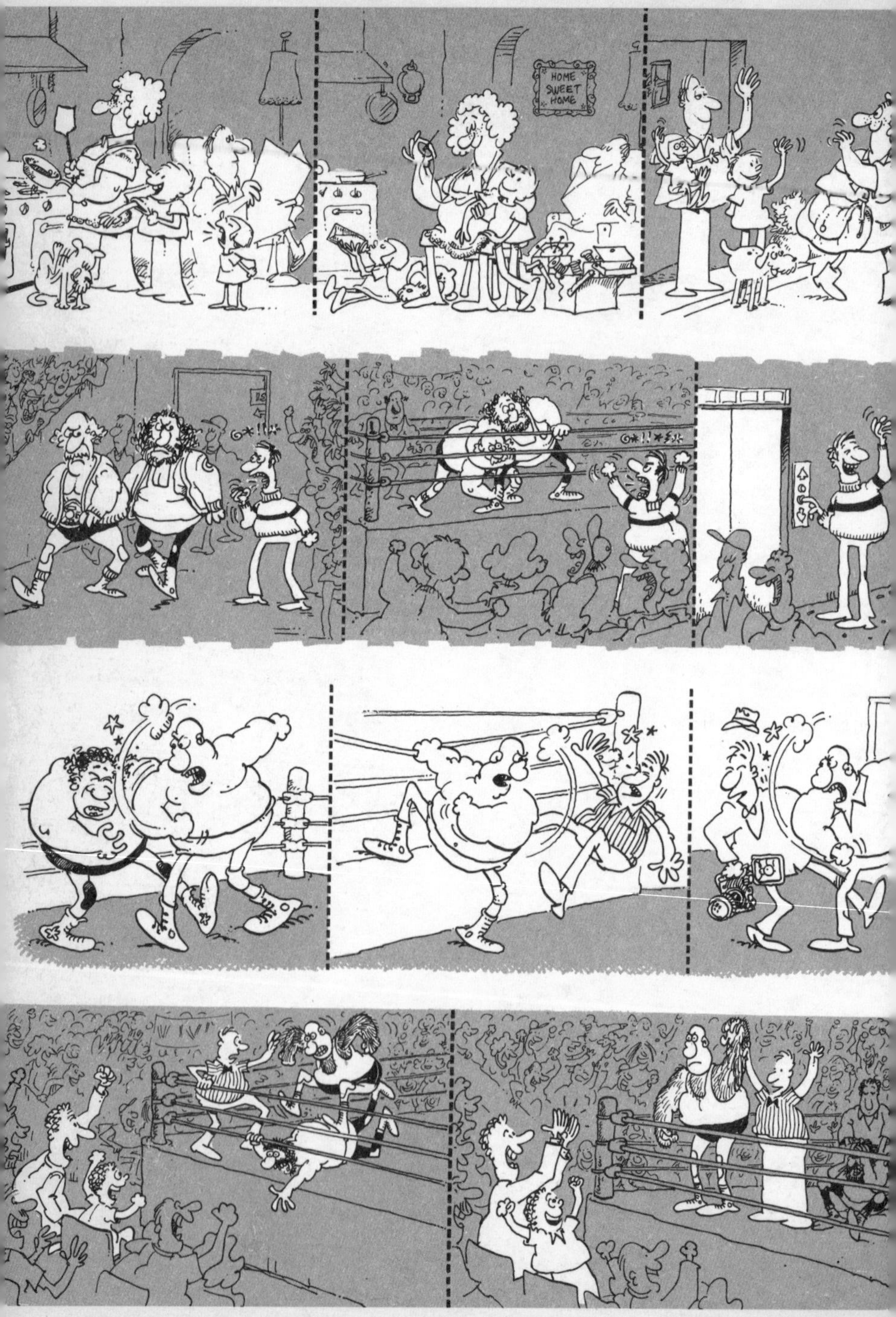
HOME SWEET HOME

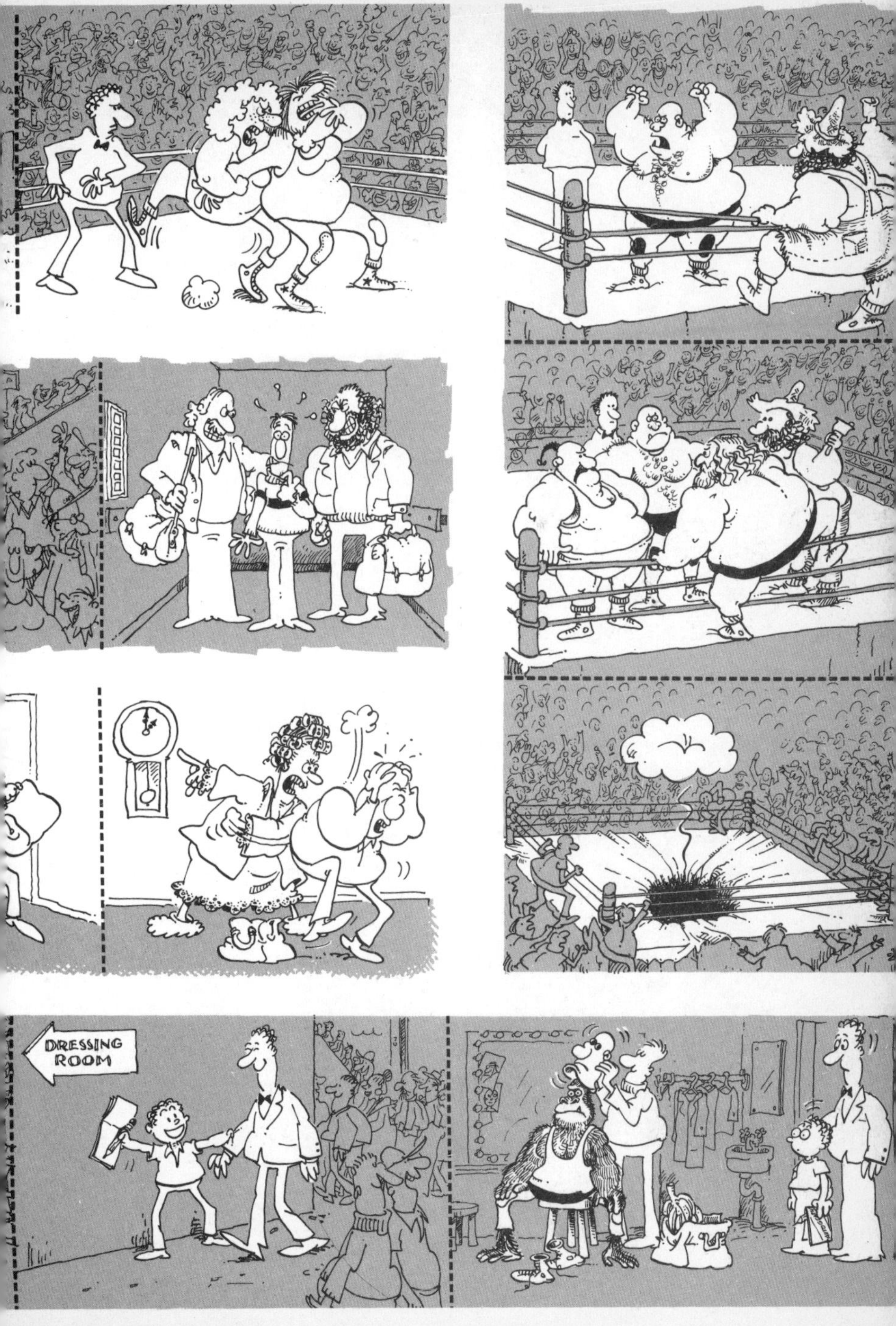
DRESSING ROOM

DON MARTIN DEPT. PART I

IN THE OPERATING RO

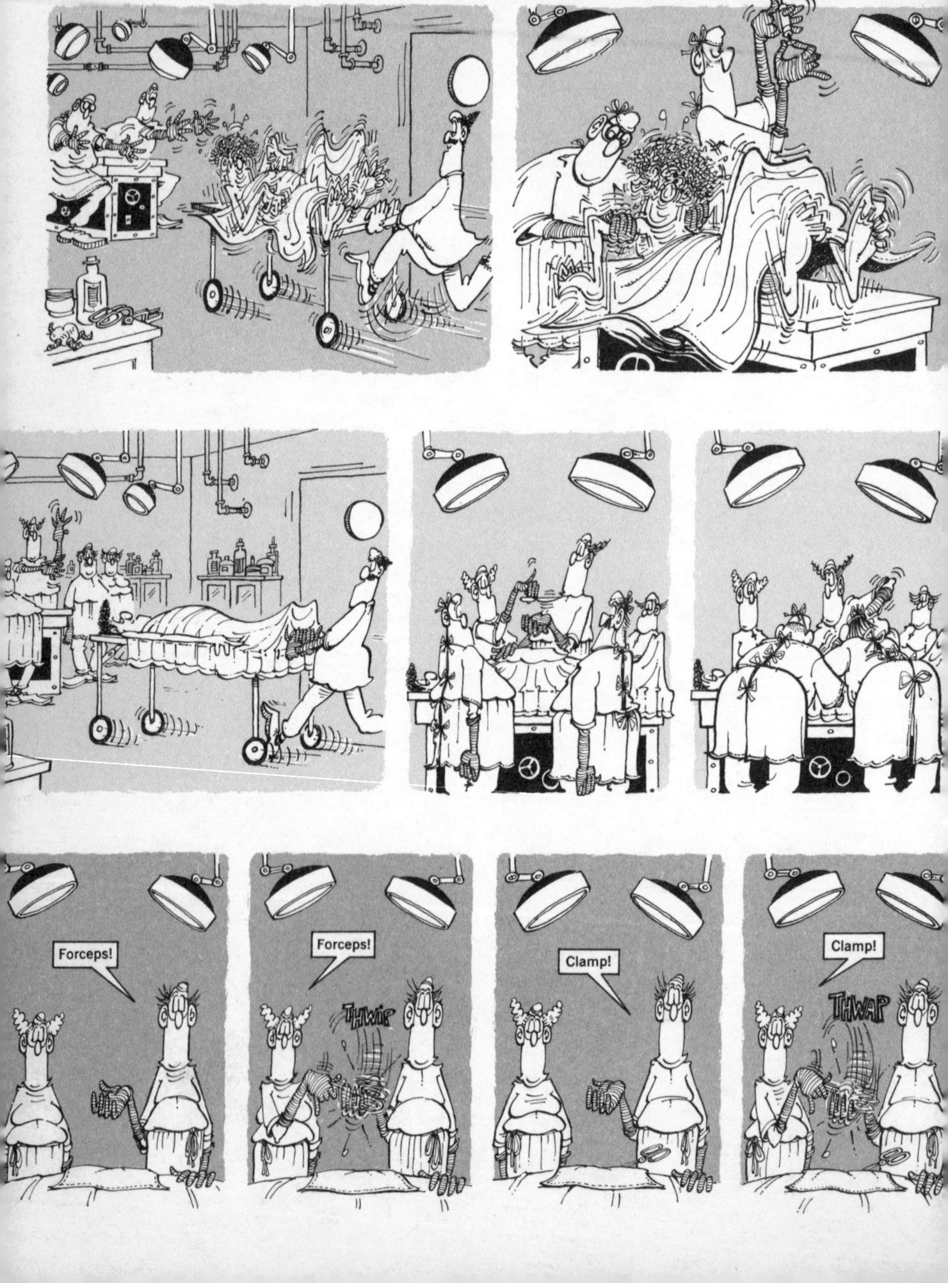

Forceps!
Forceps!
THWIP
Clamp!
Clamp!
THWAP

OM with DON MARTIN

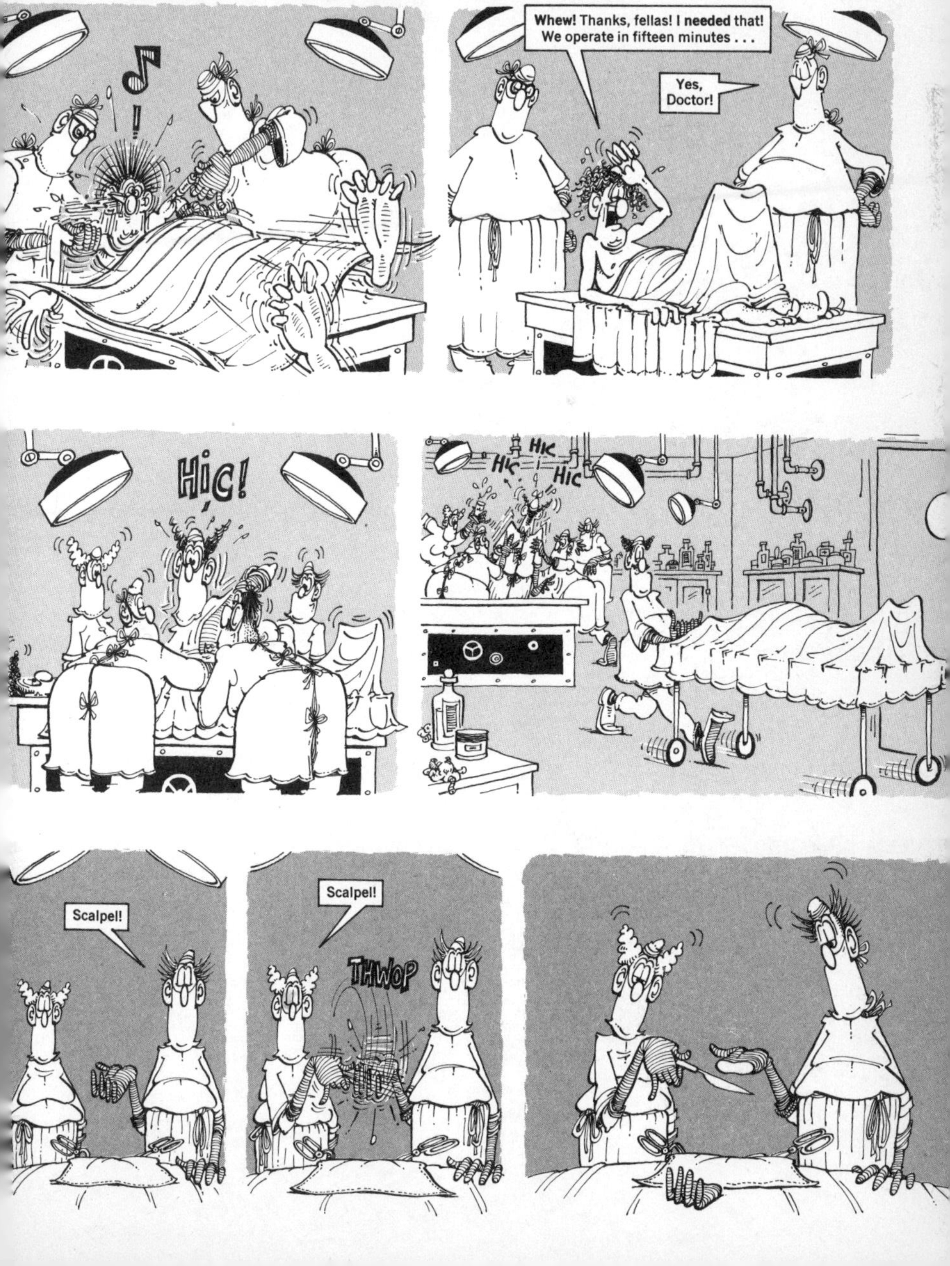
Whew! Thanks, fellas! I needed that!
We operate in fifteen minutes . . .
Yes, Doctor!
HiC!
HIC
HIC
HIC
Scalpel!
Scalpel!
THWOP

BREAKING UP

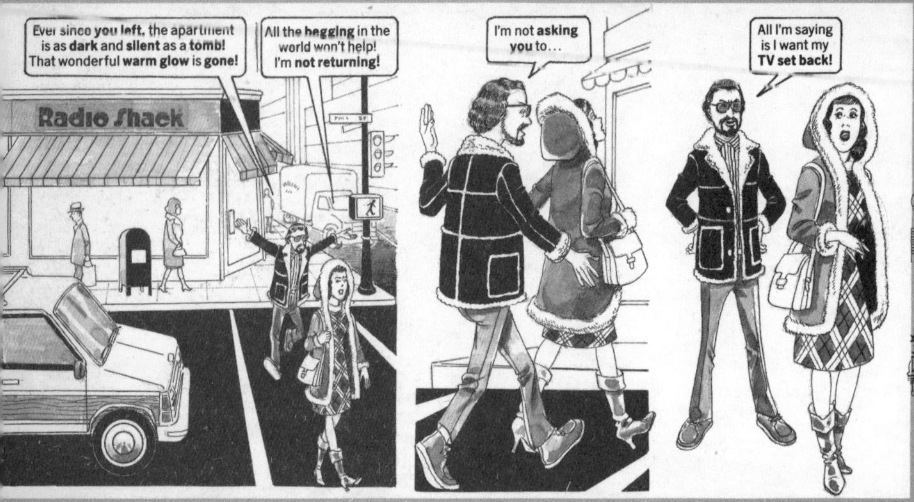

Ever since you left, the apartment is as dark and silent as a tomb! That wonderful warm glow is gone!
All the begging in the world won't help! I'm not returning!
I'm not asking you to...
All I'm saying is I want my TV set back!
Radio Shack

BERG'S-EYE VIEW DEPT.

THE LIGHTE

PRIORITIES

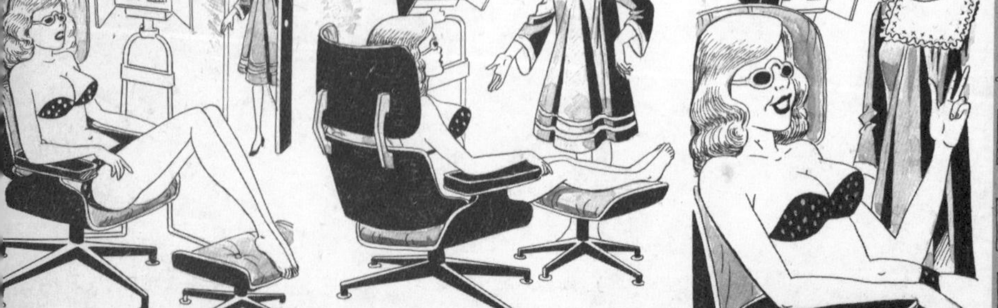

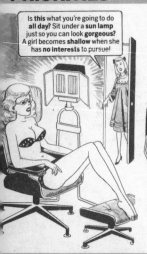

Is this what you're going to do all day? Sit under a sun lamp just so you can look gorgeous? A girl becomes shallow when she has no interests to pursue!
I'll have you know I have a very wide range of interests!
Oh, yeah? Name just five!
That's easy—John, Tom, Bill, Charlie, and Joe!

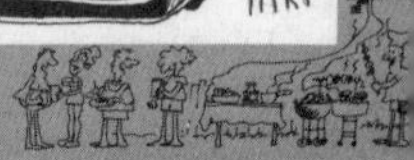

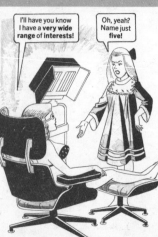

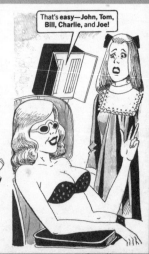

TALENT

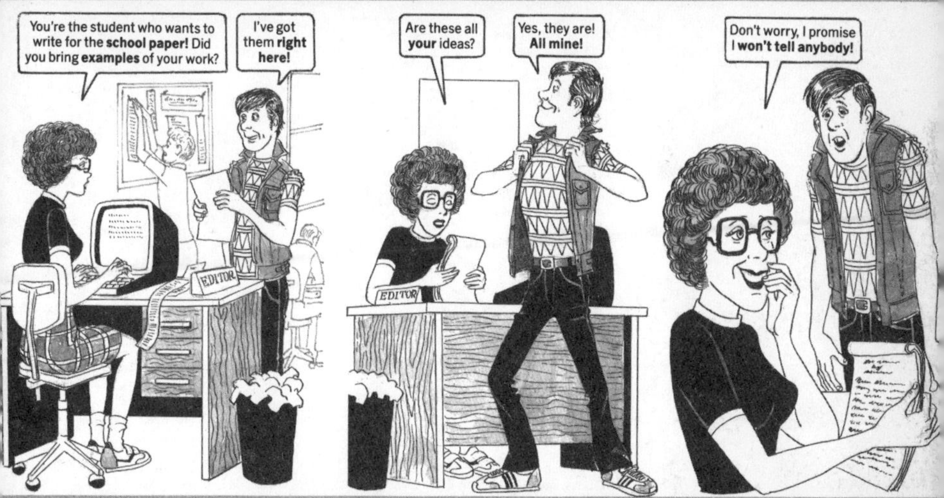

You're the student who wants to write for the **school paper!** Did you bring **examples** of your work?
I've got them **right here!**
EDITOR
Are these all **your** ideas?
Yes, they are! **All mine!**
EDITOR
Don't worry, I promise I **won't tell anybody!**

R SIDE OF...

ARTIST & WRITER:
DAVE BERG

TECHNOLOGY

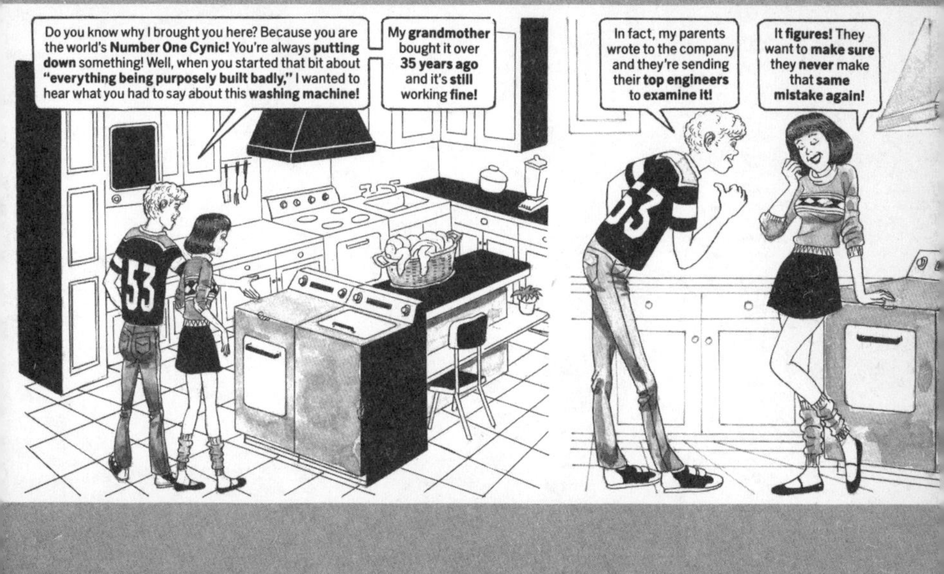

Do you know why I brought you here? Because you are the world's **Number One Cynic!** You're always **putting down** something! Well, when you started that bit about **"everything being purposely built badly,"** I wanted to hear what you had to say about this **washing machine!**
My **grandmother** bought it over **35 years ago** and it's **still** working **fine!**
53
In fact, my parents wrote to the company and they're sending their **top engineers** to **examine it!**
It **figures!** They want to **make sure** they **never** make that **same mistake again!**
53

RESTRICTIONS

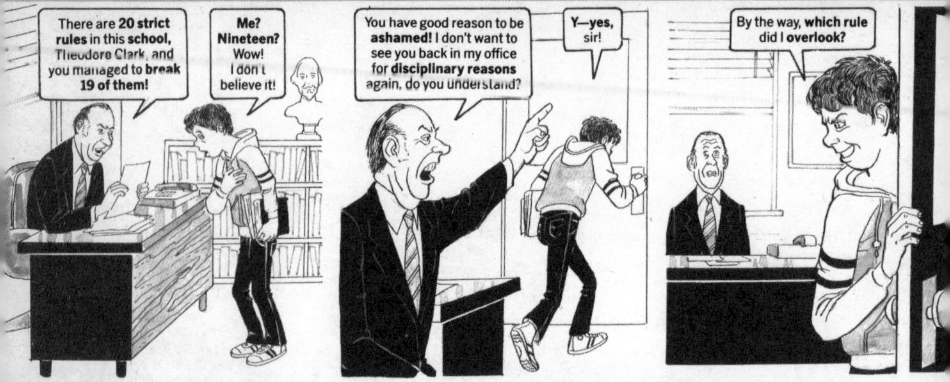

There are 20 strict rules in this school, Theodore Clark, and you managed to break 19 of them!
Me? Nineteen? Wow! I don't believe it!
You have good reason to be ashamed! I don't want to see you back in my office for disciplinary reasons again, do you understand?
Y—yes, sir!
By the way, which rule did I overlook?

SELF RELIANCE

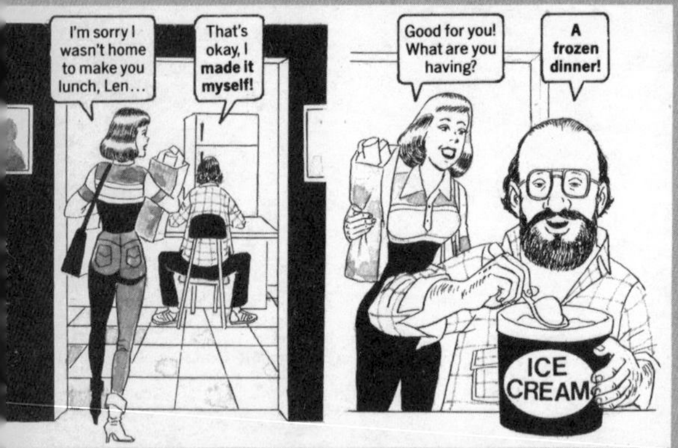

I'm sorry I wasn't home to make you lunch, Len...
That's okay, I made it myself!
Good for you! What are you having?
A frozen dinner!
ICE CREAM

EDUCATION

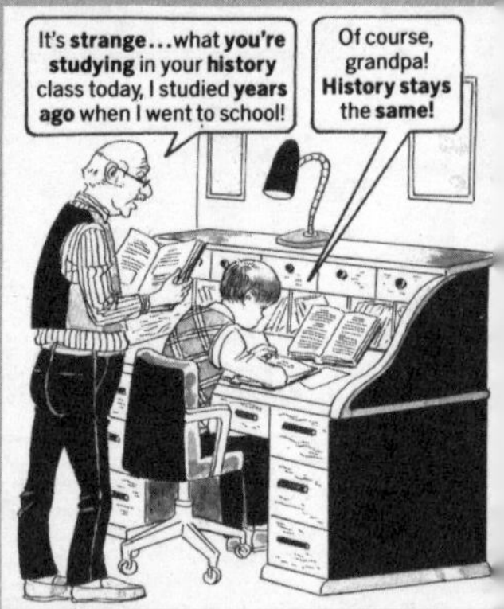

It's strange...what you're studying in your history class today, I studied years ago when I went to school!
Of course, grandpa! History stays the same!

JOB INTERVIEWS

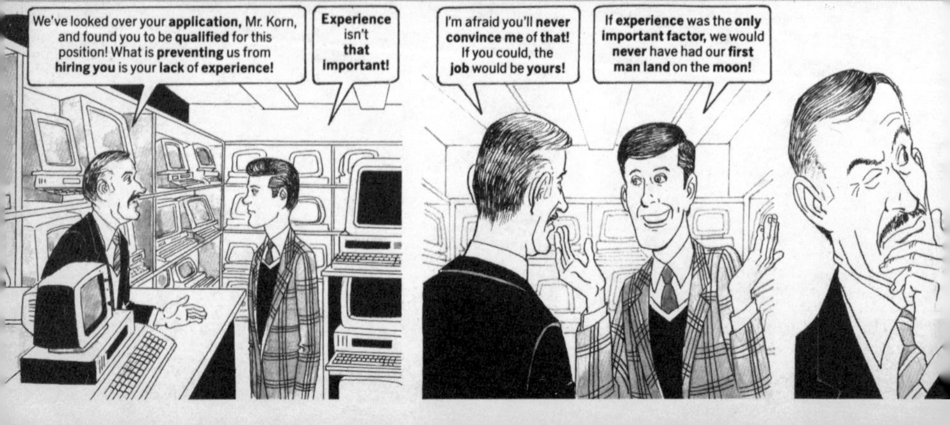

We've looked over your application, Mr. Korn, and found you to be qualified for this position! What is preventing us from hiring you is your lack of experience!
Experience isn't that important!
I'm afraid you'll never convince me of that! If you could, the job would be yours!
If experience was the only important factor, we would never have had our first man land on the moon!

RESPONSIBILITIES

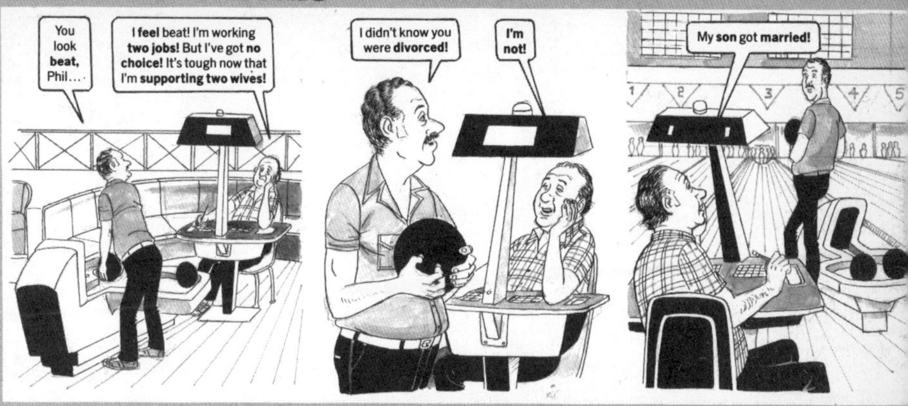
You look beat, Phil…
I feel beat! I'm working two jobs! But I've got no choice! It's tough now that I'm supporting two wives!
I didn't know you were divorced!
I'm not!
My son got married!

KID BROTHERS

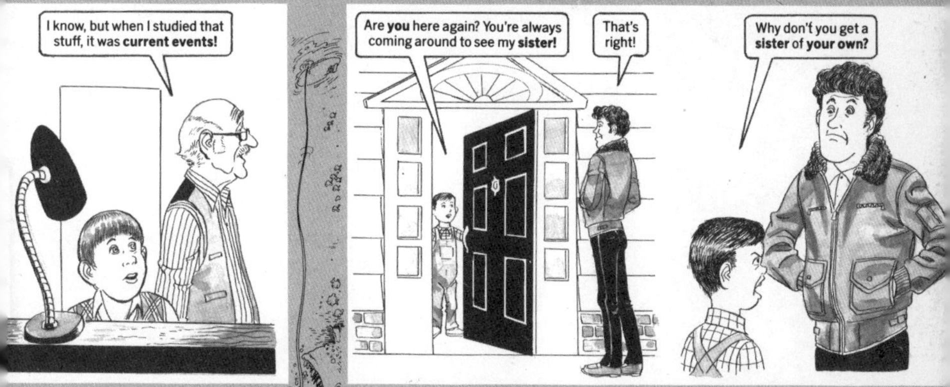
I know, but when I studied that stuff, it was current events!
Are you here again? You're always coming around to see my sister!
That's right!
Why don't you get a sister of your own?

REPUTATIONS

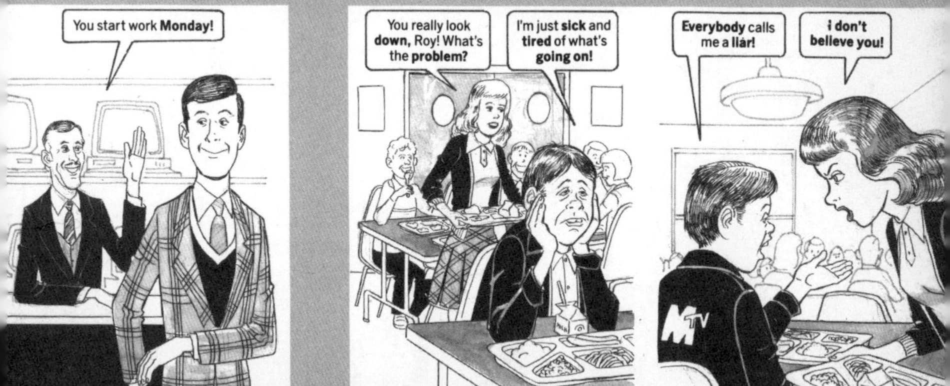
You start work Monday!
You really look down, Roy! What's the problem?
I'm just sick and tired of what's going on!
Everybody calls me a liar!
I don't believe you!

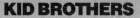

FAST CURES

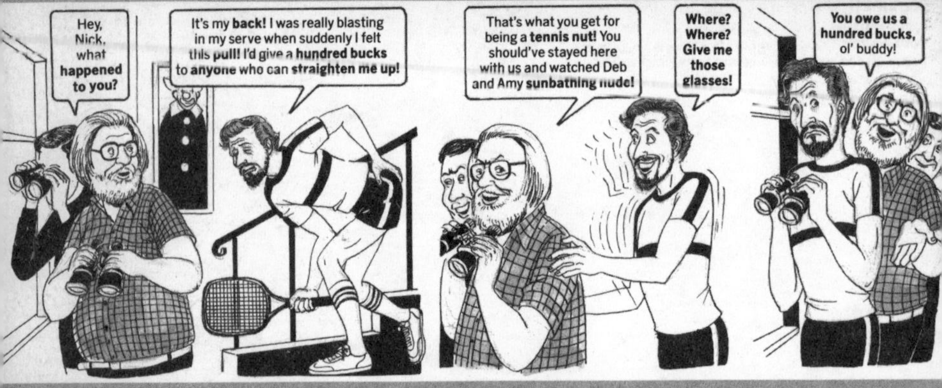

Hey, Nick, what happened to you?
It's my back! I was really blasting in my serve when suddenly I felt this pull! I'd give a hundred bucks to anyone who can straighten me up!
That's what you get for being a tennis nut! You should've stayed here with us and watched Deb and Amy sunbathing nude!
Where? Where? Give me those glasses!
You owe us a hundred bucks, ol' buddy!

MODERN INTERPRETATION

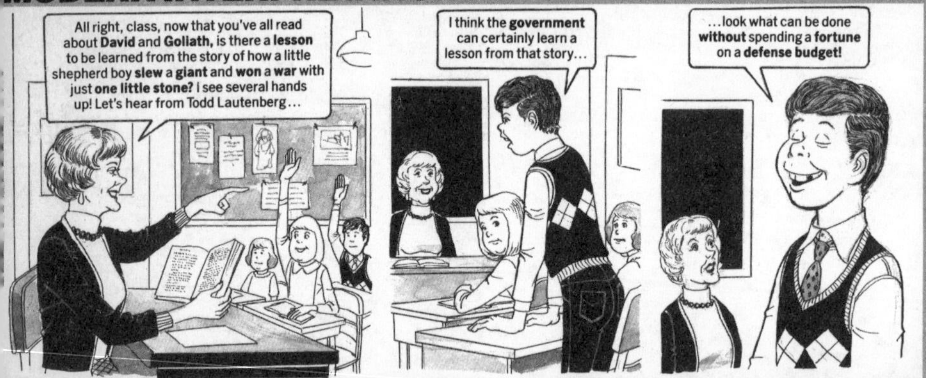

All right, class, now that you've all read about David and Goliath, is there a lesson to be learned from the story of how a little shepherd boy slew a giant and won a war with just one little stone? I see several hands up! Let's hear from Todd Lautenberg...
I think the government can certainly learn a lesson from that story...
...look what can be done without spending a fortune on a defense budget!

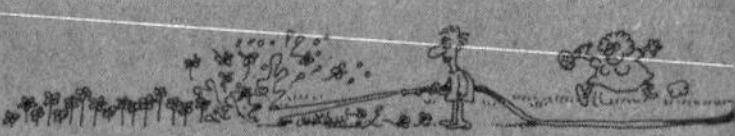

DOCTORS

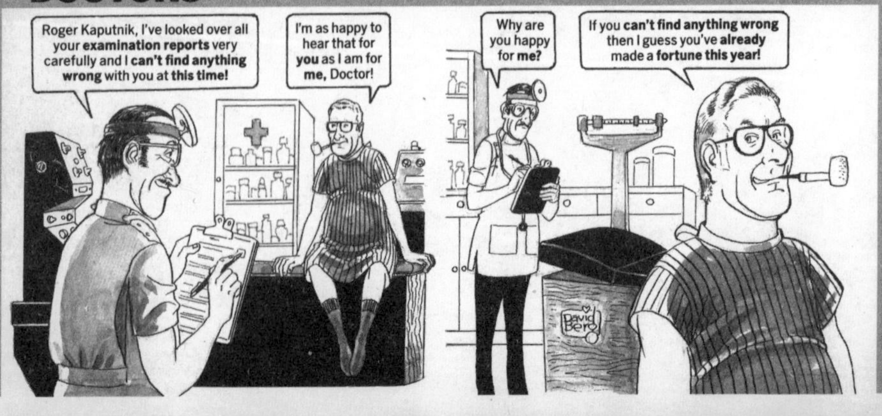

Roger Kaputnik, I've looked over all your examination reports very carefully and I can't find anything wrong with you at this time!
I'm as happy to hear that for you as I am for me, Doctor!
Why are you happy for me?
If you can't find anything wrong then I guess you've already made a fortune this year!
David Berg

DRAWING VERSE BLOOD DEPT.

It's an ugly world out there, what with wars and terrorists and muggers and all the rest. And it's time we prepared the kiddies by giving them the message as early as possible. Well, what better way to introduce them to the hard realities of life, than with Mad's...

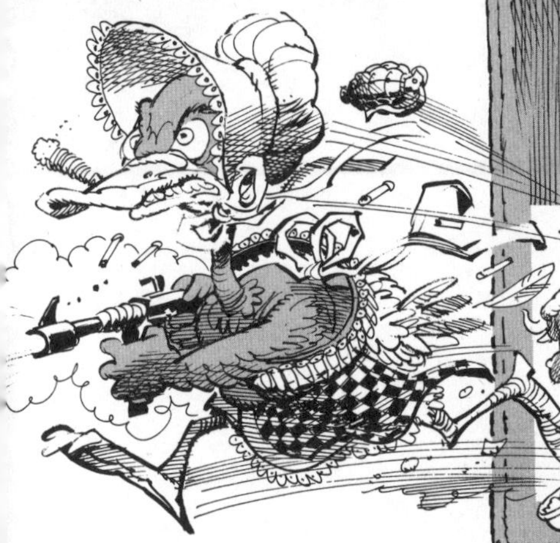

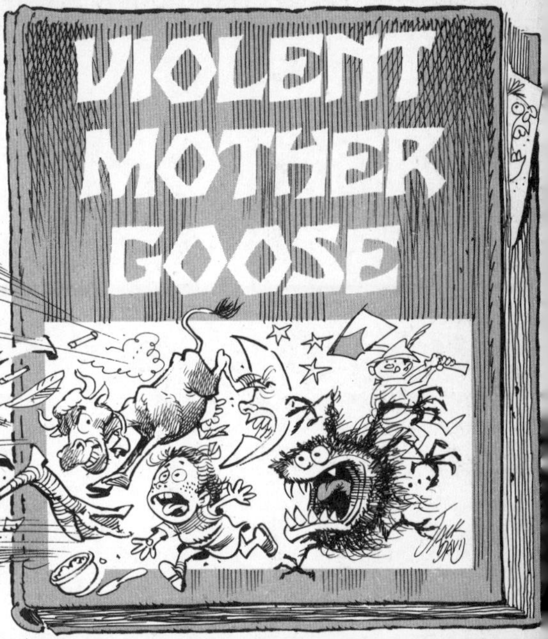
VIOLENT
MOTHER
GOOSE

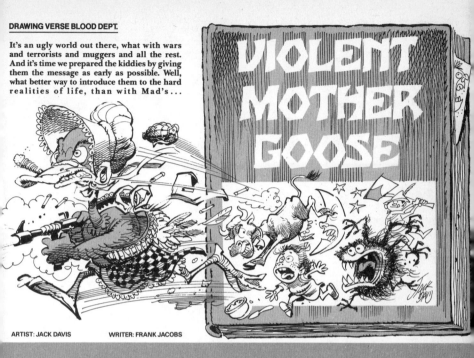

ARTIST: JACK DAVIS WRITER: FRANK JACOBS

JACK SPRAT

Jack Sprat
Can swing his bat;
His wife can spray her mace;
He'll smack her hard
When she's off-guard;
She'll spritz him in the face.

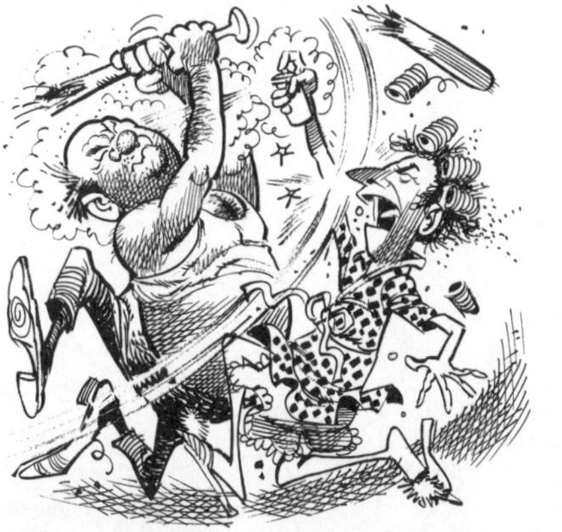

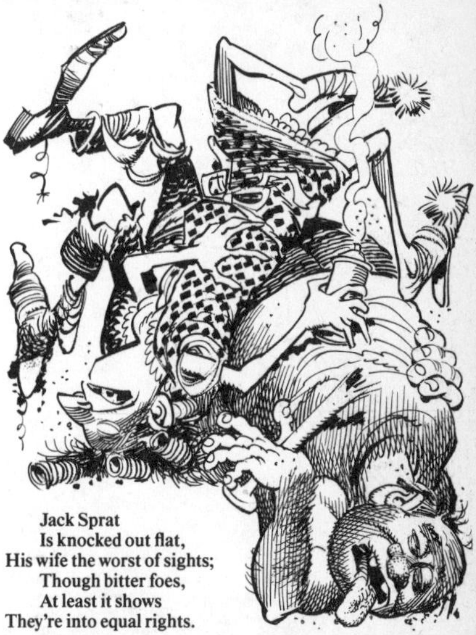

Jack Sprat
Is knocked out flat,
His wife the worst of sights;
Though bitter foes,
At least it shows
They're into equal rights.

THIS IS THE FILM THAT JACK MADE

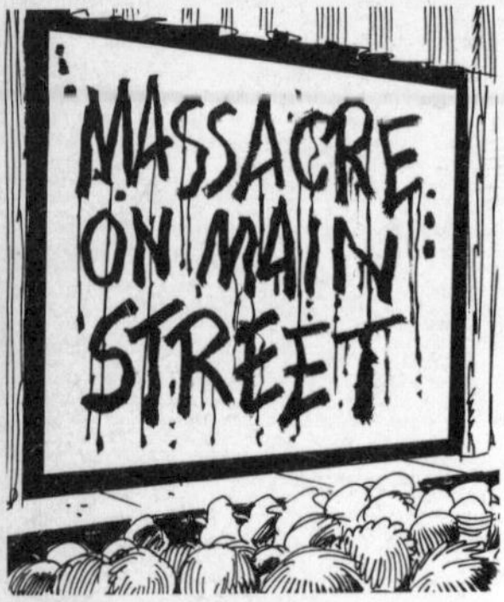
MASSACRE ON MAIN STREET

This is the film that Jack made.

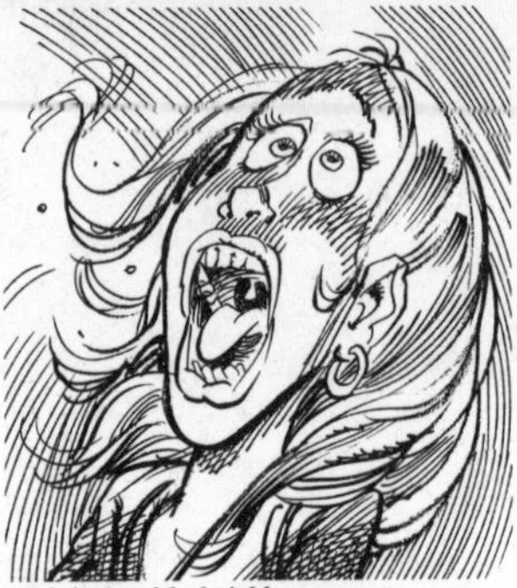

This is the girl who's blown away
who's in the film that Jack made.

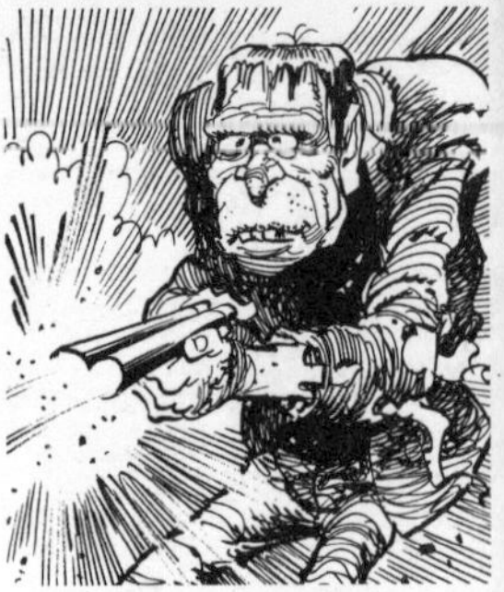

This is the creep who stalks his prey,
Who blasts the girl who's blown away,
Who's in the film that Jack made.

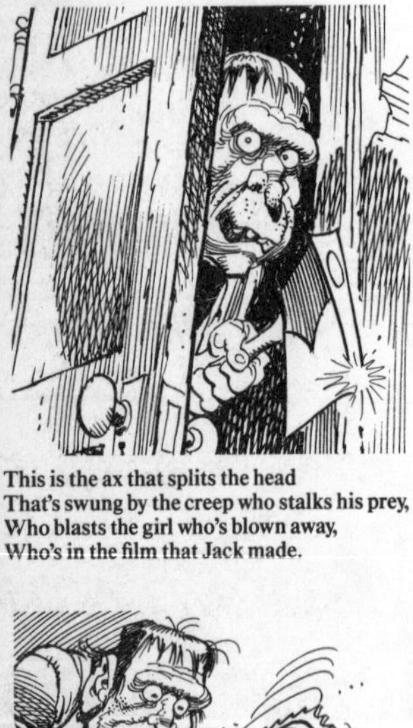

This is the ax that splits the head
That's swung by the creep who stalks his prey,
Who blasts the girl who's blown away,
Who's in the film that Jack made.

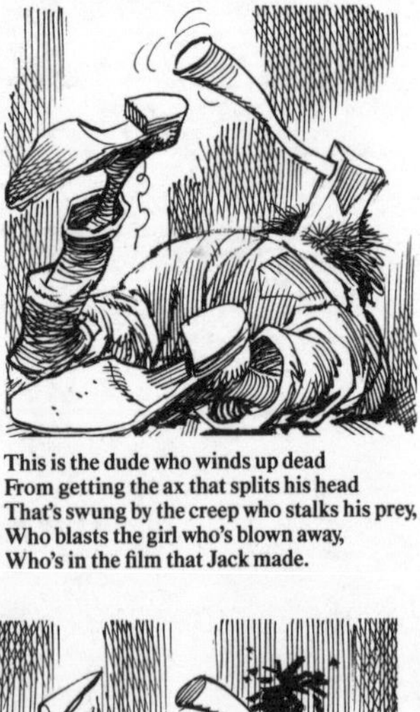

This is the dude who winds up dead
From getting the ax that splits his head
That's swung by the creep who stalks his prey,
Who blasts the girl who's blown away,
Who's in the film that Jack made.

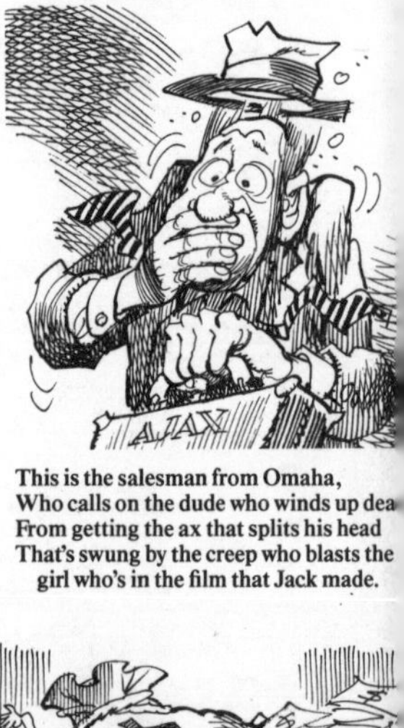
AJAX

This is the salesman from Omaha,
Who calls on the dude who winds up dea
From getting the ax that splits his head
That's swung by the creep who blasts the
girl who's in the film that Jack made.

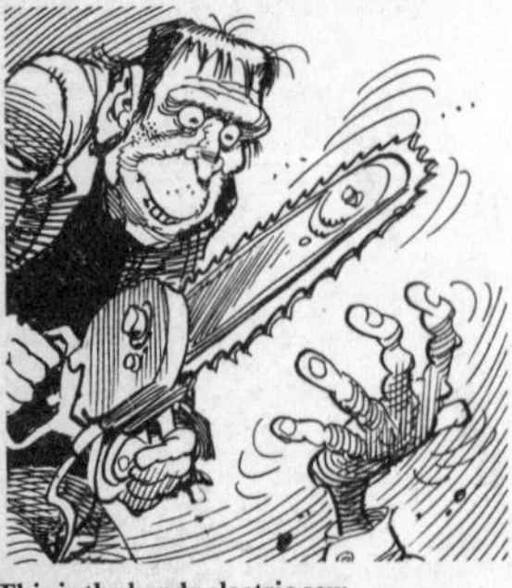

This is the handy electric saw
That slices the salesman from Omaha,
Who calls on the dude who winds up dead
From getting the ax that splits his head
That's swung by the creep who blasts the
girl who's in the film that Jack made.

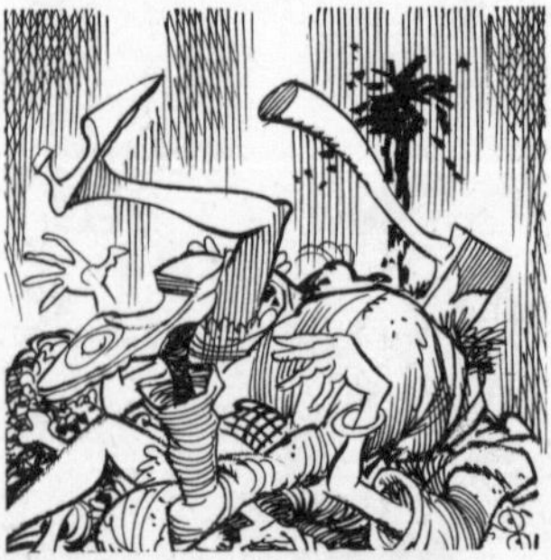

This is the carnage of blood and gore
That's made by the handy electric saw
That slices the salesman from Omaha,
Who calls on the dude who gets the ax
that's swung by the creep who blasts
the girl who's in the film that Jack made.

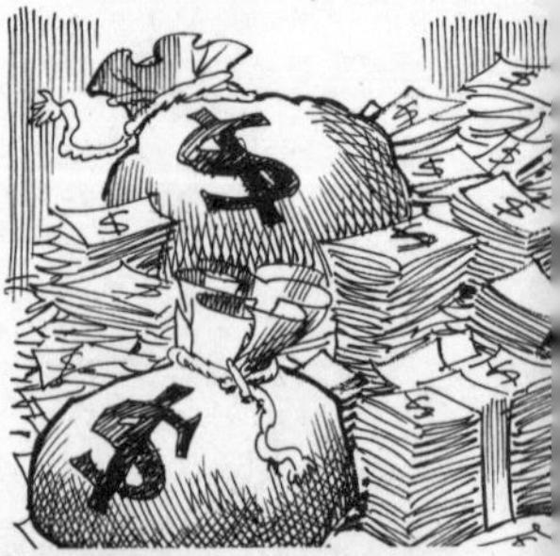

These are the profits of bucks galore
That come from the carnage of blood and gor
That's made by the handy electric saw
That slices the salesman from Omaha,
Who follows the dude who gets the ax
that's swung by the creep who blasts
the girl who's in the film that Jack made.

SING A SONG OF VIOLENCE

Sing a song of violence,
Of punks and goons and thugs,
Of homicides and gang wars,
Of corpses full of slugs.

If such atrocious doings
Are not your cup of tea,
Well, tough, that's all you're getting
Tonight on your TV.

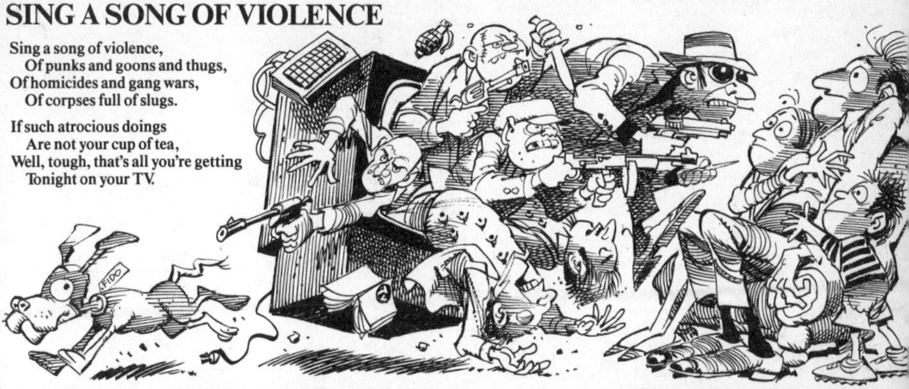
FIDO

JACK BE NIMBLE

Jack be nimble;
Jack be slick;
Jack meet mugger;
Jack give kick.

Jack show quickness;
Jack show skill;
Jack learn bullet
Quicker still.

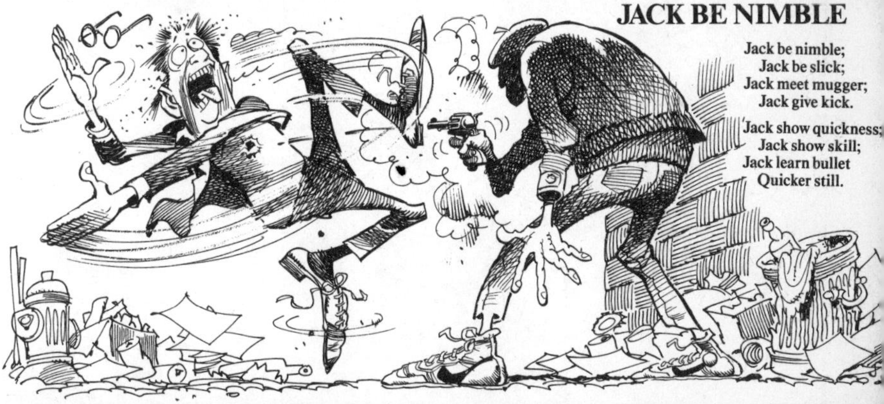

OMAR HAD A LITTLE BOMB

Omar had a little bomb;
He found it filled a need
For getting rid of all those folks
With whom he disagreed.

Omar let his bomb go off
Without the proper care;
And now we're finding little bits
Of Omar ev'rywhere.

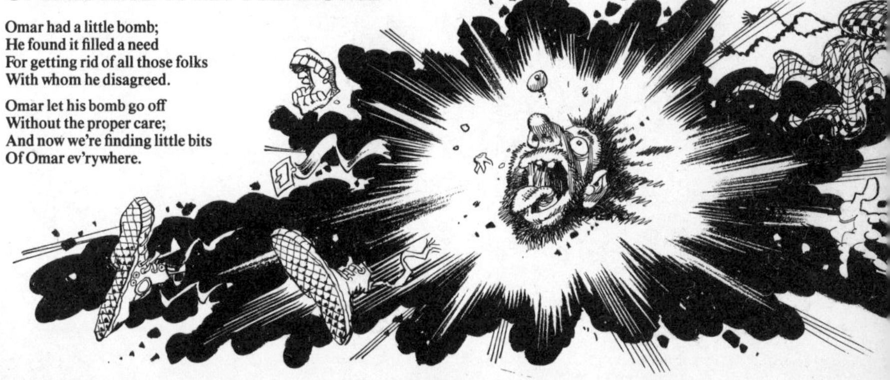

JOKE AND DAGGER DEPT.

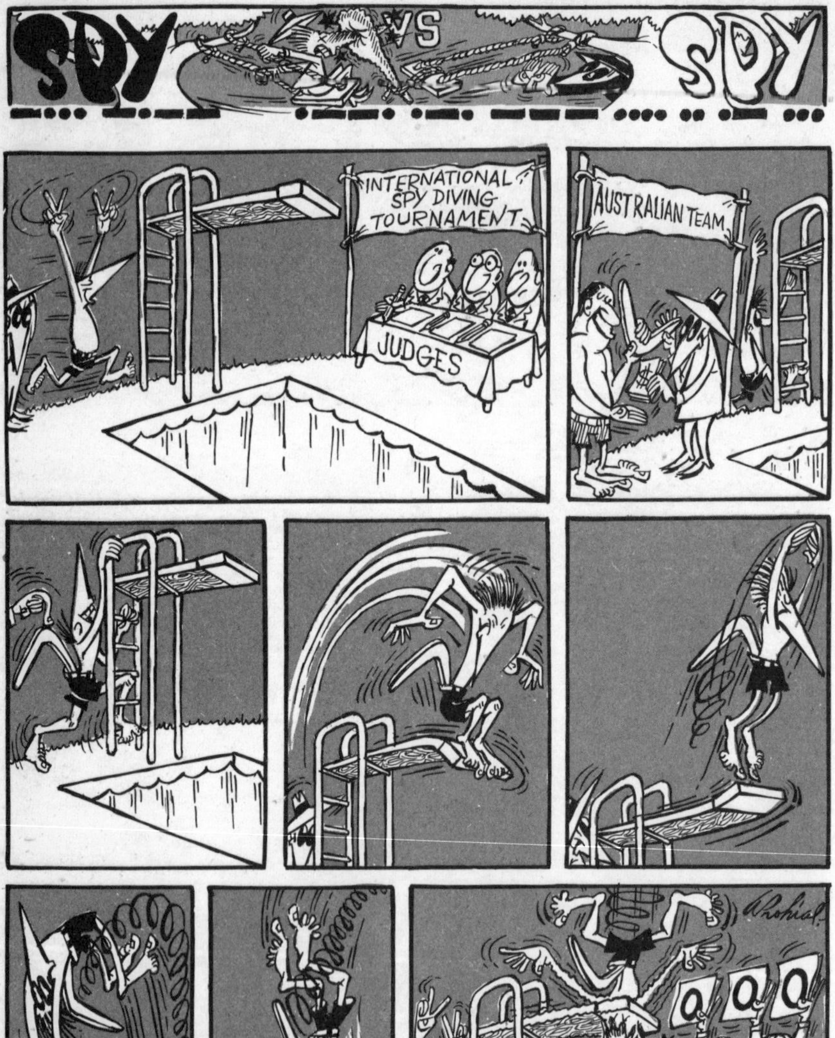
SPY
VS
SPY
INTERNATIONAL SPY DIVING TOURNAMENT
JUDGES
AUSTRALIAN TEAM
0
0
0
JUDGES
Prohias

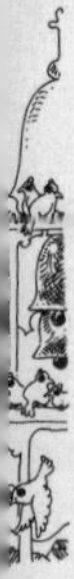

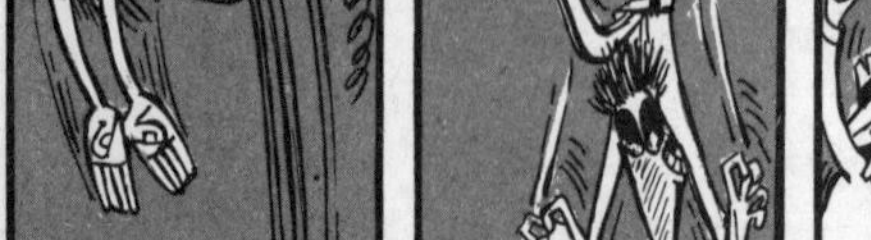

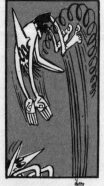

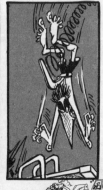

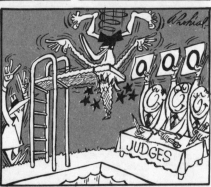

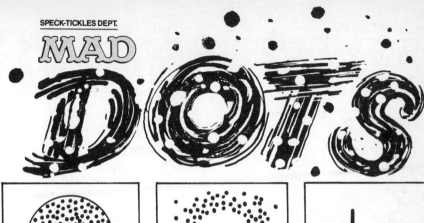

MAD DOTS

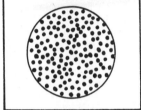

AN OVERHEAD VIEW OF
RONALD REAGAN'S
BIRTHDAY CAKE

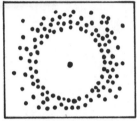

SOMEONE DYING ON A
NEW YORK CITY STREET

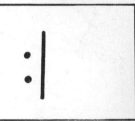

STARTING LINE AT THE FROSTBITE
FALLS, SOUTH DAKOTA ANNUAL
MARATHON

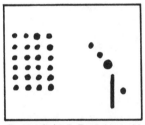

REFRIGERATOR PERRY ON THE
JOHNNY CARSON SHOW

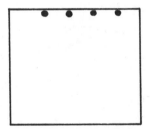

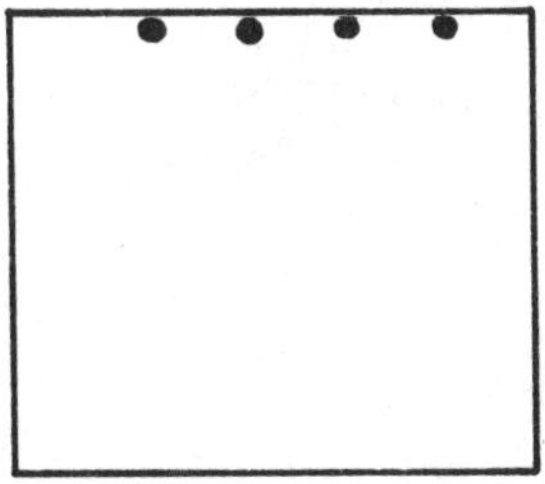

DIDN'T FEED THE FISH

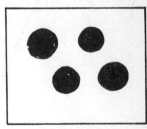

OVERFED THE FISH

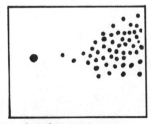

A SWARM OF PIMPLES
APPROACHING A KID
EATING A HERSHEY BAR

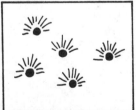

RESIDENTS OF
THREE MILE ISLAND

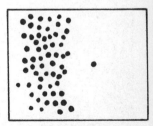

THE KLU KLUX KLAN'S IDEA
OF A FAIR FIGHT

WRITER: MAT JACOBS

SERGIO ARAGONES DEPT.

A MAD LOOK AT WATER

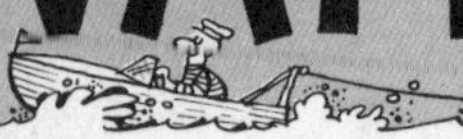

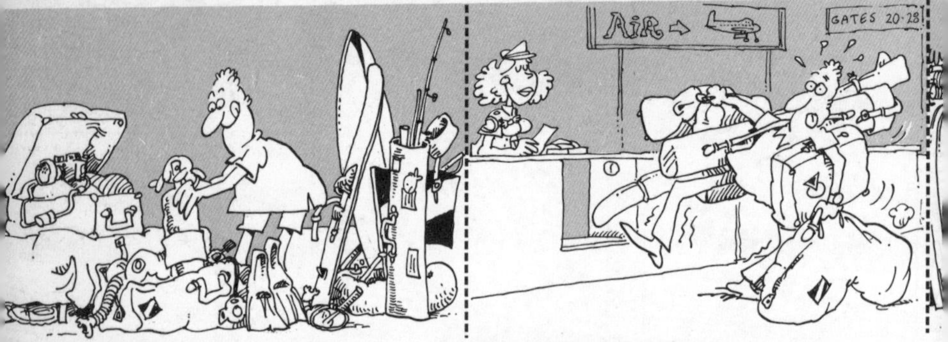

AIR
GATES 20-28

ARTIST AND WRITER: SERGIO ARAGONES

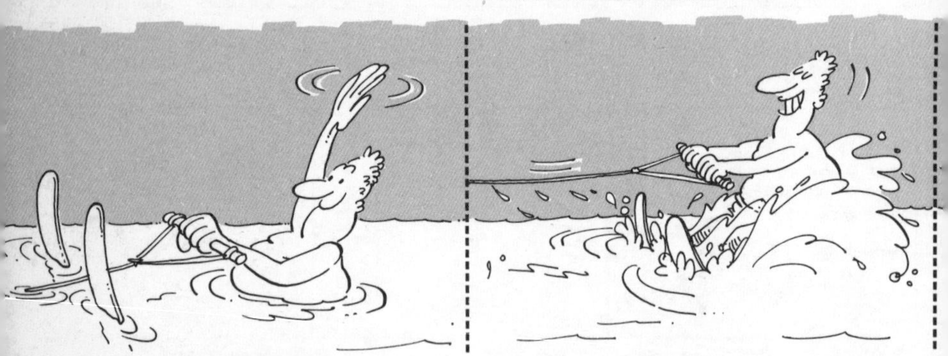

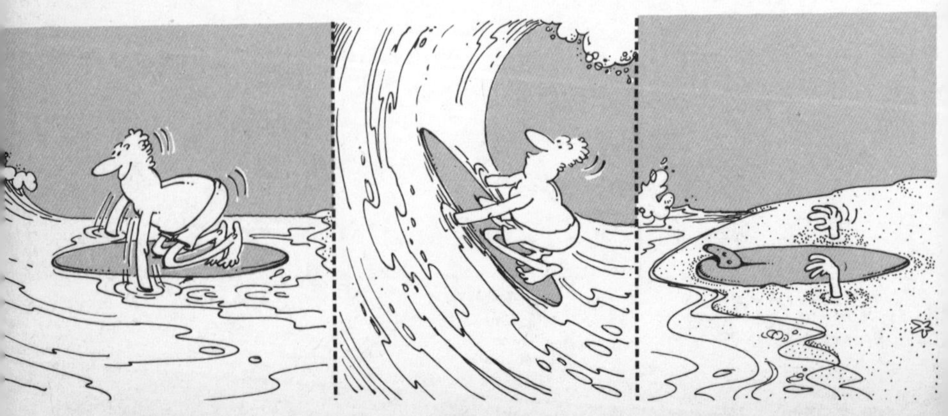

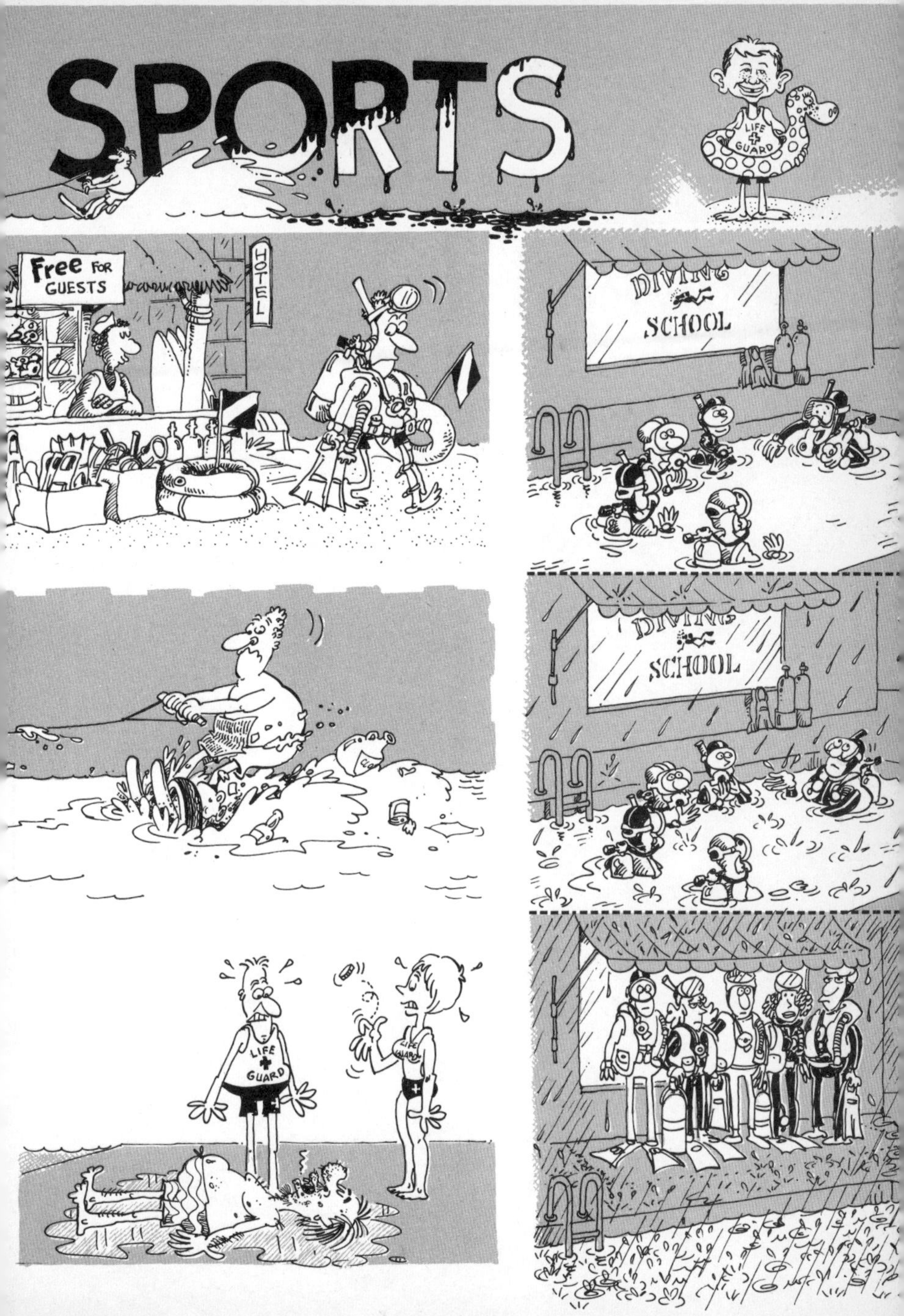
SPORTS
LIFE GUARD
Free FOR GUESTS
HOTEL
DIVING SCHOOL
DIVING SCHOOL
LIFE GUARD
LIFE GUARD

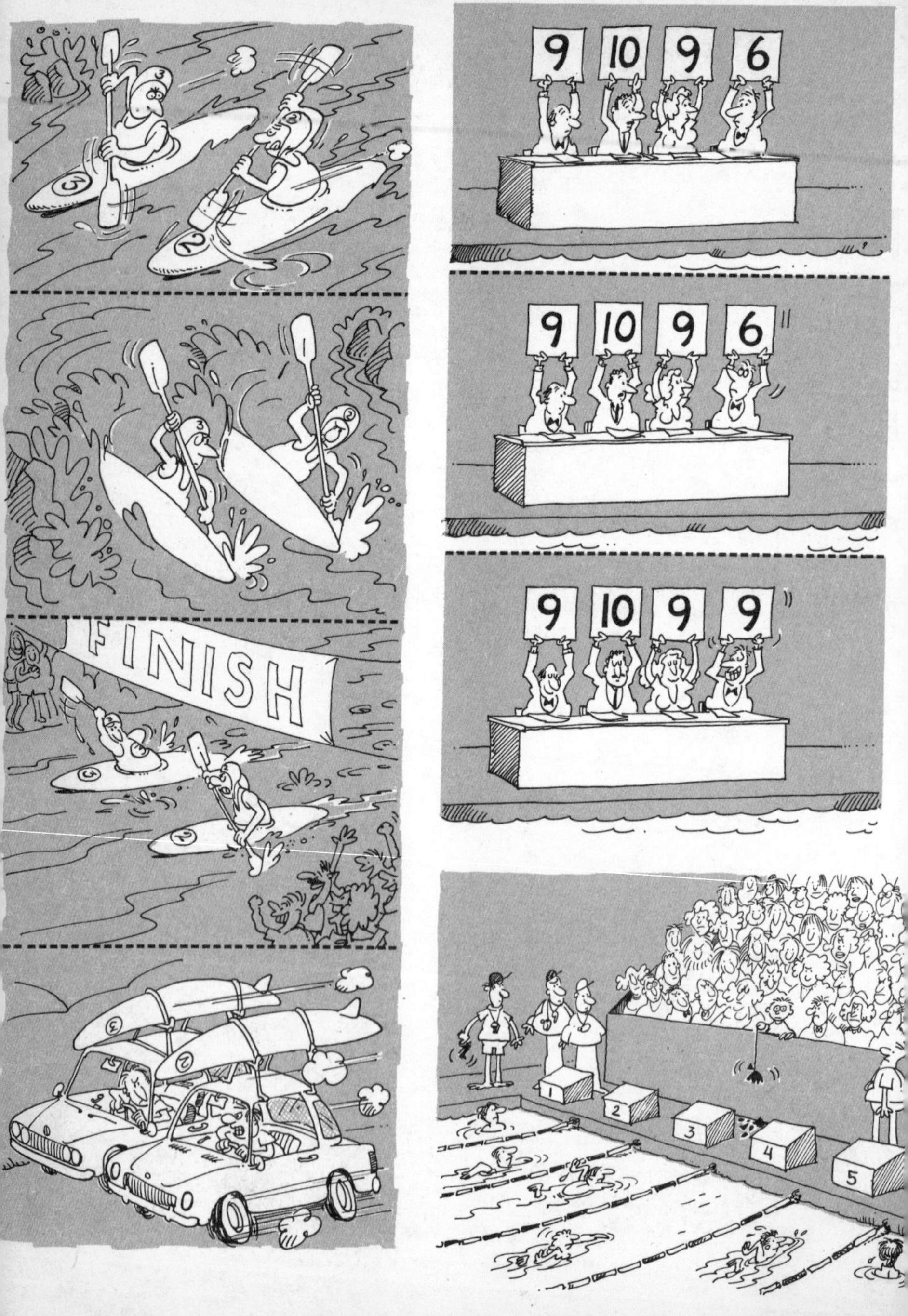

3
2
FINISH
9 10 9 6
9 10 9 6
9 10 9 9
1
2
3
4
5

DEPARTING SHOTS DEPT.

AT THE BEDSIDE, PART I

PFFT
PUFF
I tell you Phil, I **can't take** any more of this! Please, Phil, do me one last **favor. Pull the plug!**
CRUNCH
GRIND
I **can't** do **that,** Bob! That's not a decision **I** can make!
DO NOT REMOVE
But it's sheer **torture!** Can't you understand that?! If I was strong enough **I'd pull the plug** myself!
You shouldn't be **talking** that way, Bob!
DO NOT REMOVE
I can't **stand it** anymore! I'm going **nuts! Please**… I'll give you my **house**… my **car**… **anything!!! JUST PULL THE PLUG!!!**
All right! All right! **I'll pull the plug!**
WELCOME BACK TO THE WHEEL of FORTUNE

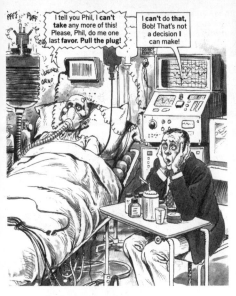

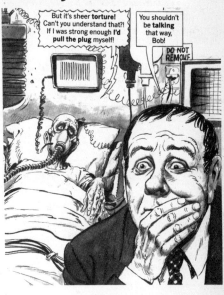

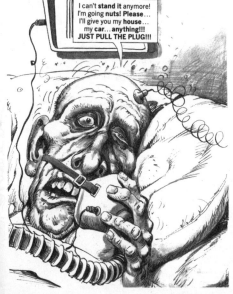

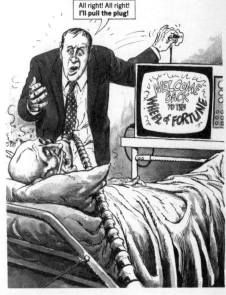

ARTIST: HARRY NORTH WRITER: CHARLIE KADAU

ROAD SCHOLAR DEPT.

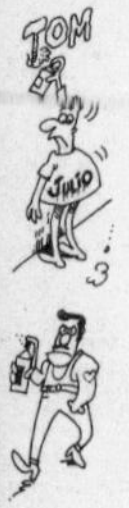

In most states, renewing your driver's license is as easy as signing your name and enclosing a check. Simple, but what this procedure doesn't do is weed out unsafe drivers—motorists who have long since forgotten everything they had to learn in order to get their first license! How about you? Are your driving skills up to par? Or have you too become sloppy and careless behind the wheel! Spend a few minutes with this quiz and see:

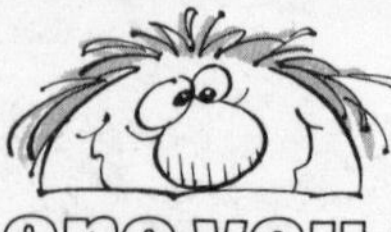

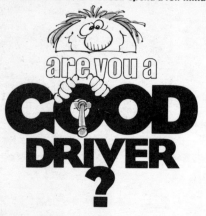

are you a GOOD DRIVER ?

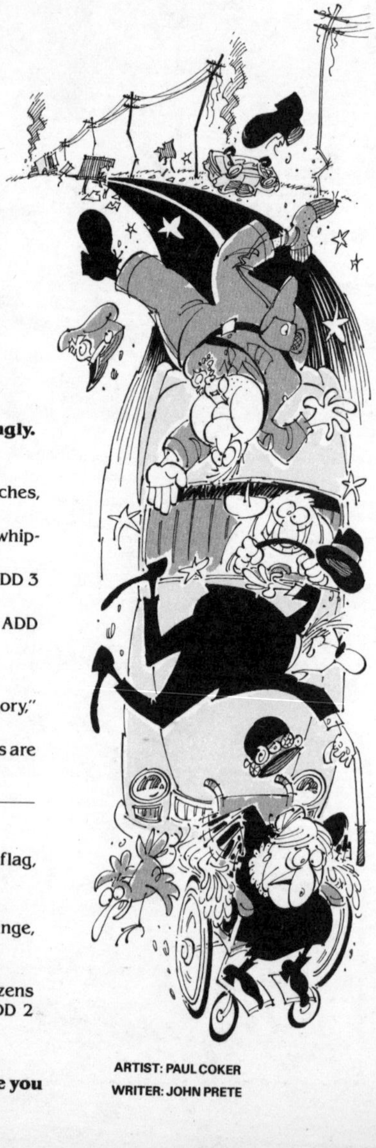

BEGIN with the national speed limit of 55 miles per hour.
ANSWER each question and add or subtract miles accordingly.

PART I—DRIVING HISTORY

1) If the statue of St. Christopher on your dashboard is on crutches, ADD 1 mile.

2) If you've ever received kickbacks from chiropractors for all the whiplash victims you send them, ADD 2 miles.

3) If Lee Iacocca has ever offered you a rebate *not* to buy a car, ADD 3 miles.

4) For each of the following that has been named in your honor, ADD accordingly:

a) A tow truck, ADD 1 mile.
b) A local demolition derby race track, ADD 2 miles.
c) A national auto insurance company's "Extra High Risk Category," ADD 5 miles.

5) On the back of your driver's license where recent traffic violations are listed, if the words "See Attached Sheets" appear, ADD 2 miles.

DRIVING HISTORY SUBTOTAL............................ ______

PART II—ON THE ROAD

1) If you start each morning by pledging allegiance to a checkered flag, ADD 1 mile.

2) If your second car is an ambulance, ADD 2 miles.

3) If, while stopped at an intersection waiting for a red light to change, you...

a) Rev your engine to intimidate those around you, ADD 1 mile.
b) Place both hands on the horn, ready to blare it at senior citizens who might still be crossing when the light turns green, ADD 2 miles.
c) Pick your nose, SUBTRACT 4 miles.

NOTE: If the above question does not apply to you because you never brake for a red light, ADD 5 miles.

ARTIST: PAUL COKER
WRITER: JOHN PRETE

4) For every time you've looked in your rear-view mirror and seen a body lying in the street, ADD 2 miles. (If you've *never* looked in your rear-view mirror, ADD 4 miles.)

5) For each of the following bumper stickers that can be found on your car, ADD 1 mile:

STOP SIGNS ARE FOR SISSIES

SEAT BELTS SUCK

NUKE THE AUTOMOBILE CLUB

HONK IF YOU LOVE HEAD-ONS

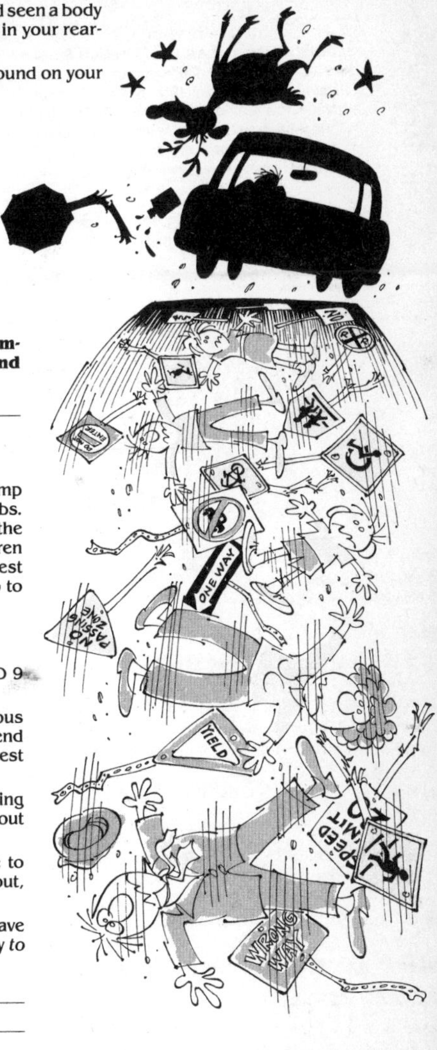
ONE WAY
YIELD
WRONG WAY

NOTE: If the message on your bumper sticker is incomprehensible because of blood splatterings and caked hair, TACK ON an additional 6 miles.

ON THE ROAD SUBTOTAL .... ______

PART III—HYPOTHETICAL SITUATIONS

1) It is a warm, sunny Sunday afternoon. You decide to jump in the car and visit your ailing Aunt Alba in the suburbs. Turning onto Aunt Alba's street, you pass a home for the blind, a "Deer Crossing" sign and a group of small children playing in the street. Which of the following comes closest in length to the skid marks you'll make as you pull up to Aunt Alba's?

a) A standard 30-foot garden hose, ADD 2 miles.

b) An unravelled wool sweater, ADD 5 miles.

c) A computer printout of Joan Collins' ex-lovers, ADD 9 miles.

2) You're sitting over at a friend's home in a semi-conscious state after hours of heavy drinking. Suddenly, your friend announces "Everybody out!" Which of the following best describes what you would do in this situation?

a) Stumble out to your car, spend 15 stupid minutes trying to insert your keys into the ignition, then finally peel out in a screeching blaze of glory, ADD 3 miles.

b) Same as "a," except that you would take the time to throw up in your friend's driveway before you peel out, ADD 4 miles.

c) If the question does not apply because you would have been involved in a drunk driving accident on your way *to* the party, ADD 7 miles.

HYPOTHETICAL QUESTIONS SUBTOTAL .... ______

GRAND TOTAL .... ______

SCORING

51—60

Your driving skills are like those of a recent graduate of a high school Driver's Ed class. In other words, you have none! You are a threat to all life.

61–70

You have the driving skills of a deaf, dumb and blind man! Walk everywhere!!

71 or Above

You have a great future ahead of you as a New York City cab driver! Apply at once!

WOMEN'S GLIB DEPT.

Back in MAD #234, we gave guys hints on "How To Pick Up Girls." Our mail response showed that liberated women of today want equal time when it comes to learning pick-up lines guaranteed to impress great hunks. So, ladies (and, ahem, certain gentlemen) we now present the following batch of ice-breakers, Your guide to...

HOW TO PICK UP GUYS

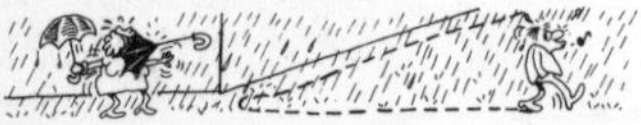

AT A FAST FOOD HANGOUT

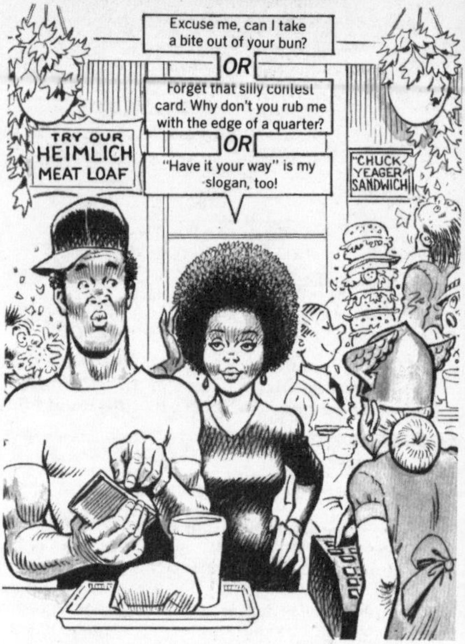
Excuse me, can I take a bite out of your bun?
OR
Forget that silly contest card. Why don't you rub me with the edge of a quarter?
OR
"Have it your way" is my slogan, too!
TRY OUR HEIMLICH MEAT LOAF
"CHUCK YEAGER SANDWICH

AT A FOOTBALL GAME

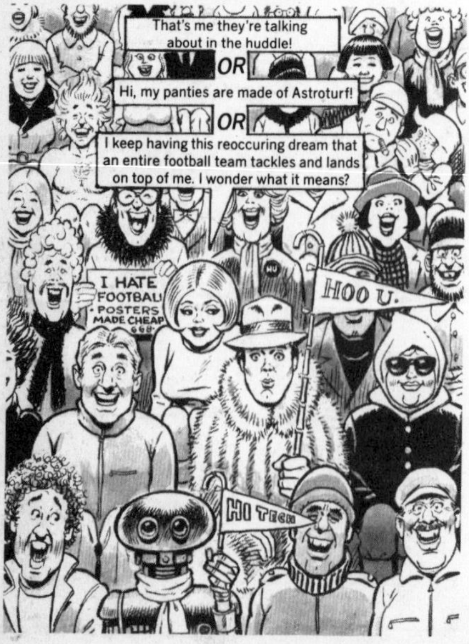
That's me they're talking about in the huddle!
OR
Hi, my panties are made of Astroturf!
OR
I keep having this reoccuring dream that an entire football team tackles and lands on top of me. I wonder what it means?
I HATE FOOTBALL POSTERS MADE CHEAP
HOO U.
HI TECH

AT A SKI RESORT

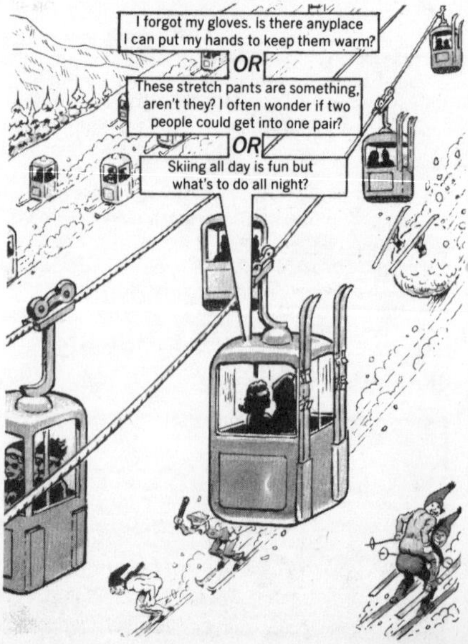
I forgot my gloves. Is there anyplace I can put my hands to keep them warm?
OR
These stretch pants are something, aren't they? I often wonder if two people could get into one pair?
OR
Skiing all day is fun but what's to do all night?

AT A PERSONAL COMPUTER STORE

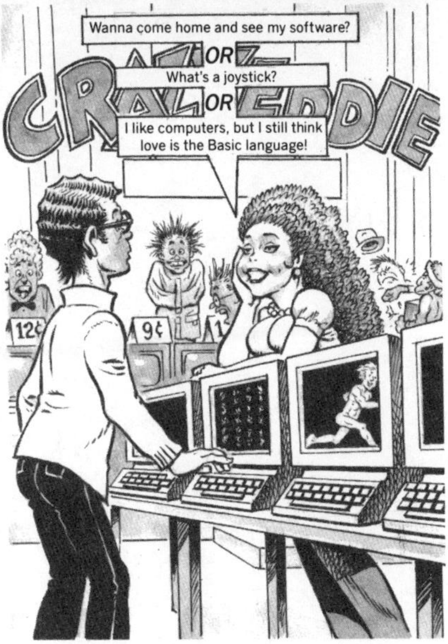
Wanna come home and see my software?
OR
What's a joystick?
OR
I like computers, but I still think love is the Basic language!
12¢
9¢

AT A HEALTH CLUB

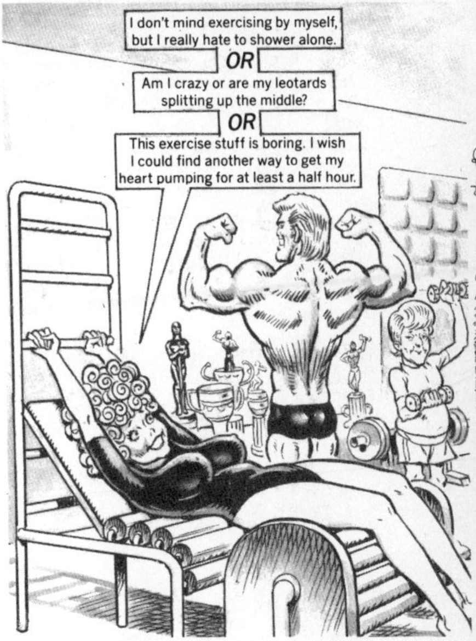
I don't mind exercising by myself, but I really hate to shower alone.
OR
Am I crazy or are my leotards splitting up the middle?
OR
This exercise stuff is boring. I wish I could find another way to get my heart pumping for at least a half hour.

ARTISTS: WILL ELDER AND HARVEY KURTZMAN WRITER: ARNIE KOGEN

AT A SUPERMARKET

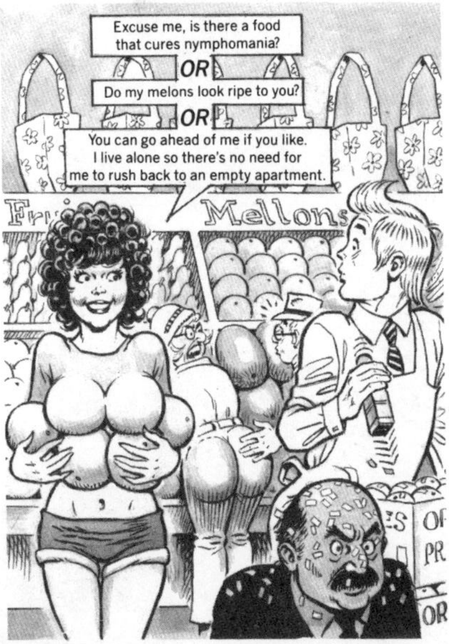
Excuse me, is there a food that cures nymphomania?
OR
Do my melons look ripe to you?
OR
You can go ahead of me if you like. I live alone so there's no need for me to rush back to an empty apartment.
Mellons

AT A BOOKSTORE

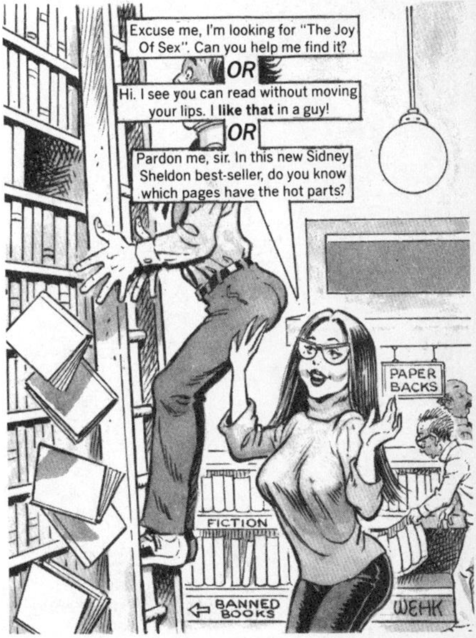
Excuse me, I'm looking for "The Joy Of Sex". Can you help me find it?
OR
Hi. I see you can read without moving your lips. I **like that** in a guy!
OR
Pardon me, sir. In this new Sidney Sheldon best-seller, do you know which pages have the hot parts?
PAPER BACKS
FICTION
BANNED BOOKS
WEHK

JOKE AND DAGGER DEPT.

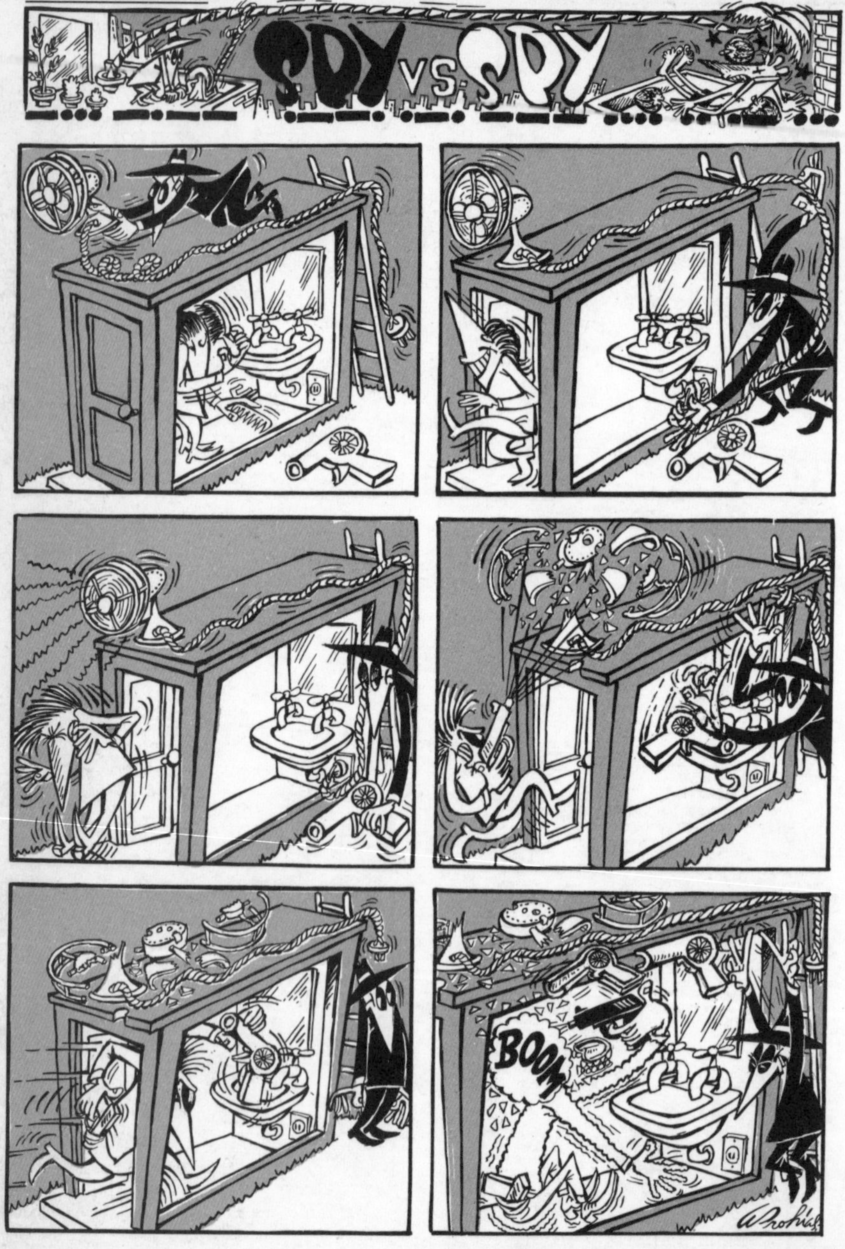
SPY VS. SPY
BOOM

WORKING OFF THE (COMIC) BOOKS DEPT.

IF SUPER-HEROES NEEDED EXTRA MONEY

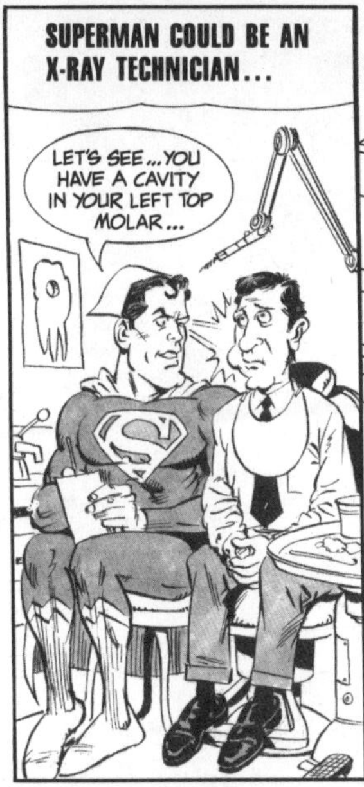
SUPERMAN COULD BE AN X-RAY TECHNICIAN...
LET'S SEE...YOU HAVE A CAVITY IN YOUR LEFT TOP MOLAR...

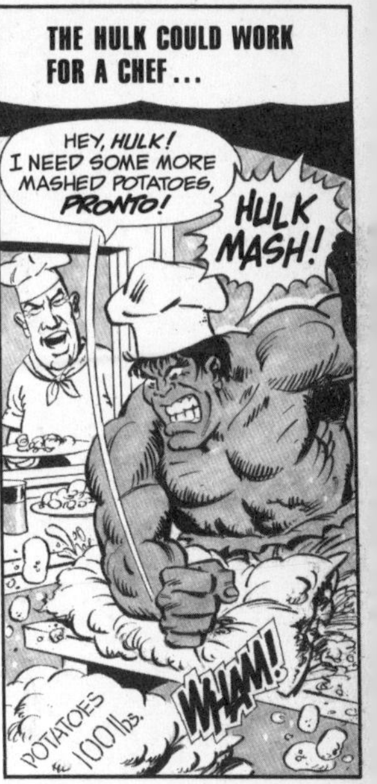
THE HULK COULD WORK FOR A CHEF...
HEY, HULK! I NEED SOME MORE MASHED POTATOES, PRONTO!
HULK MASH!
WHAM!
POTATOES 100 lbs.

ARTIST: ANGELO TORRES WRITER: BOB SUPINA

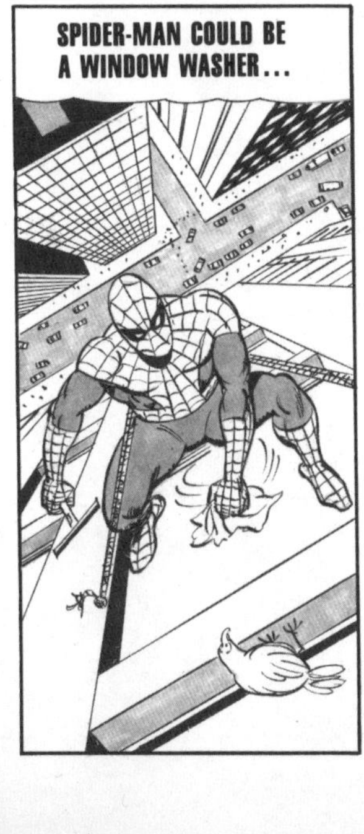
SPIDER-MAN COULD BE A WINDOW WASHER...

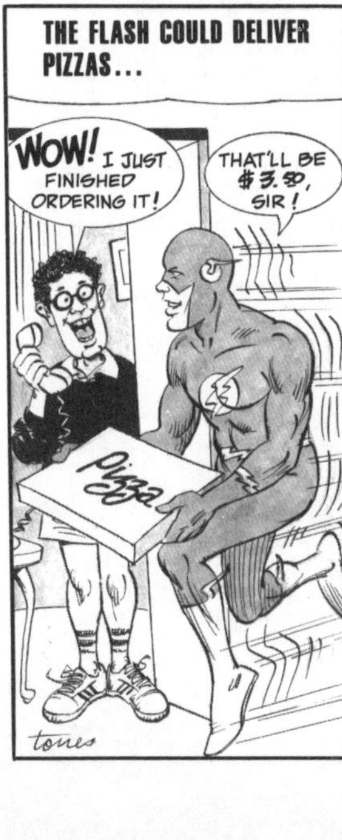
THE FLASH COULD DELIVER PIZZAS...
WOW! I JUST FINISHED ORDERING IT!
THAT'LL BE $3.50, SIR!
pizza

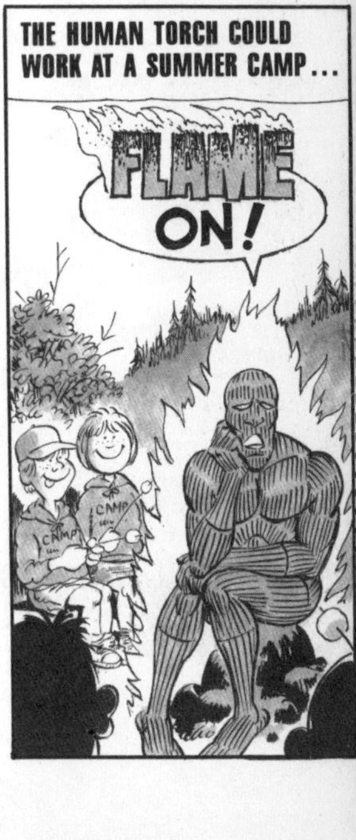
THE HUMAN TORCH COULD WORK AT A SUMMER CAMP...
FLAME ON!
CAMP
CAMP

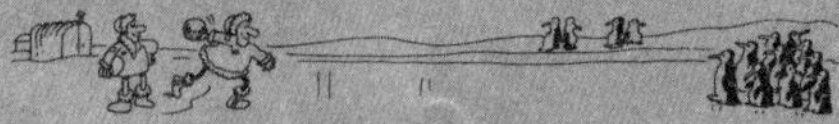

DATING

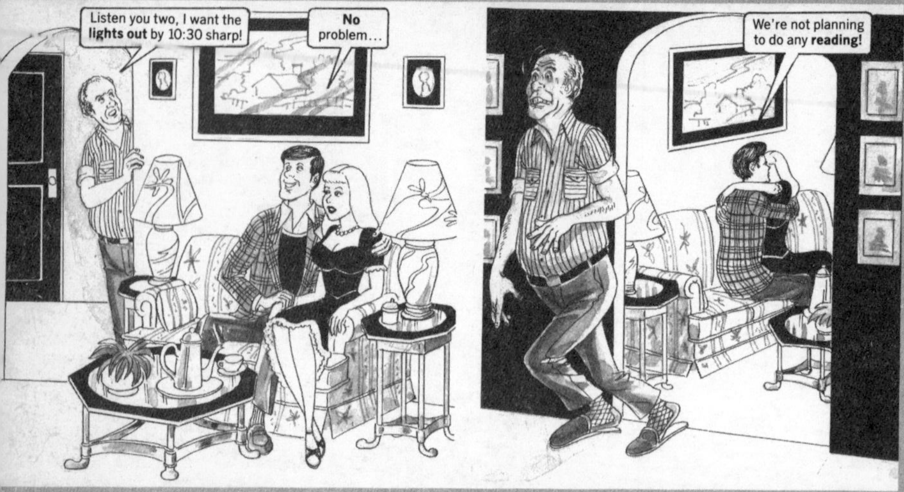

Listen you two, I want the **lights out** by 10:30 sharp!
No problem...
We're not planning to do any **reading!**

BERG'S-EYE VIEW DEPT.

THE LIGHTE

KNOWLEDGE

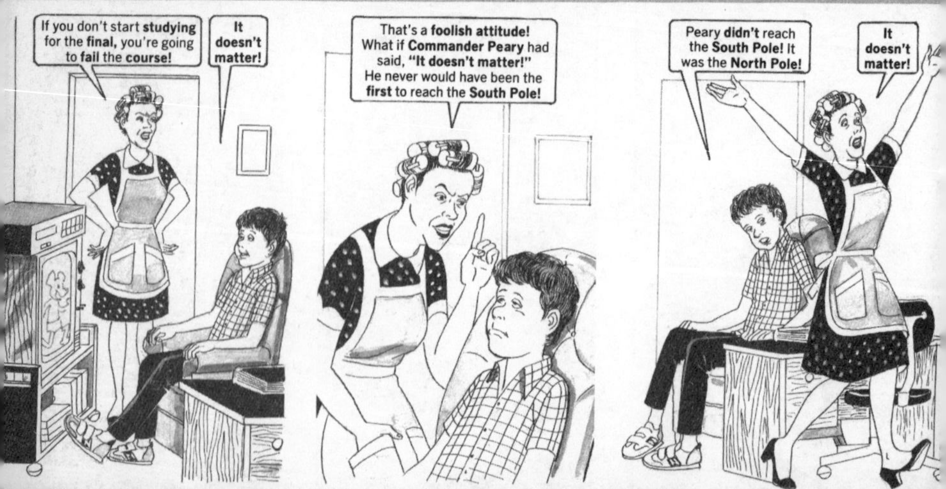

If you don't start **studying** for the **final,** you're going to **fail** the **course!**
It doesn't matter!
That's a **foolish attitude!** What if **Commander Peary** had said, **"It doesn't matter!"** He never would have been the **first** to reach the **South Pole!**
Peary **didn't** reach the **South Pole!** It was the **North Pole!**
It doesn't matter!

COLLEGE

Laura, isn't this your son's first year away at college?
Yes, he's majoring in Communications!
That's nice! How's he doing?
It's hard to say...
...he never phones or writes!

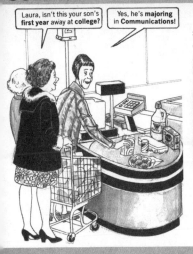

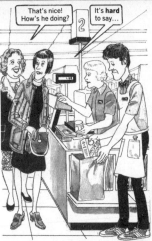

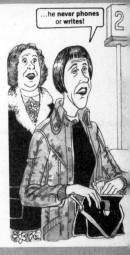

R SIDE OF...

ARTIST & WRITER:
DAVE BERG

GETTING CAUGHT

I just got nailed for reckless driving!
You gotta be kidding! What did you do?
I was driving very slowly in my convertible with the top down and Nicole La Palme sitting close beside me...
What's reckless about that?
My girlfriend saw us!

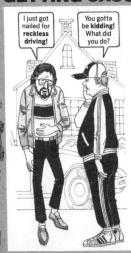

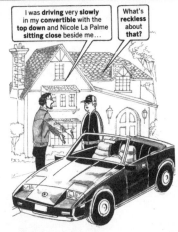

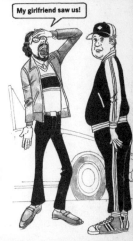

CULTURE

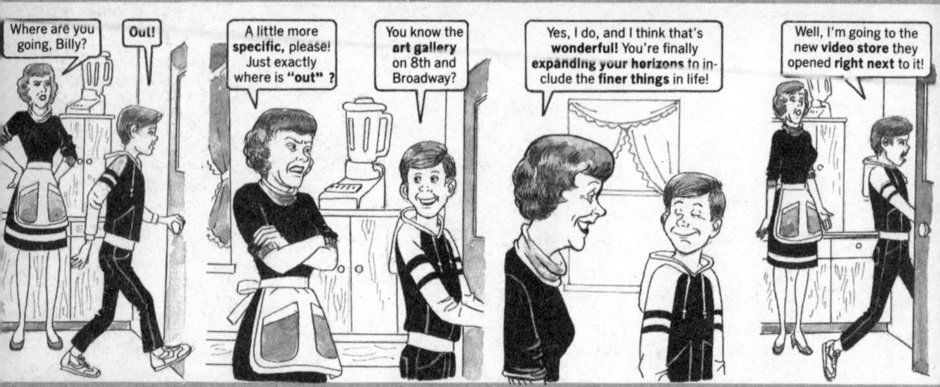

Where are you going, Billy?
Out!
A little more **specific,** please! Just exactly where is **"out"** ?
You know the **art gallery** on 8th and Broadway?
Yes, I do, and I think that's **wonderful!** You're finally **expanding your horizons** to include the **finer things** in life!
Well, I'm going to the new **video store** they opened **right next** to it!

PICKUPS

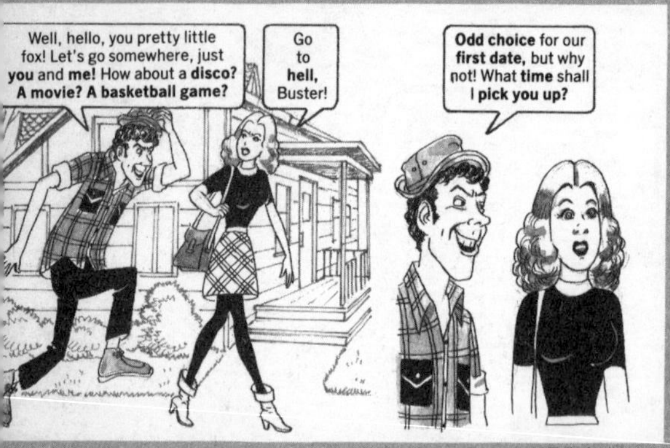

Well, hello, you pretty little fox! Let's go somewhere, just **you** and **me!** How about a **disco? A movie? A basketball game?**
Go to **hell,** Buster!
Odd choice for our **first date,** but why not! What **time** shall I **pick you up?**

ARGUMENTS

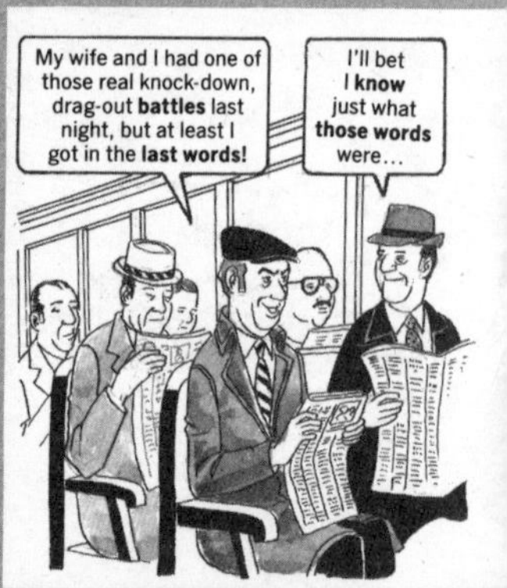

My wife and I had one of those real knock-down, drag-out **battles** last night, but at least I got in the **last words!**
I'll bet I **know** just what **those words** were...

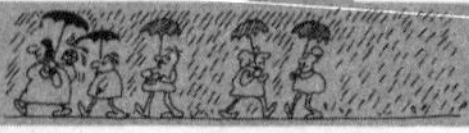

MATHEMATICS

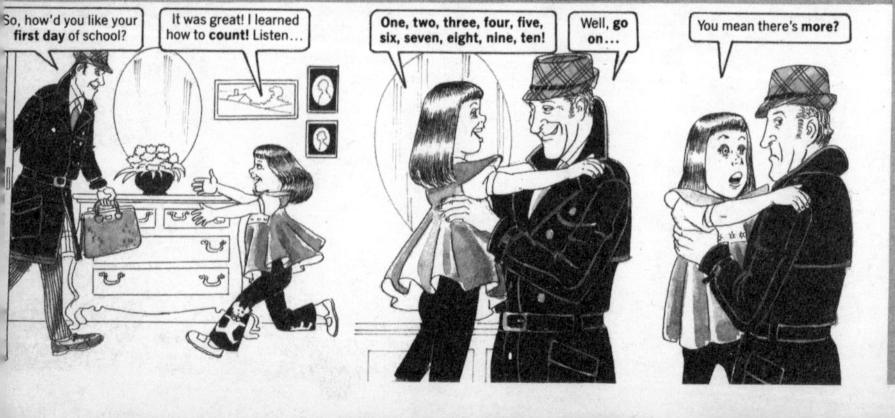

So, how'd you like your **first day** of school?
It was great! I learned how to **count!** Listen...
One, two, three, four, five, six, seven, eight, nine, ten!
Well, **go on...**
You mean there's **more?**

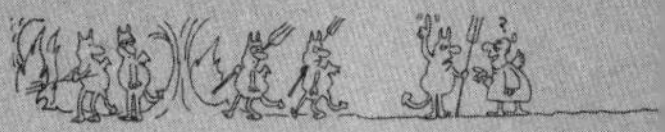

WRESTLING

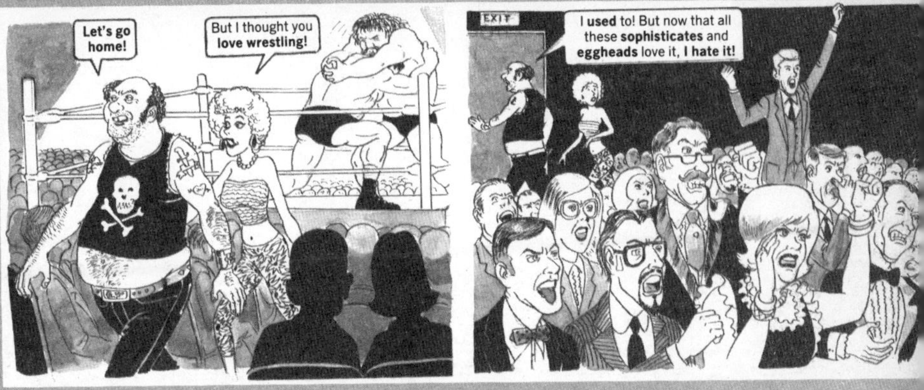
Let's go home!
But I thought you love wrestling!
EXIT
I used to! But now that all these sophisticates and eggheads love it, I hate it!

PSYCHOLOGY

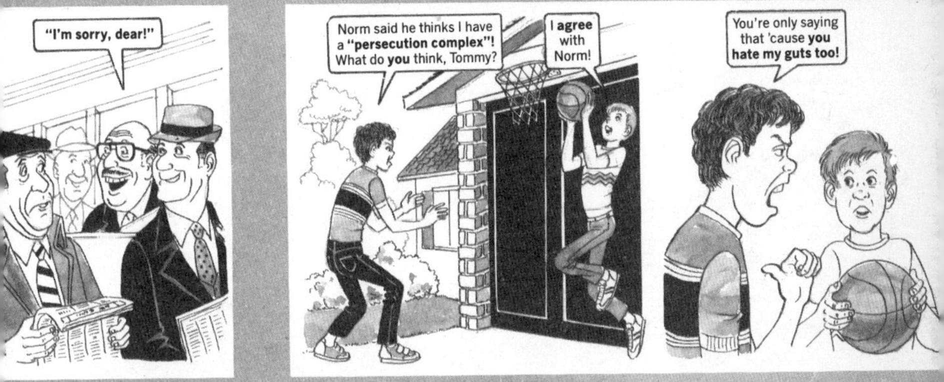
"I'm sorry, dear!"
Norm said he thinks I have a "persecution complex"! What do you think, Tommy?
I agree with Norm!
You're only saying that 'cause you hate my guts too!

MARRIAGE

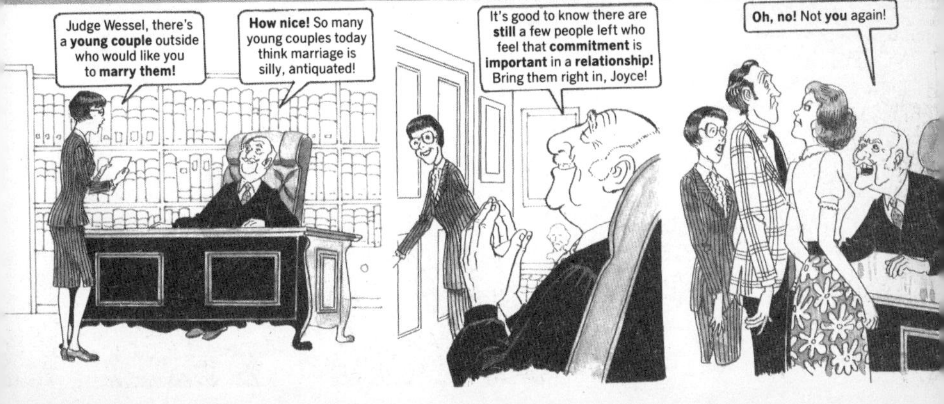
Judge Wessel, there's a young couple outside who would like you to marry them!
How nice! So many young couples today think marriage is silly, antiquated!
It's good to know there are still a few people left who feel that commitment is important in a relationship! Bring them right in, Joyce!
Oh, no! Not you again!

BEING ON TIME

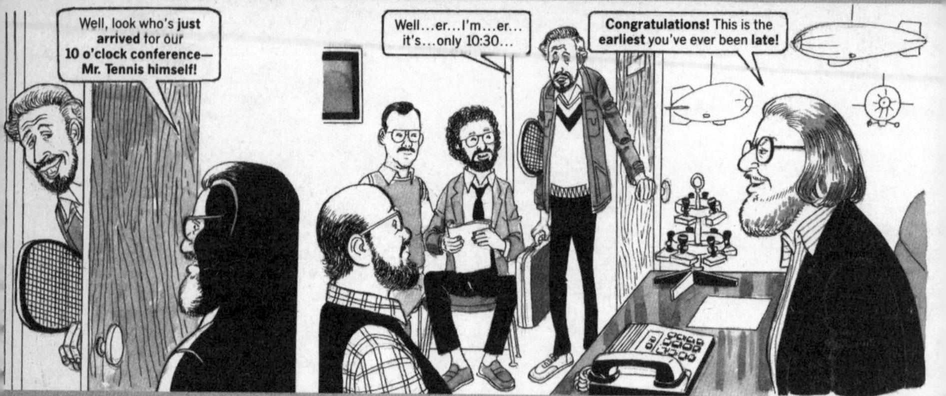
Well, look who's **just arrived** for our **10 o'clock conference—Mr. Tennis himself!**
Well...er...I'm...er... it's...only 10:30...
Congratulations! This is the **earliest** you've ever been **late!**

TRAVEL

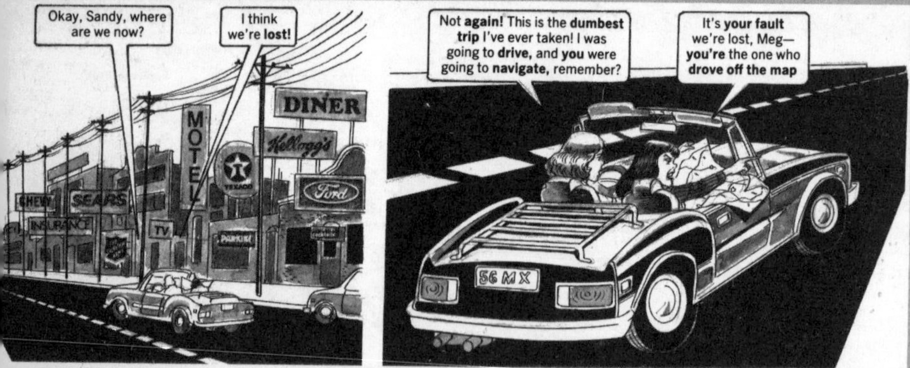
Okay, Sandy, where are we now?
I think we're **lost!**
DINER
MOTEL
Kellogg's
TEXACO
Ford
CHEVY
SEARS
INSURANCE
TV
Not **again!** This is the **dumbest trip** I've ever taken! I was going to **drive,** and **you** were going to **navigate,** remember?
It's **your fault** we're lost, Meg—**you're** the one who **drove off the map**
56 MX

DOCTORS

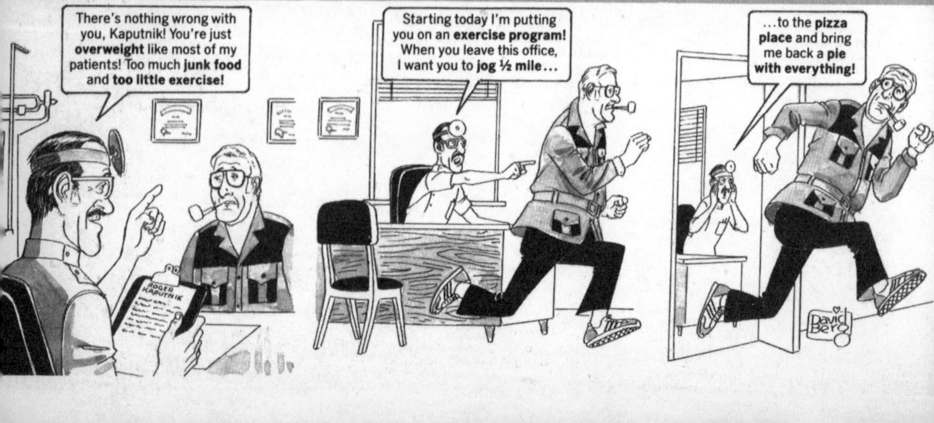
There's nothing wrong with you, Kaputnik! You're just **overweight** like most of my patients! Too much **junk food** and **too little exercise!**
ROGER KAPUTNIK
Starting today I'm putting you on an **exercise program!** When you leave this office, I want you to **jog ½ mile...**
...to the **pizza place** and bring me back a **pie with everything!**
David Berg

OUR CREATURE PRESENTATION DEPT.

HORRIFYING CRIME CLICHES...

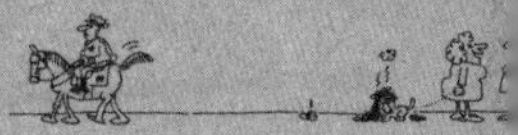

ARTIST: PAUL COKER WRITER: FRANK JACOBS

Packing A ROD

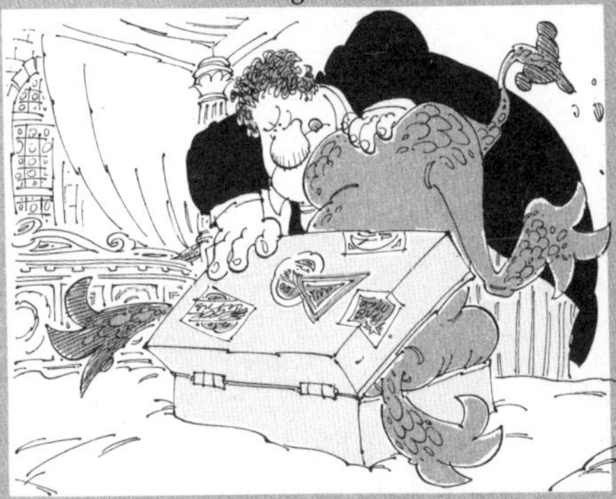

Committing A FELONY

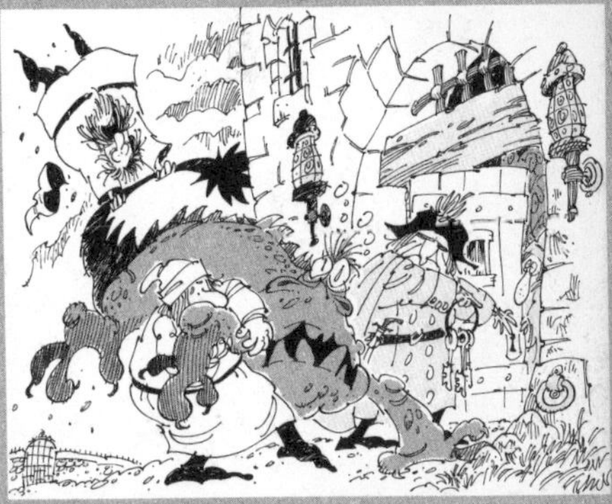

Running A RACKET

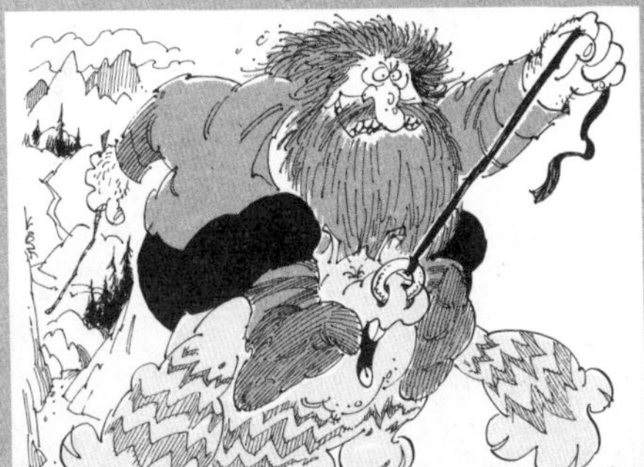

Putting Out A CONTRACT

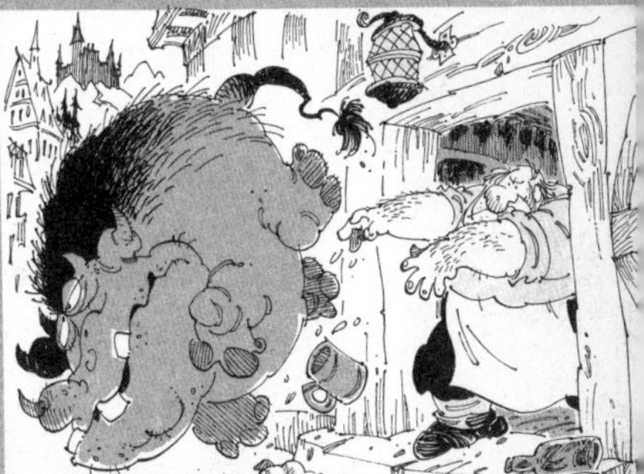

Ignoring A SUMMONS

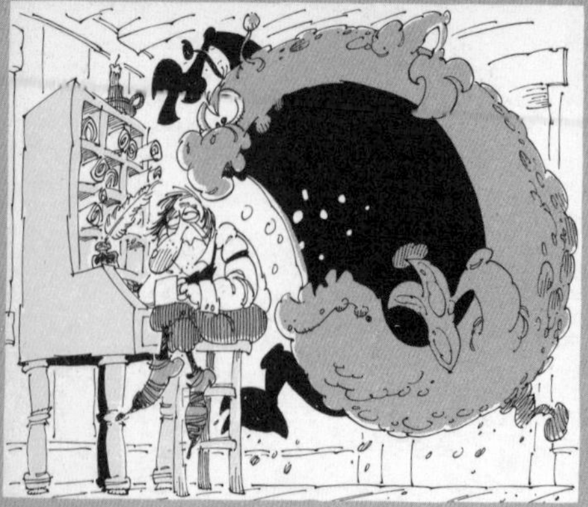

Pulling Off A CAPER

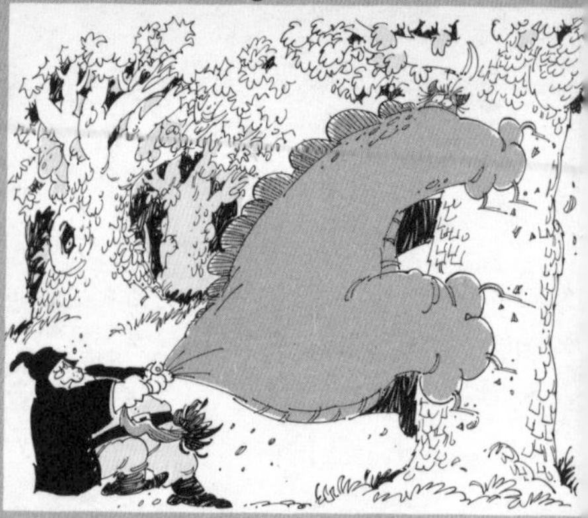

Impaneling A JURY

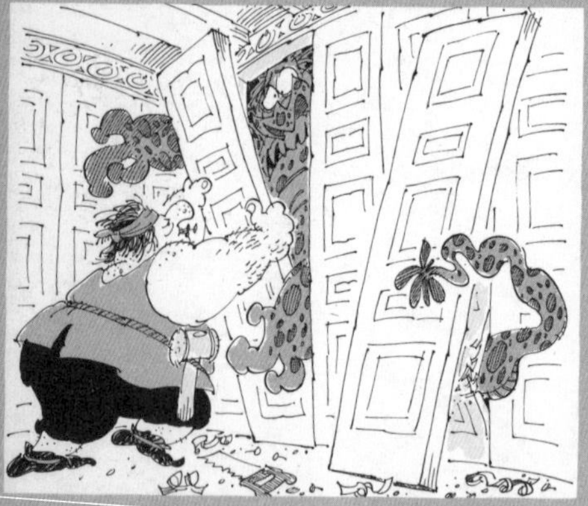

Delivering A VERDICT

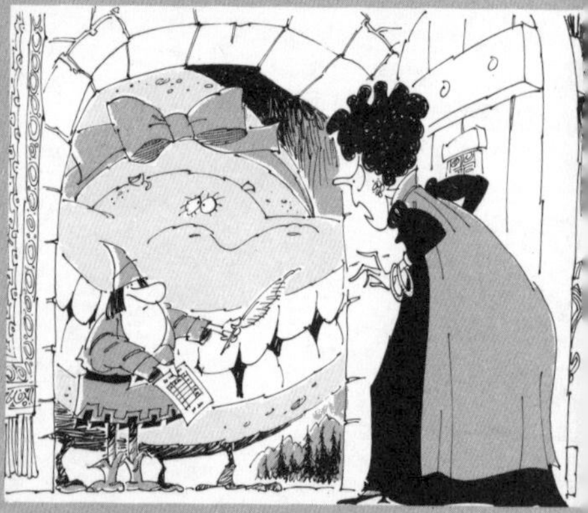

Getting Off With An ACQUITTAL

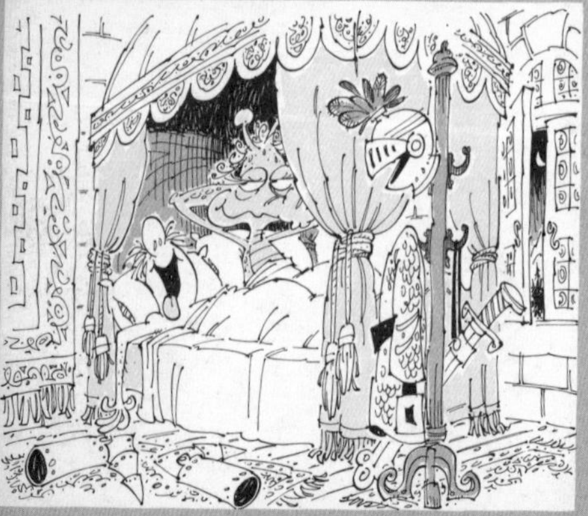

Filing An APPEAL

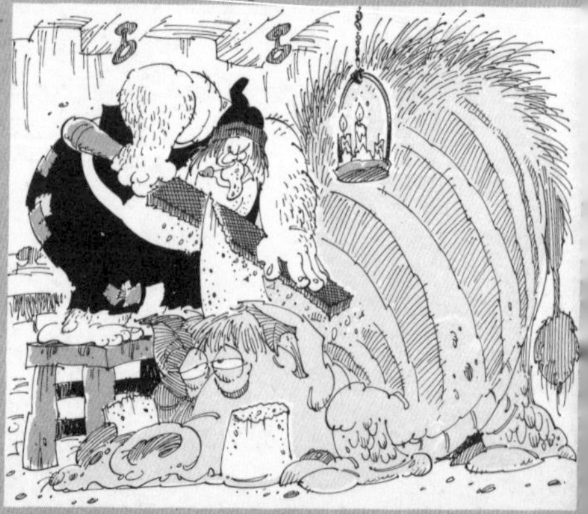

Ducking A WARRANT

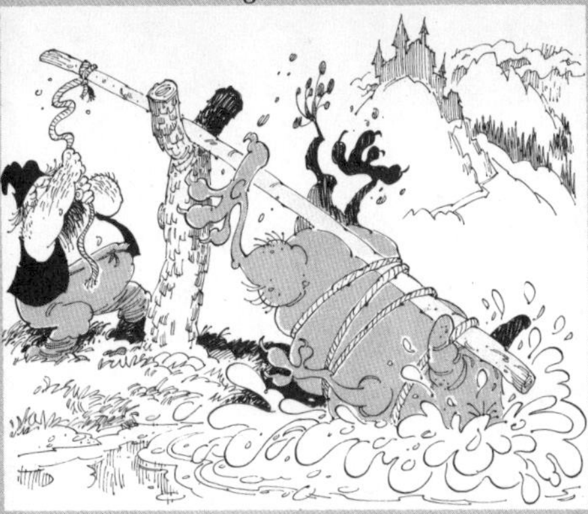

Copping A PLEA

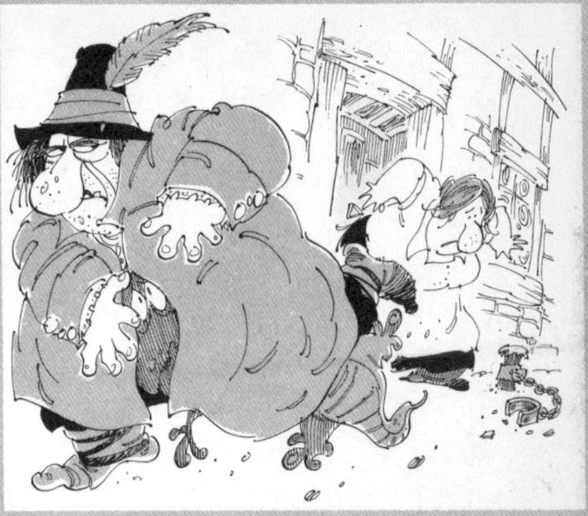

Beating A RAP

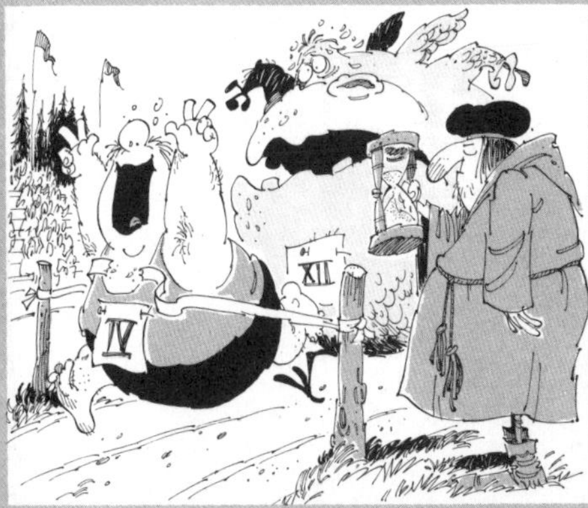
IV
XII

Suspending A SENTENCE

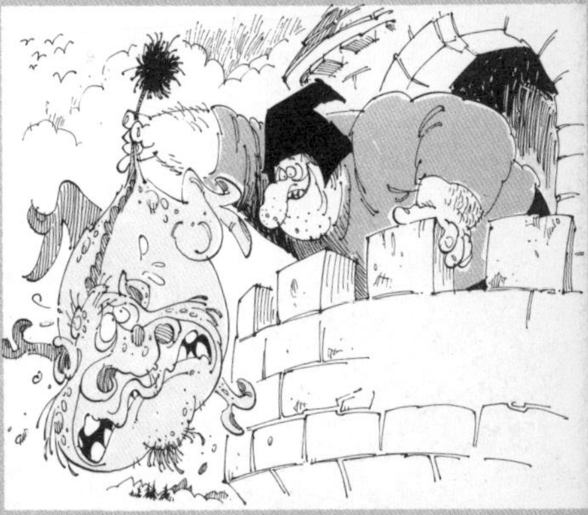

Overturning A CONVICTION

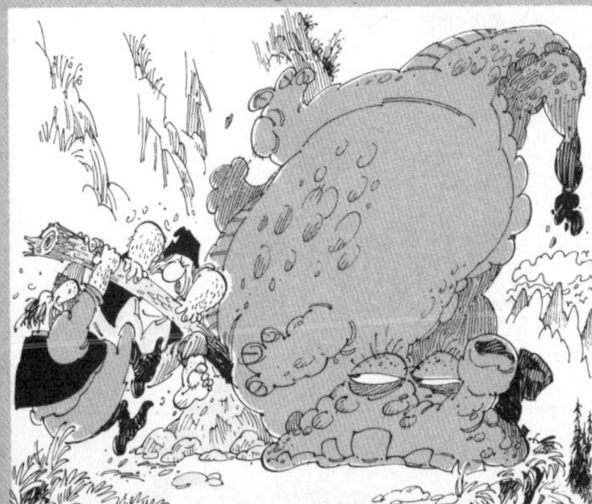

Serving A STIFF TERM

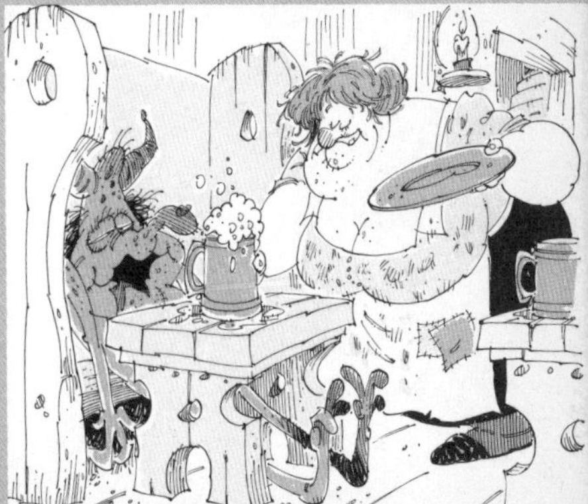

A VIEW TO A SPILL DEPT.

"Experts" say there was no damaging effect to the surrounding area when radiation accidentally

THE THREE MILE ISLA

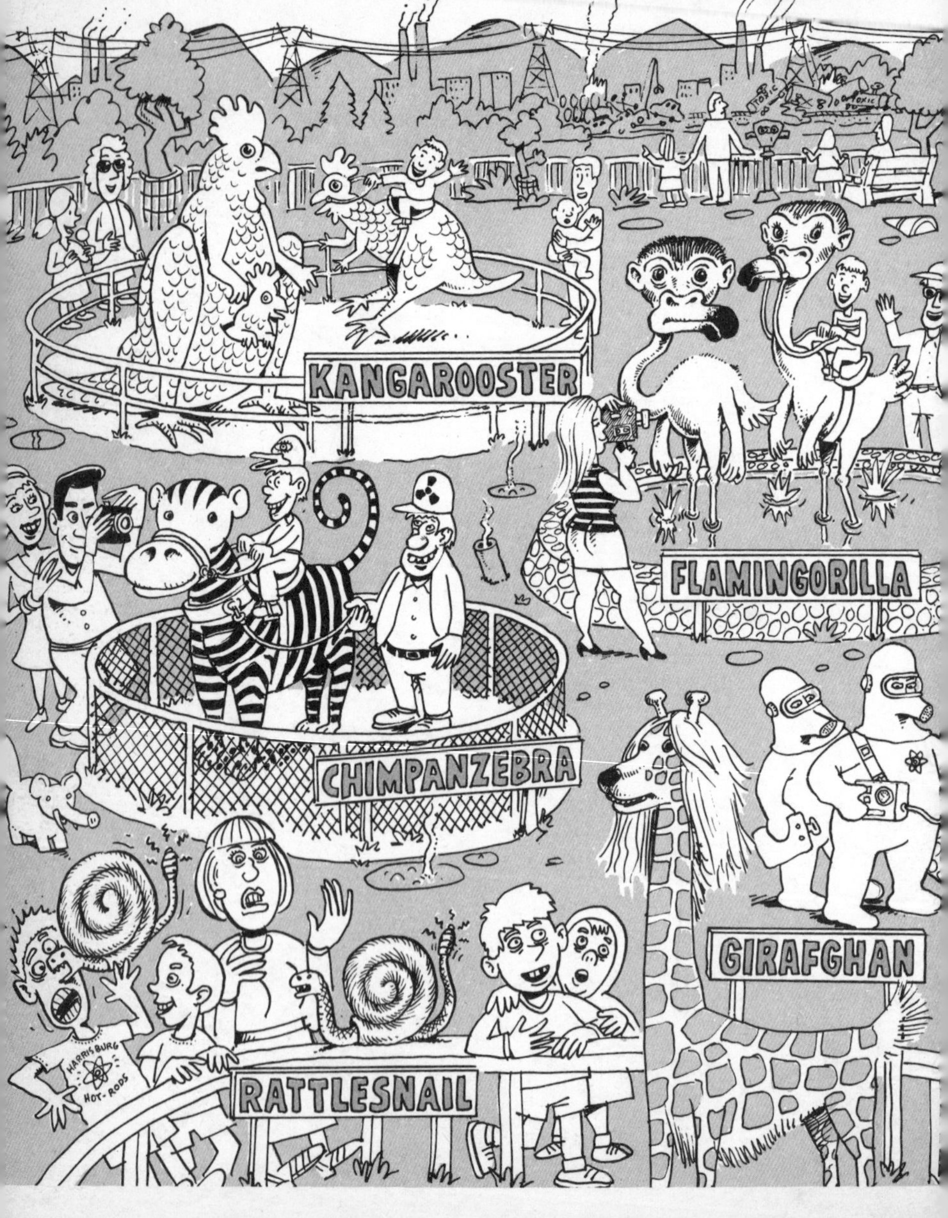

TOXIC
TOXIC
KANGAROOSTER
FLAMINGORILLA
CHIMPANZEBRA
GIRAFGHAN
HARRISBURG HOT-RODS
RATTLESNAIL

ked out at the Three Mile Island nuclear reactor. We're not so sure. Look what we found at...

ND CHILDREN'S ZOO

ARTIST AND WRITER: TOM HACHTMAN

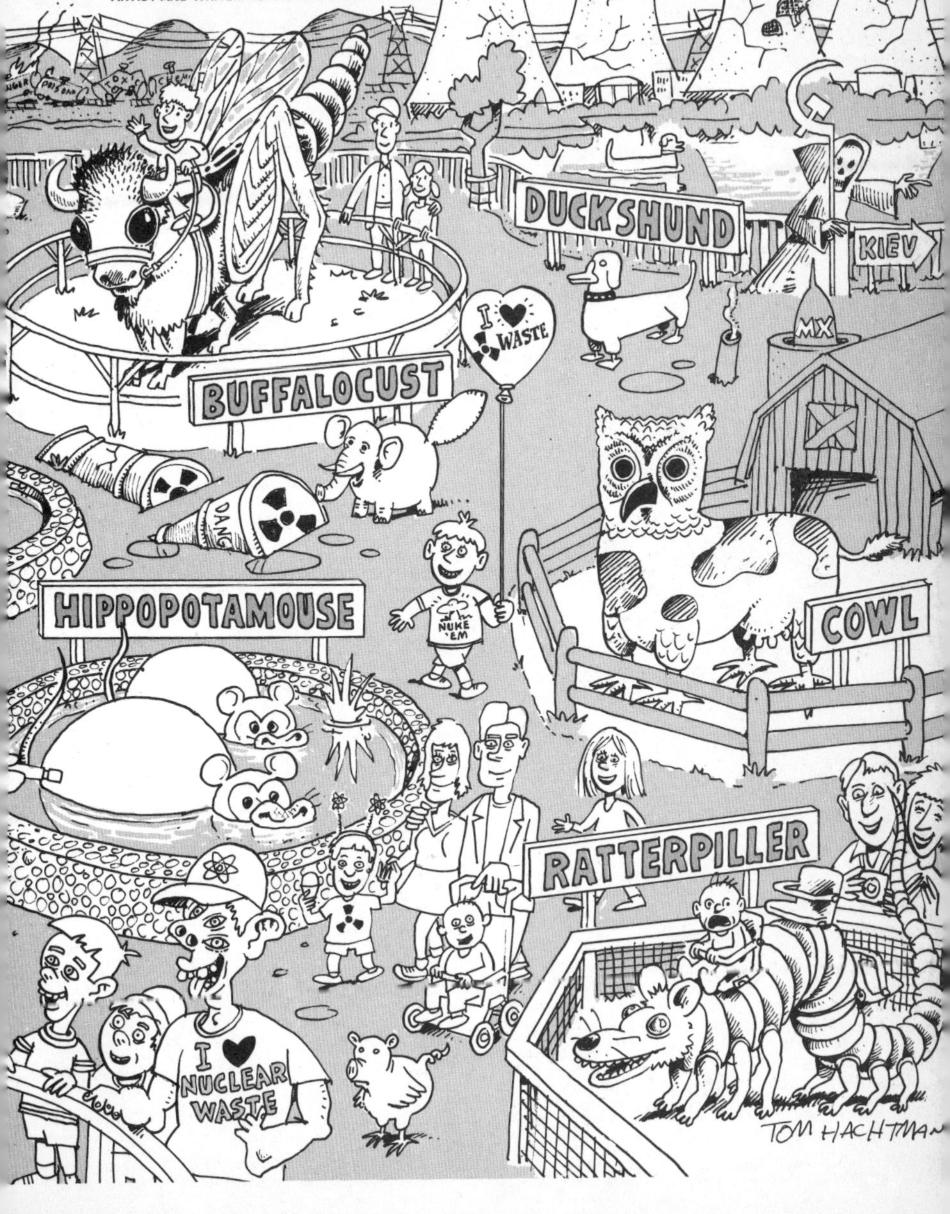

DUCKSHUND
KIEV
I ♥ WASTE
MX
BUFFALOCUST
HIPPOPOTAMOUSE
NUKE 'EM
COWL
RATTERPILLER
I ♥ NUCLEAR WASTE
TOM HACHTMAN

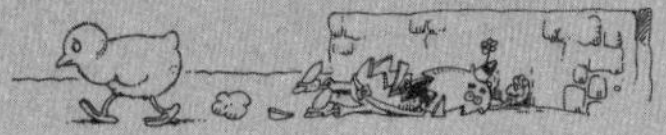

SHUNS OF PITCHES DEPT.

And now the sharp eyes of MAD take a long hard look at

Those Ridiculous lit

ARTIST: GEORGE WOODBRIDG

TV COMMERCIALS SAY RIDICULOUS THINGS LIKE

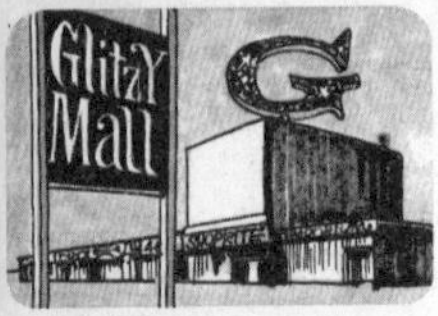
Glitzy Mall
G

The Do-It-Yourself Emporium is conveniently located in the New Glitzy Mall near East Wuthering Heights.

THINKING ABOUT IT THIS MUST MEAN...

The location is "convenient" for everyone who lives in the part of East Wuthering Heights that's near the New Glitzy Mall. From 25 miles away it's a lot less convenient, but they hope you won't realize that until you're already on the road.

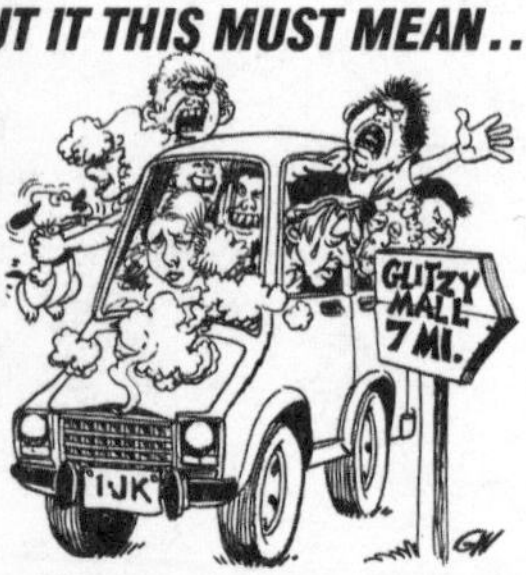
GLITZY MALL 7 MI.
IJK
GW

TV COMMERCIALS SAY RIDICULOUS THINGS LIKE

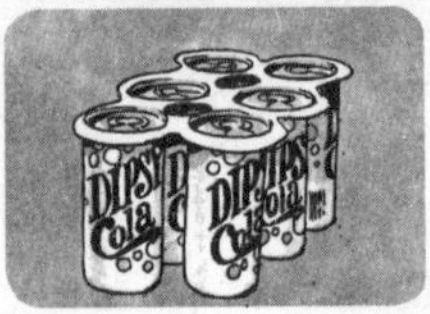
DIPSY Cola

Dipsy-Cola is now available in handy six-packs at your favorite store.

THINKING ABOUT IT THIS MUST MEAN...

They're surely aware that exclusive clothing shops and jewelry salons don't sell soft drinks, so they obviously assume your favorite store is a crowded, smelly supermarket.

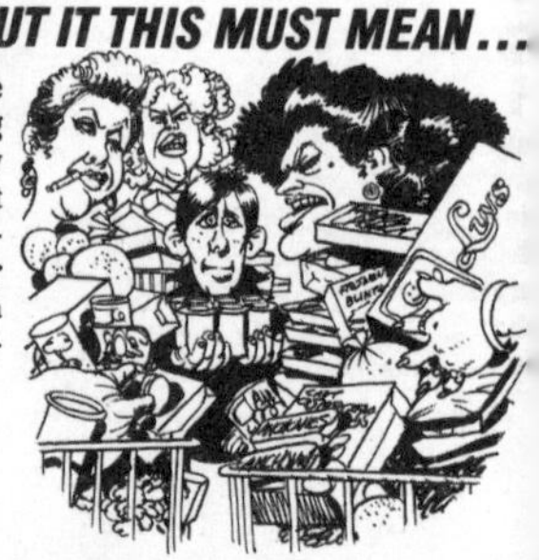

TV COMMERCIALS SAY RIDICULOUS THINGS LIKE

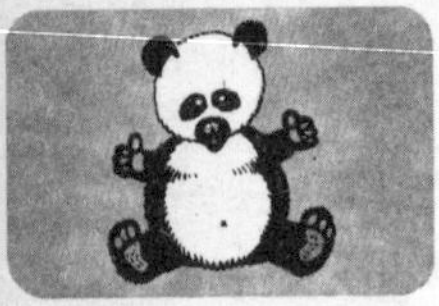

You must act quickly to get one of these gorgeous stuffed pandas because the supply is limited.

THINKING ABOUT IT THIS MUST MEAN...

Even five million lousy pandas can be considered a "limited" supply when compared to the infinite quantities of such things as outer space, rainwater, a Mother's love and the gas you get from eating baked beans.

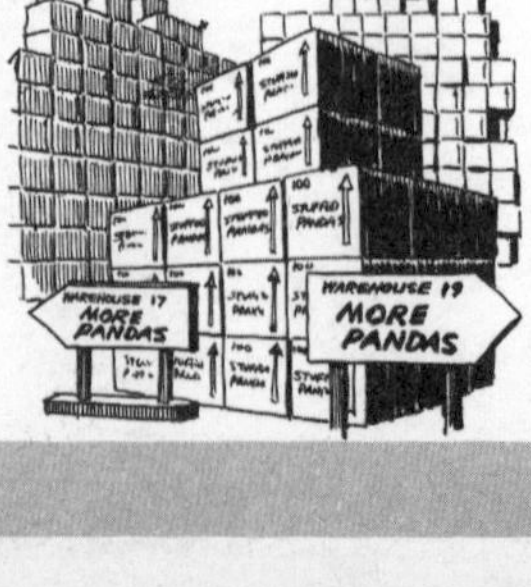
WAREHOUSE 17 MORE PANDAS
WAREHOUSE 19 MORE PANDAS

TV COMMERCIALS SAY RIDICULOUS THINGS LIKE

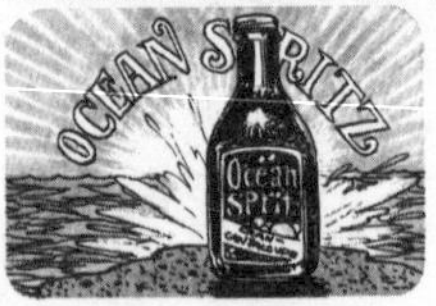
OCEAN SPRITZ
Ocean Spritz

For maximum savings, get Ocean Spritz Cran-Cantaloupe Juice in the big full quart bottle.

THINKING ABOUT IT THIS MUST MEAN...

They helpfully call it a "big full" quart bottle so you won't get it confused with some other size of quart bottle, such as the small partly empty quart bottle or the gigantic overflowing quart bottle.

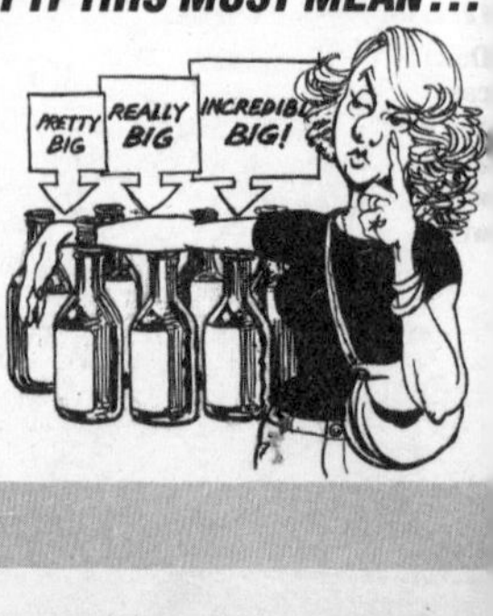
PRETTY BIG
REALLY BIG
INCREDIBL BIG!

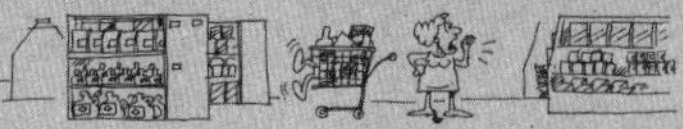

Things TV Commercials Say!

WRITER: TOM KOCH

TV COMMERCIALS SAY RIDICULOUS THINGS LIKE

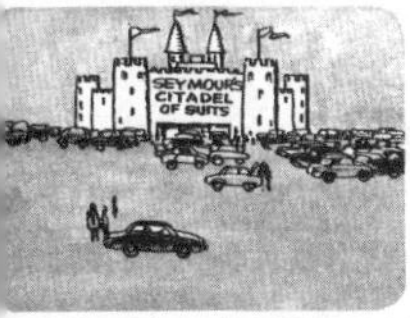
SEYMOUR'S CITADEL OF SUITS

At Seymour's Citadel of Suits, there's always a full acre of free parking.

THINKING ABOUT IT THIS MUST MEAN...

The clothing they sell may shrink, but they give you their unconditional guarantee that the size of their parking lot remains unchanged from day to day.

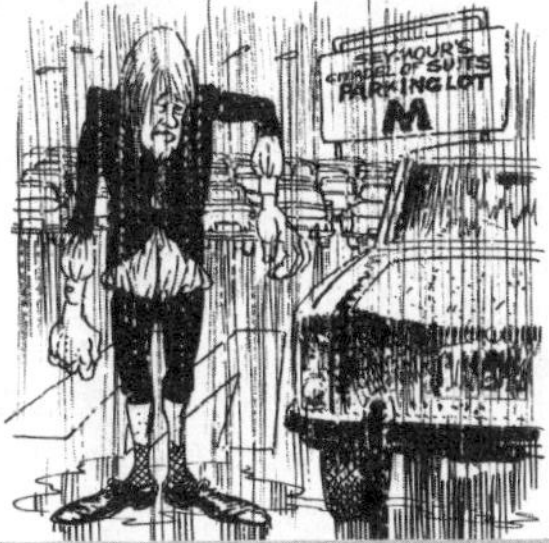
SEYMOUR'S CITADEL OF SUITS PARKING LOT
M

TV COMMERCIALS SAY RIDICULOUS THINGS LIKE

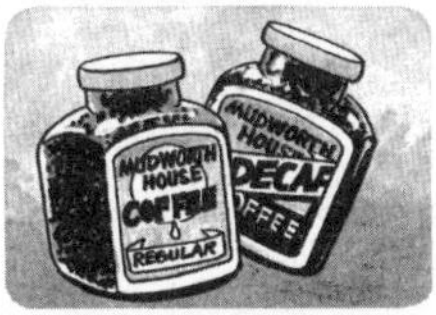
MUDWORTH HOUSE COFFEE
REGULAR
MUDWORTH HOUSE DECAF COFFEE

Mudworth House is now available in both regular blend and new decaffeinated. Ask for it by name.

THINKING ABOUT IT THIS MUST MEAN...

They prefer you ask for their product by name because it wastes too much time when you play Charades with the grocer to make him guess what it is you want.

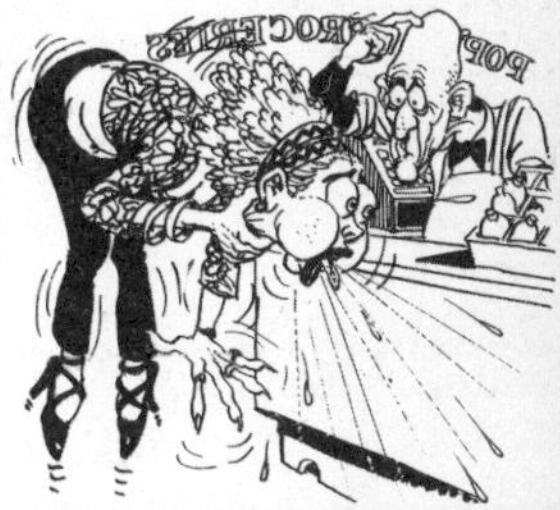
GROCERIES
POP'S

TV COMMERCIALS SAY RIDICULOUS THINGS LIKE

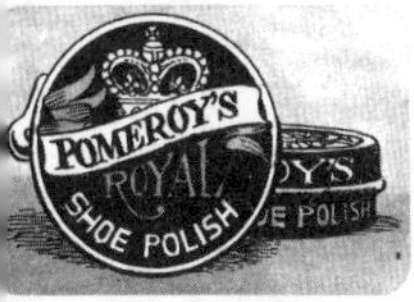
POMEROY'S
ROYAL
SHOE POLISH

Pomeroy's Shoe Polish is available at better stores everywhere.

THINKING ABOUT IT THIS MUST MEAN...

Don't blame them if you can't find it. The obvious problem is you do all your shopping at worse stores everywhere.

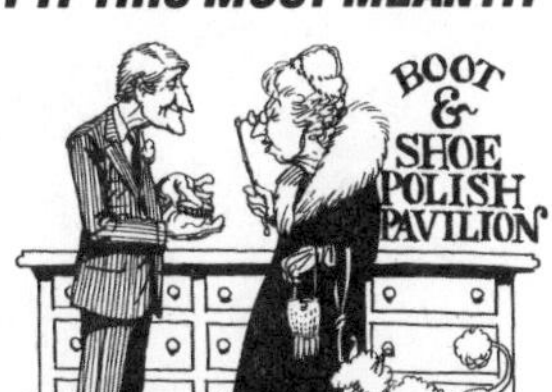
BOOT & SHOE POLISH PAVILION

TV COMMERCIALS SAY RIDICULOUS THINGS LIKE

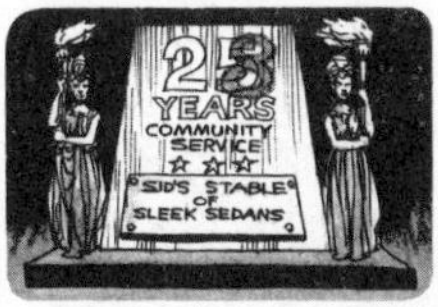
25 YEARS
COMMUNITY SERVICE
SID'S STABLE OF SLEEK SEDANS

Come see us at Smiling Sid's Stable of Sleek Sedans, where we have been serving the community since 1957.

THINKING ABOUT IT THIS MUST MEAN...

They're trying to gain your trust and regain their own self-respect with the preposterous claim that a used car lot is somehow "serving the community."

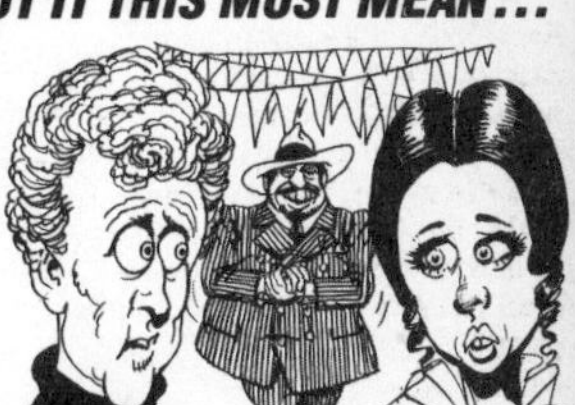

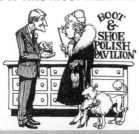

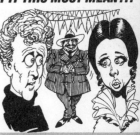

SERGIO ARAGONES DEPT.

HEAD TRIP

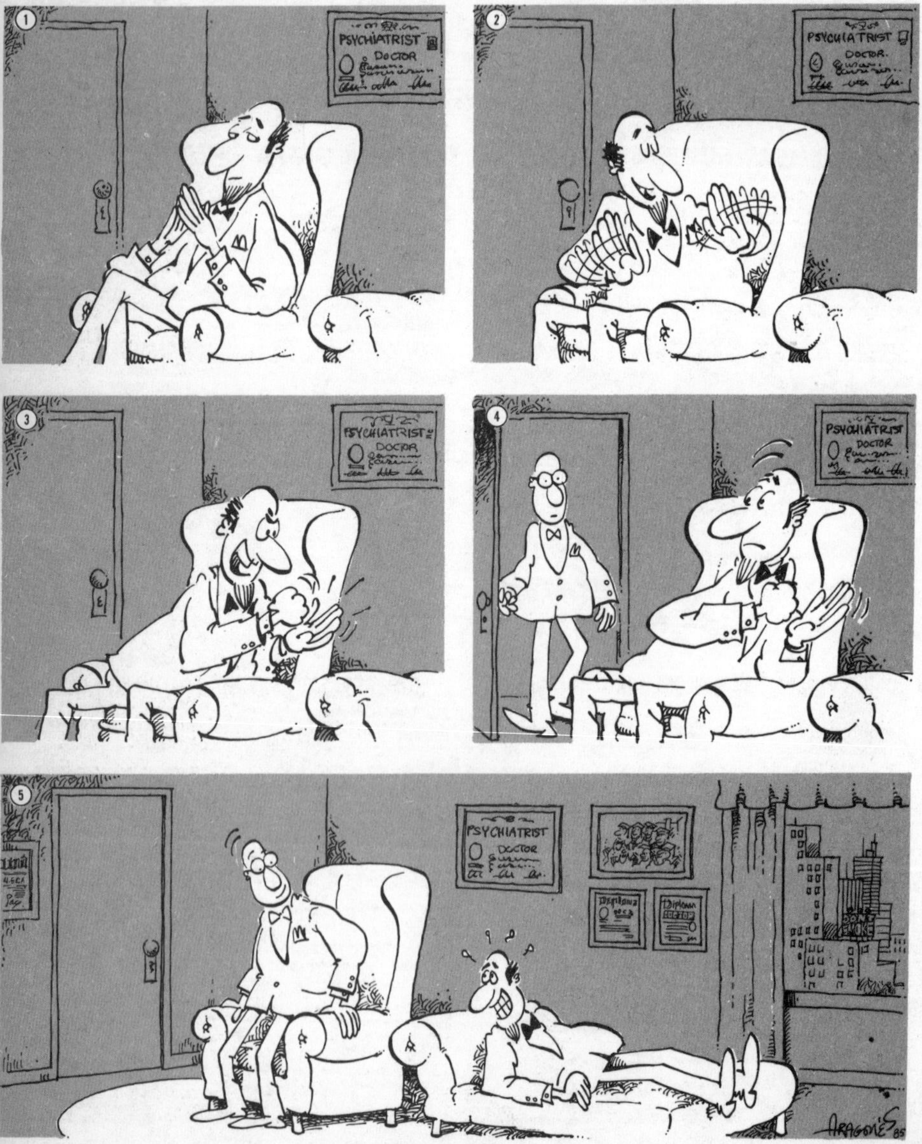
1
PSYCHIATRIST
DOCTOR
2
PSYCHIATRIST
DOCTOR.
3
PSYCHIATRIST
DOCTOR
4
PSYCHIATRIST
DOCTOR
5
PSYCHIATRIST
DOCTOR
Diploma
Diploma
ARAGONES 85

ARTIST AND WRITER: SERGIO ARAGONES

JOKE AND DAGGER DEPT.

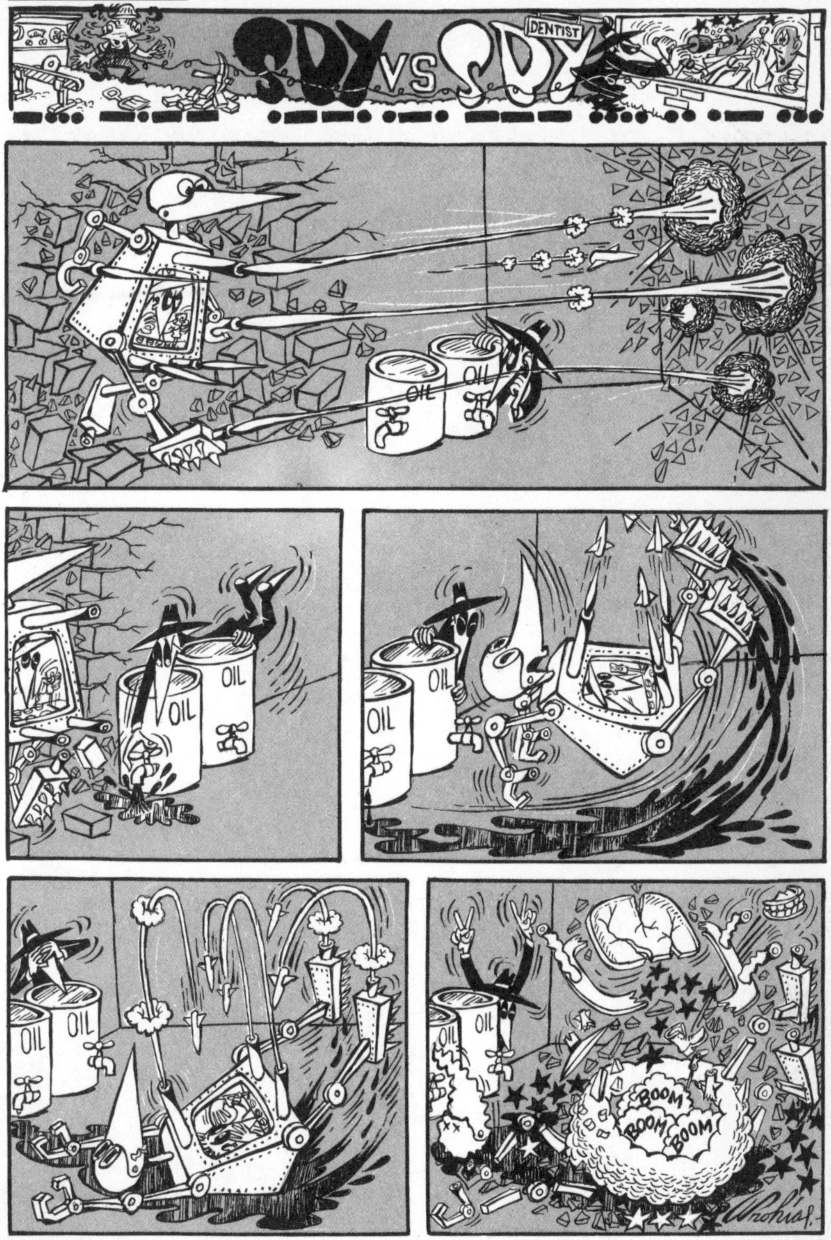
SPY VS SPY
DENTIST
OIL
OIL
OIL
OIL
OIL
OIL
OIL
OIL
OIL
BOOM
BOOM
BOOM
Prohias

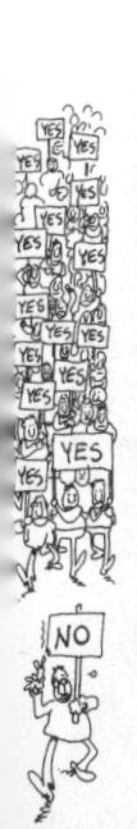
YES
NO

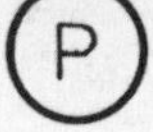
P

Use any solvent
except trichloroethyler

ZINGER AROUND THE COLLAR DEPT.

Those strange doodles shown above are some of the many "Clothing Care Symbols" found on shirts and other garments. We at MAD don't think the are very practical (especially since we neve

NEW CLOTHING CARE SYM

ARTIST: BOB CLAR

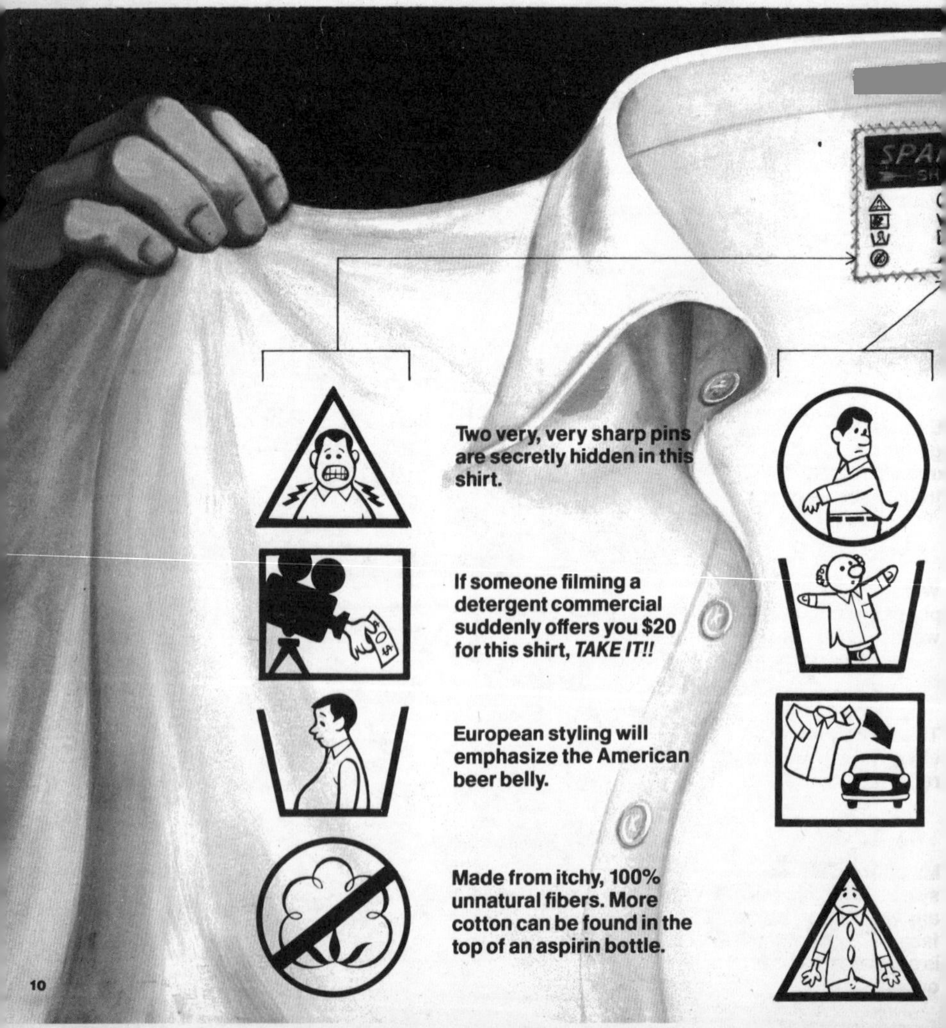
Two very, very sharp pins are secretly hidden in this shirt.
If someone filming a detergent commercial suddenly offers you $20 for this shirt, *TAKE IT!!*
European styling will emphasize the American beer belly.
Made from itchy, 100% unnatural fibers. More cotton can be found in the top of an aspirin bottle.

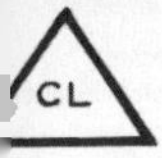

Use chlorine bleach as directed on the container label.

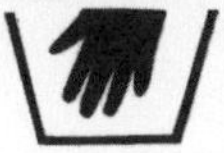

Hand washable using lukewarm water.

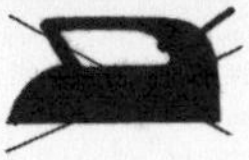

Do not press or iron.

laundry)! We think garment makers could do all a favor by using symbols for information that's *really* important! So, with that in mind, we take unusual pleasure in introducing these...

LS THAT TELL IT LIKE IT IS

RITER: CHARLIE KADAU

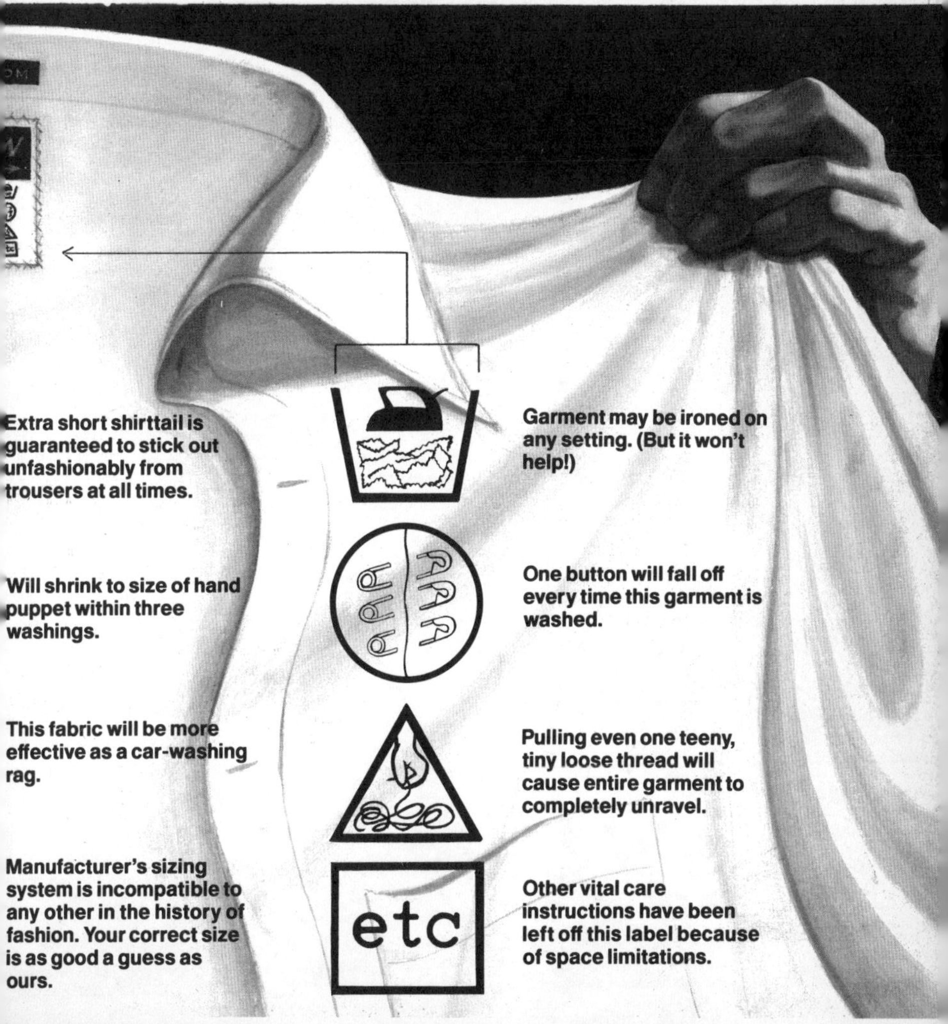

Extra short shirttail is guaranteed to stick out unfashionably from trousers at all times.

Garment may be ironed on any setting. (But it won't help!)

Will shrink to size of hand puppet within three washings.

One button will fall off every time this garment is washed.

This fabric will be more effective as a car-washing rag.

Pulling even one teeny, tiny loose thread will cause entire garment to completely unravel.

Manufacturer's sizing system is incompatible to any other in the history of fashion. Your correct size is as good a guess as ours.

Other vital care instructions have been left off this label because of space limitations.

EDICT AND WEEP DEPT.

Ever notice how strangely people behave...like saying "Thank you!" to check-out clerks in supermarkets? Ever wonder what they're thanking them for? For giving them change for their own money? For over-charging them for several items in their shopping cart? For keeping them waiting on line for twenty minutes? There are a lot of things people do that make absolutely no sense. But everyone does them because everyone ELSE does them! It's as if we're all behaving according to some "unwritten rules" of our society. Like "Don't belch in public!" or "Cover your nose when you sneeze!" Except that most of the time, these "unwritten laws" are arbitrary and silly! How silly...? Well, we'll show you how silly— as we take this MAD look at what it would be like...

IF SOCIETY'S
Unwritten

IN AN ELEVATOR...

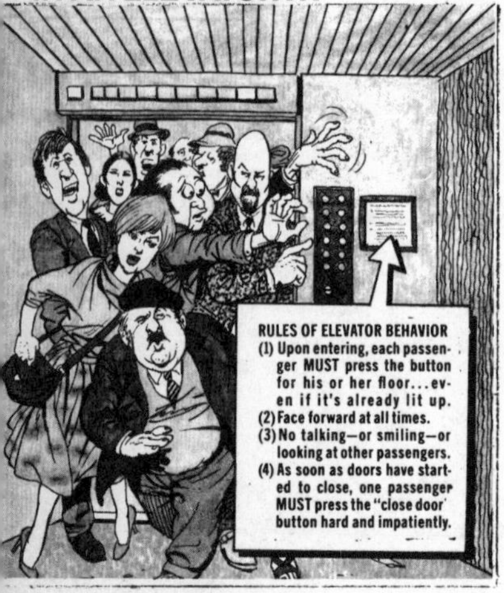
RULES OF ELEVATOR BEHAVIOR
(1) Upon entering, each passenger MUST press the button for his or her floor...even if it's already lit up.
(2) Face forward at all times.
(3) No talking—or smiling—or looking at other passengers.
(4) As soon as doors have started to close, one passenger MUST press the "close door" button hard and impatiently.

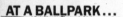

IN A HOSPITAL...

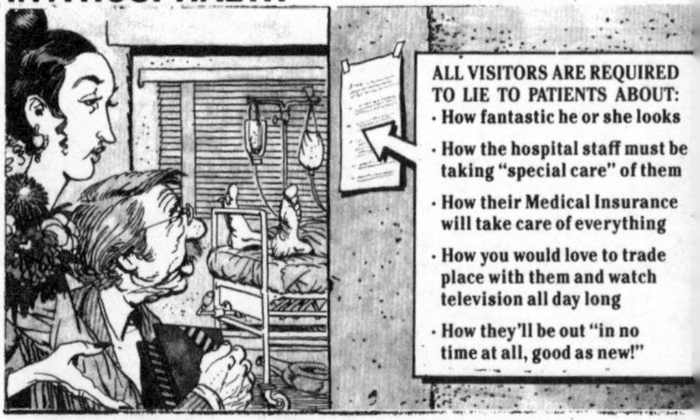
ALL VISITORS ARE REQUIRED TO LIE TO PATIENTS ABOUT:
· How fantastic he or she looks
· How the hospital staff must be taking "special care" of them
· How their Medical Insurance will take care of everything
· How you would love to trade place with them and watch television all day long
· How they'll be out "in no time at all, good as new!"

AT A FAMILY REUNION...

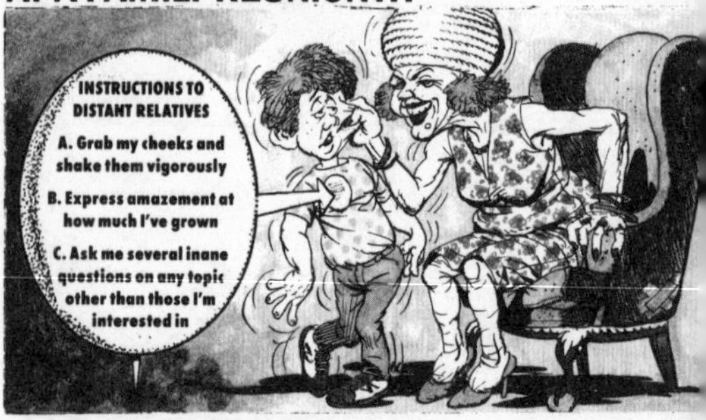
INSTRUCTIONS TO DISTANT RELATIVES
A. Grab my cheeks and shake them vigorously
B. Express amazement at how much I've grown
C. Ask me several inane questions on any topic other than those I'm interested in

AT A BALLPARK...

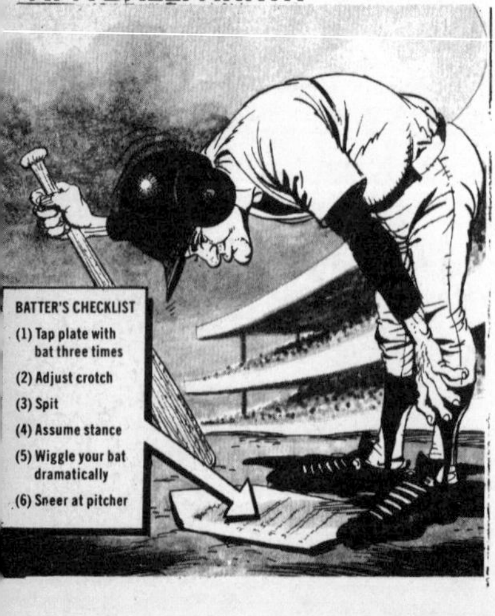
BATTER'S CHECKLIST
(1) Tap plate with bat three times
(2) Adjust crotch
(3) Spit
(4) Assume stance
(5) Wiggle your bat dramatically
(6) Sneer at pitcher

AT AN INTERSECTION...

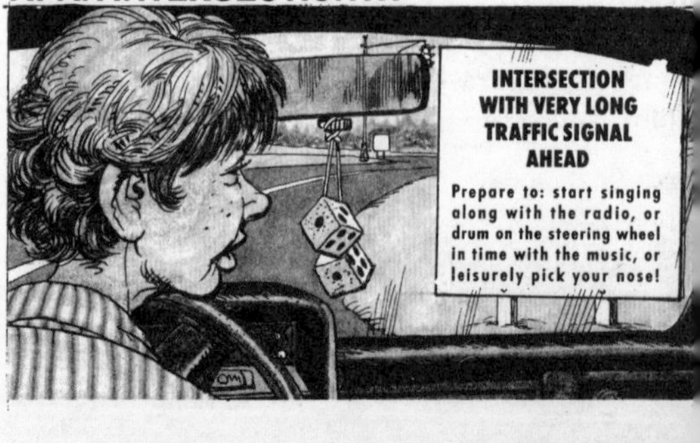
INTERSECTION WITH VERY LONG TRAFFIC SIGNAL AHEAD
Prepare to: start singing along with the radio, or drum on the steering wheel in time with the music, or leisurely pick your nose!

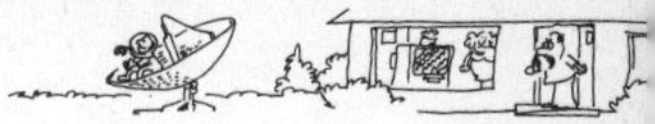

Rules of Behavior

VERE ACTUALLY WRITTEN DOWN

RTIST: GEORGE WOODBRIDGE WRITER: MIKE SNIDER

T A BUSINESS MEETING...

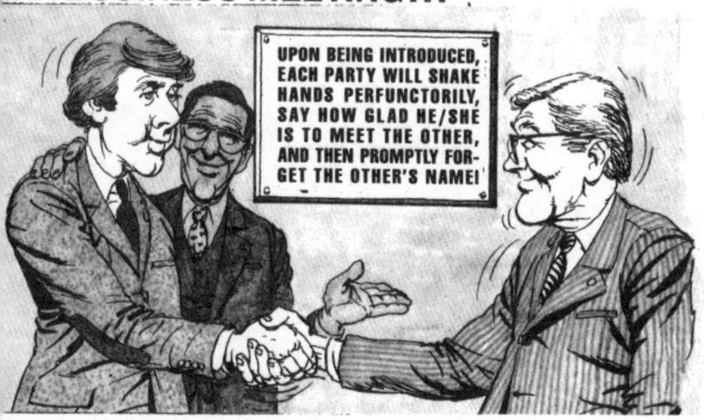
UPON BEING INTRODUCED, EACH PARTY WILL SHAKE HANDS PERFUNCTORILY, SAY HOW GLAD HE/SHE IS TO MEET THE OTHER, AND THEN PROMPTLY FORGET THE OTHER'S NAME!

T A CHECK-OUT COUNTER...

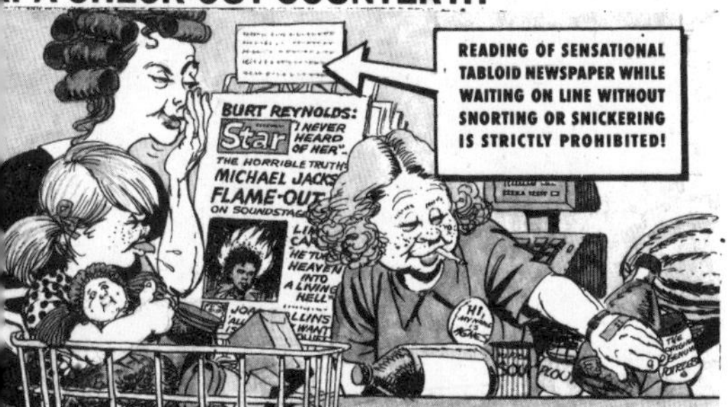
READING OF SENSATIONAL TABLOID NEWSPAPER WHILE WAITING ON LINE WITHOUT SNORTING OR SNICKERING IS STRICTLY PROHIBITED!
BURT REYNOLDS:
Star
"I NEVER HEARD OF HER"
THE HORRIBLE TRUTH:
FLAME-OUT
ON SOUNDSTAGE

N A MATERNITY FLOOR...

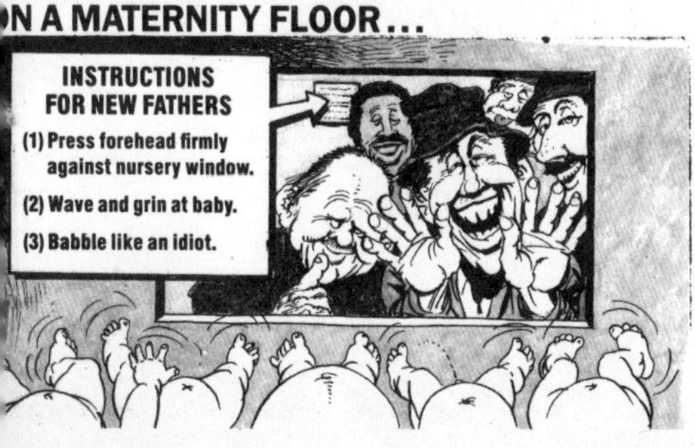
INSTRUCTIONS FOR NEW FATHERS
(1) Press forehead firmly against nursery window.
(2) Wave and grin at baby.
(3) Babble like an idiot.

AT A SPEAKER'S PLATFORM...

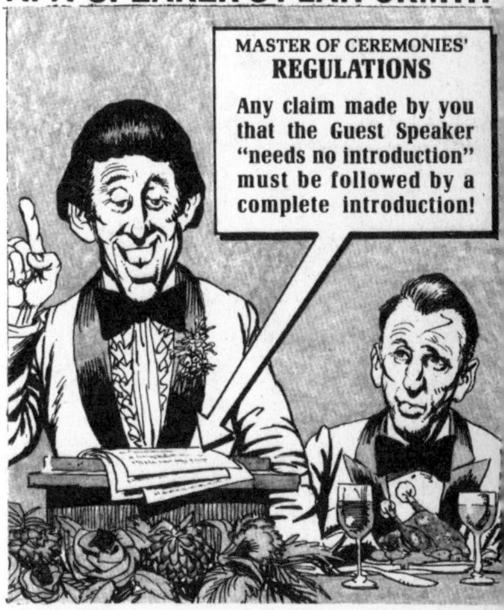
MASTER OF CEREMONIES' REGULATIONS
Any claim made by you that the Guest Speaker "needs no introduction" must be followed by a complete introduction!

IN A GARAGE...

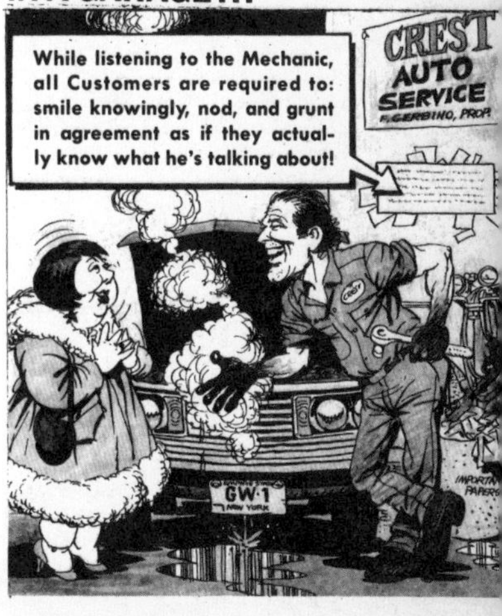
While listening to the Mechanic, all Customers are required to: smile knowingly, nod, and grunt in agreement as if they actually know what he's talking about!
CREST AUTO SERVICE
F. GERBINO, PROP.
GW-1
NEW YORK

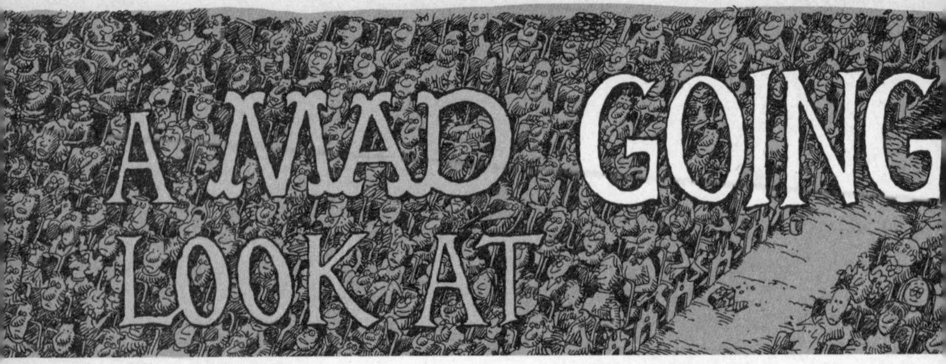
A MAD GOING
LOOK AT

SERGIO ARAGONES DEPT.

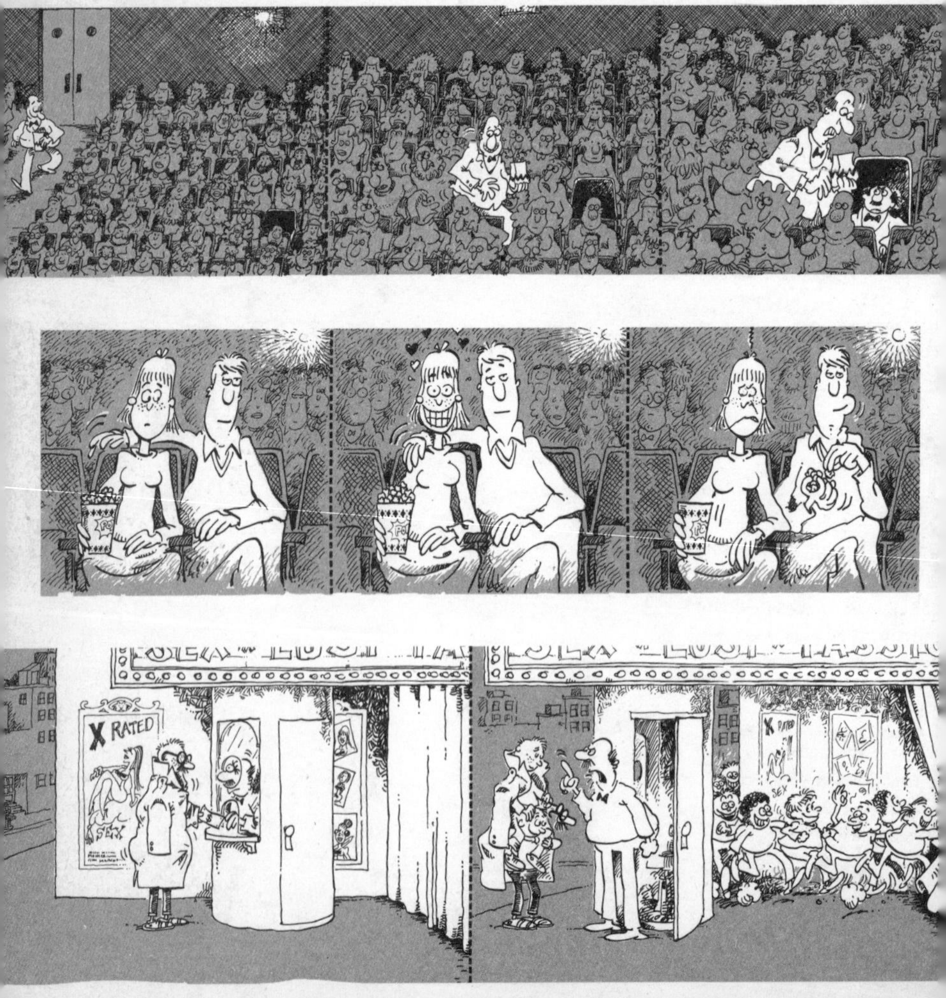
X RATED
SEX
X RATED
SEX

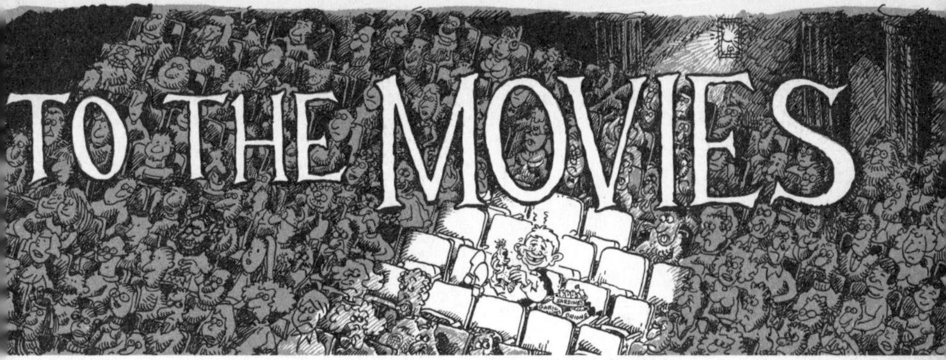
TO THE MOVIES
SARDINES

ARTIST & WRITER: SERGIO ARAGONES

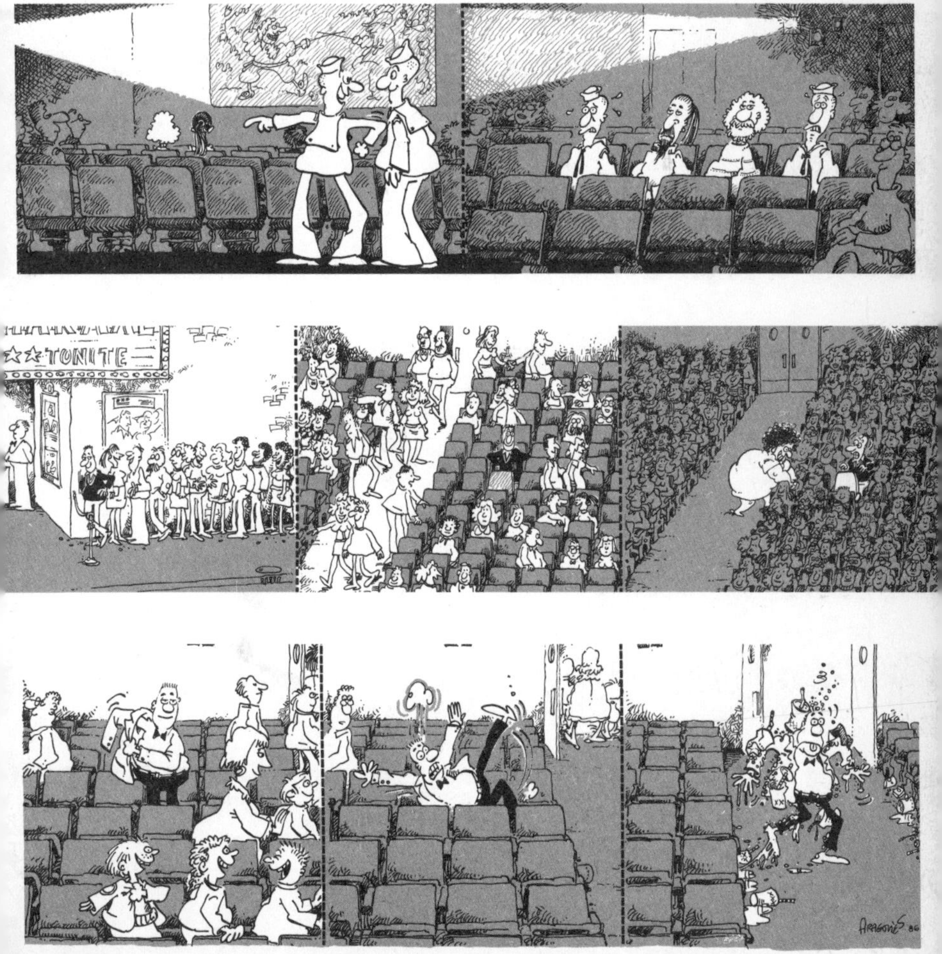
TONITE
ARAGONES 86

PERPLEX EDUCATION DEPT.

*Years ago life was easier. The most pressing problem folks seemed to face was deciding whic
radio program to tune in that evening. But times change. Life's complexities have gone wa*

MAD'S MODER

Where can you buy a winter jacket the d

remaining pleasures don't cause cancer?

divorce?

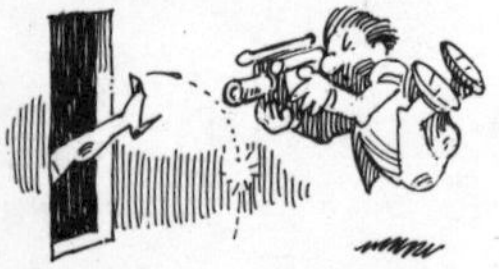

Where can you b

What do you serve your vegetarian, holi

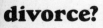

friend for dinner?

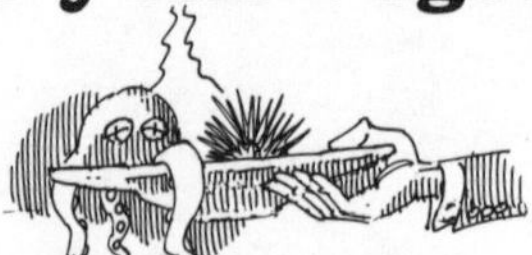

Is it po

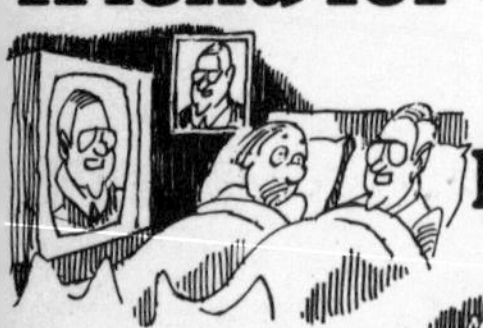

Do you have to buy earrings yo

them?

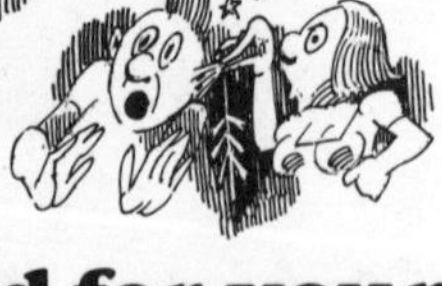

Is $1.35 still "cheap"?

Day card for your gay, transvestite step-fa

travel to where the residents don't hate o

possible to suffer from an illness that Phi

ARTIST: HARVEY KURTZMA

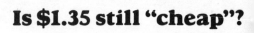

beyond just moving a little plastic marker from the morning music show to the shadow traffic report. As baffling dilemmas appear, we find ourselves searching desperately for answers to

-DAY PUZZLERS

after New Years? 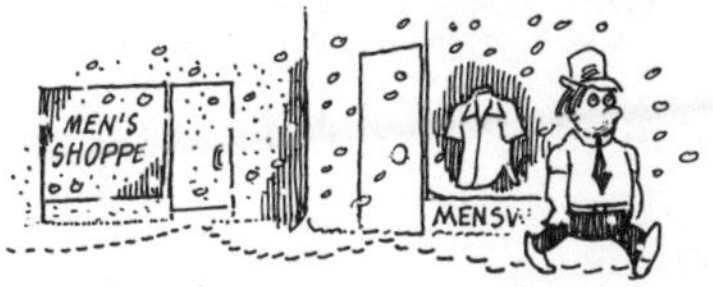
MEN'S
SHOPPE
Which

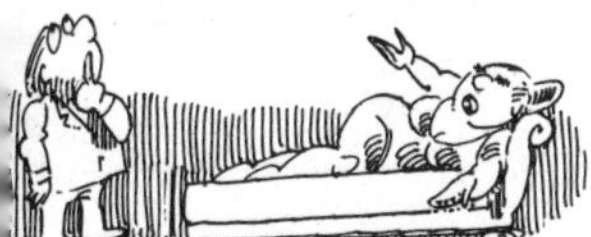

Should you video tape your

a watch that just tells time? 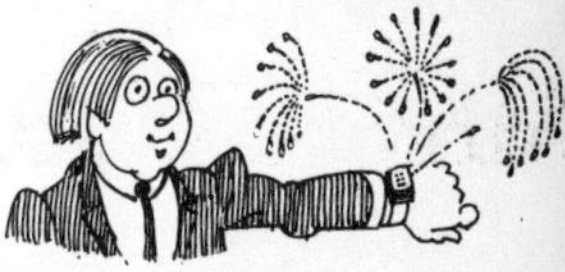

ic, new-age, buddhist, feminist, rotarian

ible to totally avoid seeing Ed McMahon?

boyfriend will like too, so you can share

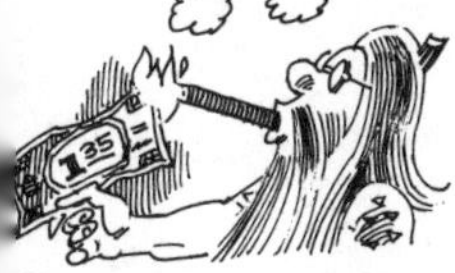

Where do you find a Mother's

ner? 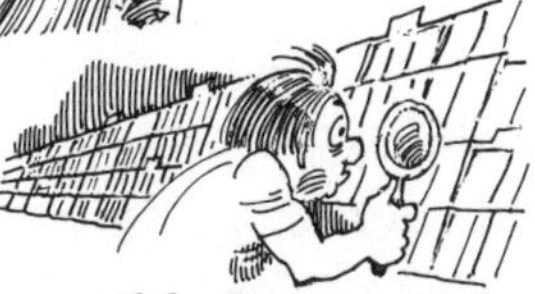 **What country can you**

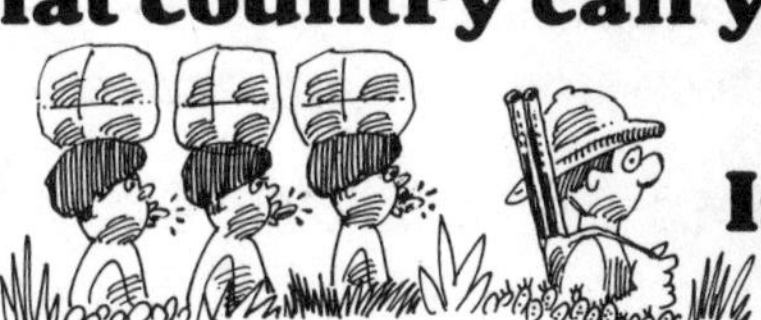

resent all Americans? **Is it**

Donahue hasn't covered yet? 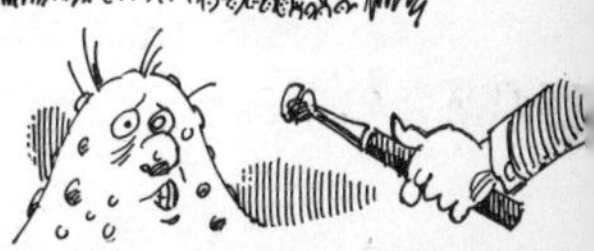

WRITER: DAVID AMES

WE'RE IN HEAT DEPT.

Budding trees signal spring, changing leaves indicate autumn, and heavy snow means winter. But what about that other season—how can we tell when it begins? Beach parties? Picnics?

SUMMER HAS A

...LITTLE KIDS SELL LEMONADE FOR 5¢ A GLASS, COMPLETE WITH SAND AND DROWNE

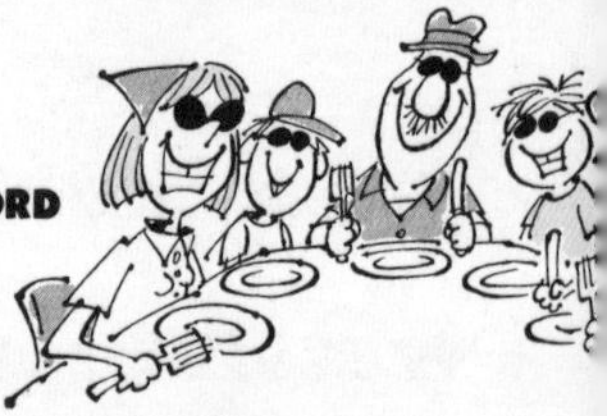

FOR FREE MEALS ENROUTE TO RESORTS YOU CAN'T AFFORD

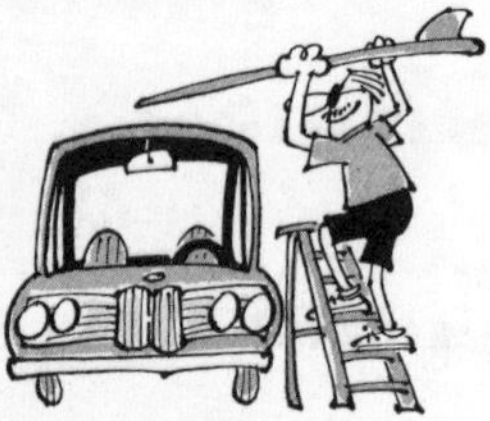

SURFBOARD **...AND YOU RUN OUT OF DENTAL FLOSS TRYIN**

FOR NO REASON EXCEPT THAT THE OIL COMPANIES KNOW YOU'LL PAY MORE IN WAR

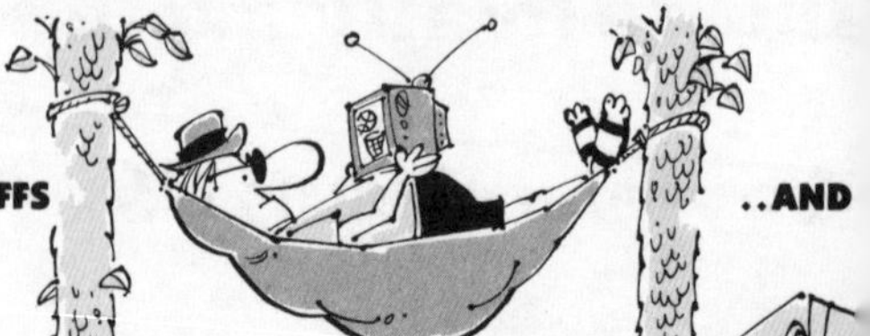

HAVE BEEN CUT FROM THE NBA PLAYOFFS **..AND**

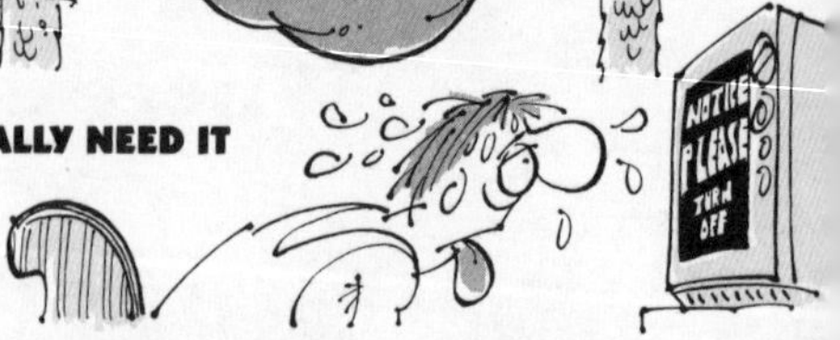
NOTICE
PLEASE
TURN
OFF

CONDITIONER ON THE FIRST DAY YOU REALLY NEED IT

UP THE STORM WINDOWS BECAUSE IT'S TIME AGAIN TO PUT UP THE SCREENS

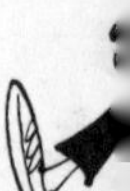

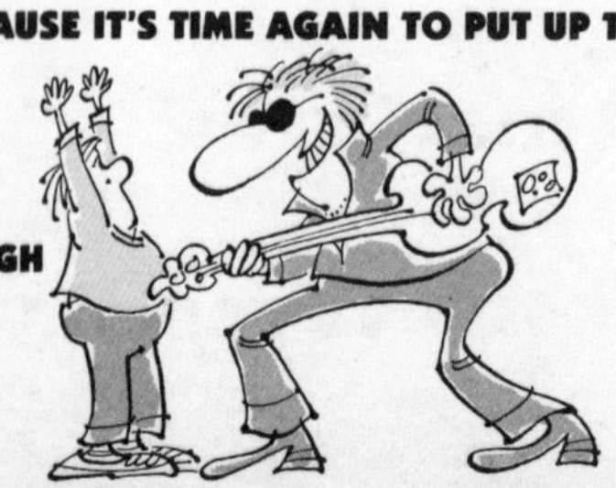

TICKET PRICES REMAIN SKY-HIGH **...AND TV NETWORK**

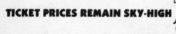

Think again! (And while you're at it, throw another shrimp on the barbie!) MAD has some other signs in mind... *warning* signs! The signs that mean three months of torture! You know that

RRIVED WHEN...

ARTIST: PAUL COKER   **WRITER: TOM KOCH**

...AND DISTANT RELATIVES UNEXPECTEDLY DROP BY

ITS

...AND YOUR LOCAL YUPPIE REPLACES THE SKI RACK ON TOP OF HIS BMW WITH A

DISLODGE PIECES OF CORN-ON-THE-COB

...AND GAS PRICES GO UP

EATHER.

YES, SUMMER'S HERE...WHEN ALL BUT 8 TEAMS

ELECTRIC CO. ASKS YOU TO HELP AVERT A POWER FAILURE BY TURNING OFF YOUR AIR

...AND YOUR FAMILY STOPS BUGGING YOU TO TAKE DOWN THE SCREENS AND PUT

...AND ROCK CONCERTS MOVE OUTSIDE TO BIG STADIUMS, BUT

GIN BRAGGING ABOUT THEIR NEW FALL LINEUP–DURING JUNKY RERUNS OF THE SHOWS

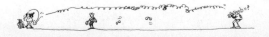

THEY RAVED ABOUT *LAST* YEAR.

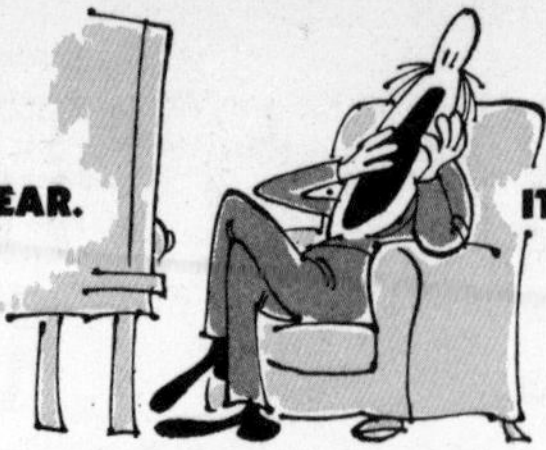

IT'S DEFINITELY SUMMER...WHEN YOU STOP SETTING YOUR ALARM FOR SCHOOL, BUT THE IDIOT NEXT DOOR WAKES YOU EVEN EARLIER WITH HIS LAWN MOWER

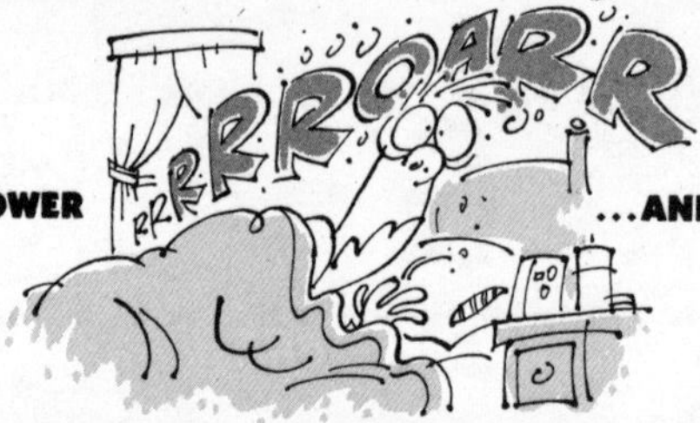
RRRRROARR

...AND YOUR ONLY POSSIBLE CONTACT WITH AN AIR CONDITIONING REPAIRMAN IS HIS ANSWERING MACHINE

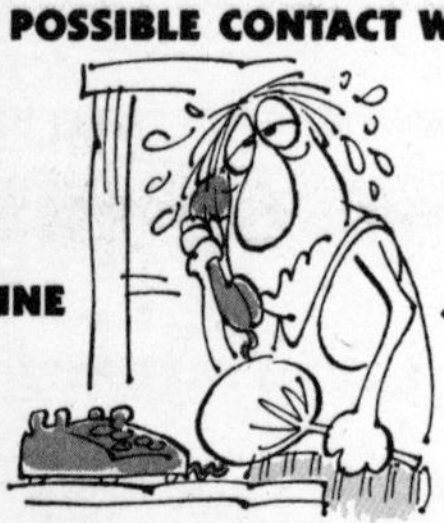

...AND DAD SAYS HE'LL SPEND HIS VACATION BECOMING YOUR PAL AS THE TWO OF YOU PAINT THE GARAGE TOGETHER

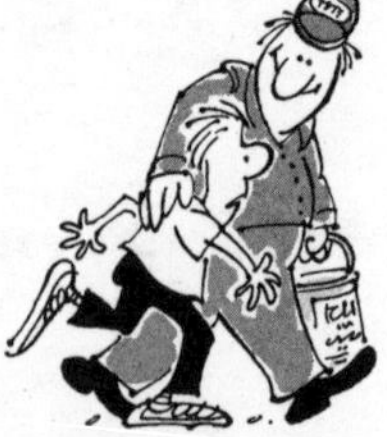

...AND PARK RANGERS REPORT THAT THE THREAT OF FLOODS HAS BEEN REPLACED BY THE THREAT OF BRUSH FIRES

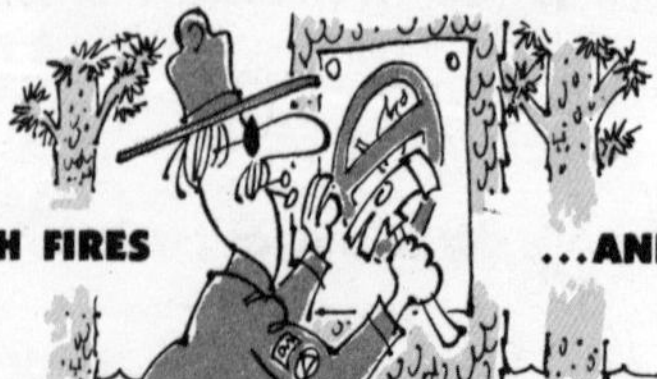

...AND OVER-EAGER MERCHANTS RUIN YOUR VACATION BY STARTING THE FIRST BACK-TO-SCHOOL SALES.

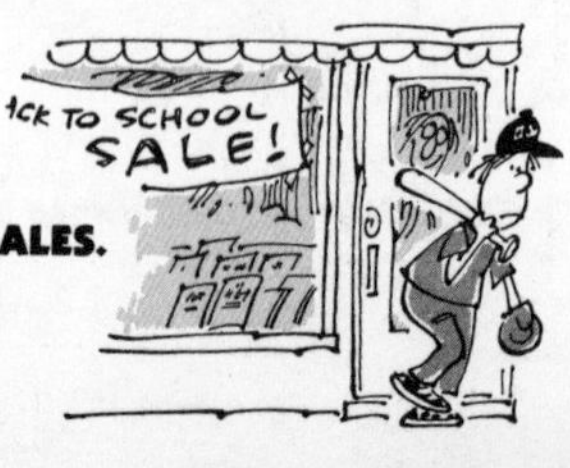
ACK TO SCHOOL
SALE!

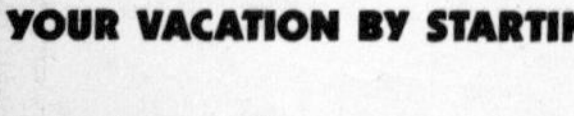

UP, UP AND OY VEY DEPT.

LIVING ON THE EDGE

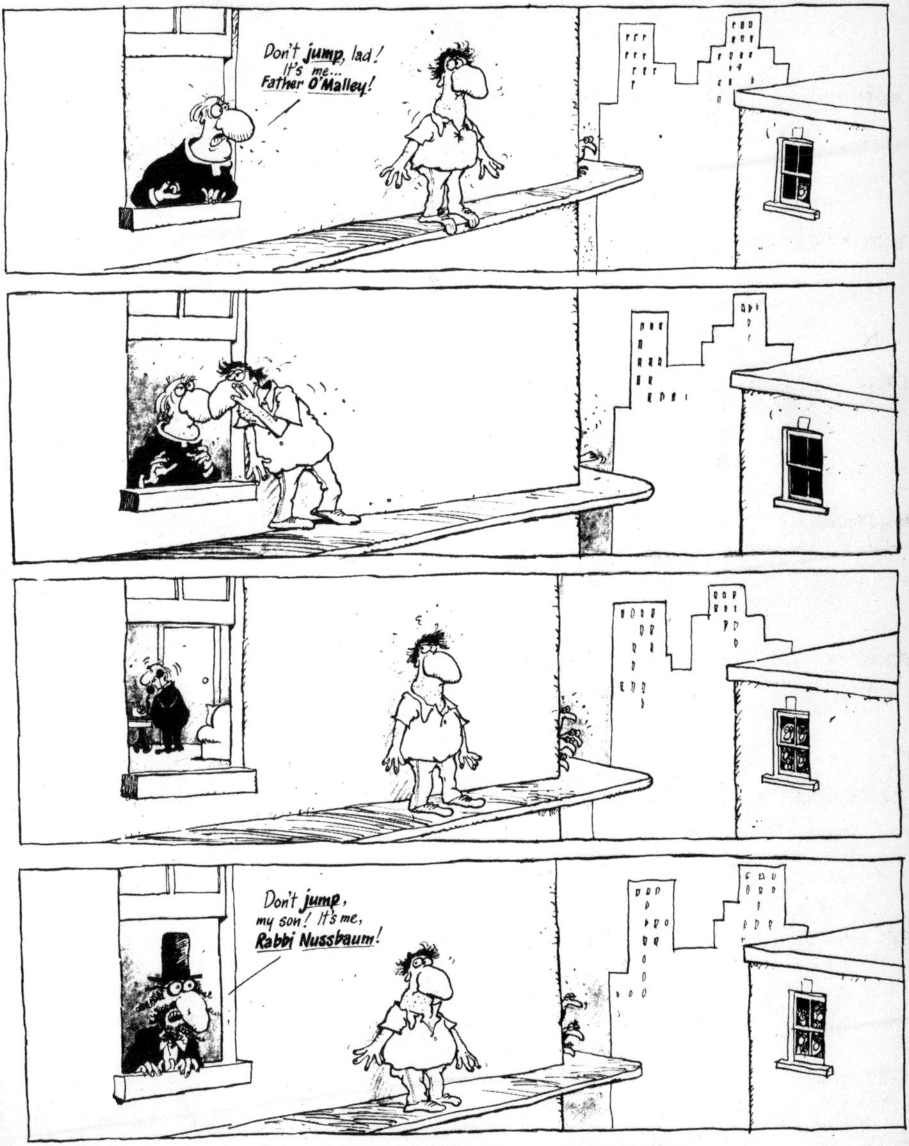
Don't jump, lad! It's me... Father O'Malley!
Don't jump, my son! It's me, Rabbi Nussbaum!

ARTISTS: DON EDWING AND HARRY NORTH WRITER: DON EDWING

SERGIO ARAGONES DEPT.

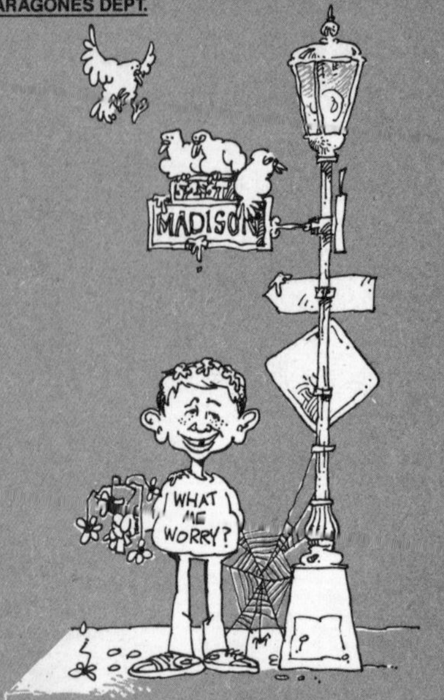
MADISON
WHAT ME WORRY?

A MAD LOOK AT DATING

ARTIST & WRITER: SERGIO ARAGONES

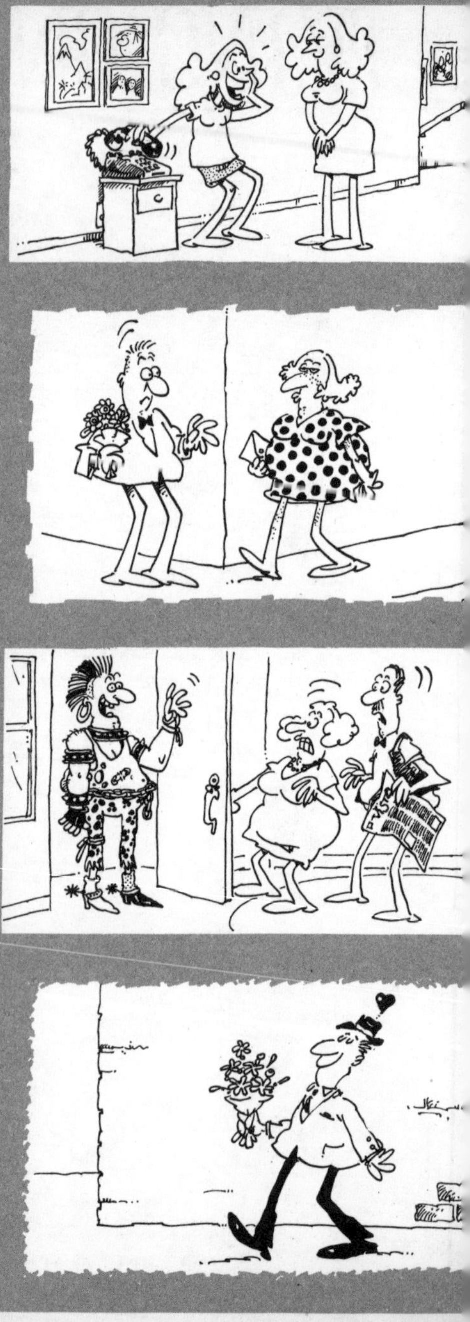

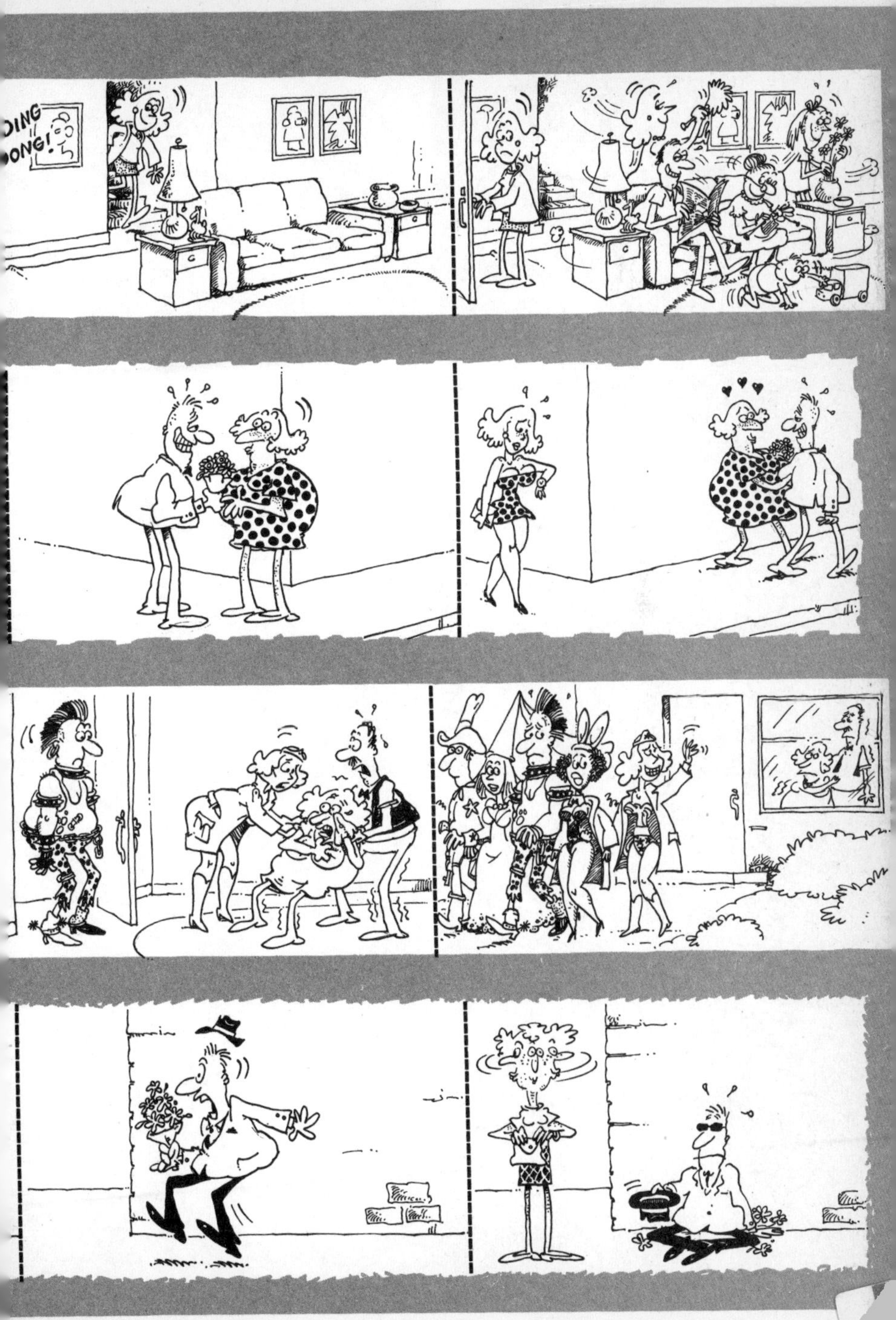
DING DONG!

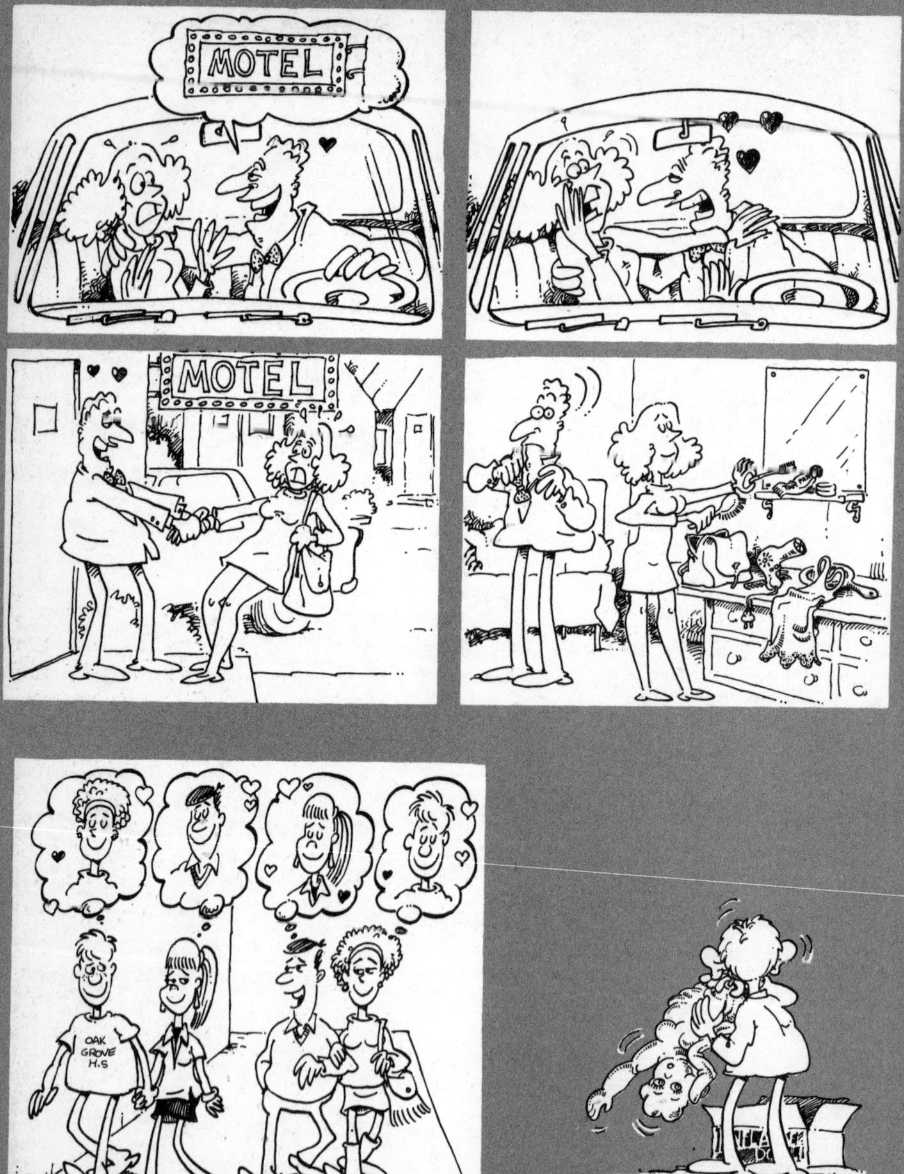
MOTEL
MOTEL
OAK GROVE H.S
ARAGONÉS 87

JOKE AND DAGGER DEPT.

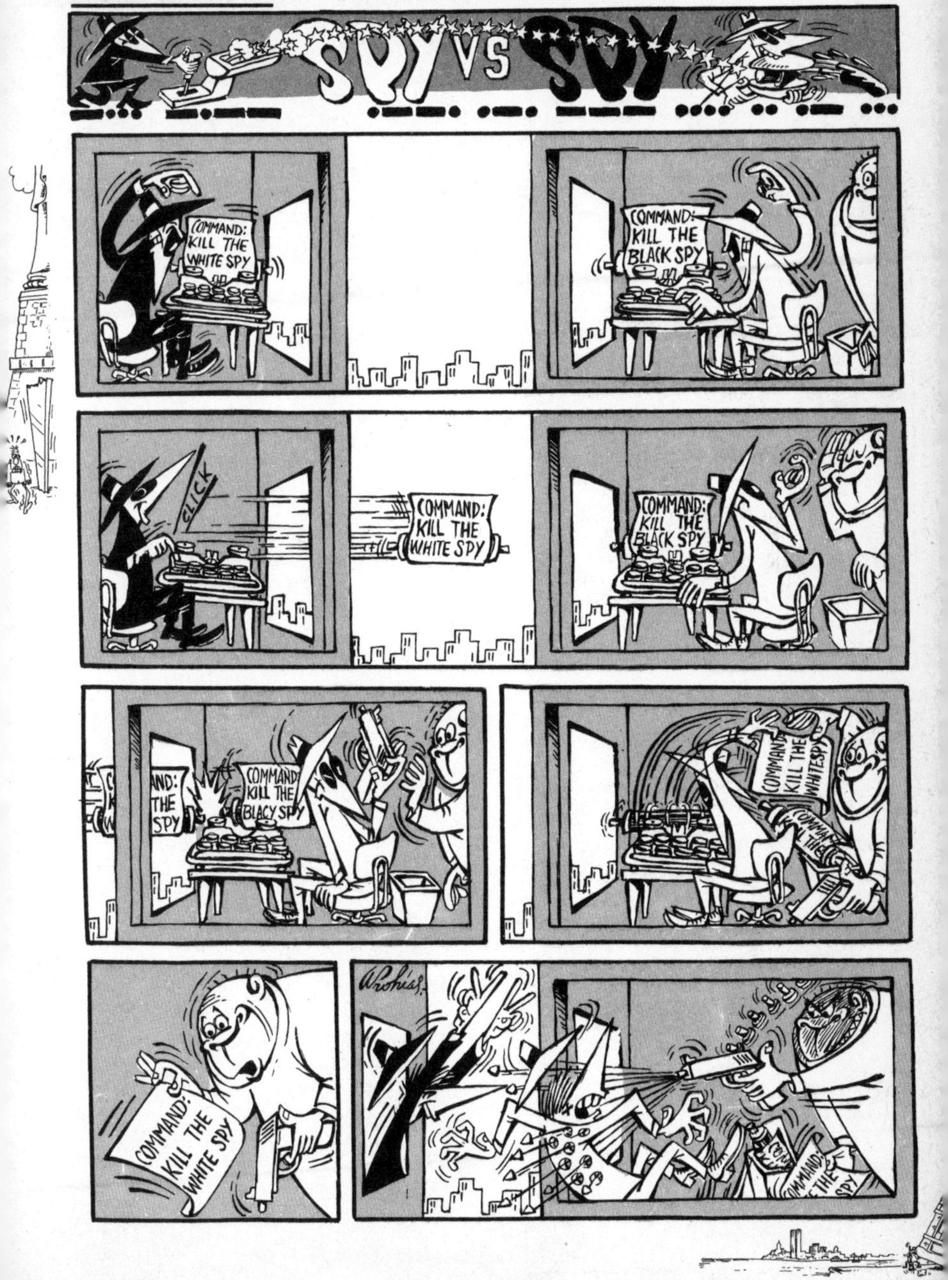
SPY VS SPY
COMMAND: KILL THE WHITE SPY
COMMAND: KILL THE BLACK SPY
CLICK
COMMAND: KILL THE WHITE SPY
COMMAND: KILL THE BLACK SPY
COMMAND: KILL THE
COMMAND: KILL THE WHITE SPY
COMMAND: KILL THE WHITE SPY
Prohias

THE PLOY'S THE THING DEPT.

CLEVER WAYS TO GET OUT OF

RUNNY NOSE

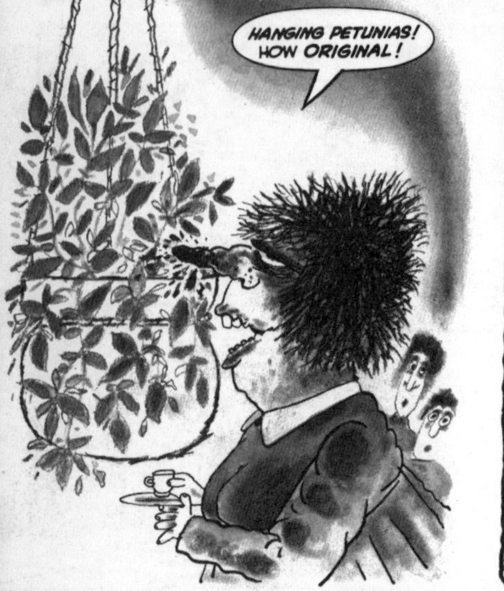
HANGING PETUNIAS! HOW ORIGINAL!

GARLIC BREATH

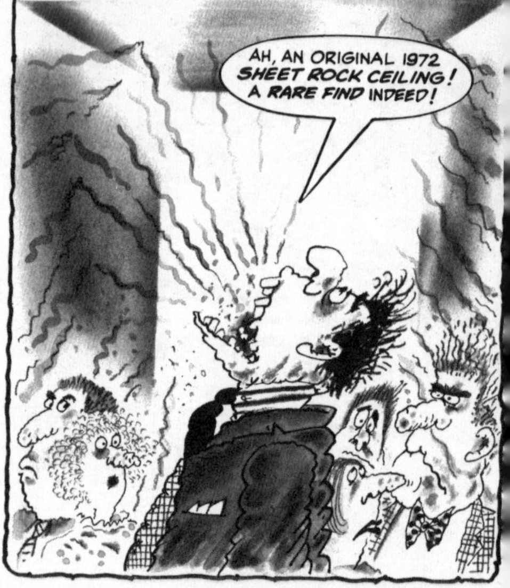
AH, AN ORIGINAL 1972 SHEET ROCK CEILING! A RARE FIND INDEED!

ARTIST AND WRITER: PAUL PETER PORGES

AN OPEN ZIPPER

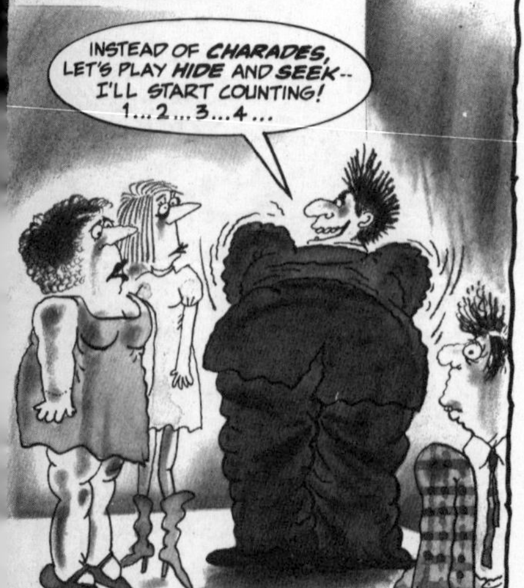
INSTEAD OF CHARADES, LET'S PLAY HIDE AND SEEK-- I'LL START COUNTING! 1...2...3...4...

DROOPY PANTYHOSE

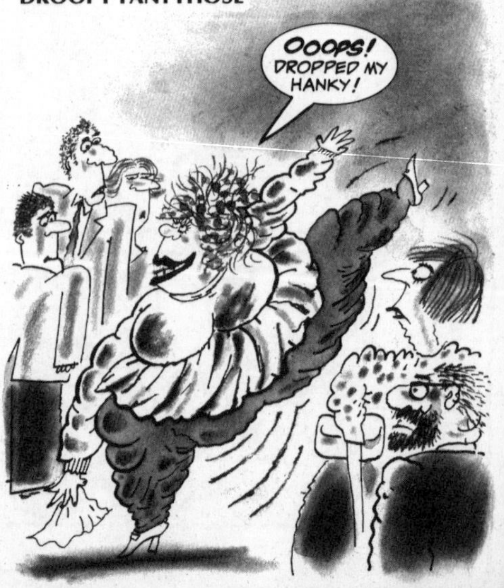
OOOPS! DROPPED MY HANKY!

EMBARRASSING SITUATIONS

DOGGY-DOO SHOES

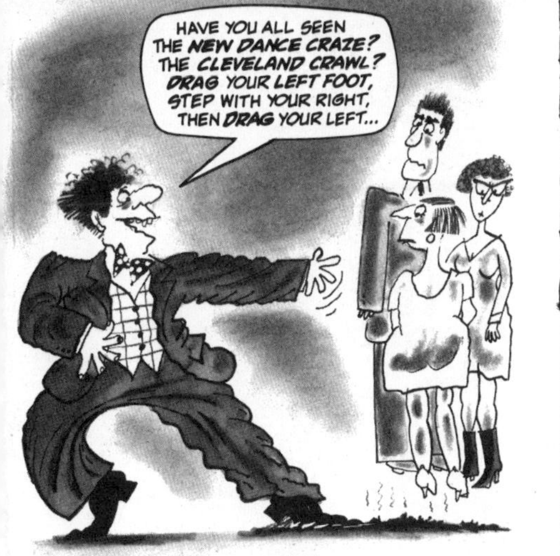
HAVE YOU ALL SEEN THE NEW DANCE CRAZE? THE CLEVELAND CRAWL? DRAG YOUR LEFT FOOT, STEP WITH YOUR RIGHT, THEN DRAG YOUR LEFT...

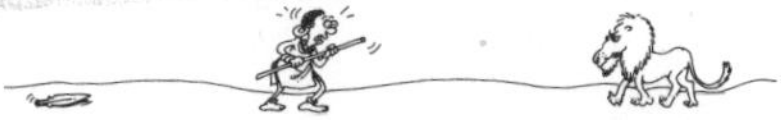

LIMITED ATHLETIC ABILITY

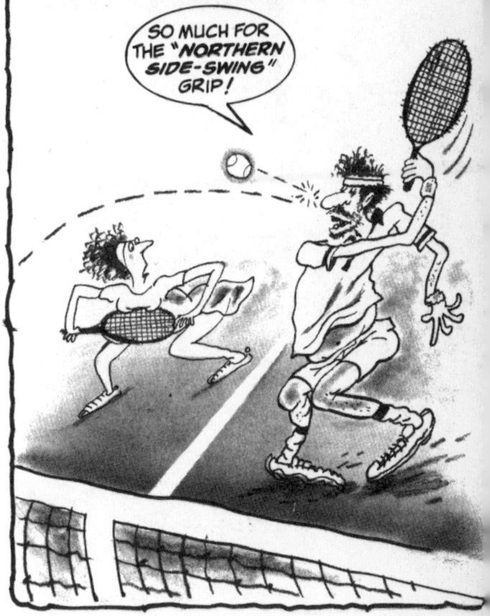
SO MUCH FOR THE "NORTHERN SIDE-SWING" GRIP!

DANDRUFF

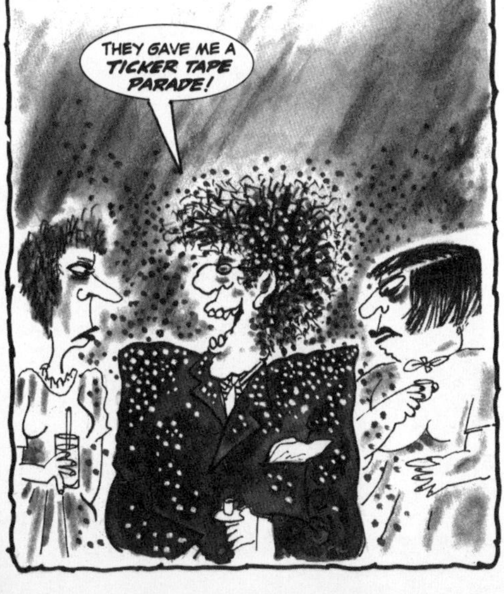
THEY GAVE ME A TICKER TAPE PARADE!

GAMY ARMPITS

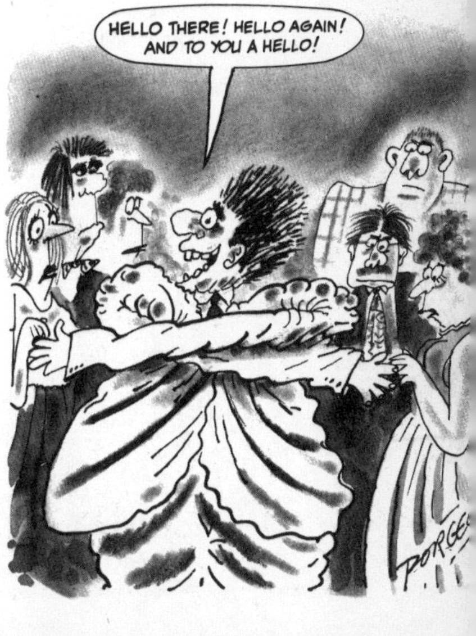
HELLO THERE! HELLO AGAIN! AND TO YOU A HELLO!

DON MARTIN DEPT. PART II

BACK IN THE OPERATING ROOM WITH DON MARTIN
DURING A HEART TRANSPLANT

SHKLIK
SHKLOP
Worst case of rejection I've ever seen!
D. MARTIN

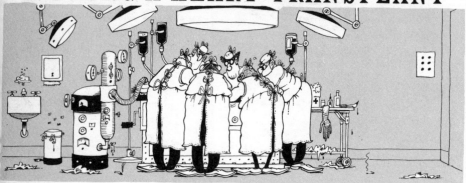

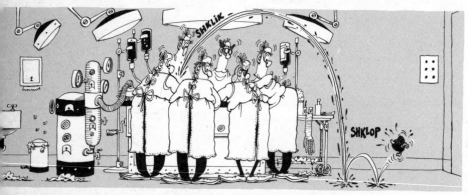

FEEBLE ATTRACTIONS DEPT.

They sit in the dark corners of shopping malls, unwanted and unloved, unable to ask for the attention they so desperately need. Who are these pitiful creatures? Pathetic K-Mart shoppers? Hardly! We're talking about mechanical ponies and rocking boats—the forgotten rides of childhood. Today's kids don't part with their quarters unless they're really stimulated! Which is why we at MAD suggest introducing these…

NEW AND IMPROVED STORE KIDDIE RIDES

ARTIST: AL JAFFEE WRITER: DAN BIRTCHER

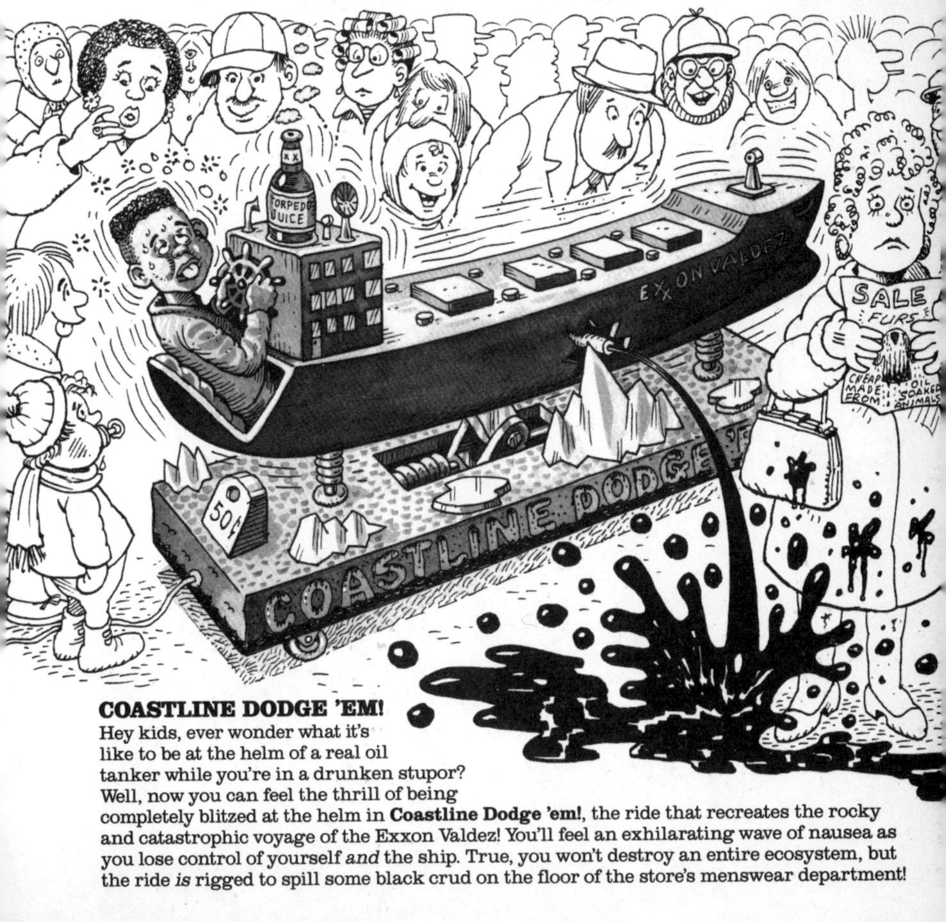

TORPEDO JUICE
XX
EXXON VALDEZ
COASTLINE DODGE 'EM
50¢
SALE
FURS
CHEAP FURS MADE FROM OIL SOAKED ANIMALS

COASTLINE DODGE 'EM!

Hey kids, ever wonder what it's like to be at the helm of a real oil tanker while you're in a drunken stupor? Well, now you can feel the thrill of being completely blitzed at the helm in **Coastline Dodge 'em!**, the ride that recreates the rocky and catastrophic voyage of the Exxon Valdez! You'll feel an exhilarating wave of nausea as you lose control of yourself *and* the ship. True, you won't destroy an entire ecosystem, but the ride *is* rigged to spill some black crud on the floor of the store's menswear department!

STREEP THROAT What's dark and deep and filled with the thundering sounds of foreign vowels? Why, it's **Streep Throat**, the amazing new ride which catapults you into the make-believe voice box of one of America's most annoying voices, Meryl Streep! You'll hear her say, "The Nazis made the Gringo take my baby to Flatbush, m'lord" in eleven different accents, including: British, Australian, Polish, Dutch, Estonian and Native Gypsy Ragpicker Dialect. You'll swear you were actually in the mouth of a FOREIGNER! (Must be under 4' 6" to clear gum line.)

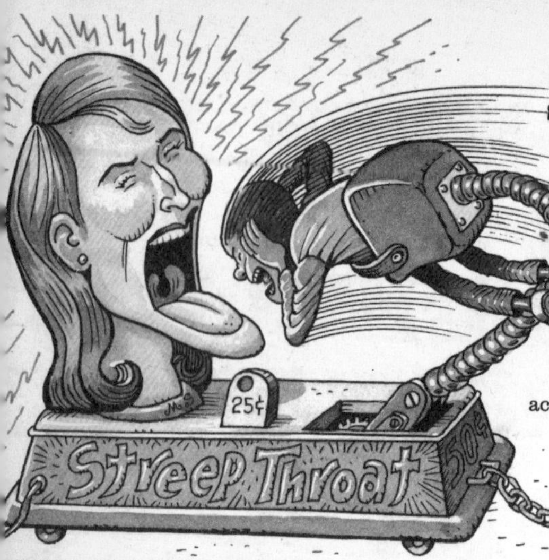
25¢
50¢
Streep Throat

PRESCRIPTION SIGNATURE In this age of fast video games and slasher movies, kids demand that their rides be fast and slashing too! That's why we've created **Prescription Signature**, the new ride in which you're strapped atop a giant ball-point pen! Feel for yourself the unpredictable jerking of a doctor's moronic scrawl! Believe us, you don't know what excitement is until you've experienced the wild scribbling of a prescription for hemorrhoids in high velocity Latin! It's stimulating, it's bizarre... it's illegible! Be sure to hang on, though, because if you fall—that's all she wrote!

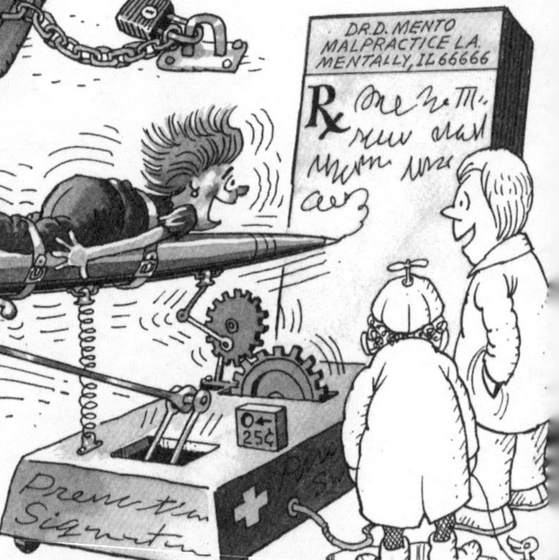
DR. D. MENTO
MALPRACTICE L.A.
MENTALLY, IL 66666
Rx
25¢

YUGO-A-GO-GO When Yugo auto sales took a nose dive, there were still hundreds of thousands of kids who never had the chance to ride in one of these Iron Curtain Wonder cars! That's where the amazing and wacky Yugo-A-Go-Go comes in! After inserting a quarter, simply climb in, turn the ignition key and experience the feeling of absolutely nothing happening...just like actual Yugo owners did! And here's an extra surprise: This ride *isn't* a toy replica! It's a real non-working, cramped and uncomfortable Yugo! Va Va Voom!

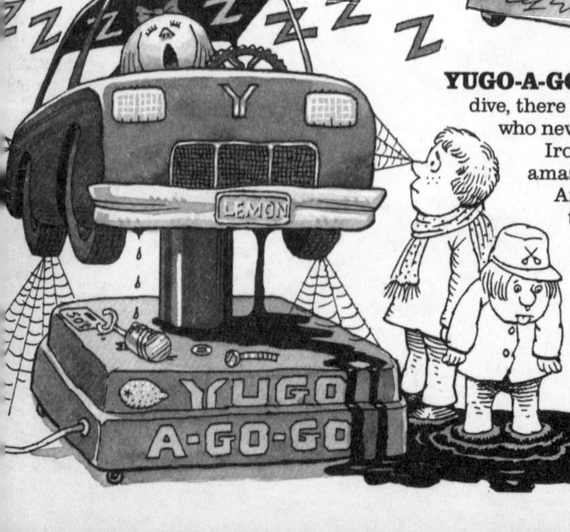
Y
LEMON
50¢
YUGO
A-GO-GO

SPACE-AGE CHECK-OUT

We've all seen a grocery clerk scan a package again and again at the check-out, desperately trying to get the bar code to register. Ever fantasized about being treated that way yourself? Then **Space-Age Check-Out** is for you! A giant mechanical hand violently lifts you from the ground and drags you against a hard glass plate. Blinding red lasers flash in your eyes as you are mistaken for an improperly coded canned ham. Ride ends when you are dropped. (Maker of ride assumes no responsibility for kidney damage.)

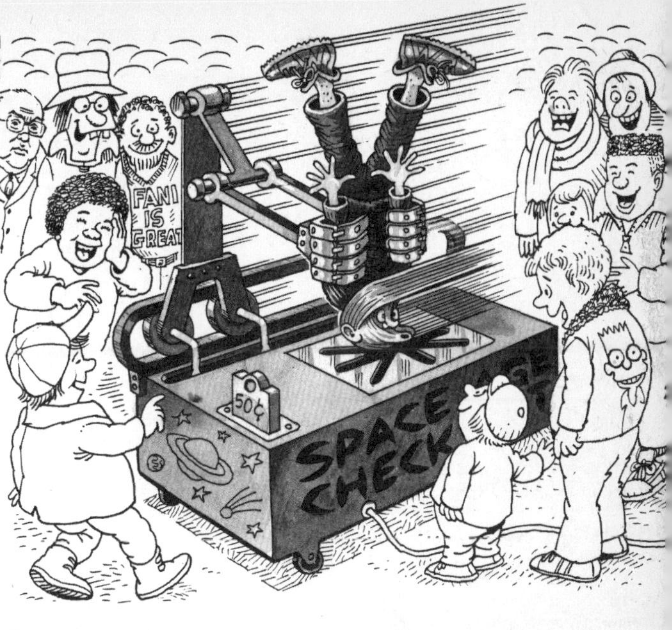

"THIS HUMOR IS OBSCENE"
Jesse Helms
FANI IS GREAT
50¢
SPACE
CHECK

SPECIAL DELIVERY Whoa-ho! It's exciting! Whoo-hoo! It's incredible! Whee-hee! It's **Special Delivery**, the wacky new ride in which you get banged around and mishandled just like a priceless breakable in the hands of an incompetent civil servant! First you're slammed and sealed in an oversized box with an inadequate amount of styrofoam peanuts. Then you're off for Cleveland from Miami Beach via Seattle with lengthy stop-offs at the Post Offices in Peewaukee, Grand Rapids, Intercourse, Wammelsdorf, Cupenluck, Wammelsdorf (again!), and Baktash, South Korea! On the other hand, you may sit around in the back room for weeks, stinking up the joint like a long-forgotten case of rotting gouda cheese!

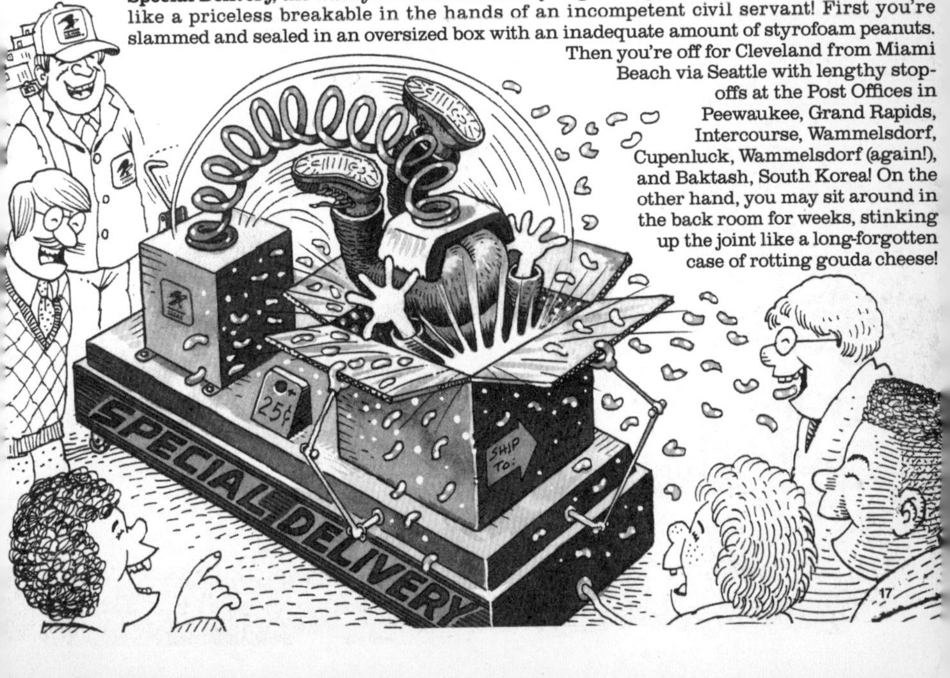

25¢
SPECIAL DELIVERY
SHIP TO:

HIGHER EDUCATION

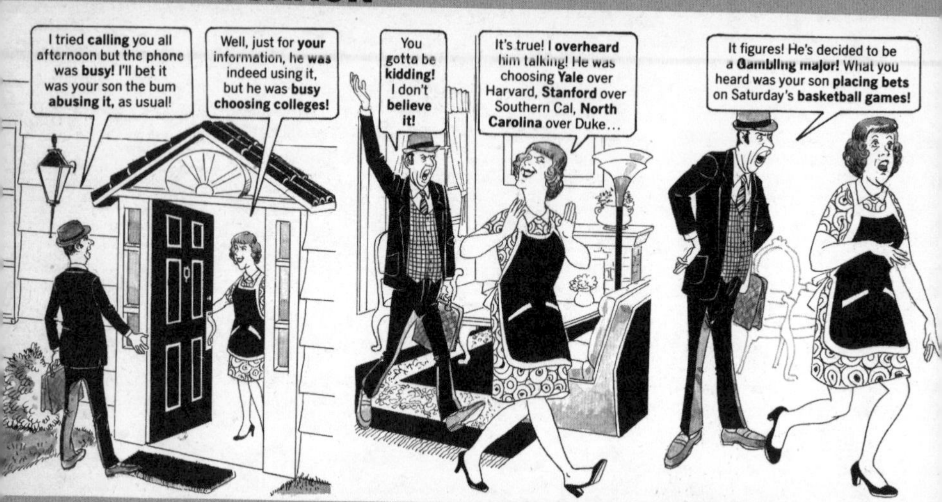
I tried calling you all afternoon but the phone was busy! I'll bet it was your son the bum abusing it, as usual!
Well, just for your information, he was indeed using it, but he was busy choosing colleges!
You gotta be kidding! I don't believe it!
It's true! I overheard him talking! He was choosing Yale over Harvard, Stanford over Southern Cal, North Carolina over Duke…
It figures! He's decided to be a Gambling major! What you heard was your son placing bets on Saturday's basketball games!

BERG'S-EYE VIEW DEPT.

THE LIGHTE

EQUALITY

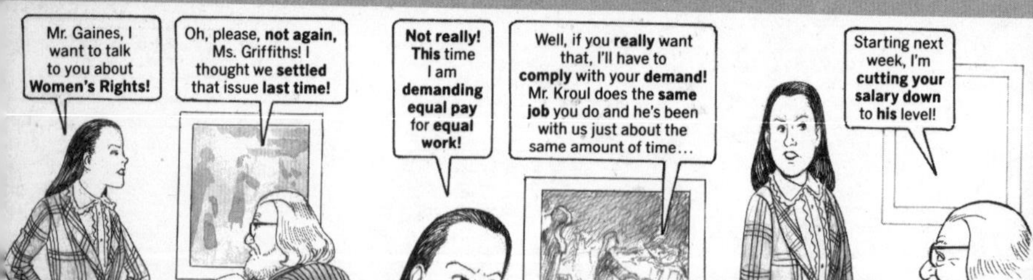
Mr. Gaines, I want to talk to you about Women's Rights!
Oh, please, not again, Ms. Griffiths! I thought we settled that issue last time!
Not really! This time I am demanding equal pay for equal work!
Well, if you really want that, I'll have to comply with your demand! Mr. Kroul does the same job you do and he's been with us just about the same amount of time…
Starting next week, I'm cutting your salary down to his level!

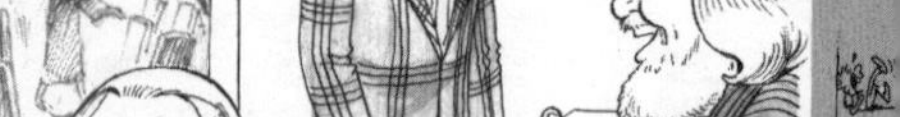
SILENCE HOSPITAL

ACCIDENTS

But officer, it's not my fault! He stepped right in **front** of my **car!**

That may be true, Miss...

...but after all, it is his backyard!

R SIDE OF...

ARTIST & WRITER:
DAVE BERG

RUNNING

This is **rough!** What am I doing running in a **marathon?** Who **started** these **stupid things?**

Actually, it all started in **ancient Greece** when a soldier ran **26 miles** to deliver a message!

Well, it's a **helluva lot easier** when there's an army with **pointy spears** running **behind you!**

JUSTICE

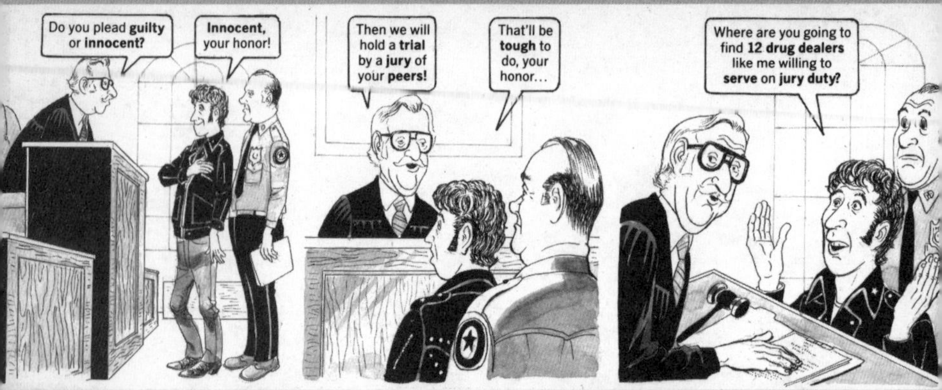
Do you plead **guilty** or **innocent?**
Innocent, your honor!
Then we will hold a **trial** by a **jury** of your **peers!**
That'll be **tough** to do, your honor…
Where are you going to find **12 drug dealers** like me willing to **serve** on **jury duty?**

DINNER

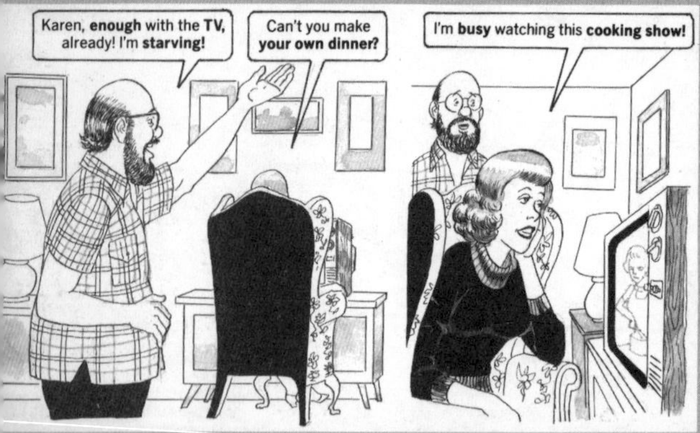
Karen, **enough** with the **TV,** already! I'm **starving!**
Can't you make **your own dinner?**
I'm **busy** watching this **cooking show!**

FINANCES

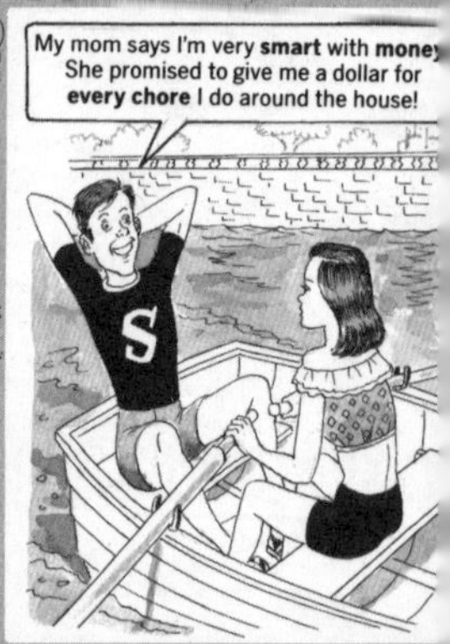
My mom says I'm very **smart** with **money** She promised to give me a dollar for **every chore** I do around the house!

BEHAVIOR

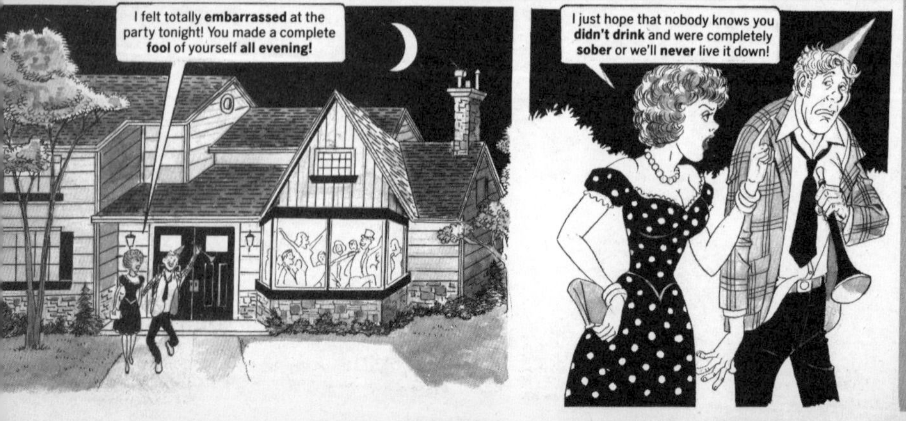
I felt totally **embarrassed** at the party tonight! You made a complete **fool** of yourself **all evening!**
I just hope that nobody knows you **didn't drink** and were completely **sober** or we'll **never** live it down!

FAST LIVING

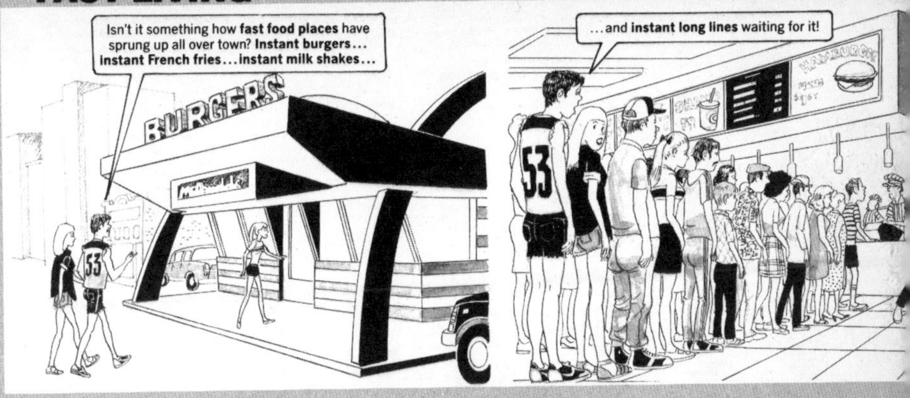
Isn't it something how **fast food places** have sprung up all over town? **Instant burgers... instant French fries... instant milk shakes...**
BURGERS
53
...and **instant long lines** waiting for it!
53

INTERVIEWS

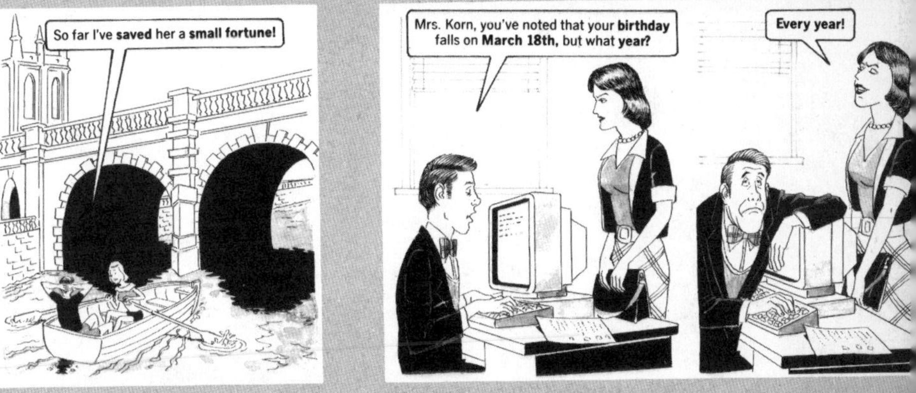
So far I've **saved** her a **small fortune!**
Mrs. Korn, you've noted that your **birthday** falls on **March 18th,** but what **year?**
Every year!

MODERN MORALS

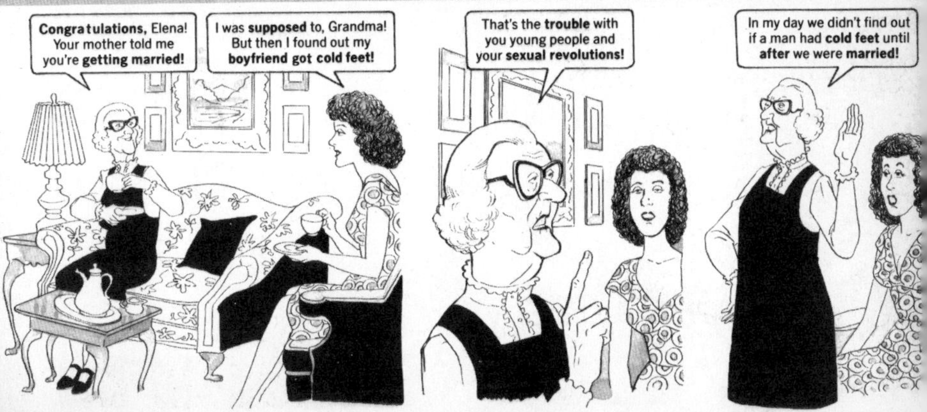
Congratulations, Elena! Your mother told me you're **getting married!**
I was **supposed** to, Grandma! But then I found out my **boyfriend got cold feet!**
That's the **trouble** with you young people and your **sexual revolutions!**
In my day we didn't find out if a man had **cold feet** until **after** we were **married!**

CHOICES

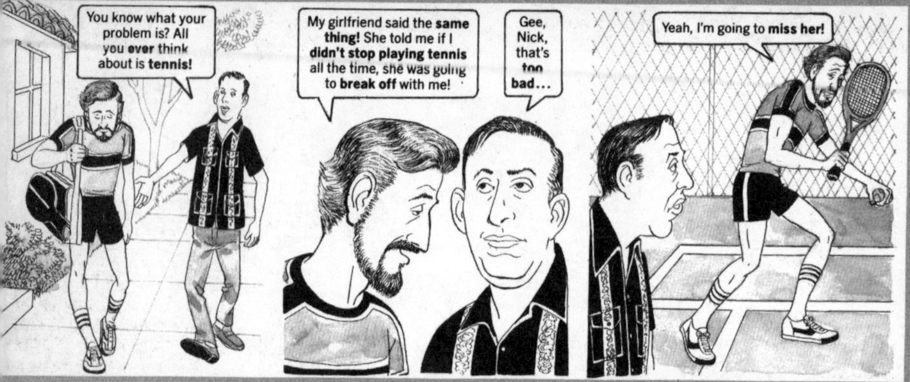

You know what your problem is? All you **ever** think about is **tennis**!
My girlfriend said the **same thing**! She told me if I **didn't stop playing tennis** all the time, she was going to **break off** with me!
Gee, Nick, that's **too bad**...
Yeah, I'm going to **miss her**!

PETS

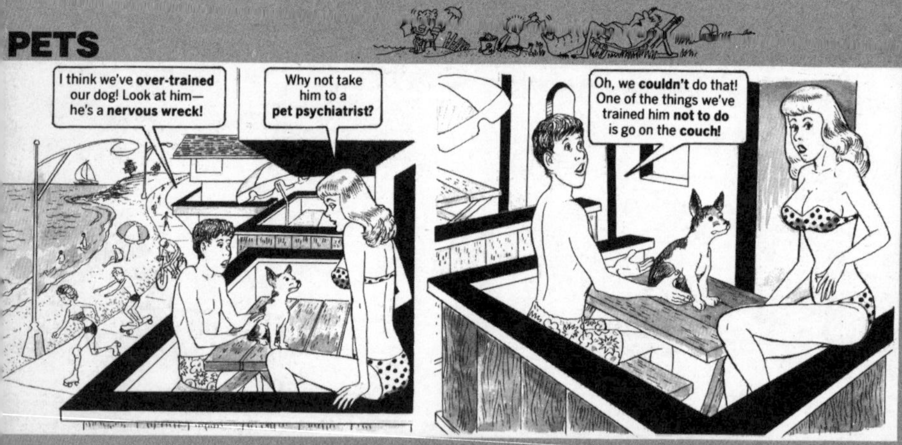

I think we've **over-trained** our dog! Look at him—he's a **nervous wreck**!
Why not take him to a **pet psychiatrist**?
Oh, we **couldn't** do that! One of the things we've trained him **not to do** is go on the **couch**!

DOCTORS

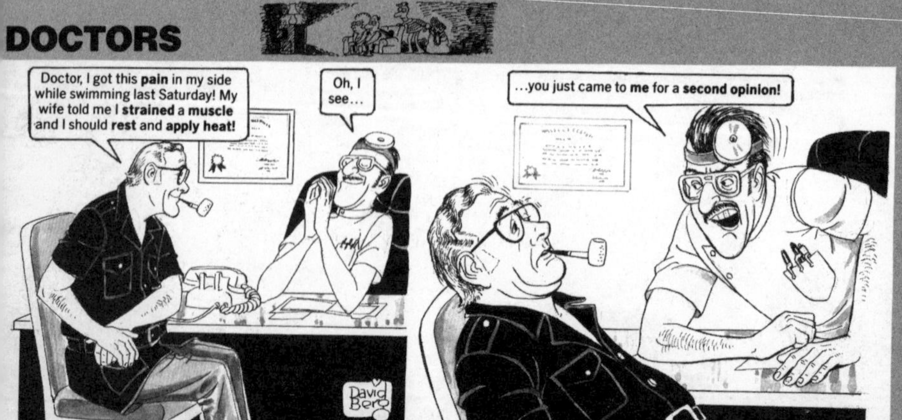

Doctor, I got this **pain** in my side while swimming last Saturday! My wife told me I **strained** a **muscle** and I should **rest** and **apply heat**!
Oh, I see...
...you just came to **me** for a **second opinion**!
David Berg

WAKE WATCHERS DEPT.

ABRA-CADAVER

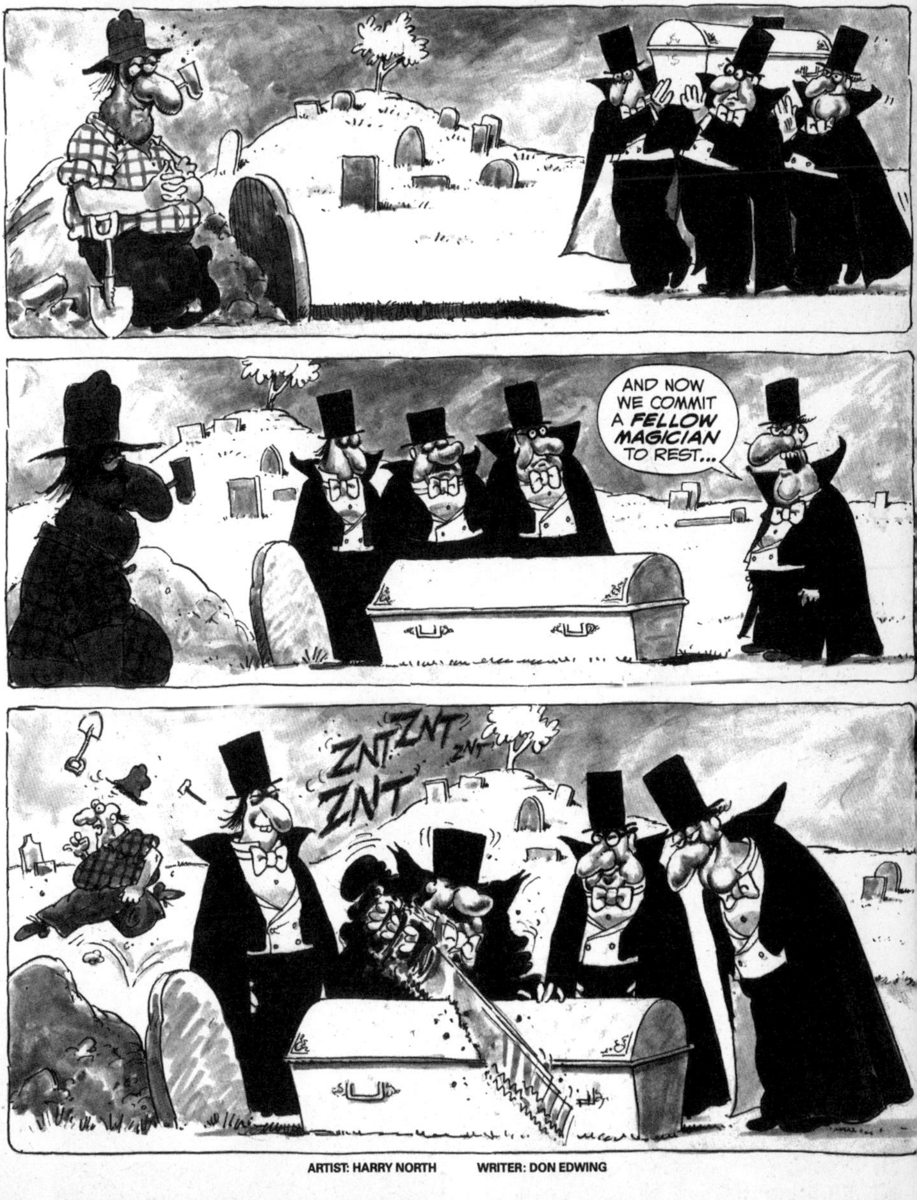

AND NOW WE COMMIT A FELLOW MAGICIAN TO REST...
ZNT ZNT ZNT ZNT ZNT

ARTIST: HARRY NORTH WRITER: DON EDWING

SERGIO ARAGONES DEPT.

A MAD LOOK AT BASEBALL

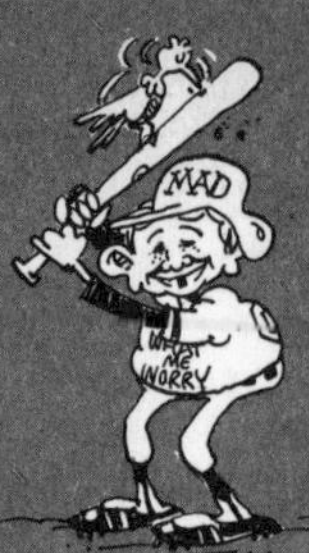
MAD
WHAT ME WORRY

ARTIST AND WRITER: SERGIO ARAGONES

TOP OF THE FIRST...

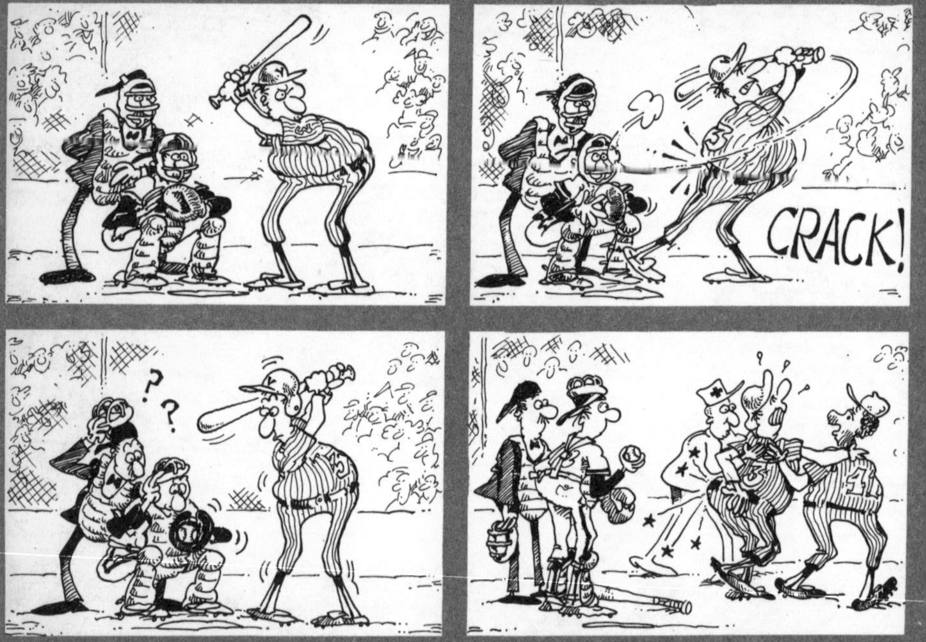
CRACK!

BOTTOM OF THE FIRST...

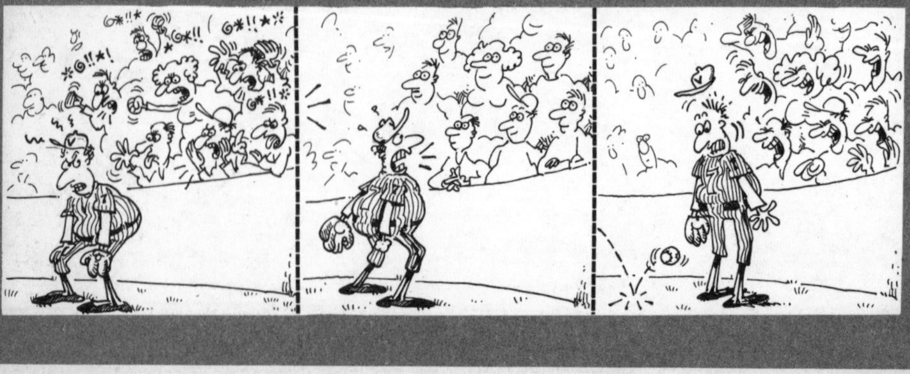

MAD BASEBALL BOTTOM OF THE SECOND—STILL SCORELESS

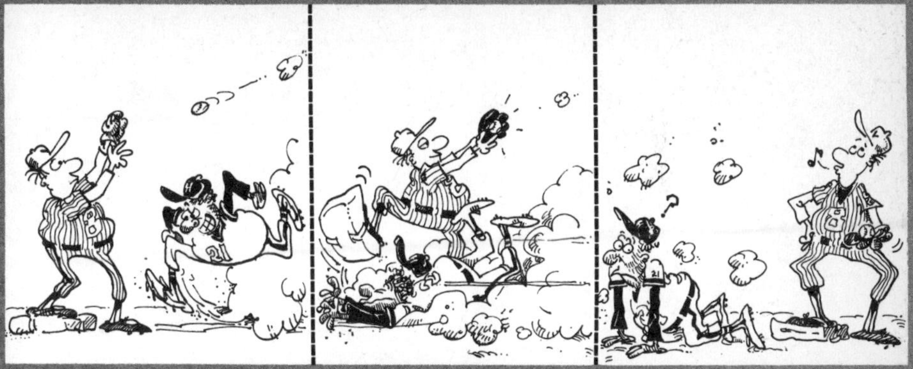

BOTTOM OF THE THIRD—SCORE TIED 1-1...

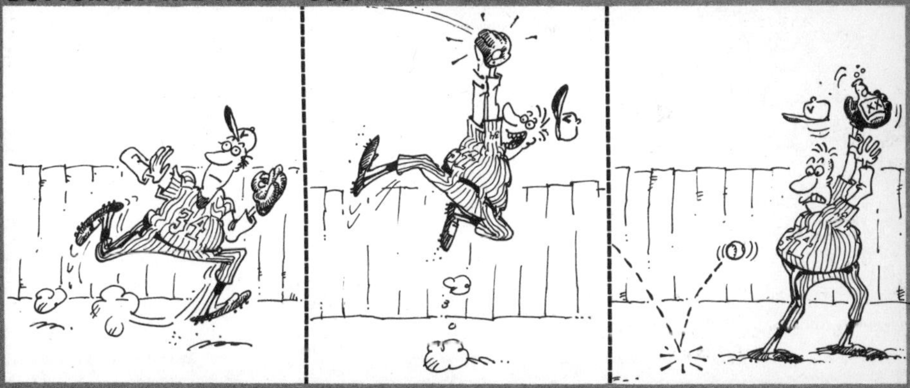

TOP OF THE FOURTH—PRESS COVERAGE

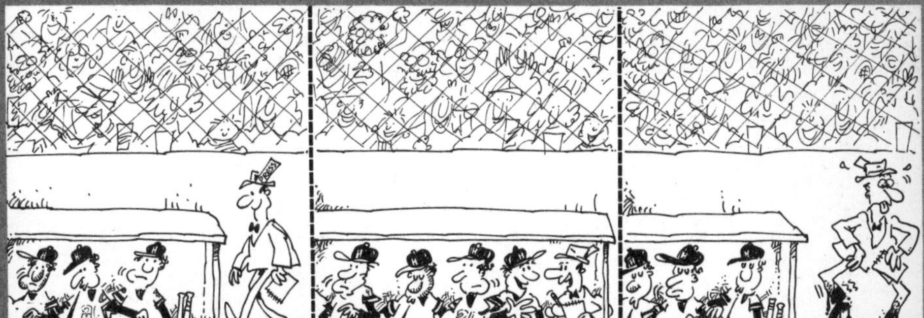

SPITOO!
SPITZZ!
SPITOO!!

ARTIST AND WRITER: SERGIO ARAGONES

MAD BASEBALL TOP OF THE FIFTH—LOADED BASES...

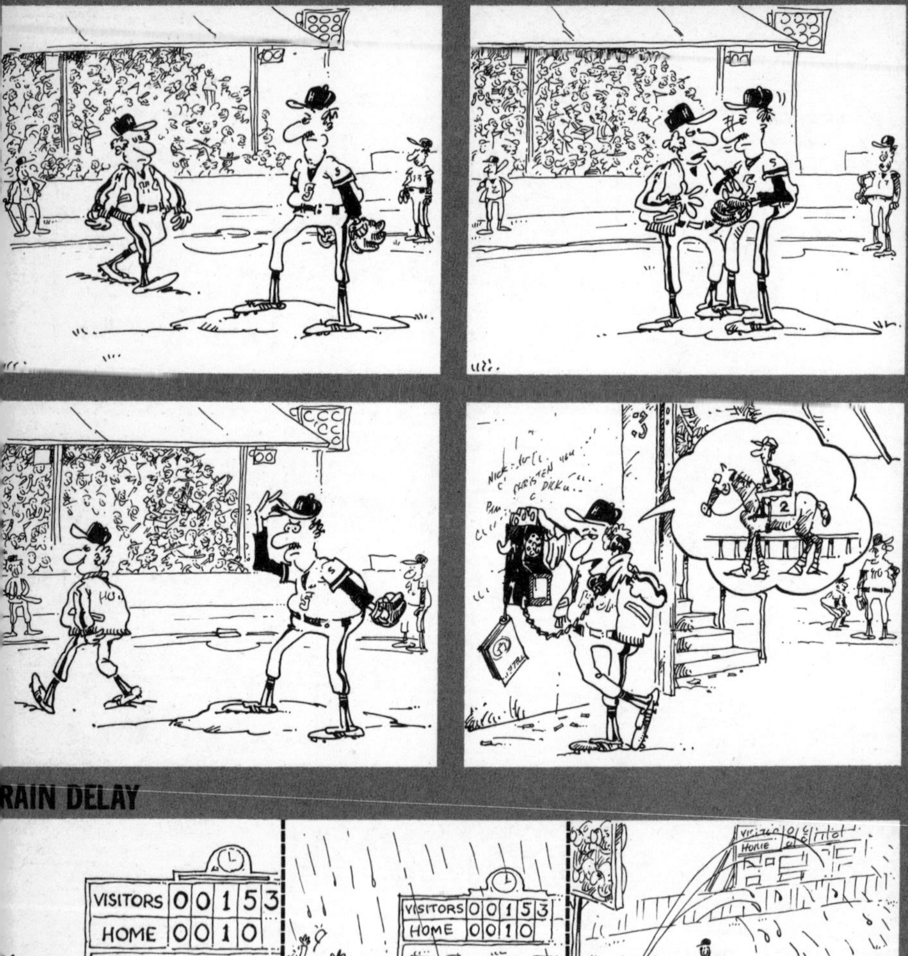

NICK
CHRISTEN 464
DICK
PAM
2

RAIN DELAY

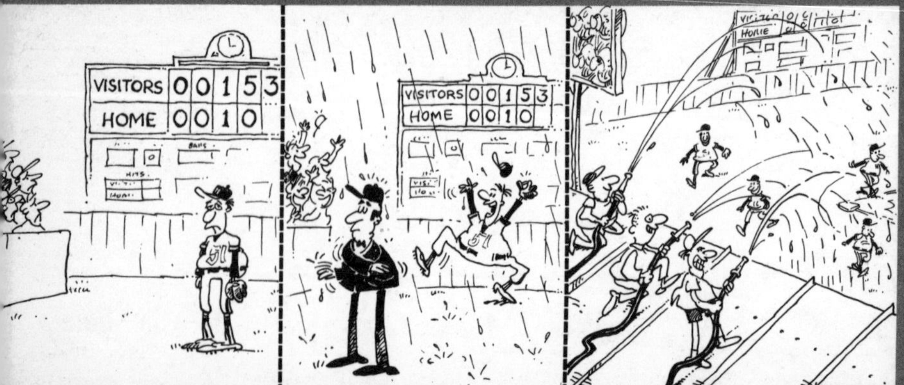

VISITORS 0 0 1 5 3
HOME 0 0 1 0
VISITORS 0 0 1 5 3
HOME 0 0 1 0

ARTIST AND WRITER: SERGIO ARAGONES

MAD BASEBALL WORLD CHAMPS!

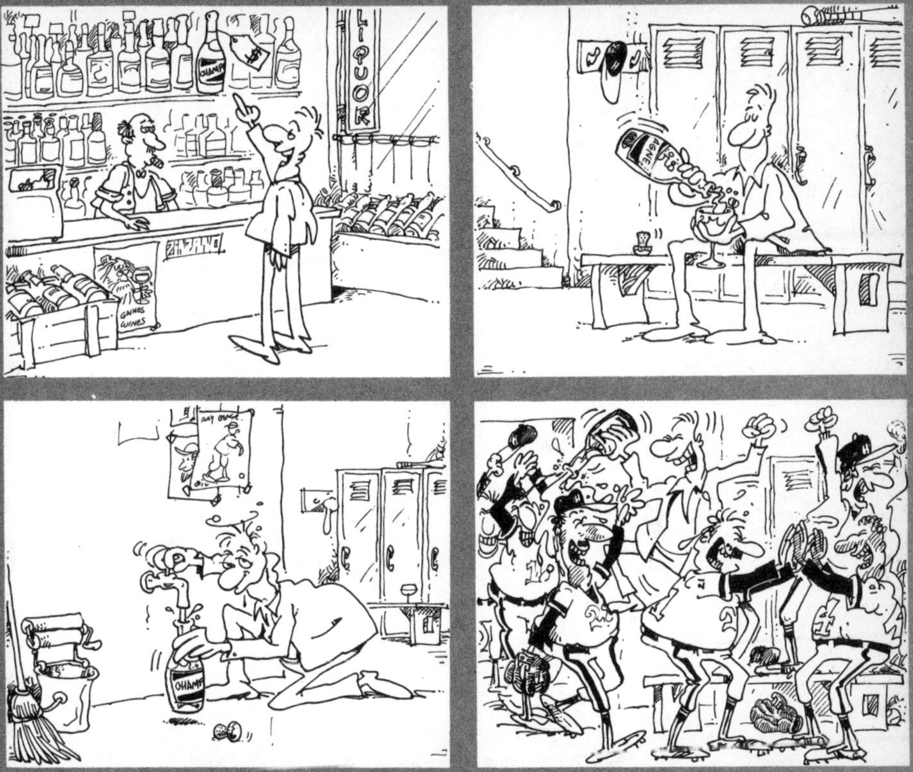
LIQUOR
CHAMP
CHAMP

OPENING DAY—THE FOLLOWING SEASON...

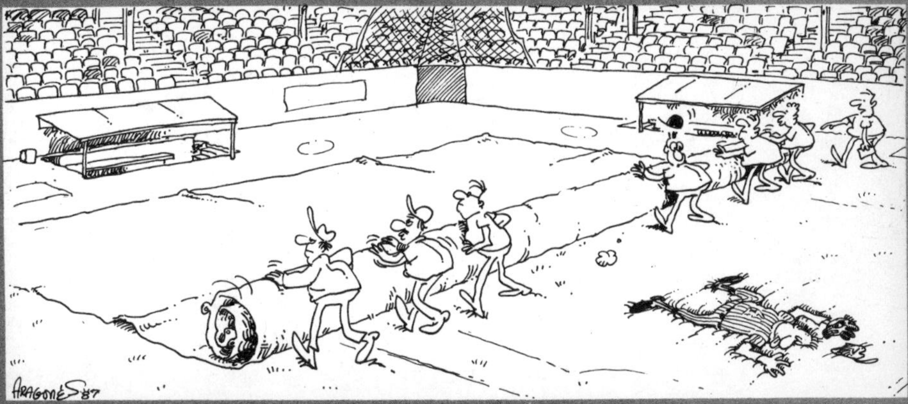
ARAGONES '87

ARTIST AND WRITER: SERGIO ARAGONES

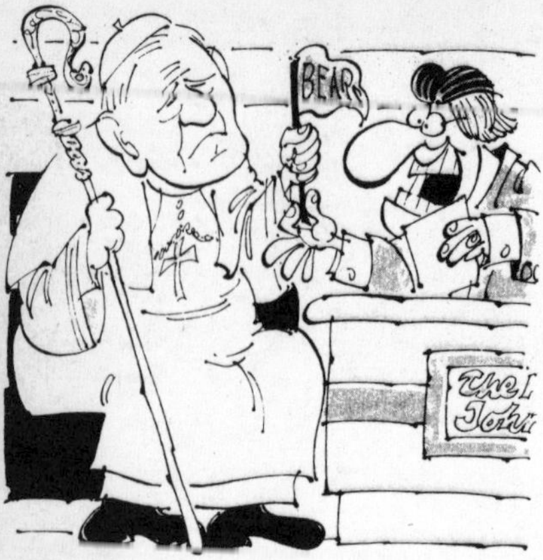
BEARS

EVERY GUEST ON EVERY TALK SHOW getting asked to give his Super Bowl "pick."

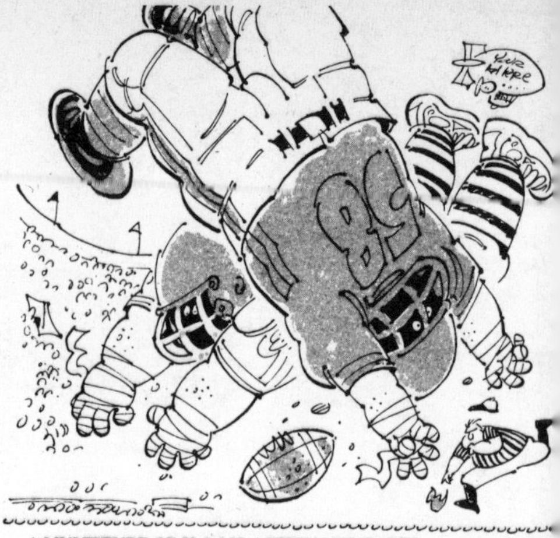

A MULTITUDE OF SLO-MO ACTION MONTAGES, shown over and over, all accompanied by Sinatra's version of "The Winners."

CERTAIN-T-FORMATIONS DEPT.

Aren't you sick of Super Bowl hype? We are! Every year's the same! Dull and predictable! Who wants to see another "sports profile" about 300-lb. linebackers who knit? We wish they'd cook up some new angles, because otherwise (unless you fall asleep!)...

EVERY SUPE

ARTIST: PAUL COK

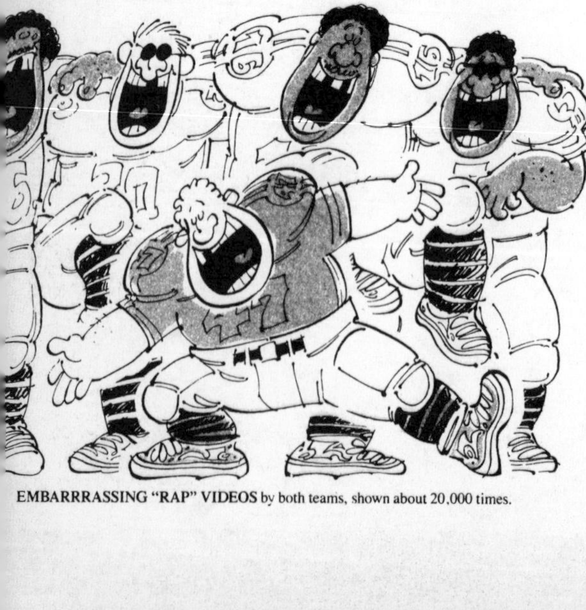

EMBARRRASSING "RAP" VIDEOS by both teams, shown about 20,000 times.

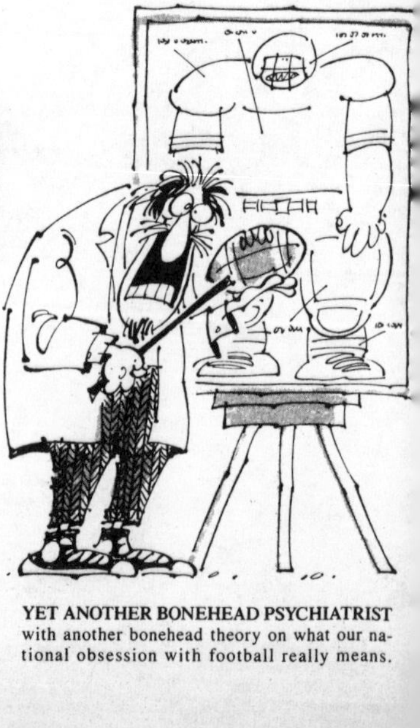

YET ANOTHER BONEHEAD PSYCHIATRIST with another bonehead theory on what our national obsession with football really means.

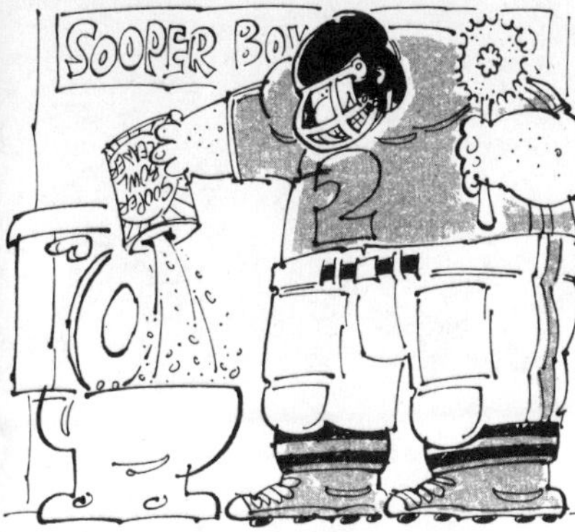
SOOPER BOW

DOZENS OF CHEAP ATTEMPTS to "cash in" on the Super Bowl hype, made by businesses not even remotely connected with football.

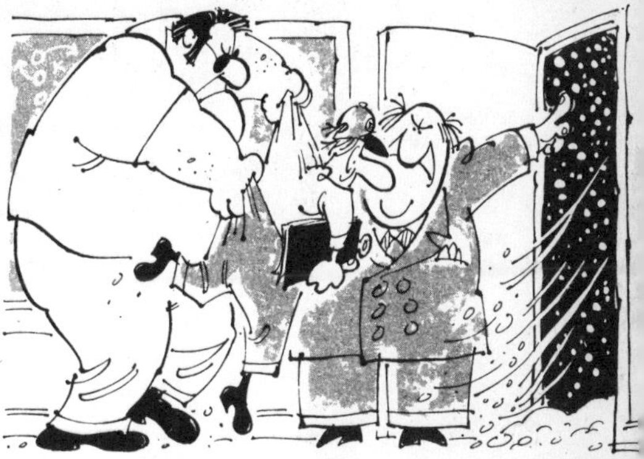

THE UNCEREMONIOUS FIRING of half of the NFL coaches who just didn't make it to the Super Bowl.

R BOWL WEEK YOU'RE SURE OF SEEING...

RITER: MIKE SNIDER

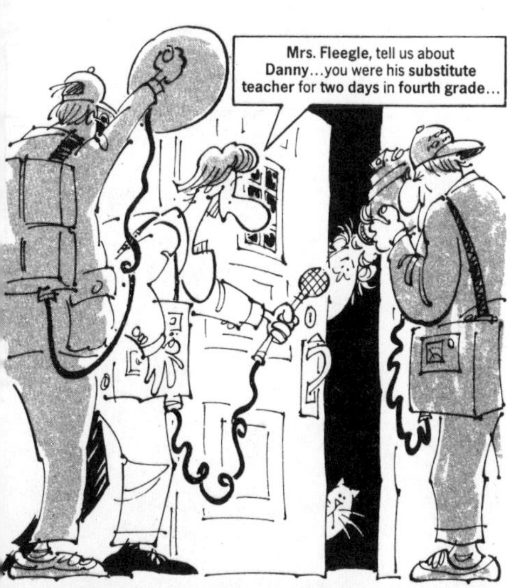
Mrs. Fleegle, tell us about Danny...you were his substitute teacher for two days in fourth grade...

MORE BIOGRAPHICAL INFORMATION on the two opposing quarterbacks than even their own mothers could stand.

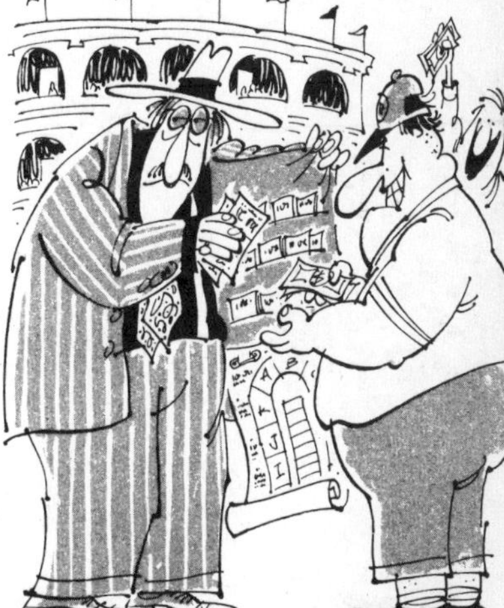

THE SAME STORIES ABOUT TICKET SCALPING —with the exact same prices—that you remember seeing the year before—and the year before that.

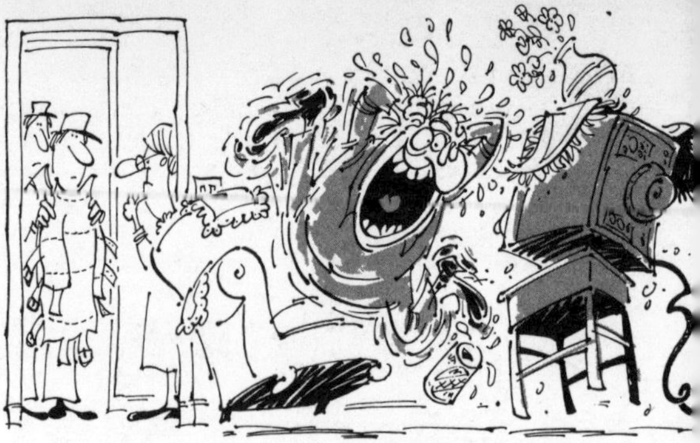

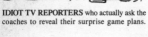

HUNDREDS OF "SUPER BOWL MOMENTS" on TV that make the previous Super Bowls look a lot more exciting than anything you remember.

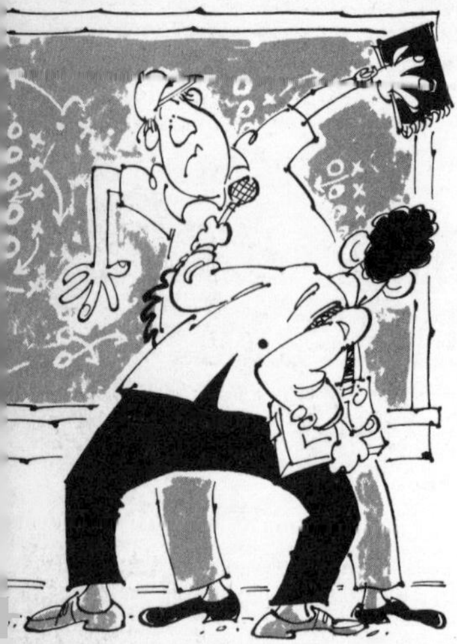

IDIOT TV REPORTERS who actually ask the coaches to reveal their surprise game plans.

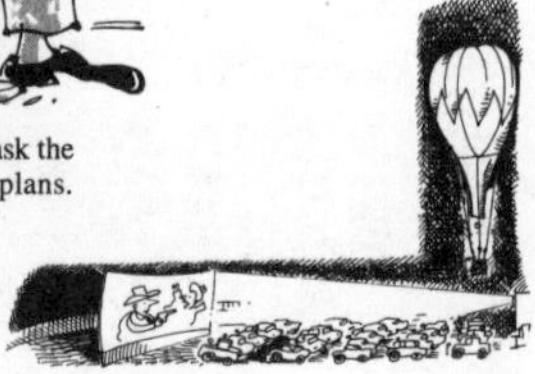

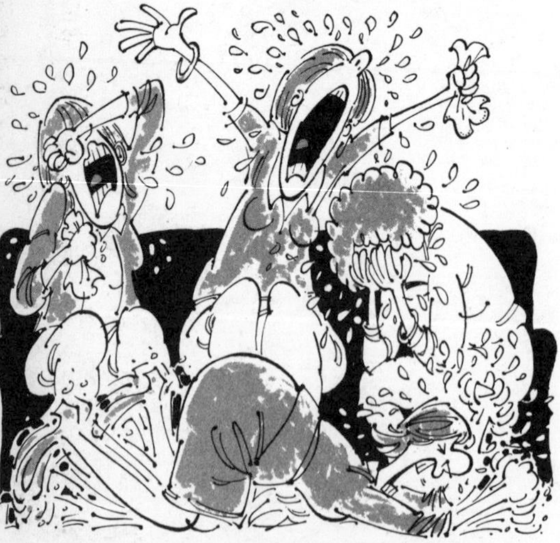

PANELS OF WHINY "FOOTBALL WIDOWS" who get together on the Phil Donahue and Oprah Winfrey shows.

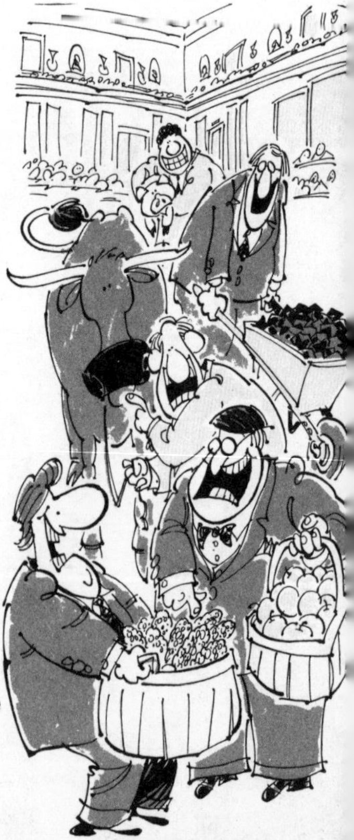

SENATORS WASTING VALUABLE TIME IN CONGRESS with goofy penny ante bets.

RENTING AND RAVING DEPT.

Many cheered the arrival of the video cassette recorder as another great invention—like the electric toothbrush and the coin machine that dispenses live bait. But now, some are openly questioning the VCR's value to society. Is its ability to bring recent movies into the home such a boon to mankind? Saturday night on the town—at the movies—is an *American tradition*.. Do we really want to throw over a cherished custom for some cheap little tape in a plastic box? Of course!! So pause, eject your better judgement, and fast-forward through...

WHY OWNING A VCR IS BETTER THAN GOING TO THE MOVIES

ARTIST: HARVEY KURTZMAN WRITER: TOM KOCH

To go to a movie, you must beg for the family car, which your parents often use on Saturday nights.

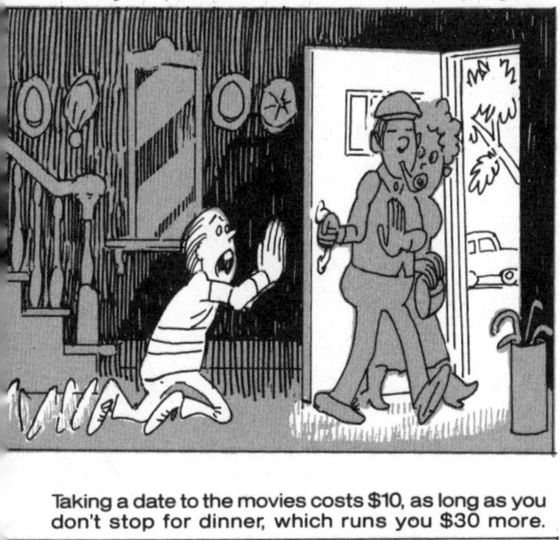

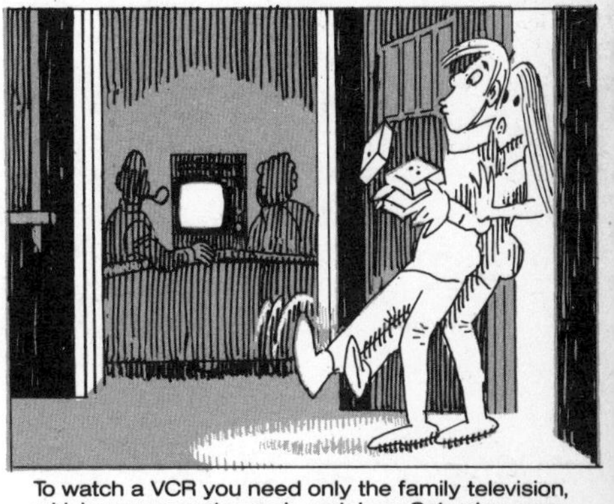

To watch a VCR you need only the family television, which your parents rarely watch on Saturday evenings—except when they're not out using the car.

Taking a date to the movies costs $10, as long as you don't stop for dinner, which runs you $30 more.

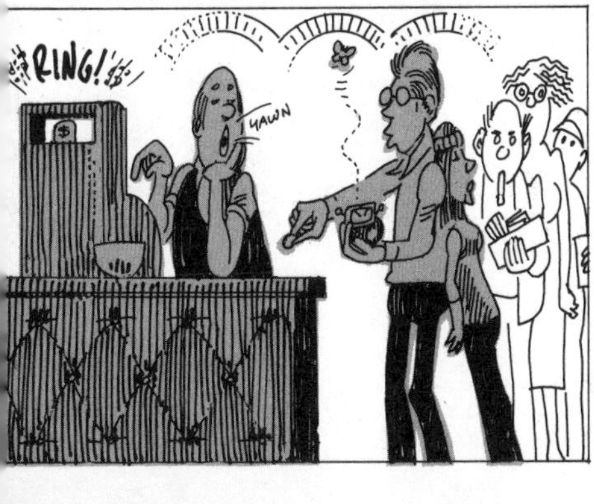
$RING!$
YAWN

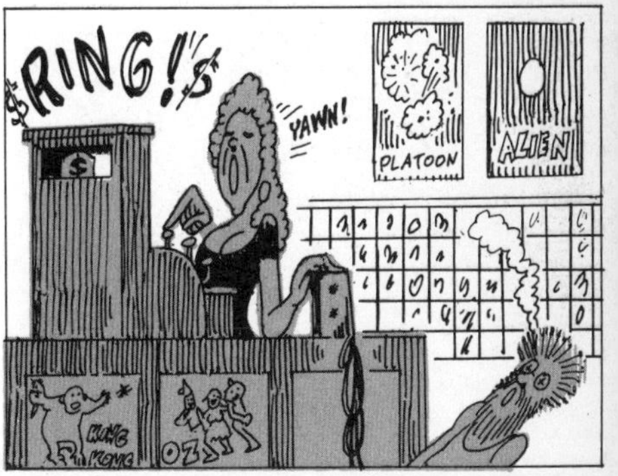
$RING!$
YAWN!
PLATOON
ALIEN
KING KONG
OZ

Renting a video tape costs only $2.00, as long as you don't lose it or damage it (assuming it was OK to begin with!), otherwise it runs you $79.95 more.

Driving to the movies on a Saturday night can turn into a frustrating waste of time that leaves you stranded in traffic for almost an hour.

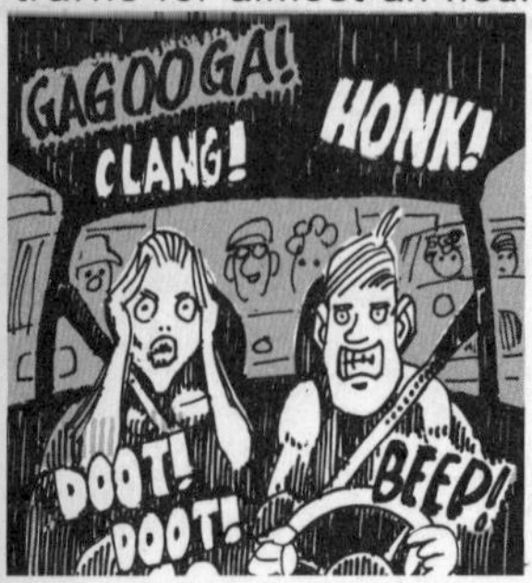
GAGOOGA!
CLANG!
HONK!
DOOT! DOOT!
BEEP!

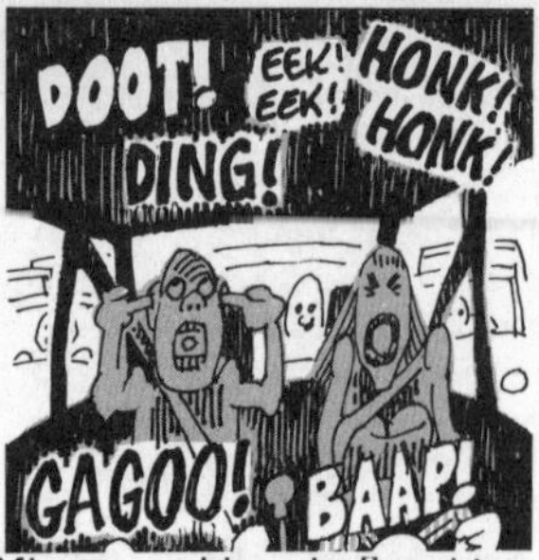
DOOT!
EEK! EEK!
HONK! HONK!
DING!
GAGOO!
BAAP!

Afternoon drives to the video store are never frustrating, provided you enjoy waiting 45 minutes for service that gets you out just in time for the Saturday night traffic jam.

As a movie-goer, on Saturday nights you have to watch whatever the theatre owner decides to present, even when it is a "Teenage Slasher Film Festival."

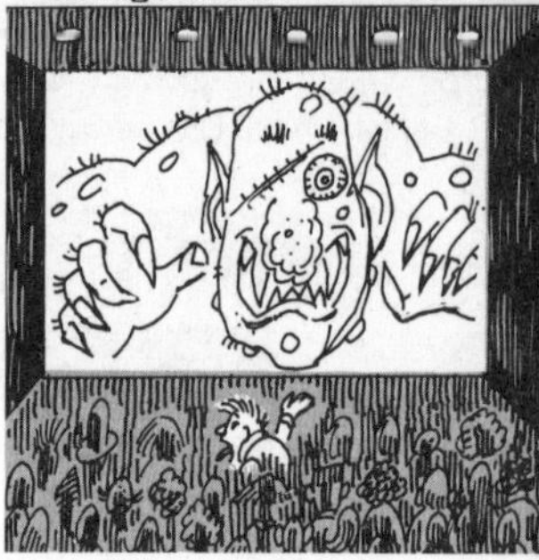

Wedging yourself for two hours into a cramped, food-stained theatre seat can lead to spine misalignment and sticky pants.

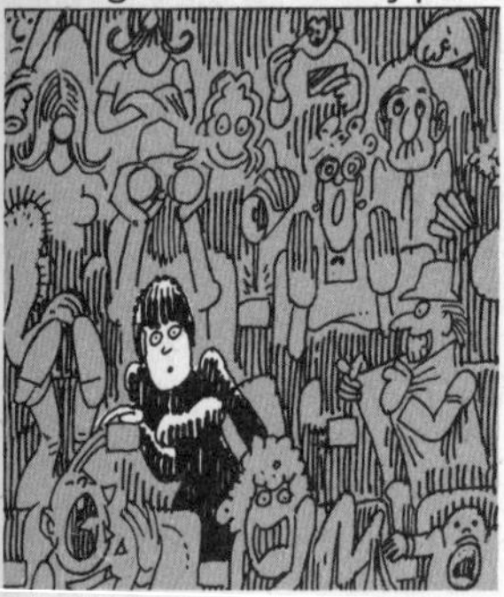

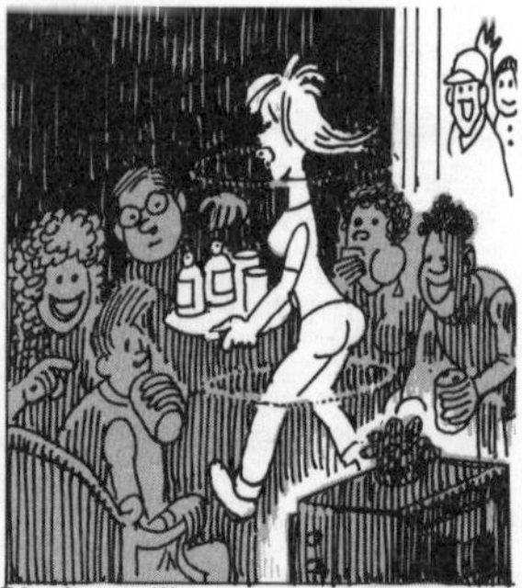

Chairs will never cause problems in your comfortable home. Uninvited guests will keep you so busy fixing food that you'll never have time to sit down.

At the movies, your enjoyment of the film is always disrupted by lots of people climbing over you to reach their seats.

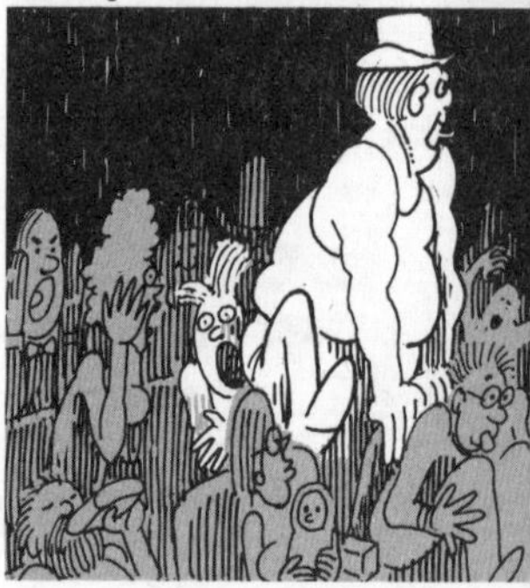

If you and your date get too personally involved at a movie, you may be interrupted by an usher swinging a flashlight.

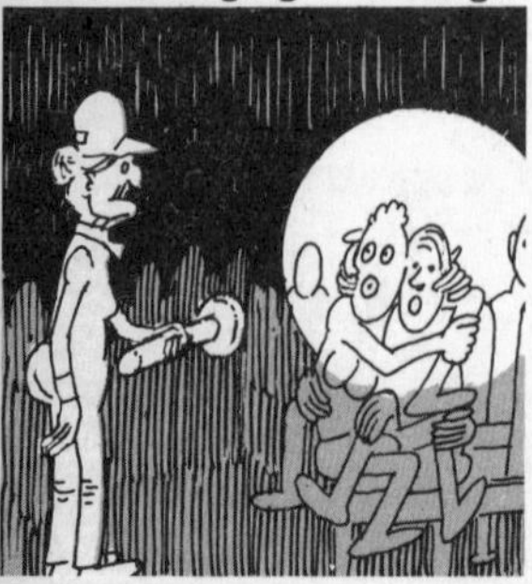

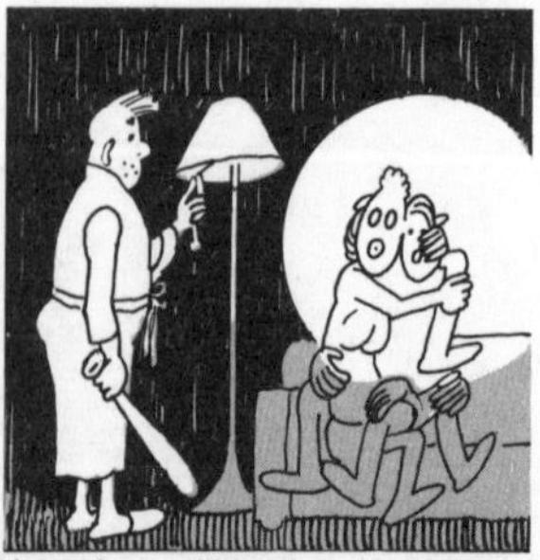

No usher will bother the two of you in front of a VCR. However, you may be interrupted by your parents, who frequently swing objects larger than flashlights.

After you've finished a late Saturday night at the movies, you must face the drudgery of driving all the way back home.

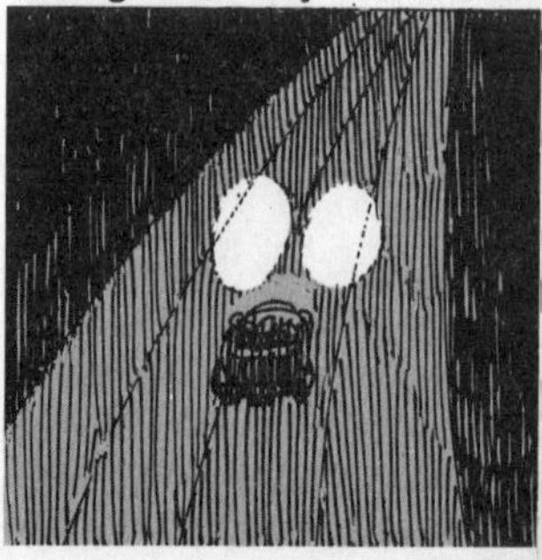

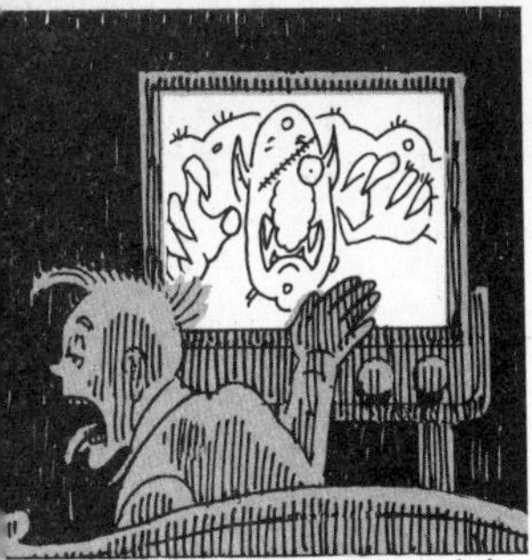

As a VCR owner you can watch anything you want—except on weekends, when the only tapes still available are "Friday the 13th Parts III, IV and V."

Before a movie begins you must first sit through boring reminders not to talk, litter or smoke, and previews that can drag on for fifteen minutes.

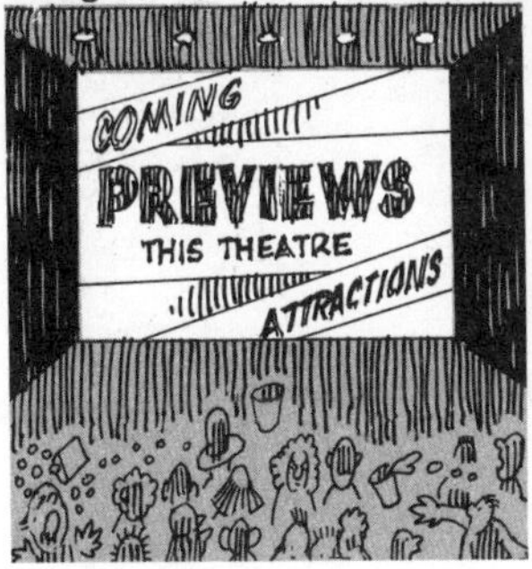
COMING
PREVIEWS
THIS THEATRE
ATTRACTIONS

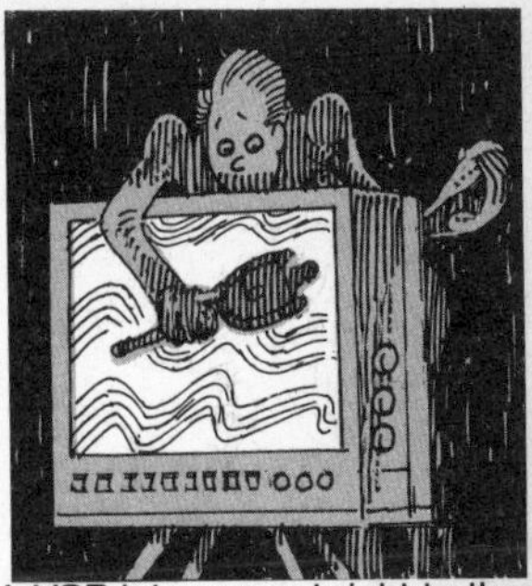

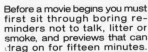

A VCR lets you get right to the feature, just as soon as you adjust the contrast, brightness, color and tint, which rarely takes more than half an hour.

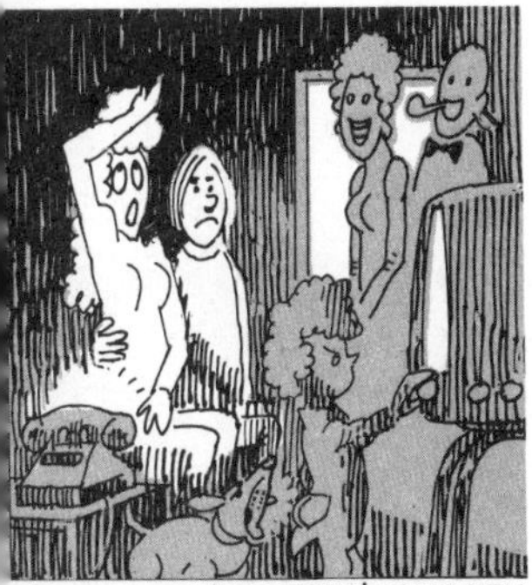

People seldom crawl over you when you're home with a VCR. They simply ring your doorbell and telephone every ten minutes.

In a public theatre you never know if the stranger next to you is a demented weirdo who's planning to stab you to death.

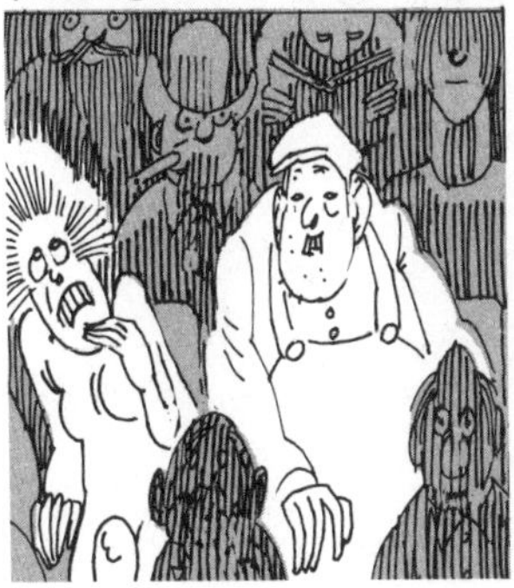

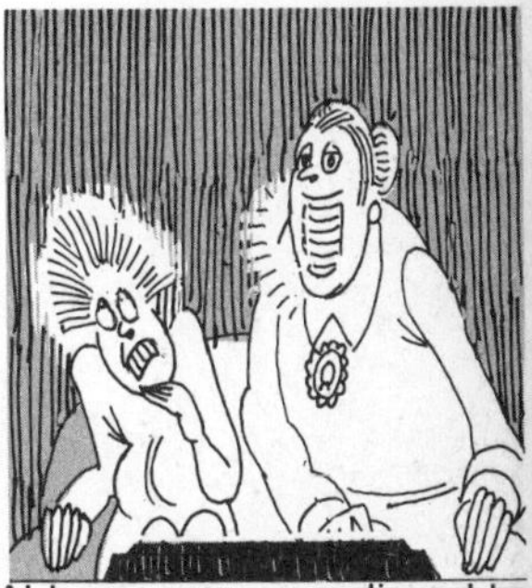

At home, you are relieved to know that the person next to you is just a demented friend or relative who's merely capable of boring you to death.

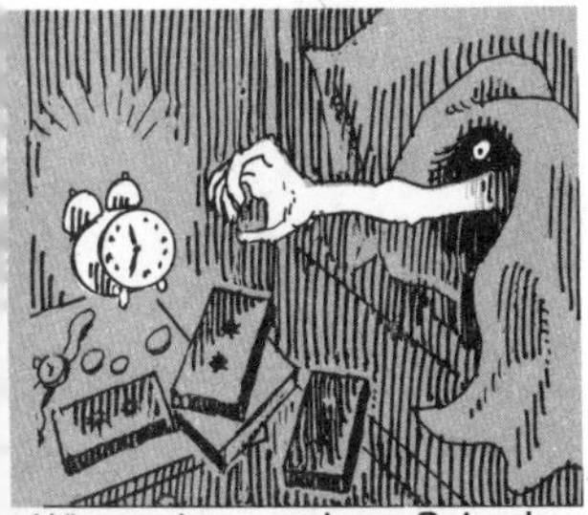

When a tape ends on Saturday night, you're already home—at least until Sunday morning, when you must face the drudgery of schlepping it back by 10 AM—or pay for an extra day.

Attending a popular first-run movie on the weekend gives you just one thing to discuss with your friends on Monday morning.

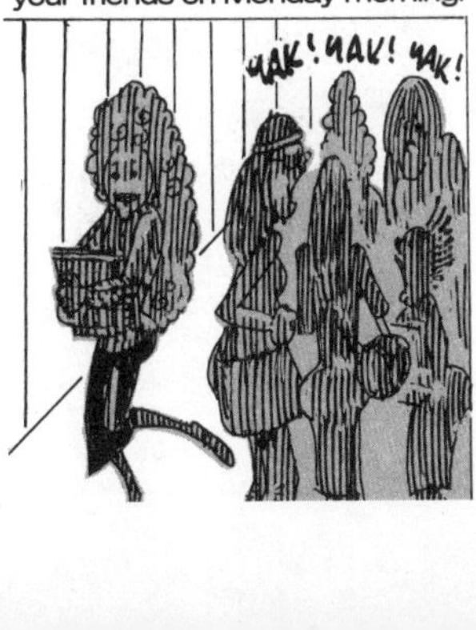
YAK! YAK! YAK!

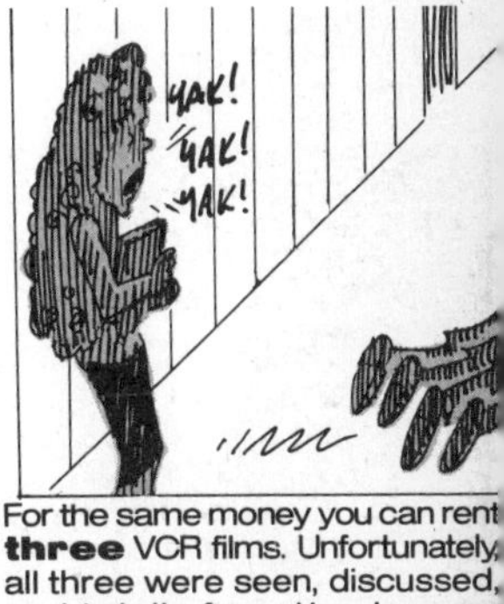
YAK!
YAK!
YAK!

For the same money you can rent **three** VCR films. Unfortunately, all three were seen, discussed, and totally forgotten by your friends about six months ago.

ALLEY OOPS! DEPT.

DRAMA ON PAGE 98

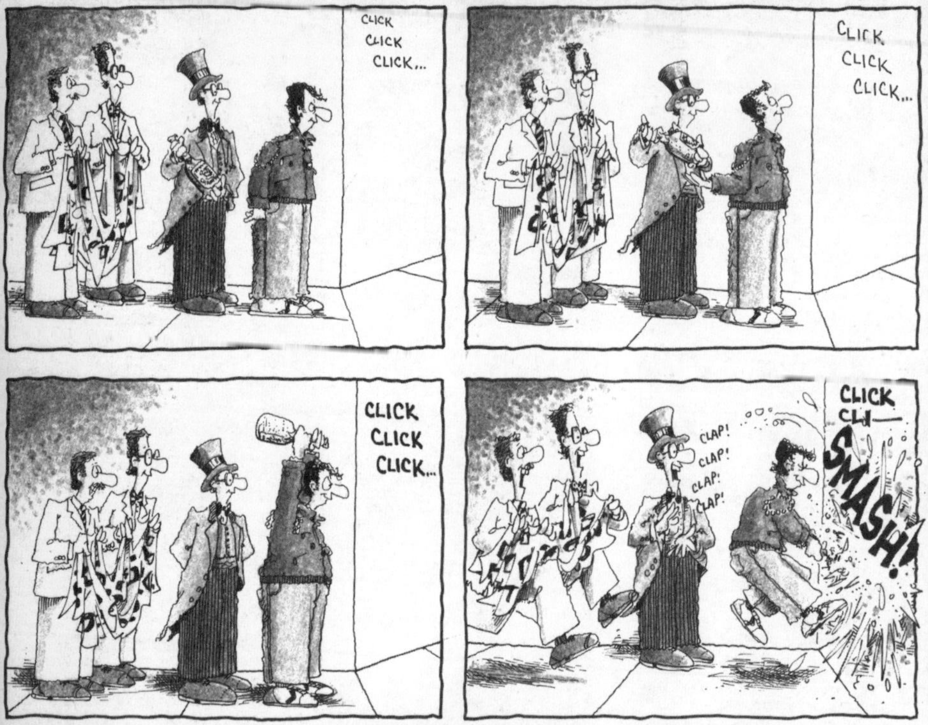
CLICK
CLICK
CLICK...
CLICK
CLICK
CLICK...
CLICK
CLICK
CLICK...
CLICK
CLI—
CLAP!
CLAP!
CLAP!
CLAP!
SMASH!

ARTIST AND WRITER: JOHN CALDWELL

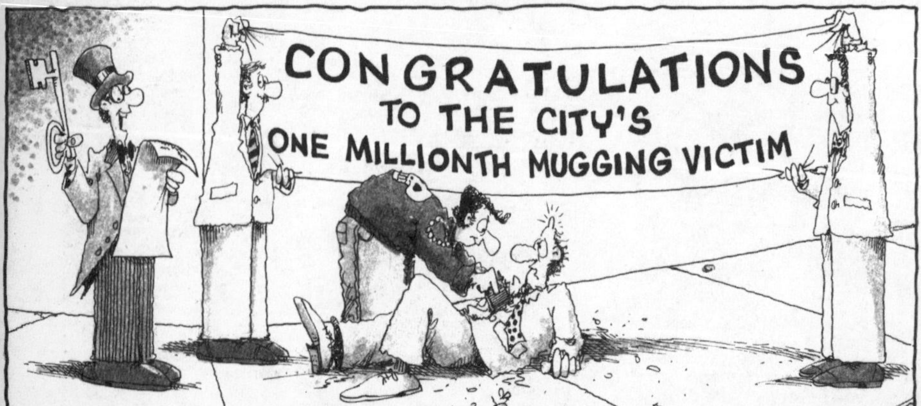
CONGRATULATIONS
TO THE CITY'S
ONE MILLIONTH MUGGING VICTIM
CALDWELL

JOKE AND DAGGER DEPT.

SPY vs SPY

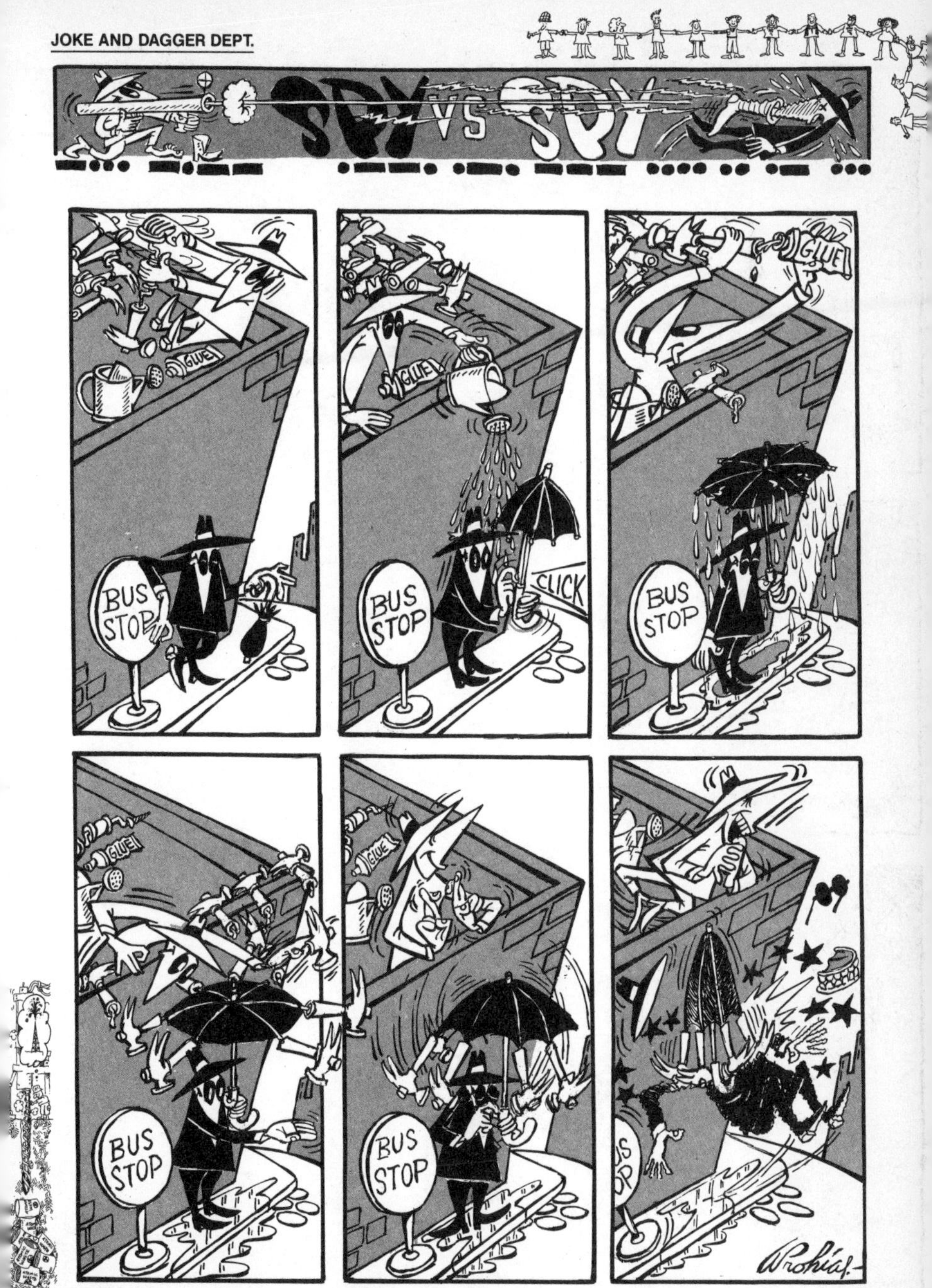
GLUE
BUS STOP
GLUE
CLICK
BUS STOP
GLUE
BUS STOP
GLUE
BUS STOP
GLUE
BUS STOP
Prohías

TALES FROM THE DUCK SIDE DEPT.

THE COLOSSAL COURTROOM CONFRONTATION

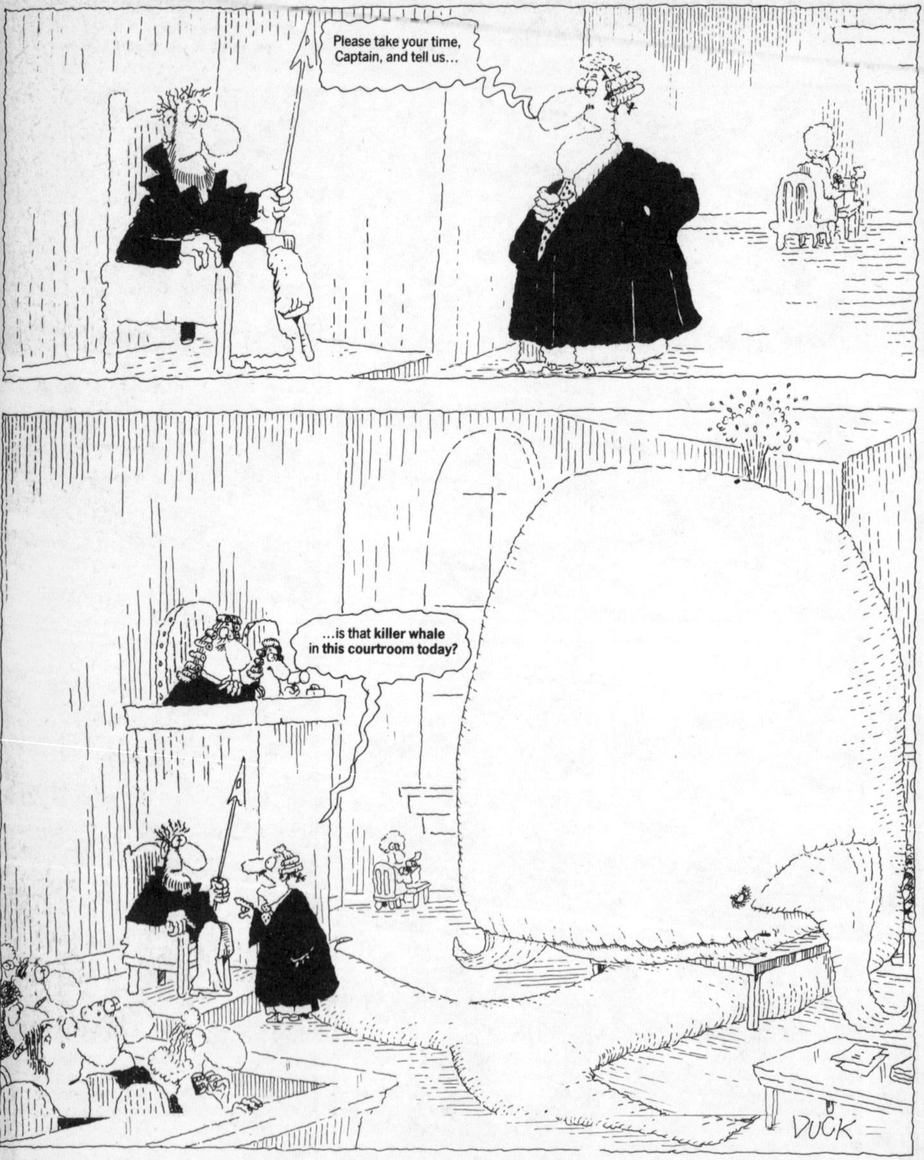
Please take your time, Captain, and tell us…
…is that killer whale in this courtroom today?
DUCK

ARTIST AND WRITER: DUCK EDWING

THE ENVELOPE, SLEAZE! DEPT.

You probably know loads of people who receive fat envelopes in the mail that are filled with chances to win fantastic prizes and mucho bucks if they will only send in the entry form (and hopefully order some dumb magazines as well). But, how many people do you know who have actually been a winner in one of these cockamamie contests? Well, we don't know any either! And we thought it was about time we got even with the creeps who keep sending out this stupid trash. So without further ado,

MAD OPENS A TYPICAL MAGAZINE SWEEPSTAKES PACKAGE

YOU CAN WIN THESE GRAND PRIZES!

Super Spectacular Grand Prize #1

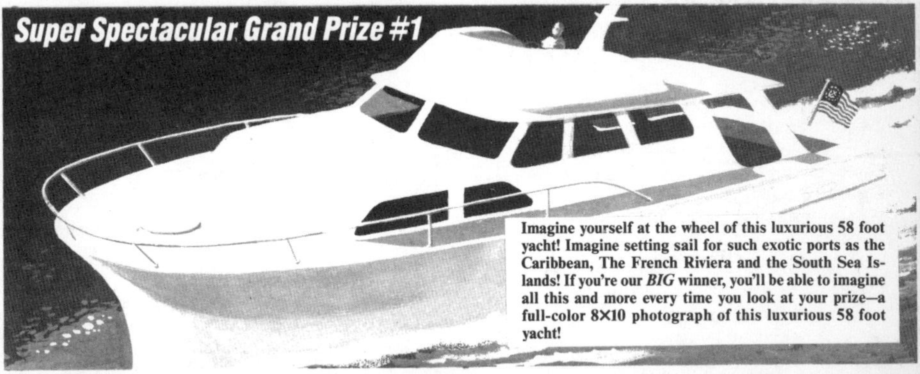

Imagine yourself at the wheel of this luxurious 58 foot yacht! Imagine setting sail for such exotic ports as the Caribbean, The French Riviera and the South Sea Islands! If you're our *BIG* winner, you'll be able to imagine all this and more every time you look at your prize—a full-color 8X10 photograph of this luxurious 58 foot yacht!

Wild Incredible Grand Prize #2

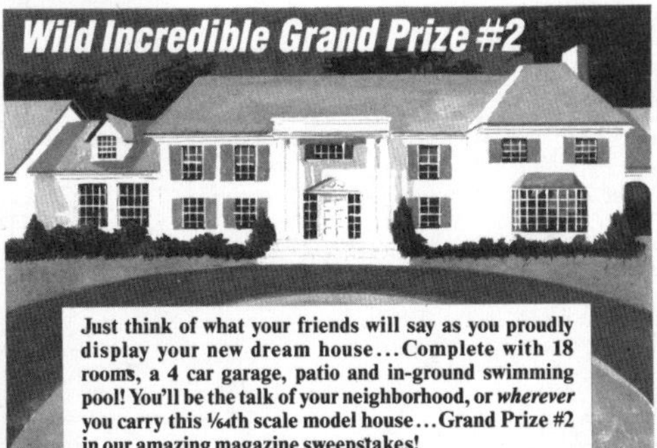

Just think of what your friends will say as you proudly display your new dream house... Complete with 18 rooms, a 4 car garage, patio and in-ground swimming pool! You'll be the talk of your neighborhood, or *wherever* you carry this 1/64th scale model house... Grand Prize #2 in our amazing magazine sweepstakes!

Utterly Unbelievable Grand Prize #3

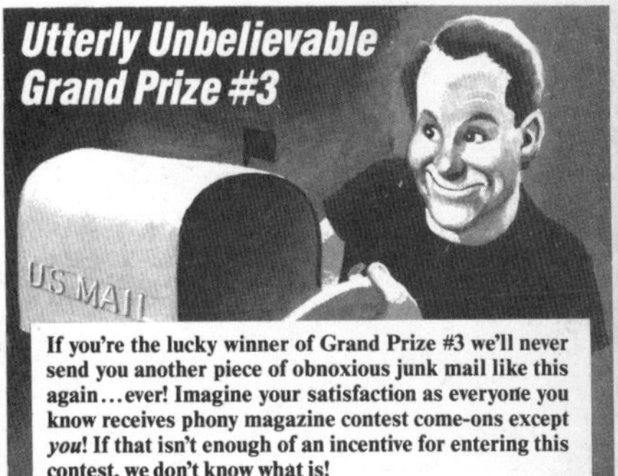
US MAIL

If you're the lucky winner of Grand Prize #3 we'll never send you another piece of obnoxious junk mail like this again... ever! Imagine your satisfaction as everyone you know receives phony magazine contest come-ons except *you*! If that isn't enough of an incentive for entering this contest, we don't know what is!

WHO CAN ENTER

Our 5 Million Dollar Bonus Sweepstakes is open to all residents of the United States and Canada with the following exceptions: Anyone under the age of 18, women, left-handed people, good dancers, wristwatch owners, taxidermists, circus midgets, football fans, ex-members of Menudo, wax fruit manufacturers, Christians, and men.

If you've decided not to order...

please read this!

Dear Friend:

If you've decided you don't want to take advantage of our incredibly spectacular and truly amazing magazine buys, YOU CAN STILL ENTER OUR SWEEPSTAKES *EVEN IF YOU DON'T BUY ANYTHING*! But remember: for some unexplainable reason, a person's chances of winning seem to increase when they buy lots and lots of magazines from us. I'm not saying you *have* to buy magazines in order to win anything, but I can't think of a single winner we've had who didn't buy multi-year subscriptions to several dozen of our fine magazines!

What do you take me for, a blithering idiot? Only a moron would give away hundreds of thousands of
jerks who think they can
and ugly as sin to boot.
ought to be shot!

Fondly,

Emerson L. Bunk
President
Fat Chance Publishers

HALF OFF
Potholder Monthly
From the publishers of Cardboard Illustrated
Only $23.40

83¢ A COPY
Illegal Business Week
Only $11.95

HALF OFF
OUCH!
The Magazine of Painful Dentistry
Only $14.97

58¢ OFF
ALL ADS
We dare you to find an article
Only $48.50

58¢ A COPY
VD Guide
Where It Is and How To Avoid It
Only $13.32

$8.00 OFF
Better Avocado
(Includes our Annual Guacamole Issue)
Only $14.99

This Check Could

Fat Chance Publishers
12 Bogus Boulevard
Shady Groves, Connecticut

Pay To the Order Of Mr. Occupant and
Five Million 00/xx

First National Void Bank

Official Signature Here

Only $23.40

in every issue)
Only $9.99

Only $48.50

$3.05 OFF
MAD
Winner of the VEEKO Award

GOOD VALUE
Sports Titillated
52 Swimsuit Issues A Year!
$62.79

GOOD VALUE
Teen Rabbi
The Magazine for Everyone!
Only $20.00

ES
AN
Journal for
ss Executives)
ly $44.56

HALF OFF
CREATIVE TERRORISM
Free Hostage with Paid Subscription! 12 Explosive Issues
Only $29.99

A Personal Note From Fat Chance Publishers

Dear Mr. Occupant,

You may already be the winner of our 5 Million Dollar Bonus Prize...and not even know it!

Just think of what 5 Million Dollars could do for the Occupant **family...A mink coat for** Mrs. Occupant**...A college education for the** Occupant **children...Yes,** Mr. Occupant, **you could be**

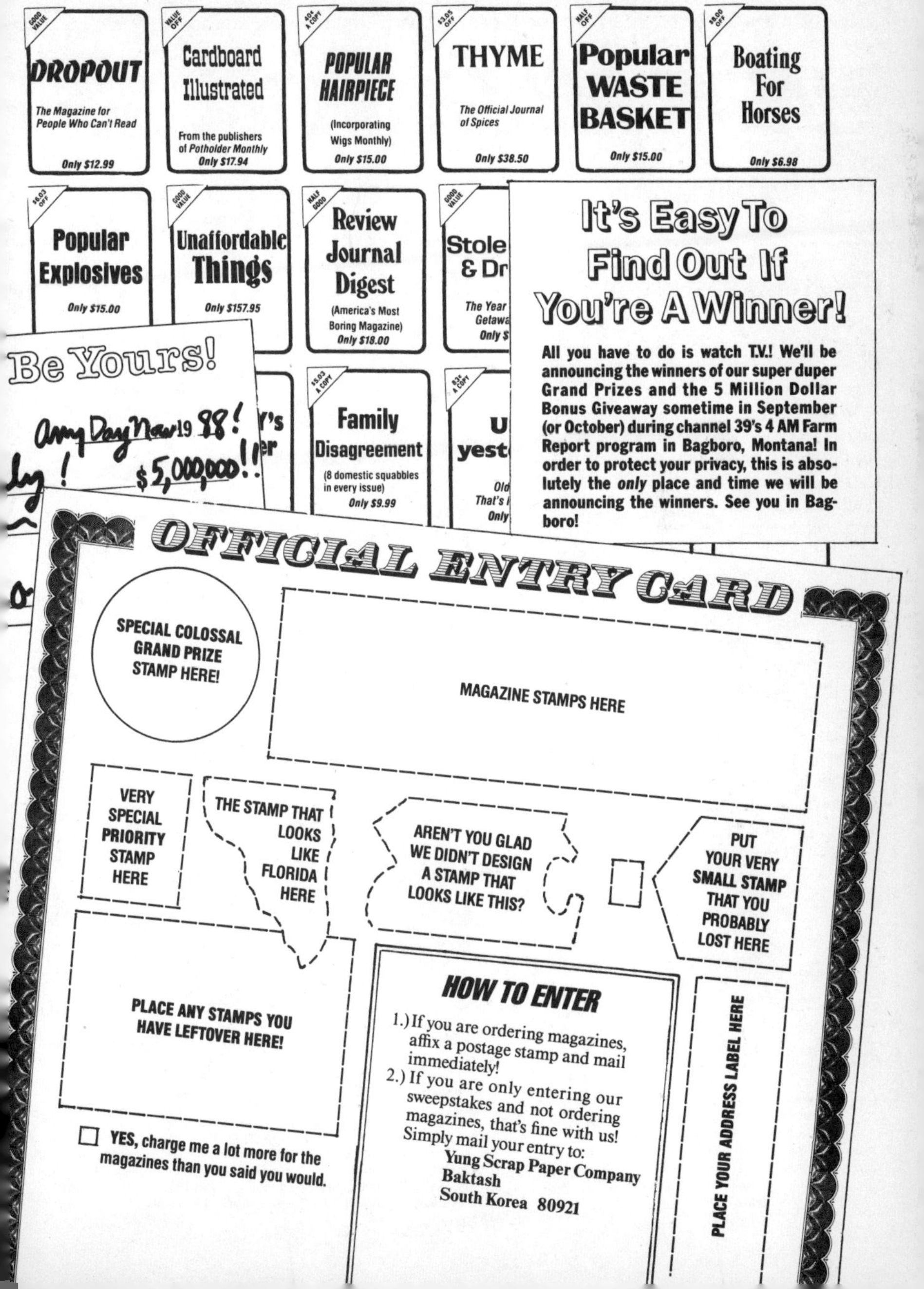
GOOD VALUE
DROPOUT
The Magazine for People Who Can't Read
Only $12.99
VALUE OFF
Cardboard Illustrated
From the publishers of Potholder Monthly
Only $17.94
40¢ A COPY
POPULAR HAIRPIECE
(Incorporating Wigs Monthly)
Only $15.00
$3.05 OFF
THYME
The Official Journal of Spices
Only $38.50
HALF OFF
Popular WASTE BASKET
Only $15.00
$8.00 OFF
Boating For Horses
Only $6.98
$6.03 OFF
Popular Explosives
Only $15.00
GOOD VALUE
Unaffordable Things
Only $157.95
HALF GOOD
Review Journal Digest
(America's Most Boring Magazine)
Only $18.00
$5.03 A COPY
Family Disagreement
(8 domestic squabbles in every issue)
Only $9.99
83¢ A COPY
Be Yours!
Any Day Now 19 88!
$5,000,000!!
It's Easy To Find Out If You're A Winner!
All you have to do is watch T.V.! We'll be announcing the winners of our super duper Grand Prizes and the 5 Million Dollar Bonus Giveaway sometime in September (or October) during channel 39's 4 AM Farm Report program in Bagboro, Montana! In order to protect your privacy, this is absolutely the only place and time we will be announcing the winners. See you in Bagboro!
OFFICIAL ENTRY CARD
SPECIAL COLOSSAL GRAND PRIZE STAMP HERE!
MAGAZINE STAMPS HERE
VERY SPECIAL PRIORITY STAMP HERE
THE STAMP THAT LOOKS LIKE FLORIDA HERE
AREN'T YOU GLAD WE DIDN'T DESIGN A STAMP THAT LOOKS LIKE THIS?
PUT YOUR VERY SMALL STAMP THAT YOU PROBABLY LOST HERE
PLACE ANY STAMPS YOU HAVE LEFTOVER HERE!
YES, charge me a lot more for the magazines than you said you would.
HOW TO ENTER
1.) If you are ordering magazines, affix a postage stamp and mail immediately!
2.) If you are only entering our sweepstakes and not ordering magazines, that's fine with us! Simply mail your entry to:
Yung Scrap Paper Company
Baktash
South Korea 80921
PLACE YOUR ADDRESS LABEL HERE

CHORE-FIRE SOLUTIONS DEPT.

What's a working mother to do? She makes breakfast, sends the kids to school, cleans the hous and then rushes to the office where she types, prepares reports and attends business meetings

DUAL-PURPOSE OFFICE SUPP

ARTIST: AL JAFFE

SIDE-BY-SIDE FILE CABINETS AND WASHER/DRYER

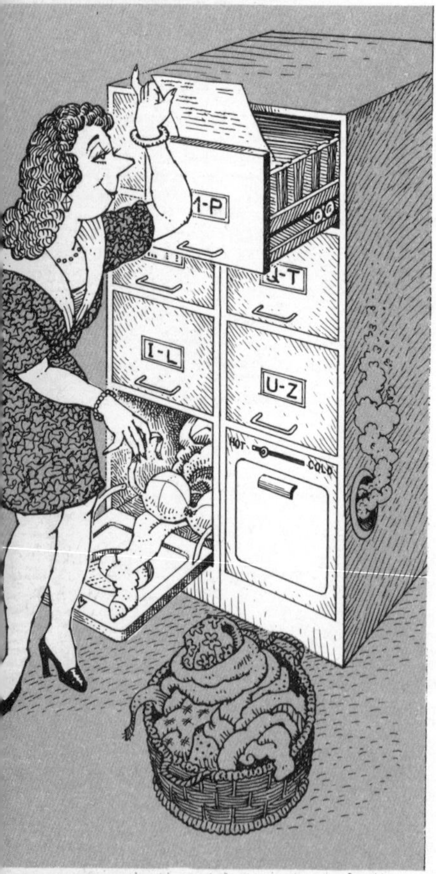

I-L
U-Z
HOT
COLD

Color-coordinated to fit any decor, each of these stainless steel file cabinets houses a full-load capacity washer and dryer. Whether washing your kid's grungiest clothes or just a handful of dainties, you'll be able to do a week's worth of laundry and file those important contracts all at the same time. As a bonus, you can file detergent under "D," fabric softener under "F," etc.

COMPUTER TERMINAL/MAKEUP MIRROR

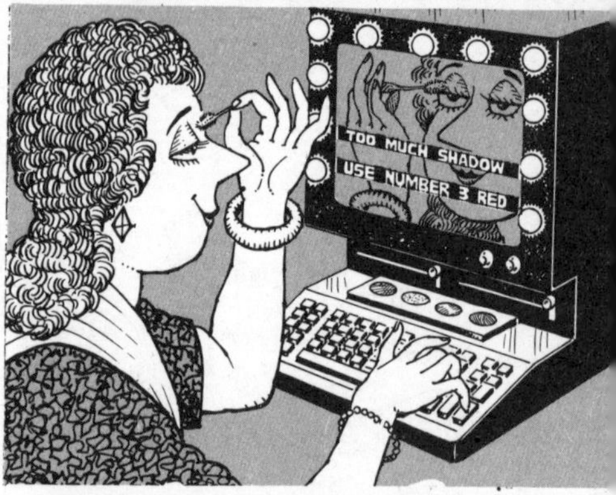

TOO MUCH SHADOW
USE NUMBER 3 RED

Finally, a way to apply your morning makeup *and* word process at the same time! Each of these powerful 20 megabyte PCs is connected to a central mainframe and comes with a highly reflective monitor scree with adjustable makeup lights. Peripherals include the disk drive/nail polish dryer and the cosmetic tray/letter quality printer.

PAPER SHREDDER/PASTA MAKER

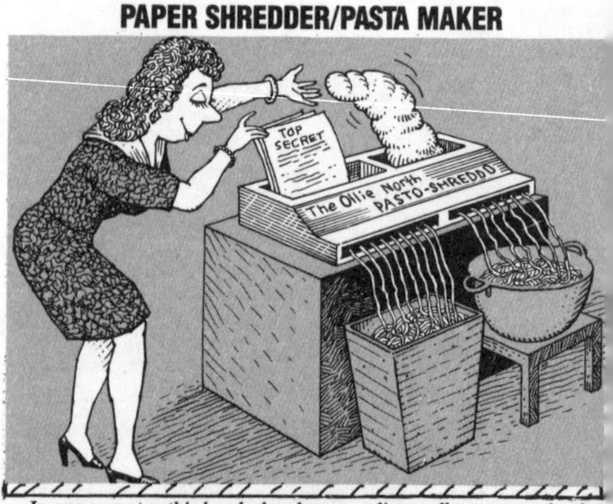

TOP SECRET
The Ollie North PASTO-SHREDDO

In one easy step this handy, handsome appliance allows you to shred confidential documents *and* add bulk to your family's diet! The stainless steel cutting edges never need sharpening and each unit includes settings for making rigatoni, ravioli and fettucine, as well as destroying photos, blueprints and other top secret memoranda.

Wouldn't it be great if she could do her office work at home or her house work at the office? Yes! That's why MAD envisions in the not-too-distant future a catalogue full of new and innovative...

IES FOR WORKING MOTHERS

WRITER: JOHN RIOS

EXECUTIVE DESK/IRONING BOARD

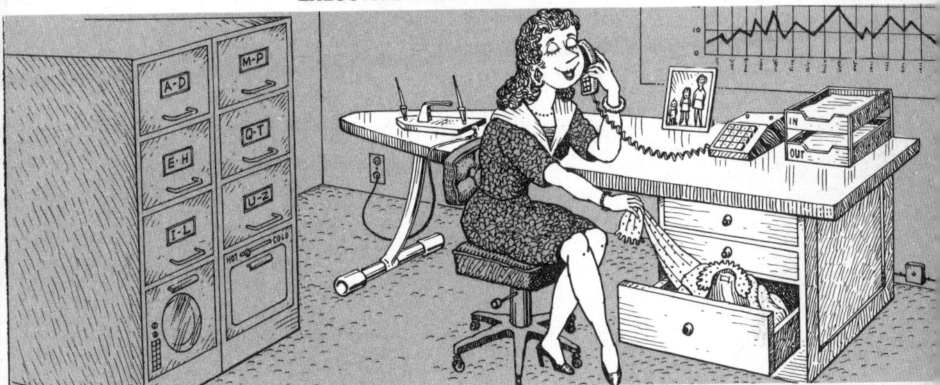
A-D
M-P
E-H
Q-T
I-L
U-Z
HOT
COLD
IN
OUT

A handsome in-laid mahogany base topped off by a smart, fire-retardant ironing board. Its extra large surface means you'll never have to be more than an arm's length from office reports, balance sheets and wrinkled blouses and skirts. The three drawers (with solid brass handles) can accommodate office supplies, stationery and spray starches.

PEN AND PENCIL SET/STEAM IRON

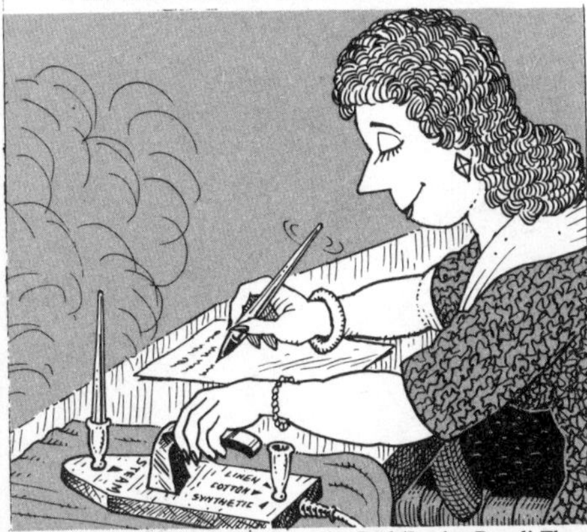
STEAM
LINEN
COTTON
SYNTHETIC

The perfect accessory for the Executive Desk/Ironing Board! The base of this attractive gold-plated pen and pencil set is a heavy-duty steam iron. Adjust the pen position for "linen," "cotton" or "synthetics," and push the pencil to the left for "steam." Guaranteed not to scorch, drag or leak ink.

STAMP PAD/SPICE RACK

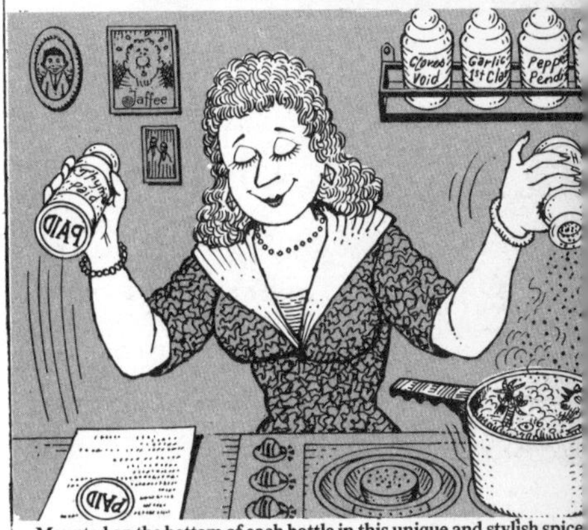
Cloves
Void
Jaffee
PAID
PAID

Mounted on the bottom of each bottle in this unique and stylish spice rack is a durable rubber stamp. Season your recipes and stamp office correspondence accordingly! Each set includes Thyme/Paid, Cloves/Void, Pepper/Pending, Garlic Powder/First Class, Bay Leaves/Received and Basil/Cancel.

ALL JAFFEE DEPT.

Embarrassing situations can happen at any time. Like right now—this article. Mostly, however, they happen when you put your big foot

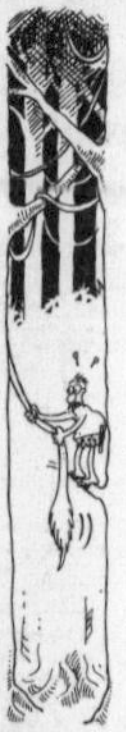

QUICK RECO
EMBARRASSIN

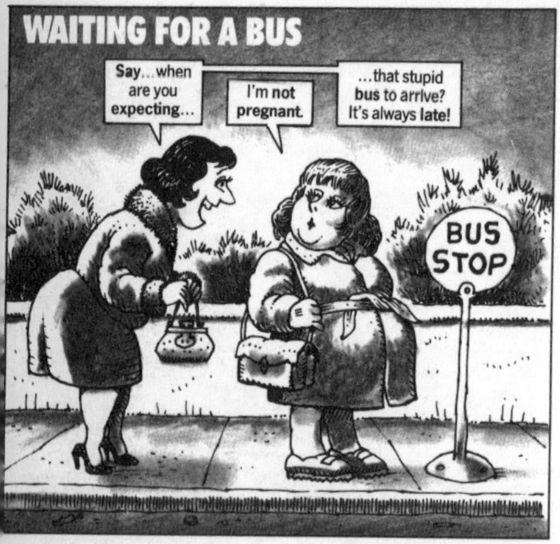
WAITING FOR A BUS
Say...when are you expecting...
I'm not pregnant.
...that stupid bus to arrive? It's always late!
BUS STOP

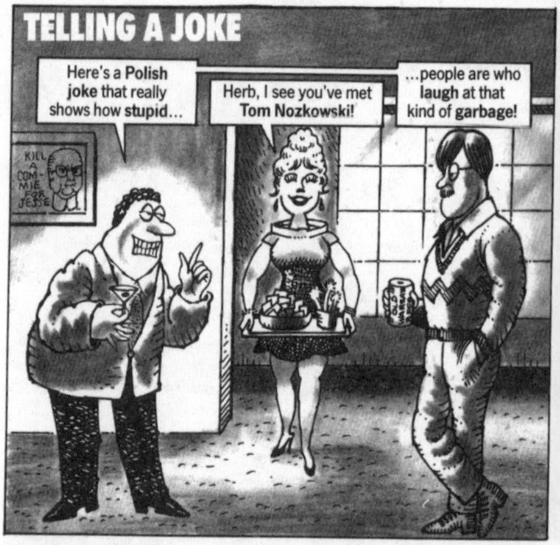
TELLING A JOKE
Here's a Polish joke that really shows how stupid...
Herb, I see you've met Tom Nozkowski!
...people are who laugh at that kind of garbage!
KILL A COM-MIE FOR JESSE

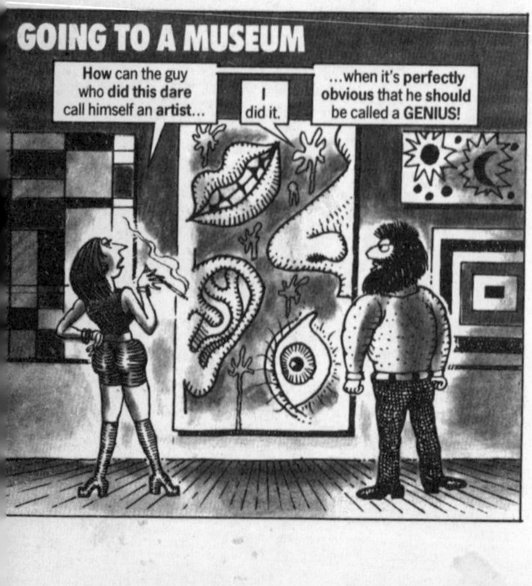
GOING TO A MUSEUM
How can the guy who did this dare call himself an artist...
I did it.
...when it's perfectly obvious that he should be called a GENIUS!

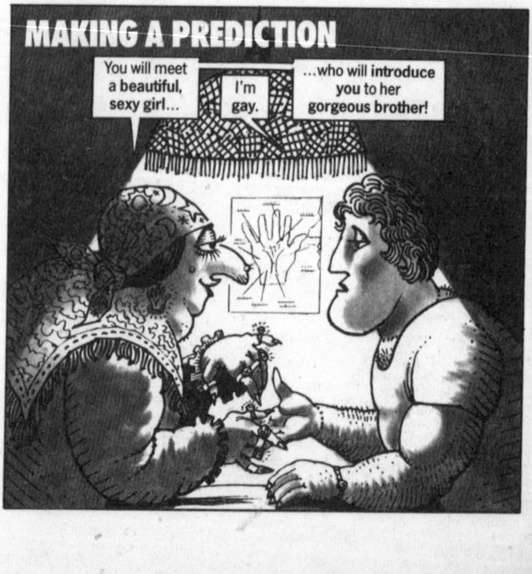
MAKING A PREDICTION
You will meet a beautiful, sexy girl...
I'm gay.
...who will introduce you to her gorgeous brother!

ɨrmly into your big mouth. But there is a way out. All you have
o do is study the examples shown here and you'll learn to make...

)VERIES FOR
G SITUATIONS

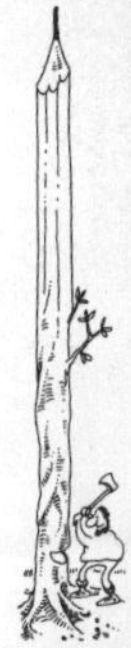

ARTIST AND WRITER: AL JAFFEE

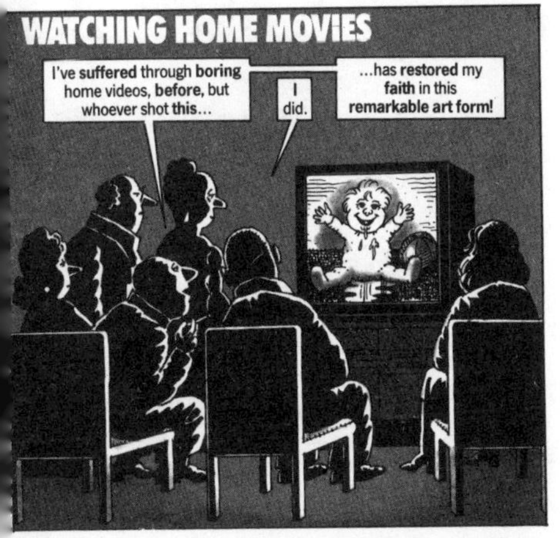
WATCHING HOME MOVIES
I've suffered through boring home videos, before, but whoever shot this...
I did.
...has restored my faith in this remarkable art form!

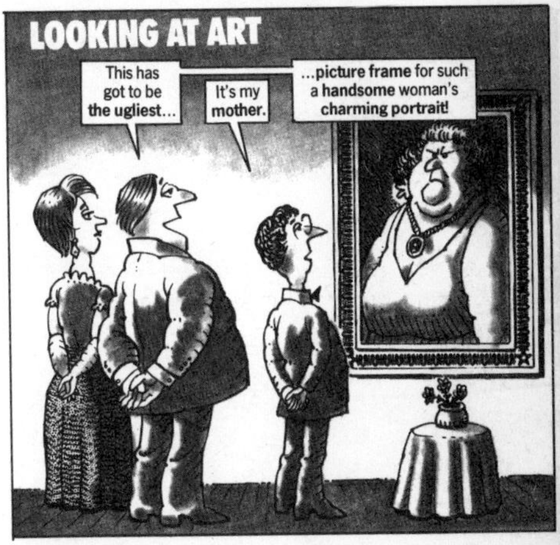
LOOKING AT ART
This has got to be the ugliest...
It's my mother.
...picture frame for such a handsome woman's charming portrait!

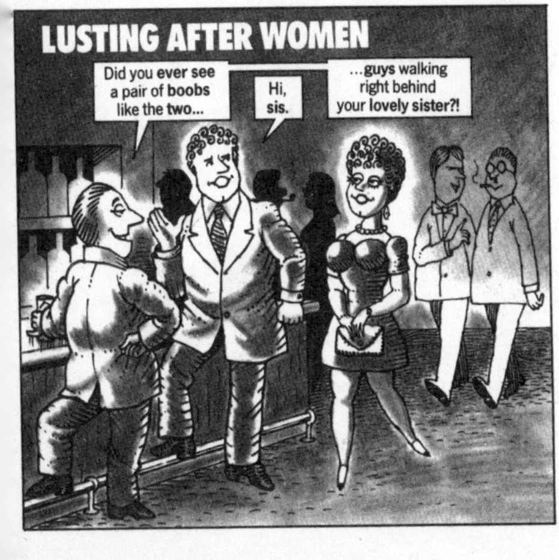
LUSTING AFTER WOMEN
Did you ever see a pair of boobs like the two...
Hi, sis.
...guys walking right behind your lovely sister?!

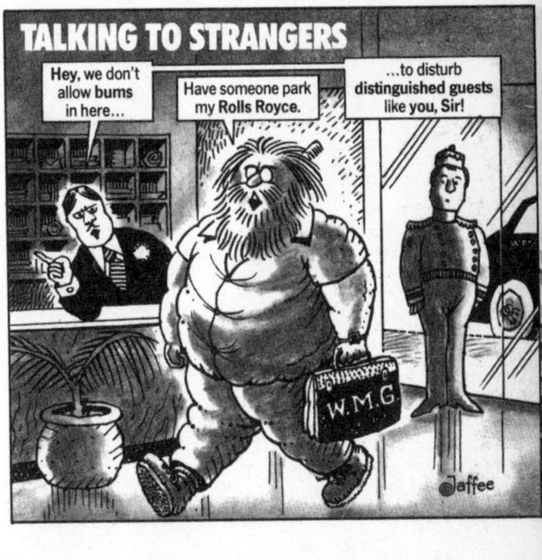
TALKING TO STRANGERS
Hey, we don't allow bums in here...
Have someone park my Rolls Royce.
...to disturb distinguished guests like you, Sir!
W.M.G
©Jaffee

CLOCK WATCHING

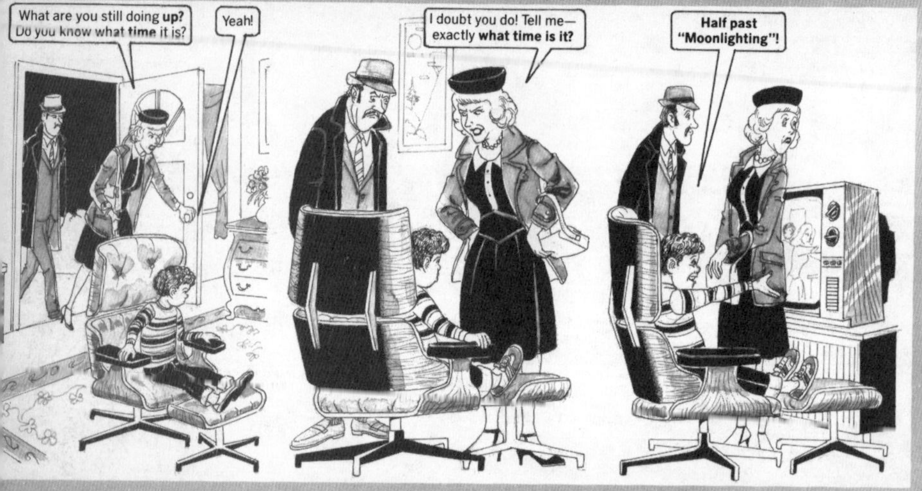

What are you still doing **up?** Do you know what **time** it is?
Yeah!
I doubt you do! Tell me—exactly **what time is it?**
Half past "Moonlighting"!

BERG'S-EYE VIEW DEPT.

THE LIGHTE

FIDELITY

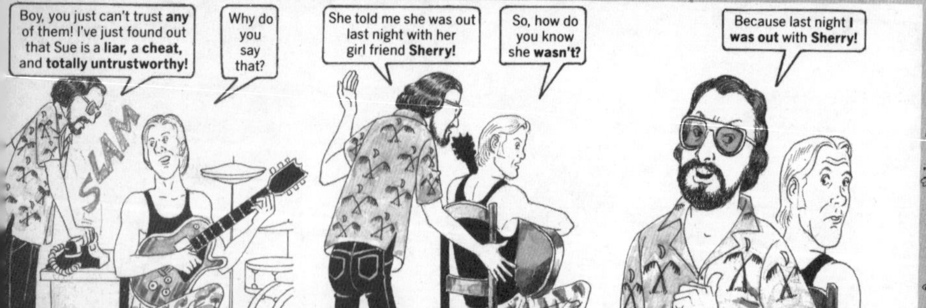

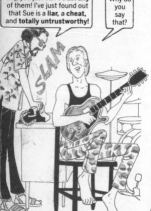

Boy, you just can't trust **any** of them! I've just found out that Sue is a **liar,** a **cheat,** and **totally untrustworthy!**
SLAM
Why do you say that?
She told me she was out last night with her girl friend **Sherry!**
So, how do you know she **wasn't?**
Because last night **I was out** with **Sherry!**

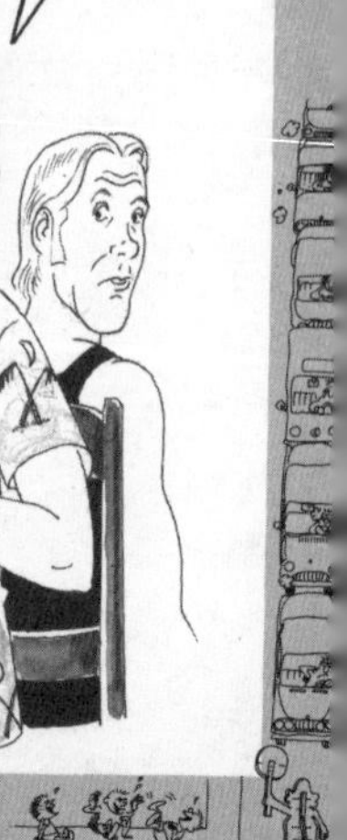

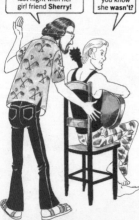

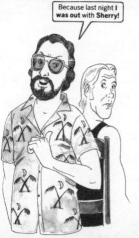

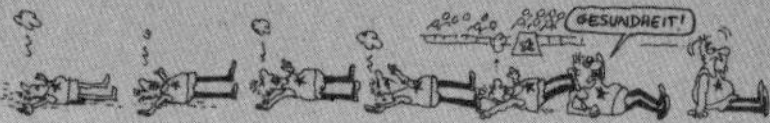
GESUNDHEIT!

FINANCES

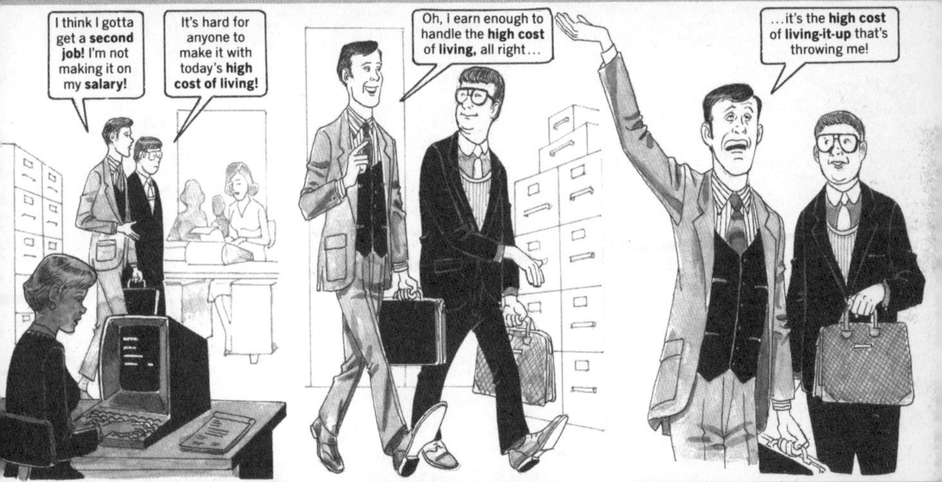
I think I gotta get a **second job!** I'm not making it on my **salary!**
It's hard for anyone to make it with today's **high cost of living!**
Oh, i earn enough to handle the **high cost** of **living,** all right...
...it's the **high cost** of **living-it-up** that's throwing me!

R SIDE OF...

ARTIST & WRITER:
DAVE BERG

INSECTS

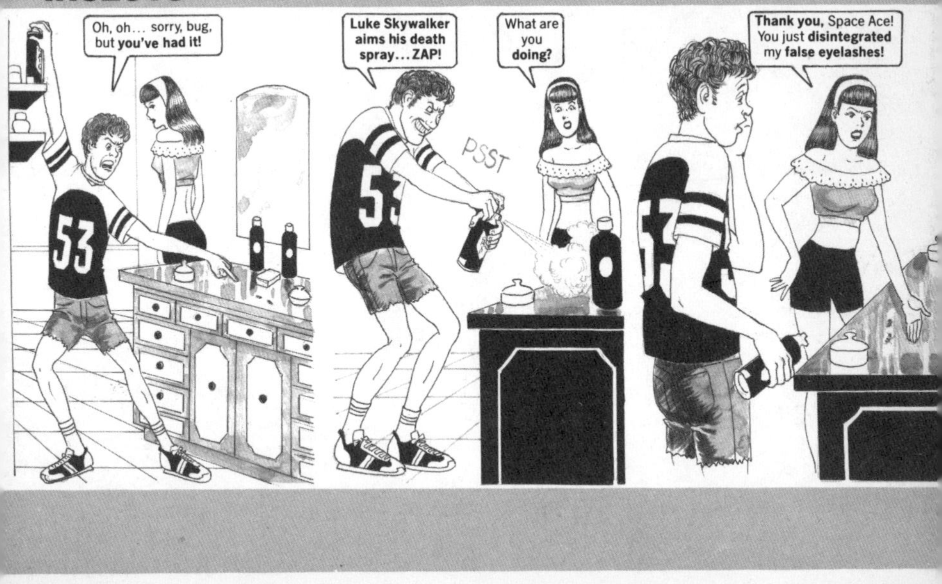
Oh, oh... sorry, bug, but **you've had it!**
53
Luke Skywalker aims his death spray... ZAP!
PSST
What are you **doing?**
Thank you, Space Ace! You just **disintegrated** my **false eyelashes!**

CARS

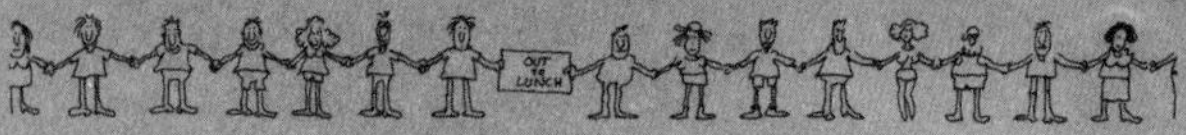

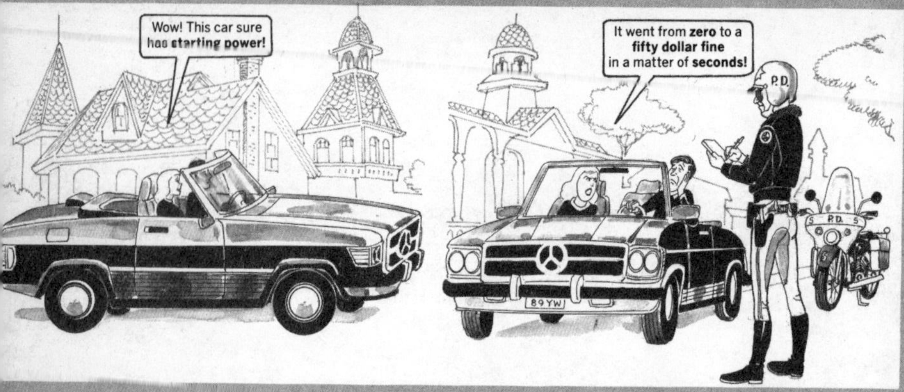

Wow! This car sure has starting power!
It went from zero to a fifty dollar fine in a matter of seconds!
P.D.
89 YW

BRAGGING

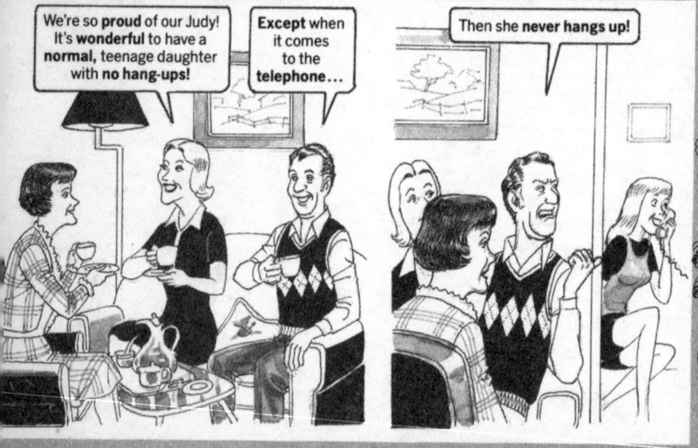

We're so proud of our Judy! It's wonderful to have a normal, teenage daughter with no hang-ups!
Except when it comes to the telephone...
Then she never hangs up!

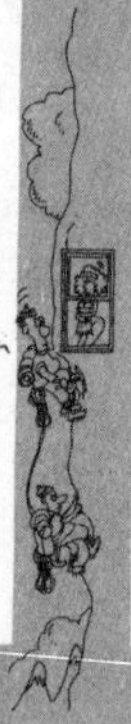

GIFT-GIVING

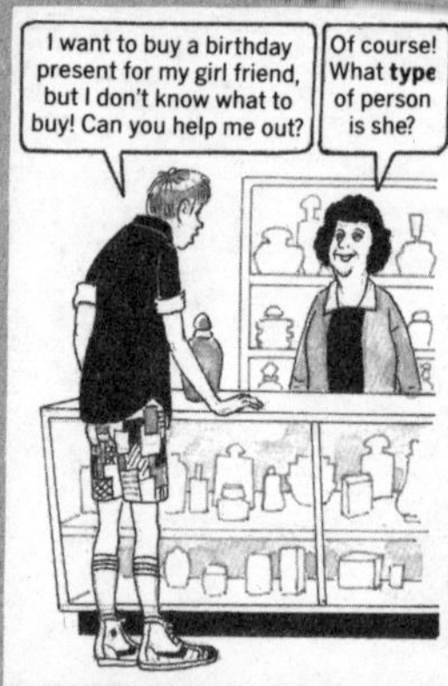

I want to buy a birthday present for my girl friend, but I don't know what to buy! Can you help me out?
Of course! What type of person is she?

ON-THE-JOB TRAINING

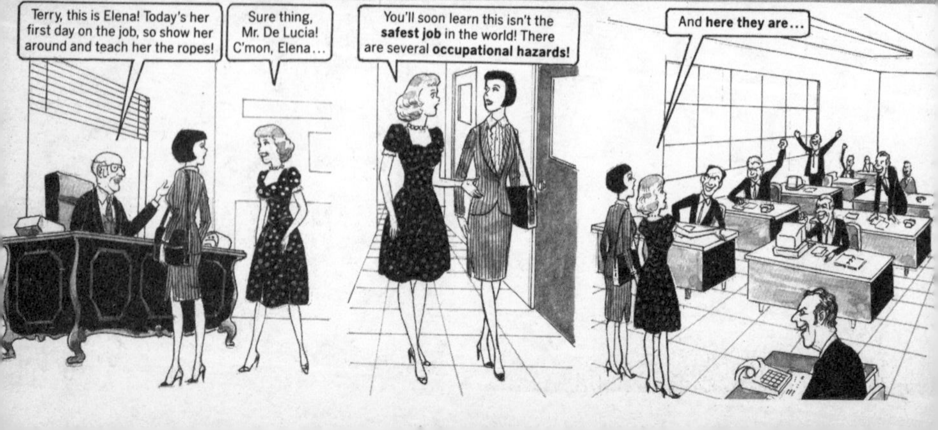

Terry, this is Elena! Today's her first day on the job, so show her around and teach her the ropes!
Sure thing, Mr. De Lucia! C'mon, Elena...
You'll soon learn this isn't the safest job in the world! There are several occupational hazards!
And here they are...

POPULARITY

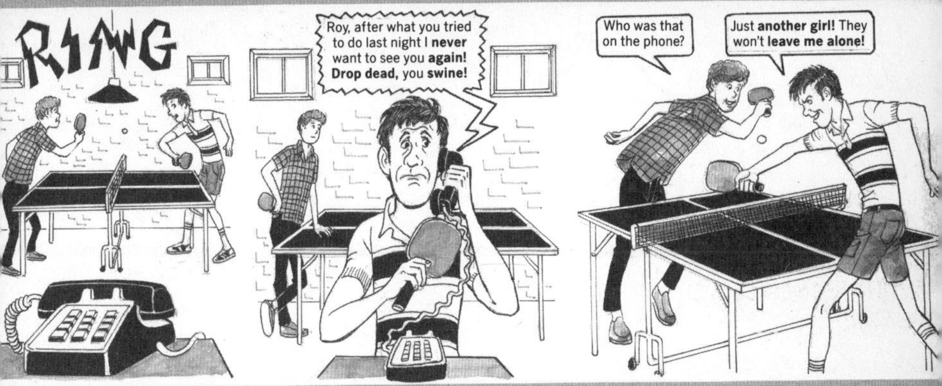

RING
Roy, after what you tried to do last night I never want to see you again! Drop dead, you swine!
Who was that on the phone?
Just another girl! They won't leave me alone!

FADS

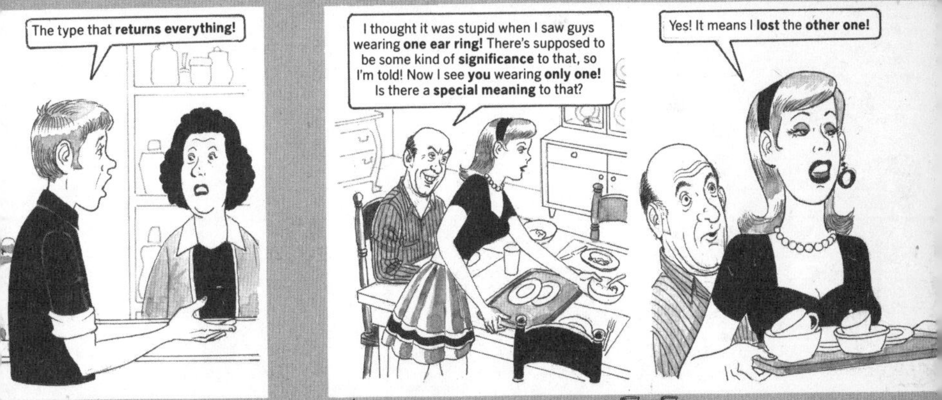

The type that returns everything!
I thought it was stupid when I saw guys wearing one ear ring! There's supposed to be some kind of significance to that, so I'm told! Now I see you wearing only one! Is there a special meaning to that?
Yes! It means I lost the other one!

CAUTION

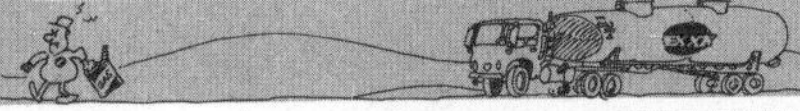

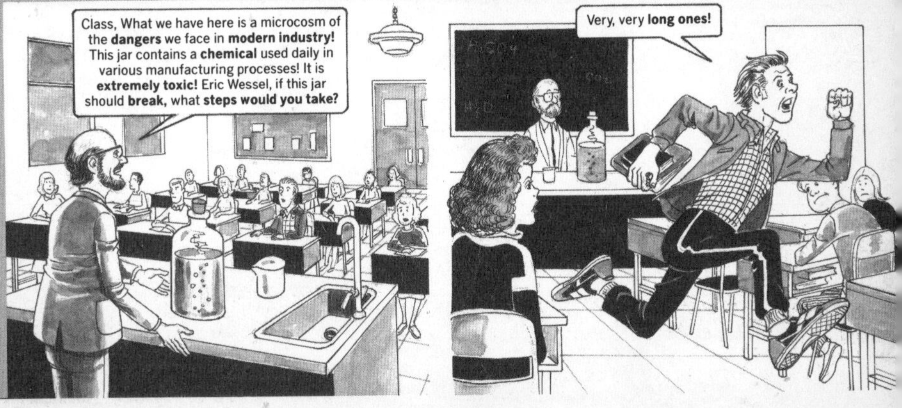

Class, What we have here is a microcosm of the dangers we face in modern industry! This jar contains a chemical used daily in various manufacturing processes! It is extremely toxic! Eric Wessel, if this jar should break, what steps would you take?
Very, very long ones!

HOT WEATHER

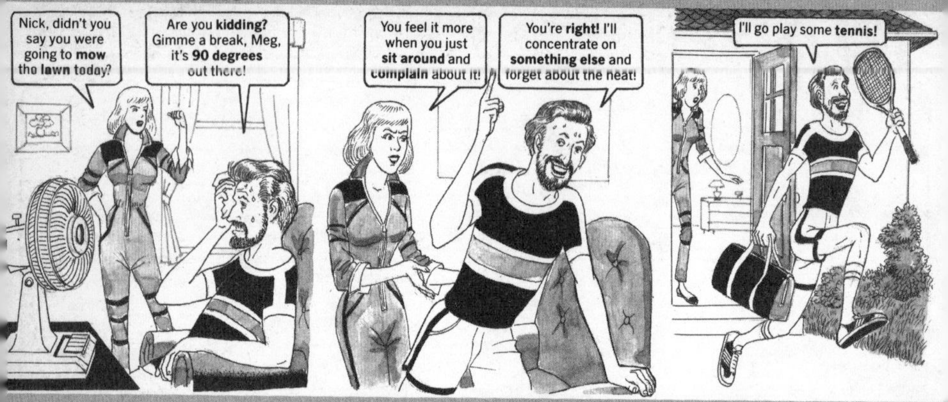

Nick, didn't you say you were going to mow the lawn today?
Are you kidding? Gimme a break, Meg, it's 90 degrees out there!
You feel it more when you just sit around and complain about it!
You're right! I'll concentrate on something else and forget about the heat!
I'll go play some tennis!

KNOWLEDGE

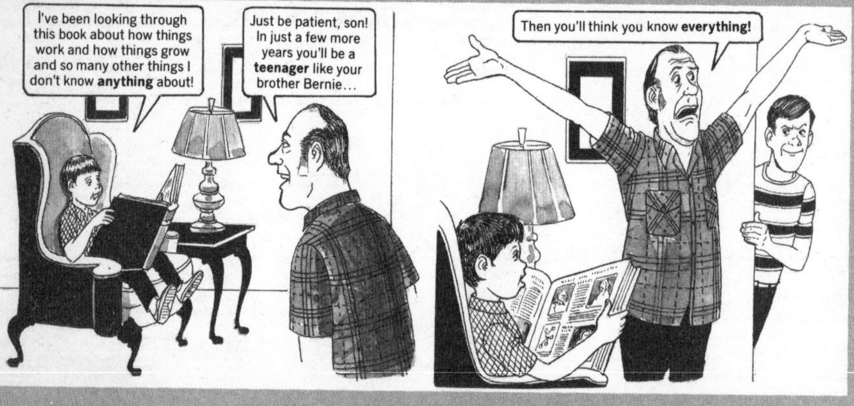

I've been looking through this book about how things work and how things grow and so many other things I don't know anything about!
Just be patient, son! In just a few more years you'll be a teenager like your brother Bernie…
Then you'll think you know everything!

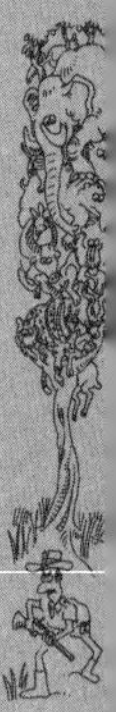

DOCTORS

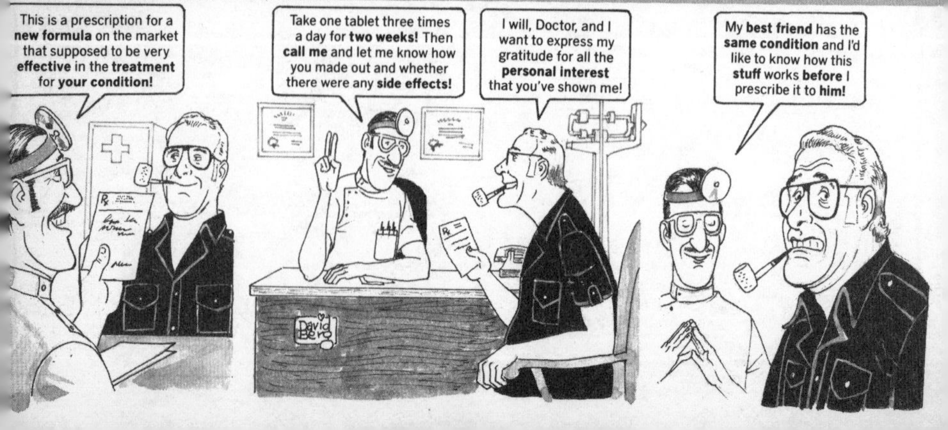

This is a prescription for a new formula on the market that supposed to be very effective in the treatment for your condition!
Take one tablet three times a day for two weeks! Then call me and let me know how you made out and whether there were any side effects!
I will, Doctor, and I want to express my gratitude for all the personal interest that you've shown me!
My best friend has the same condition and I'd like to know how this stuff works before I prescribe it to him!
David Berg

TALES FROM THE DUCK SIDE DEPT.

THE STUPEFYING SUICIDE SITUATION

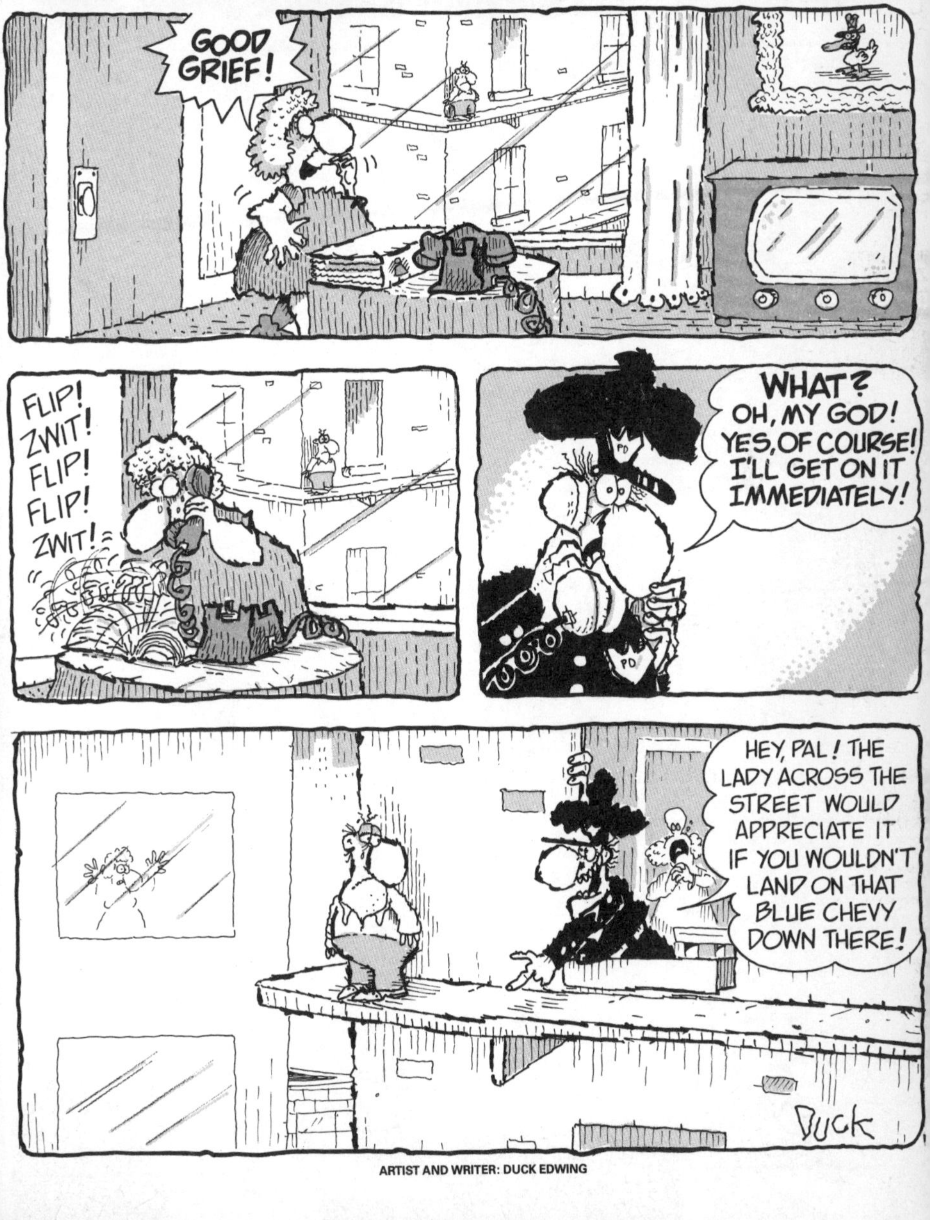
GOOD GRIEF!
FLIP! ZWIT! FLIP! FLIP! ZWIT!
WHAT? OH, MY GOD! YES, OF COURSE! I'LL GET ON IT IMMEDIATELY!
PD
HEY, PAL! THE LADY ACROSS THE STREET WOULD APPRECIATE IT IF YOU WOULDN'T LAND ON THAT BLUE CHEVY DOWN THERE!
DUCK

ARTIST AND WRITER: DUCK EDWING

WIDE WORLD OF DORKS DEPT.

DANGEROUS SP

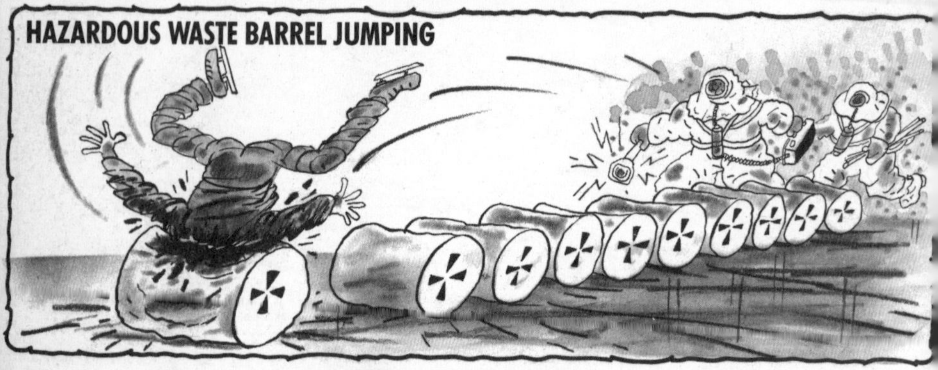

HAZARDOUS WASTE BARREL JUMPING

ARTIST AND WRITER: PAUL PETER PORGES

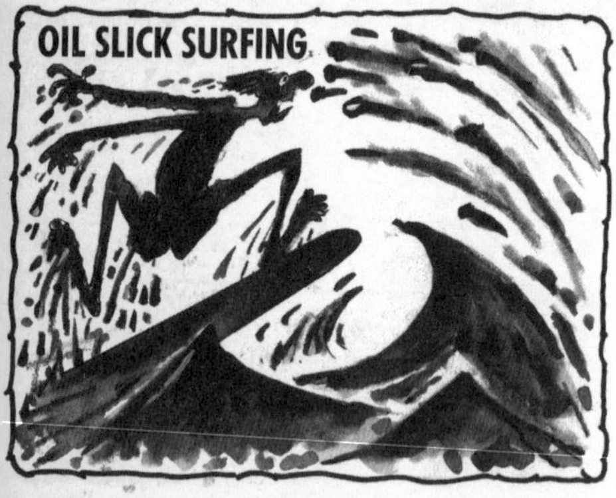

OIL SLICK SURFING

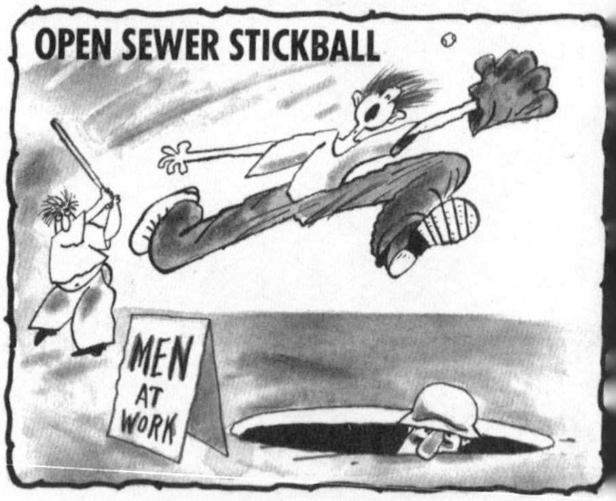
MEN AT WORK

OPEN SEWER STICKBALL

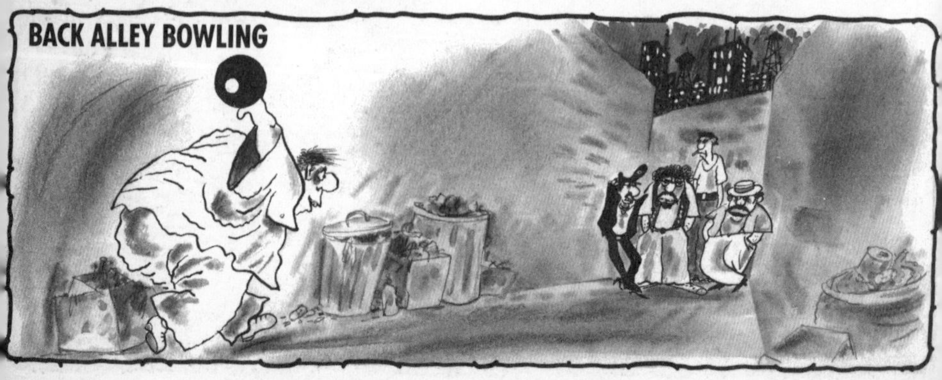

BACK ALLEY BOWLING

ORTS FOR THE VERY DARING AND THE SUPER STUPID

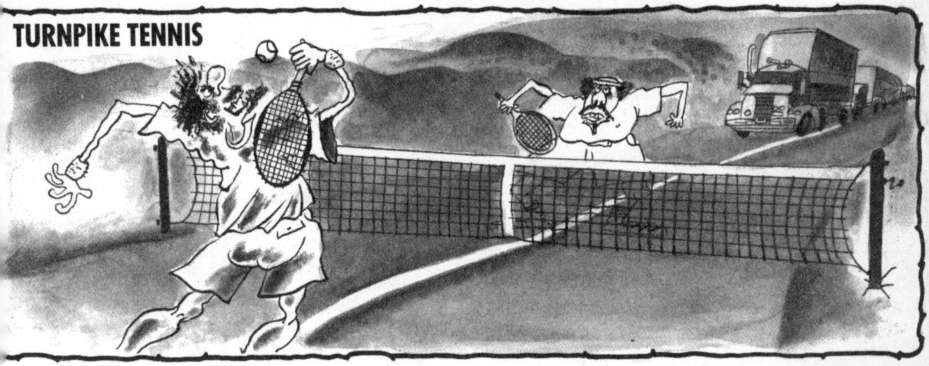
TURNPIKE TENNIS

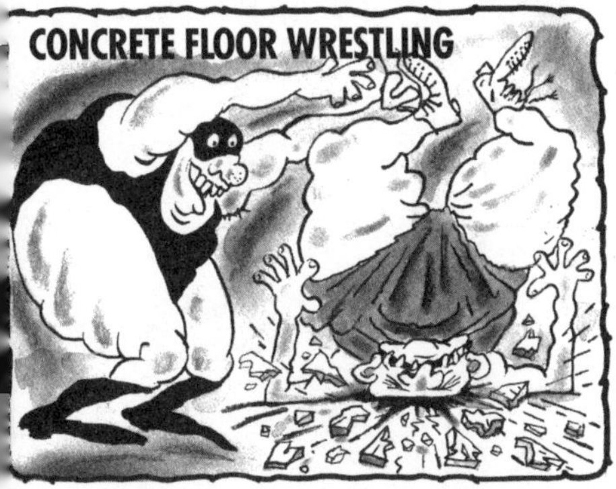
CONCRETE FLOOR WRESTLING

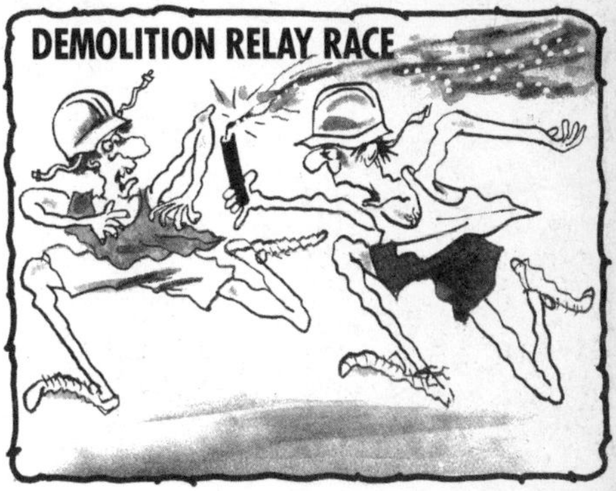
DEMOLITION RELAY RACE

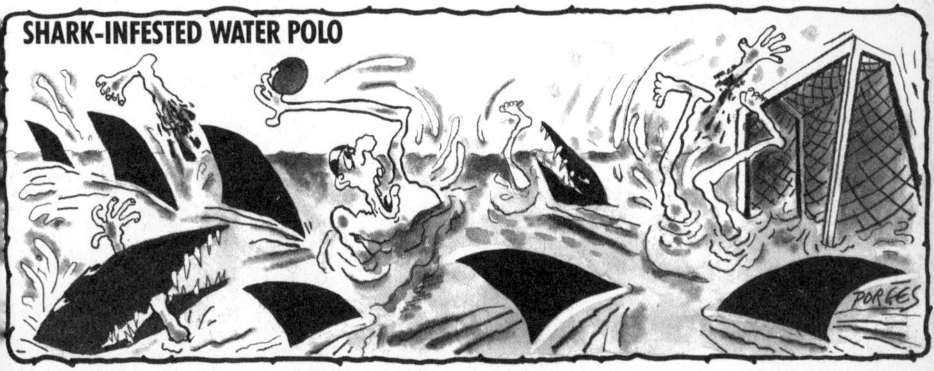
SHARK-INFESTED WATER POLO
PORGES

A BAD CASE OF CONSTELLATION DEPT.

Every year, thousands of long-winded Astrology books are sold which describe the personalities and habits of people born under the 12 Signs of the Zodiac. Well, now there's no need to wad

MAD'S INSTA

Z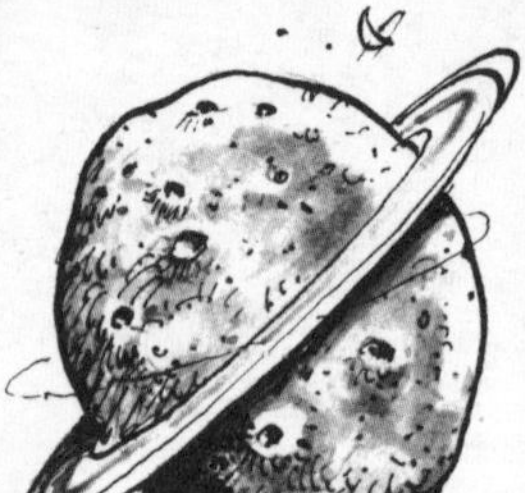DIA

ARTIST: HARRY NORT

ARIES

Aries people (Mar. 21–Apr. 20) are bold, fearless, rebellious and pioneering. You know this from the way they:

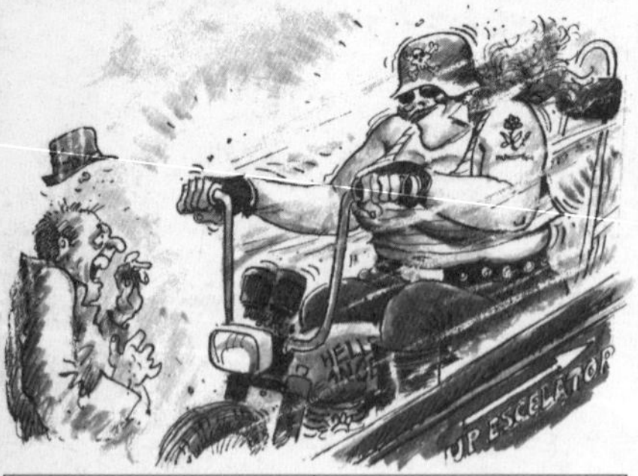
UP ESCELATOR

Tattoo their neighbors' children.	Punch out their UPS delivery men.
Jog underwater.	Train their parakeets to maim.
Put tabasco sauce on their ice cream.	Turn over broiling barbecue steaks with their bare hands.
Act nonchalant after walking through plate glass windows.	Entertain guests with color slides of accident victims.

TAURUS

Taurus people (Apr. 21–May 21) are patient, practical, serious and solemn. This is evident from the way they:

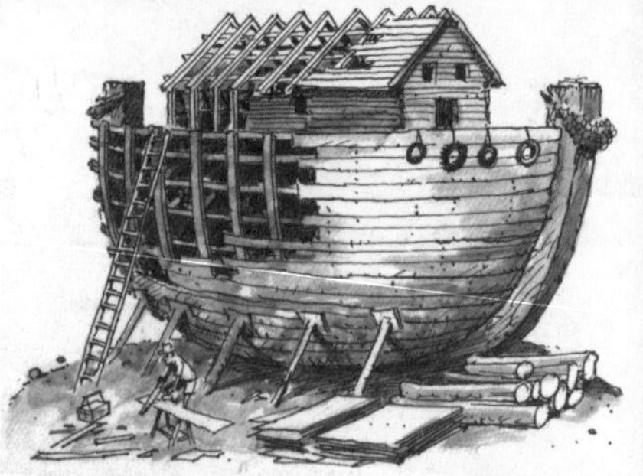

Describe the 100-Years' War battle by battle.	Bore their computers.
Show a passionate interest in storage batteries.	Count cows while driving cross-country.
Are mistaken for mummies.	Frame Tommy Hearns witticisms above their fireplaces.
Take long weekends in their cellars.	Turtle Wax their shoe trees.

through all those pages just to find out if your Aquarian sweetheart is the girl of your dreams, or if your Capricorn brother is the schmuck you think he is. You can find out fast by using...

NT GUIDE TO C TYPES

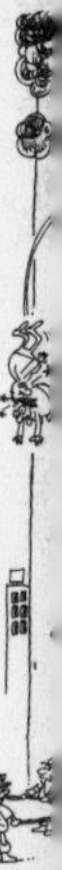

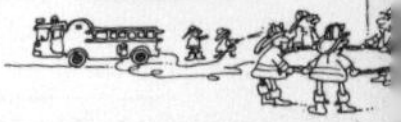

WRITER: FRANK JACOBS

GEMINI

Gemini people (May 22–June 21) are restless, versatile, quick-witted and inventive. You know it from the way they:

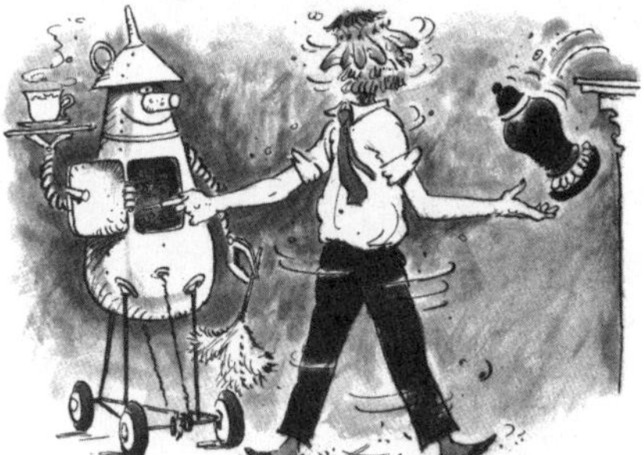

Carpet their floors with used toupees.	Are adept at juggling semi-soft cheeses.
Jump out of cakes at funerals.	Perform surgery while sky-diving.
Build giant sculptures out of hard-boiled egg yolks.	Serve Count Chocula at formal dinners.
Share their condominiums with live-in Pygmies.	Decorate their toenails with Smurf decals.

CANCER

Cancer people (June 22–July 23) are emotional, thrifty, nostalgic and home-loving. This is clear by the way they:

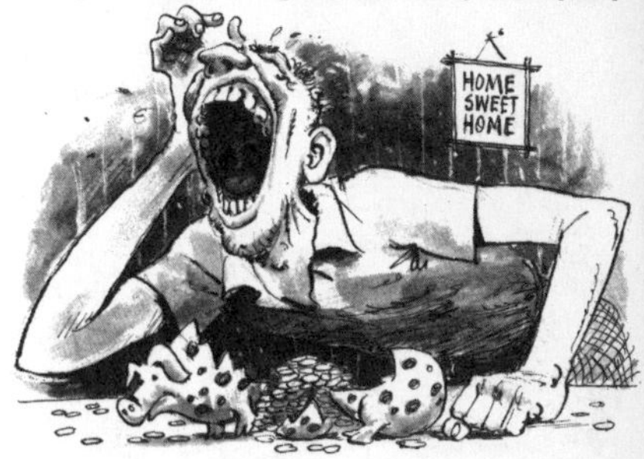
HOME SWEET HOME

Cry during Mel Brooks movies.	Bronze their baby teeth.
Feel "that way" about fan belts.	Bathe with their sheepdogs.
Save old kitchen sponges for their sentimental value.	Feel their pulse racing at garage sales.
Inscribe inspirational sayings on toilet paper.	Join hands while watching Oprah Winfrey.

Leo

Leo people (July 24–Aug. 23) are regal, commanding, egotistical and gregarious. You know this from the way they:

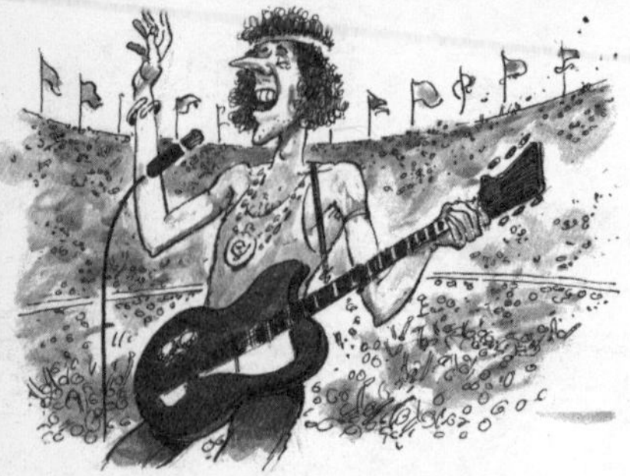

Monogram their dentures.	Send mash-notes to themselves.
Are proud to park in spaces reserved for the handicapped.	Instruct their wives to address them as "Bwana."
Train their pit bulls to curtsey.	Demand tribute from their Street-Cleaners.
Show movies of their appendectomies on giant screens.	Wear designer hearing aids.

Virgo

Virgo people (Aug. 24–Sept. 23) are proper, painstaking, fastidious and discriminating. You know from the way they:

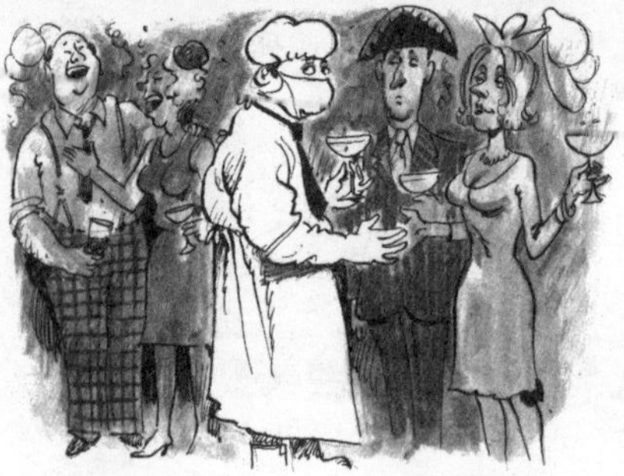

Shower after shaking hands.	Slipcover their houses.
Exhibit collections of finely mounted gnats.	Videotape test patterns.
Save sunburn peelings.	Launder Kleenex before using.
Make love fully clothed.	Introduce themselves to their children.

Sagittarius

Sagittarius people (Nov. 23–Dec. 21) are adventurous, outspoken and unpredictable. You can see by the way they:

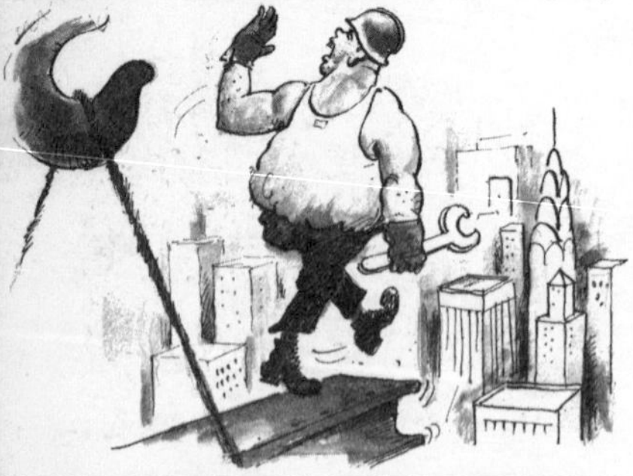

Decorate their Christmas trees with shrunken heads.	Make obscene phone calls to their Congressmen.
Throw up during soft drink commercials.	Housebreak ostriches.
Sleep on all fours.	Do warm-ups for terrorists.
Enjoy group sex in hammocks.	Catch Frisbees with their teeth.

Capricorn

Capricorn people (Dec. 22–Jan. 20) are traditional, set in their ways, loyal and solemn. You know by the way they:

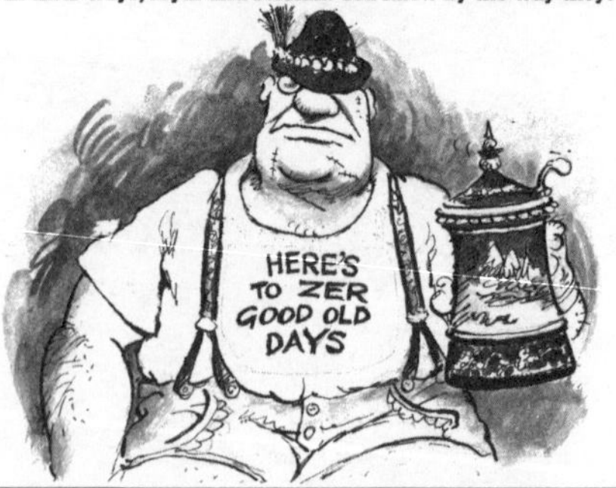
HERE'S TO ZER GOOD OLD DAYS

Gargle in waltz time.	Still support Judge Bork.
Feel at home with bison.	Mourn the current lack of interest in Lincoln Logs.
Place fig leaves over pictures of Donald Duck.	Perspire freely while watching "The People's Court."
Molt after they reach 50.	Display the earwax of their ancestors in mason jars.

LIBRA

Libra people (Sept. 24–Oct. 23) are helpful, indecisive, undemanding and peace-loving. This is evident because they:

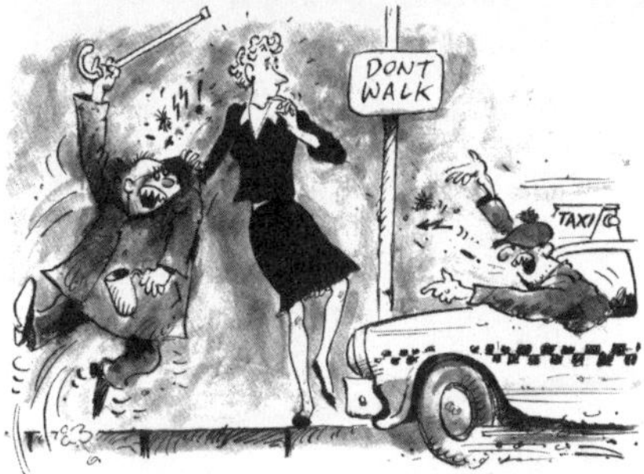
DONT WALK
TAXI

Get lost in closets.	Take the person who mugged them to lunch.
Dial "Weather" and are put on hold.	Turn themselves in for jaywalking.
Find momentary beauty in quicksand pools.	Are usually mistaken for large shrubs.
Grovel before busboys.	Floss the teeth of stray dogs.

SCORPIO

Scorpio people (Oct. 24–Nov. 22) are powerful, secretive, intense and possessive. You know from the way they:

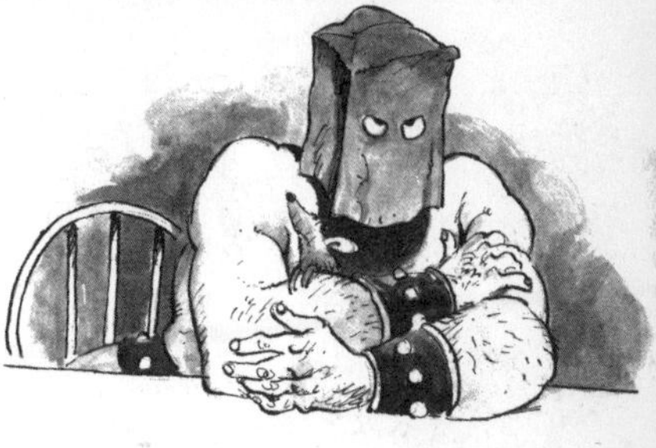

Fingerprint their children.	Outstare killer whales.
Put out contracts on yodelers.	Mutter to "The Battle Hymn of the Republic."
Spoon-feed their cobras.	Run in marathons wearing jack-boots.
Crouch in swamps during the full moon.	Plant land mines in their front lawns.

AQUARIUS

Aquarius people (Jan. 21–Feb. 19) are unconventional, creative and open minded. You can tell from the way they:

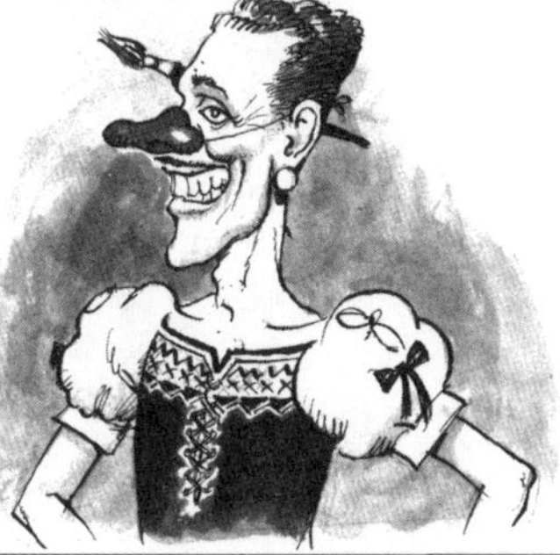

Watch "60 Minutes" naked.	Root for the werewolf in horror films.
Swallow billiard cues.	Ward off disease by wearing garlic Speedstick.
Have grandparents who are into leather.	Meet their lovers in the rear of Chinese laundries.
Fit out their giraffes with mesh stockings.	Vacation in wind tunnels.

PISCES

Pisces people (Feb. 20–Mar. 20) are dreamy, unambitious, mystical and vulnerable. This is evident by the way they:

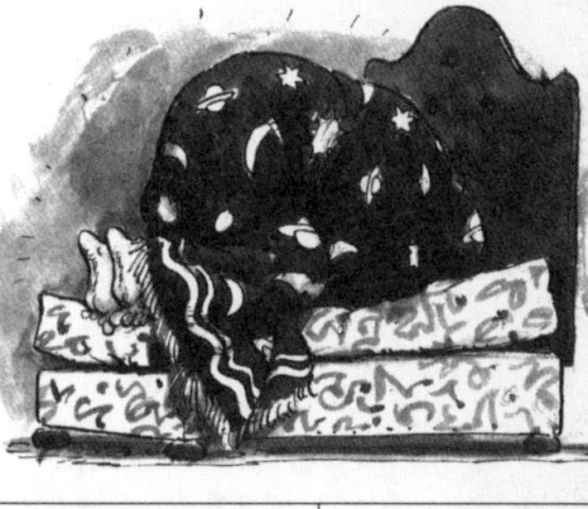

Describe in detail their past lives as pigeons.	Get trampled on escalators.
Are used as surfboards by Scorpios.	Fail as derelicts.
Flavor their Big Macs with incense.	Pray in public bathrooms.
Keep warm in winter by covering themselves with topsoil.	Study to become human sacrifices.

THE FUNNY FORM DEPT.

According to a recent study 76.4% of all MAD readers think 48.9% of all MAD intros are funnier than the articles they introduce. We figure this means one of two things: either 48.9% of our articles are absolute clinkers or 76.4% of our intros are masterful works of comic

TELL-TALE COMIC STRIP

ARTIST: BOB CLARKE

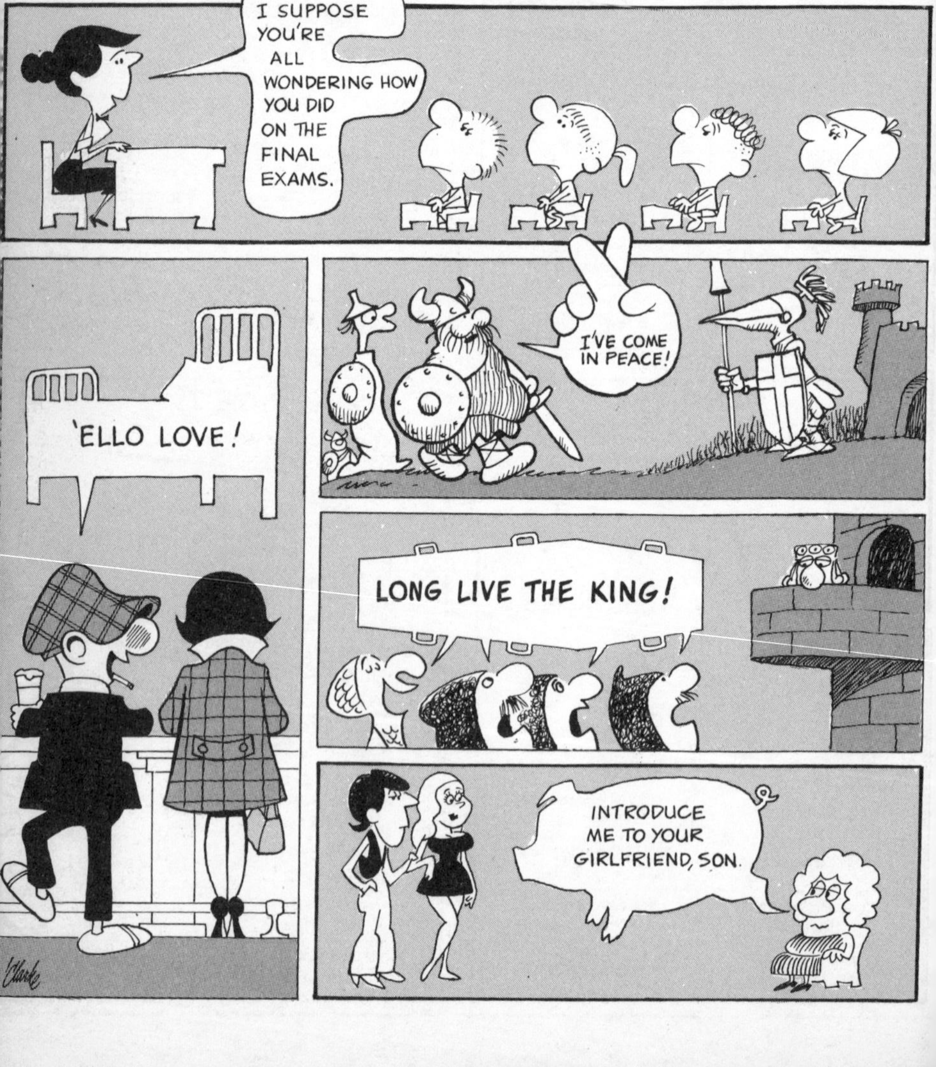

I SUPPOSE YOU'RE ALL WONDERING HOW YOU DID ON THE FINAL EXAMS.
'ELLO LOVE!
I'VE COME IN PEACE!
LONG LIVE THE KING!
INTRODUCE ME TO YOUR GIRLFRIEND, SON.
Clarke

genius. Whatever the case, we worked very hard at keeping this intro especially uninteresting and bland so the article which follows will seem clever and witty in comparison. But the only way you'll know whether we were successful in achieving this is by taking a look at…

BALLOONS [The Sequel]

WRITER: DUCK EDWING

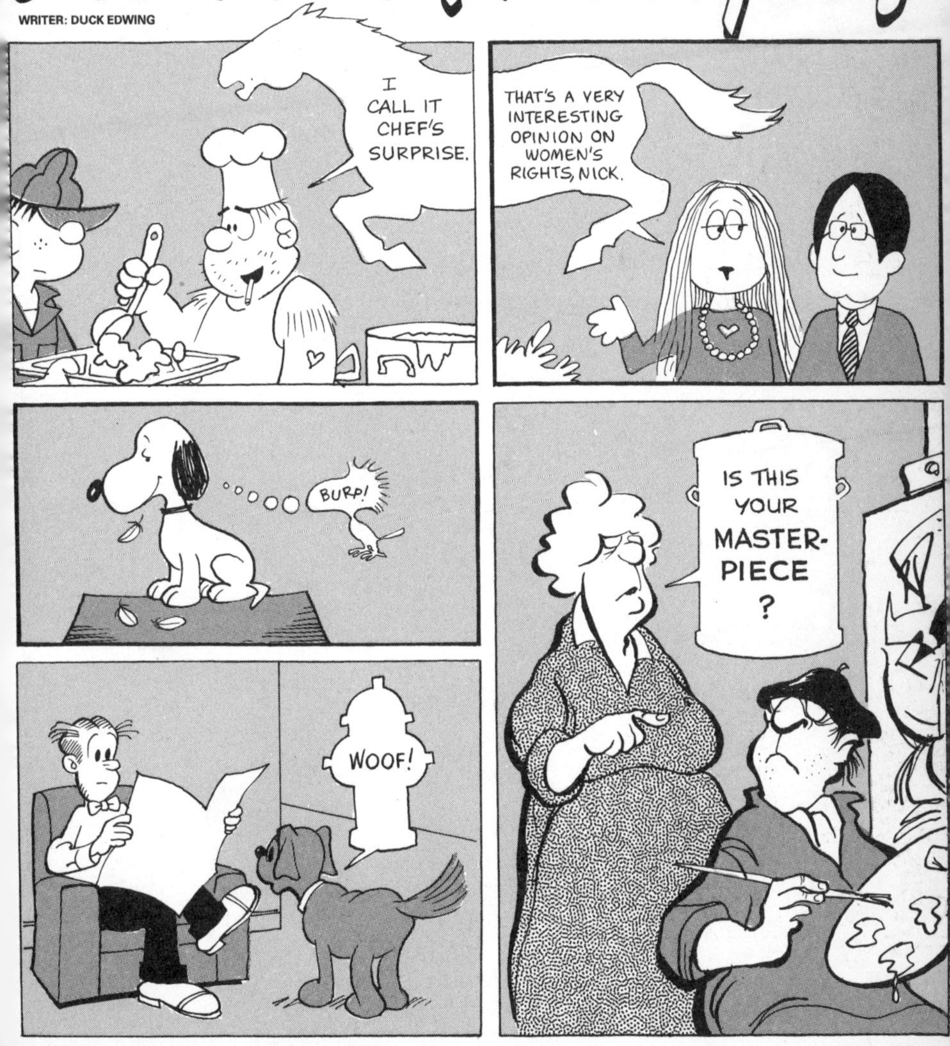
I CALL IT CHEF'S SURPRISE.
THAT'S A VERY INTERESTING OPINION ON WOMEN'S RIGHTS, NICK.
BURP!
IS THIS YOUR MASTER-PIECE ?
WOOF!

NONE DARE CALL IT REASON DEPT.

We all know how the government works—wait! That's a contradiction in terms! Maybe we shou

A MAD LOOK AT REAL-LI

ARTIST: HARRY NORT

GOVERNMENT "LOGIC" is...

...passing a "tax simplification" act...

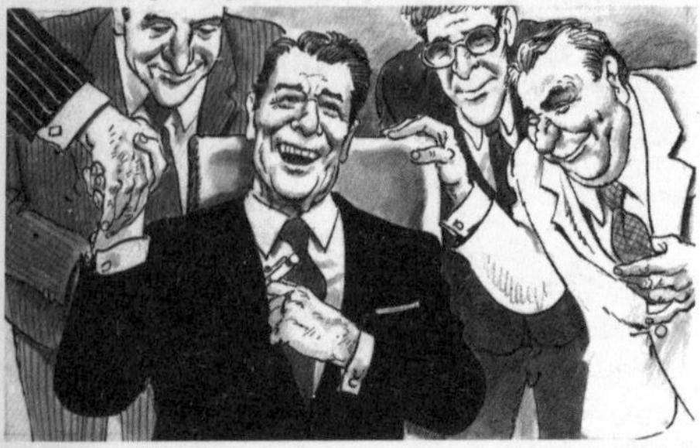

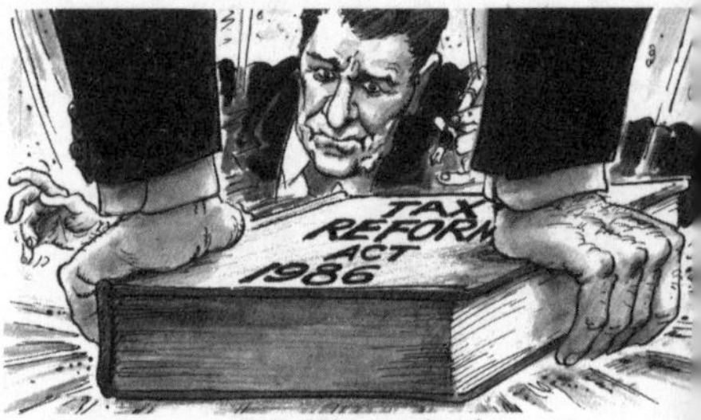
TAX REFORM ACT 1986

...that's 850 pages long!

GOVERNMENT "LOGIC" is...

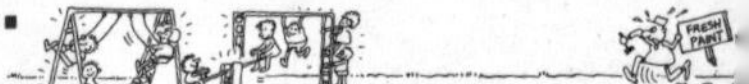
FRESH PAINT

...continuing to promote nuclear power plants as "totally safe"...

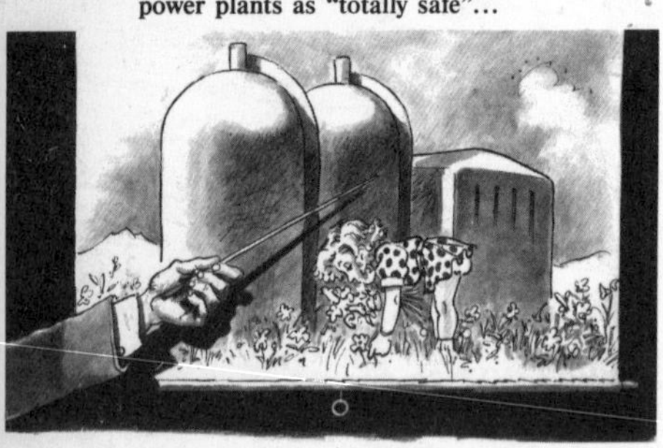

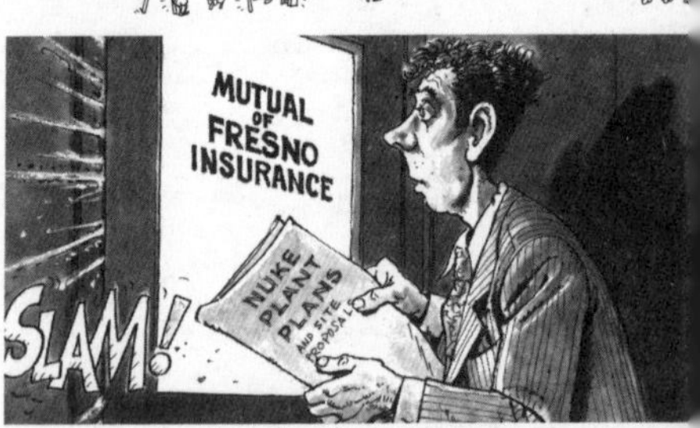
MUTUAL OF FRESNO INSURANCE
SLAM!
NUKE PLANT PLANS

...even though no insurance company will insure them—at any price!

GOVERNMENT "LOGIC" is...

...requiring competitive bids on government contracts...

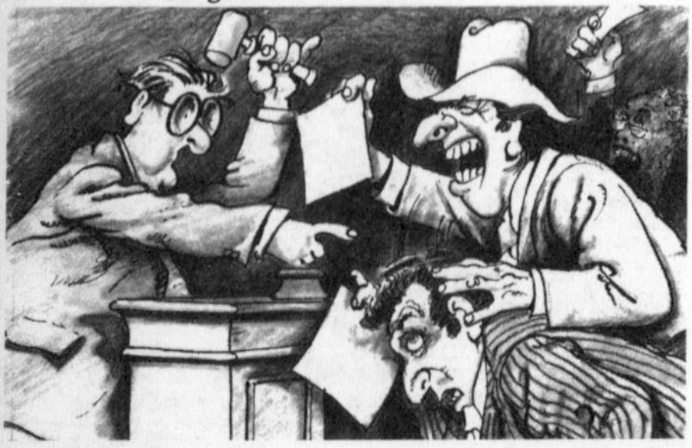

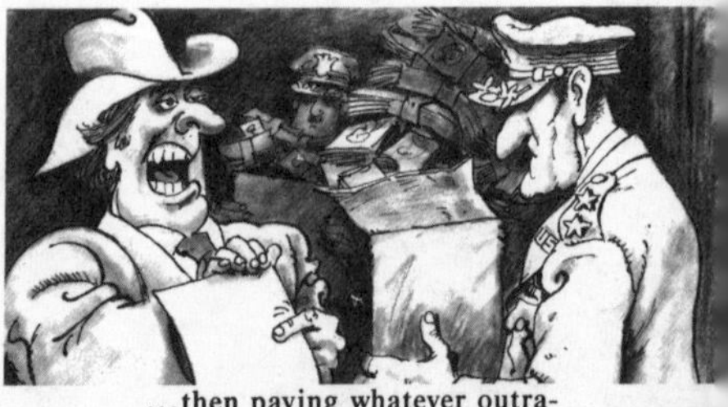

...then paying whatever outrageous "cost overruns" contractors can claim with a straight face!

"…how the government *thinks*"—naw, they don't do that either! See what we mean as we take

E GOVERNMENT "LOGIC"

RITER: MIKE SNIDER

GOVERNMENT "LOGIC" is…

…saving other countries from the oppression of left-wing dictatorships…

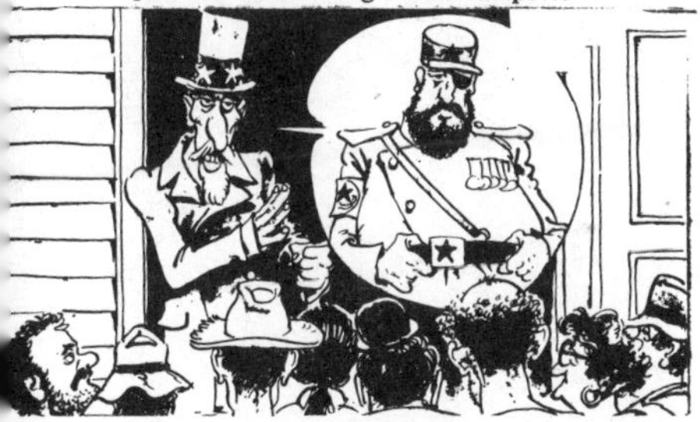

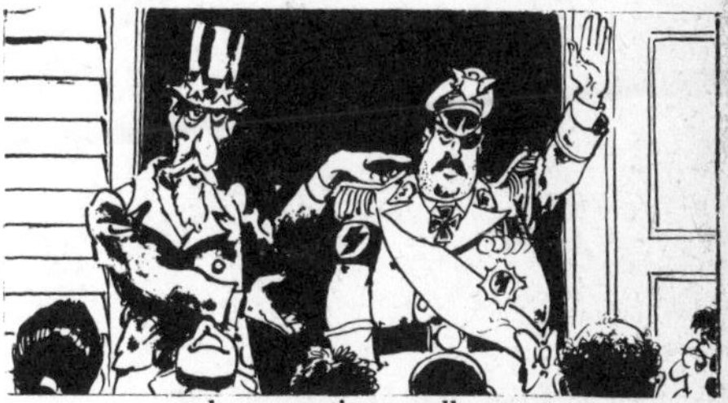

…by supporting equally oppressive right-wing dictatorships!

GOVERNMENT "LOGIC" is…

…entrusting the protection of our national parks and wilderness areas…

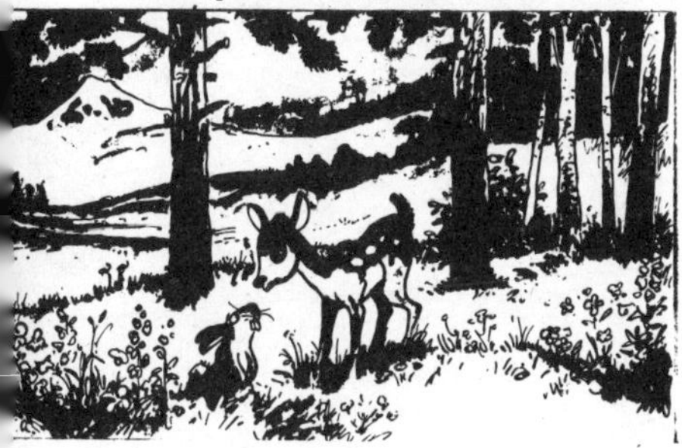

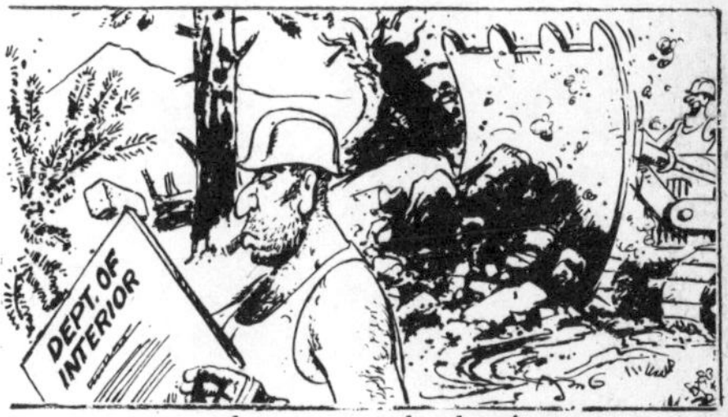
DEPT. OF INTERIOR

…to the same people who give out strip-mining and oil-drilling rights!

GOVERNMENT "LOGIC" is…

…turning down a plan that would eliminate all nuclear missiles…

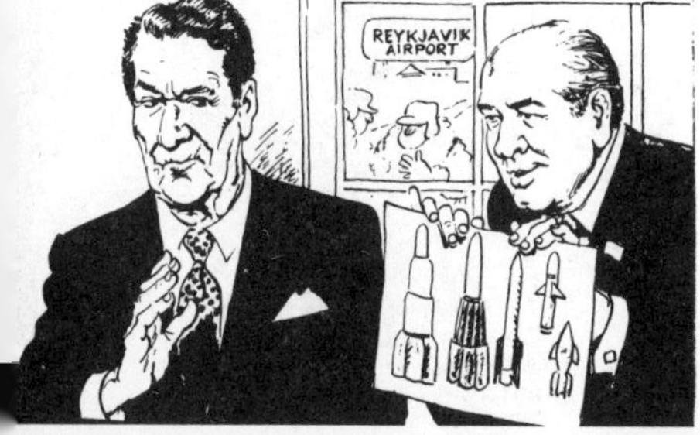
REYKJAVIK AIRPORT

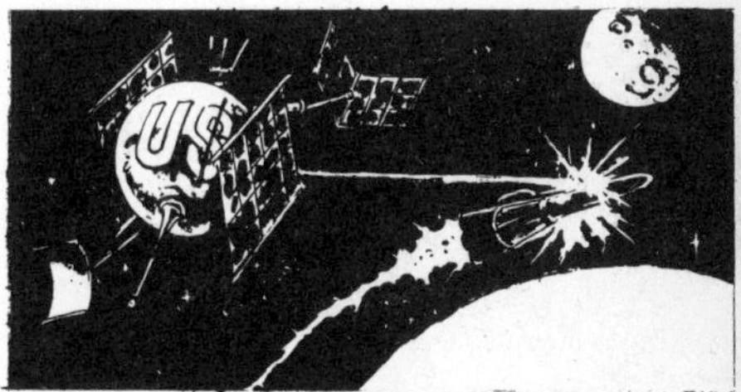
US

…so that we can build a trillion-dollar "star wars" system to defend us from the very missiles we could have eliminated!

GOVERNMENT "LOGIC" is...

...diligently keeping "undesirables" out of the U.S....

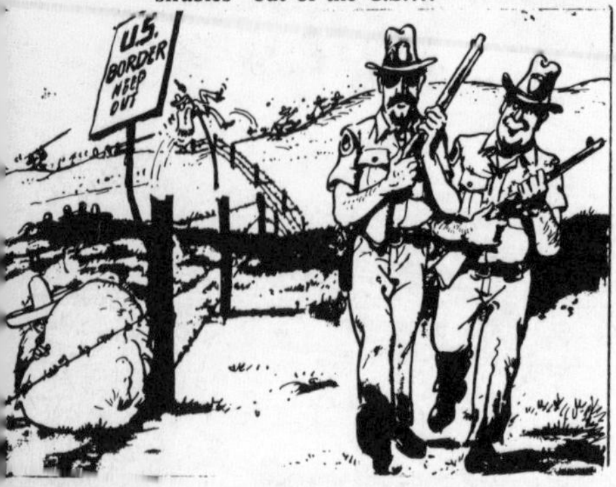
U.S.
BORDER
KEEP
OUT

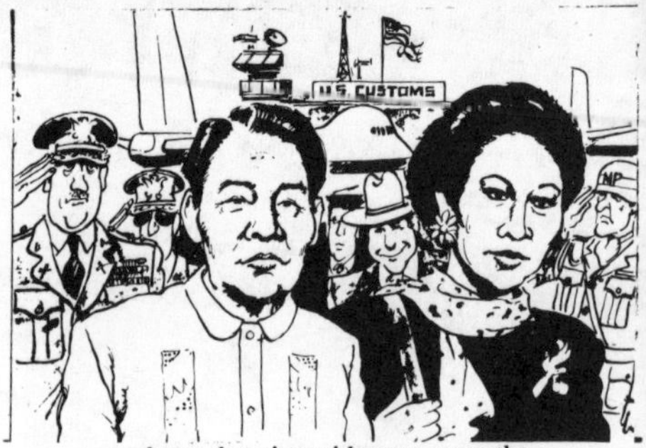
U.S. CUSTOMS
MP

...but welcoming with open arms the likes of Ferdinand and Imelda Marcos!

GOVERNMENT "LOGIC" is...

...punishing states with too many speeders...

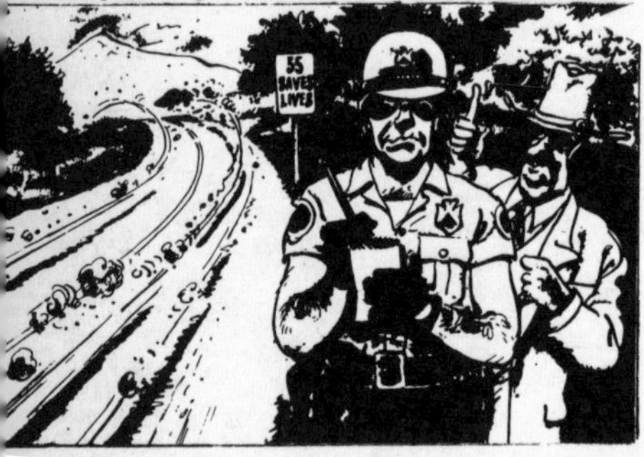
55
SAVES
LIVES

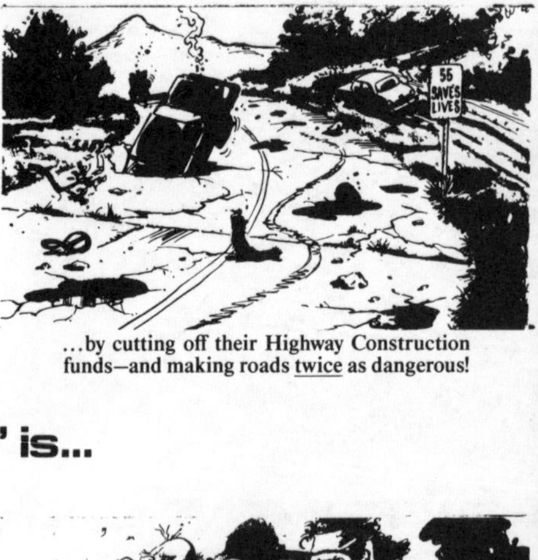
55
SAVES
LIVES

...by cutting off their Highway Construction funds—and making roads <u>twice</u> as dangerous!

GOVERNMENT "LOGIC" is...

...maintaining public health and safety by regulating everything under the sun...

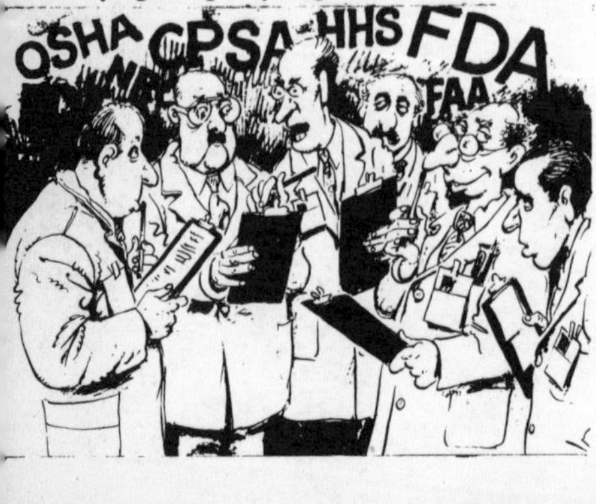
OSHA
CPSA
HHS
FDA
FAA

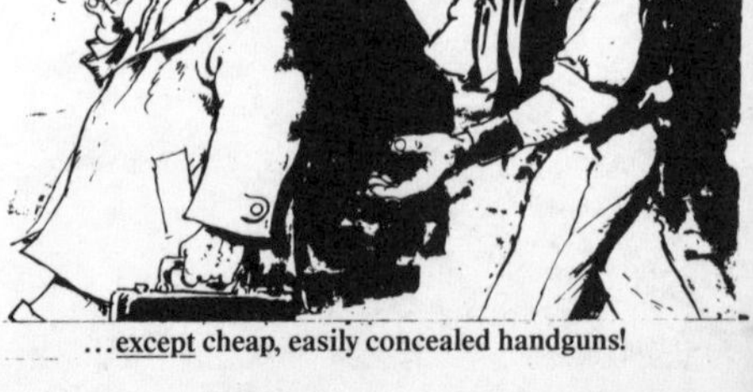

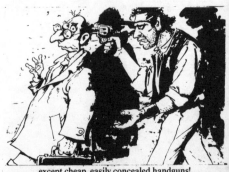

...<u>except</u> cheap, easily concealed handguns!

DON MARTIN DEPT.

ONE EVENING AT A MASQUERADE PARTY

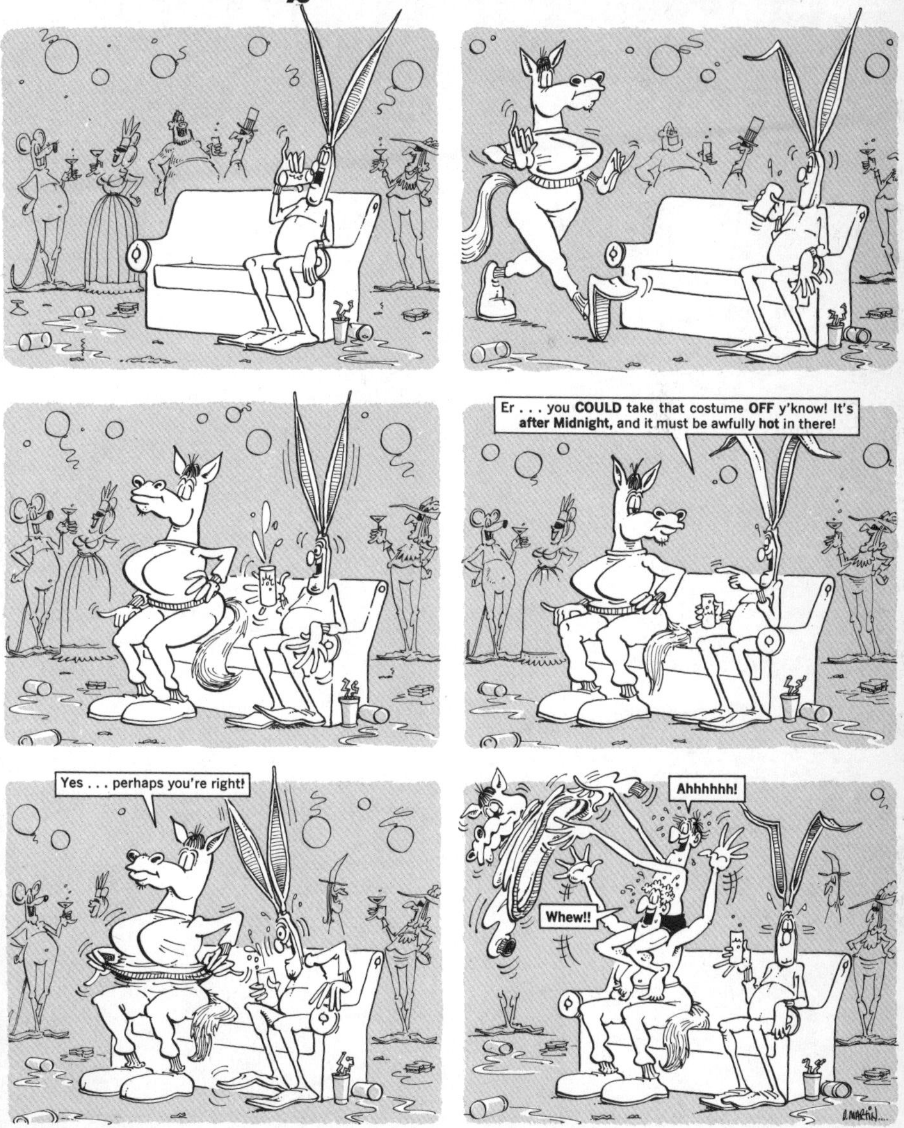
Er . . . you **COULD** take that costume **OFF** y'know! It's **after Midnight,** and it must be awfully **hot** in there!
Yes . . . perhaps you're right!
Ahhhhhh!
Whew!!
D. MARTIN...

IFS, ANDS AND BUTTS DEPT.

If you think the Surgeon General's Warning printed on cigarette packages still only says "Smoking May Be Hazardous To Your Health," think again! That line's as outdated as a 50¢ pack of menthols. Smoking hasn't gotten safer—ha!—just the opposite. These days it's so hazardous that just one warning isn't enough! That's why the Surgeon

NEW CIGARETTE WARNING L

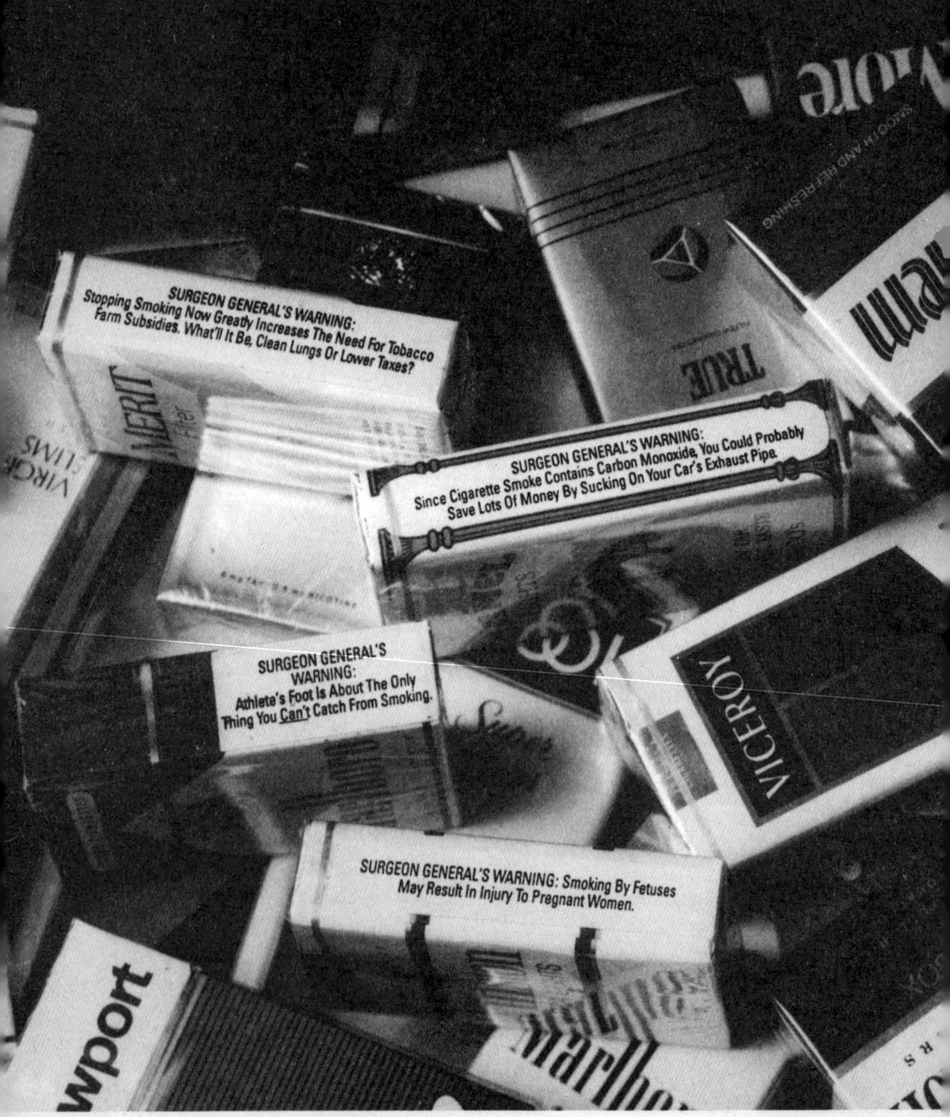

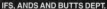

SURGEON GENERAL'S WARNING:
Stopping Smoking Now Greatly Increases The Need For Tobacco Farm Subsidies. What'll It Be, Clean Lungs Or Lower Taxes?
TRUE
SURGEON GENERAL'S WARNING:
Since Cigarette Smoke Contains Carbon Monoxide, You Could Probably Save Lots Of Money By Sucking On Your Car's Exhaust Pipe.
SURGEON GENERAL'S WARNING:
Athlete's Foot Is About The Only Thing You Can't Catch From Smoking.
VICEROY
SURGEON GENERAL'S WARNING: Smoking By Fetuses May Result In Injury To Pregnant Women.

eneral introduced a series of new, harsher warnings (some of which you may have al-
eady seen) to be placed on all cigarette packs. Of course, the tobacco companies
vould prefer you not even think about this, but we at Mad care! Remember, if you
nust get a bad taste in your mouth, you don't have to smoke—you just have to read...

BELS YOU MAY HAVE MISSED

PHOTOGRAPHER: IRVING SCHILD IDEA: ANNE GAINES WRITERS: JOE RAIOLA & CHARLIE KADAU

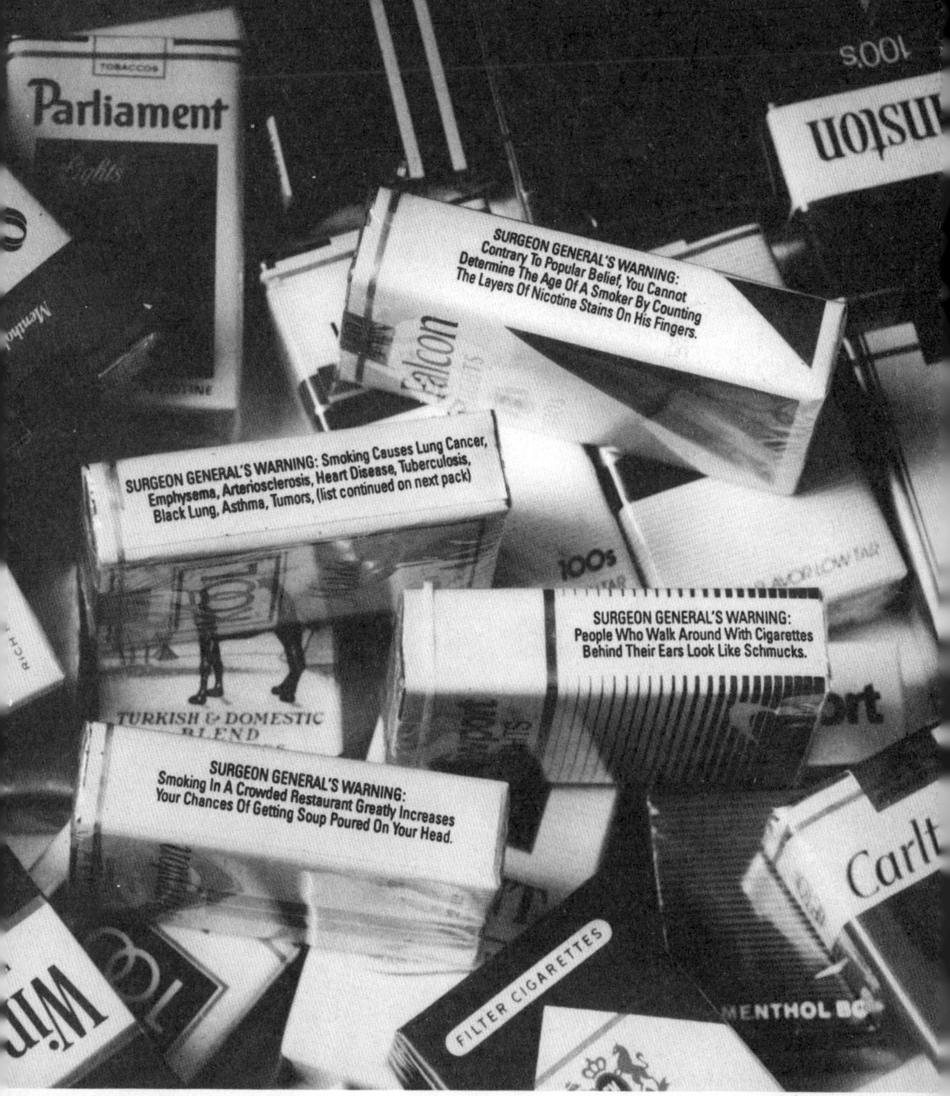

Parliament
SURGEON GENERAL'S WARNING: Contrary To Popular Belief, You Cannot Determine The Age Of A Smoker By Counting The Layers Of Nicotine Stains On His Fingers.
SURGEON GENERAL'S WARNING: Smoking Causes Lung Cancer, Emphysema, Arteriosclerosis, Heart Disease, Tuberculosis, Black Lung, Asthma, Tumors, (list continued on next pack)
SURGEON GENERAL'S WARNING: People Who Walk Around With Cigarettes Behind Their Ears Look Like Schmucks.
SURGEON GENERAL'S WARNING: Smoking In A Crowded Restaurant Greatly Increases Your Chances Of Getting Soup Poured On Your Head.
TURKISH & DOMESTIC BLEND
FILTER CIGARETTES
MENTHOL
100s

ALL THE NUKES THAT'S FIT TO PRINT DEPT.

What would happen if they dropped The Bomb? (No, not the next issue of MAD! Idiot! We mean the *nuclear* bomb!) Our government assures us that life would go on—just as soon as the Feds reinstated mail delivery and taxes! Right! Like we'd really be looking forward to squatting in our shelters, eating Spam and waiting to hear from the IRS!!! It takes *years* for radiation to leave the environment—that's a lot of Spam! So we'd need something to help pass the time...like some magazines! And we can guess what they'd be like! (After all, who knows more about the trashy future of publishing than us?!) So here's a selection of

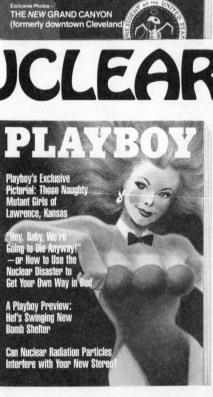

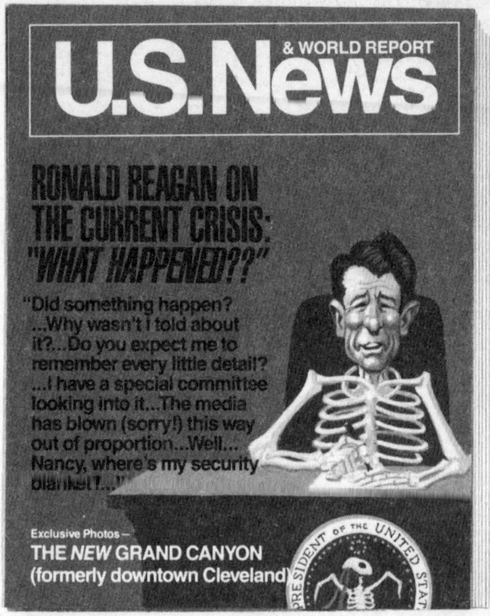
U.S. News
& WORLD REPORT
RONALD REAGAN ON THE CURRENT CRISIS: "WHAT HAPPENED??"
"Did something happen? ...Why wasn't I told about it?...Do you expect me to remember every little detail? ...I have a special committee looking into it...The media has blown (sorry!) this way out of proportion...Well... Nancy, where's my security blanket?..."
Exclusive Photos—
THE *NEW* GRAND CANYON (formerly downtown Cleveland)
PRESIDENT OF THE UNITED STATES

MAD'S POST-NUCLEAR

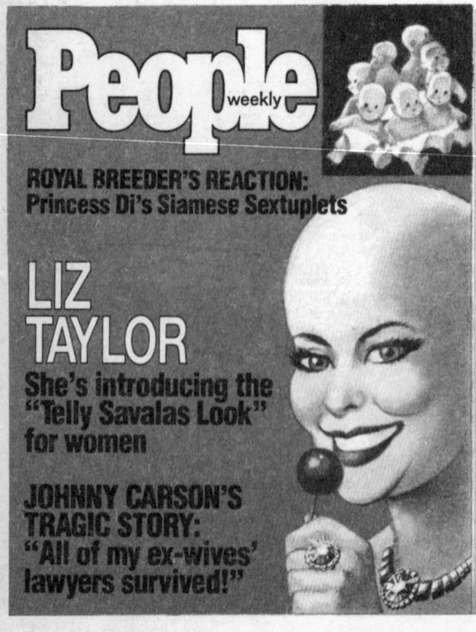
People
weekly
ROYAL BREEDER'S REACTION: Princess Di's Siamese Sextuplets
LIZ TAYLOR
She's introducing the "Telly Savalas Look" for women
JOHNNY CARSON'S TRAGIC STORY: "All of my ex-wives' lawyers survived!"

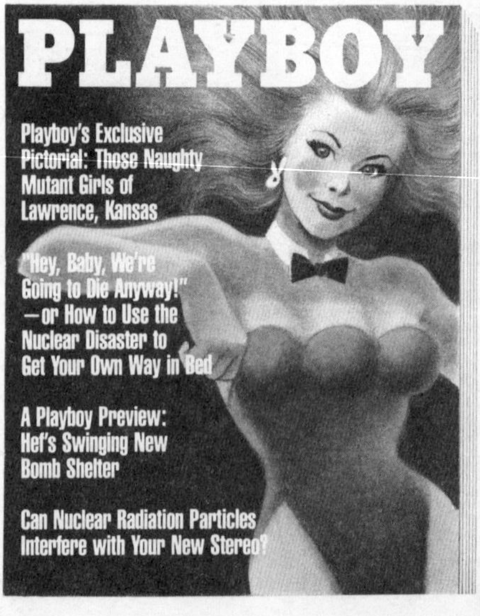
PLAYBOY
Playboy's Exclusive Pictorial: Those Naughty Mutant Girls of Lawrence, Kansas
"Hey, Baby, We're Going to Die Anyway!" —or How to Use the Nuclear Disaster to Get Your Own Way in Bed
A Playboy Preview: Hef's Swinging New Bomb Shelter
Can Nuclear Radiation Particles Interfere with Your New Stereo?

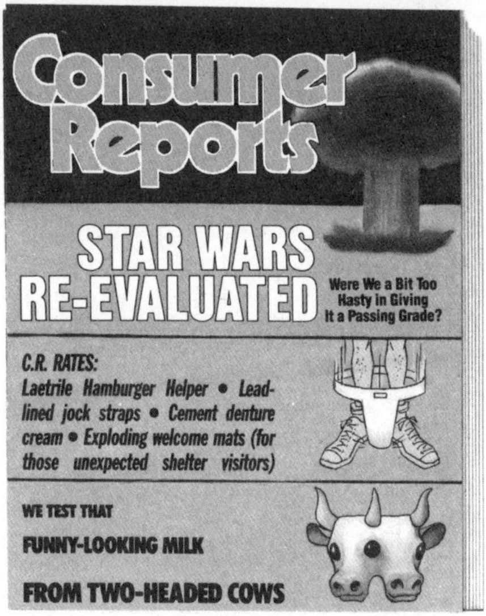
Consumer Reports
STAR WARS RE-EVALUATED
Were We a Bit Too Hasty in Giving It a Passing Grade?
C.R. RATES:
Laetrile Hamburger Helper • Lead-lined jock straps • Cement denture cream • Exploding welcome mats (for those unexpected shelter visitors)
WE TEST THAT
FUNNY-LOOKING MILK
FROM TWO-HEADED COWS

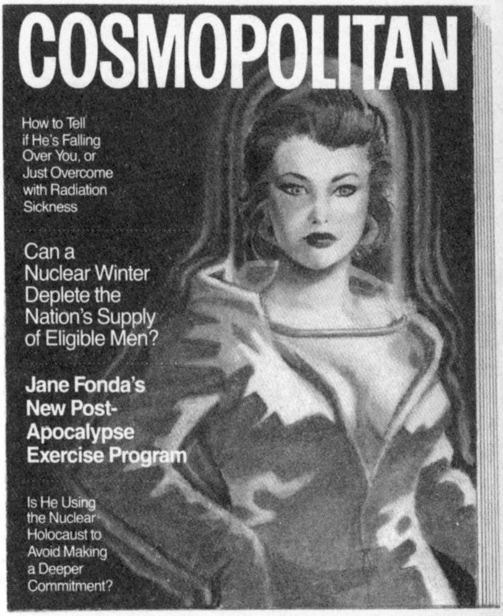
COSMOPOLITAN
How to Tell if He's Falling Over You, or Just Overcome with Radiation Sickness
Can a Nuclear Winter Deplete the Nation's Supply of Eligible Men?
Jane Fonda's New Post-Apocalypse Exercise Program
Is He Using the Nuclear Holocaust to Avoid Making a Deeper Commitment?

PUBLICATIONS

ARTIST: BOB CLARKE WRITER: BARRY LIEBMAN

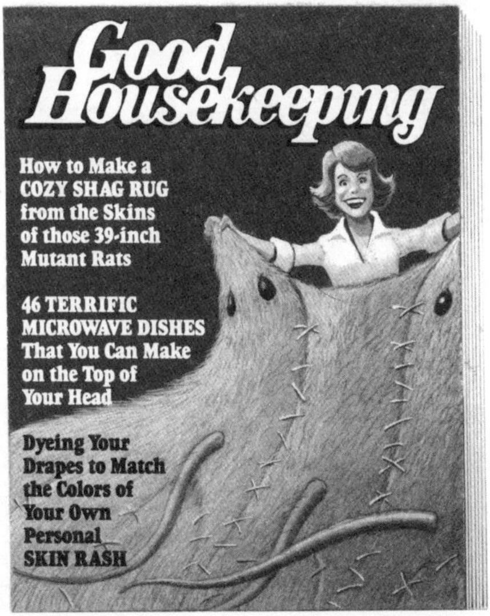
Good Housekeeping
How to Make a COZY SHAG RUG from the Skins of those 39-inch Mutant Rats
46 TERRIFIC MICROWAVE DISHES That You Can Make on the Top of Your Head
Dyeing Your Drapes to Match the Colors of Your Own Personal SKIN RASH

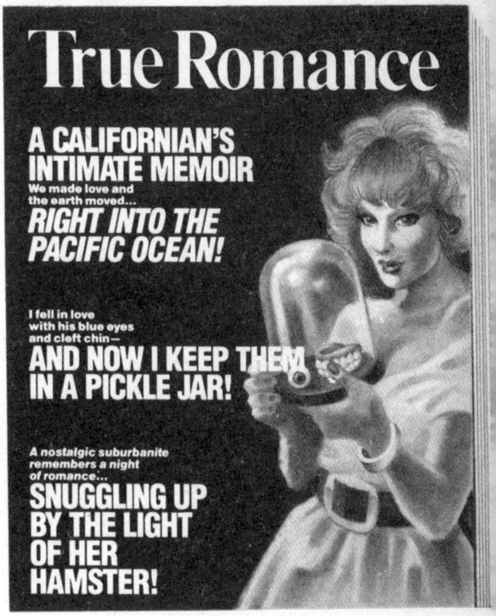
True Romance
A CALIFORNIAN'S INTIMATE MEMOIR
We made love and the earth moved...
RIGHT INTO THE PACIFIC OCEAN!
I fell in love with his blue eyes and cleft chin—
AND NOW I KEEP THEM IN A PICKLE JAR!
A nostalgic suburbanite remembers a night of romance...
SNUGGLING UP BY THE LIGHT OF HER HAMSTER!

SERGE-IN GENERAL DEPT.

A MAD LOOK AT GARA

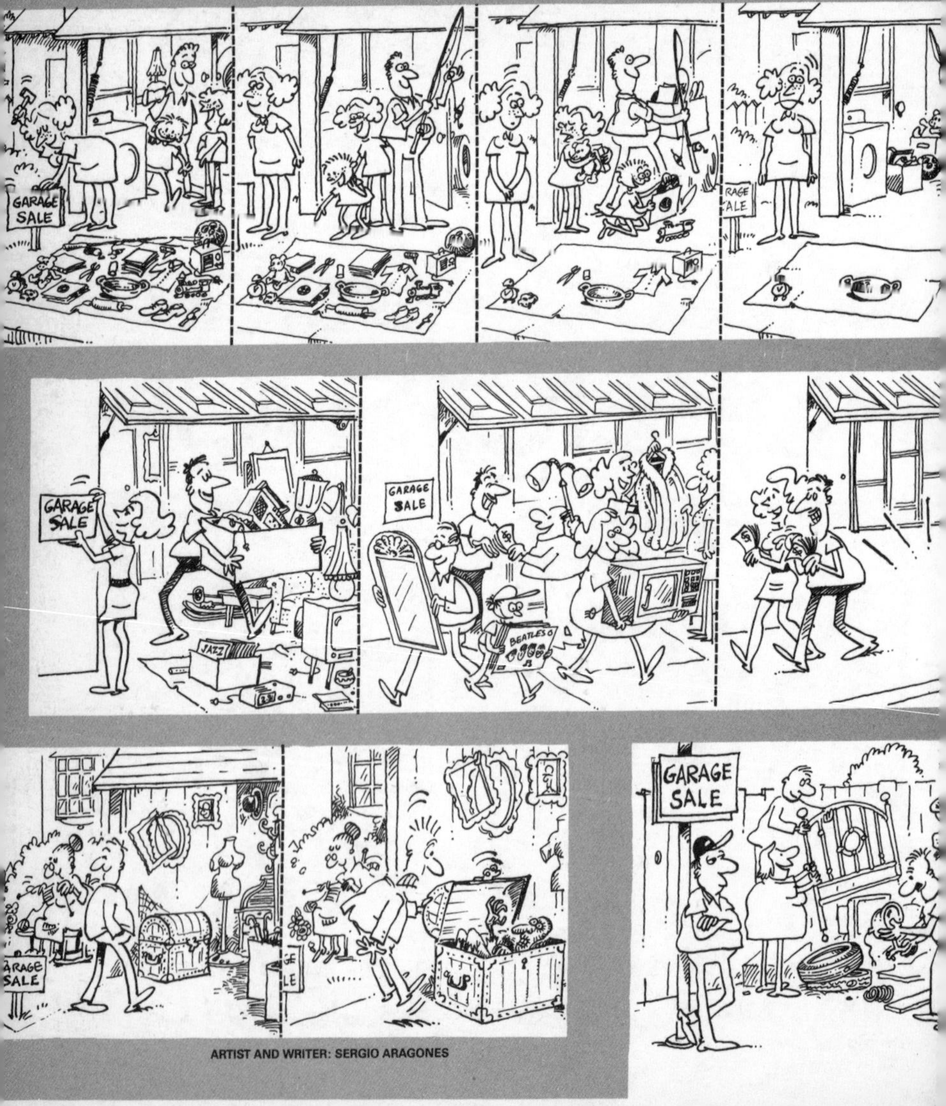
GARAGE SALE
GARAGE SALE
JAZZ
GARAGE SALE
BEATLES
GARAGE SALE
UP
GARAGE SALE

ARTIST AND WRITER: SERGIO ARAGONES

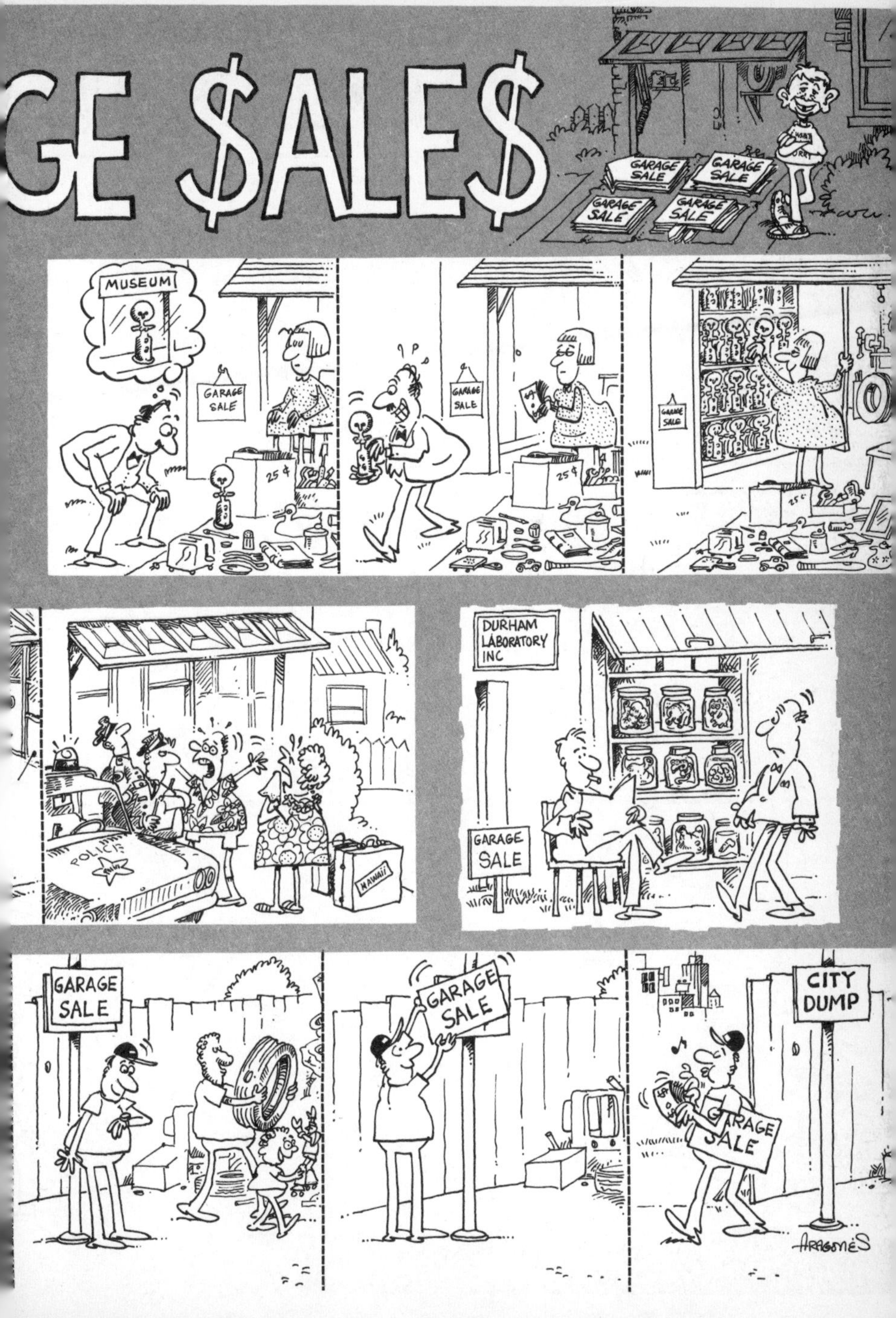
GE ALE
GARAGE SALE
GARAGE SALE
GARAGE SALE
GARAGE SALE
MUSEUM
GARAGE SALE
25¢
GARAGE SALE
25¢
GARAGE SALE
25¢
POLICE
HAWAII
DURHAM LABORATORY INC
GARAGE SALE
GARAGE SALE
GARAGE SALE
CITY DUMP
GARAGE SALE
ARAGONÉS

TALES FROM THE DUCK SIDE DEPT.

THE DISASTROUS DESERT DRAMA

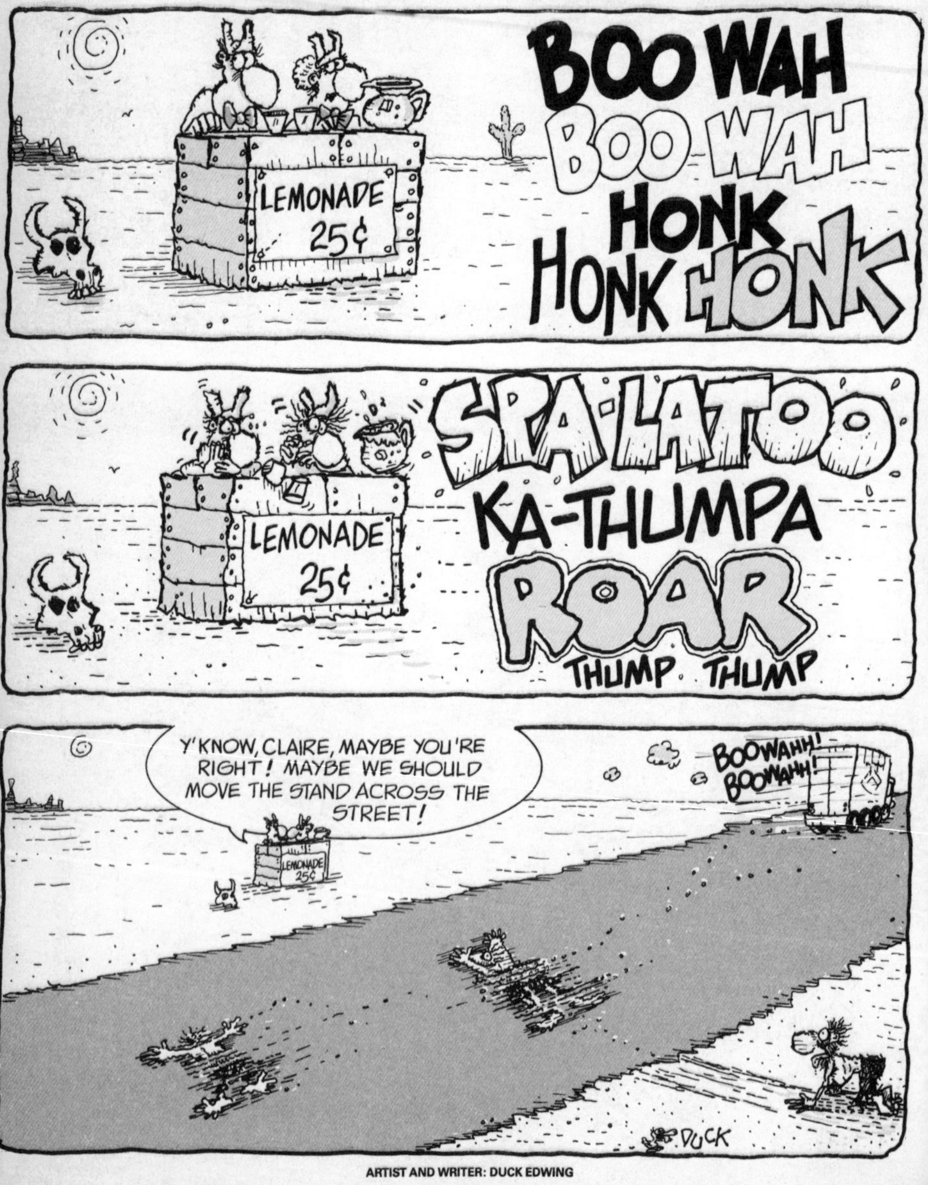
LEMONADE 25¢
BOO WAH
BOO WAH
HONK
HONK HONK
LEMONADE 25¢
SPA-LATOO
KA-THUMPA
ROAR
THUMP THUMP
Y'KNOW, CLAIRE, MAYBE YOU'RE RIGHT! MAYBE WE SHOULD MOVE THE STAND ACROSS THE STREET!
BOOWAHH! BOOWAHH!
LEMONADE 25¢
DUCK

ARTIST AND WRITER: DUCK EDWING

JOKE AND DAGGER DEPT.

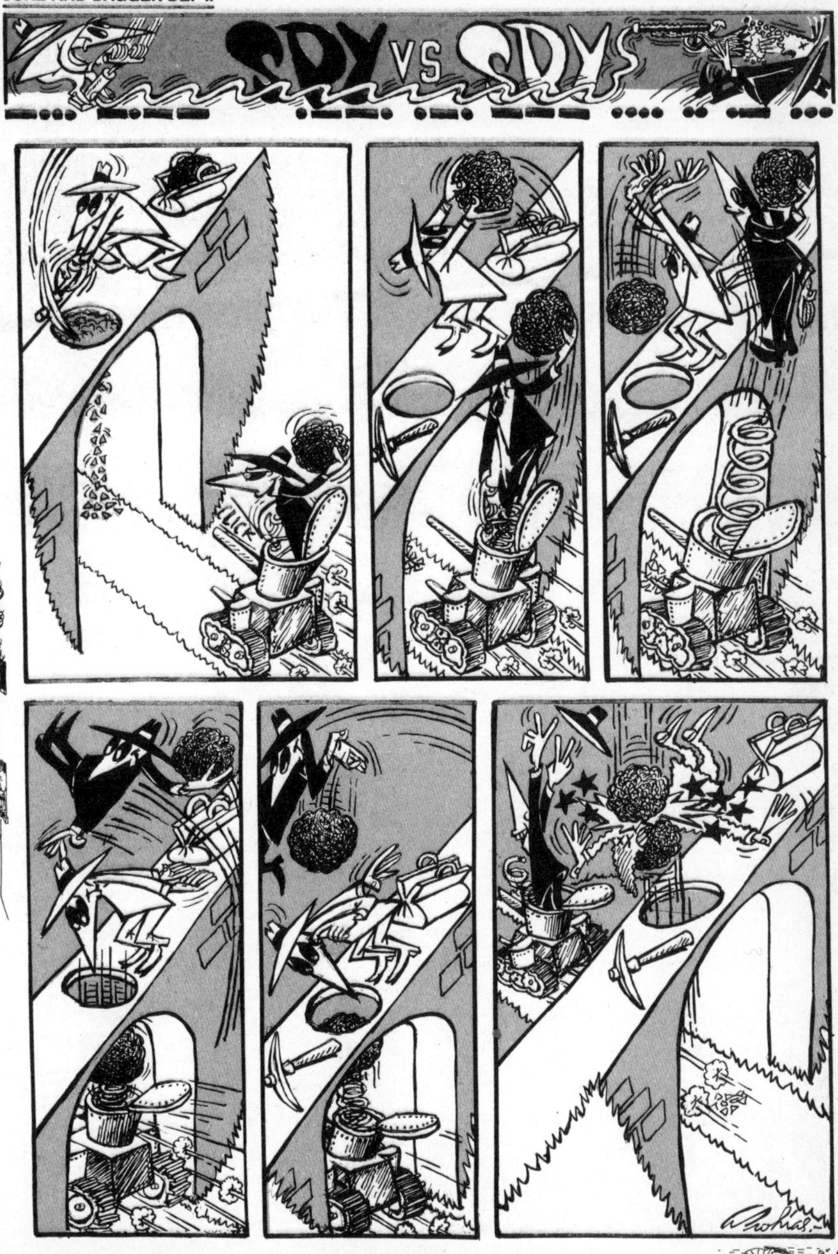
SPY vs SPY
CLICK
Prohias

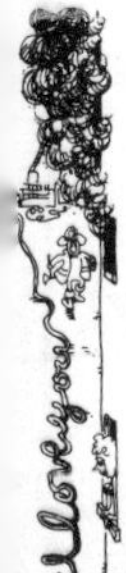

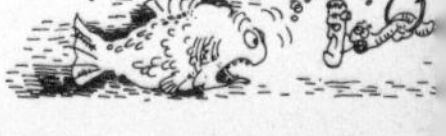

DRUM SCHTICK DEPT.

DRAMA ON PAGE 134

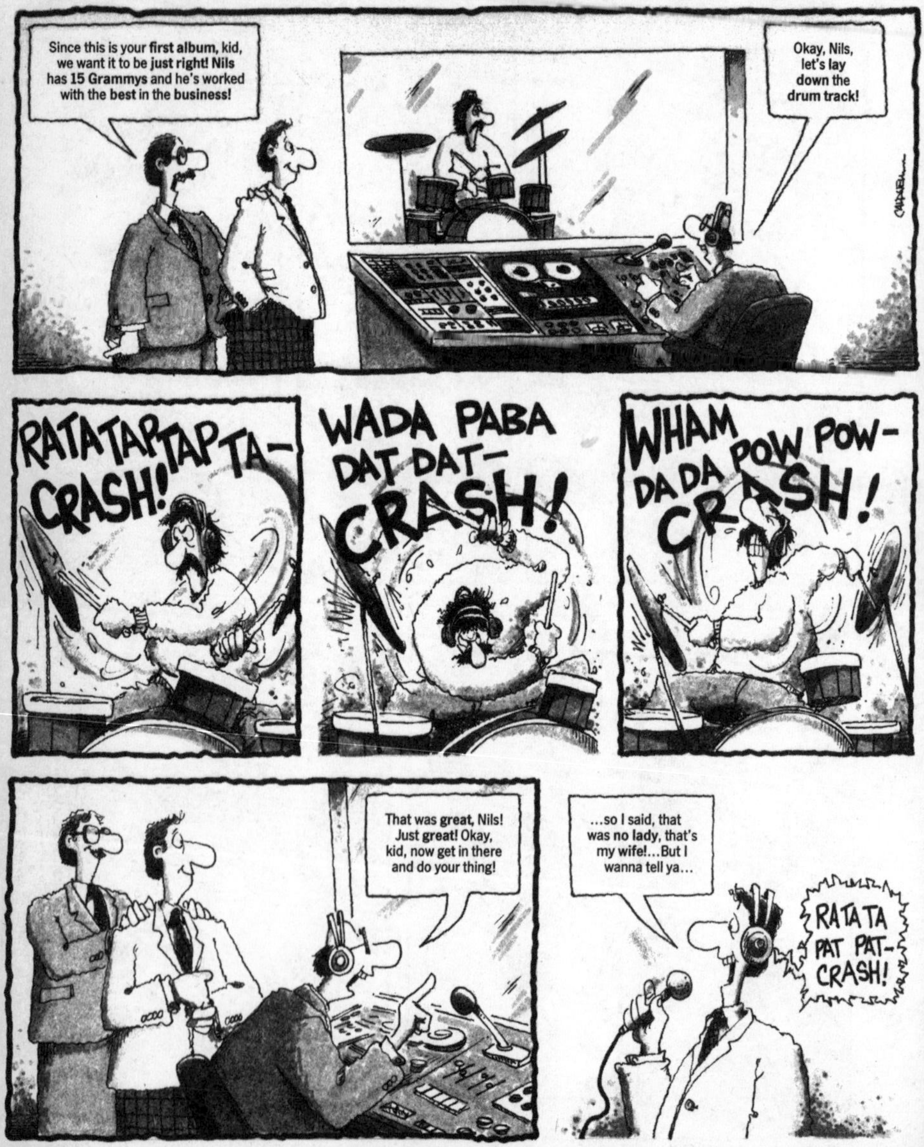
Since this is your first album, kid, we want it to be just right! Nils has 15 Grammys and he's worked with the best in the business!
Okay, Nils, let's lay down the drum track!
RATATAP TAP TA- CRASH!
WADA PABA DAT DAT- CRASH!
WHAM DA DA POW POW- CRASH!
That was great, Nils! Just great! Okay, kid, now get in there and do your thing!
...so I said, that was no lady, that's my wife!...But I wanna tell ya...
RATATA PAT PAT- CRASH!

ARTIST & WRITER: JOHN CALDWELL

SCHTICK IT IN YOUR EAR DEPT.

And now, as a public service to all you would-be artists out there, MAD Magazine, in cooperation with the Famous Artists' School of Wammelsdorf, now proudly presents...

A BEGINNERS GUIDE TO CARTOON SOUND EFFECTS

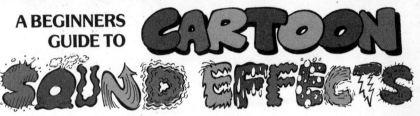

ARTIST: PAUL COKER WRITER: DUCK EDWING

aaaGOOiNTSHhhh

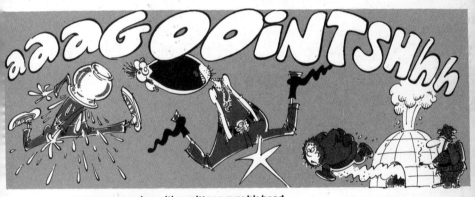

...someone sneezing with a spittoon over his head.
...a push button switchblade accidentally opening in a punk's front pocket.
...someone using a flamethrower to flush an Eskimo from his igloo.

PLOP PLOP KaBLOOiE!

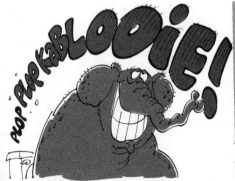

...an elephant experiencing relief.

KSSHFFWOOWAT

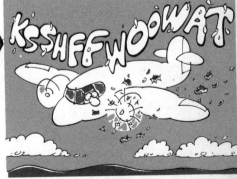

...a skydiver getting caught in a plane's propeller.

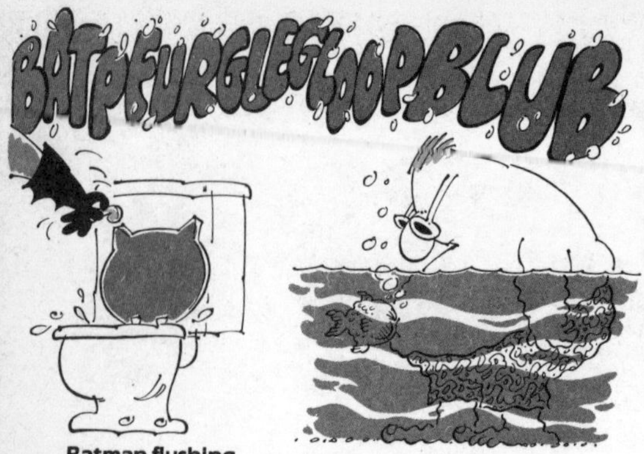
BATPFURGLEGLOOPBLUB

...Batman flushing.
...a fish blowing air bubbles into a fat man's navel.

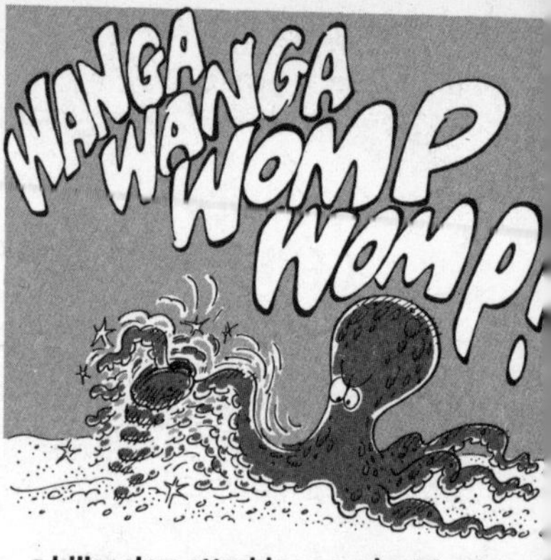
WANGANGA
WANGA
WOMP
WOMP!

...a killer clam attacking a sunburnt octopus

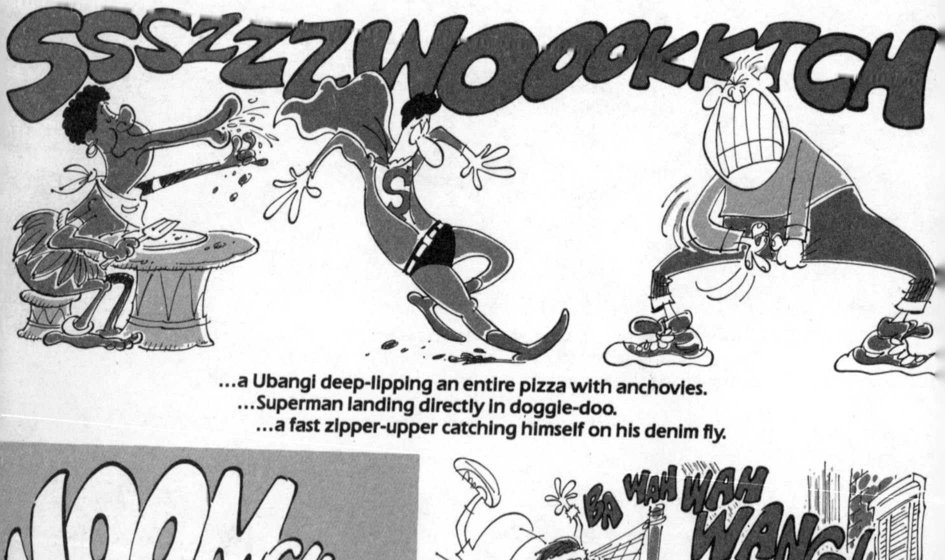
SSSZZZWOOOKKTCH

...a Ubangi deep-lipping an entire pizza with anchovies.
...Superman landing directly in doggie-doo.
...a fast zipper-upper catching himself on his denim fly.

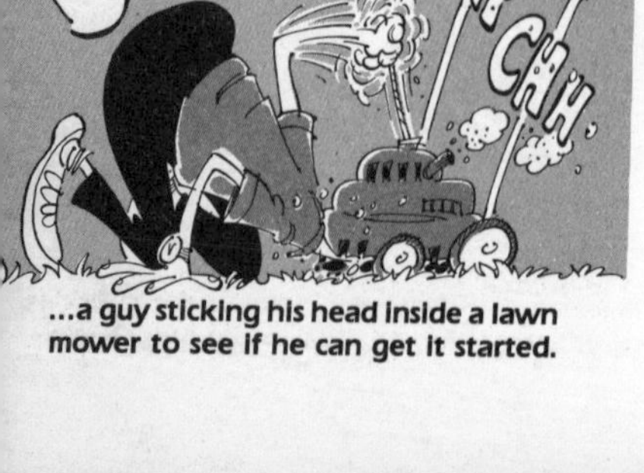
VOOM
CHH
CHH
CHH

...a guy sticking his head inside a lawn mower to see if he can get it started.

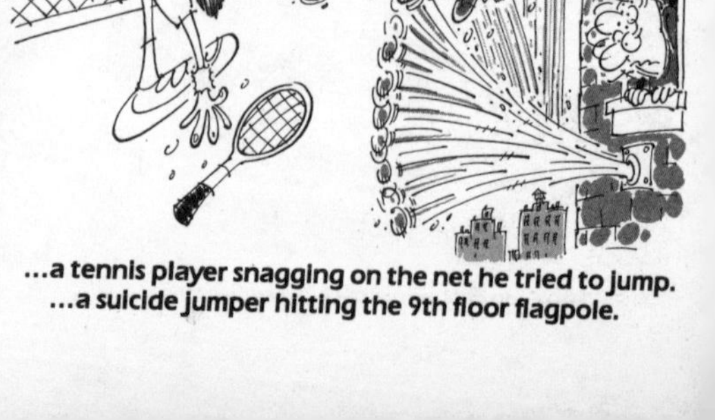
BA
WAH WAH
WANG!

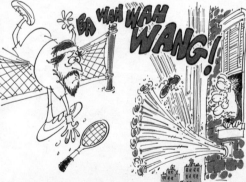

...a tennis player snagging on the net he tried to jump.
...a suicide jumper hitting the 9th floor flagpole.

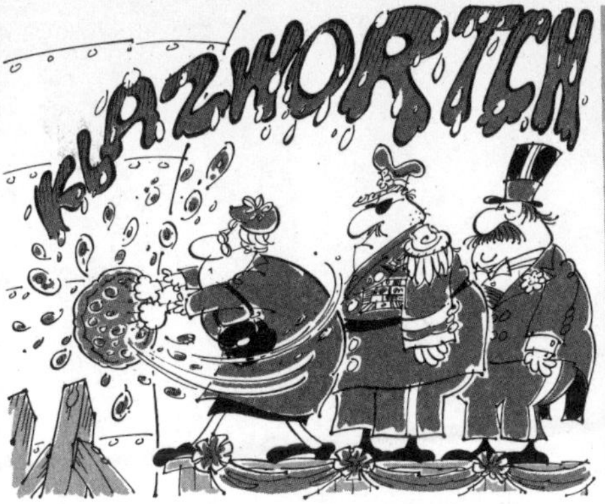
KLAZHORTCH

...an Italian ship being christened with a pizza.

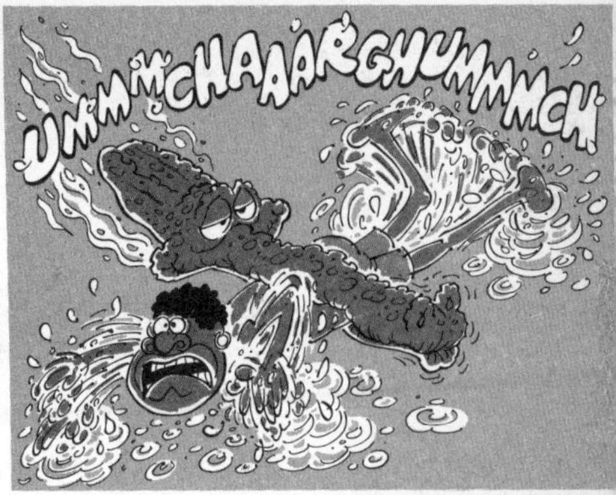
UMMMCHAAARGHUMMMCH

...an elderly crocodile gumming a frantic native.

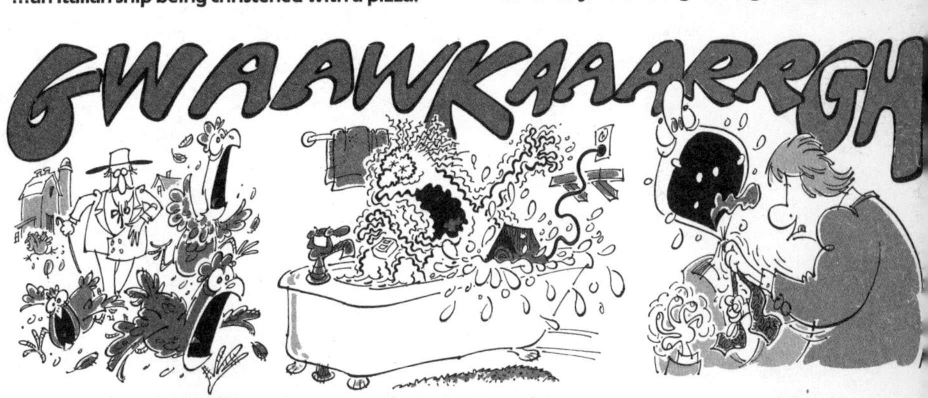
GWAAWKAAARRGH

...a Col. Sanders look-a-like visiting a chicken farm.
...a teenager accidentally knocking his radio into the bathtub.
...an apprentice tie salesman tying a Windsor knot for his first customer.

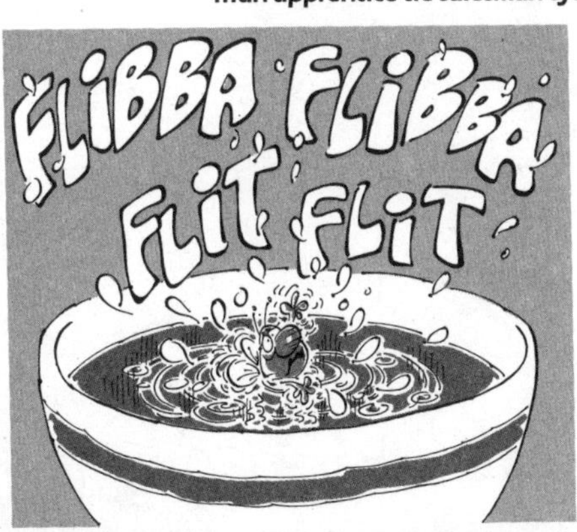
FLIBBA FLIBBA
FLIT FLIT

...a horsefly landing in a bowl of semi-cooled Jello.

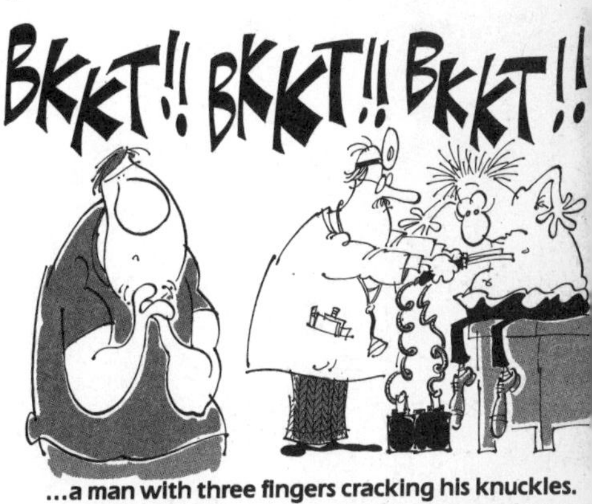
BKKT!! BKKT!! BKKT!!

...a man with three fingers cracking his knuckles.
...a doctor trying to jump-start a pacemaker.

SERGE-IN GENERAL DEPT.

A MAD LOOK AT STAY

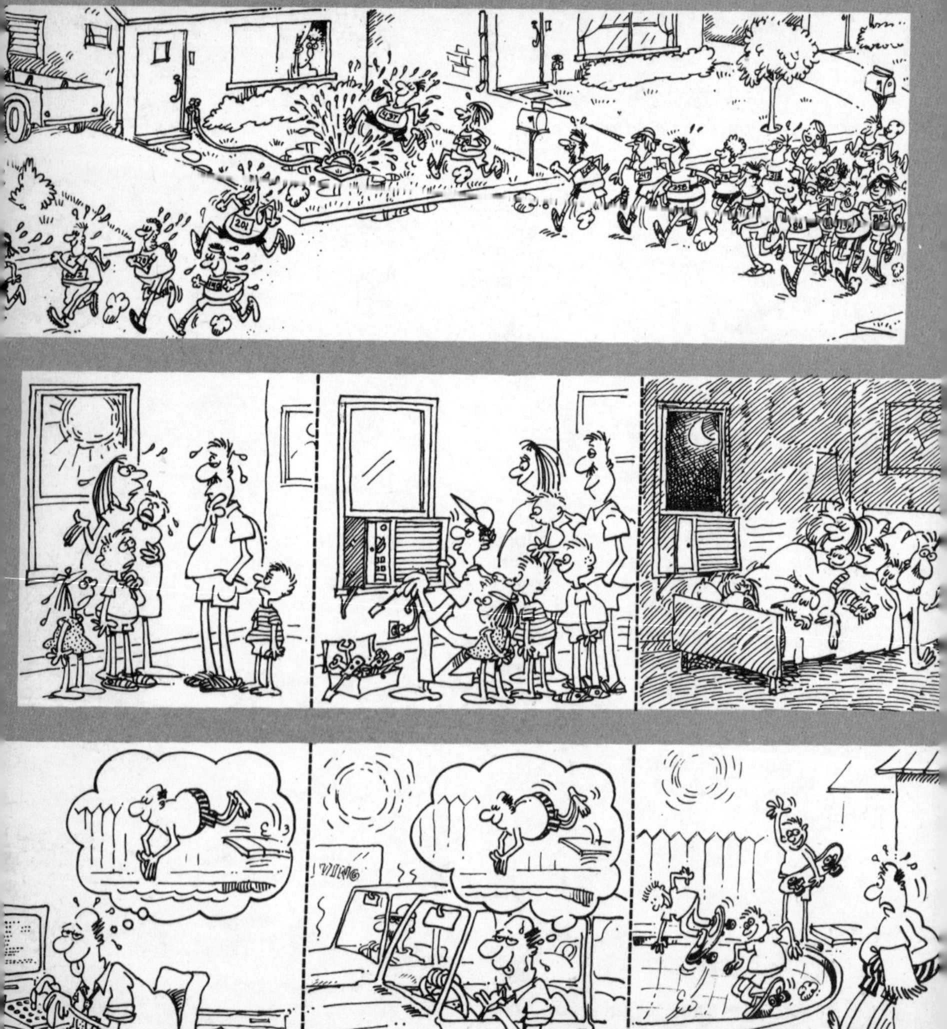

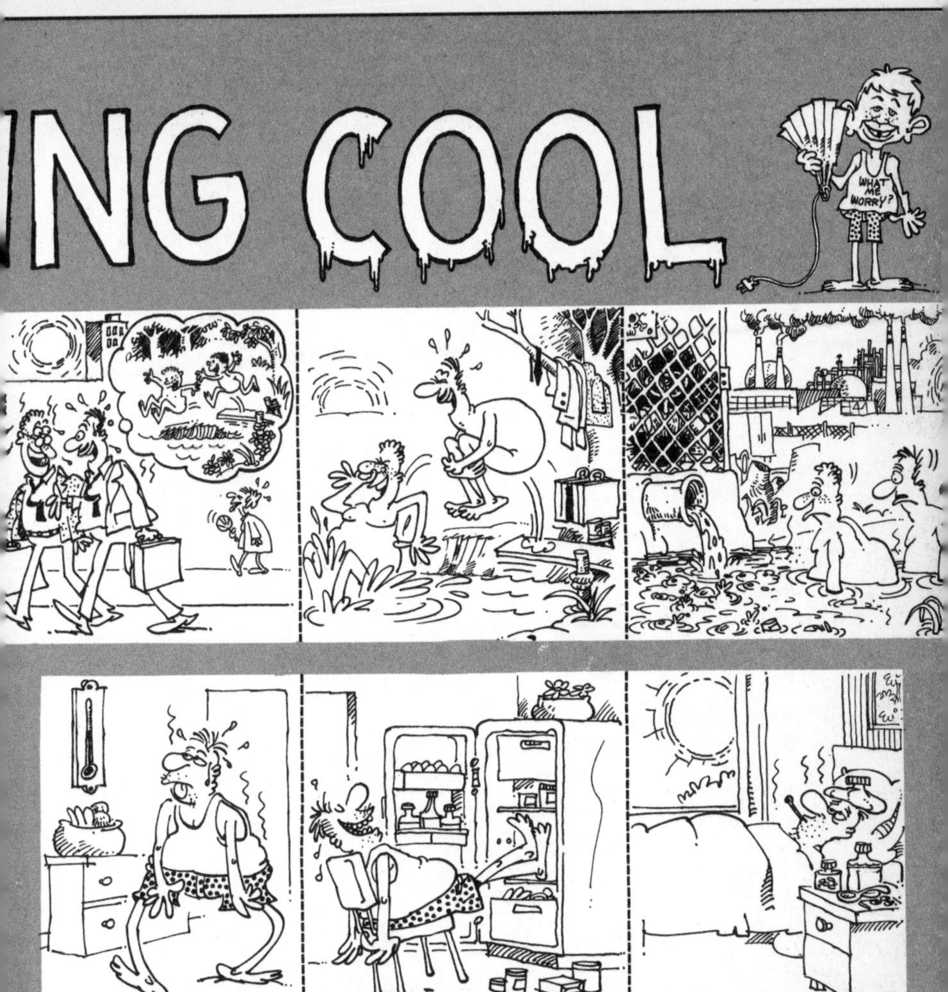
NG COOL
WHAT ME WORRY?

ARTIST AND WRITER: SERGIO ARAGONES

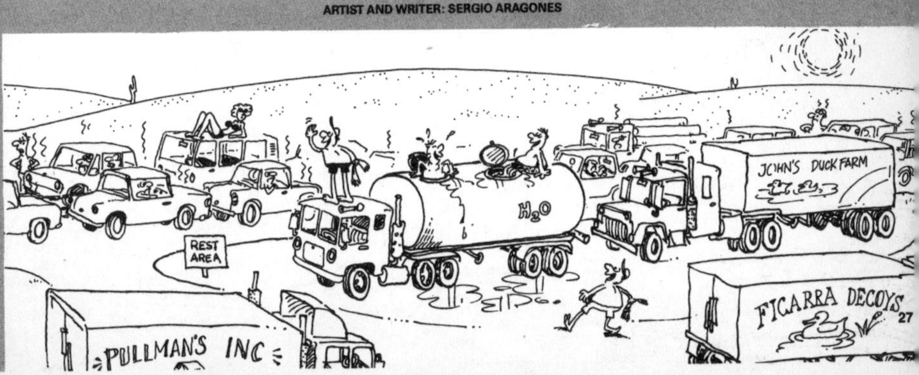
REST AREA
H2O
JOHN'S DUCK FARM
FICARRA DECOYS
PULLMAN'S INC

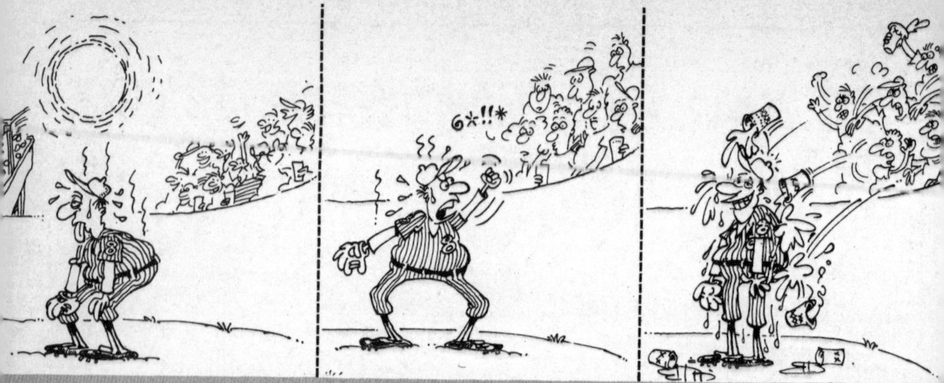

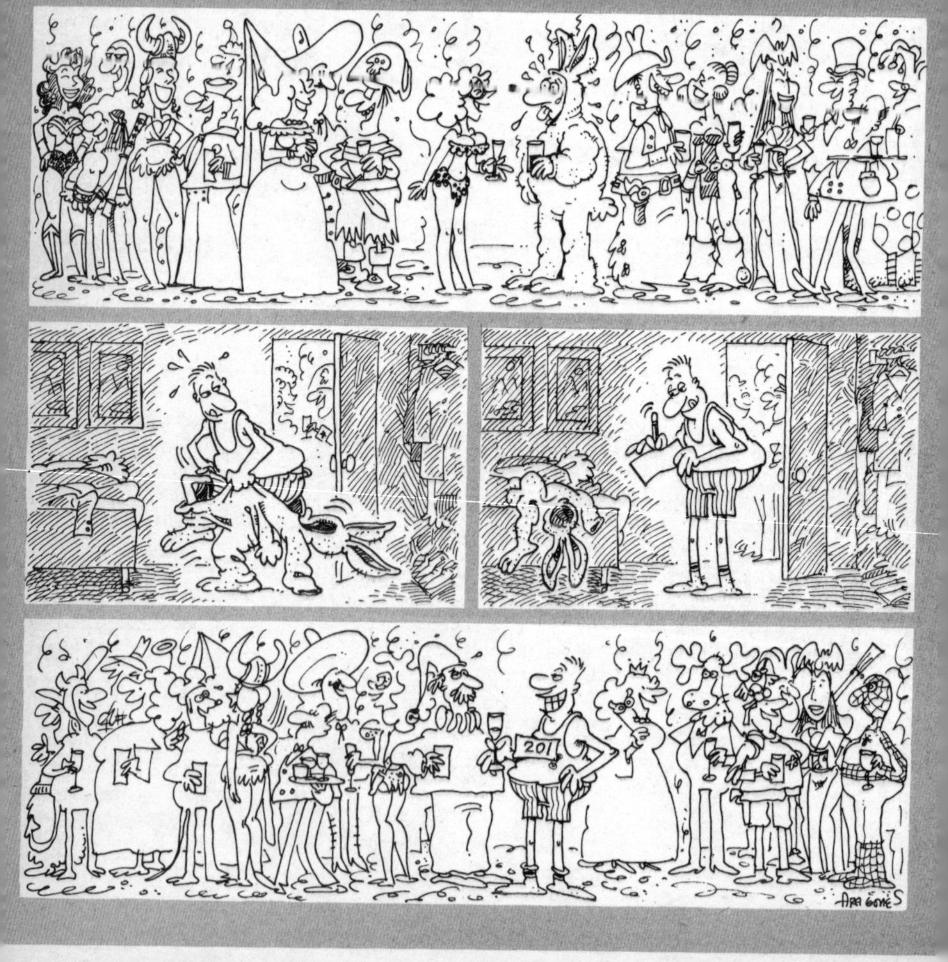
201
ARAGONÉS

TALES FROM THE DUCK SIDE DEPT.

THE MANHATTAN MONSTER MONKEYSHINE

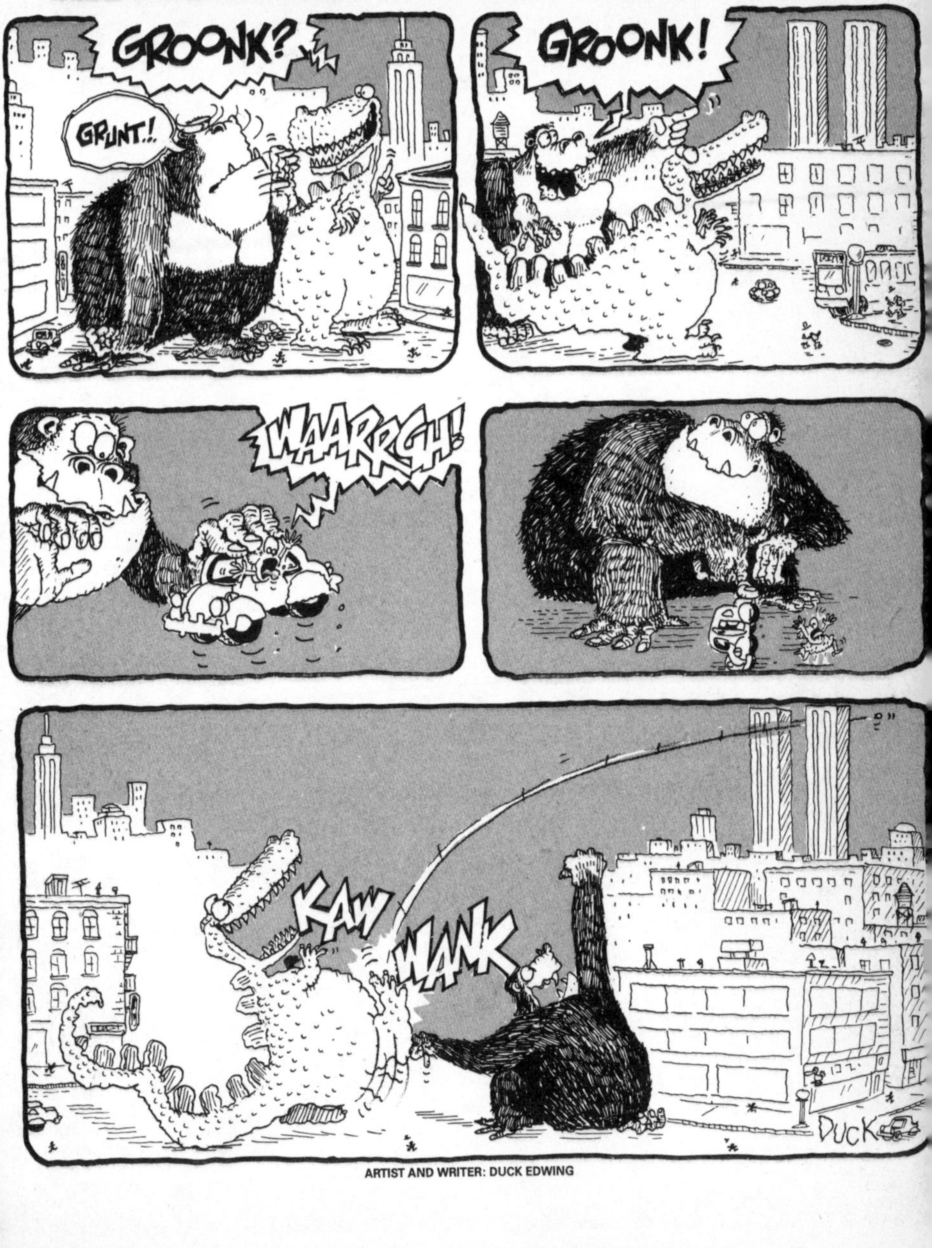
GROONK?
GRUNT.!
GROONK!
WAARRGH!
KAW
WANK
DUCK

ARTIST AND WRITER: DUCK EDWING

JUST A PHRASE WE'RE GOING THROUGH DEPT.

Words are funny little creatures. They can bring joy or sadness, hope or despair. And often it doesn't matter what the words are, as much as

SAME WORDS...*DIFFER*

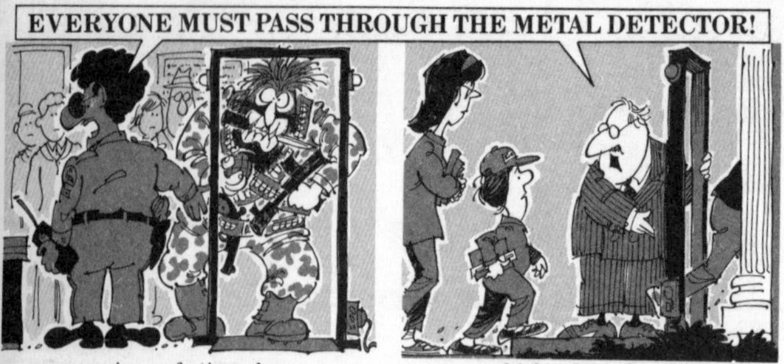
EVERYONE MUST PASS THROUGH THE METAL DETECTOR!

...is comforting when entering an airport.

...frightening when entering your high school!

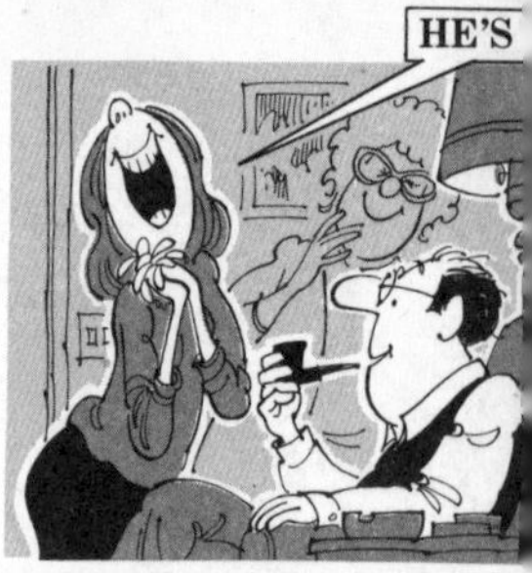
HE'S

...is terrific when your girlfriend is describing you to her parents

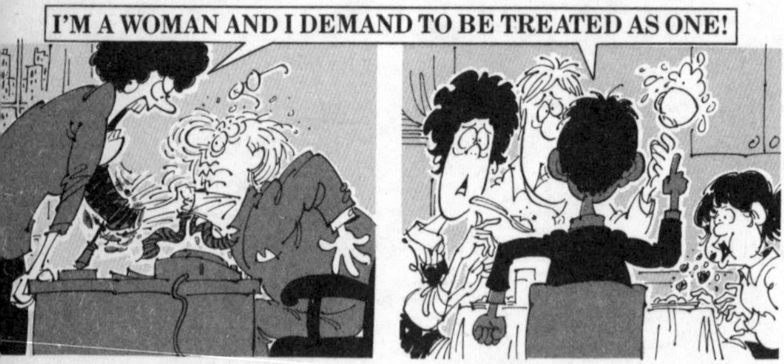
I'M A WOMAN AND I DEMAND TO BE TREATED AS ONE!

...is encouraging when it's your daughter fighting for equality at her work place.

...discouraging when it's your son making an announcement at the dinner table!

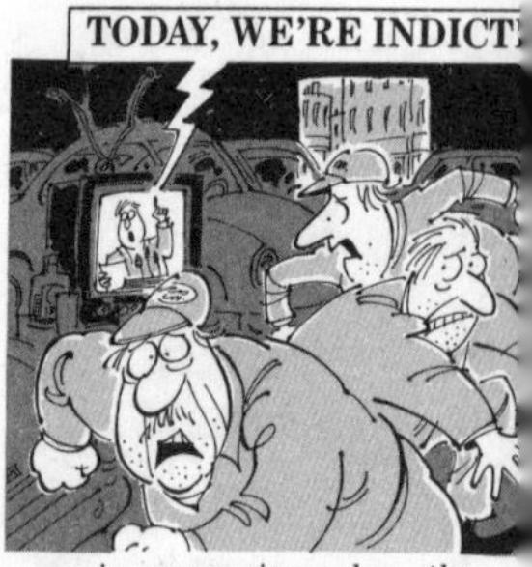
TODAY, WE'RE INDICT

...is reassuring when the D.A. is prosecuting members of a local auto theft ring.

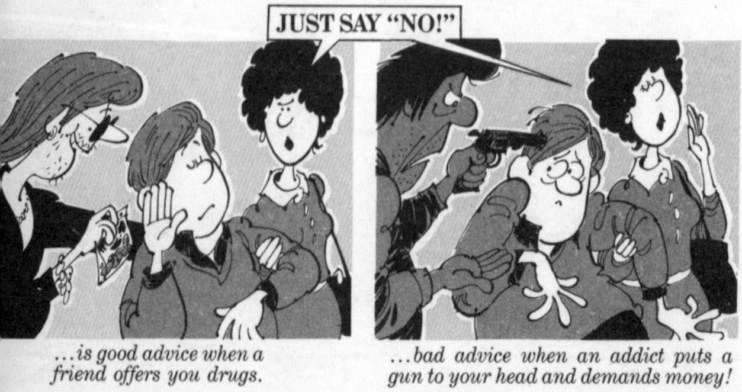
JUST SAY "NO!"

...is good advice when a friend offers you drugs.

...bad advice when an addict puts a gun to your head and demands money!

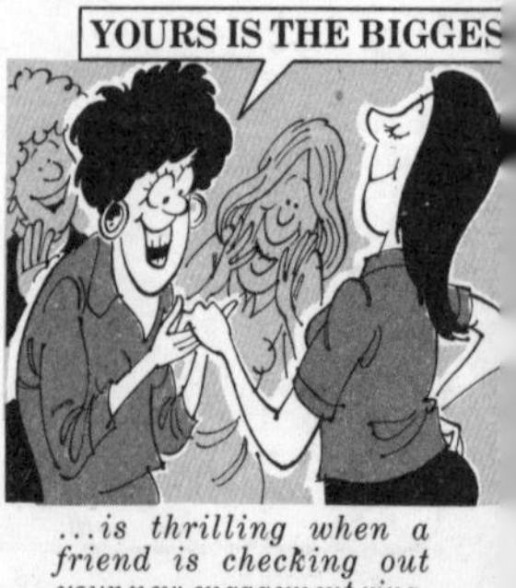
YOURS IS THE BIGGES

...is thrilling when a friend is checking out your new engagement ring.

who's saying them and to whom they are referring. Get it? Neither did we, until one of our hack writers came up with this MAD guide to...

ENT CIRCUMSTANCES!

ARTIST: PAUL COKER WRITER: J. PRETE IDEA: CHRISTOPHER ALLEN

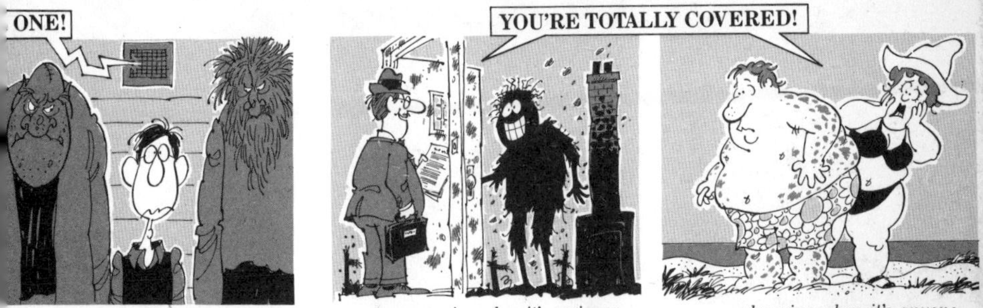
ONE!
YOU'RE TOTALLY COVERED!

...not so terrific when you're standing in a police line-up!

...is reassuring when it's an insurance agent discussing your claim.

...alarming when it's anyone discussing your burning rash!

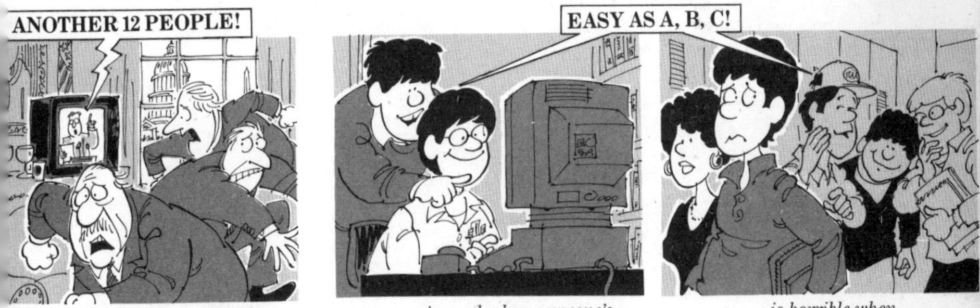
ANOTHER 12 PEOPLE!
EASY AS A, B, C!

...less reassuring when the D.A. is prosecuting members of the White House staff!

...is good when someone's talking about the computer program you just bought.

...is horrible when someone's talking about your sister!

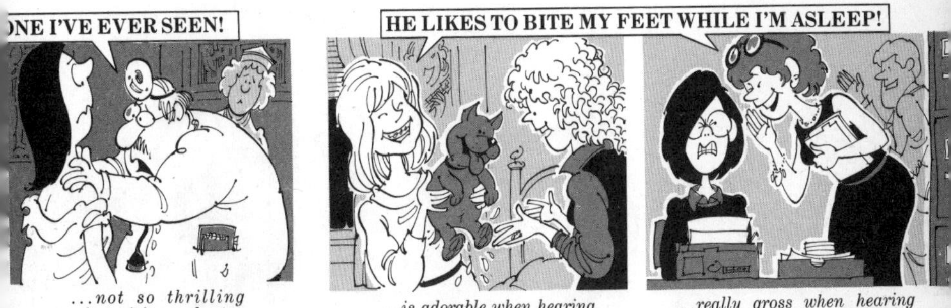
ONE I'VE EVER SEEN!
HE LIKES TO BITE MY FEET WHILE I'M ASLEEP!

...not so thrilling when it's a doctor examining your goiter!

...is adorable when hearing about someone's new puppy.

...really gross when hearing about someone's new boyfriend!

SERGE-IN GENERAL DEPT.

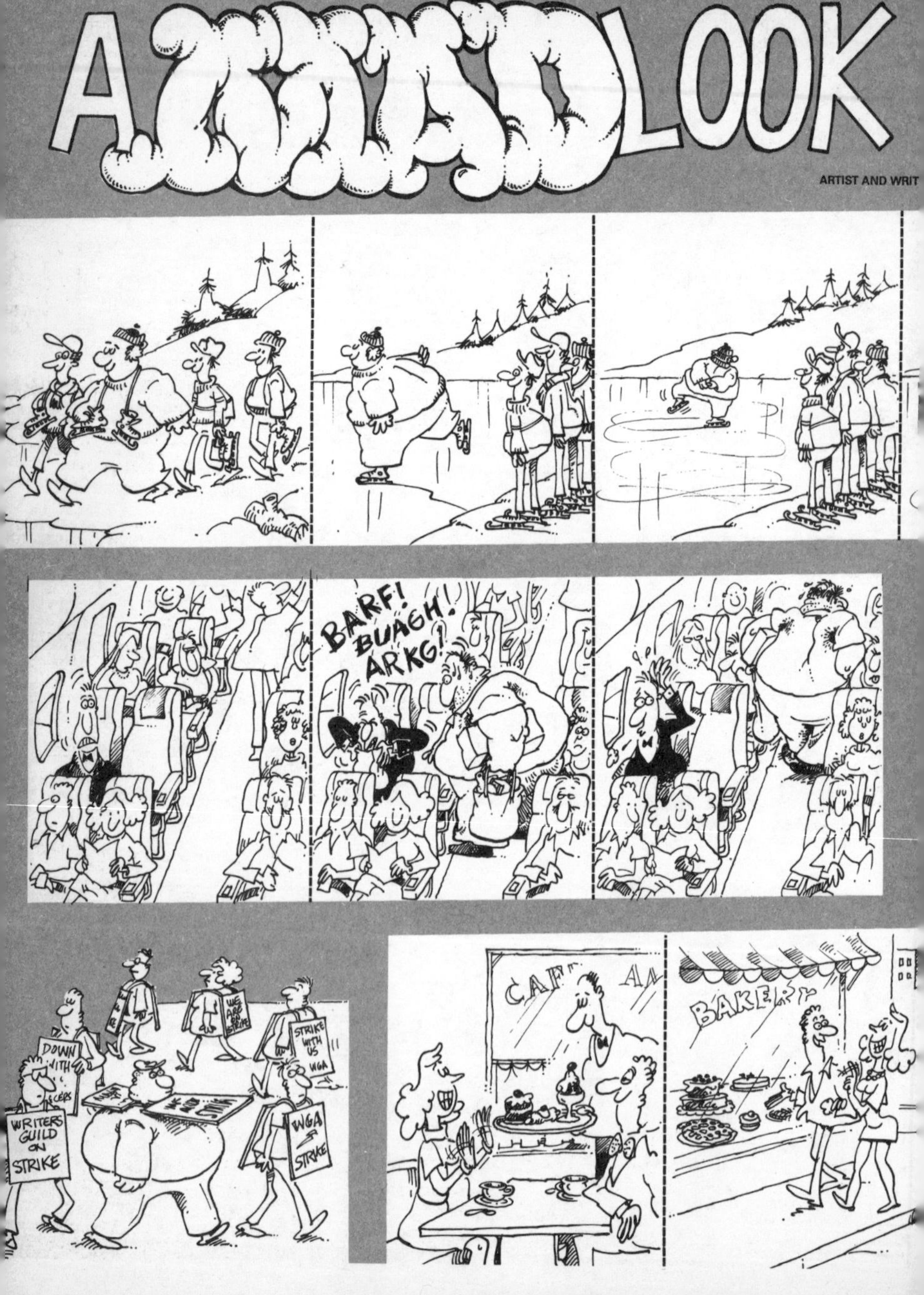
A
LOOK
ARTIST AND WRIT
BARF! BUAGH! ARKG!
DOWN WITH
WE ARE ON STRIKE
STRIKE WITH US WGA
WRITERS GUILD ON STRIKE
WGA STRIKE
BAKERY

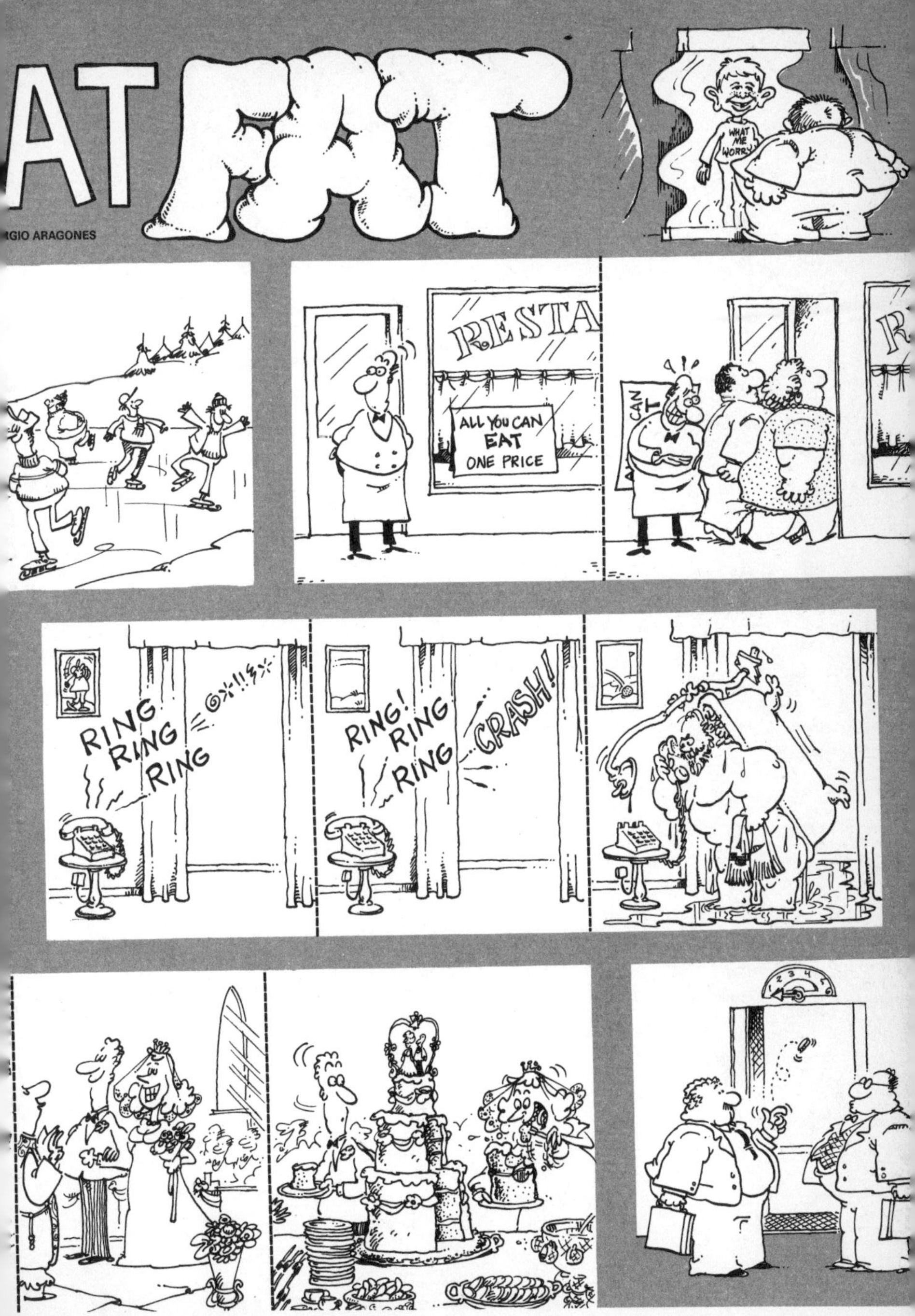AT FAT
WHAT ME WORRY
RGIO ARAGONES
RESTA
ALL YOU CAN EAT ONE PRICE
CAN
RING RING RING
RING! RING RING
CRASH!
1 2 3 4 5

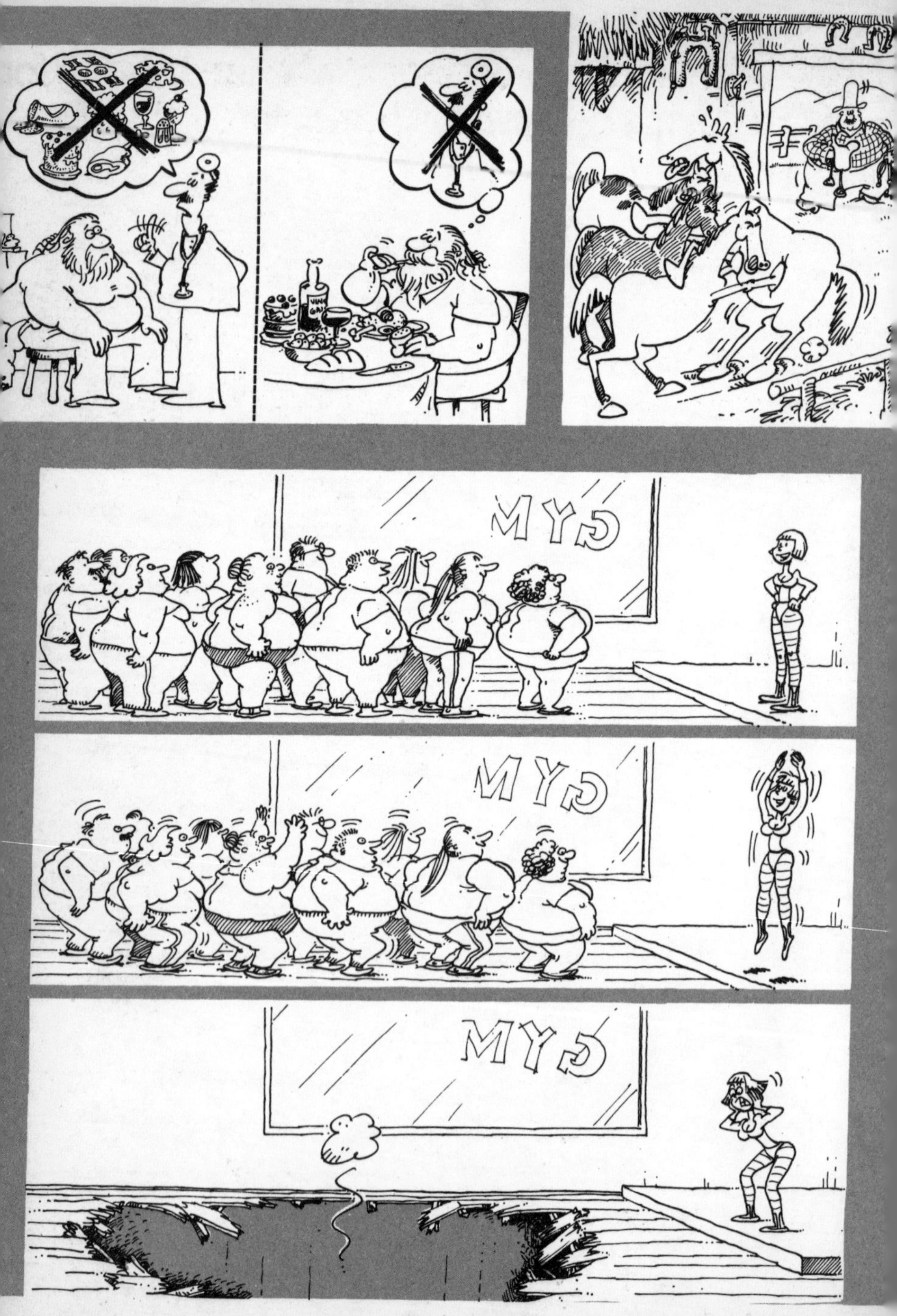

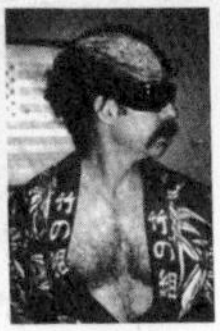

We're looking for people who are looking for a course on how to write children's books.

By Chic Glitz
Dean of Words

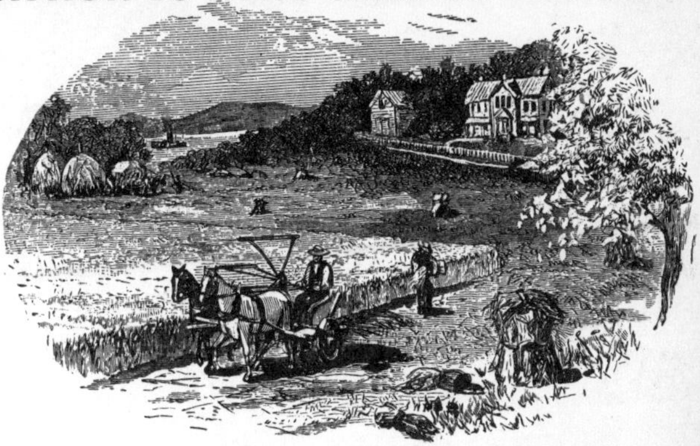

Home of the Home Study Institute for the Discovery of Hidden Talents in the Field of Writing Children's Books deep in the Connecticut woods. The Institute is located in a dilapidated shack behind this Victorian mansion.

RECENT GOVERNMENT FIGURES INDICATE there's now a better than 50/50 chance that everyone reading this ad was once a child. That means you've already done all the necessary research needed to create a child's book. Now all you have to do is write one!

Writing children's books is as easy as A, B, 3! Kids don't know from grammar, punctuation and style. To them, a book is just a string of words on pages. You don't have to use big words *or* know how to spell correctly!

Important details

Of course, there *are* fine points to be learned before writing children's books. Should you submit your story in crayon on white paper or type it on a brown paper bag? Who should you submit it to? General Motors or a book publisher? Should your book be illustrated, or maybe have drawn pictures?

That's where we come in. We're the Home Study Institute for the Discovery of Hidden Talents in the Field of Writing Children's Books. We're listed in the Guinness Book of World Records as the learning institution with the longest name! What better reference is there than that?

Lingering doubts?

You may still ask yourself: Am I qualified to be a writer? If you can write a check in the amount of $350—and the bank is so moved by your writing that they pay the amount of the check to us, then you're qualified!

After receiving Lesson One, "How to Sharpen a Pencil," you will be able to say to your friends, "Hey, I'm a writer"! Then, we will send you (at additional cost, of course) your own business card that says: WRITER. If you so desire, you can add other information like your name, address and phone number, also at an additional cost.

Learn writing "tricks"

Above all, we'll teach you to be original and avoid common clichés, which is easy as pie! We pledge the grass won't be greener on the other side of the fence any more for you! But, since even the longest journey starts with one step and today is the first day of the rest of your life, remember: He who hesitates is lost! Fill out and mail in the attached coupon now!

If you want to start on the fabulous road to becoming a famous author EVEN FASTER and earn big bucks to help pay off the charges we'll put on your credit card, then call 1-800-WRITER *this second* and give us your VISA, MASTERCARD or AMERICAN EXPRESS number. SPECIAL OFFER: Give us all three credit card numbers and learn three times faster!

Satisfied students

Here are some comments from our graduates:

"I could hardly believe it when I opened the publisher's envelope and a check fell out! My first sale after mailing out 6,735 submissions! I'll be taking a break from my writing now to decide how to spend my $5 check!!"
—N.M., Poor, NM

"I used to waste valuable time doing nothing. But now, thanks to the Institute, I now waste valuable time writing unpublished kid's books!" —J.W., Skank, OR

"The Home Study Institute for the discovery of Hidden Talents in the Field of Writing Children's Books is the best course in the entire world! I never, ever thought I'd be paid for my writing, but I just got my first check for writing this favorable quote for them to use in their ad!!!" —D.D., Boatbasin, NY

Don't think, do it!

Our course will get you started on the road to becoming an author of children's books, or children's stories, or maybe just a single children's word. We GUARANTEE you that after taking the course no more than five times, you will definitely be published, or at the very least, xeroxed!

The Home Study Institute for the Discovery of Hidden Talents in the Field of Writing Children's Books
11 Verb Place Noun, Alaska

Dear Mr. Glitz: Enclosed is my check for $350, which covers EVERYTHING you can think of for the moment. But being extremely creative, I know I can expect many future charges. I understand that once my check clears, I am under no obligation whatsoever to even open my study-at-home course.

Mr. Mrs. Ms. Miss

____
Please circle one and print name clearly

____
Street

____
City

____
State **Zip**

NEW CARS

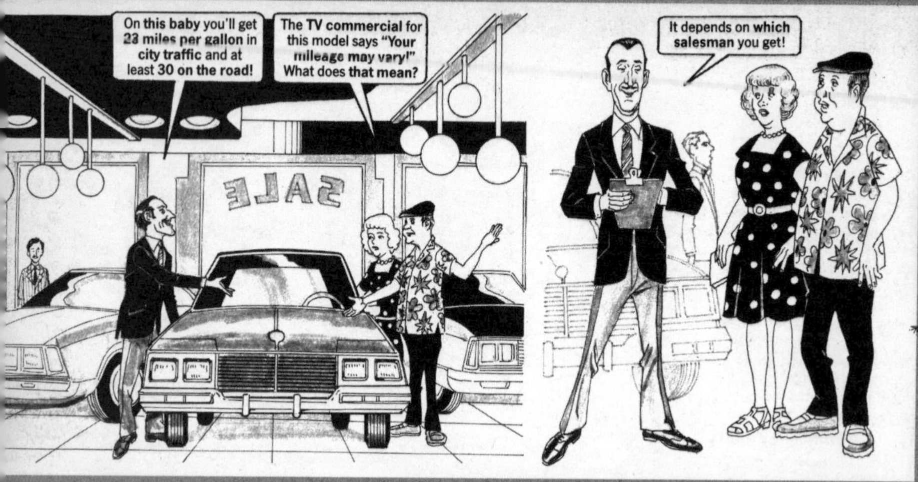
On this baby you'll get 23 miles per gallon in city traffic and at least 30 on the road!
The TV commercial for this model says "Your mileage may vary!" What does that mean?
SALE
It depends on which salesman you get!

BERG'S-EYE VIEW DEPT.

THE LIGHTE

OLD FRIENDS

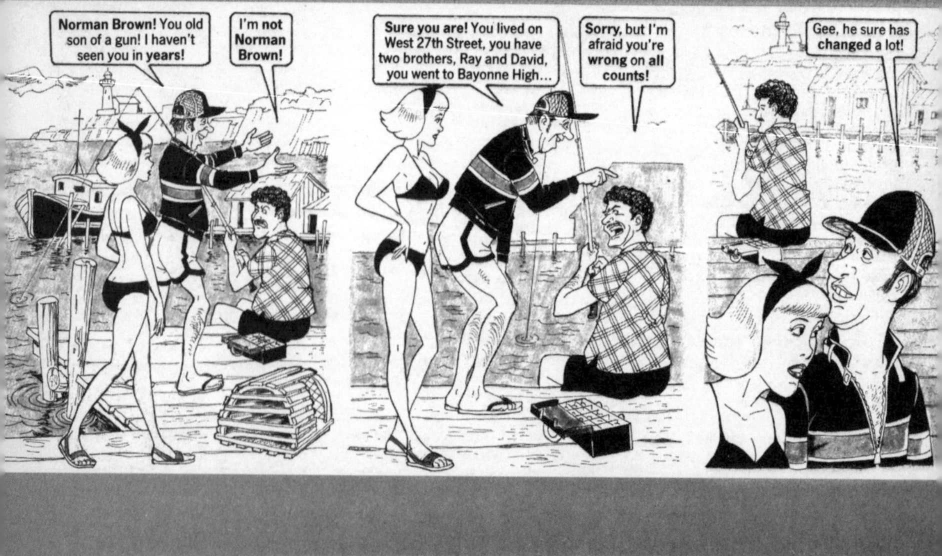
Norman Brown! You old son of a gun! I haven't seen you in years!
I'm not Norman Brown!
Sure you are! You lived on West 27th Street, you have two brothers, Ray and David, you went to Bayonne High...
Sorry, but I'm afraid you're wrong on all counts!
Gee, he sure has changed a lot!

Grandpa, I can't figure out this math **problem.** Can you help me?

Hmm, maybe you don't understand this "**bushels of apples**" and "**bales of hay**" business! Let's try it this way — "If one girl pays $50 each for three pairs of **designer jeans** and another girl spends $80 to have her **hair** and **nails** done, how much…"

Were you able to help Lisa with her homework?

Yep! It's **easy** when you know the **new math!**

R SIDE OF...

ARTIST & WRITER:
DAVE BERG

PRIORITIES

Hey, Tommy, I'm having a **party** at my house **Saturday night!** Lotsa girls, lotsa beer, lotsa laughs! Can you make it?

Hold on while I **check** my appointment book!

STATE

TV GUIDE

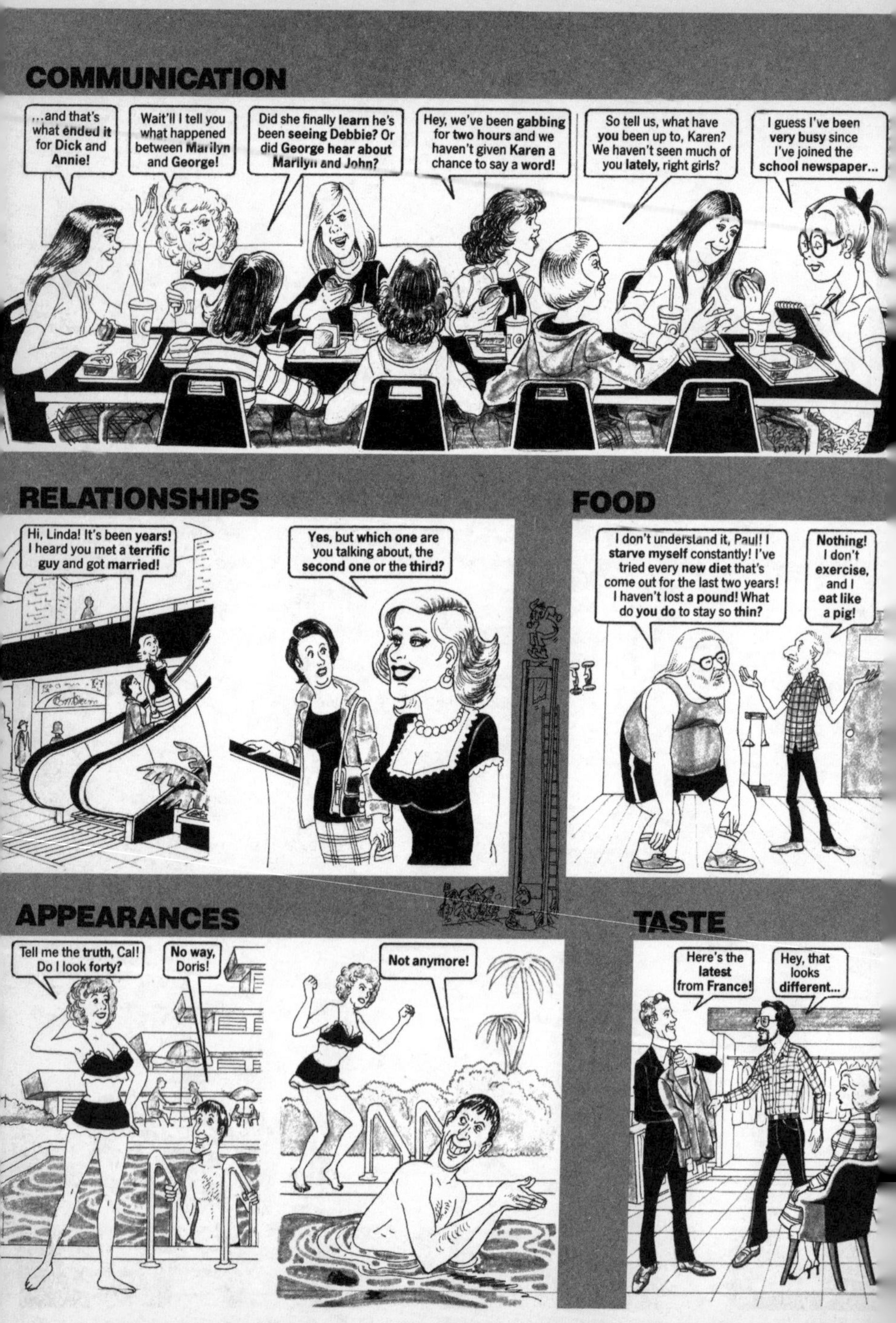
COMMUNICATION
...and that's what ended it for Dick and Annie!
Wait'll I tell you what happened between Marilyn and George!
Did she finally learn he's been seeing Debbie? Or did George hear about Marilyn and John?
Hey, we've been gabbing for two hours and we haven't given Karen a chance to say a word!
So tell us, what have you been up to, Karen? We haven't seen much of you lately, right girls?
I guess I've been very busy since I've joined the school newspaper...
RELATIONSHIPS
Hi, Linda! It's been years! I heard you met a terrific guy and got married!
Yes, but which one are you talking about, the second one or the third?
FOOD
I don't understand it, Paul! I starve myself constantly! I've tried every new diet that's come out for the last two years! I haven't lost a pound! What do you do to stay so thin?
Nothing! I don't exercise, and I eat like a pig!
APPEARANCES
Tell me the truth, Cal! Do I look forty?
No way, Doris!
Not anymore!
TASTE
Here's the latest from France!
Hey, that looks different...

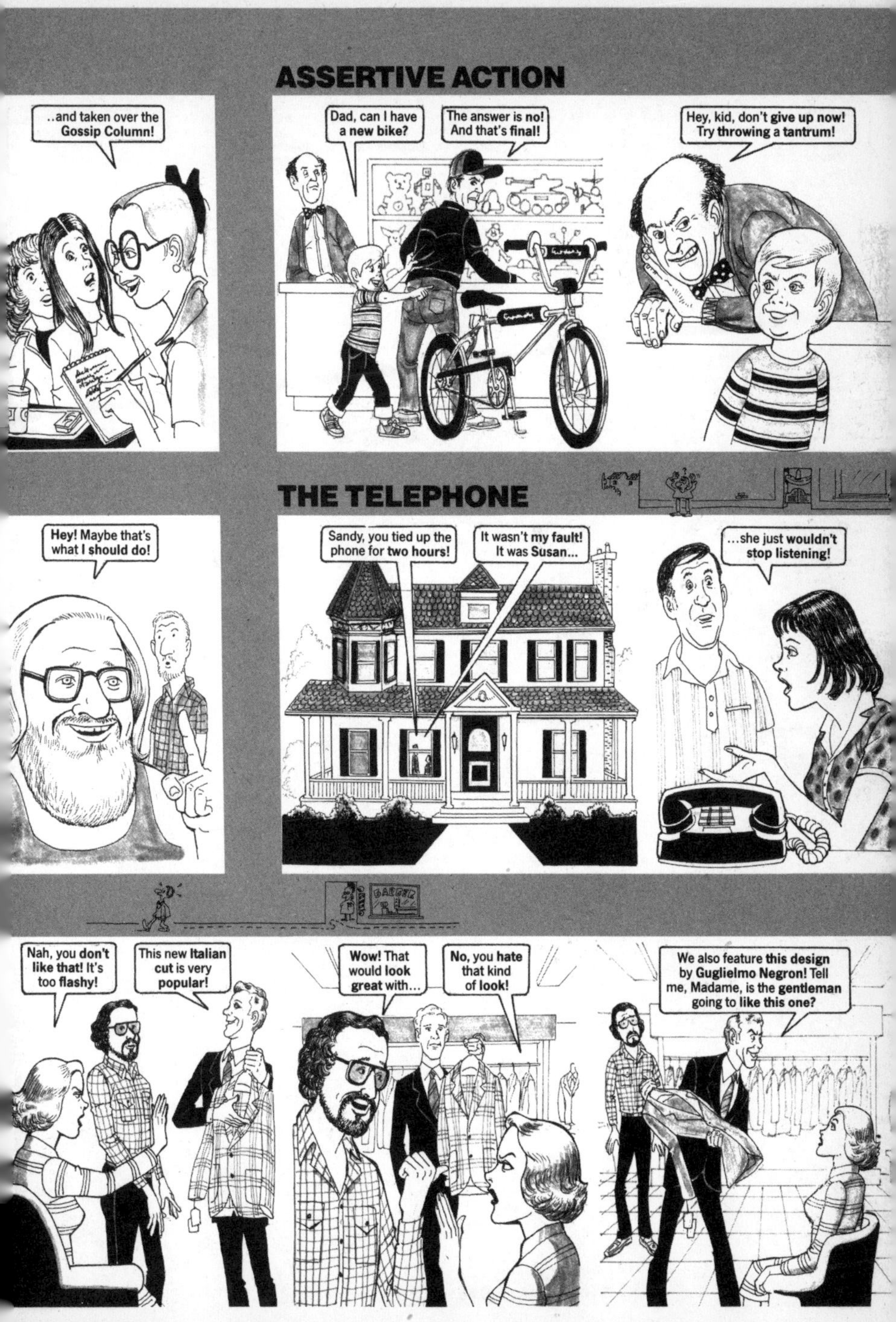
..and taken over the Gossip Column!
ASSERTIVE ACTION
Dad, can I have a new bike?
The answer is no! And that's final!
Hey, kid, don't give up now! Try throwing a tantrum!
Hey! Maybe that's what I should do!
THE TELEPHONE
Sandy, you tied up the phone for two hours!
It wasn't my fault! It was Susan...
...she just wouldn't stop listening!
Nah, you don't like that! It's too flashy!
This new Italian cut is very popular!
Wow! That would look great with...
No, you hate that kind of look!
We also feature this design by Guglielmo Negron! Tell me, Madame, is the gentleman going to like this one?

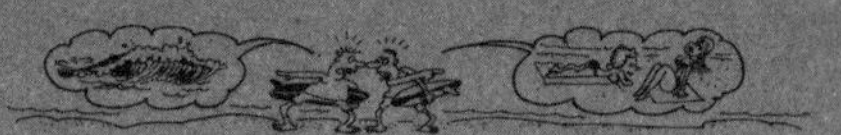

ACHES AND PAINS

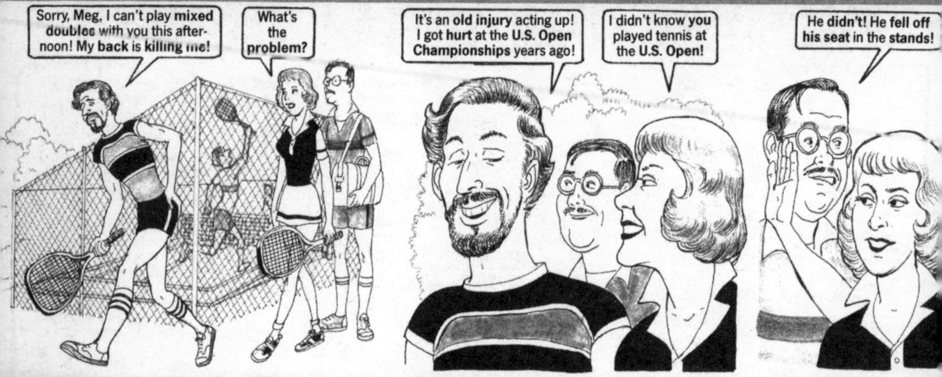
Sorry, Meg, I can't play mixed doubles with you this afternoon! My back is killing me!
What's the problem?
It's an old injury acting up! I got hurt at the U.S. Open Championships years ago!
I didn't know you played tennis at the U.S. Open!
He didn't! He fell off his seat in the stands!

GUILT

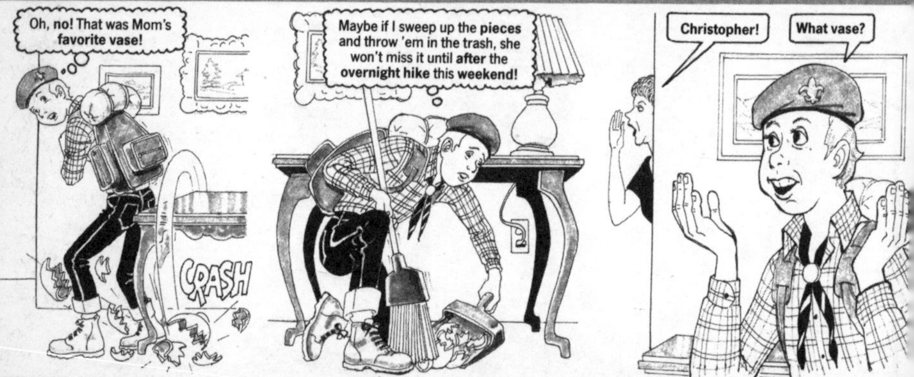
Oh, no! That was Mom's favorite vase!
CRASH
Maybe if I sweep up the pieces and throw 'em in the trash, she won't miss it until after the overnight hike this weekend!
Christopher!
What vase?

DOCTORS

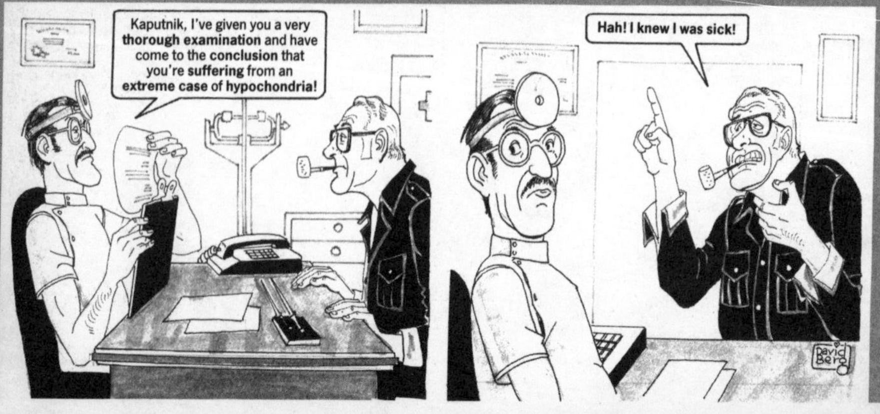
Kaputnik, I've given you a very thorough examination and have come to the conclusion that you're suffering from an extreme case of hypochondria!
Hah! I knew I was sick!
David Berg

TALES FROM THE DUCK SIDE DEPT.

THE TERRIBLE TOILET TRAUMA

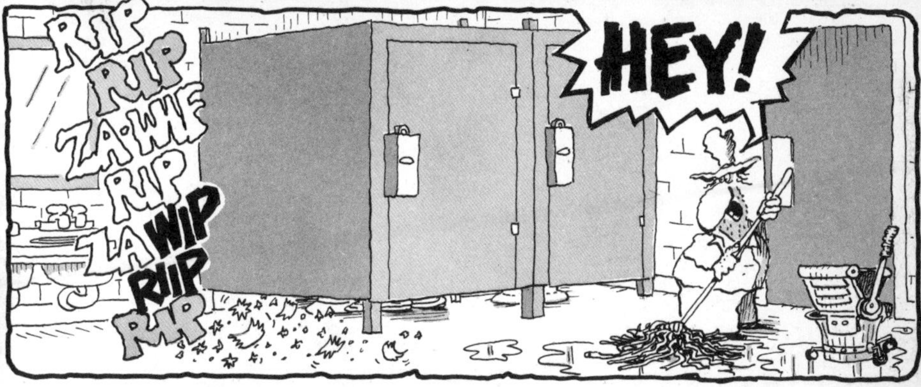
RIP
RIP
ZA·WIF
RIP
ZA WIP
RIIP
RIP
HEY!

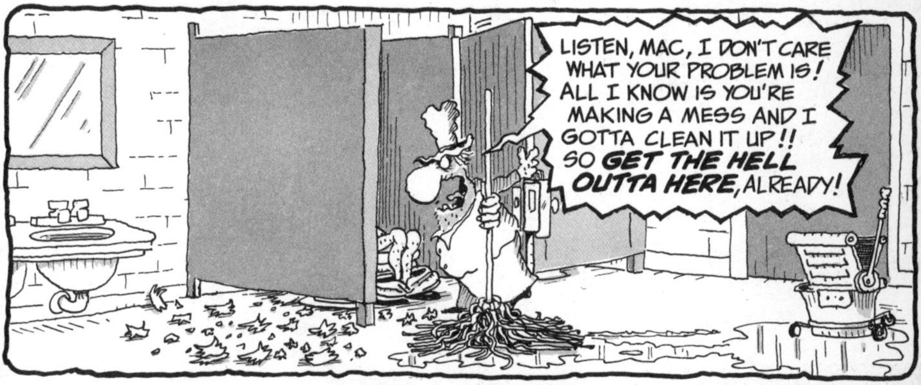
LISTEN, MAC, I DON'T CARE WHAT YOUR PROBLEM IS! ALL I KNOW IS YOU'RE MAKING A MESS AND I GOTTA CLEAN IT UP!! SO **GET THE HELL OUTTA HERE,** ALREADY!

ARTIST AND WRITER: DUCK EDWING

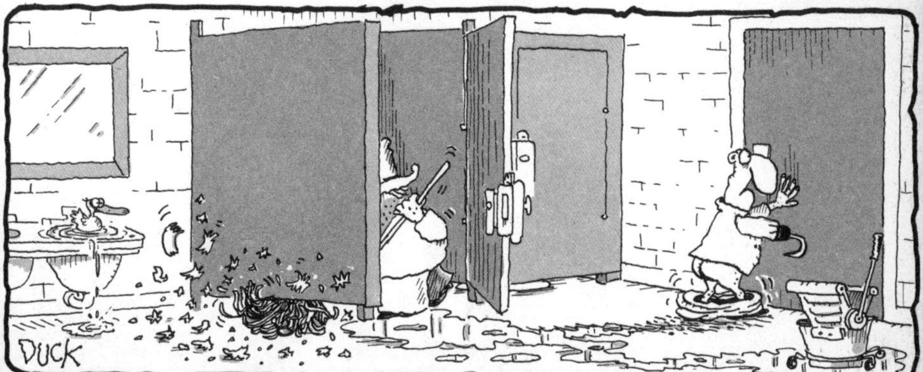
DUCK

THE KING IS BLED DEPT.

Elvis Presley died in 1977. At least, that's what most people believe. But there's still a bunch of kooks who think he faked his death and is really alive. Not to mention the fast-buck hucksters living off the Presley legend. Which makes us ask: "What would Elvis say about all this?" Most likely, he'd pick up his guitar and sing...

"DON

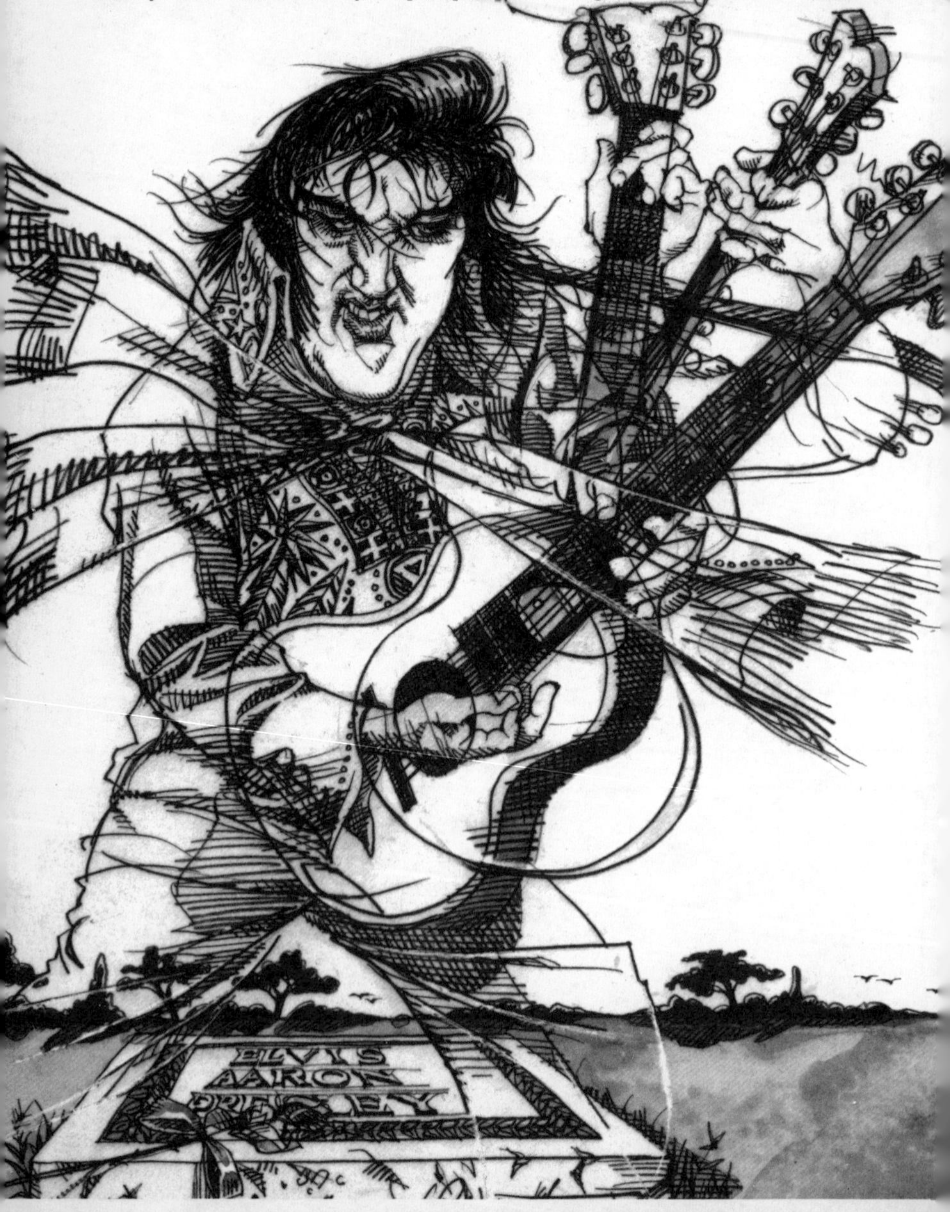

ELVIS
AARON
PRESLEY

T BE FOOLED”

(sung to the tune of “Don’t Be Cruel”)

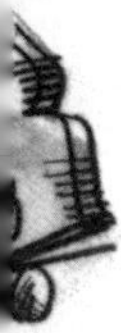

There’s a number folks..are..cal-lin’
(and you know it’s not..toll-free)
With a tape of some guy..drawl-in’,
Who is claim-in’ to..be..me.
DON’T BE FOOLED!
’Cause it just ain’t true!

There’s a girl in San..Di-e-go,
Who’s convinced that I..ain’t..dead;
Says I drive a Win-ne-ba-go
With a para-keet..named..Fred.
DON’T BE FOOLED!
That’s a rip-off too!

They’re just play-in’ with..your..head;
Ev’rybody..knows
The King is dead!

There’s a load of im-i-tat-ors
Comin’ off as El-vis..clones—
Mainly crum-my second..rat-ers.
Makin’ mon-ey off..my..bones.
DON’T BE FOOLED!
That ain’t noth-in’ new!

Makes no diff-rence how..they..sound;
I’m still bur-ied
Six feet underground!

There’s a book by an..ad-mir-er,
Says I live in Mam-moth..Cave,
And she swears in..the..“En-quir-er”
Jimmy Hoffa’s in..my..grave.
DON’T BE FOOLED!
Not a word is true!

You can tell the tab-loid..press,
The King’s got no
Fowarding address!

If you want an ex-plan-a-tion
For the stor-ies they..contrive,
Check the rise in..cir-cu-la-tion
Ev’ry time I’m “proved”..a-live.
DON’T BE FOOLED!
They’re all conning you!

Don’t let it break..your..heart;
Where..I’ve..gone
There’s no Top Forty Chart!

Yes, I’m push-in’ up..the..dai-sies,
But the uproar just..won’t..cease,
’Cause the world is full of..cra-zies
Who won’t let me rest..in..peace!
DON’T BE FOOLED!
This I’m tellin’ you!
DON’T BE FOOLED!
What they say ain’t true!

ARTIST: GERRY GERSTEN WRITER: FRANK JACOBS

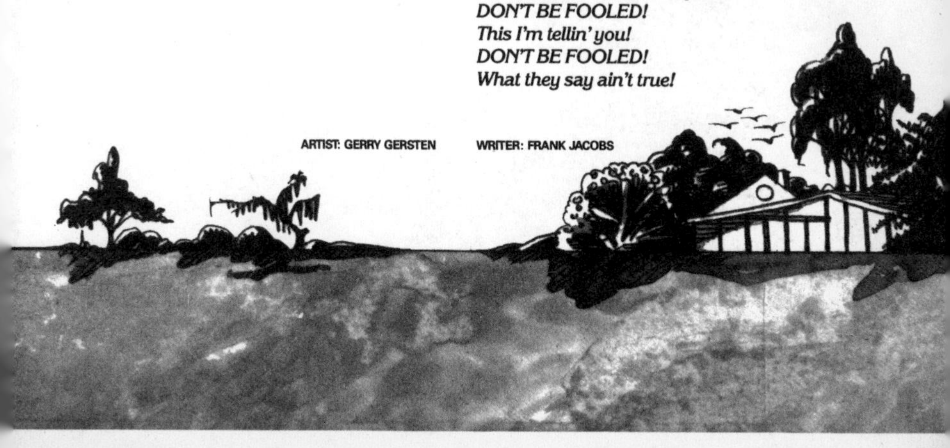

McDonald's "McD.L.T." (which keeps the lettuce and tomato cool and the hamburger hot) was promoted as a great new idea in hamburger technology. But isn't this how all burgers are *supposed* to be? Are we so used to lousy goods and services that a company raising its standards to "merely adequate" can claim to be doing us a favor? If so, we hope they introduce...

OTHER McD.L.T. TYPE IDEAS WE'D LIKE TO SEE FROM McDONALD'S

ARTIST: AL JAFFEE WRITER: MIKE SNIDER

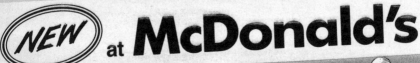

NEW at McDonald's

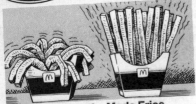

McRecently-Made Fries

Now, have it two ways... *Regular or Fresh and Hot!*

McGrease

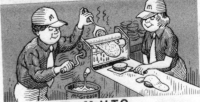

The McH.T.G.

One McDonald's burger: "Hold The Grease!"

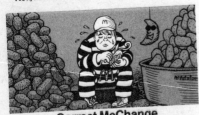

Correct McChange

Any employee caught skimming is now immediately transferred to the kitchen crew! No exceptions!

McBag

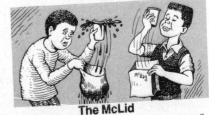

The McLid

The latest in liquid-containment technology...it actually keeps your soft drink contained in the cup!

McIQ 90
McIQ 89⅞
YOU'RE McFIRED

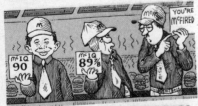

Semi-McLiterate Counterpersons

We've increased our minimum IQ to 90...And—no more droolers!

McJohn
McPot

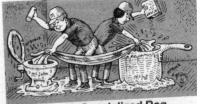

The McSpecialized Rag

Now, a separate rag for each of our cleanup chores!

TALES FROM THE DUCK SIDE DEPT.

THE PESKY PECKER PUZZLER

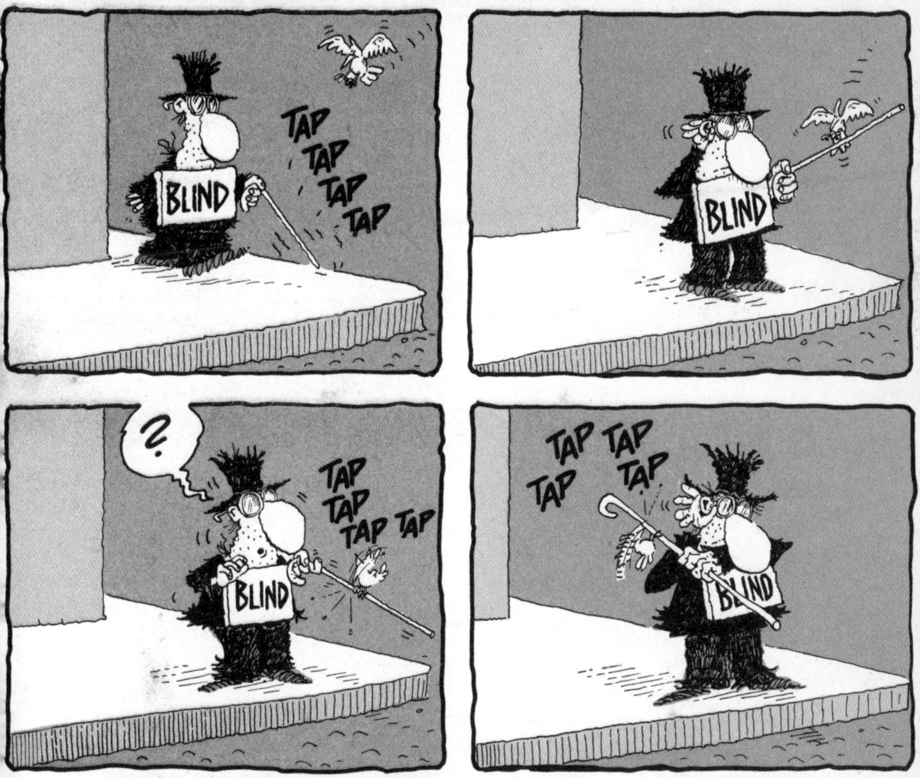
BLIND
TAP TAP TAP TAP
BLIND
?
TAP TAP TAP TAP
BLIND
TAP TAP TAP TAP
BLIND

ARTIST AND WRITER: DUCK EDWING

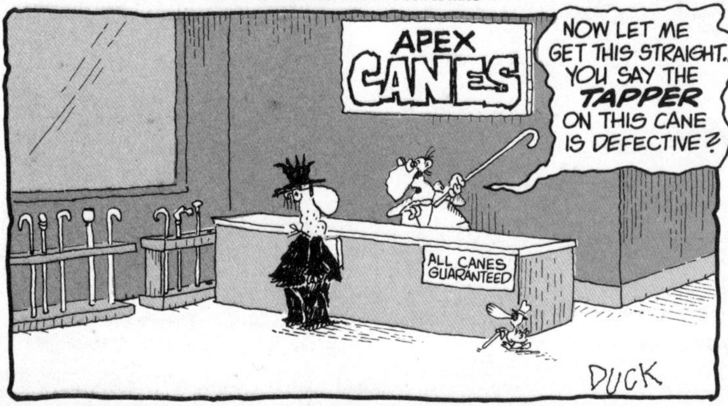
APEX CANES
NOW LET ME GET THIS STRAIGHT... YOU SAY THE *TAPPER* ON THIS CANE IS DEFECTIVE?
ALL CANES GUARANTEED
DUCK

TOYS "R" U

BIG DISCOUNTS! **HU SELEC**

BOINNNG!
JACKO IN THE BOX
ENERGIZER

Muttel
JACKO-IN-THE-BOX
Kids love to wind box until the obnoxious Austrailian battery pitchman pops out! Repulsive. Ages 3¼–3½.
(One oversized Energizer battery not included)

9.99

Unintendo
EXCITING UNINTENDO GAME CARTRIDGES
50 titles to choose from! All basically the same game. Ages 8–death.
(Two LL batteries not included)

59.95 Each

50 EXCITING TITLES

TYSON VS GIVENS

SUPER DELUXE
OPERATION
GAME

Porker Brothers
SUPER DELUXE OPERATION GAME
You be the doctor! Improved version of this classic skill gam[e] uses real human organs. Refrigerator required. Ages Pleistocene-Bronze.
(Four F batteries not included)

139.99

Kennerd
TRANSROBONAUTS ACTION ASSORTMENT SET
Clicks, snaps and interchanges with Technobugs, Dinotron Slimemasters and Transrodent Reptobots to form a pile of rubble you won't know what to do with! Ages 8–8.
(Three D, twelve C, thirty-nine AA batteries not included)

48.99

Wiltin' Badley
JUNIOR TATTOO SET
No paint! No ink! No dye! These tattoos are permanent, so they won't wash off! Includes needles and stencils for battleship, heart, "mom," hula girl, others. Ages 3–up.
(One dry cell battery not included)

19.79

BZZZZZZZZ...

Ohio Aren't
EASY-DOES-IT NO SWEAT JIGSAW PUZZLE
Molded four-piece jigsaw puzzl[e] actually looks like 2,060 pieces! Assembles in 12 seconds. Illustrated instructions make for even easier assemblage. Gives you a false sense of accomplishment! Ages 45–up.
(A,E,I,O,U batteries not included)

9.95

FOR MORE TOY BARGAINS TURN TO BACK COVER

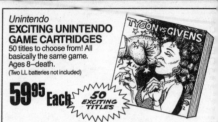

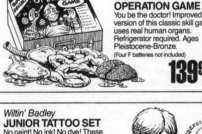

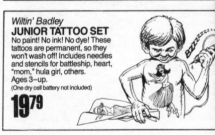

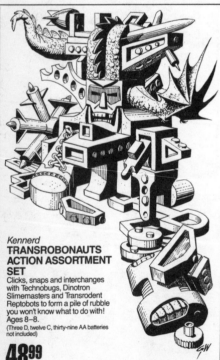

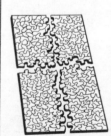

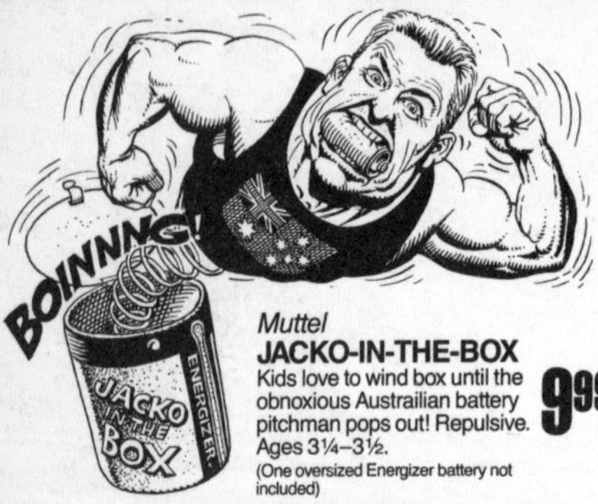

NS! NO GUARANTEES! TOYS"R"U

emcoma

OYS AND GIRLS UTHENTIC GUN EPLICA OLLECTION

enuine, life-size copies of .38 ecial, .44 Magnum and wed-off Shotgun look exactly e the real things! Fools erybody, even jumpy police icers! Ages 6–down.

(ne hundred and seven 9V batteries not uded)

18⁹⁹

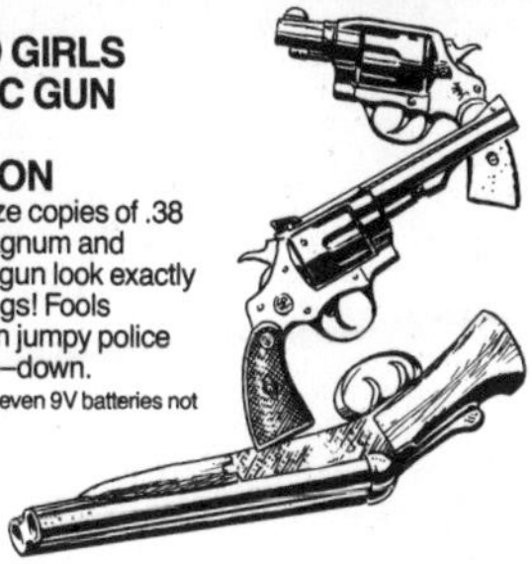

ARTIST: GEORGE WOODBRIDGE

WRITERS: CHARLIE KADAU & JOE RAIOLA

Playskull

SHIFTY SHELDON THE CORRUPT ACCOUNTANT

Computerized learning tool teaches preschoolers about tax evasion, double ledger entries and embezzling. Ages Conception–burial.

(One car battery not included)

219⁹⁹

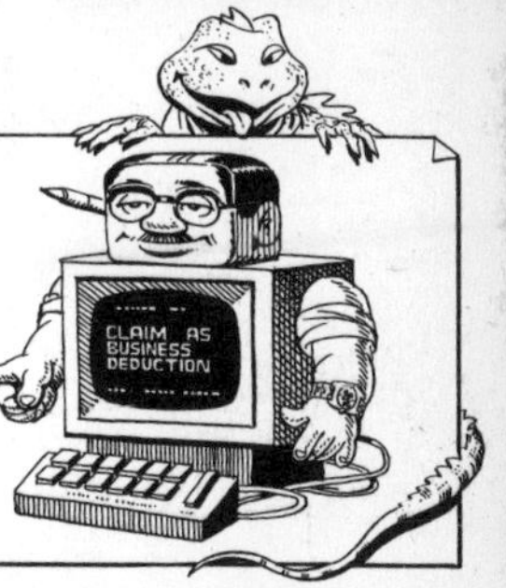
CLAIM AS
BUSINESS
DEDUCTION

IG Toys

SNURF PLAY FIGURES

ll new collection of those cuddly, dorable Snurfs including lasher, Pimp, Junkie, Mugger, thers. Ages mixed-up.

(our AC/DC batteries not included)

6⁹⁹ Each

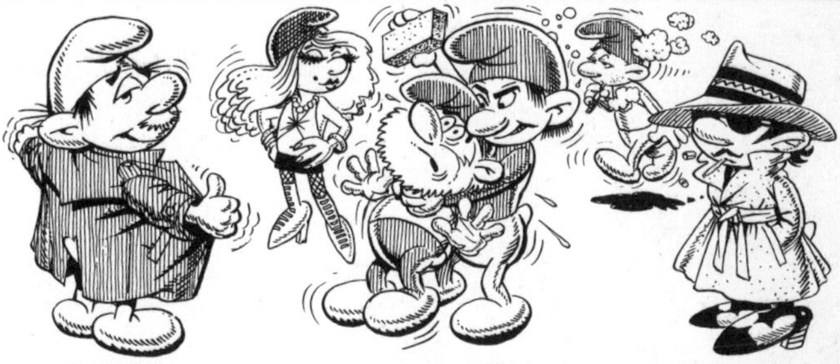

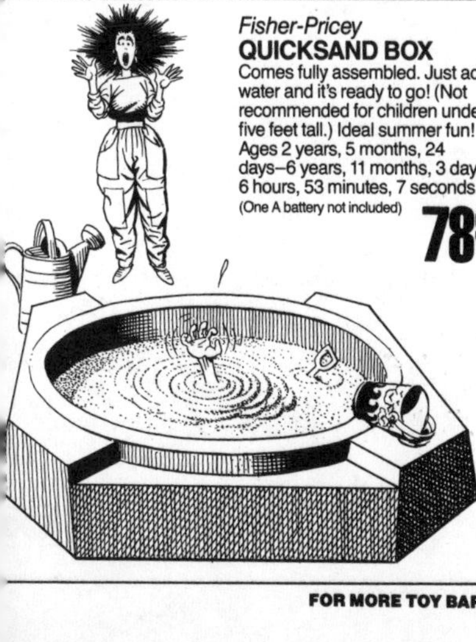

Fisher-Pricey

QUICKSAND BOX

Comes fully assembled. Just add water and it's ready to go! (Not recommended for children under five feet tall.) Ideal summer fun! Ages 2 years, 5 months, 24 days–6 years, 11 months, 3 days, 6 hours, 53 minutes, 7 seconds.

(One A battery not included)

78⁹⁷

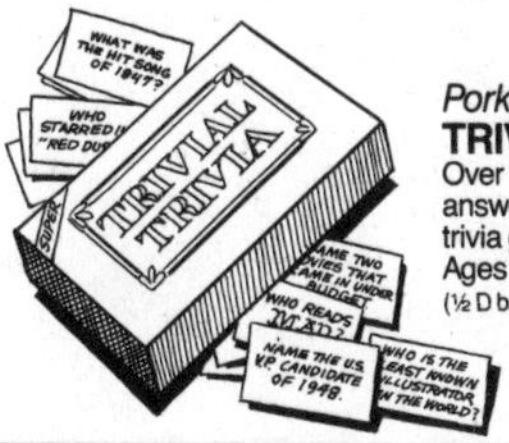
WHAT WAS THE HIT SONG OF 1947?
TRIVIAL TRIVIA
WHO READS MAD
NAME THE U.S. V.P. CANDIDATE OF 1948.
WHO IS THE LEAST KNOWN ILLUSTRATOR IN THE WORLD?

Porker Brothers

TRIVIAL TRIVIA

Over 1,000 questions and answers ripped off from other trivia games better than this one! Ages Birth–up.

(½ D battery not included)

99⁹⁹

Guffy

GUMBO GUMBY

Obese, unhappy version of everyone's favorite clay figure! Unbendable. Ages 7–up.

(Four AA batteries not included)

28⁹⁹

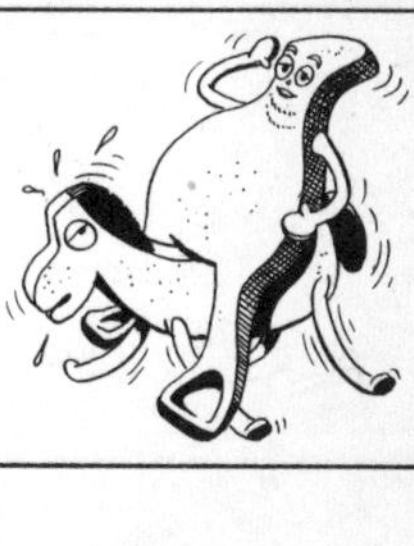

FOR MORE TOY BARGAINS TURN TO BACK COVER

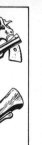

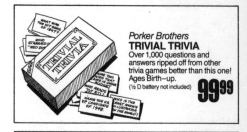

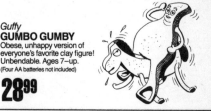

BLADDER UP! DEPT.

Attention all you Couch Potatoes with weak Bladders! Do you need more breaks than ju the usual commercial interruptions for your bodily functions? Thanks to the followi

IT'S SAFE TO GO TO T

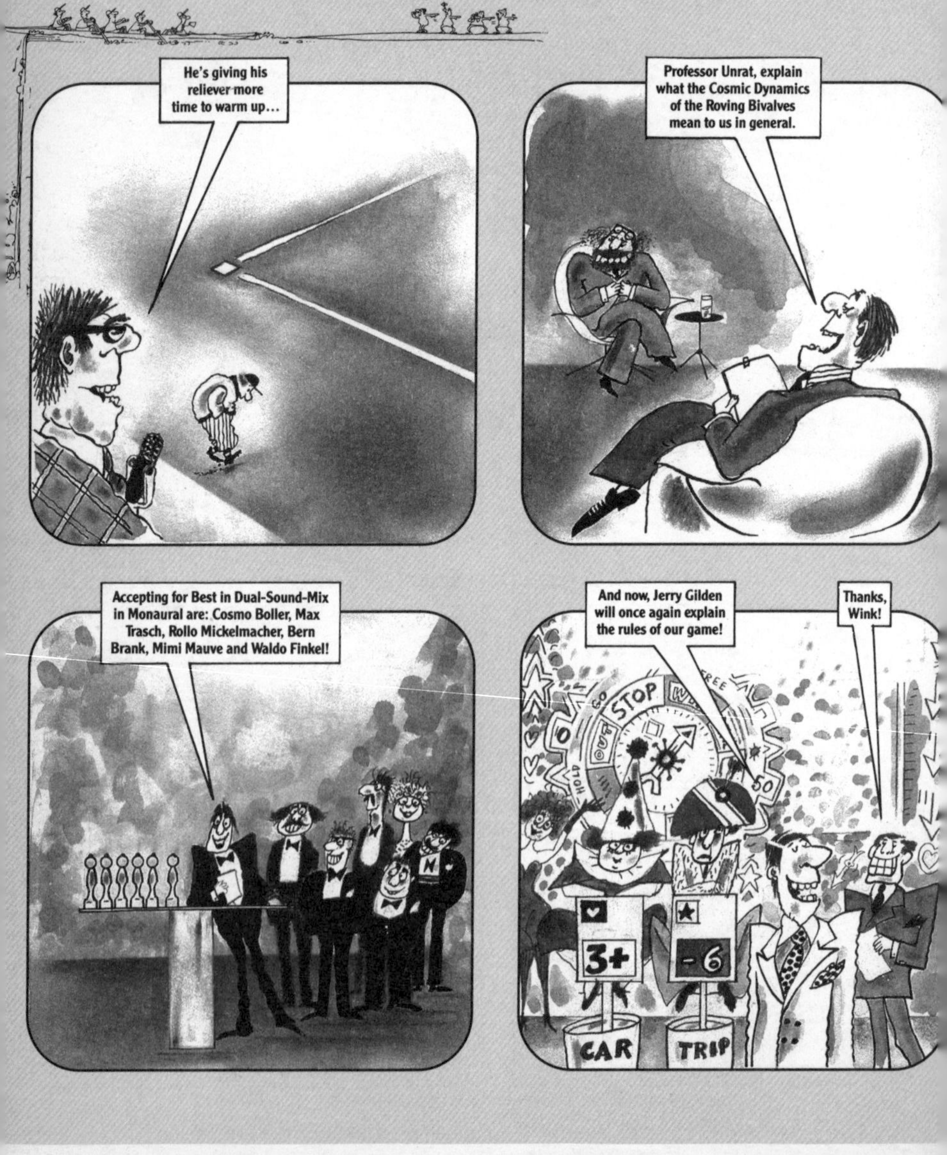

He's giving his reliever more time to warm up...
Professor Unrat, explain what the Cosmic Dynamics of the Roving Bivalves mean to us in general.
Accepting for Best in Dual-Sound-Mix in Monaural are: Cosmo Boller, Max Trasch, Rollo Mickelmacher, Bern Brank, Mimi Mauve and Waldo Finkel!
And now, Jerry Gilden will once again explain the rules of our game!
Thanks, Wink!
STOP
OUT
50
3+
-6
CAR
TRIP

rticle, now you can be sure you won't miss anything important on TV while you're "takin' are of business!" Just what in God's name are we claiming in this introduction? Simply...

E BATHROOM WHEN...

RTIST AND WRITER: PAUL PETER PORGES

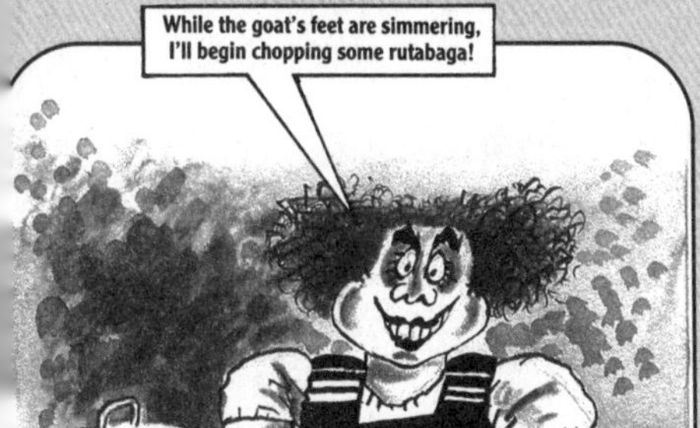
While the goat's feet are simmering, I'll begin chopping some rutabaga!

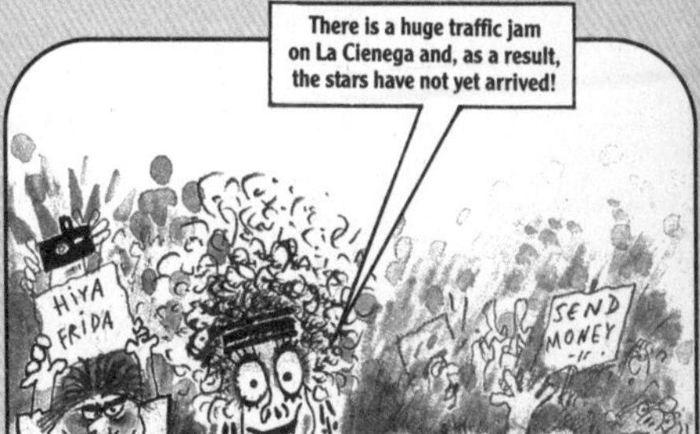
There is a huge traffic jam on La Cienega and, as a result, the stars have not yet arrived!
HIYA FRIDA
SEND MONEY

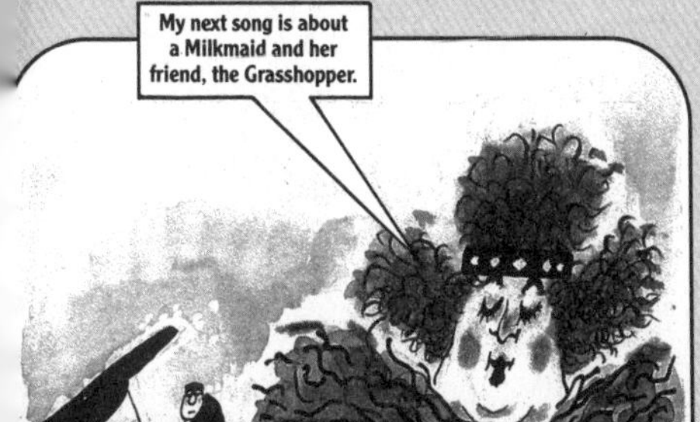
My next song is about a Milkmaid and her friend, the Grasshopper.

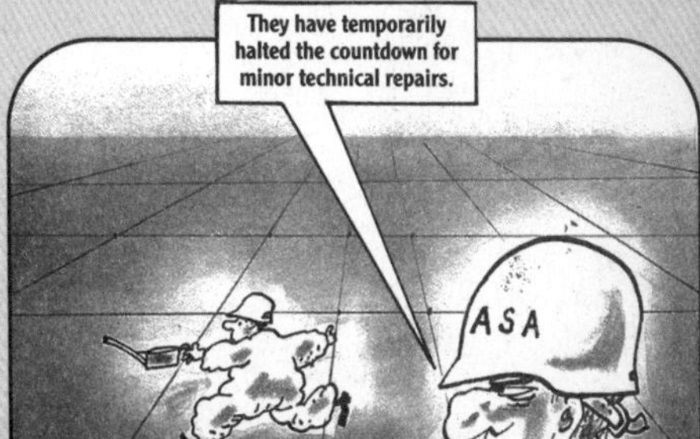
They have temporarily halted the countdown for minor technical repairs.
ASA

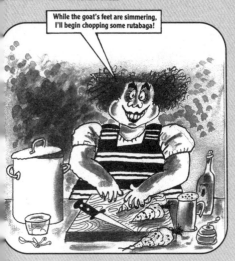

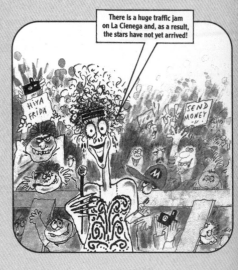

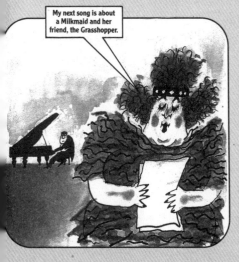

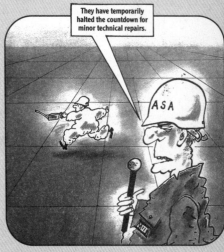

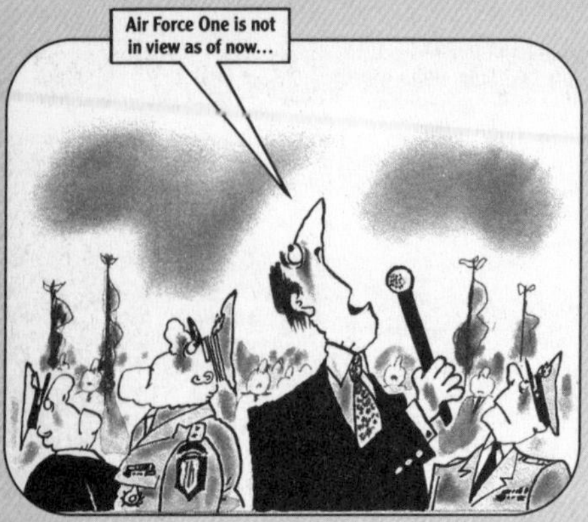
Air Force One is not in view as of now…

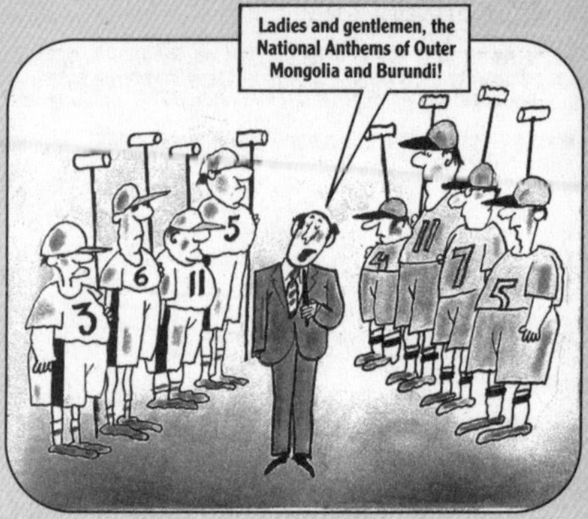
Ladies and gentlemen, the National Anthems of Outer Mongolia and Burundi!

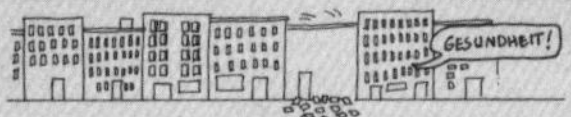
GESUNDHEIT!

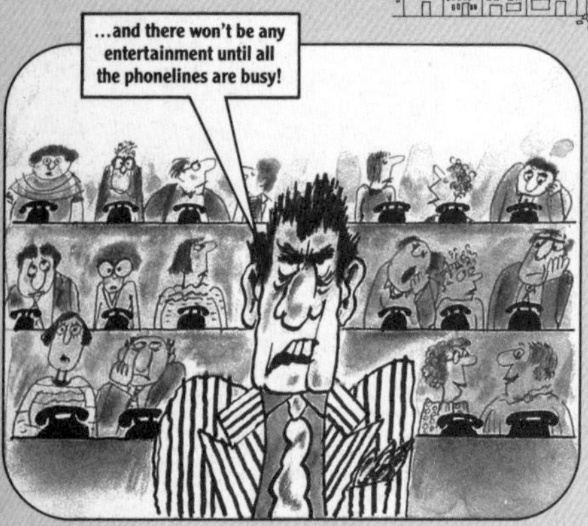
…and there won't be any entertainment until all the phonelines are busy!

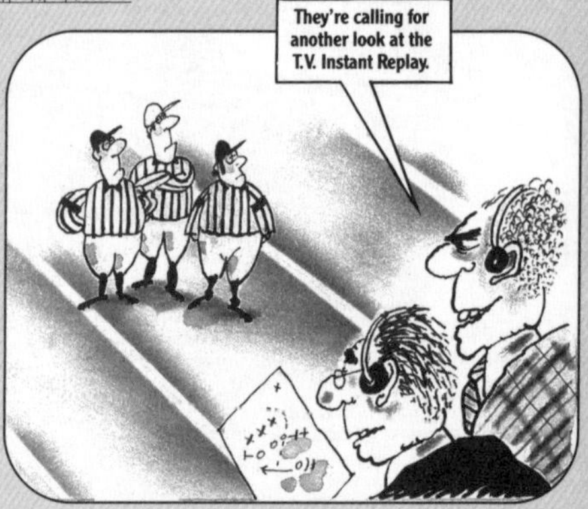
They're calling for another look at the T.V. Instant Replay.

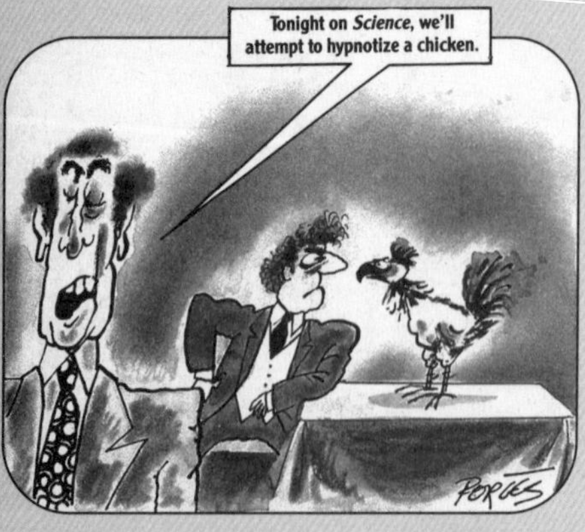
Tonight on *Science*, we'll attempt to hypnotize a chicken.
PORGES

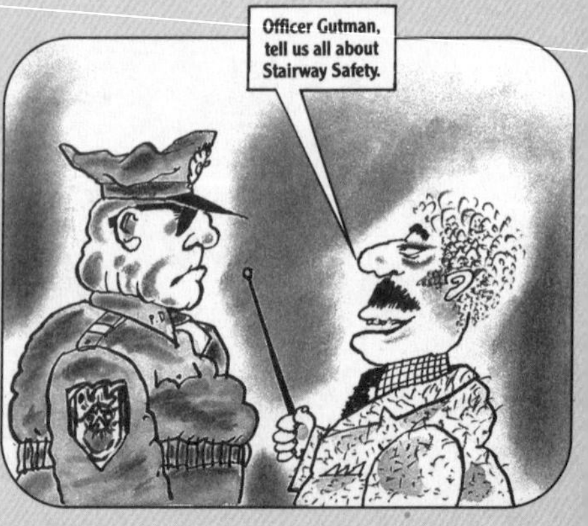
Officer Gutman, tell us all about Stairway Safety.

SERGE-IN GENERAL DEPT.

HAND-ME-DOWN

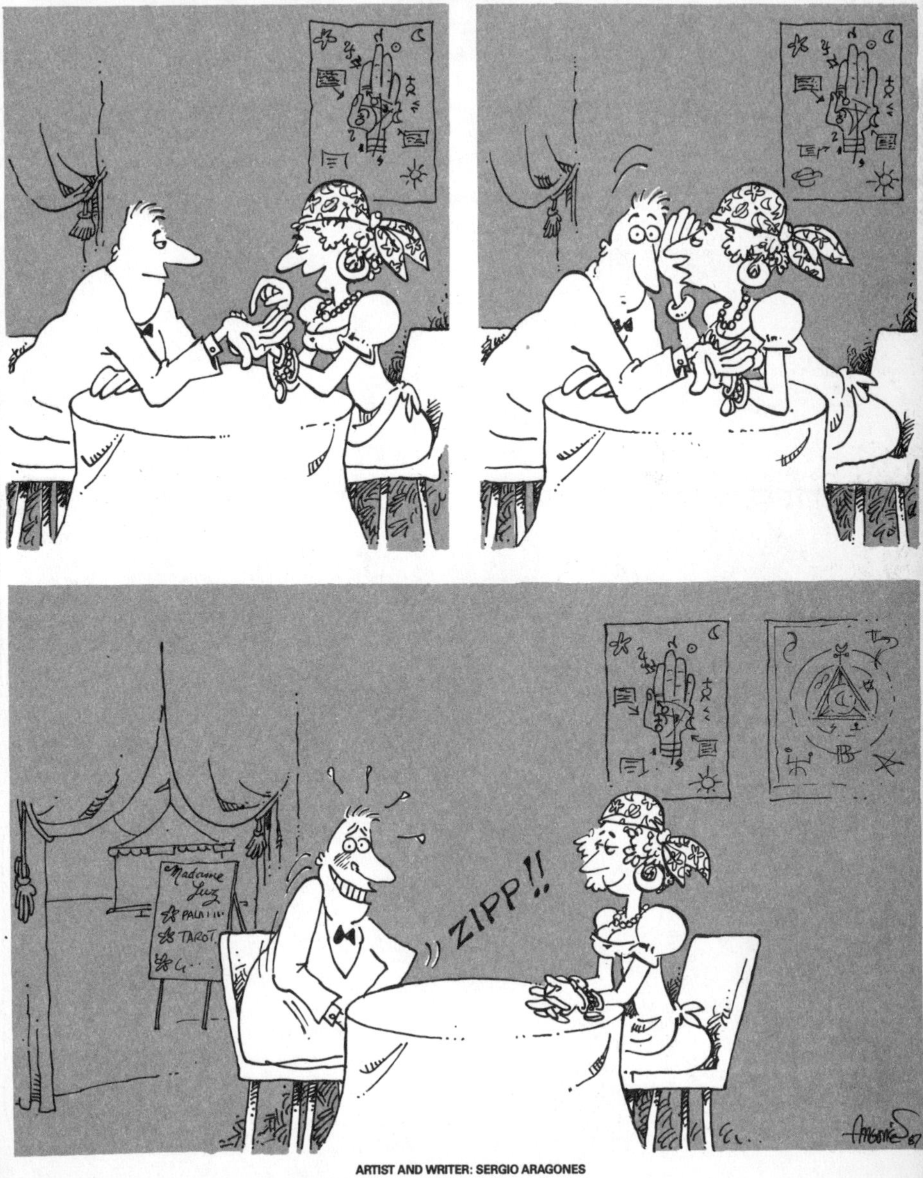

Madame Luz
TAROT.
ZIPP!!

ARTIST AND WRITER: SERGIO ARAGONES

COMMON CENTS DEPT.

MORE YOU'D BE RICH IF YOU HAD A

ARTIST: PAUL COKER WRITER: CHARLIE KADAU

MEXICO 1986

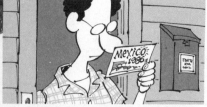

...For every vacation postcard you send to friends that arrives long after you've already come home.

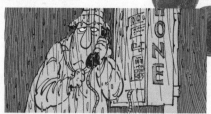

...For every telephone receptionist who asks if you can "hold" and then puts you on "hold" before you can answer.

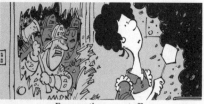

...For every time you set off your smoke detector just by cooking.

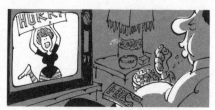

...For every health club ad that says this is your last chance to join before the rates go up.

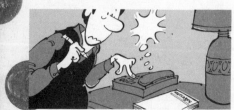

...For every message on your answering machine that turns out to be a recording of someone hanging up.

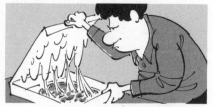

...For every take-out pizza you get where there's more cheese stuck to the box than on the pizza.

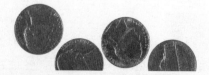

NICKEL...

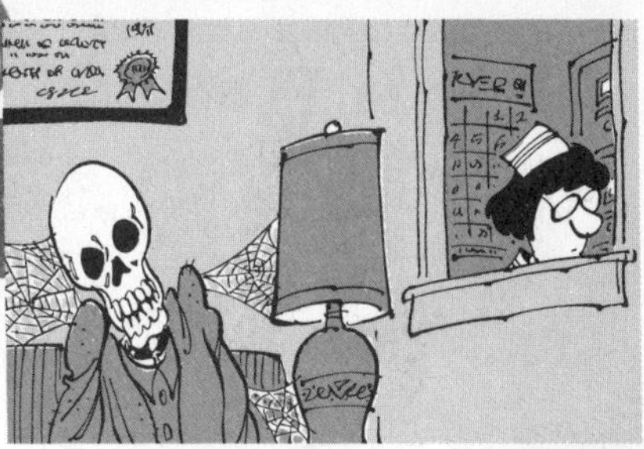

...For every minute you waste in a doctor's waiting room beyond your scheduled appointment time.

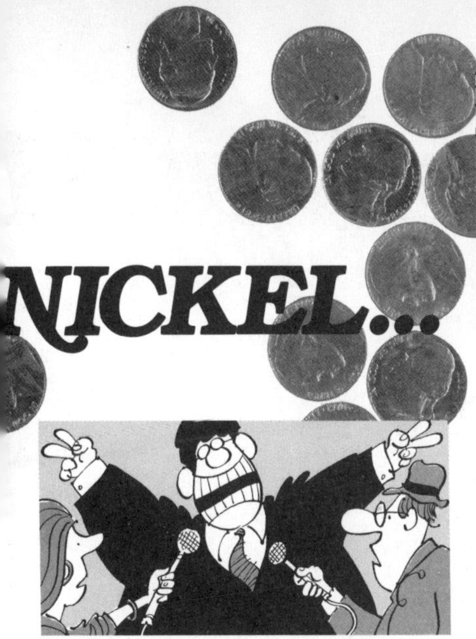

...For every politician who claims victory in a primary, even when he finishes second, third, or worse.

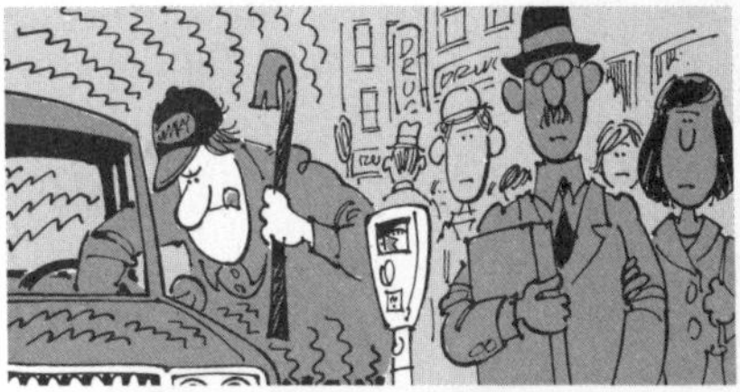

...For every blaring car burglar alarm that people completely ignore.

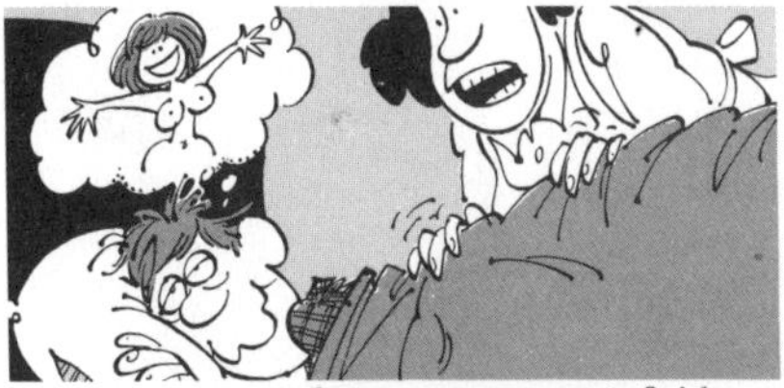

...For every great dream you never get to finish because somebody wakes you right at the best part.

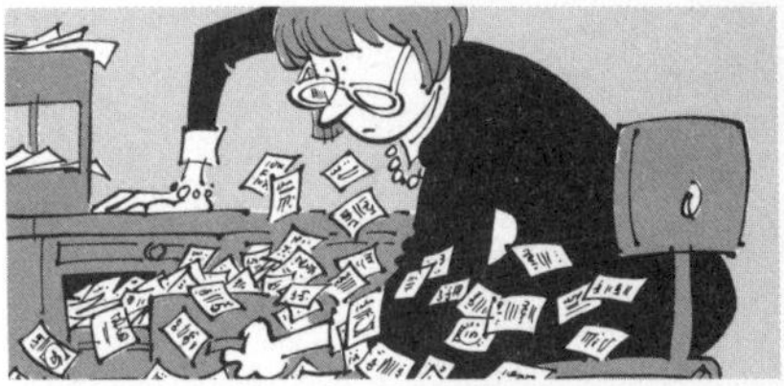

...For every old packet of salt, ketchup, soy sauce and Sweet 'N Low stashed away in your desk drawer.

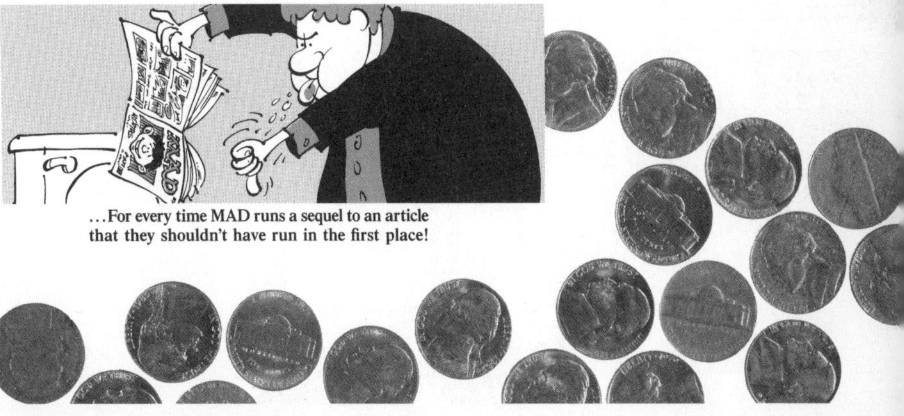
MAD

...For every time MAD runs a sequel to an article that they shouldn't have run in the first place!

GOING OUT IN A BLAZE OF GORY DEPT.

DUCK EDWING CONTEMPLATES SUICIDE

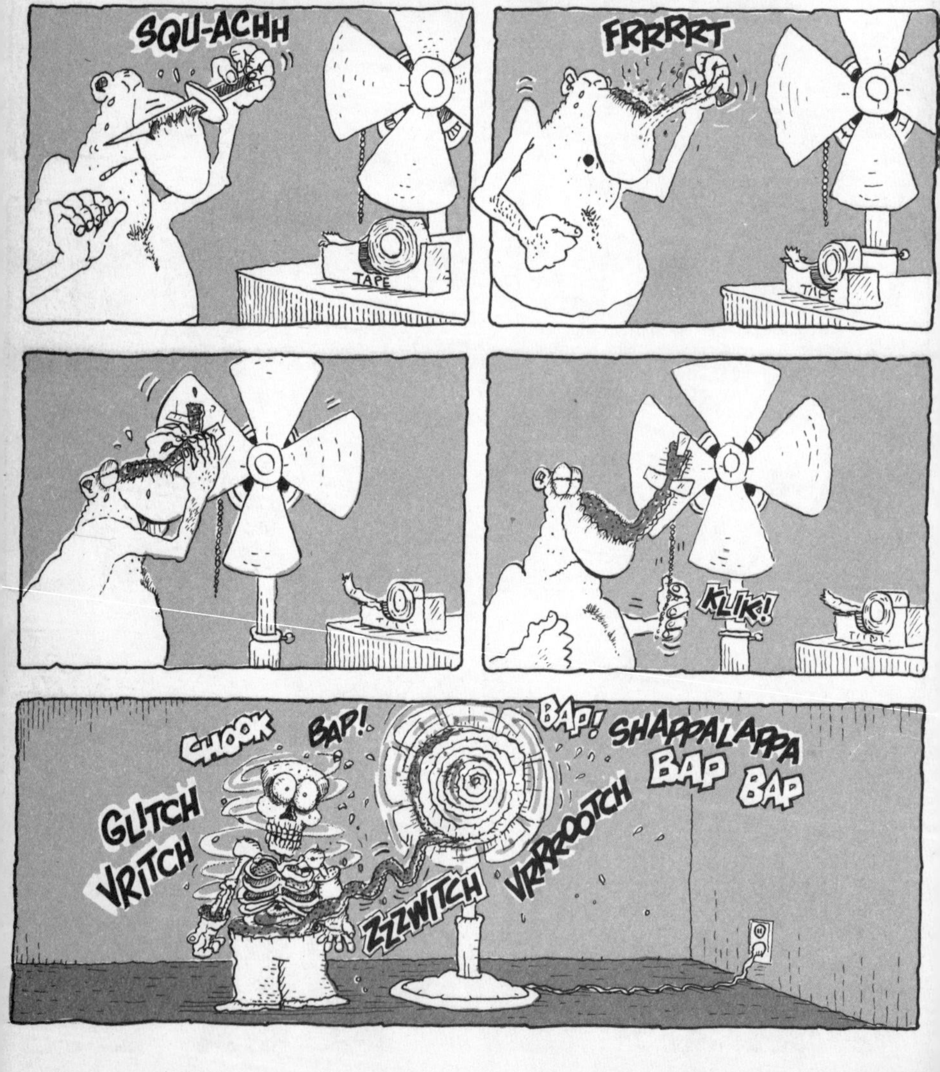
SQU-ACHH
TAPE
FRRRRT
KLIK!
CHOOK
BAP!
BAP!
SHAPPALAPPA
BAP
BAP
GLITCH
VRITCH
ZZZWITCH
VRRROOTCH

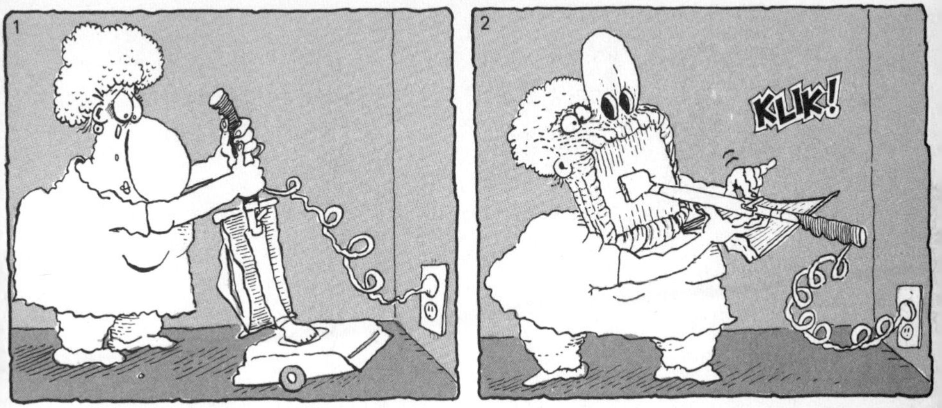
1
2
KLIK!

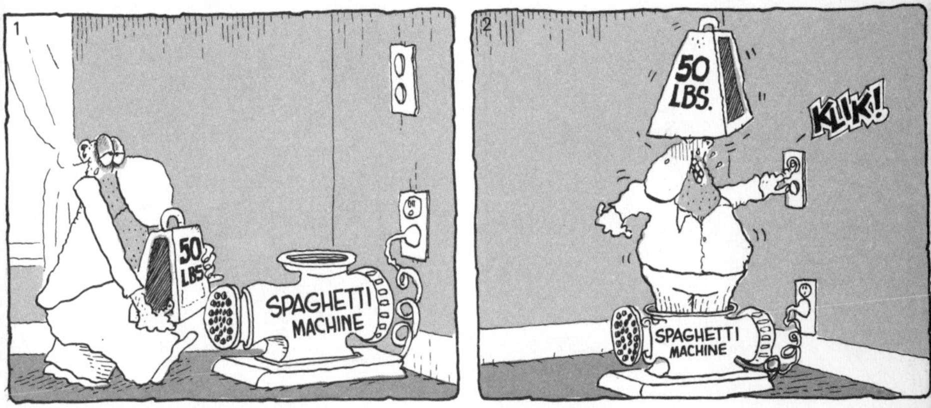
1
50 LBS
SPAGHETTI MACHINE
2
50 LBS.
KLIK!
SPAGHETTI MACHINE

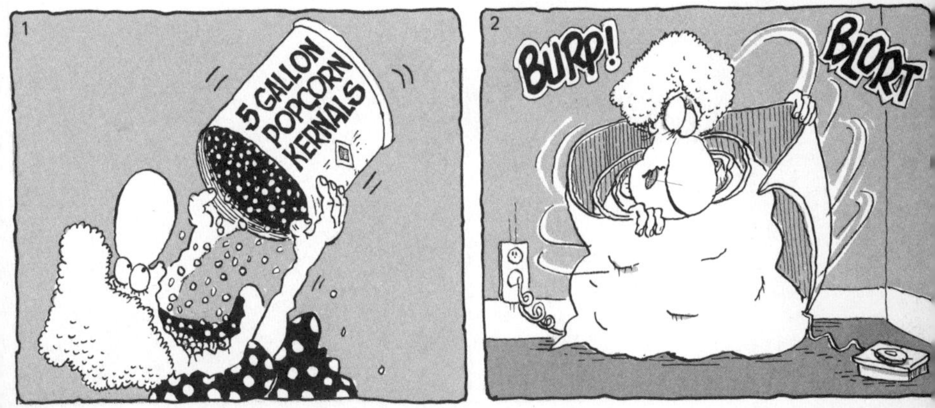
1
5 GALLON POPCORN KERNALS
2
BURP!
BLORT

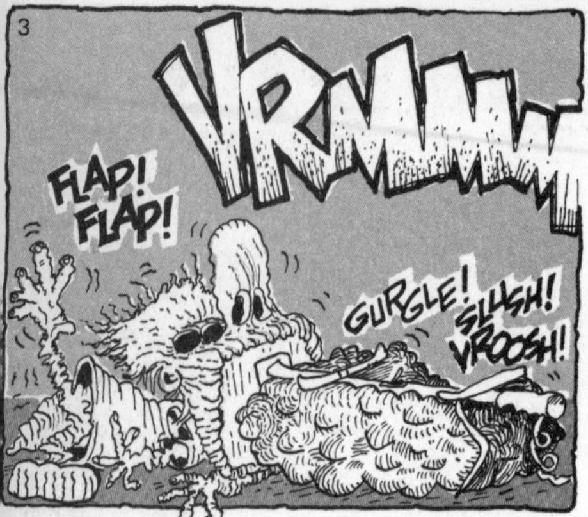
VRMMMM
FLAP! FLAP!
GURGLE! SLUSH! VROOSH!

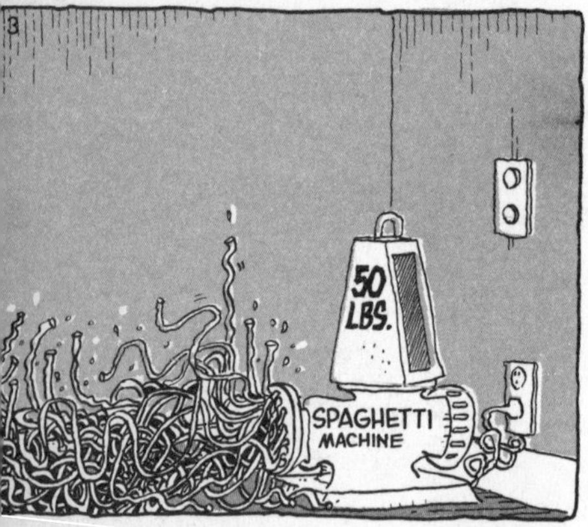
50 LBS.
SPAGHETTI MACHINE

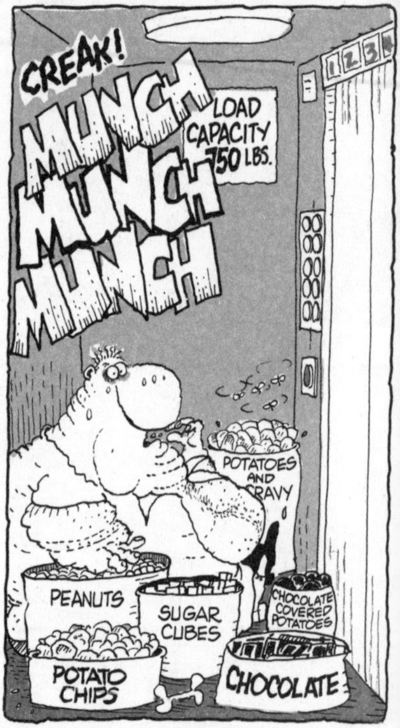
CREAK!
MUNCH MUNCH MUNCH
LOAD CAPACITY 750 LBS.
1 2 3
POTATOES AND GRAVY
PEANUTS
SUGAR CUBES
CHOCOLATE COVERED POTATOES
POTATO CHIPS
CHOCOLATE

ARTIST AND WRITER: DUCK EDWING

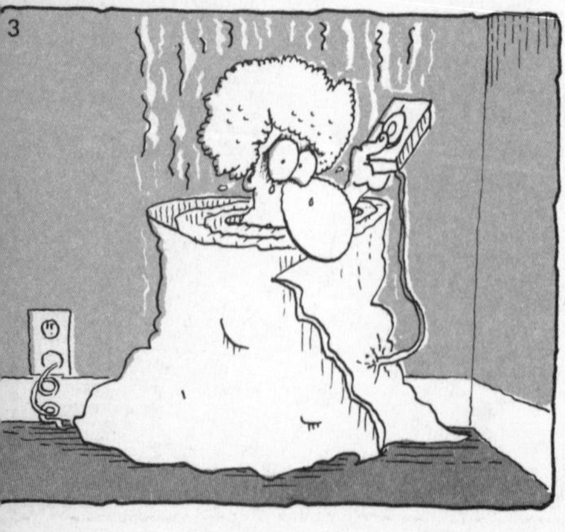

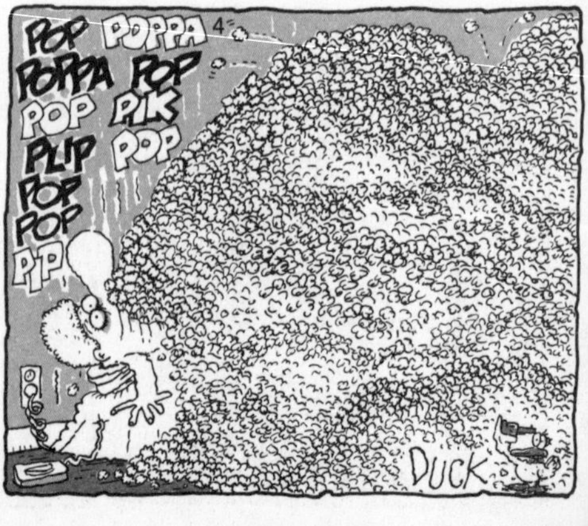
POP POPPA
POPPA POP
POP PIK
PLIP POP
POP
POP
PIP
DUCK

DON MARTIN DEPT.

ONE EVENING IN SPAIN

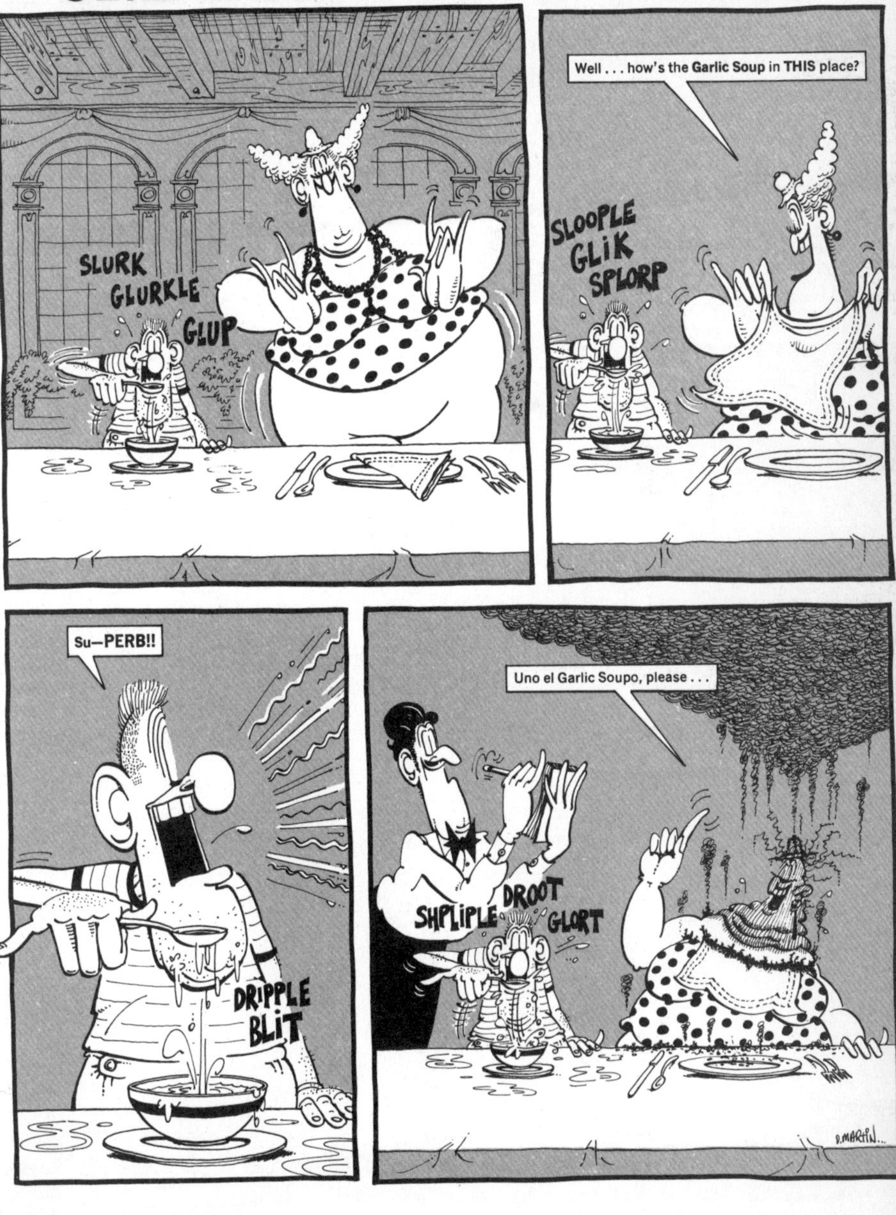
SLURK
GLURKLE
GLUP
Well . . . how's the Garlic Soup in THIS place?
SLOOPLE
GLIK
SPLORP
Su—PERB!!
DRIPPLE
BLIT
Uno el Garlic Soupo, please . . .
SHPLIPLE
DROOT
GLORT
D. MARTIN...

SERGE-IN-GENERAL DEPT.

A MAD LOOK AT FEMALE

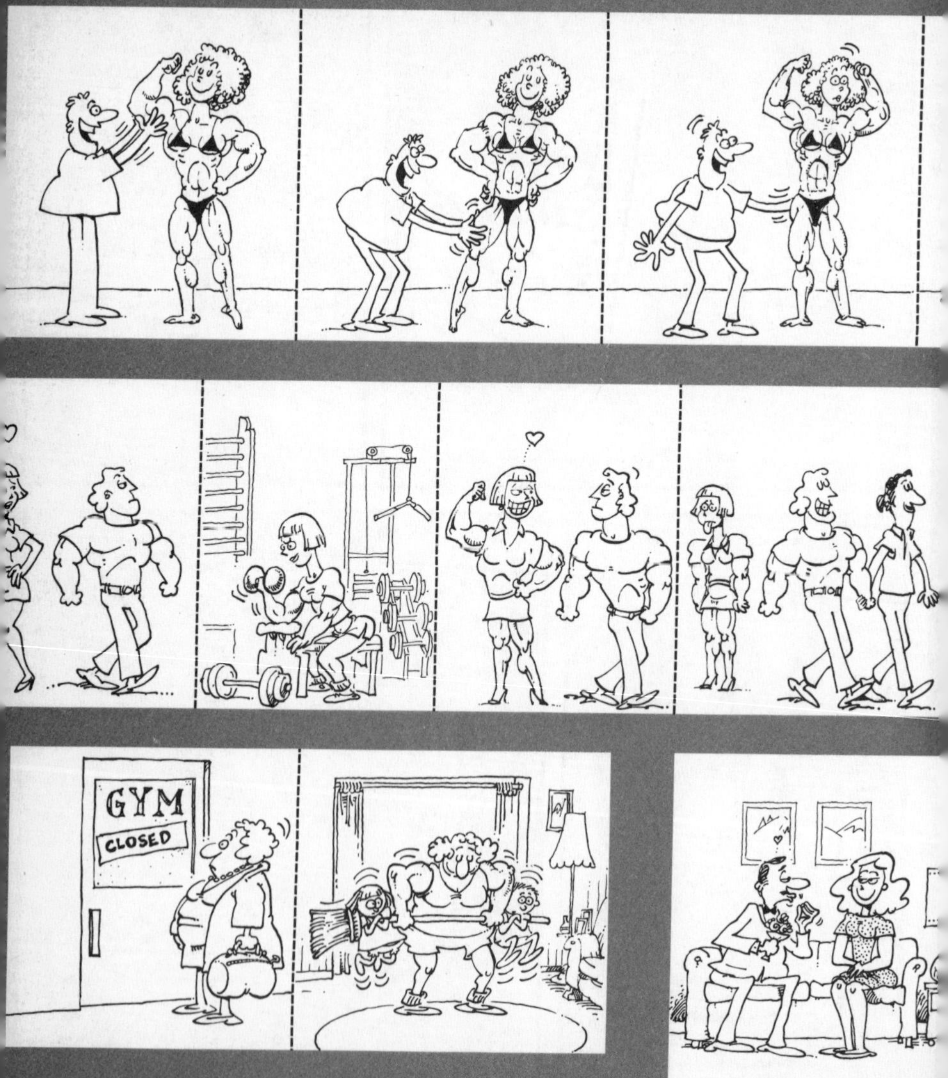
GYM
CLOSED

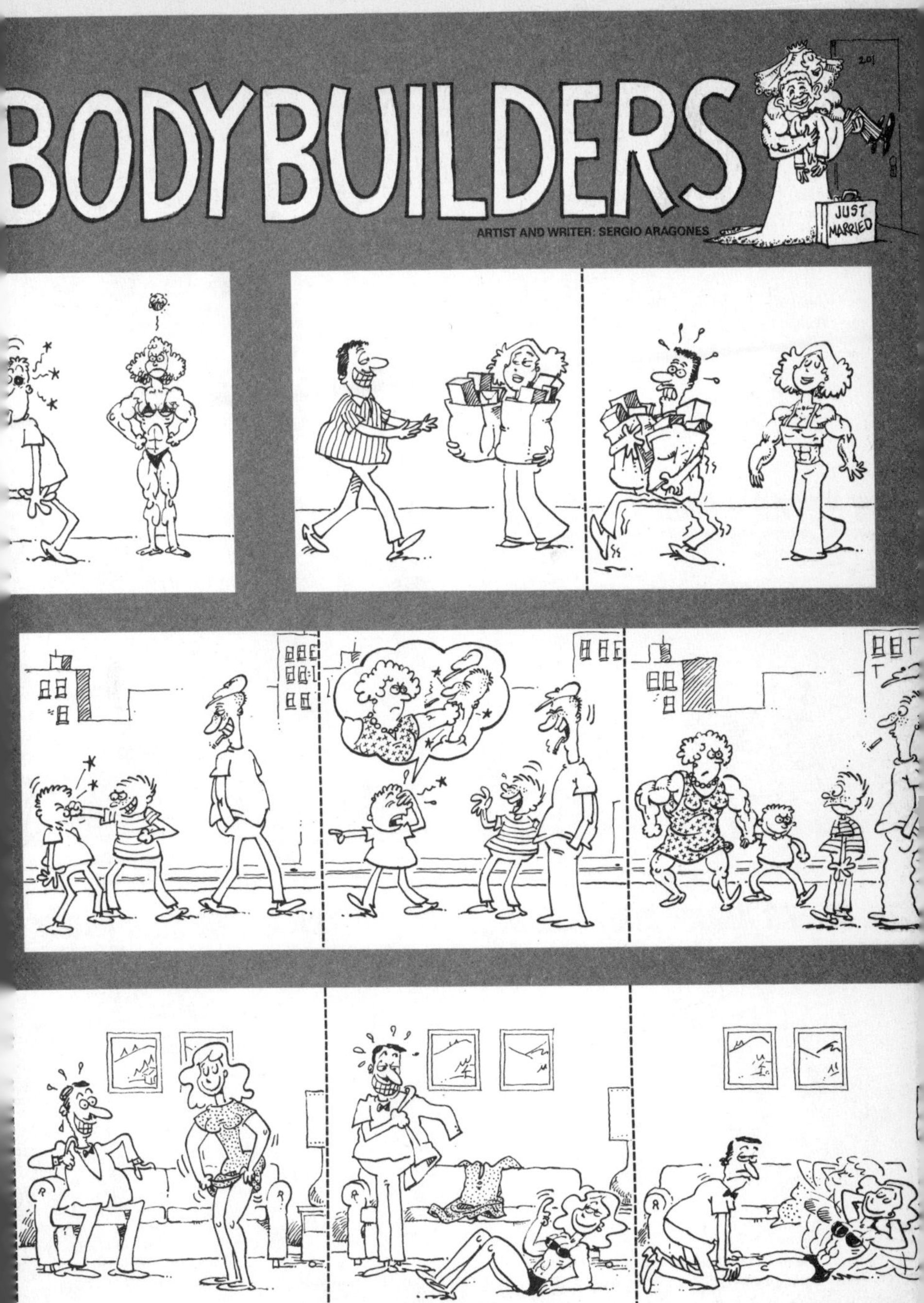
BODYBUILDERS
ARTIST AND WRITER: SERGIO ARAGONES
201
JUST MARRIED

HARDEE-HAR-HARBINGERS DEPT.

For the keenly aware in the world, there are little warning signs everywhere—nuances that some kind of trouble, be it big or small, lies ahead. Unfortunately, it's rare that the average MAD reader is keenly aware of anything! Which is why we thought it necessary to compile the following list of...oh, let's call them "tipoffs"...that all is not well in your little corner of the world. Read it carefully and see if (for once) you don't agree with us that...

IT'S NEVER

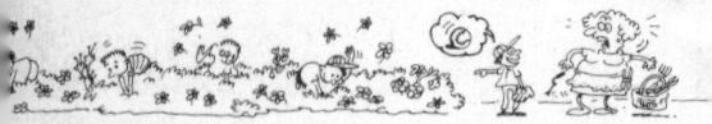

IT'S NEVER A GOOD SIGN WHEN...

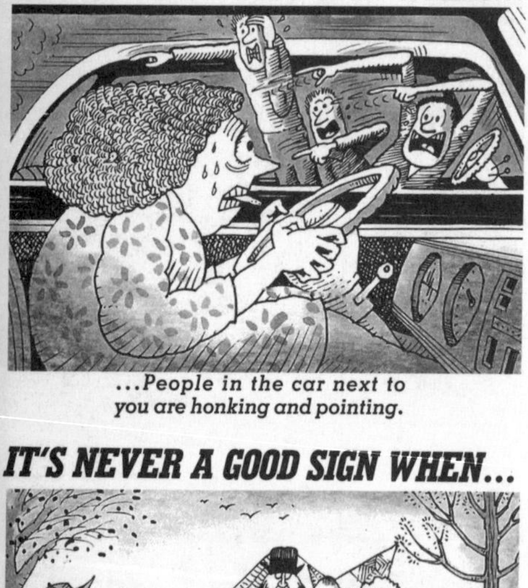

...People in the car next to you are honking and pointing.

IT'S NEVER A GOOD SIGN WHEN...

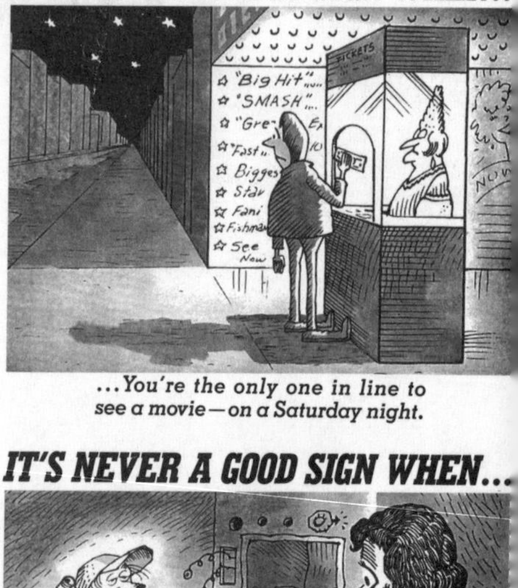
TICKETS
"Big Hit"
"SMASH"
See Now

...You're the only one in line to see a movie—on a Saturday night.

IT'S NEVER A GOOD SIGN WHEN...

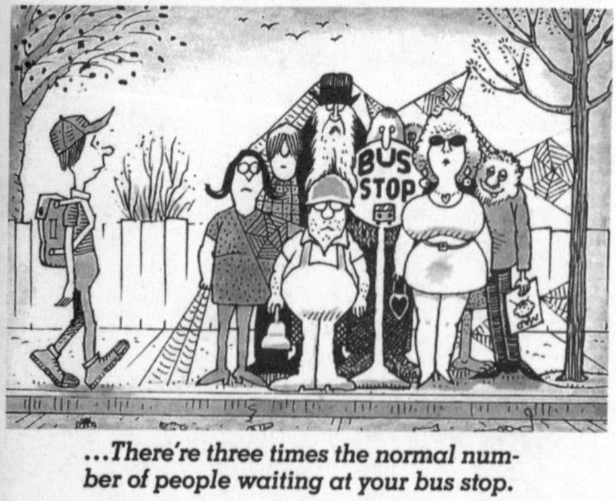
BUS STOP

...There're three times the normal number of people waiting at your bus stop.

IT'S NEVER A GOOD SIGN WHEN...

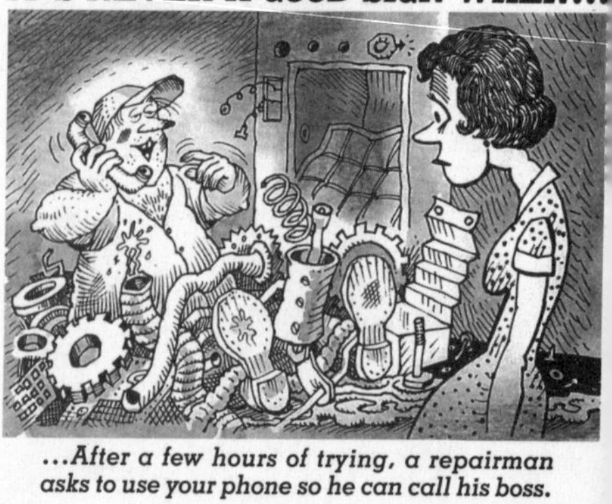

...After a few hours of trying, a repairman asks to use your phone so he can call his boss.

A GOOD SIGN WHEN...

IT'S NEVER A GOOD SIGN WHEN...

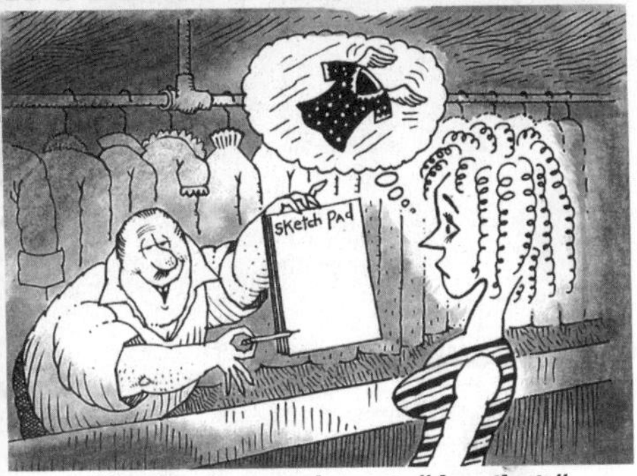
Sketch Pad

...Your dry cleaner asks you to "describe it."

IT'S NEVER A GOOD SIGN WHEN...

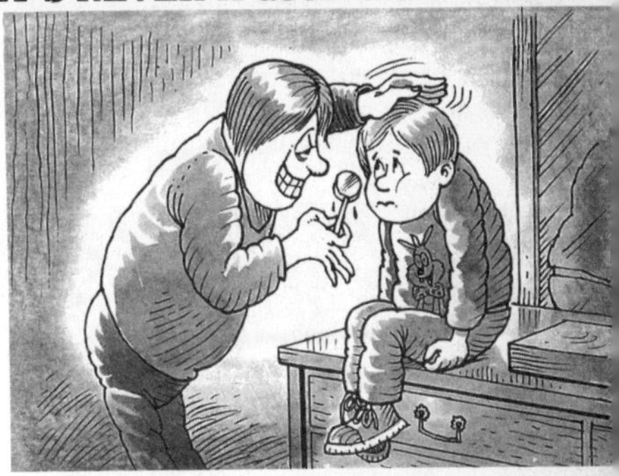

...Your older brother starts treating you "nice."

IT'S NEVER A GOOD SIGN WHEN...

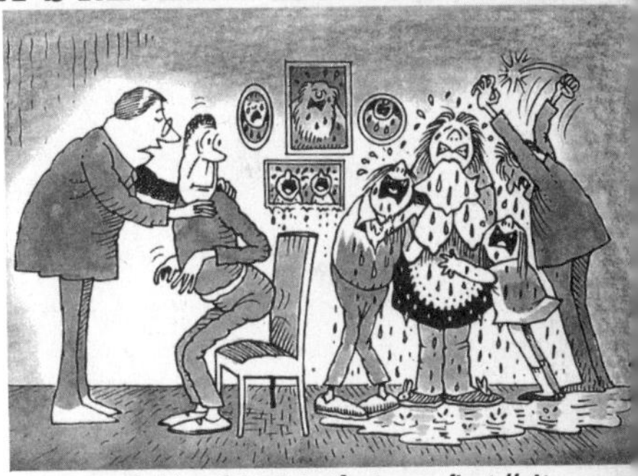

...A friend insists that you first "sit down" before he'll tell you something.

IT'S NEVER A GOOD SIGN WHEN...

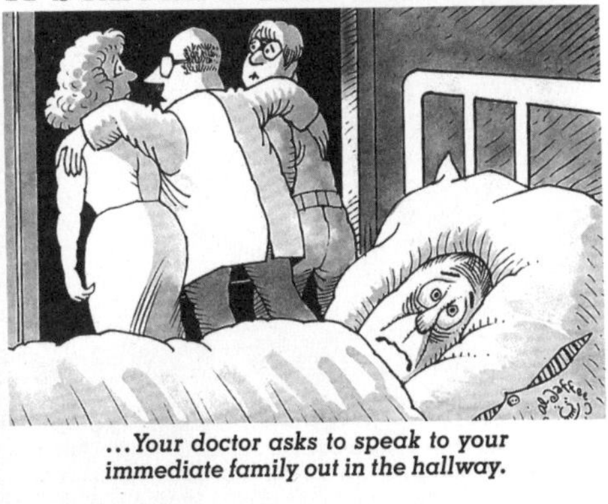

...Your doctor asks to speak to your immediate family out in the hallway.

ARTIST: AL JAFFEE WRITER: J. PRET

PROGRESS RETORT DEPT.

They say you can't stop progress. But we say, TOO BAD! The alleged "progress" we've seen has resulted in more suffering and misery than it has in benefits to mankind! To prove it, here's just a smattering of...

SCIENTIF

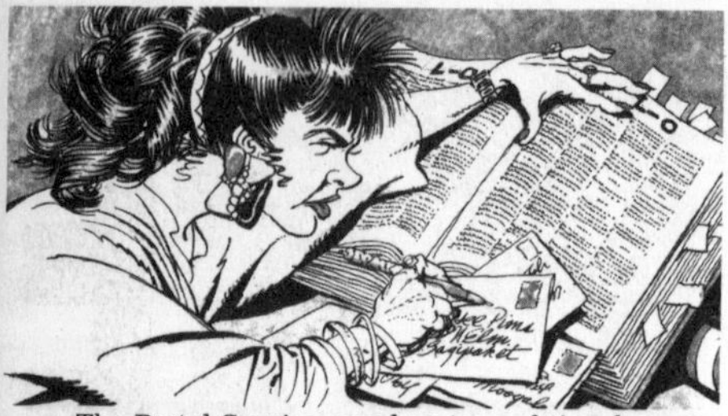

The Postal Service saved us tons of time by shortening the abbreviation for Michigan from "Mich." to "MI." Now we waste even more time trying to figure out whether "MI" stands for Michigan, Minnesota, Mississippi or Missouri.

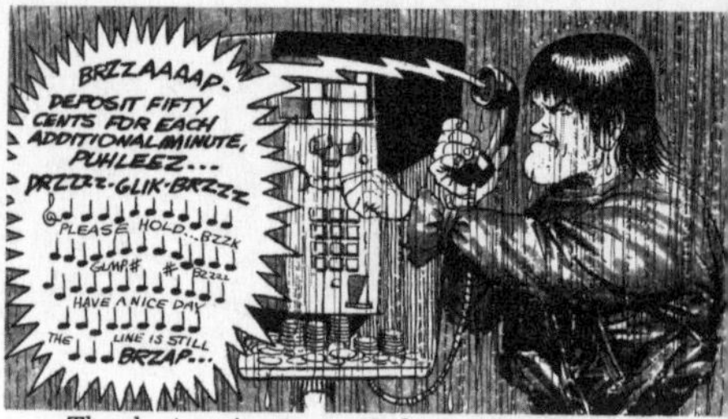
BRZZAAAAP-
DEPOSIT FIFTY CENTS FOR EACH ADDITIONAL MINUTE, PUHLEEZ...
DRZZZZ-GLIK-BRZZZZ
PLEASE HOLD...BZZK
HAVE A NICE DAY
THE LINE IS STILL BRZAP...

Thanks to science, we no longer get a grating busy signal when we call an overloaded office phone number. Instead, we're put on "hold," and are forced to listen to some bad recorded music, often at a toll charge of fifty cents per minute.

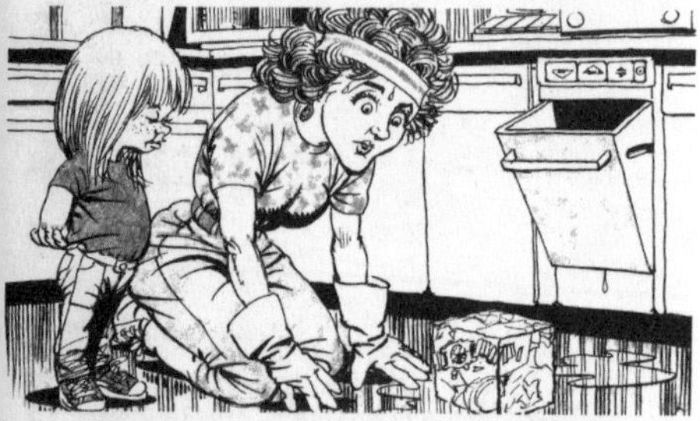

The trash compactor is a modern wonder that makes it unnecessary for us to hunt for valuables we threw away by mistake, because we know, even if we find them, they'll be crushed.

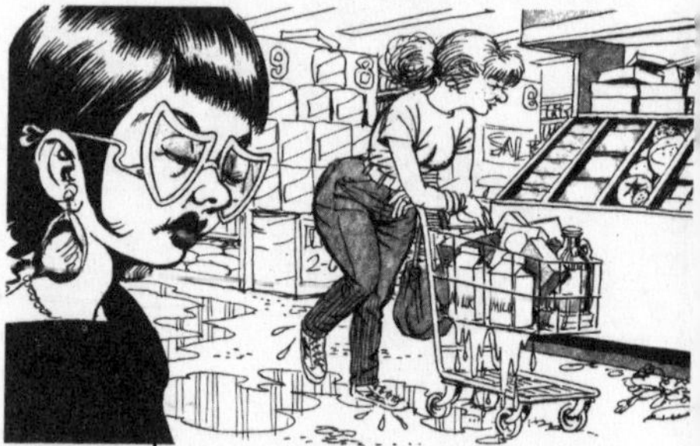

Glass milk bottles that occasionally broke have now been universally replaced by cardboard milk cartons that virtually always leak.

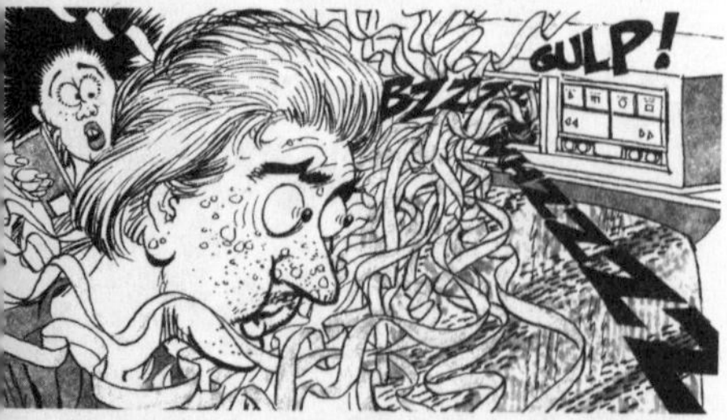
GULP!

Automated manufacturing has enabled the retail price of the cheapest VCRs to drop well below $200. Interestingly, the cheapest VCRs soon require the services of a repairman who is *un*automated and whose price has risen well above $200.

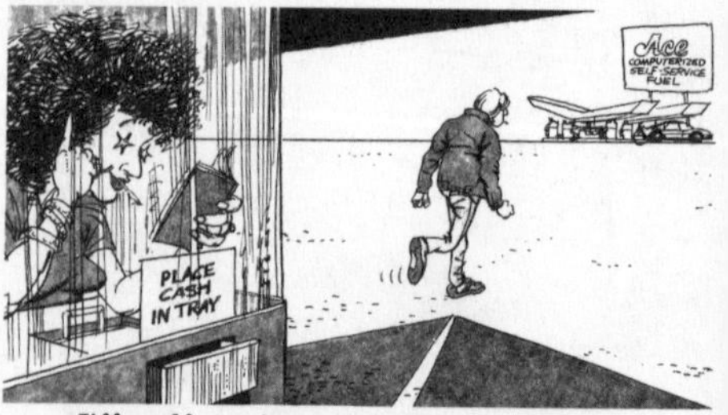
Ace
COMPUTERIZED SELF-SERVICE FUEL
PLACE CASH IN TRAY

Jiffy self-service gas stations let you speed up to the pump, walk over and give the cashier your money, walk back to pump your gas, walk back to collect your change and then walk back to your car again—all in less than an hour.

C ADVANCES THAT UNIMPROVE OUR LIVES!

ARTIST: GEORGE WOODBRIDGE

WRITER: TOM KOCH

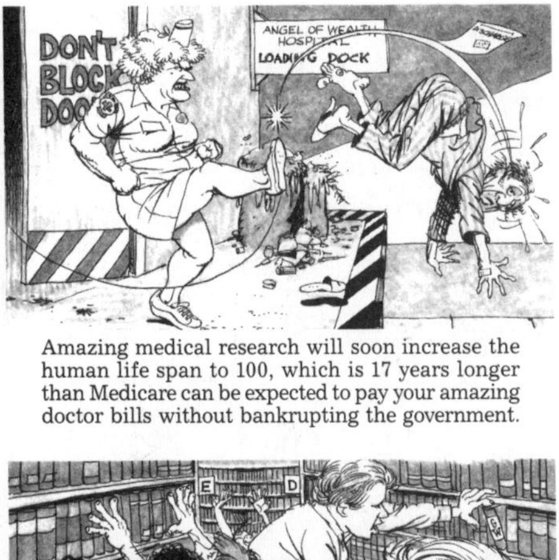
DON'T
ANGEL OF WEALTH

Amazing medical research will soon increase the human life span to 100, which is 17 years longer than Medicare can be expected to pay your amazing doctor bills without bankrupting the government.

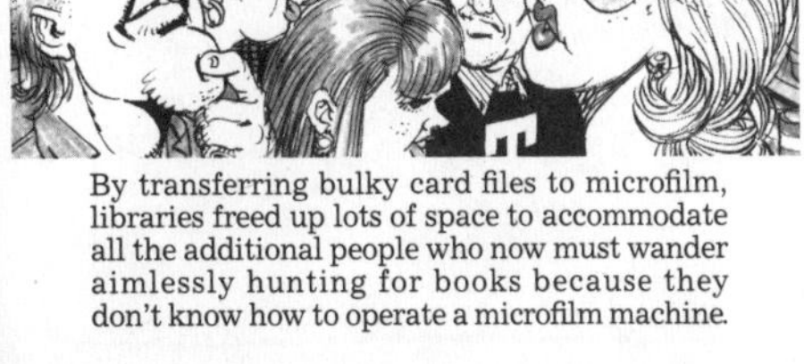

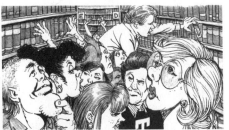

By transferring bulky card files to microfilm, libraries freed up lots of space to accommodate all the additional people who now must wander aimlessly hunting for books because they don't know how to operate a microfilm machine.

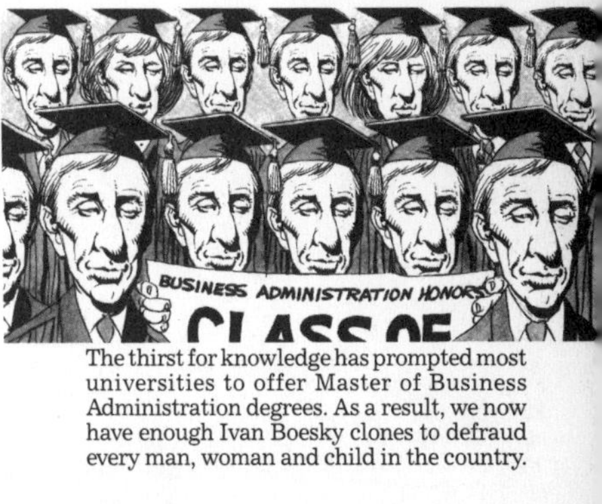
BUSINESS ADMINISTRATION HONORS

The thirst for knowledge has prompted most universities to offer Master of Business Administration degrees. As a result, we now have enough Ivan Boesky clones to defraud every man, woman and child in the country.

TALES FROM THE DUCK SIDE DEPT.

THE EXQUISITE EXECUTION EXPERIMENT

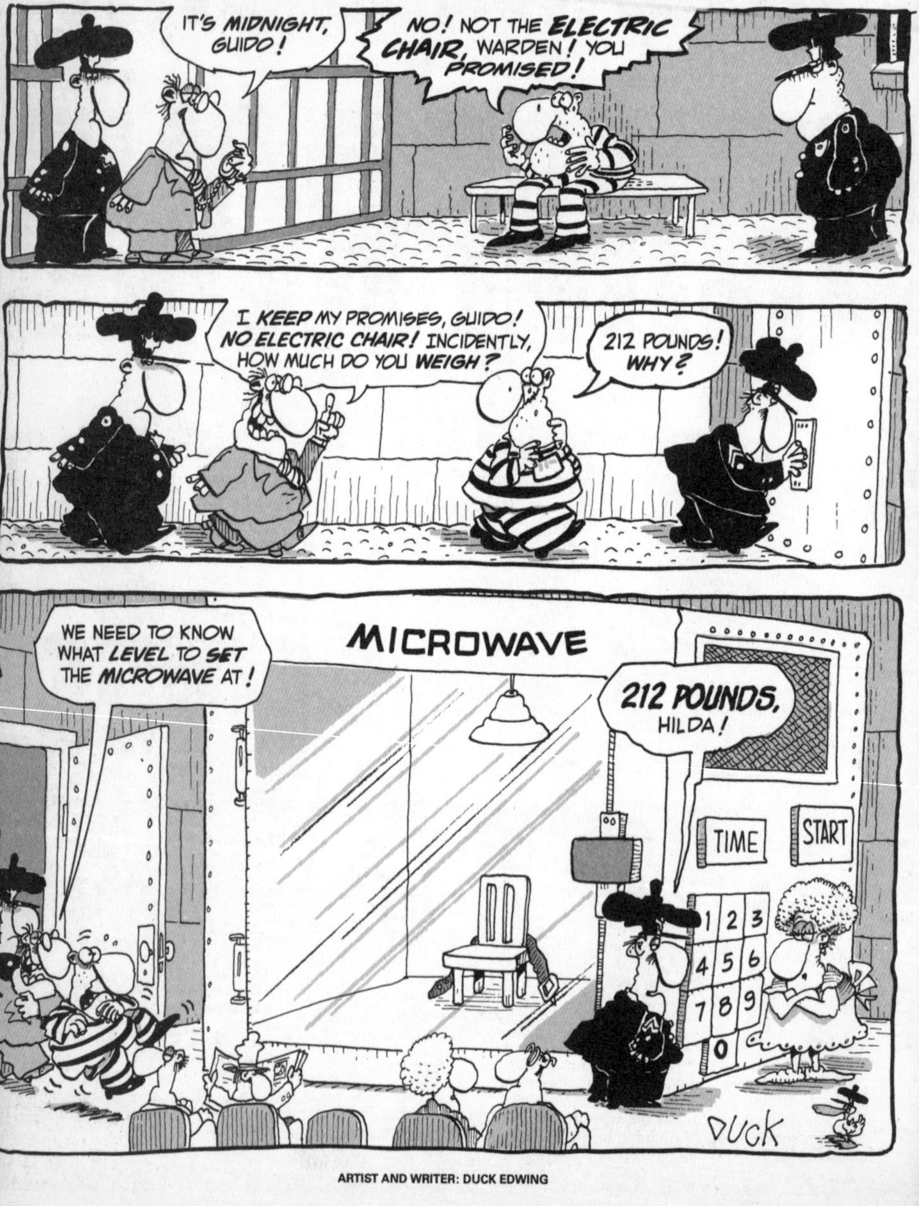

IT'S MIDNIGHT, GUIDO!
NO! NOT THE ELECTRIC CHAIR, WARDEN! YOU PROMISED!
I KEEP MY PROMISES, GUIDO! NO ELECTRIC CHAIR! INCIDENTLY, HOW MUCH DO YOU WEIGH?
212 POUNDS! WHY?
WE NEED TO KNOW WHAT LEVEL TO SET THE MICROWAVE AT!
MICROWAVE
212 POUNDS, HILDA!
TIME
START
1 2 3
4 5 6
7 8 9
0
DUCK

ARTIST AND WRITER: DUCK EDWING

ALL JAFFEE DEPT.

These days, our postal system is clogged with millions of slick, four color catalogs from The Sharper Image, Brookstone, Hammacher Schlemmer and other upscale mailorder companies. They're filled with unusual gadgets, exotic tools and strange contraptions that all have two things in common: They're incredibly overpriced and totally useless! Who needs a $200 computerized cheese scale anyway?? It would be a joy if we could go to our mailbox just once and find a catalog filled with *useful* tools and truly novel inventions. Perhaps a catalog just like...

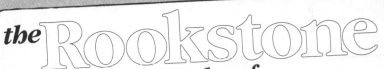

the Rookstone
catalog of
Really Useful Tools, Nifty Gadgets,
Hi-Tech Thingamajigs and Crafty Geegaws
NEW!
"Wear" Your Tools And You'll Always Know "Where" They Are!
FRONT
BACK
PLANS BUILD AN AFFORDABLE HOUSE
FRONT VIEW
SIDE VIEW
MATERIALS
Rookstone introduces its exclusive Complete Tool Shop Belt! No more fumbling for the right tool...it's always just an arm's length away! Clips, loops, hooks and pockets provide space for 110 tools. This is one tool belt you'll want to wear everywhere!
#455342 $1,098.98

ARTIST AND WRITER: AL JAFFEE

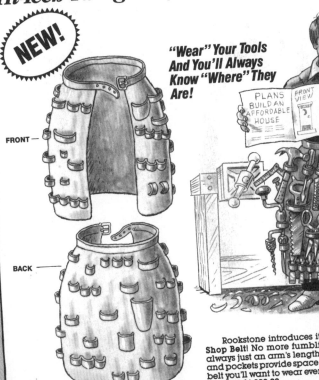

Our New Key Will Send Your Locksmith To Intensive Care!

Your locksmith will have a fit when you show him your **Lifetime Key Supply!** If you lose or bend a key, break off another one from the solid brass block of 24 key slugs, snap it into the key head and start unlocking those doors!

#28599899 $124.95

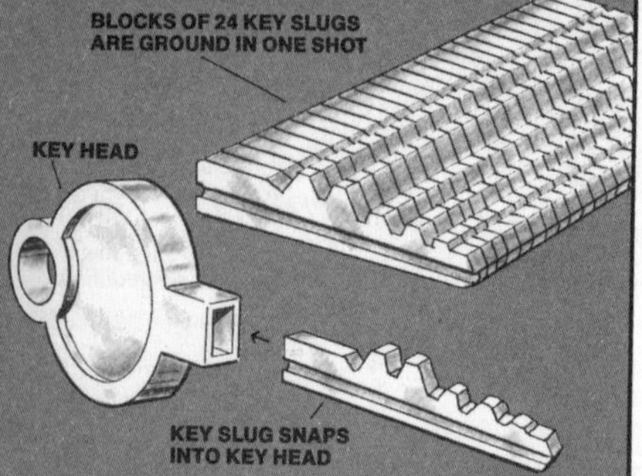
BLOCKS OF 24 KEY SLUGS
ARE GROUND IN ONE SHOT
KEY HEAD
KEY SLUG SNAPS
INTO KEY HEAD

Third Hand Puts Getting A Grip On Things Within Your Grasp

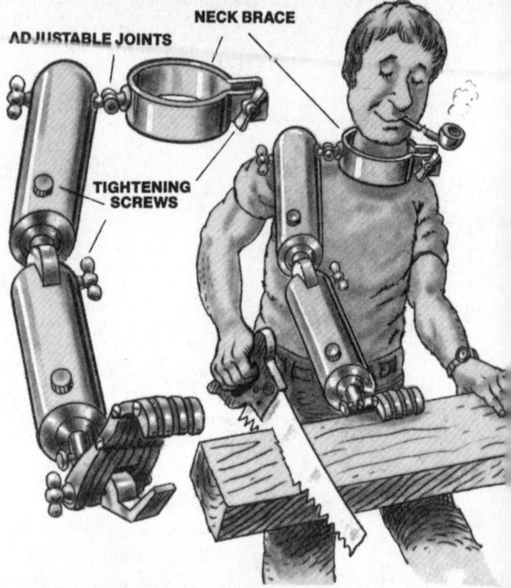
NECK BRACE
ADJUSTABLE JOINTS
TIGHTENING
SCREWS

Made of strong, lightweight plastic, the **Third Hand** eliminates the need for bulky workbenches. Specify right or left hand model. Not recommended for any obscene use in a sexual context.

#877639 $139.99

New Two-way Tool Gets Your Shoes, Toilet Bowl Clean (And Vice Versa)

Save valuable workshop space with this perky **Shoe Buffer/Toilet Bowl Cleaner!** Quiet two horsepower motor drives 100% lamb's wool brush at 2,500 RPM. We strongly recommend you buff your shoes *before* cleaning your toilet.

#2 $99.99

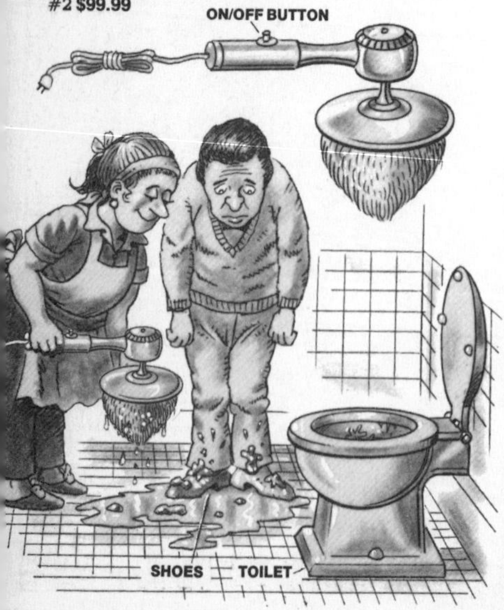
ON/OFF BUTTON
SHOES
TOILET

Spiffy Product Turns Your Screen Holes Into Whole Screens

Using scotch tape technology, our **Screen Patch Tape's** adhesive/mesh design allows screen fix-ups in a jiffy. Once and for all, you can prove to mosquitos and other insects that you are superior!

#19 $88.99

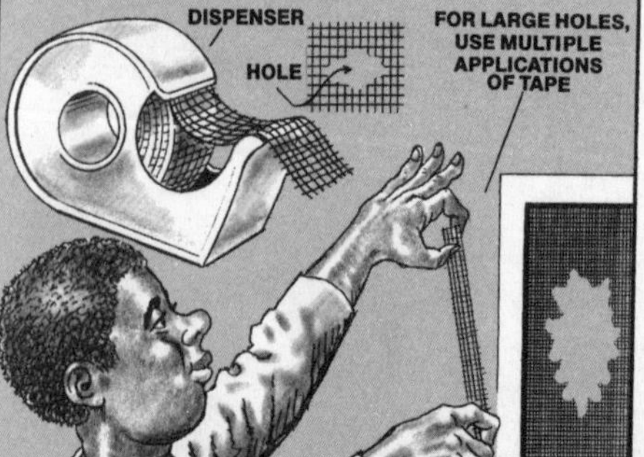
DISPENSER
HOLE
FOR LARGE HOLES,
USE MULTIPLE
APPLICATIONS
OF TAPE

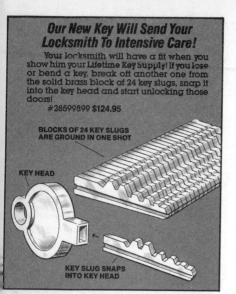

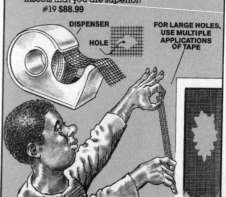

"Telescopic" Legs Turn Your Hovel Into A Mansion

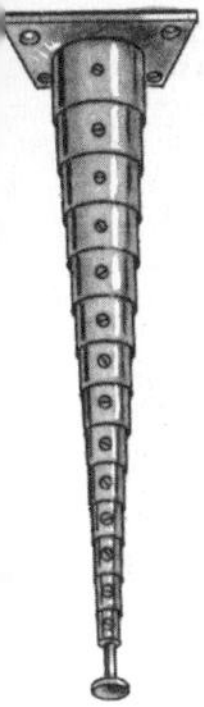

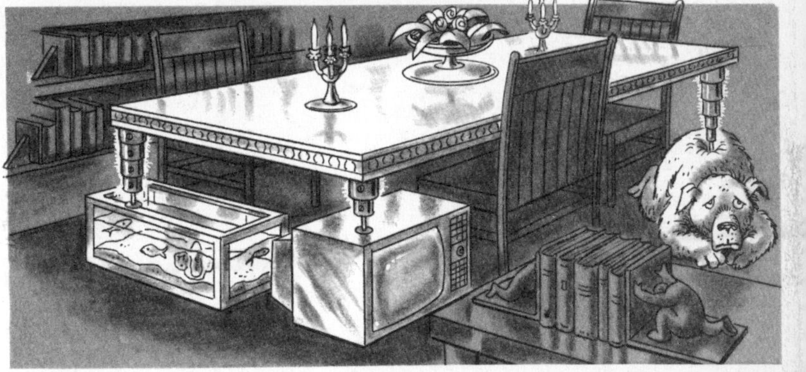

Cramped city apartment living can no longer prevent you from owning large, regal furniture. By adding these **super adjustable table legs**, you'll be able to fit even the largest sculpted mahogany banquet table into the smallest one-room apartment!

#786512 $735.00

Stick It On Your Wall In Style!

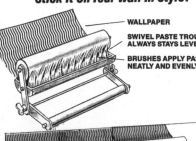

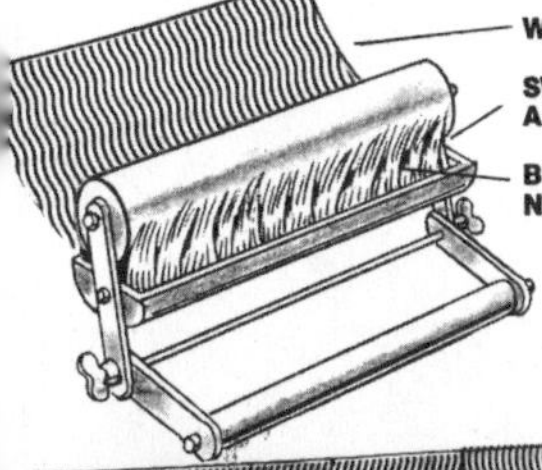
WALLPAPER
SWIVEL PASTE TROUGH ALWAYS STAYS LEVEL
BRUSHES APPLY PASTE NEATLY AND EVENLY

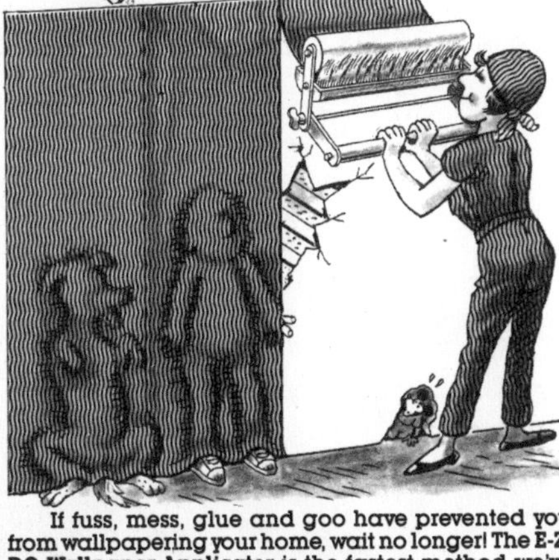

If fuss, mess, glue and goo have prevented you from wallpapering your home, wait no longer! The **E-Z-DO Wallpaper Applicator** is the fastest method we've found! Imported from Chad.

#675 $299.95

You've Heard Of Snap-On Tools, Now Take A Look At Snap-off Tools!

Snap-Off Screws and Nuts eliminate the need for greasy, dangerous tools! After using them, "snap off" the installation appendage and toss it. Never buy another expensive gimmicky tool again!

#1 $94.95

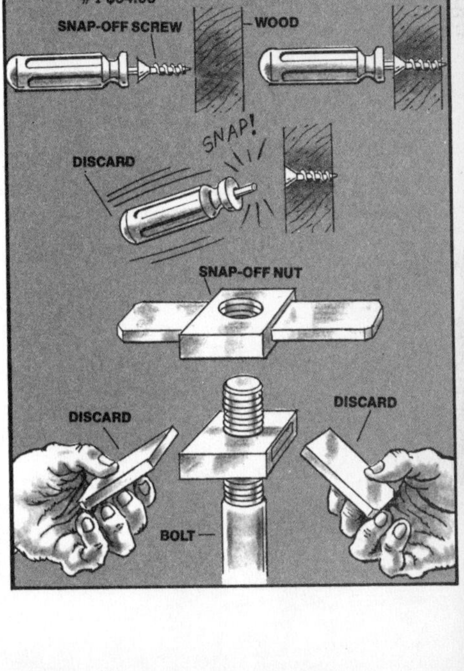
SNAP-OFF SCREW
WOOD
SNAP!
DISCARD
SNAP-OFF NUT
DISCARD
DISCARD
BOLT

10-in-1 Bit Gives You The Drill Of Your Life

Borrowing an idea from Medieval England, what looks like a jouster's lance is actually the **All-In-One-Drill Bit**. Just keep drilling until you reach the hole diameter you want! What you put into the hole is entirely up to you!
#555 $198.98

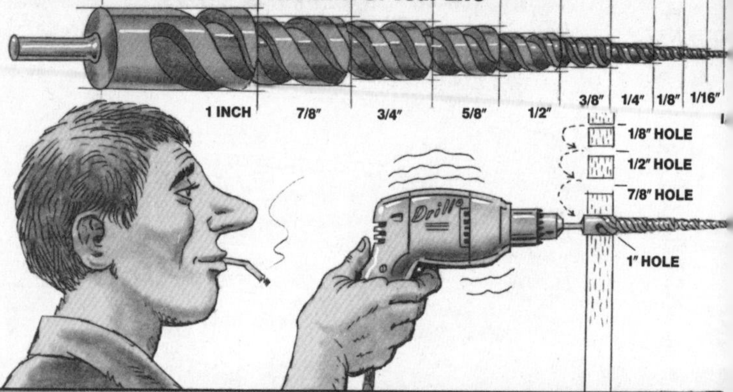
1 INCH
7/8"
3/4"
5/8"
1/2"
3/8"
1/4"
1/8"
1/16"
Drill
1/8" HOLE
1/2" HOLE
7/8" HOLE
1" HOLE

Nifty Hammer With Nail "File" Proves Three Heads Are Better Than Two!

The handle of this ingenious **Multi-Hammer/Nail Dispenser** holds four types of nails and the threaded hammerhead and claw modules form nine different combinations. Odorless.
#78864 $249.99

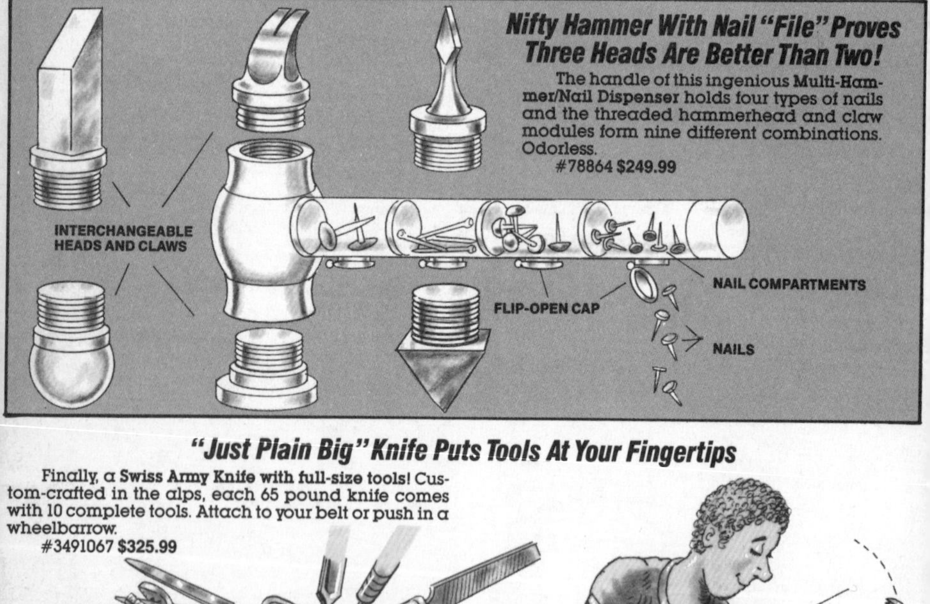
INTERCHANGEABLE HEADS AND CLAWS
NAIL COMPARTMENTS
FLIP-OPEN CAP
NAILS

"Just Plain Big" Knife Puts Tools At Your Fingertips

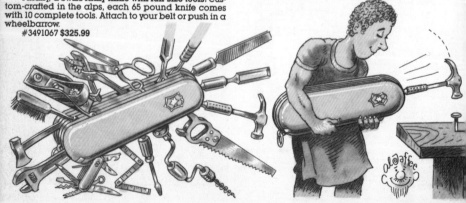

Finally, a **Swiss Army Knife** with full-size tools! Custom-crafted in the alps, each 65 pound knife comes with 10 complete tools. Attach to your belt or push in a wheelbarrow.
#3491067 $325.99

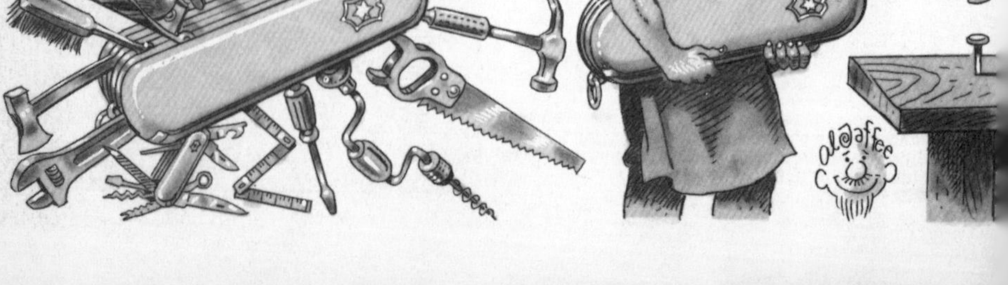

SERGE-IN GENERAL DEPT.

A MAD LOOK AT DRIVER'S ED

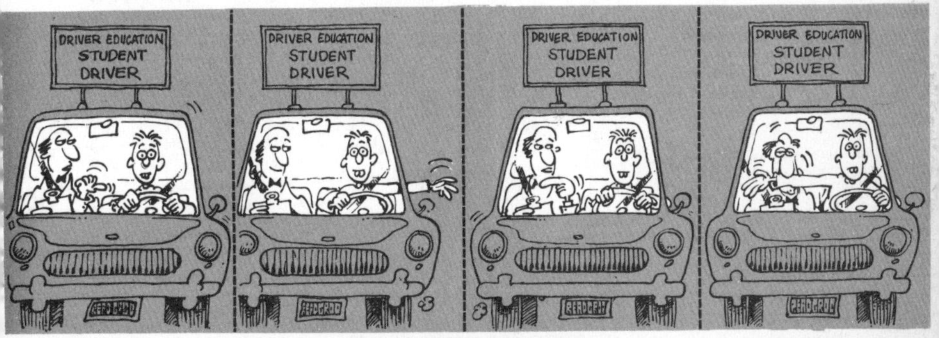
DRIVER EDUCATION
STUDENT
DRIVER
DRIVER EDUCATION
STUDENT
DRIVER
DRIVER EDUCATION
STUDENT
DRIVER
DRIVER EDUCATION
STUDENT
DRIVER

ARTIST AND WRITER: SERGIO ARAGONES

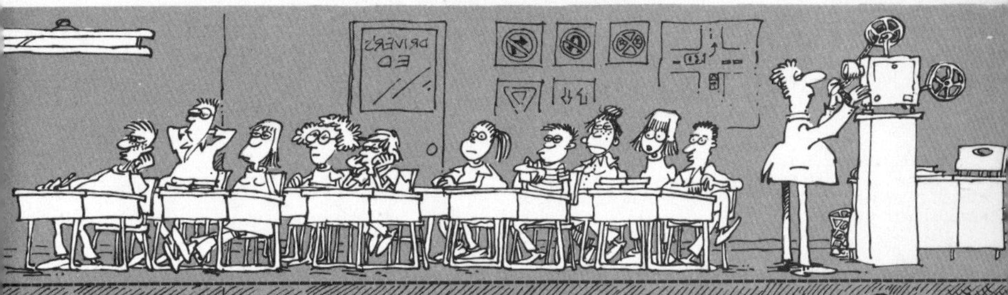
DRIVER'S
ED

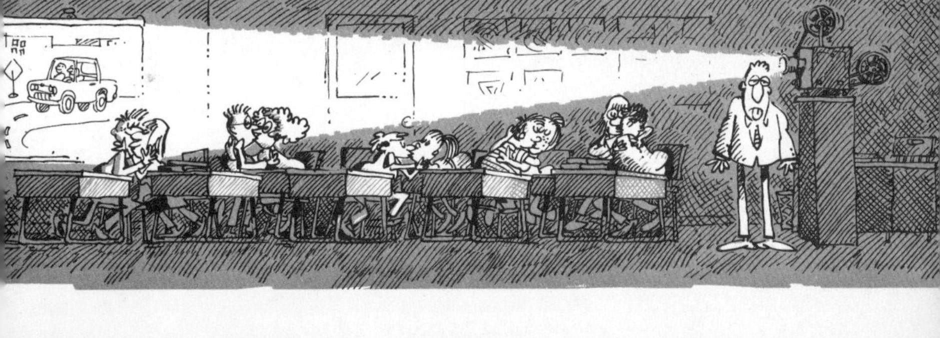

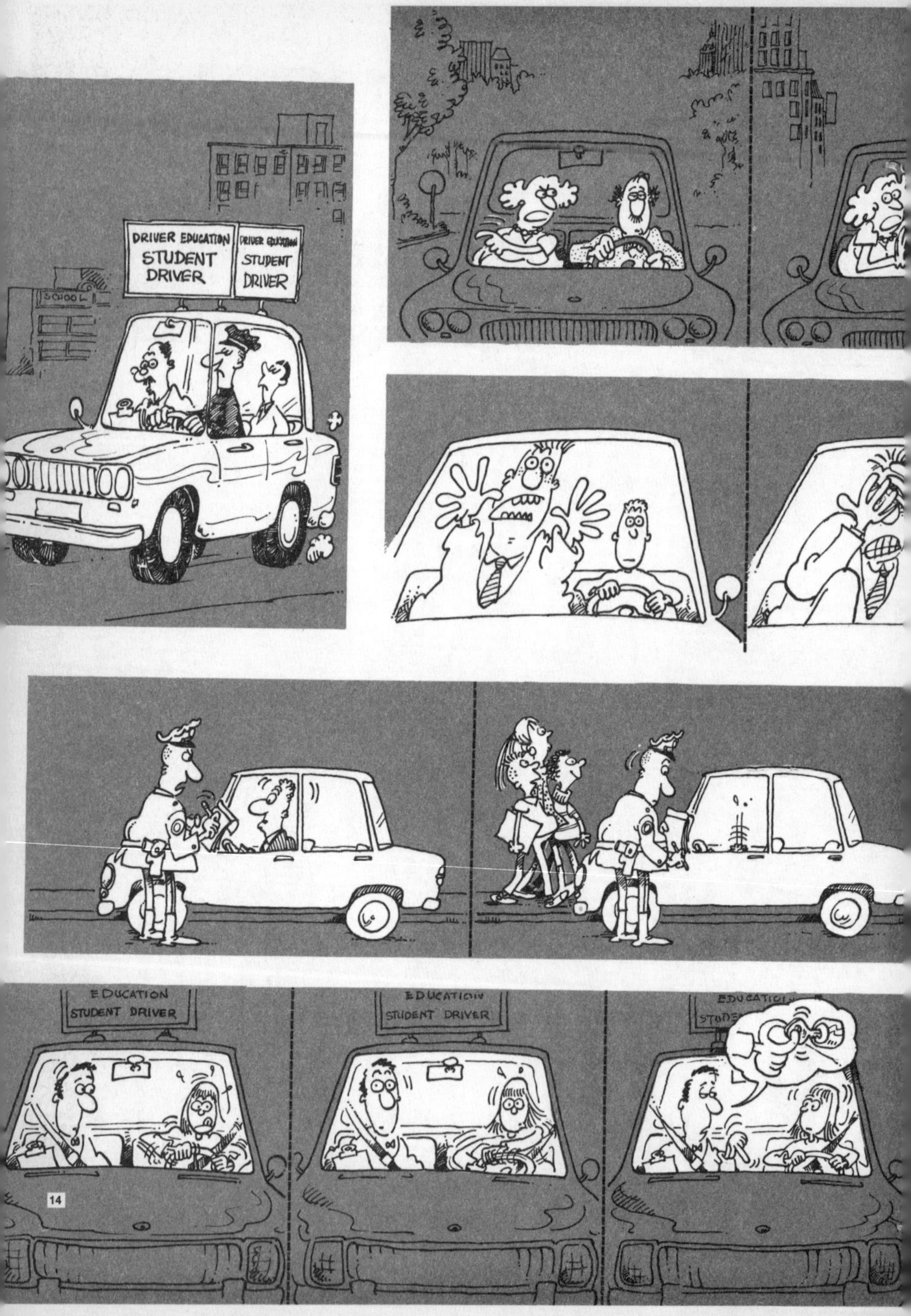
DRIVER EDUCATION
STUDENT
DRIVER
DRIVER EDUCATION
STUDENT
DRIVER
SCHOOL
EDUCATION
STUDENT DRIVER
EDUCATION
STUDENT DRIVER

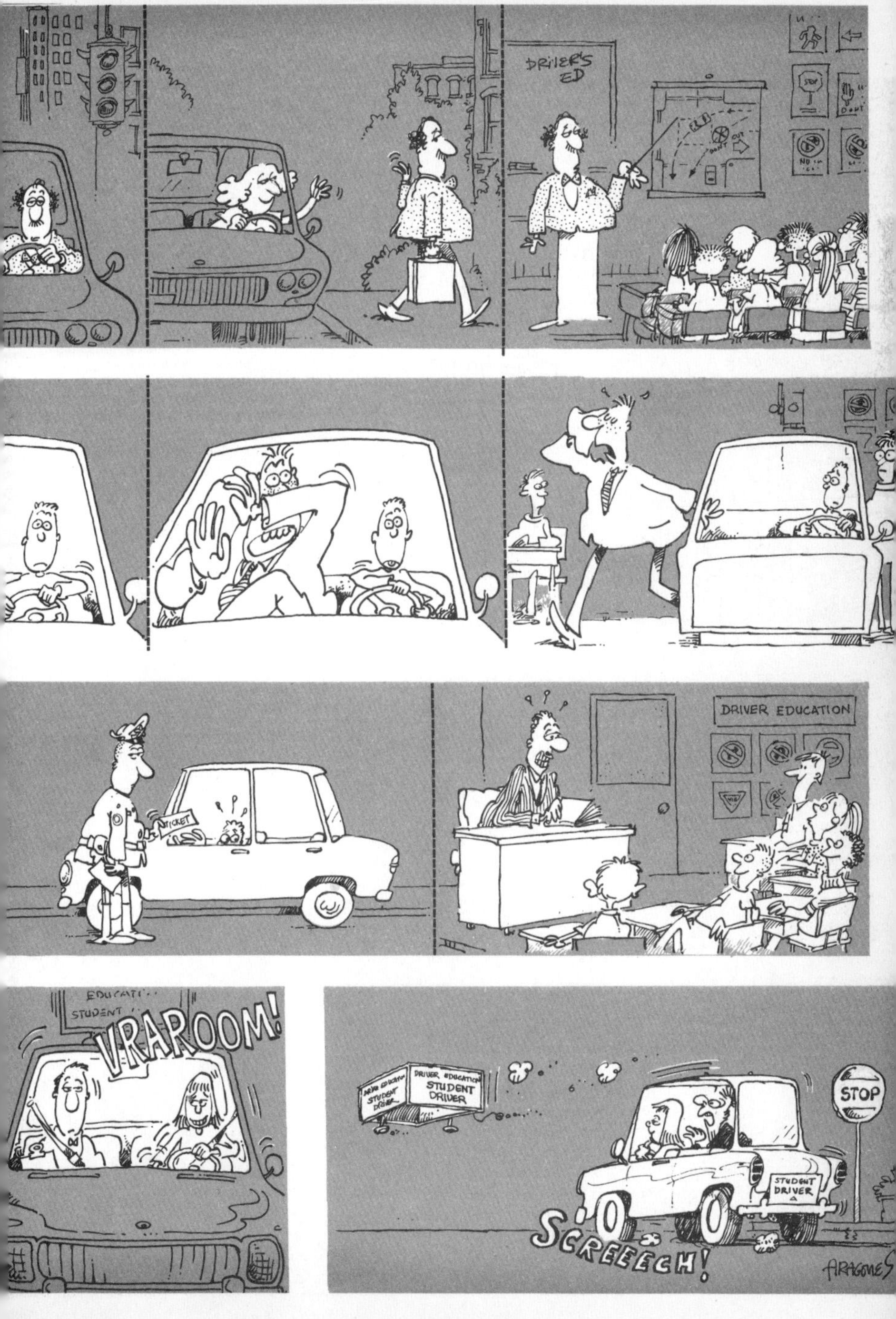
DRIVER'S ED
TICKET
DRIVER EDUCATION
VRAROOM!
DRIVER EDUCATION
STUDENT DRIVER
STOP
STUDENT DRIVER
SCREEECH!
ARAGONES

FRANK ON A ROLL DEPT.

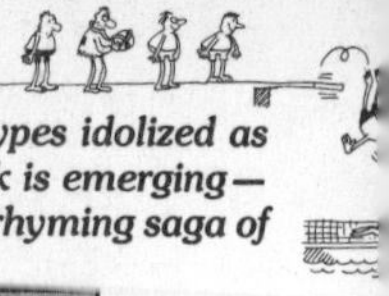

Legend has it that college athletes once were clean-living, law-abiding types idolized as role models. But with all the recent scandals, it seems a new breed of jock is emerging—one who's more a role model for aspiring criminals! Which leads us to this rhyming saga of

TEN COLLEGE ATHLETES

ARTIST: JACK DAVIS WRITER: FRANK JACOBS

Ten college athletes,
The best the school could sign;
One punched out a campus cop—
Slam! Bam! We're down to nine.

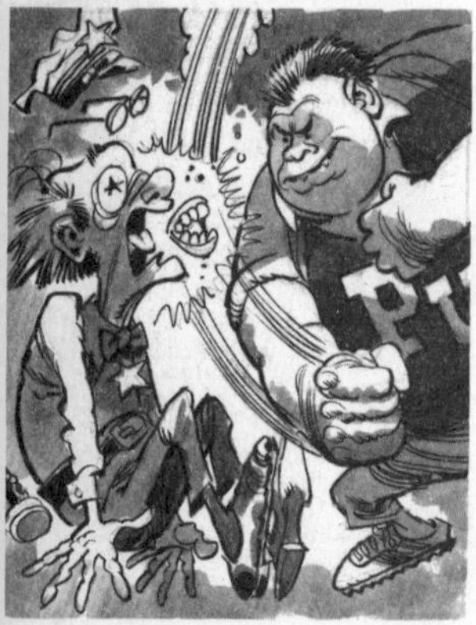

Nine freshmen athletes,
Beefed up and looking great;
One OD'd on steroid shots—
He's stiff, which leaves us eight.

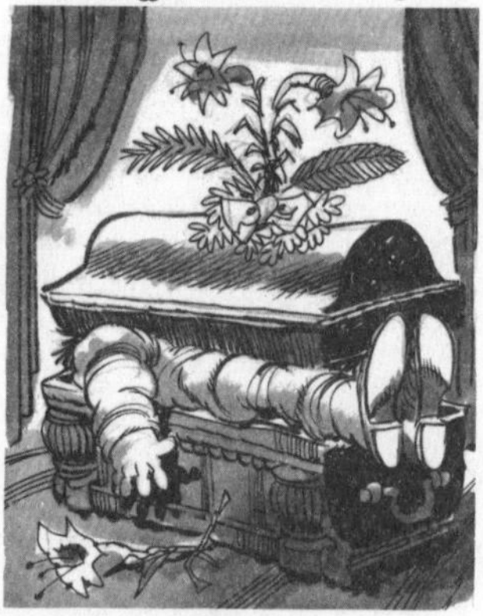

Eight freshmen athletes,
With juiced-up Porsches revvin';
One was driving stolen wheels—
Beep-beep—we're down to seven.

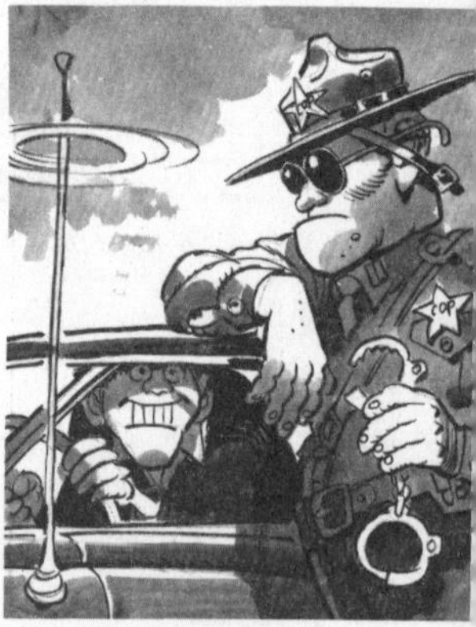

COP

Four junior athletes,
Unleashed and running free;
One shot up a bar and grill—
Boom! Boom! We're down to three.

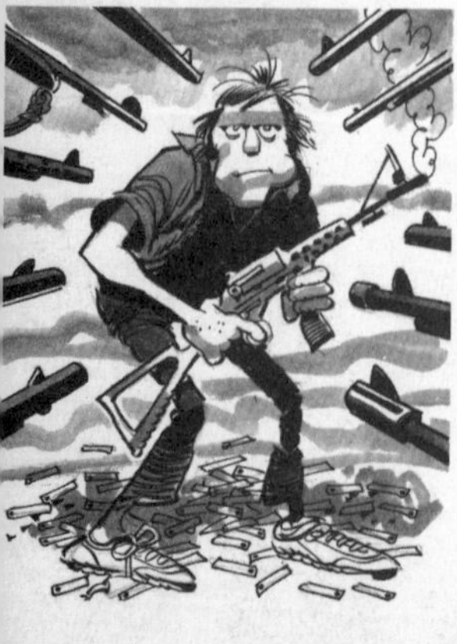

Three senior athletes,
In class, without a clue;
One flunked out and stabbed his prof—
Point made—which leaves us two.

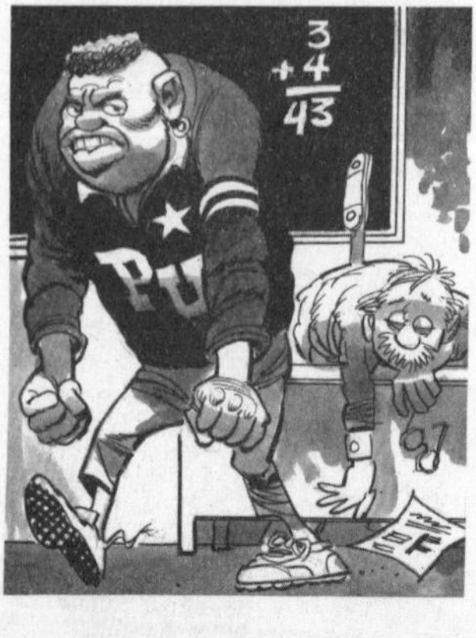

3
+4
43
PU
F

Two senior athletes,
Their school-days nearly done;
One got nailed for coed rape—
School's out—we're down to one.

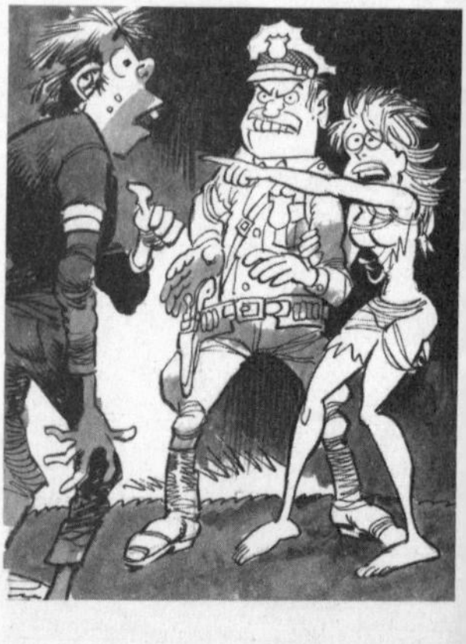

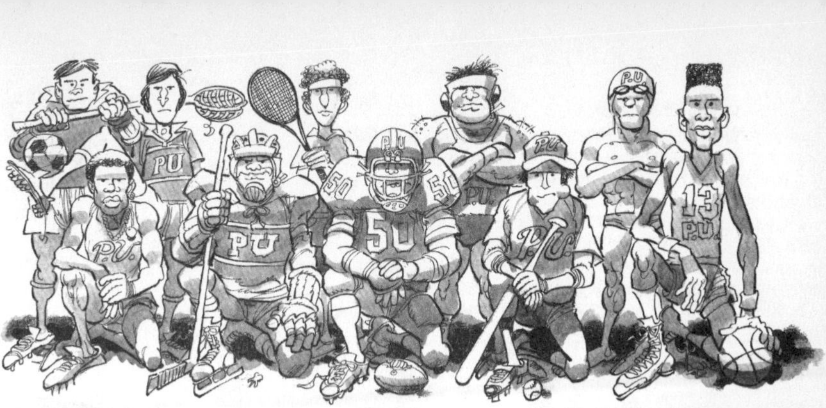
PU
P.U.
50
13
P.U.

Seven soph'more athletes,
Big spenders with the chicks;
One took payoffs from alums –
Bye, guy – that leaves us six.

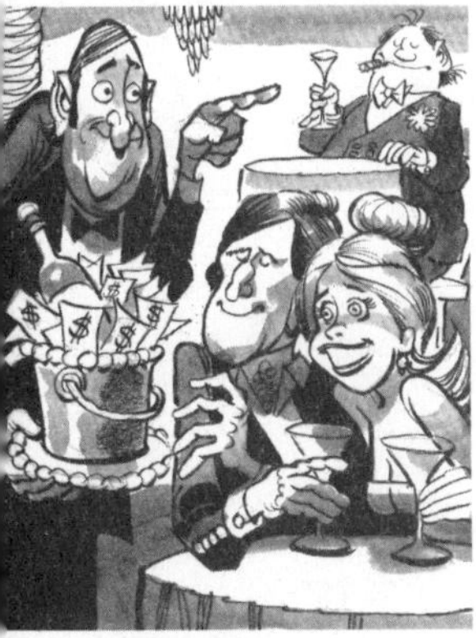

Six soph'more athletes,
Each betting he'll survive;
One helped gamblers fix a game –
Bet's off – we're down to five.

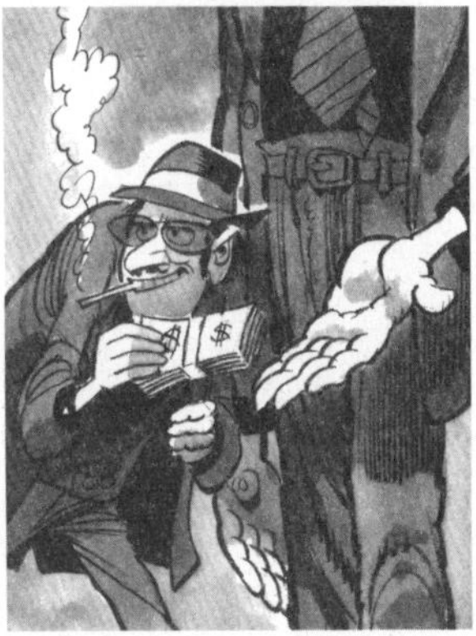

Five junior athletes,
Hot stuff and out to score;
One got busted dealing coke –
Toot-toot – that leaves us four.

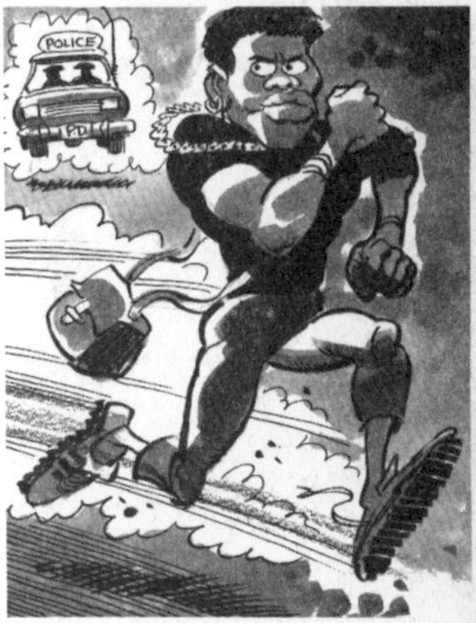
POLICE
PD

One college athlete,
Respected, clean, sincere;
My gosh, he's gonna graduate!
Hey! What's he doing here?

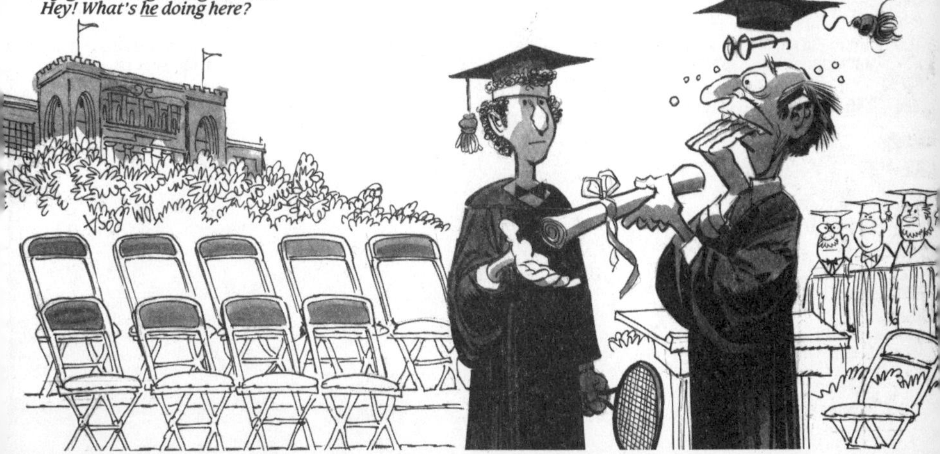

FOR YOU PRIZE ONLY DEPT.

WHY
TO
MAGA
S

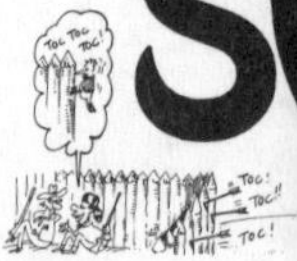

Look carefully at the Publishers' Sweepstakes envelope below. You probably get one every year, and you probably trash it! You think it's junk mail, and besides, the odds must be crazy that you, out of millions, could be the big winner, right? Wrong! The truth is many people fail to receive their notices. And those who do either trash them or screw up the forms so badly that they're eliminated! So what are you waiting for? Go through your garbage! Get back that entry form and check every box, affix every stupid sticker and rush it in, because MAD has assembled the figures to prove convincingly...

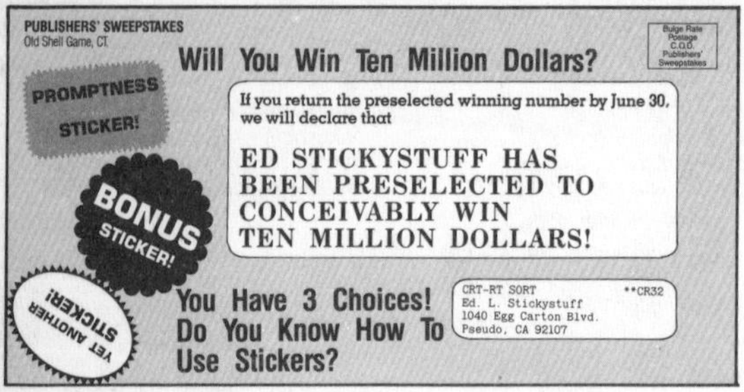

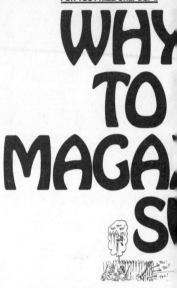

PUBLISHERS' SWEEPSTAKES
Old Shell Game, CT
Bulge Rate Postage C.O.D. Publishers' Sweepstakes
Will You Win Ten Million Dollars?
PROMPTNESS STICKER!
If you return the preselected winning number by June 30, we will declare that
ED STICKYSTUFF HAS BEEN PRESELECTED TO CONCEIVABLY WIN TEN MILLION DOLLARS!
BONUS STICKER!
YET ANOTHER STICKER!
You Have 3 Choices! Do You Know How To Use Stickers?
CRT-RT SORT **CR32
Ed. L. Stickystuff
1040 Egg Carton Blvd.
Pseudo, CA 92107

Among 50,000,000 entries sent out...

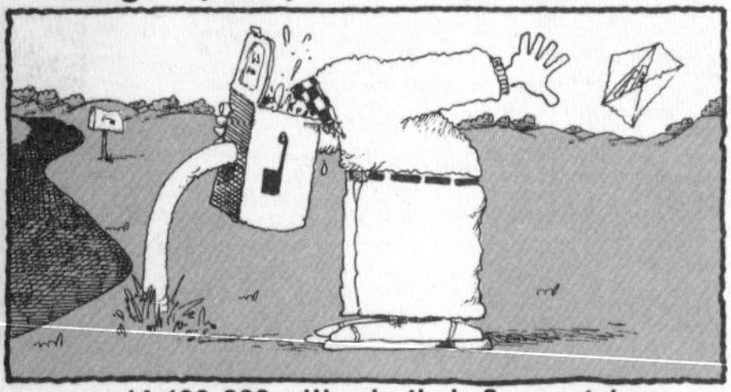

...14,168,000 will ruin their Sweepstakes entry forms by throwing up all over them the moment they see the picture of Ed McMahon.

Of the remaining 35,832,000...

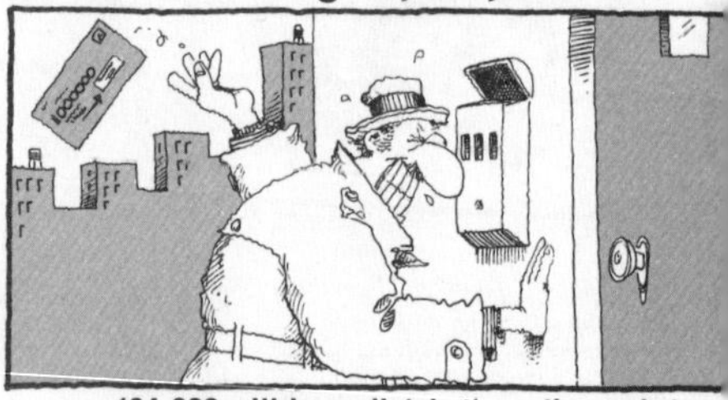

...184,000 will immediately throw the packet away after discovering that no hard core pornographic magazines are among those being offered.

Of the remaining 30,886,951...

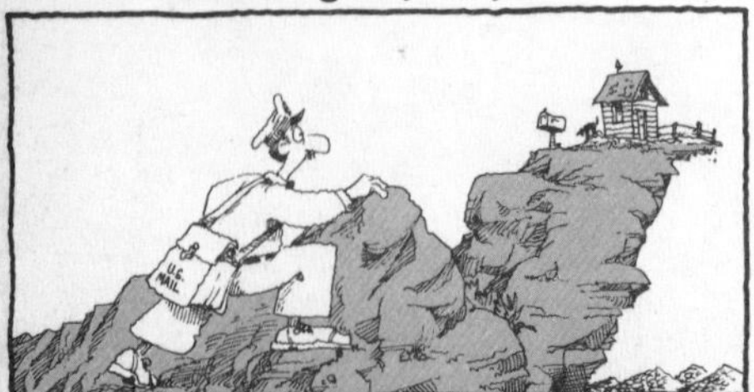

U.S. MAIL

...3,800,957 will be farmers and yahoos living so far out in the sticks that the mailman can't get through until two weeks after the deadline.

Of the remaining 27,085,994...

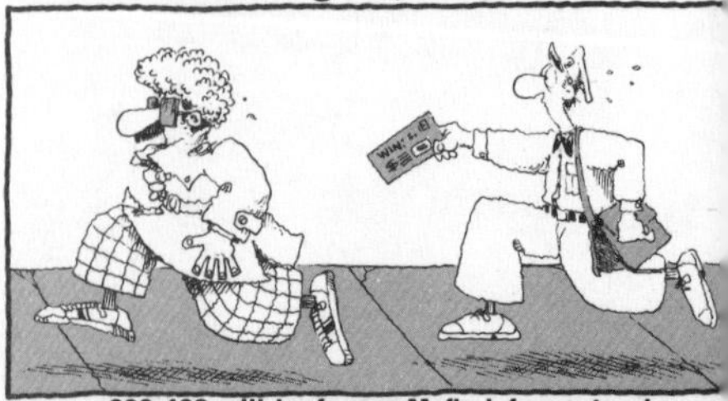

...622,460 will be former Mafia informants who got new identities from the F.B.I. and who are afraid to claim mail addressed to their real names.

YOU ARE SURE
VIN THE NEXT
INE PUBLISHERS'
EEPSTAKES

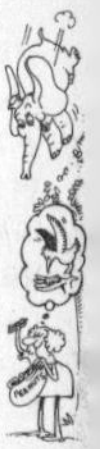

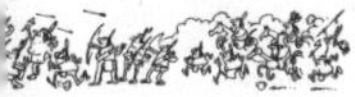

ARTIST: JOHN CALDWELL WRITER: TOM KOCH

Of the remaining 35,648,000...

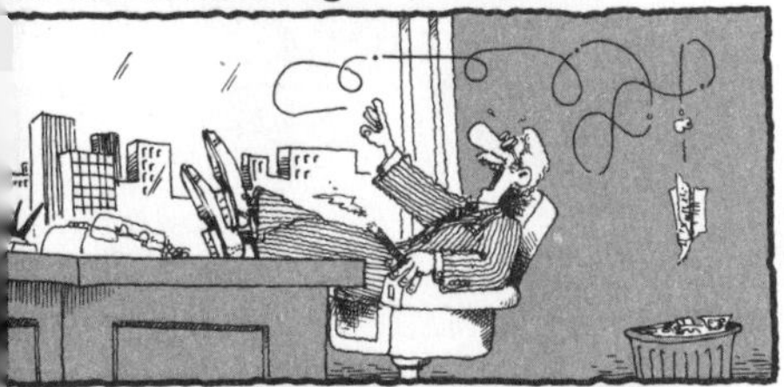

...2,300,049 will be wealthy Wall Street wheeler-dealers and real estate brokers who don't think prizes of yachts or houses are valuable enough to waste time trying to win.

Of the remaining 33,347,951...

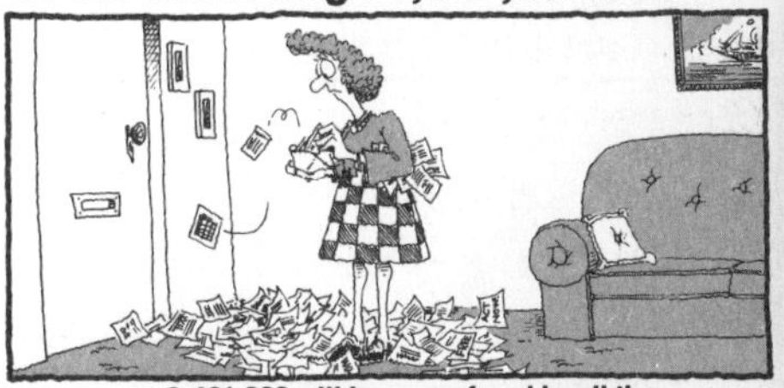

...2,461,000 will be so confused by all the stickers, form letters, bonus seals, and other garbage that they'll give up without ever finding the Sweepstakes entry form.

Of the remaining 26,463,534...

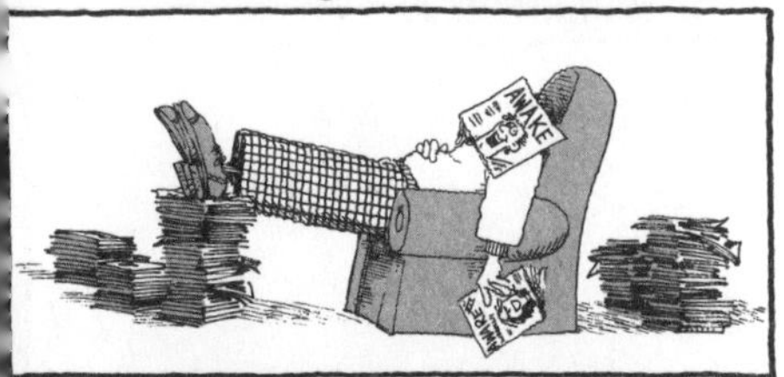
AWAKE

...16,917,540 will be so busy reading the magazines that they subscribed to last year in hopes of winning that they won't have time to open this year's contest packet.

Of the remaining 9,545,994...

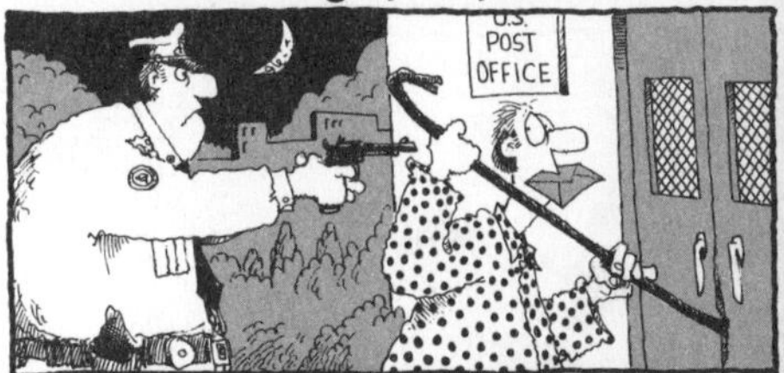
U.S. POST OFFICE

...924,875 will be so intent on winning the Promptness Bonus by mailing before "midnight tonight" that they'll be arrested for breaking into the Post Office before "midnight tonight."

Of the remaining 8,621,119...

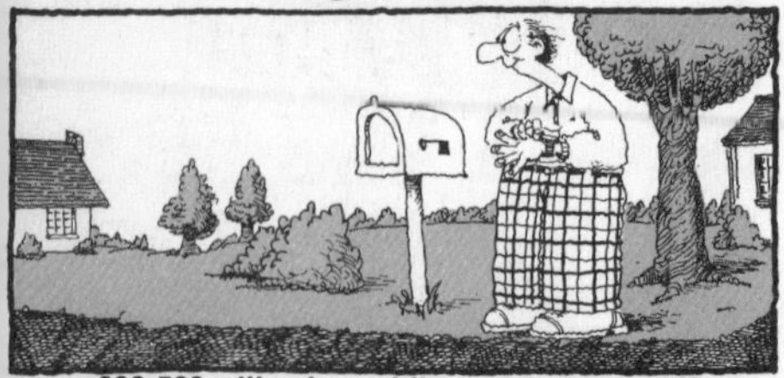

...892,500 will only read the part that says, "You may have already won $1,000,000!" and assume they don't have to do anything but wait for the money.

Of the remaining 7,728,619...

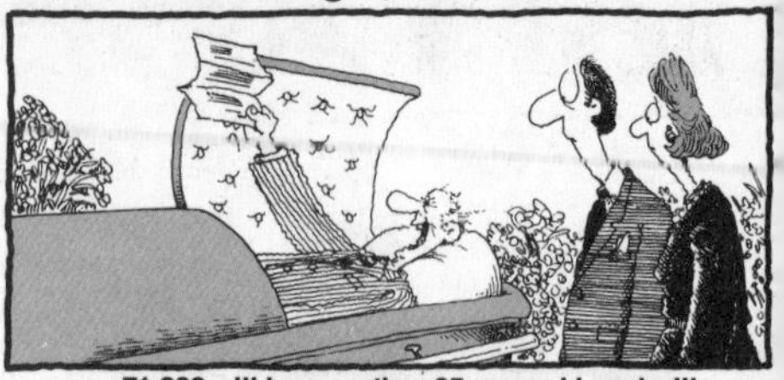

...71,000 will be more than 95 years old, and will reason that it's just plain goofy to go after prize money that's paid out in 30 annual installments.

Of the remaining 7,657,619...

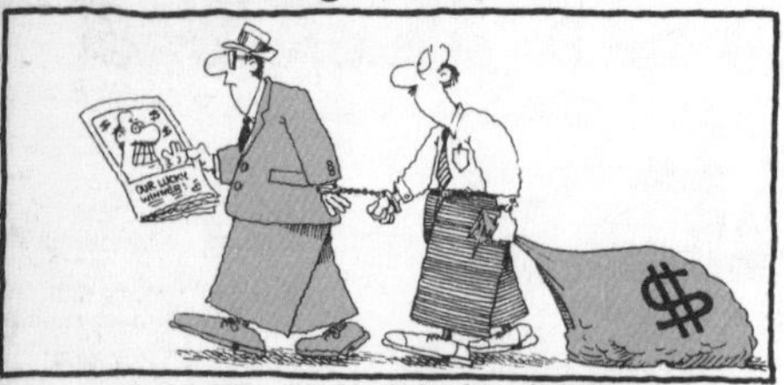
OUR LUCKY WINNERS!

...2,194,350 will skip it for fear that the publicity of a big contest win might cause the I.R.S. to notice that they've never filed a tax return.

Of the remaining 5,463,269...

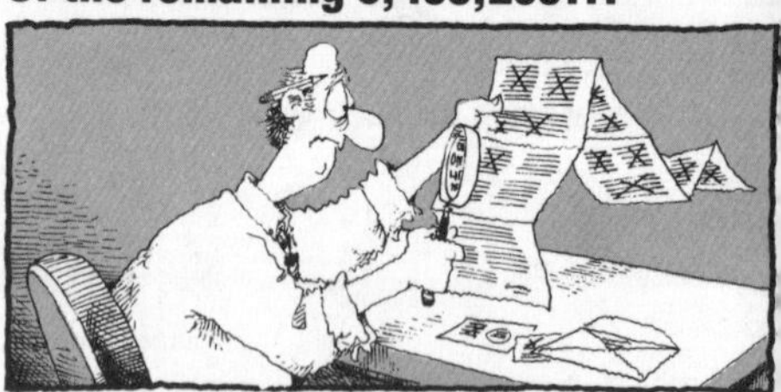

...2,432,005 will fail to participate because they can't find the only obscure option among 85 possibilities that lets you enter without buying anything.

Of the remaining 3,031,264...

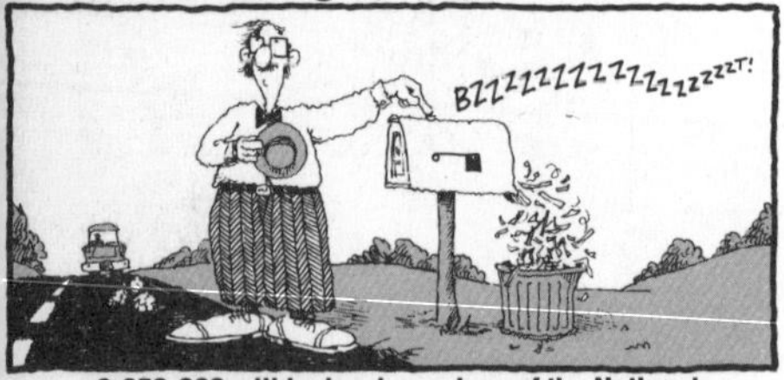
BZZZZZZZZZZzzzzzzzT!

...2,350,000 will be loyal members of the National Society To Wipe Out Junk Mail, and are bound by oath to destroy Sweepstakes envelopes on sight.

Of the remaining 681,264...

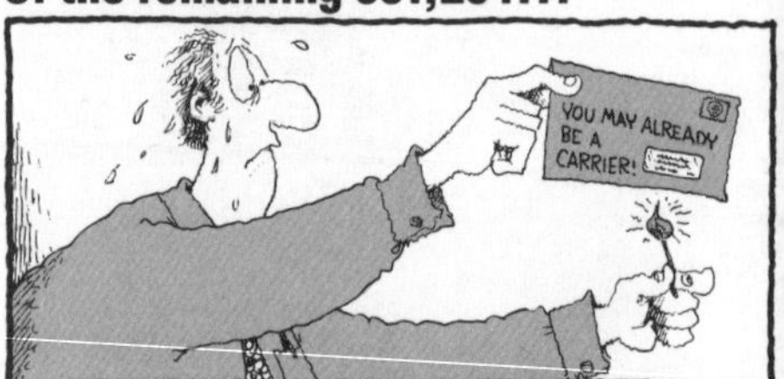
YOU MAY ALREADY BE A CARRIER!

...1,868 will consult numerologists who tell them that their assigned numbers are so unlucky that using them could touch off an epidemic of cholera.

Of the remaining 679,396...

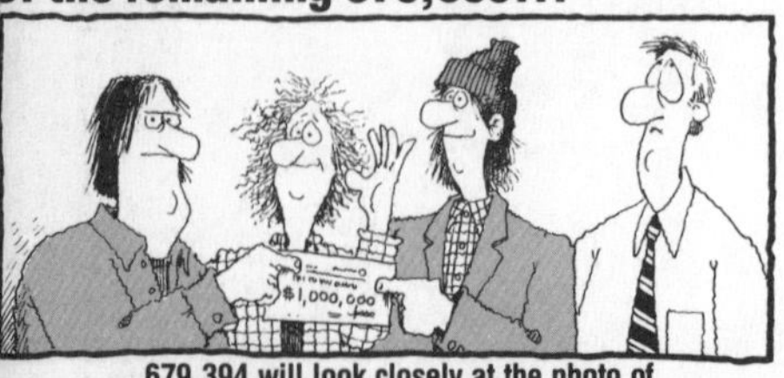
$1,000,000

...679,394 will look closely at the photo of last year's winners and decide that they'd rather lose $1,000,000 than risk being seen with this year's roundup of goons and fools.

Of the remaining 2...

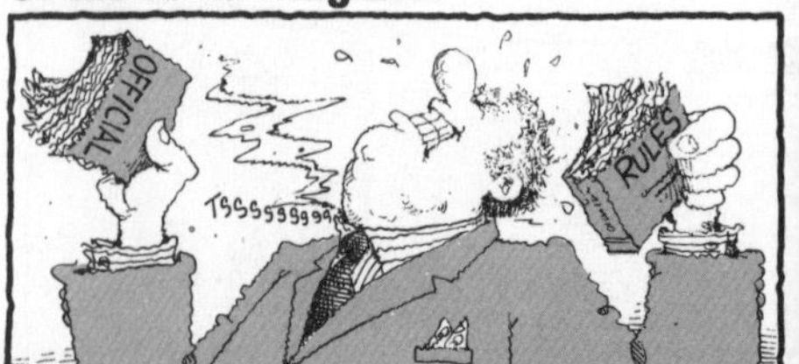
OFFICIAL
TSSSSSSSSS
RULES

...1 will be none other than prizemeister Ed McMahon, who is ineligible to win his own contest, thus leaving *you* as the only possible choice for first prize!!

TALES FROM THE DUCK SIDE DEPT.

THE UNNERVING UNDERTAKER'S UNDERTAKING

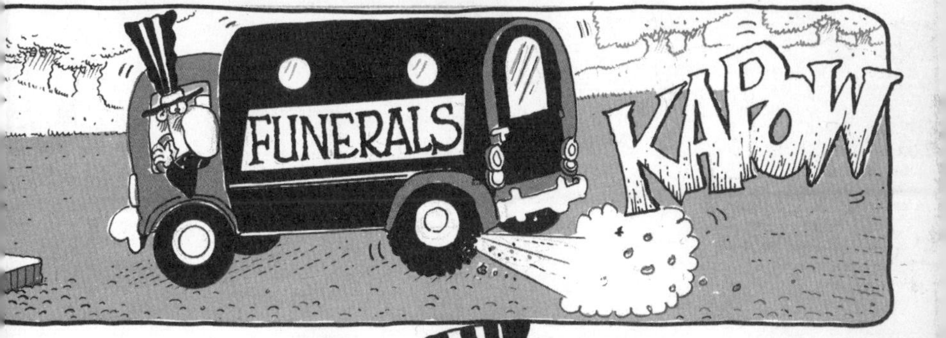
FUNERALS
KAPOW

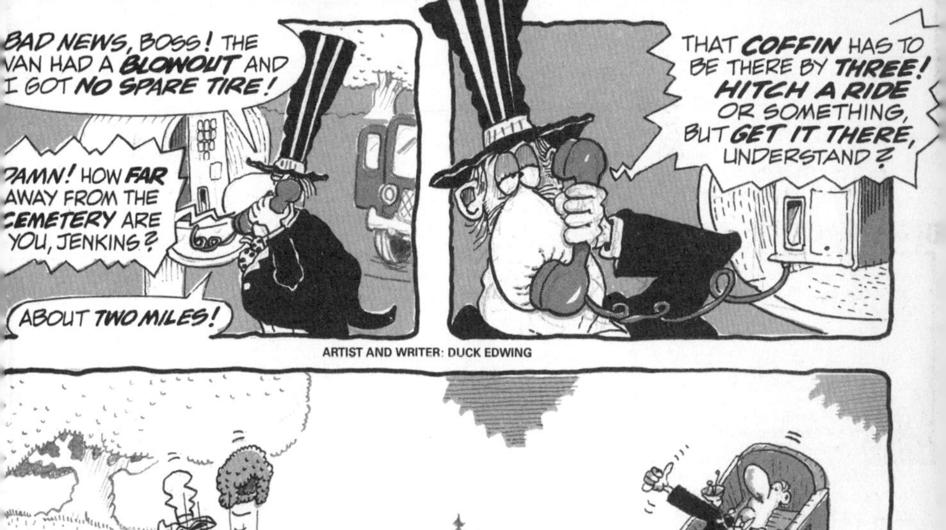
BAD NEWS, BOSS! THE VAN HAD A BLOWOUT AND I GOT NO SPARE TIRE!
DAMN! HOW FAR AWAY FROM THE CEMETERY ARE YOU, JENKINS?
ABOUT TWO MILES!
THAT COFFIN HAS TO BE THERE BY THREE! HITCH A RIDE OR SOMETHING, BUT GET IT THERE, UNDERSTAND?

ARTIST AND WRITER: DUCK EDWING

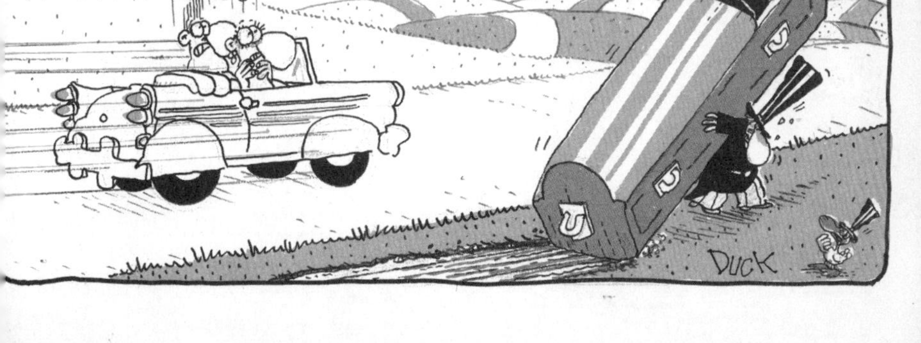
DUCK

DEFLATER MOUTH DEPT.

When we're young, we all play fun party game like "Pin the Tail on the Donkey" and "Beat th Crap Out of Phil." But when we get older, som people start playing other games, like "Impress

MA BIG BUS

ARTIST: AL JAFFEE

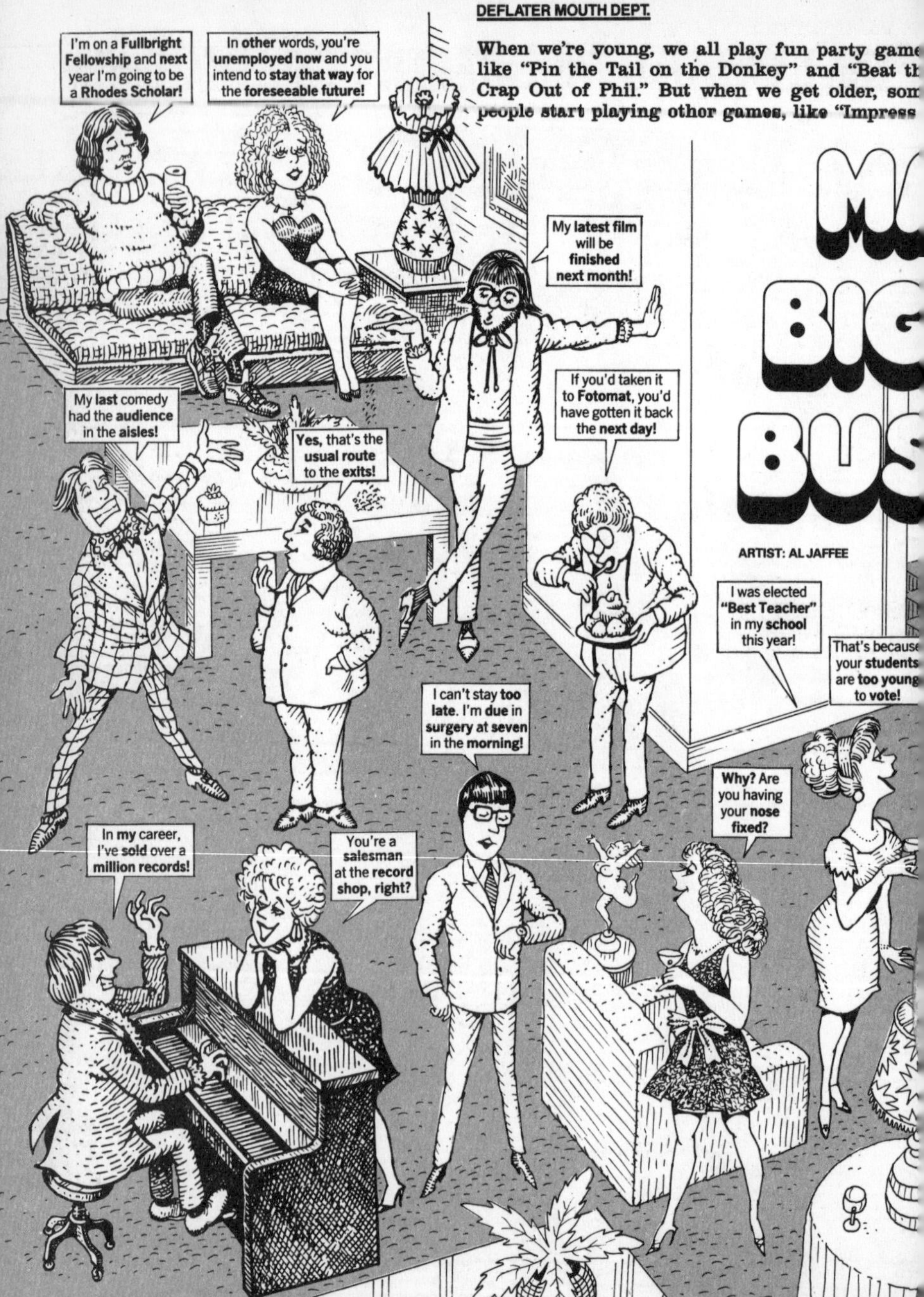

I'm on a **Fullbright Fellowship** and **next** year I'm going to be a **Rhodes Scholar!**
In **other** words, you're **unemployed now** and you intend to **stay that way** for the **foreseeable future!**
My **latest film** will be **finished next month!**
If you'd taken it to **Fotomat**, you'd have gotten it back the **next day!**
My **last** comedy had the **audience** in the **aisles!**
Yes, that's the **usual route** to the **exits!**
I was elected **"Best Teacher"** in my **school** this year!
That's because your **students** are **too young** to **vote!**
I can't stay **too late**. I'm **due** in **surgery** at **seven** in the **morning!**
Why? Are you having your **nose fixed?**
In **my** career, I've **sold** over a **million records!**
You're a **salesman** at the **record shop, right?**

Stranger" and "Stab Phil in the Back." So much for fun! But you can still enjoy yourself when you're surrounded by party-going blowhards (Phil! Are you paying attention?!!) by being prepared with

D'S EGO TERS

WRITER: STAN HART

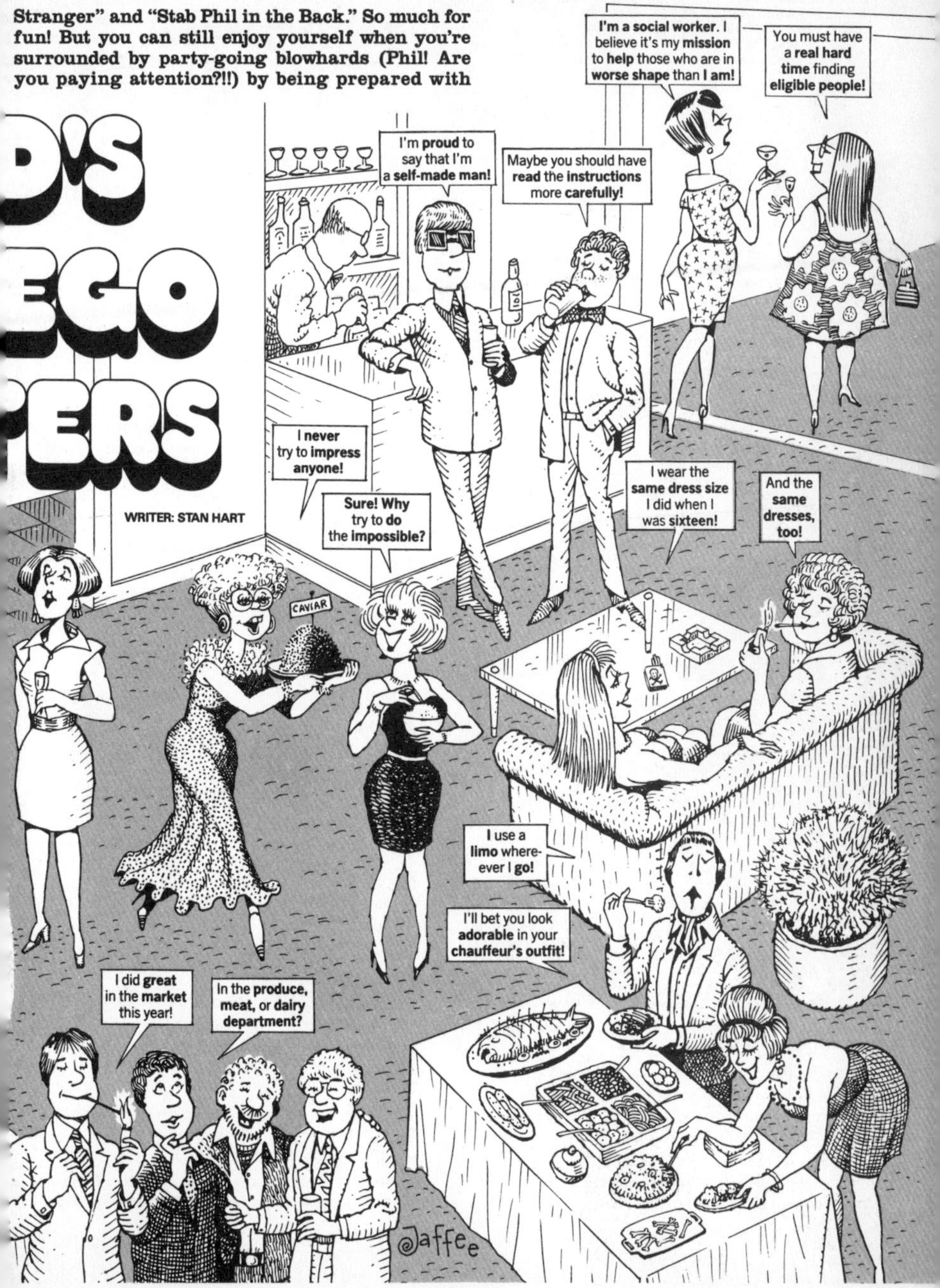

I'm a social worker. I believe it's my mission to help those who are in worse shape than I am!
You must have a real hard time finding eligible people!
I'm proud to say that I'm a self-made man!
Maybe you should have read the instructions more carefully!
I never try to impress anyone!
Sure! Why try to do the impossible?
I wear the same dress size I did when I was sixteen!
And the same dresses, too!
CAVIAR
I use a limo wherever I go!
I'll bet you look adorable in your chauffeur's outfit!
I did great in the market this year!
In the produce, meat, or dairy department?
Jaffee

OUR DAILY DREAD DEPT.

As we travel through life, we begin to see emerging patterns that occur with eerie regularity. If you don't believe us, check your calendar as we review...

THE MAD WEEK

ARTIST: PAUL COKER WRITER: CHARLIE KADAU

ON SUNDAYS...

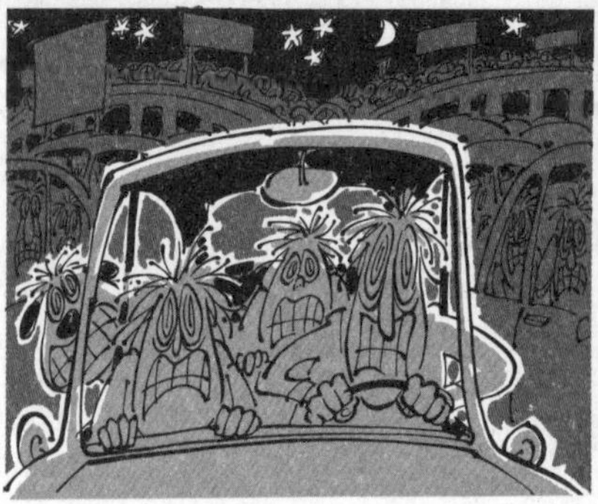

...You stay out late to miss the end-of-weekend traffic jam, only to wind up in a traffic jam of other people who stayed out late for the same reason.

...At about 10:30 p.m. you decide it's time to start working on your weekend homework assignment.

...You add the six sections you "still haven't gotten to" to the pile of Sunday newspaper sections you still haven't gotten to from the past 18 weeks.

ON WEDNESDAYS...

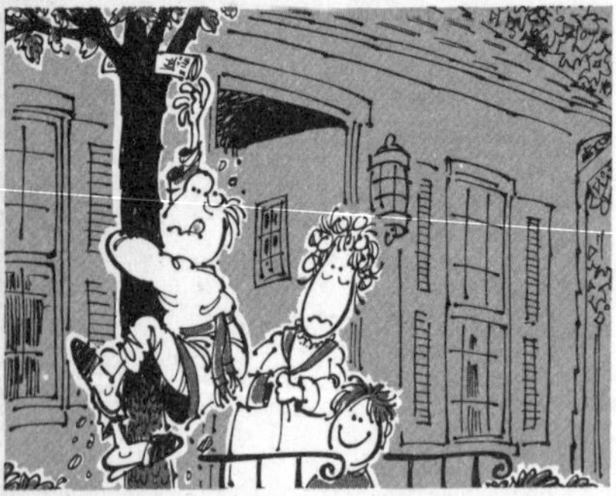

...You step out your door and finally find where the paperboy threw Monday's newspaper.

...You make the unbelievable discovery that every bookstore in town is sold out of the *Cliff's Notes* of the novel you haven't read a page of yet, but have to hand in a book report on by Friday.

...You make a silent pledge to yourself that by the end of this week you'll finish all the work you had pledged to finish by the end of *last* week.

ON THURSDAYS...

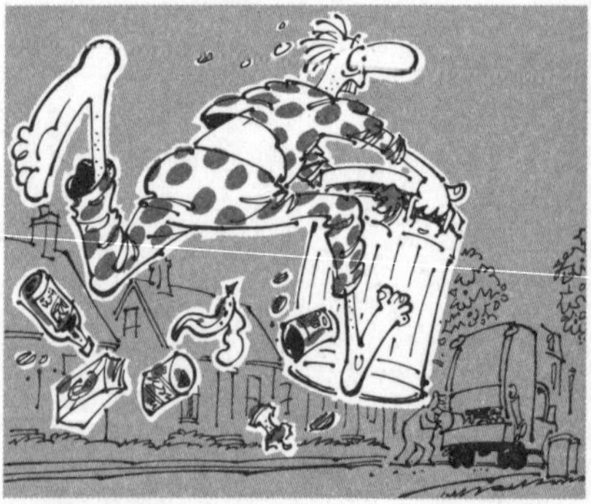

...At about 4:30 a.m., the sound of garbage trucks reminds you that you didn't put the trash out the night before.

...You finally get up enough nerve to ask someone for a date on Saturday night, only to discover they made other plans yesterday.

...You remember that you still haven't returned the video you rented that was due back last Monday.

DEPT.

...sgusting!! Loathesome!!!"
...wait! Before you respond
...to something, you should
...alternative. It may be even
...so don't just sit there—get
...ercise your decision skills!
...ome ugly choices to make as...

MAD A...
THE LESSER...

ARTIST: PAUL COK...

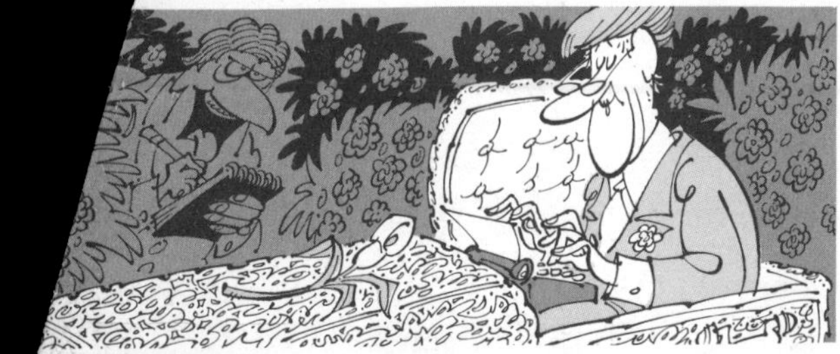

Sleazy "unauthorized biographies" that trash the reputations of defenseless dead celebrities... **OR** ...the sickeningly pompous "vanity books" celebrities write about themselves while they're still alive?!!

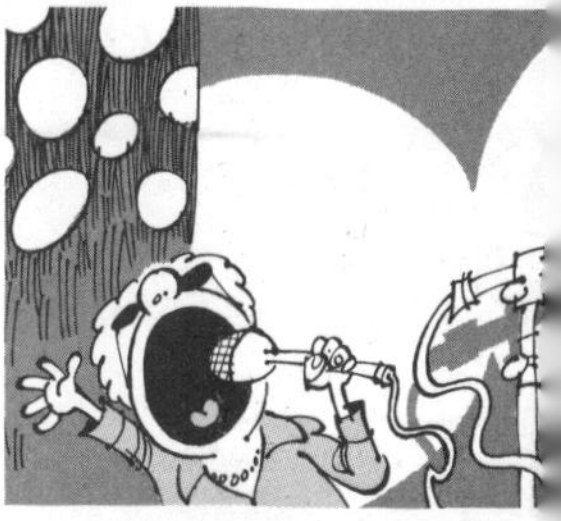

Young pop singers closer to infancy than puberty who are crooning about love and sex...

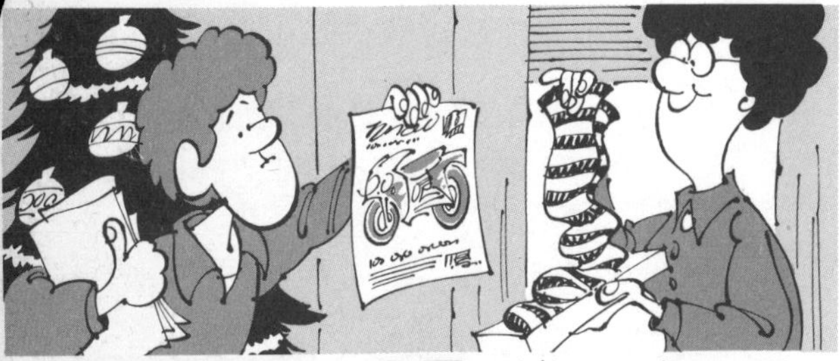

Issuing a "Christmas Wish List" of what you really want—and looking like a greedy, materialistic pig... **OR** ...taking your chances—and bracing for an onslaught of socks, underwear and fountain pens?!!

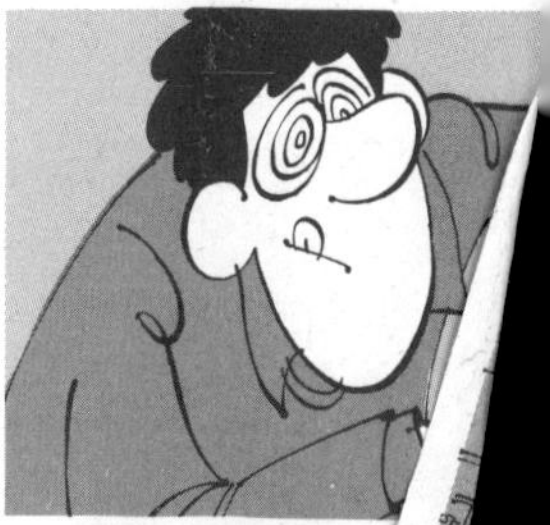

Coin-operated video g... addictive, you wind up... all your spare cash o...

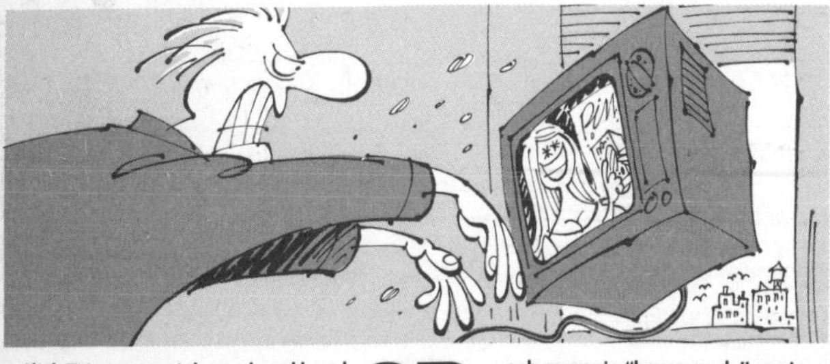

Slick TV commercials produced by ad agency weasels who know all of the "subliminal tricks" in the book... **OR** ...sub-moronic "home-made" spots put together in a half hour by the company president's brain-dead son-in-law?!!

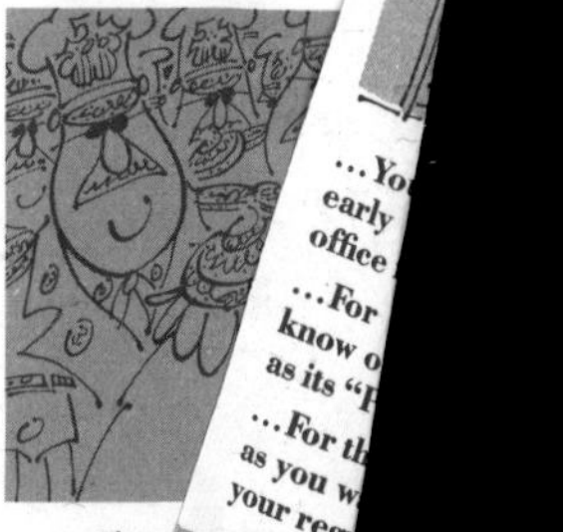

...You
early
office
...For
know o
as its "
...For th
as you w
your reg

The re...
assoc...
"nat...

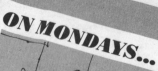

ON MONDAYS...

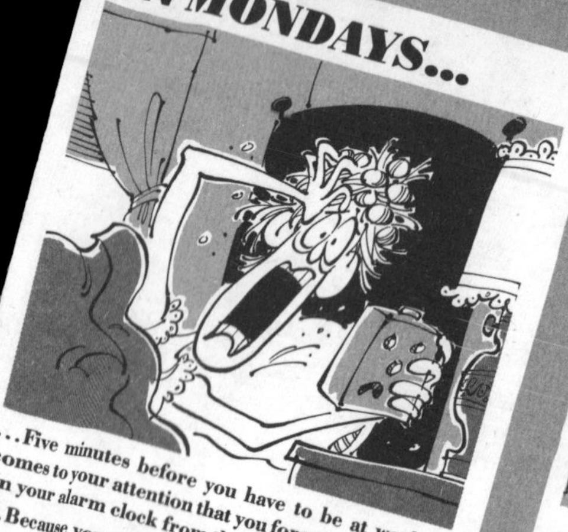

...Five minutes before you have to be at work, it comes to your attention that you forgot to click back on your alarm clock from the weekend.

...Because you never got around to doing the laundry you have to fish underwear out of the hamper.

...You step out your door to discover that the weather is a lot better than it was all weekend.

O

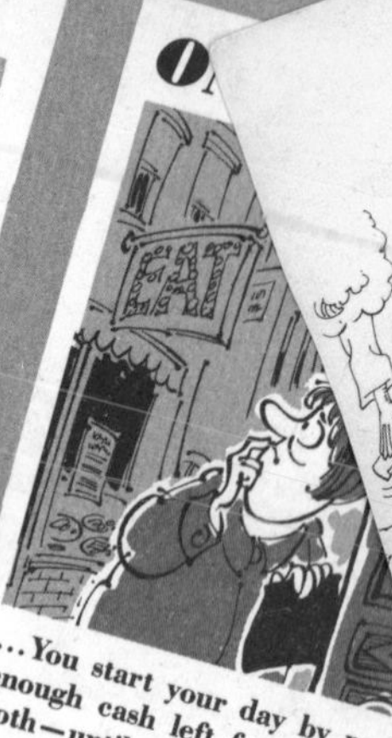
EAT

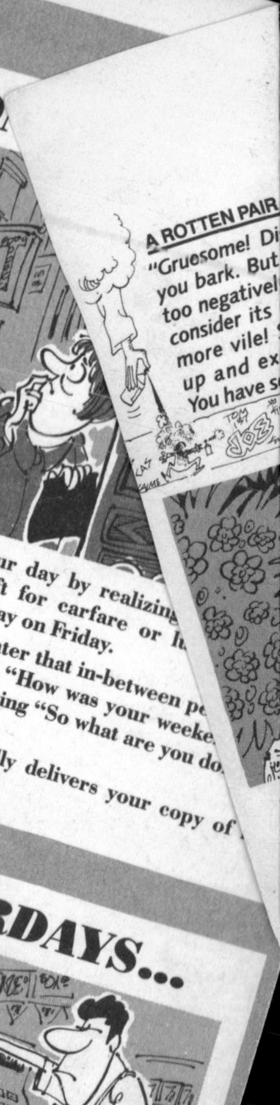
A ROTTEN PAIR
"Gruesome! Di
you bark. But
too negativel
consider its
more vile!
up and ex
You have s
TOM '87
JOB

...You start your day by realizing enough cash left for carfare or l both—until payday on Friday.

...At work, you enter that in-between pe people stop asking "How was your weeke have yet to start asking "So what are you do weekend?"

...The mailman finally delivers your copy of week's *TV Guide*.

ON FRIDAYS...

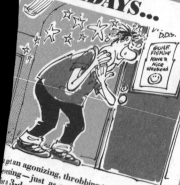

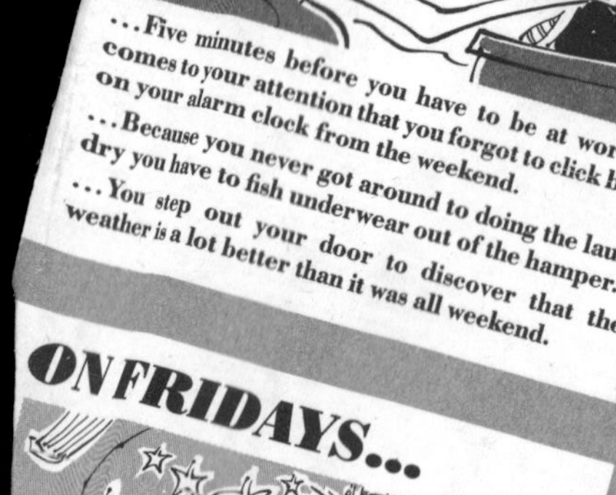
D.D.S.
GONE FISHIN'
Have a Nice Weekend

u get an agonizing, throbbing toothache in the evening—just as your dentist is leaving his for a 3-day weekend.

the umpteenth Friday in a row, you don't care *who* ABC News is planning to choose erson of the Week."

first time all week, you can stay up as late nt—but you get drowsy and fall asleep at lar time anyway.

ON SATURDAYS...

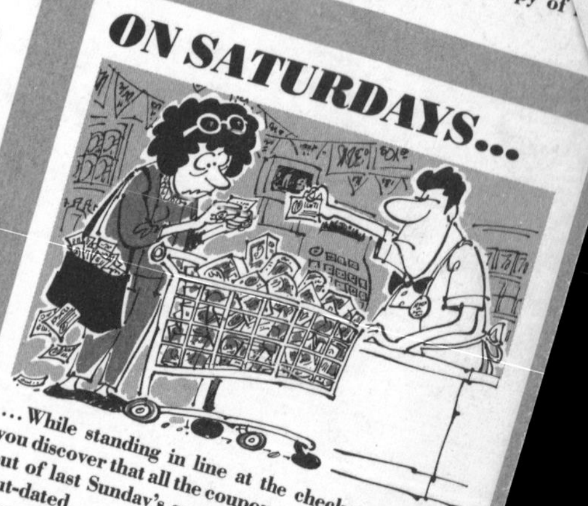

...While standing in line at the checkout counter you discover that all the coupon specials you clipped out of last Sunday's supermarket circular are now out-dated.

...Dozens of nuisance chores once again prevent you from watching the hours and hours of video tapes you've recorded over the last two months.

..You make it a point to get home in time to catch "Saturday Night Live" only to be disappointed by the show yet again.

SKS: WHICH IS
OF TWO EVILS???

WRITER: MIKE SNIDER

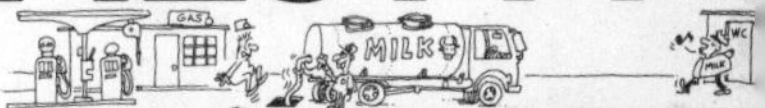

GAS
MILK
WC

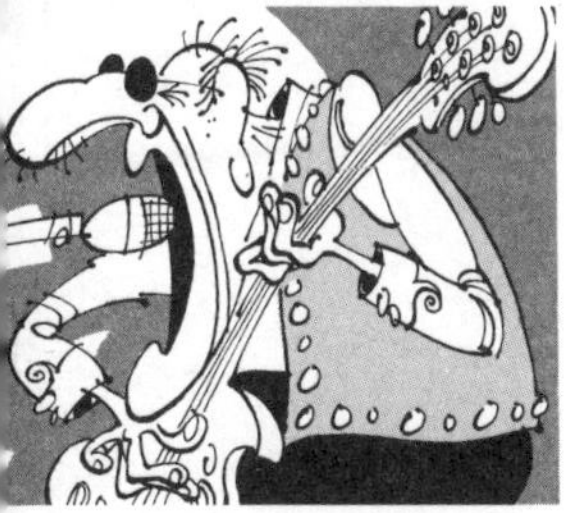

R …way-past-their-prime "legends of rock-n-roll" who expect us to believe they're still sixteen?!!

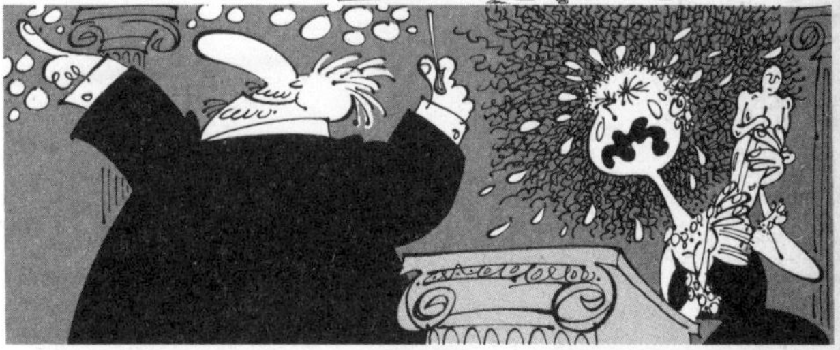

Academy-Award Show production numbers that prove Hollywood has more than its share of tone-deaf clods… **OR** …the too-horrible-to-contemplate alternative—an evening of uninterrupted acceptance speeches?!!

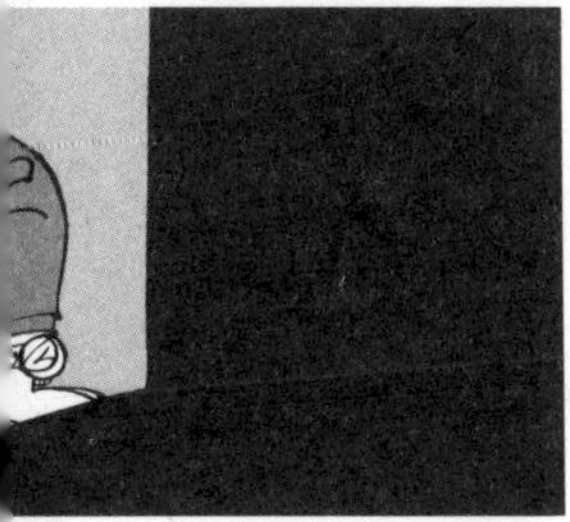

R Nintendo home versions of the same arcade favorites that merely consume all of your spare time?!!

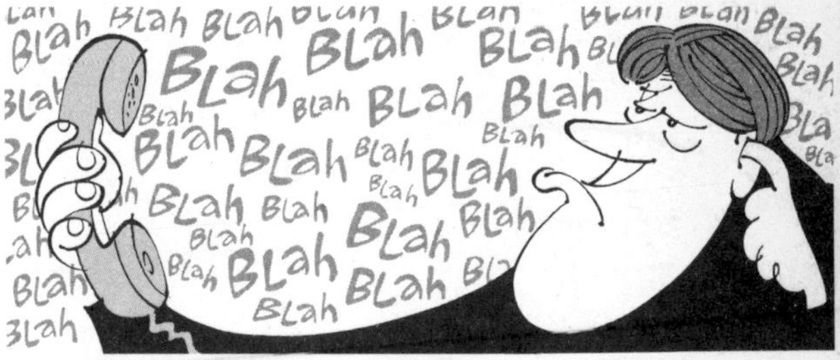

Blah Blah Blah Blah Blah
Blah Blah Blah Blah Blah
Blah Blah Blah Blah Blah
Blah Blah Blah Blah Blah

Missing important calls because bird-brain friends and relatives are always tying up your line… **OR** …getting Call Waiting—and constantly having your important calls interrupted by the same boobs?!!

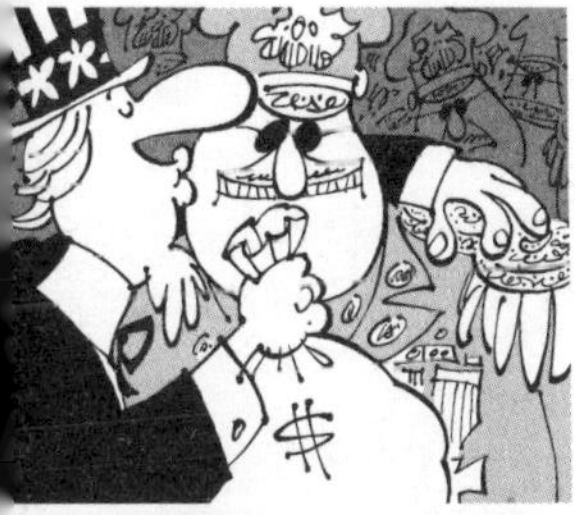

R …the even more loathsome vermin who usually wind up replacing the dictator when he's overthrown?!!

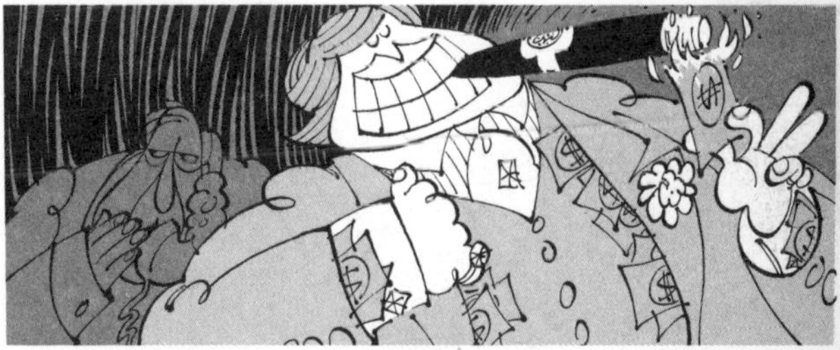

Secretive capitalists who wheel and deal in back rooms, away from the scrutiny of the public eye… **OR** …self-promoting ego-maniacs of high finance who won't stay out of the public eye for a minute?!!

THE DIABOLICAL DUNGEON DECEPTION

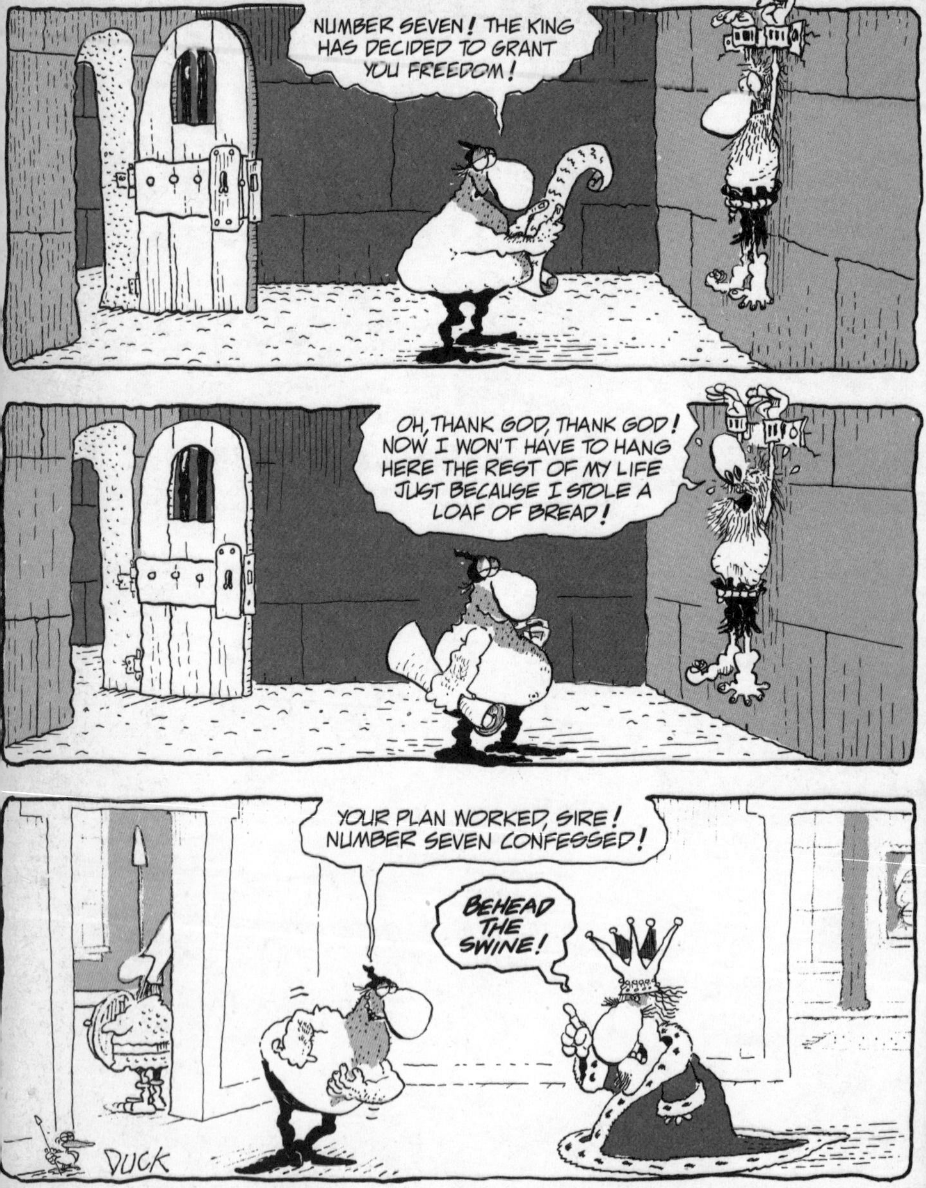
NUMBER SEVEN! THE KING HAS DECIDED TO GRANT YOU FREEDOM!
OH, THANK GOD, THANK GOD! NOW I WON'T HAVE TO HANG HERE THE REST OF MY LIFE JUST BECAUSE I STOLE A LOAF OF BREAD!
YOUR PLAN WORKED, SIRE! NUMBER SEVEN CONFESSED!
BEHEAD THE SWINE!
DUCK

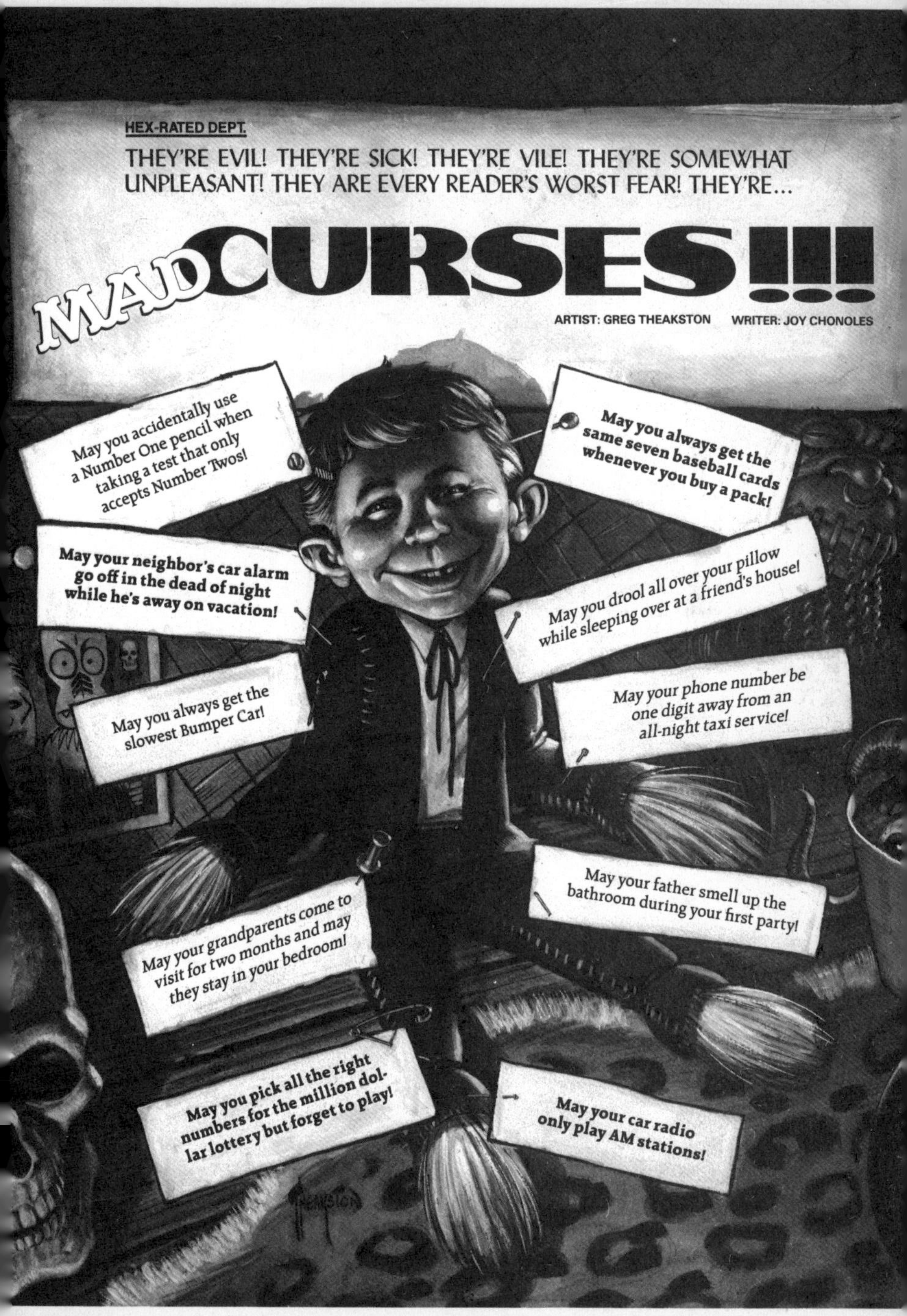
HEX-RATED DEPT.
THEY'RE EVIL! THEY'RE SICK! THEY'RE VILE! THEY'RE SOMEWHAT UNPLEASANT! THEY ARE EVERY READER'S WORST FEAR! THEY'RE...
MAD CURSES!!!!
ARTIST: GREG THEAKSTON WRITER: JOY CHONOLES
May you accidentally use a Number One pencil when taking a test that only accepts Number Twos!
May you always get the same seven baseball cards whenever you buy a pack!
May your neighbor's car alarm go off in the dead of night while he's away on vacation!
May you drool all over your pillow while sleeping over at a friend's house!
May you always get the slowest Bumper Car!
May your phone number be one digit away from an all-night taxi service!
May your father smell up the bathroom during your first party!
May your grandparents come to visit for two months and may they stay in your bedroom!
May you pick all the right numbers for the million dollar lottery but forget to play!
May your car radio only play AM stations!
THEAKSTON

A *MAD* LOOK AT SELF-

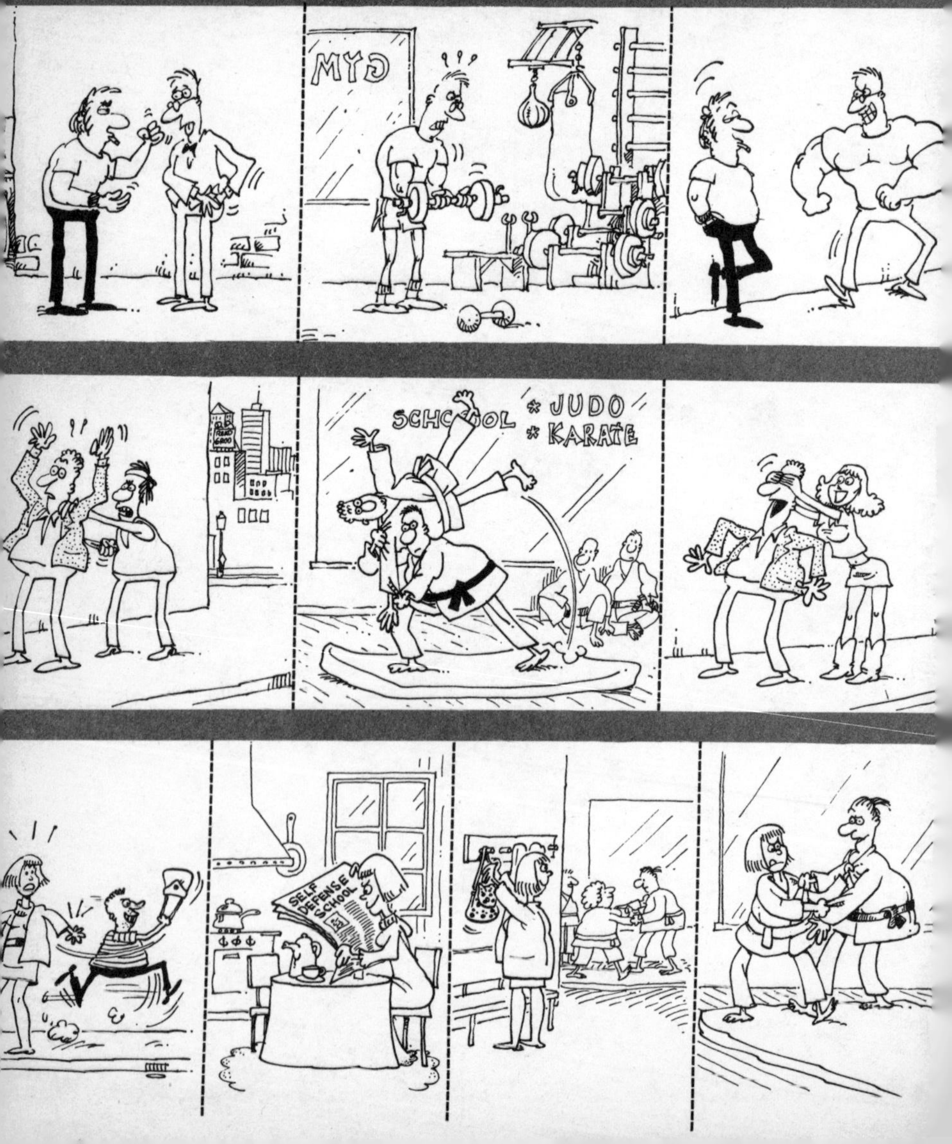
GYM
SCHOOL
* JUDO
* KARATE
SELF DEFENSE SCHOOL

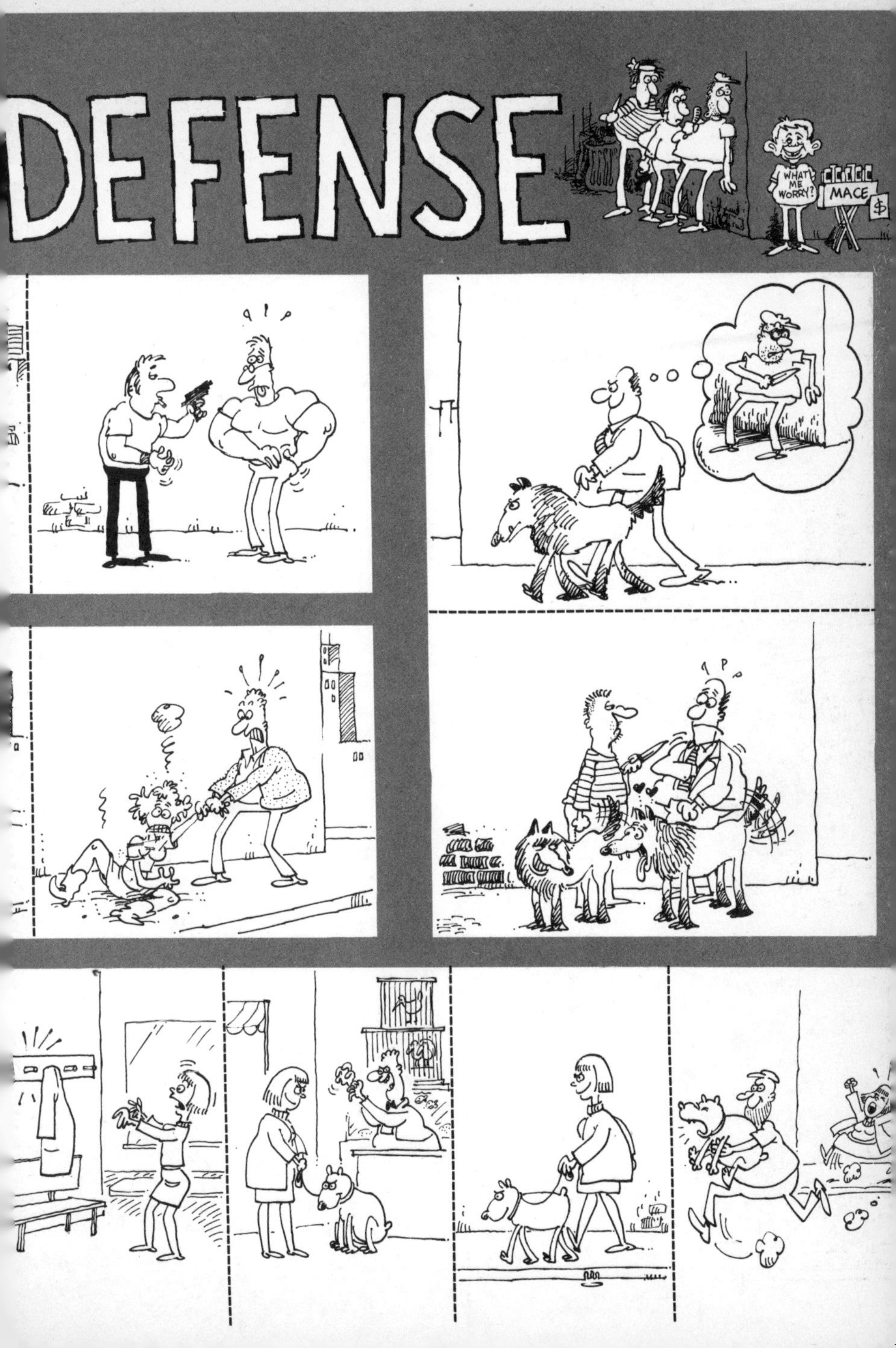

DEFENSE
WHAT ME WORRY?
MACE
$

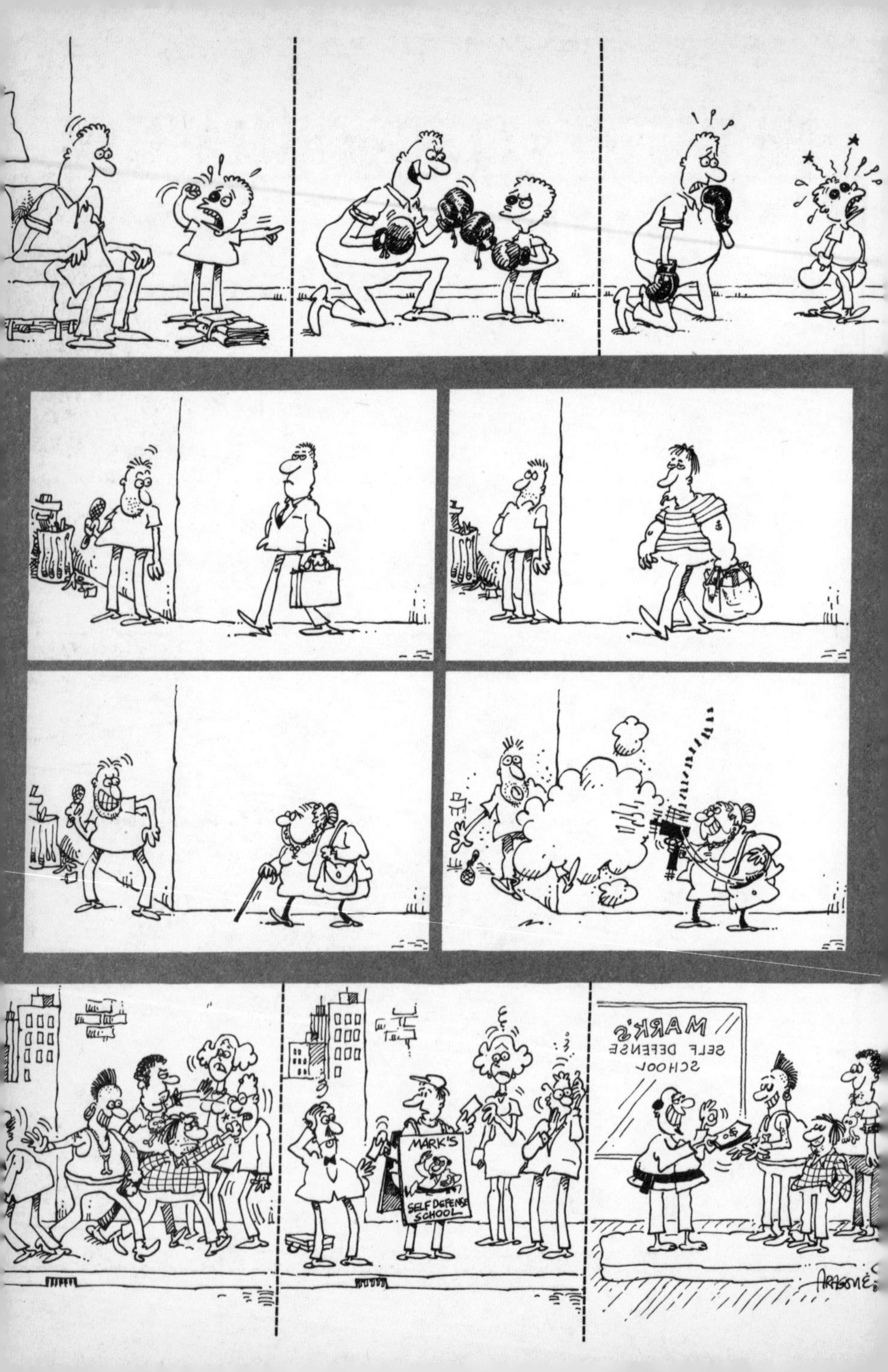
MARK'S
SELF DEFENSE
SCHOOL

TALES FROM THE DUCK SIDE DEPT.

THE HAUNTING HUNTING HULLABALOO

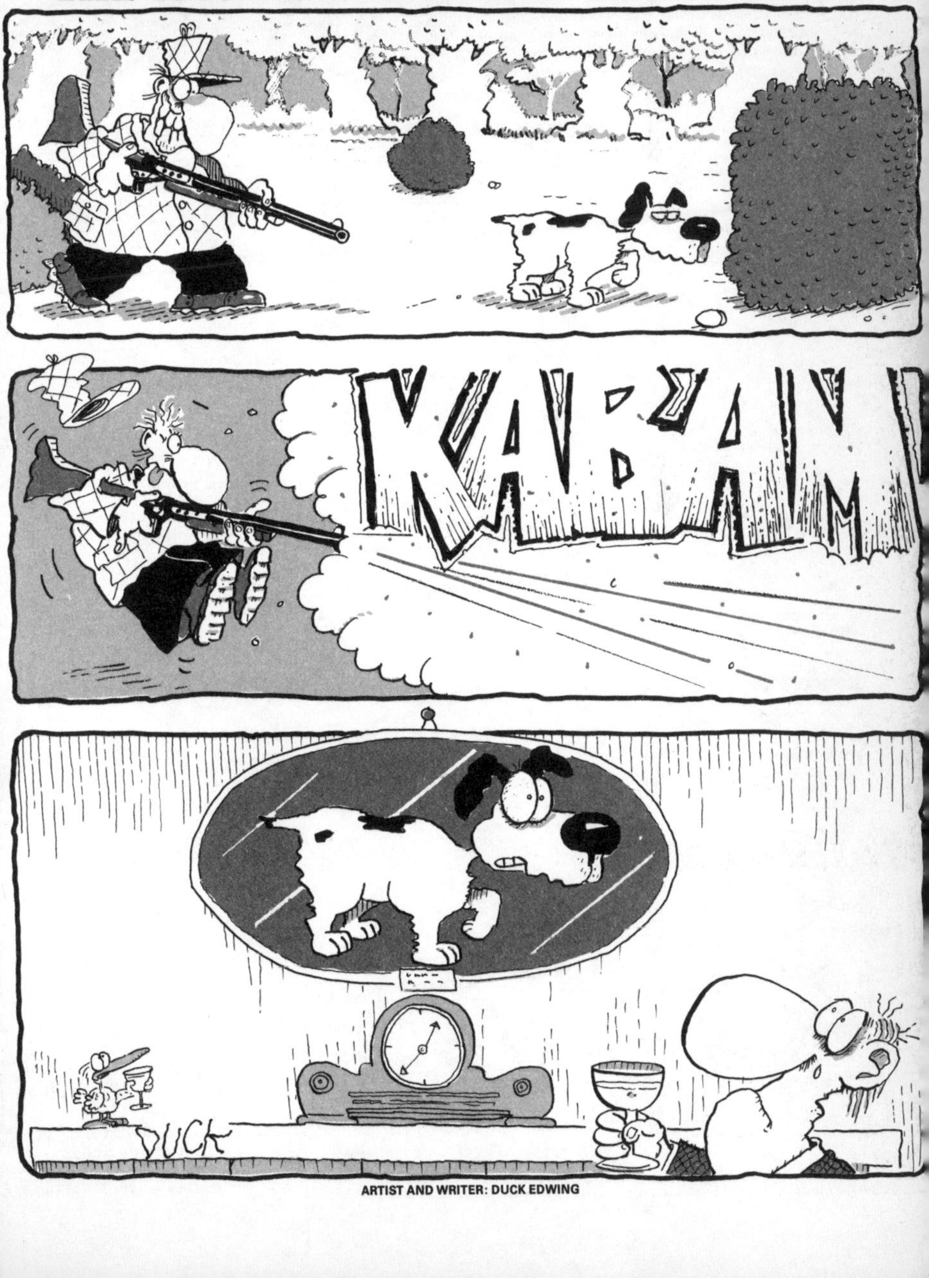
KABAM
DUCK

ARTIST AND WRITER: DUCK EDWING

FACTS EVASION DEPT.

These days we're bombarded with information from TV, books, movies, parents, teachers and even worthless humor magazines! Most times, the information is either stupid, useless, embarrassing or too late to do you any good! To see what we mean, think back and consider all of the information you were given lately. Then sit back and ask yourself...

Do You RE

ARTIST: AL JAFFE

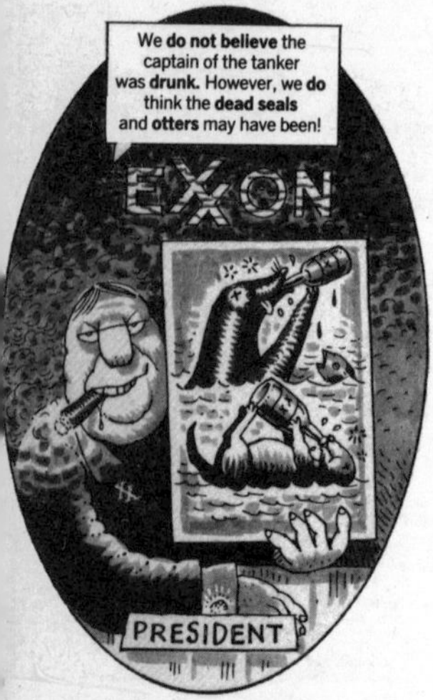

We do not believe the captain of the tanker was drunk. However, we do think the dead seals and otters may have been!
EXON
PRESIDENT

...Exxon's side of the oil spill story?

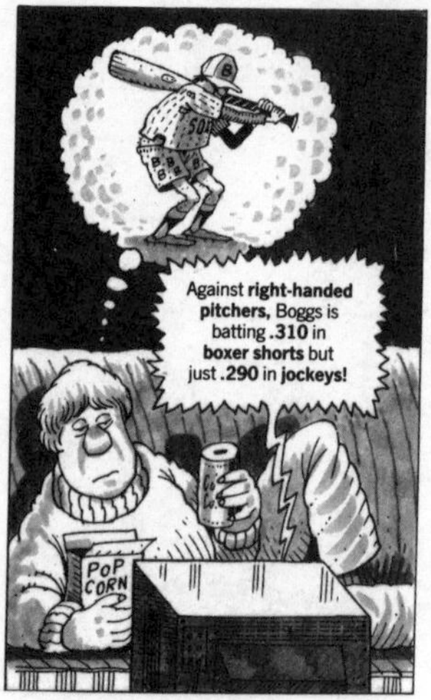

Against right-handed pitchers, Boggs is batting .310 in boxer shorts but just .290 in jockeys!
POP CORN

...most of the statistics that baseball announcers spew at you?

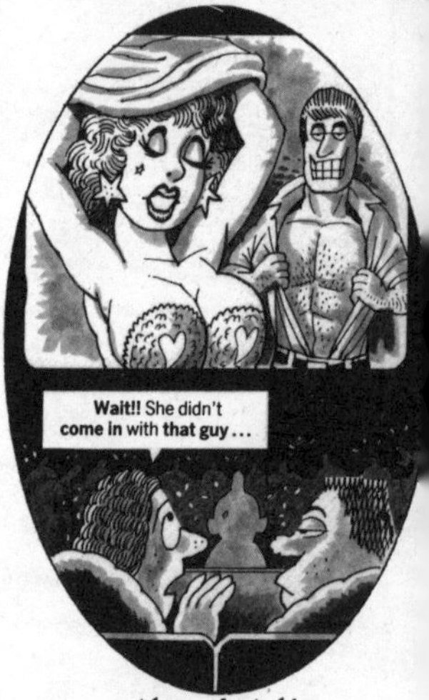

Wait!! She didn't come in with that guy...

...the plot line in a porno movie?

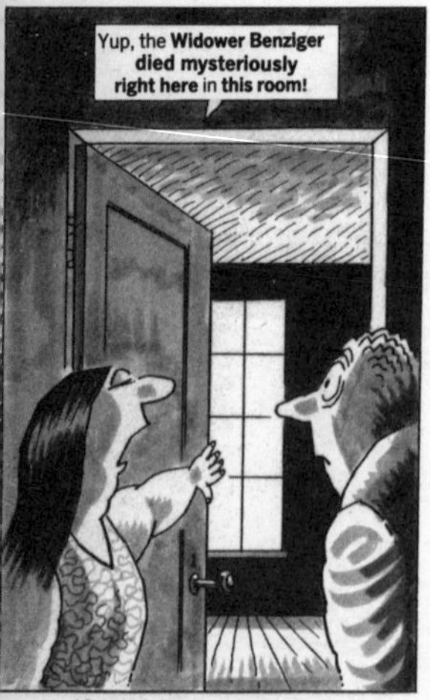

Yup, the Widower Benziger died mysteriously right here in this room!

...that some guy died in the bedroom of the apartment you just rented?

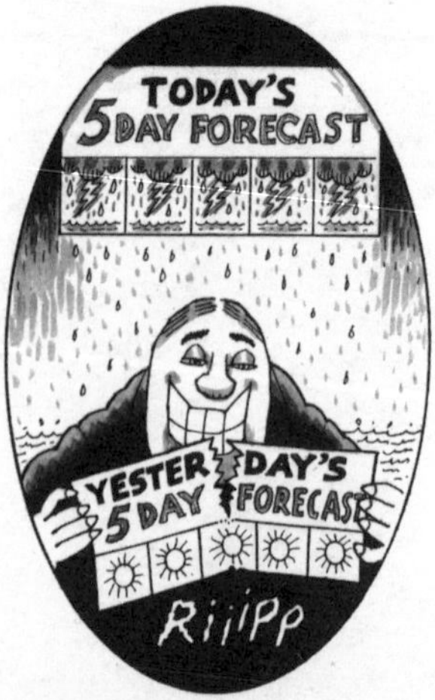

TODAY'S 5 DAY FORECAST
YESTERDAY'S 5 DAY FORECAST
RiiIPP

...the weatherman's five-day forecast, when he usually can't get it right for just one day?

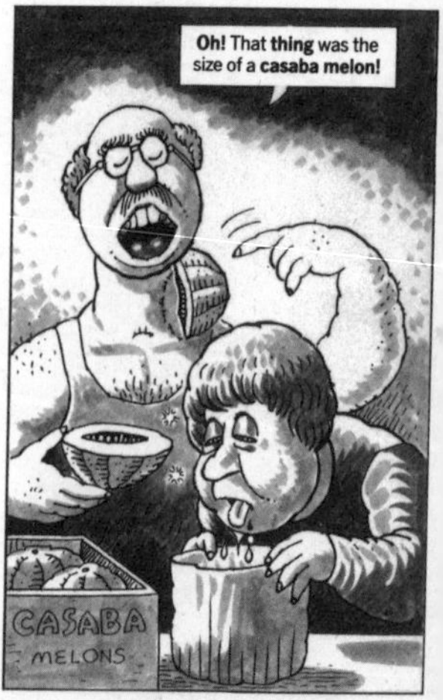

Oh! That thing was the size of a casaba melon!
CASABA MELONS

...anything about your Uncle Beppe's goiter operation?

ALLY Need To Know...

IDEA: MARY PAT LINDL WRITER: J. PRETE

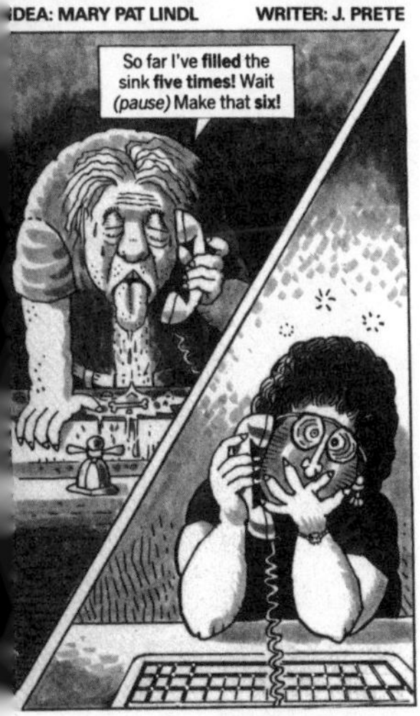

So far I've **filled** the sink **five times!** Wait *(pause)* Make that **six!**

... how many times a co-worker calling in sick threw up?

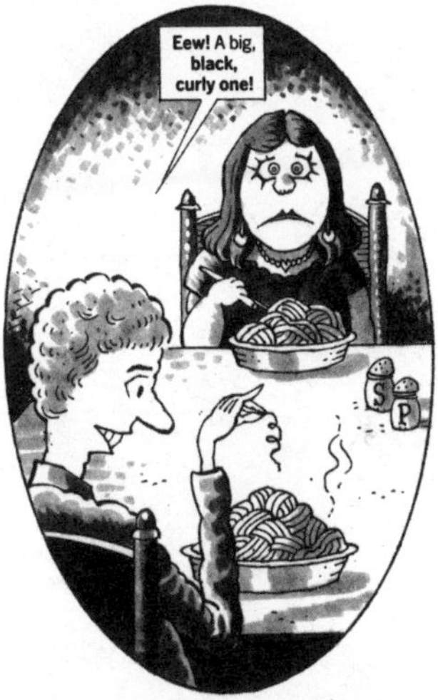

Eew! A big, **black, curly one!**
S
P

... that your dinner companion found a hair in his linguini?

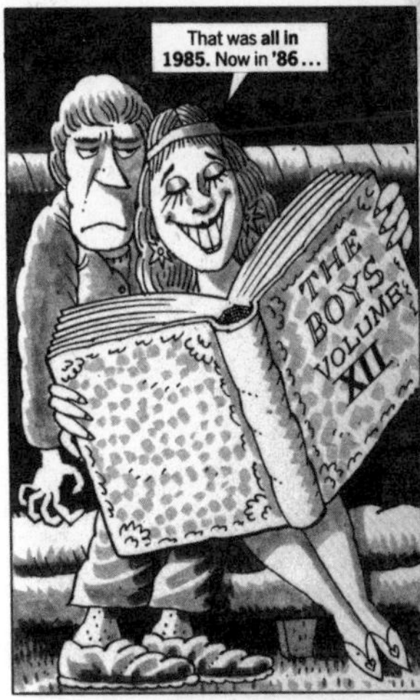

That was **all in 1985.** Now in **'86 ...**
THE BOYS VOLUME XII

... the number of guys your girl was with before you?

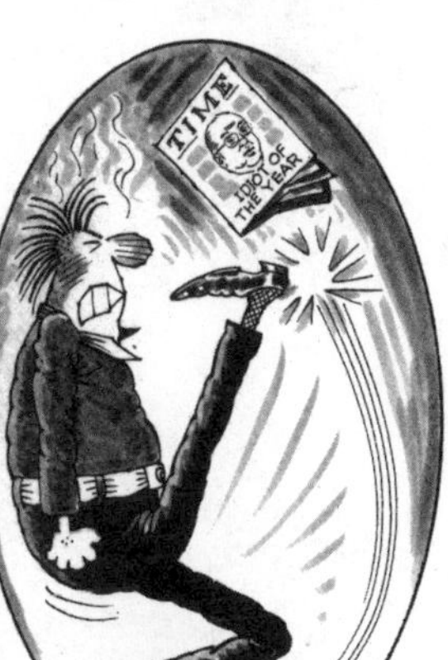

TIME
IDIOT OF THE YEAR

... that your subscription to Time magazine runs out in just 113 more issues?

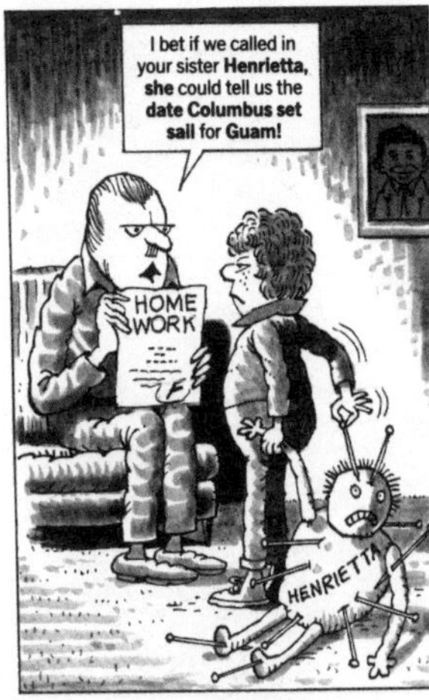

I bet if we called in your sister **Henrietta, she** could tell us the **date Columbus set sail for Guam!**
HOME WORK
F
HENRIETTA

... how much better a student your older sister was than you?

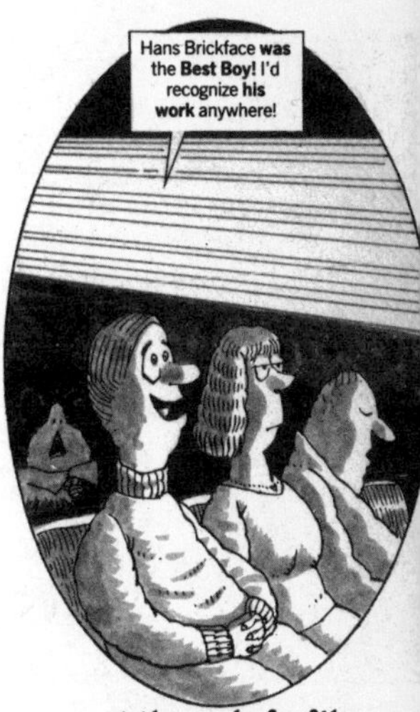

Hans Brickface **was** the **Best Boy!** I'd recognize **his work** anywhere!

... at the end of a film, who the "Best Boy" was?

BLUNDER ENLIGHTENING DEPT.

Way back in MAD #254, we presented chapter one of "The MAD 'DON'T' Book," a feature created to explain the value in knowing what not to do in a given situation. We also promised to

THE MAD "D

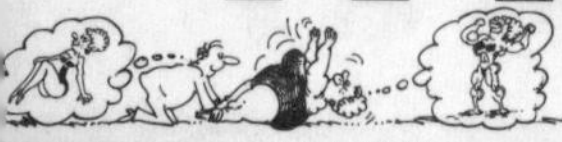

(Chapt

CHAPTER 2:
WHAT NOT TO DO ON A FIRST DATE

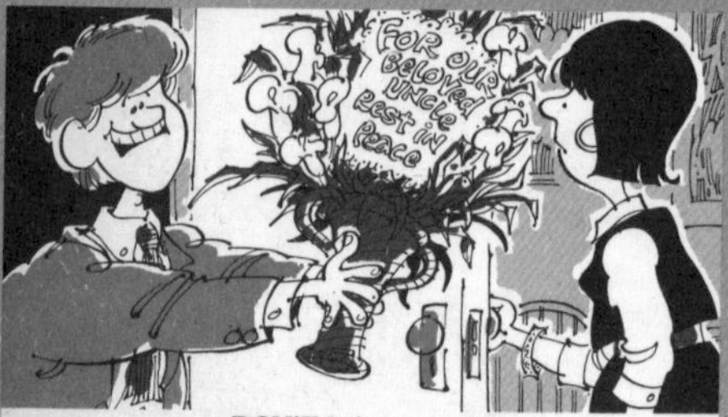
FOR OUR Beloved Uncle Rest in Peace

DON'T bring your date second-hand flowers.

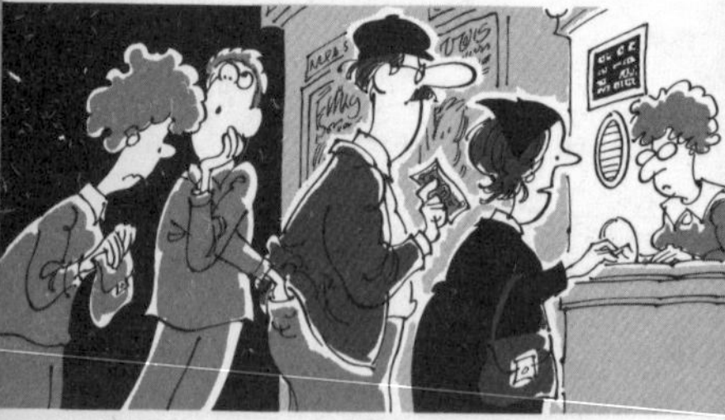

DON'T try to earn the admiration of your date by exhibiting your pickpocketing skills.

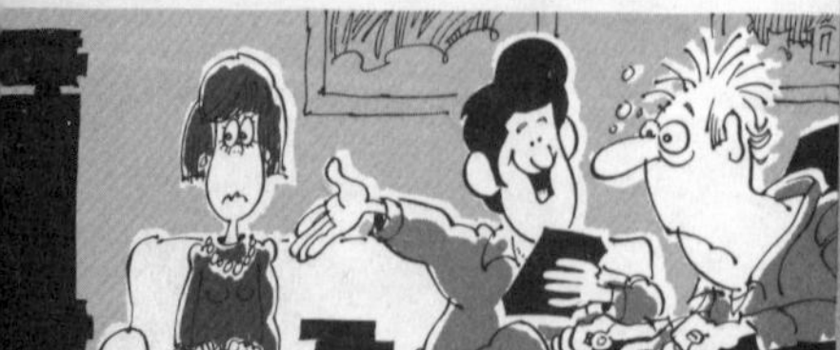

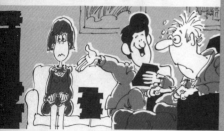

DON'T try to get on the good side of your date's father by showing off your extensive knowledge of pornographic films.

CHAPTER 3:
WHAT NOT TO DO AT A HOSPITAL

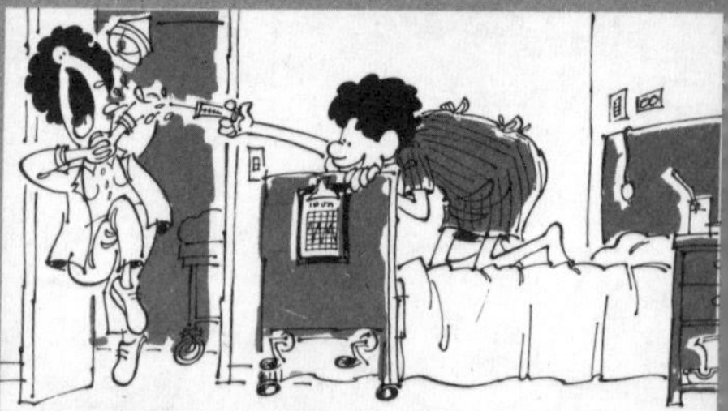

DON'T take used hypodermic needles from the trash and fashion makeshift "squirt toys" out of them.

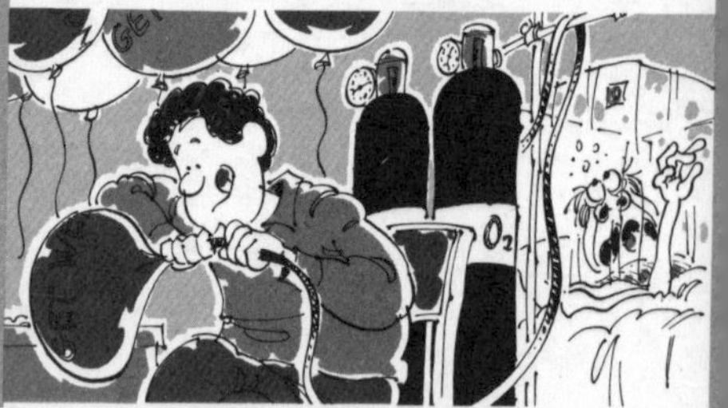

DON'T use a patient's oxygen tank to inflate a bunch of "Get Well Soon" balloons.

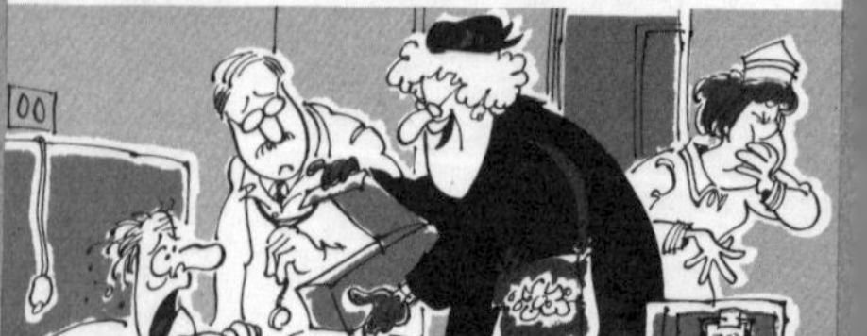

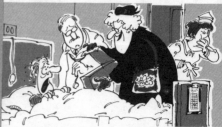

DON'T try to cheer up a convalescing friend by giving them a cake baked in the shape of the diseased organ they just had removed.

resent additional chapters in future issues, although we desperately tried not to do so! 3ut sadly, recently passed "Truth in Magazine" legislation forces us to finally publish...

ON'T" BOOK

ARTIST: PAUL COKER WRITERS: CHARLIE KADAU AND JOE RAIOLA

s 2–5)

CHAPTER 4: WHAT NOT TO DO IN A CROWDED ELEVATOR

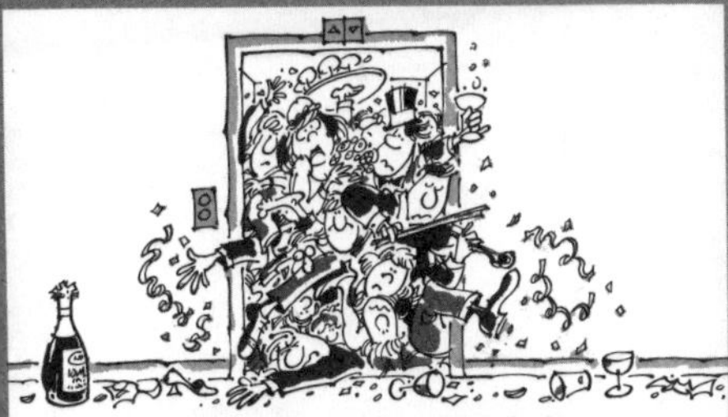

DON'T use the elevator as an intimate catering hall for your wedding reception.

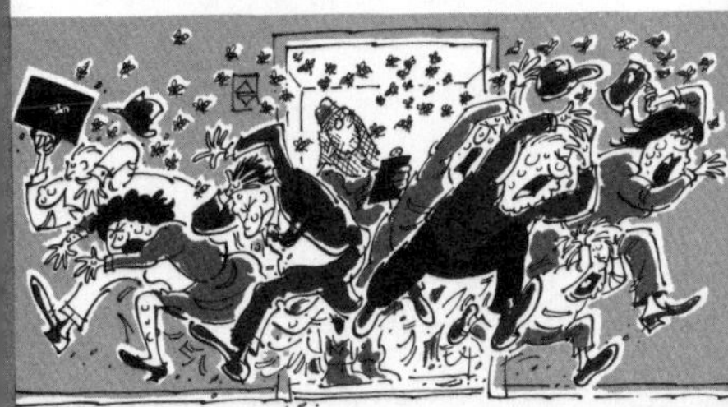

DON'T use the elevator to do research for your term paper, "The Study of Hornets in a Closed Environment."

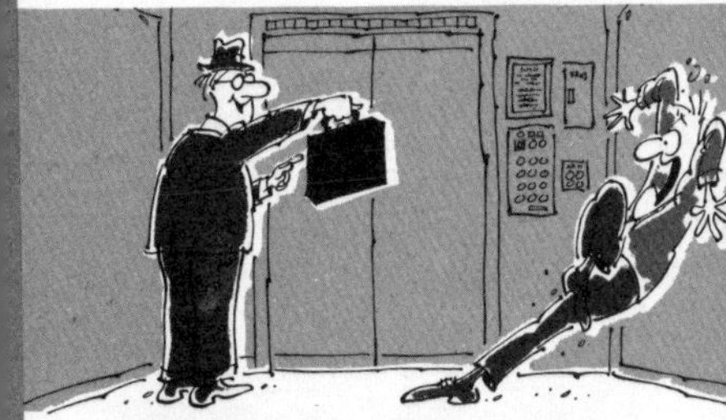

DON'T tell a stranger that the last elevator you rode in was so shaky it released all of the toxic gases you carry in your briefcase.

CHAPTER 5: WHAT NOT TO DO IN A COURTROOM

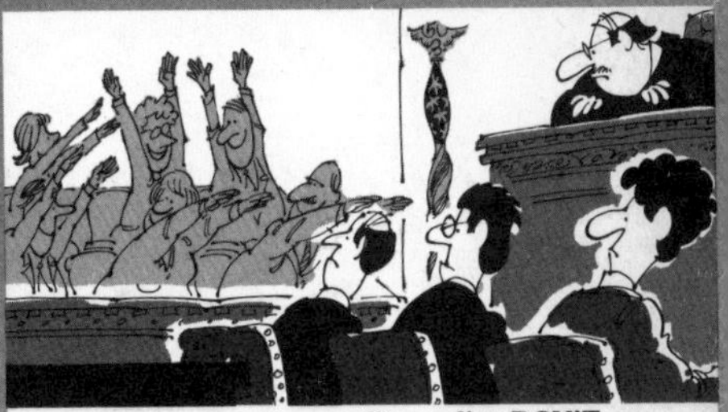

Just before declaring a guilty verdict, DON'T convince fellow jurors to join you in doing the "wave."

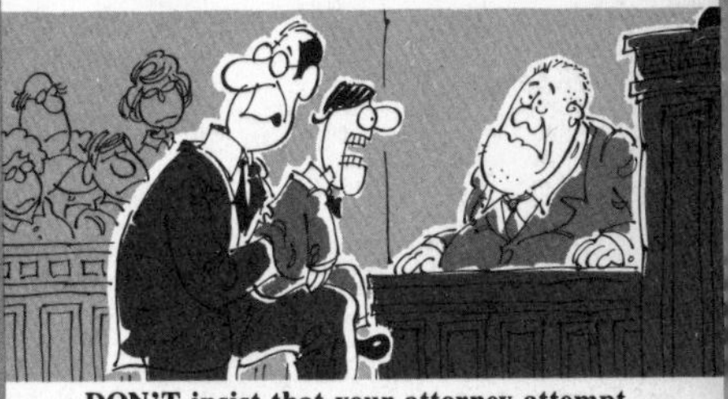

DON'T insist that your attorney attempt to trick a stubborn witness by cross-examining him with a ventriloquist's dummy.

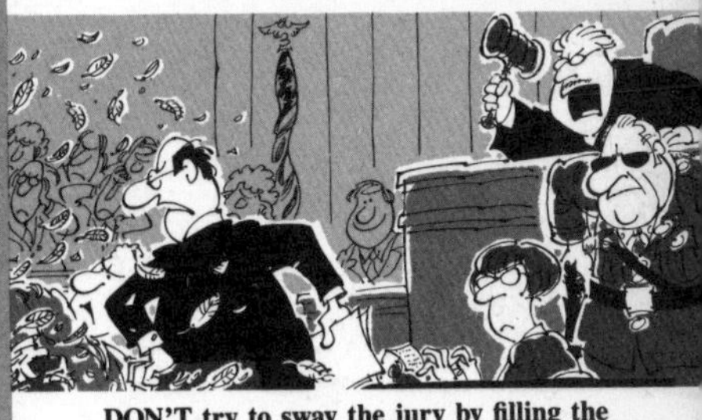

DON'T try to sway the jury by filling the courtroom with a flock of parrots, all of whom have been trained to say "not guilty."

TALES FROM THE DUCK SIDE DEPT.

THE DREADED DENTAL DEBACLE

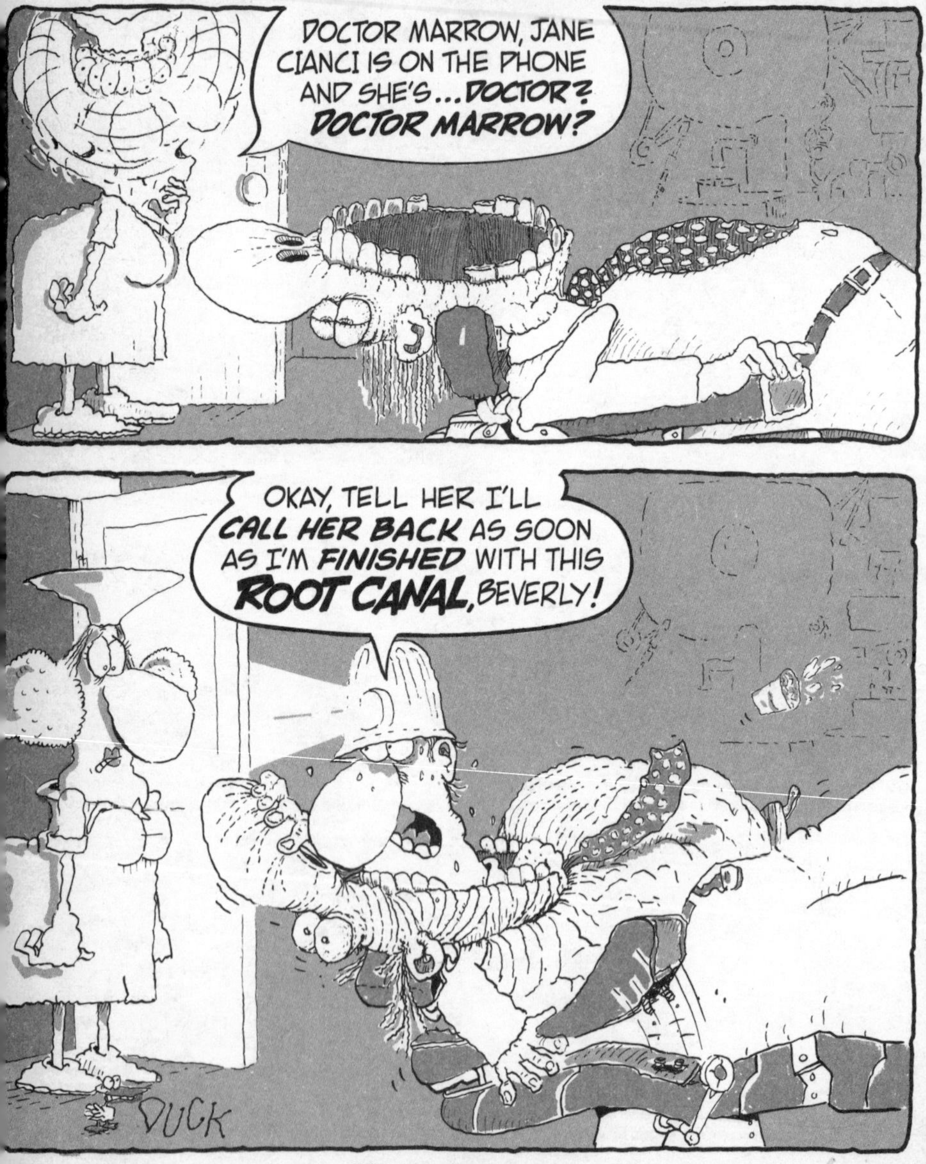
DOCTOR MARROW, JANE CIANCI IS ON THE PHONE AND SHE'S...DOCTOR? DOCTOR MARROW?
OKAY, TELL HER I'LL CALL HER BACK AS SOON AS I'M FINISHED WITH THIS ROOT CANAL, BEVERLY!
DUCK

ARTIST AND WRITER: DUCK EDWING

IT BLURTS SO BAD DEPT.

Today, government agencies, private business and frazzled individuals all have a lot of bad news to dish out that they don't want us to hear. How, then, do they do it? Simple! They bury the negative facts under a heavy layer of positive hot air! This technique of putting us in a good mood before they hit us with the awful truth is a sneaky skill that all MAD readers should learn to recognize—mainly so they can employ the same techniques themselves when the occasion arises. So join us now as we carefully examine some blatant examples we've collected of:

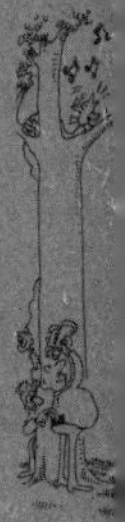

THE ART OF BREAKING BAD NEWS GENTLY

WRITER: TOM KOCH

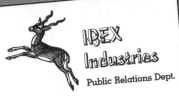

IBEX Industries

Public Relations Dept.

To All News Editors
FOR IMMEDIATE RELEASE

Ibex Industries is delighted to announce the appointment of Harley J. Pitlik, Jr., to the office of Chairman of the Board. Mr. Pitlik, a loving father as well as a college graduate, replaces C.J. Winterhorn, who retired recently after 36 years of devoted service to the company.

Ibex spokesmen said that Former Chairman Winterhorn is now enjoying a well deserved vacation in Brazil. He has purchased a comfortable villa near Rio de Janeiro with part of the $6,000,000 in company funds that he apparently saw fit to take with him.

HAVE YOUR OLD FROSTY FRIDGE SERVICED FREE

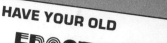

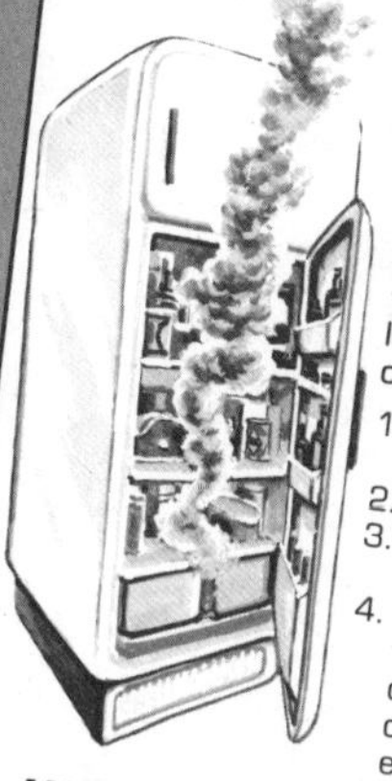

Most refrigerator companies would charge $50 or more to inspect and service their old 1988 models. Not Frosty Fridge! We don't forget our friends just because their warranties have expired. So hire a truck to bring in your old Frosty Fridge—and just look at what you'll receive with our compliments:

1. **FREE** inspection of all moving parts.
2. **FREE** oiling of door hinges.
3. **FREE** water to refill ice cube trays.
4. **FREE** replacement of N-16 valve, which the government claims is defective and could cause your refrigerator to explode.

HURRY! THIS GENEROUS OFFER MADE FOR A LIMITED TIME ONLY!

Mandamus & Fleece
Attorneys at Law

Mr. Jimmy Joe Boxford
c/o Shorty's Pinball Arcade
Beachfront Park

Dear Mr. Boxford:

Did you know that your blood type (J-Negative) is so rare that it can prove kinship to lost relatives you didn't even know you had? A Michigan judge recently decided a $500,000 inheritance case in favor of a lad like you, just because he and his uncle both had J-Negative blood.

Based on that Michigan decision, we soon hope to unite you legally with your "missing" infant son. His mother's paternity suit against you, which will bring about that happy event, begins at 10 A.M. on Sept. 23 in Circuit Court. Please be there so I can congratulate you personally on becoming a father.

Yours truly,

Fillmore Fleece

Fillmore Fleece

Deer Mom and Dad,
I am fine. The reeson ͡
boam to go Camping our ͡
me desert with sum guys ͡
met. They are neet guys. ͡
Cook meels for ~~xx~~ me ou ͡
Also, they say you shoo ͡
Put $50,000 in the Fon ͡
booth by the Bus Stashio ͡
~~at~~ wonce. If you doant, ͡
They say they will stop cook ͡
Meals for me outdoors and wil ͡
leave me hear to rot. ͡
Luv, Sto

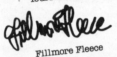

AMERICAN OINTMENT WORKS, INC.
REPORT TO STOCKHOLDERS-
A MESSAGE
FROM YOUR PRESIDENT

Successful efforts by Management to slash plant maintenance and operating costs highlighted the brilliant fiscal year just completed by American Ointment. Target goals were far surpassed as the annual outlay for utility service was cut by 87 per-cent. Similar encouraging reductions were made in purchases of washroom towels and new pencils.

The deep cuts were primarily attributable to the permanent closing of our main factory in April. Department heads optimistically look forward to even bigger cost reductions this year, once our company has gone out of business altogether.

**WHILE YOU
WERE OUT**

TIME
12:30 pm

MESSAGE

Your wife wants
you to bring home
romantic incense,
wine and a Phil
Collins CD. She
says they'll help
you make out with
some new babe,
now that she's
leaving you.

PUBLIC NOTICE

Commuting time between this locality and downtown will soon be cut in half, thanks to construction of the projected Suburbia Freeway. Surveys indicate that the easier access will cause most home values in this area to double. The few homes which will not enjoy this phenomenal increase are those which must be torn down to make room for the Freeway. Fortunately, that only includes the homes in this block. Please be a good neighbor and move your junk out by Thursday so the bulldozer crews can begin their community improvement work.

FORDYCE PLANCHET CORP.
ELKPATH, IDAHO

OFFICE OF THE PRESIDENT

Dear Employee:

Sometimes, it pays to count our blessings. That's why I am taking a moment to remind you that the community where we all work is in the heart of a natural wonderland that abounds in fish and game.

If you're like me, you probably wish you had more time to enjoy outdoor pursuits. Now, thanks to the loss of the Snively Lumber account, you'll have unlimited free time following your early retirement. I'll be filled with envy as I picture you cleaning out your locker and leaving this stuffy building forever by 5 P.M. next Friday.

J. L. Fordyce III

Signed by Emma Lu Vitsman for Mr. Fordyce, who is out of town on vacation

A WARM INVITATION TO ALL!!!

Local residents are cordially invited to a free lecture by Police Chief Hugh Newby at the High School next Tuesday evening. The Chief's subject will be, "Making Your Home More Secure." Cookies and Dr. Pepper will be served afterward.

This helpful talk consists of easy-to-follow advice for installing dead bolts, window latches and similar home improvements that may protect citizens from the four maniacs who escaped from the State Work Farm last night and reportedly are heading this way.

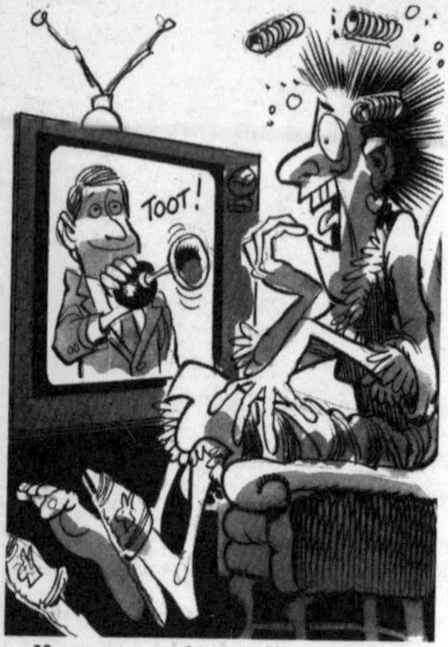
TOOT!

If you get goosebumps when a *Home Shopping Network* seller gives you a "toot"... ***GET A LIFE!!!!!!!!!!!!***

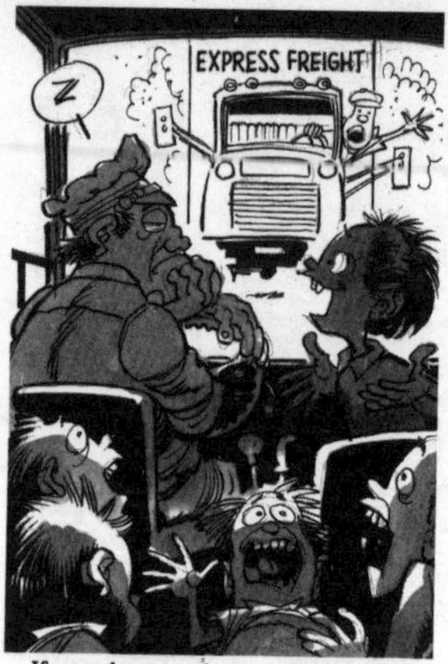
Z
EXPRESS FREIGHT

If you always make it a point to sit up front on a bus so you can "chat" with the driver... ***GET A LIFE!!!!!!!!***

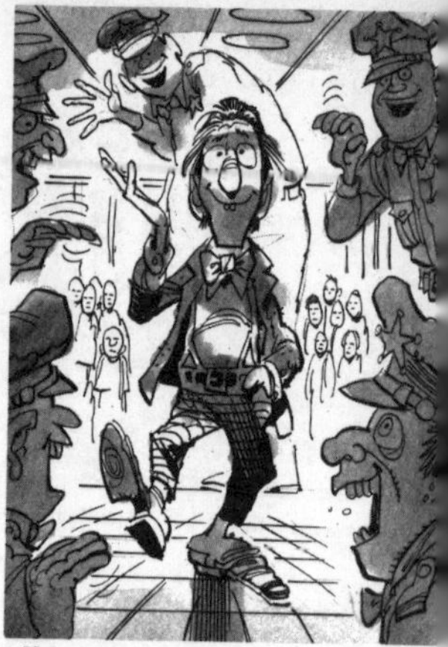

If you are on a first-name basis with all of the security guards at your local shopping mall... ***GET A LIFE!!!!!***

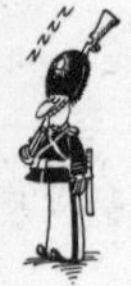

TAKING A SCHLEP IN THE RIGHT DIRECTION DEPT.

There are basically two kinds of people in the world: those who lead rich, exciting lives and those who do not. What group are you in? We're betting, based on the fact you're reading this intro, that you're part of the group that does not—the losers, the sticks-in-the-mud... the dull dweebs! Well, MAD wants to help you change! We're offering the following examples in the hope that they will motivate you to finally get off your butt, hold your head high and go out there and...

GET

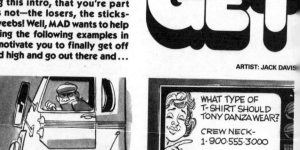

ARTIST: JACK DAVIS

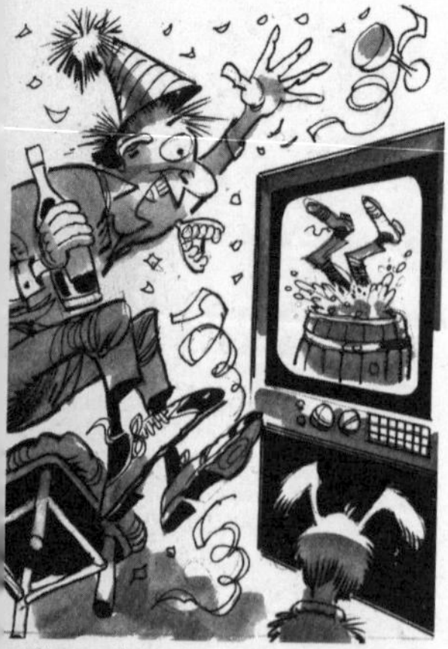

If you only need to catch the episode where Mr. Drysdale falls into Granny's vat of homemade possum-fat soap to complete your "Beverly Hillbillies" checklist... ***GET A LIFE!!!!!!!!!!!!!***

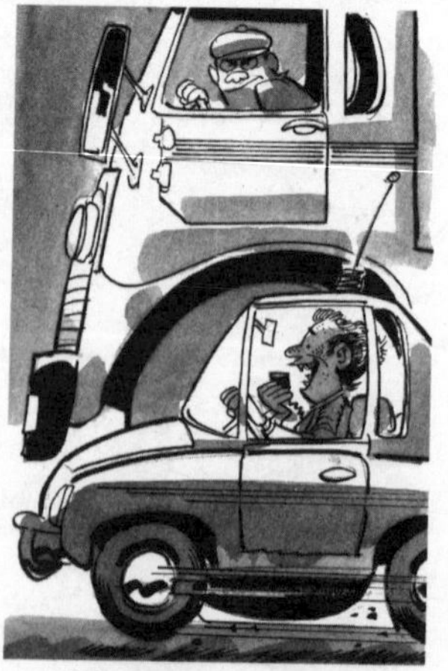

If you still own and operate a C.B. radio and you are not a licensed, interstate truck driver... ***GET A LIFE!!!!!!!!!***

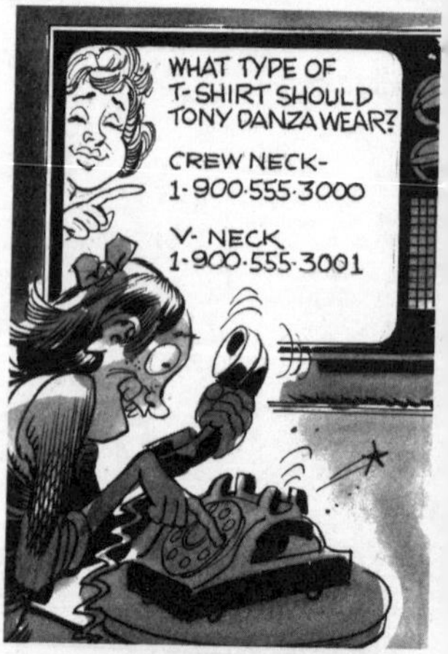
WHAT TYPE OF T-SHIRT SHOULD TONY DANZA WEAR?
CREW NECK- 1-900-555-3000
V- NECK 1-900-555-3001

If your monthly phone bill includes over $75 worth of calls to "Entertainment Tonight" 900# Opinion Polls... ***GET A LIFE!!!!!!!!!!!!!!!***

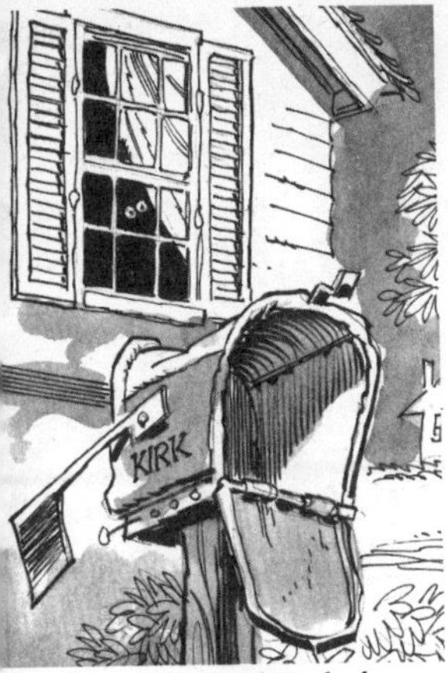
KIRK

If you eagerly anticipate the day your jury duty notice arrives in the mail . . . ***GET A LIFE!!!!!!!!!!!!***

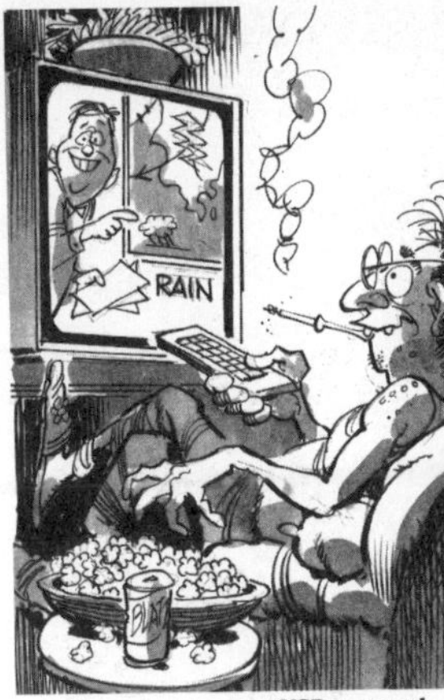
RAIN

If you program your VCR to record *The Weather Channel* while you're not at home . . . ***GET A LIFE!!!!!!!!!***

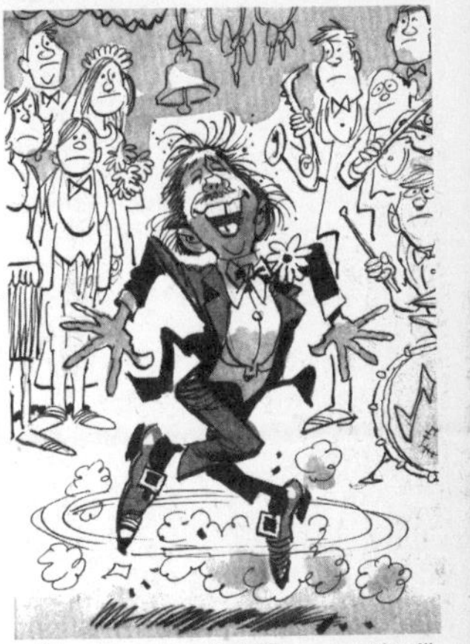

If you've ever yelled "One more time!" to a wedding band that just finished playing "The Alley Cat" . . . ***GET A LIFE!!***

A LIFE !!!!!!!!!

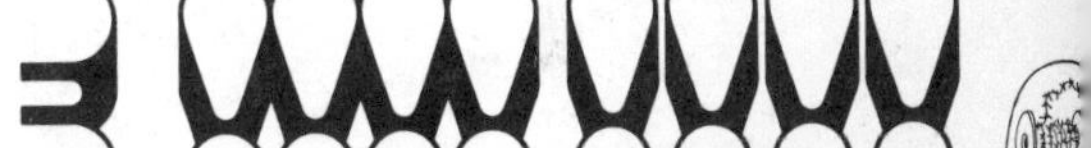
NYLON
NYLON

WRITER: CHARLIE KADAU

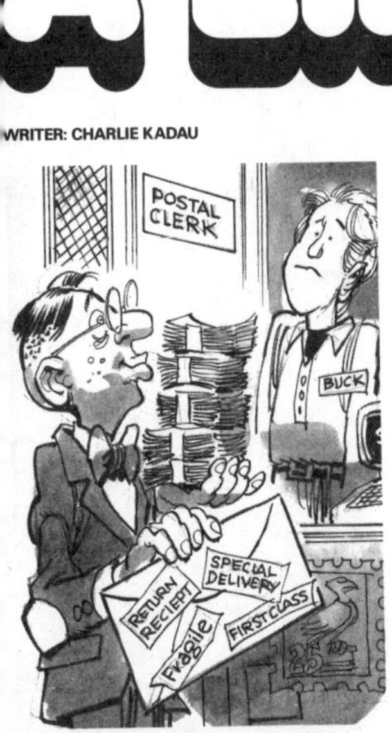
POSTAL CLERK
BUCK
SPECIAL DELIVERY
RETURN RECIEPT
Fragile
FIRST CLASS

If you mail back your Publisher's Clearing House Sweepstakes entry form registered, return receipt requested . . . ***GET A LIFE!!!!!!!!!!***

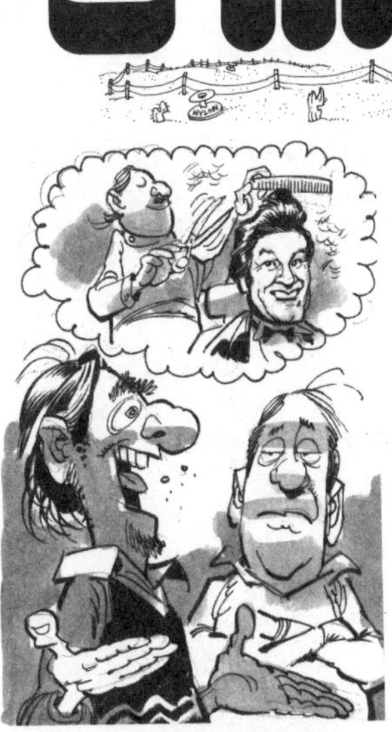

If you've ever bragged to anyone that your next door neighbor's best friend is Wink Martindale's barber . . . ***GET A LIFE!!!!!!!!!!!!***

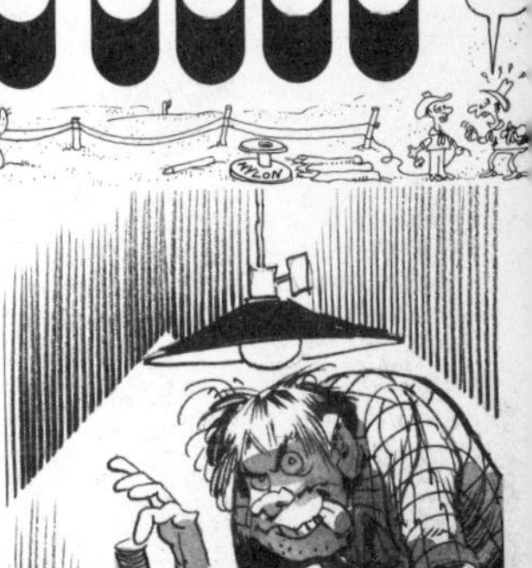

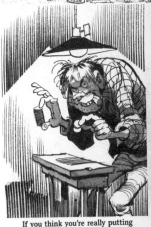

If you think you're really putting one over on your bank by cleverly placing two Canadian cents in the centers of your rolls of saved-up pennies . . . ***GET A LIFE!!!!!!!!!!!!!!!***

RECALL WAITING DEPT.

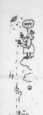

Spend two minutes with your grandparents and you realize their favorite phrase is "When I Was Your Age..." They can drive you nuts with their recollections! But here's the problem: EVERY generation likes to talk about when they were young! And in just a scant 40-50 years, today's youngsters will be the babblers—boring kids with *their* reminiscing! What will their stories be like? Here's...

"WHEN I W

TODAY'S KIDS W

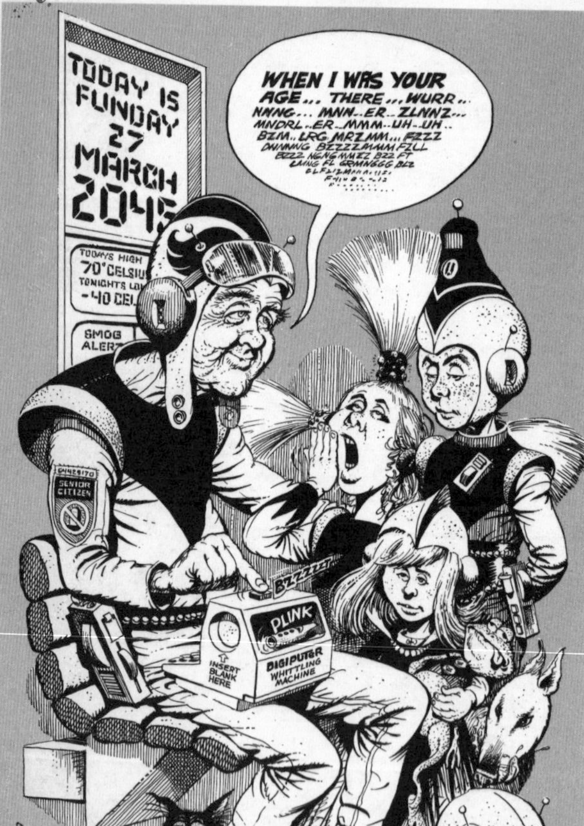
TODAY IS FUNDAY 27 MARCH 2045
TODAYS HIGH 70° CELSIU
TONIGHTS LO -40 CEL
SMOG ALERT
WHEN I WAS YOUR AGE... THERE... WURR.. NNNG... MNN..ER..ZLNNZ... MNDRL..ER..MMM..UH..UH.. BZM..LRG MRZMM... FZZZ DNNNNG BZZZZMMM FZLL BZZZ NGNGMMZZ BZZ FT
SENIOR CITIZEN
BZZZZZT
PLINK
INSERT BLANK HERE
DIGIPUTER WHITTLING MACHINE
G. WOODBRIDGE

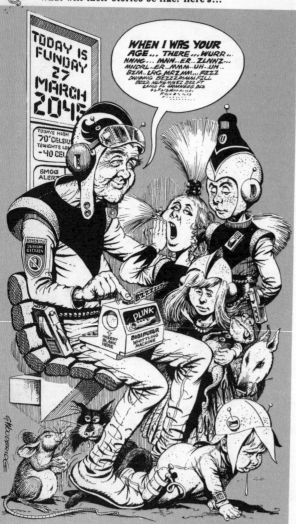

ARTIST: GEORGE WOODBRIDGE **WRITER: MIKE SNIDER**

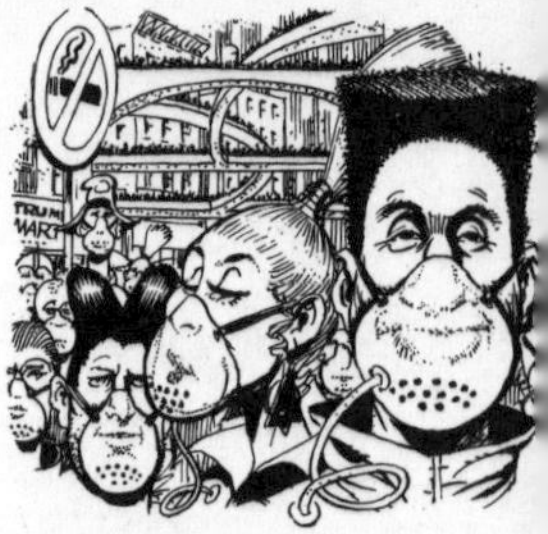

When I Was Your Age...oxygen masks were things only sick people wore!

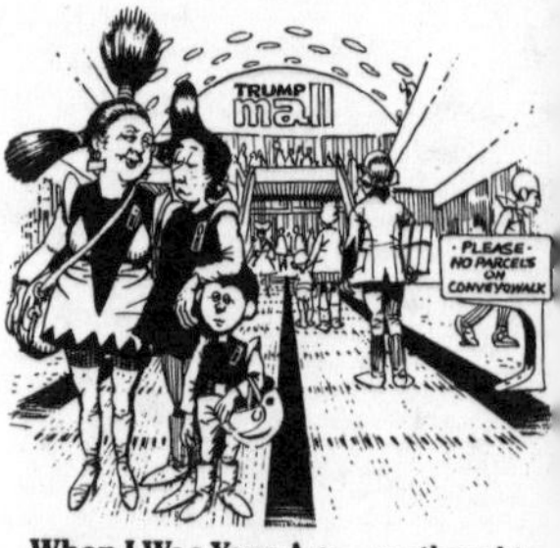
TRUMP mall
PLEASE NO PARCELS ON CONVEYOWALK

When I Was Your Age...we thought nothing of walking from one end of the mall to the other!

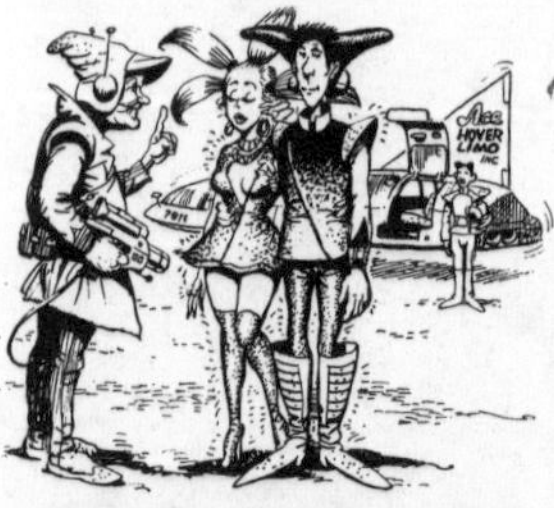
Ace HOVER LIMO INC.

When I Was Your Age...I spent only $1,000 on Prom Night—and had just as good a time as the kids who spent the big bucks!

S YOUR AGE..." STORIES BE TELLING THEIR GRANDCHILDREN

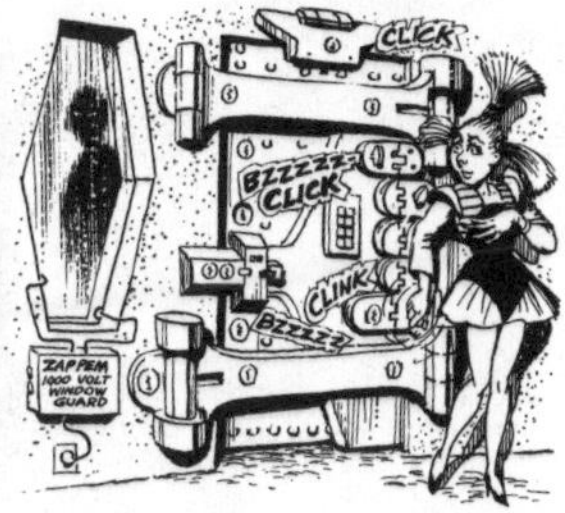
CLICK
BZZZZZ CLICK
CLINK
BZZZZZ
ZAPPEM 1000 VOLT WINDOW GUARD

When I Was Your Age...folks only needed **three** deadbolts to lock their doors!

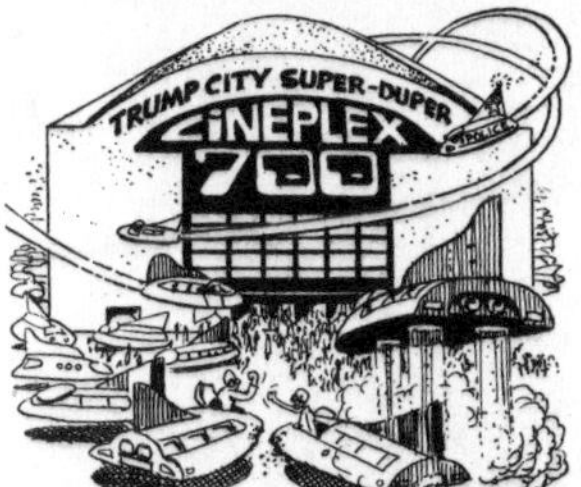
TRUMP CITY SUPER-DUPER
CINEPLEX
700

When I Was Your Age...they only had **ten** movie screens in one theatre!

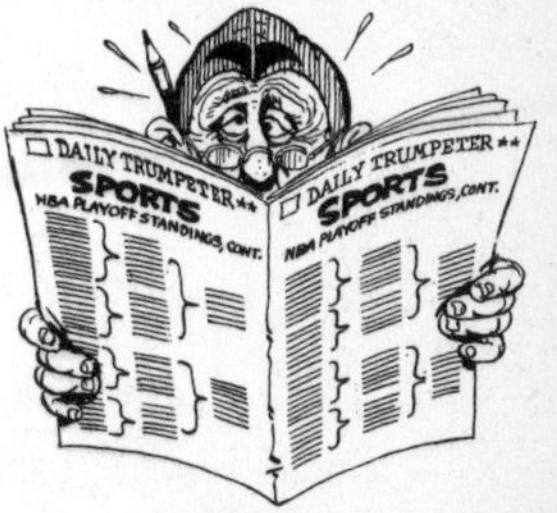
DAILY TRUMPETER
SPORTS
NBA PLAYOFF STANDINGS, CONT.
DAILY TRUMPETER
SPORTS
NBA PLAYOFF STANDINGS, CONT.

When I Was Your Age...only **½** the teams in the NBA made it to the playoffs!

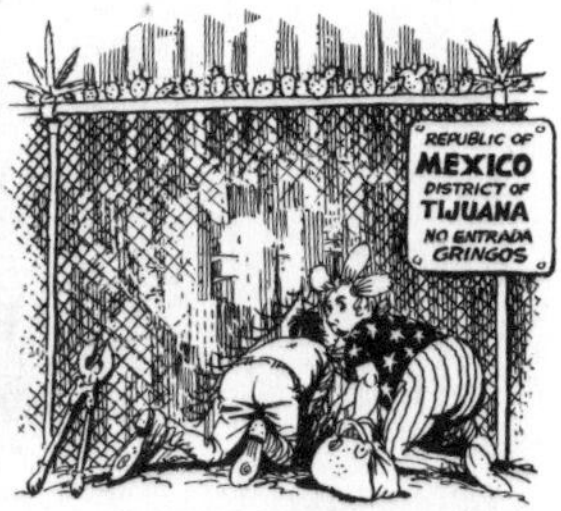
REPUBLIC OF
MEXICO
DISTRICT OF
TIJUANA
NO ENTRADA
GRINGOS

When I Was Your Age...it was the **Mexicans** who snuck into **America** to get the decent-paying jobs!

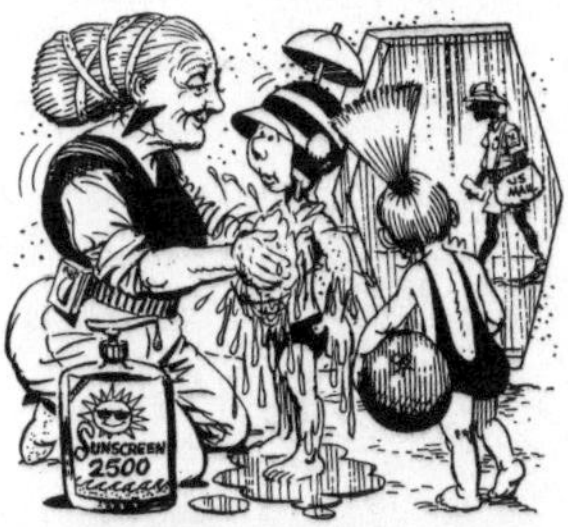
SUNSCREEN
2500

When I Was Your Age...we had a thing called **"the ozone layer"** to protect us from the sun!

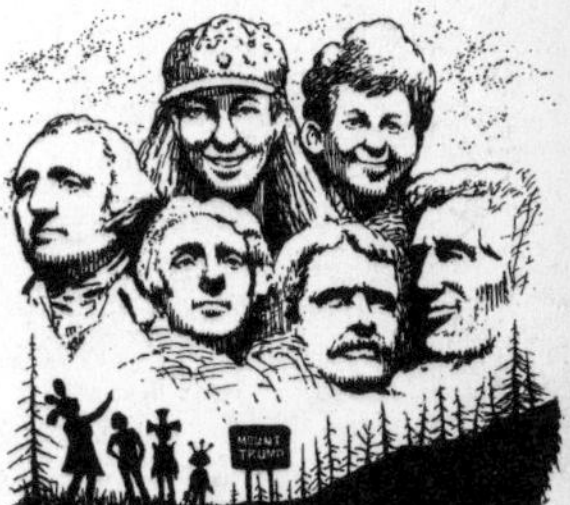
MOUNT TRUMP

When I Was Your Age...Debbie Gibson and Fred Savage hadn't even **gotten** into **politics** yet!

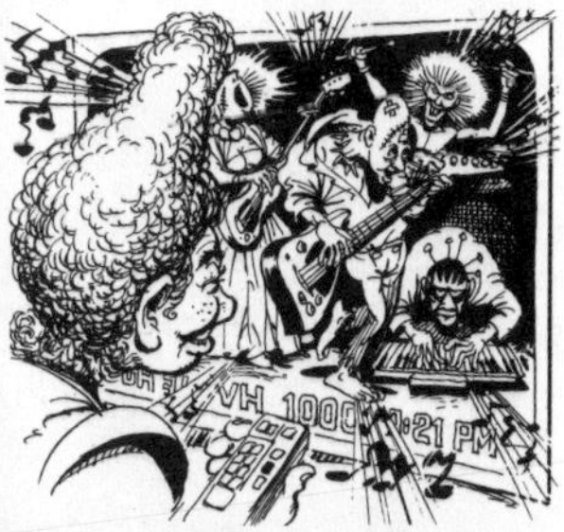
VH 1000

When I Was Your Age...we had Tone Loc, DJ Jazzy Jeff and the Beastie Boys—now there were some **great songwriters**!

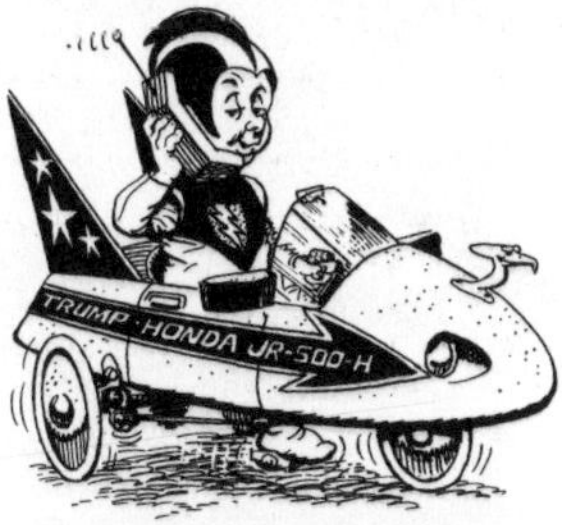
TRUMP-HONDA JR-500-H

When I Was Your Age...our family was so poor, we could only afford to put a phone in **one** of our cars!

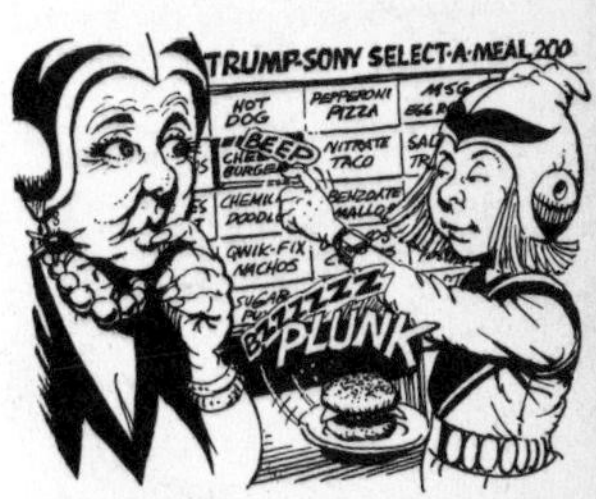
TRUMP-SONY SELECT-A-MEAL 200
HOT DOG
PEPPERONI PIZZA
NITRATE TACO
BEEP
QUIK-FIX NACHOS
PLUNK

When I Was Your Age...Mom **always** made us home-cooked meals—no matter **how** many minutes she had to sweat over the microwave!!!

"You gotta be in it to win it," "All you need is a dollar and a dream," and o and on. Lotteries are big business these days and they run catchy slogans t get you to play. "For a buck, what the—heck!" Well, you've got nothing (much

Some Truly Joy Could Do If You

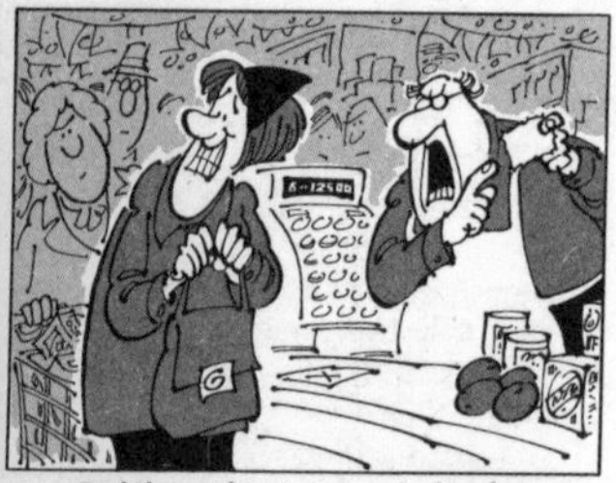

End the embarrassment of trying to pass "10¢ OFF" coupons that you know have already expired.

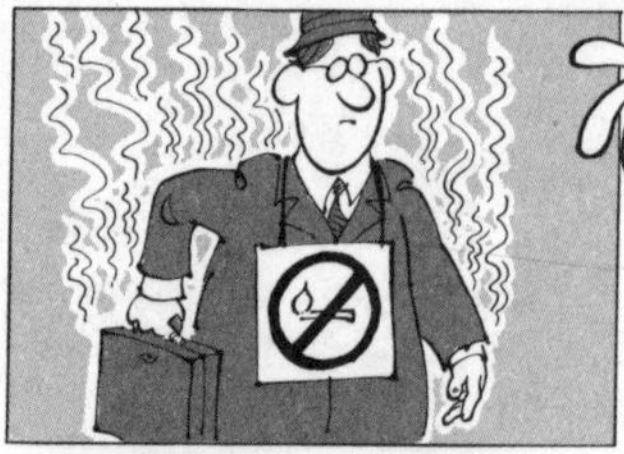

Spend 40¢ a gallon more for what is laughingly called "Full Service" so that you won't have to walk around all day reeking of gasoline.

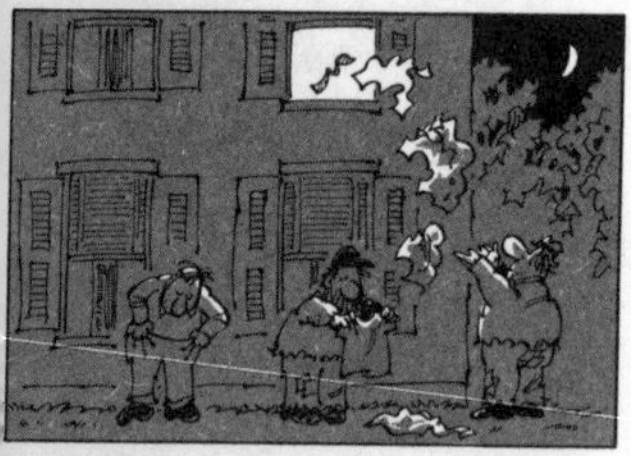

Wear your clothes once. Then throw them out and buy new ones, so you can avoid those weirdos you meet late at night at the laundromat.

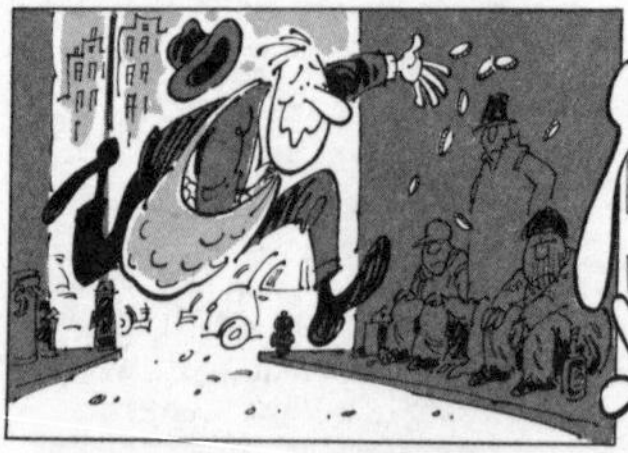

Give every beggar you encounter a quarter to lessen the chances that he will suddenly snap and strangle you for rejecting him.

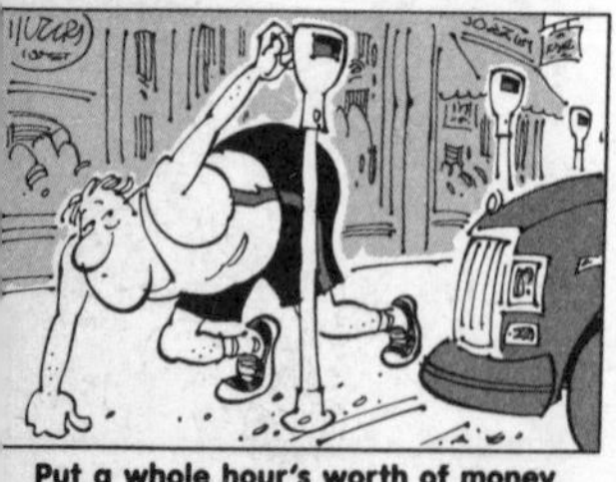

Put a whole hour's worth of money in the parking meter to escape the pressure of trying to finish all your Saturday errands in 12 minutes.

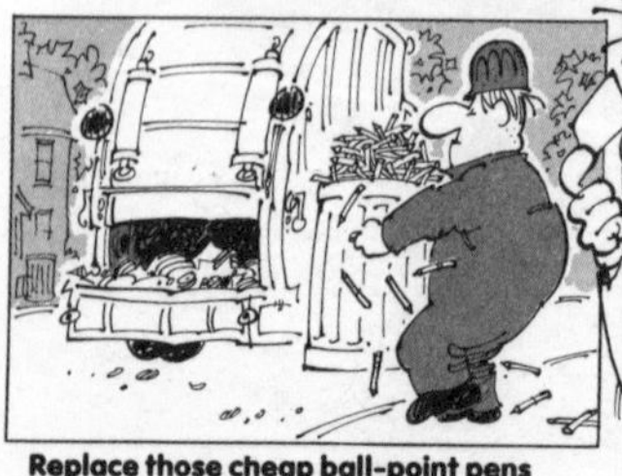

Replace those cheap ball-point pens in your kitchen drawer that refuse to work until you make a whole page of ovals just to get them started.

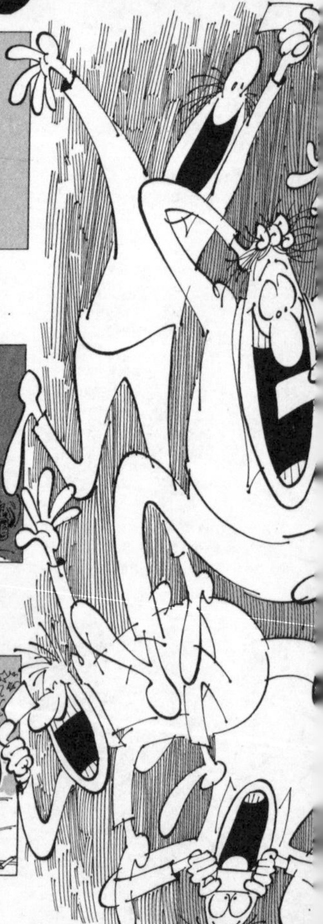

o lose. And you might even win! Then you could sail around the world and buy veryone you know a house. And when you tired of that mindless extravagance and vanted to buy *real* happiness, then you could consider our MAD suggestions for..

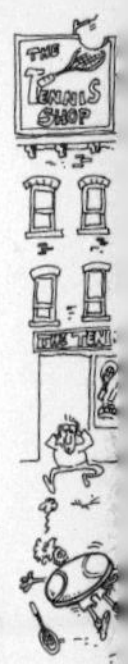

ous Things You on The Lottery

ARTIST: PAUL COKER WRITER: TOM KOCH

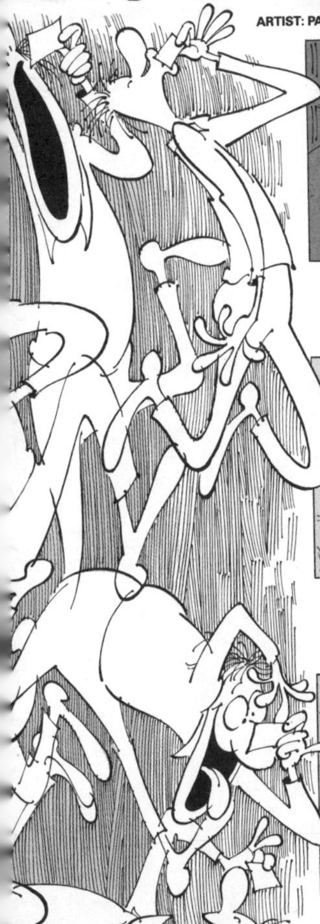

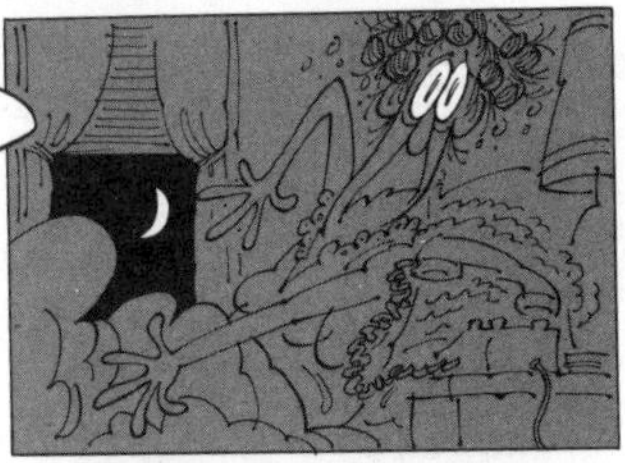

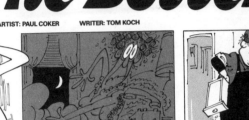

This year, stop waking up your poor mother at 2 a.m. to wish her Happy Birthday just because the long distance rates are lower then.

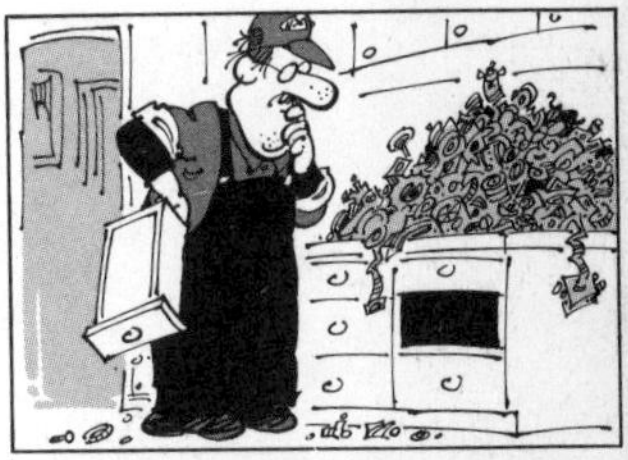

Hire a fix-it man to figure out where to put that drawerful of parts you have been saving because you assume they fell off something important.

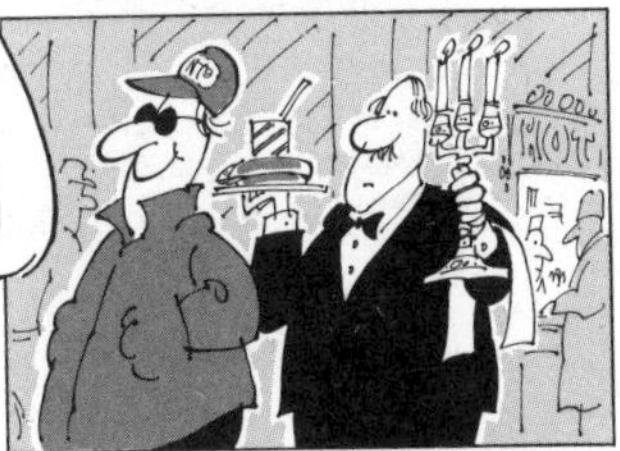

Rejoice that you can now afford to buy 2 hot dogs, a large soda, and a pretzel at an N.F.L. game and still have enough money to buy a ticket.

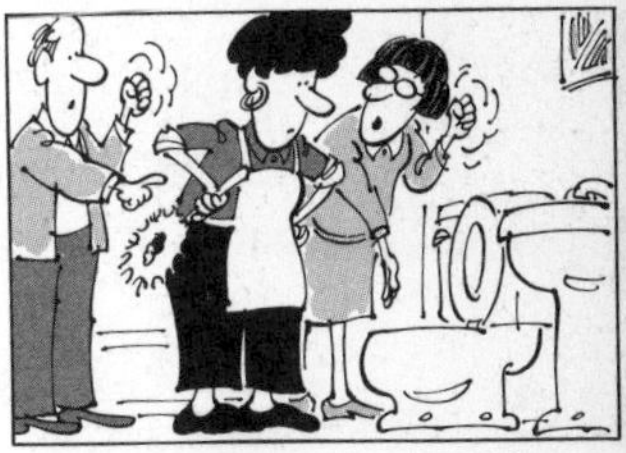

Hire a cleaning lady. Then hire a translator to help you communicate with your cleaning lady in whatever language it is that she understands.

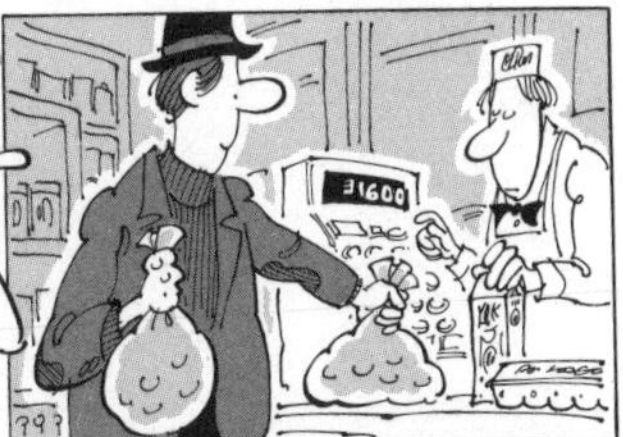

Avoid those long supermarket check-out lines by shopping exclusively at 7-Eleven, since now you can afford to pay their usual double-mark-up prices.

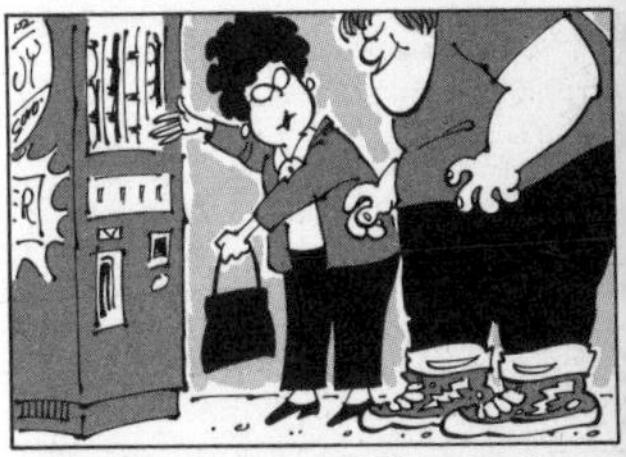

Stop wasting energy kicking vending machines that take your money and don't give anything back. (Hire a hefty teenager to kick them for you.)

ALL JAFFEE DEPT.

You've done it again—you've said the wrong thing. You've offended someone. And now he's goin to punch your lights out. Should you clam up? No! Keep talking! If You keep talking you mig

MORE QUICK
EMBARRASSI

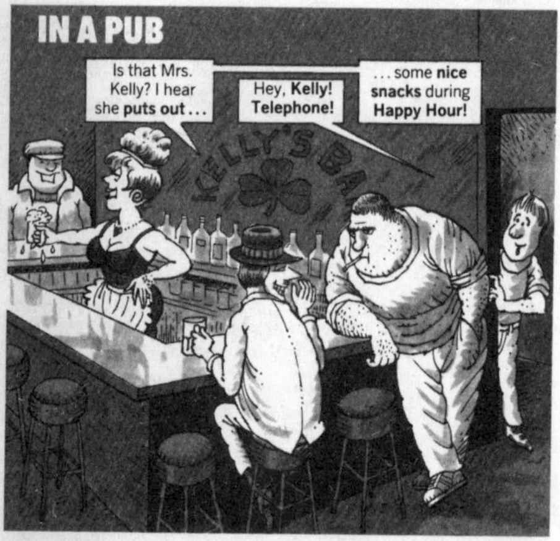
IN A PUB
Is that Mrs. Kelly? I hear she **puts out...**
Hey, **Kelly! Telephone!**
...some **nice snacks** during **Happy Hour!**

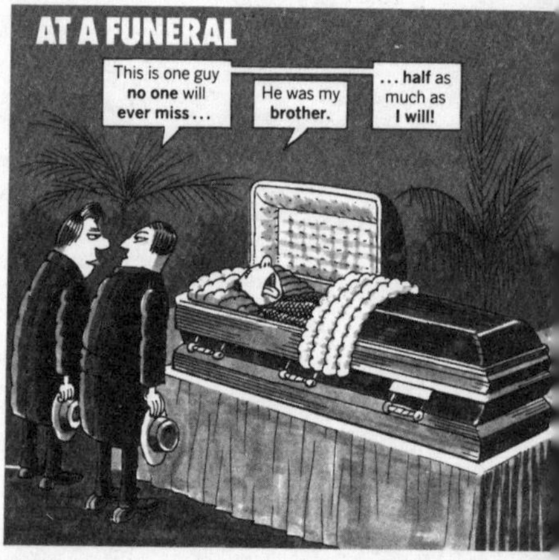
AT A FUNERAL
This is one guy **no one** will **ever miss...**
He was my **brother.**
...half as much as **I will!**

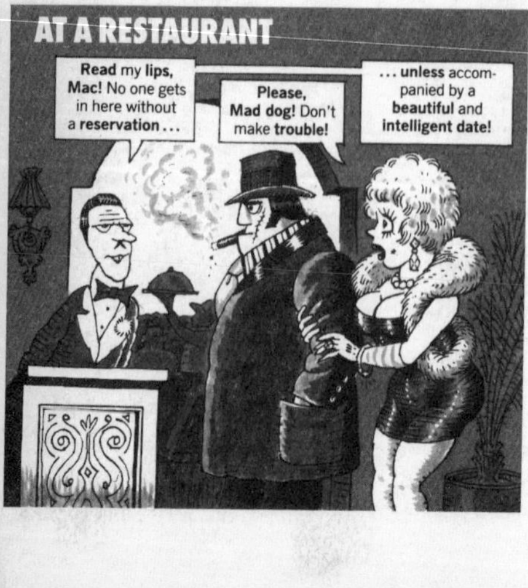
AT A RESTAURANT
Read my **lips, Mac!** No one gets in here without a **reservation...**
Please, Mad dog! Don't make **trouble!**
...unless accompanied by a **beautiful** and **intelligent date!**

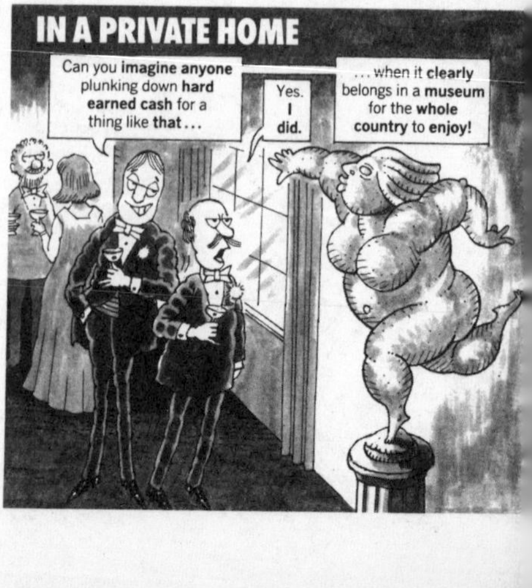
IN A PRIVATE HOME
Can you **imagine anyone** plunking down **hard earned cash** for a thing like **that...**
Yes. **I did.**
...when it **clearly** belongs in a **museum** for the **whole country** to **enjoy!**

et out of trouble. (Then again, you might get smashed in the face!) We offered this advice efore (MAD #278)—did it help? Oh. Well—you have nothing to lose! That's why we're giving you

-COVERIES FOR
G SITUATIONS

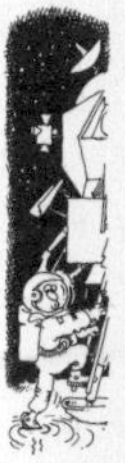

ARTIST AND WRITER: AL JAFFEE

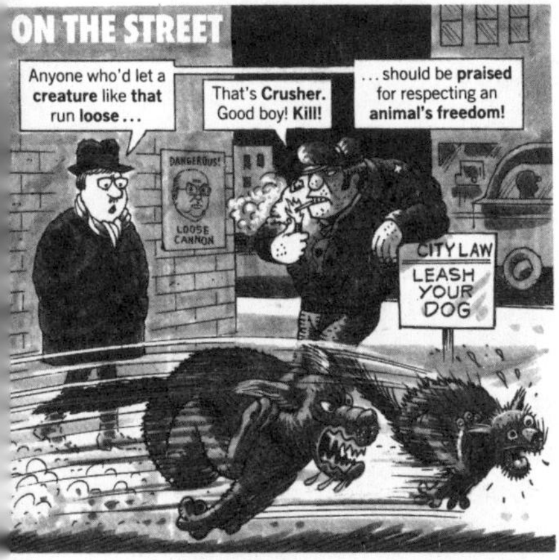
ON THE STREET
Anyone who'd let a **creature** like **that** run **loose** . . .
That's **Crusher.** Good boy! **Kill!**
. . . should be **praised** for respecting an **animal's freedom!**
DANGEROUS!
LOOSE CANNON
CITY LAW
LEASH YOUR DOG

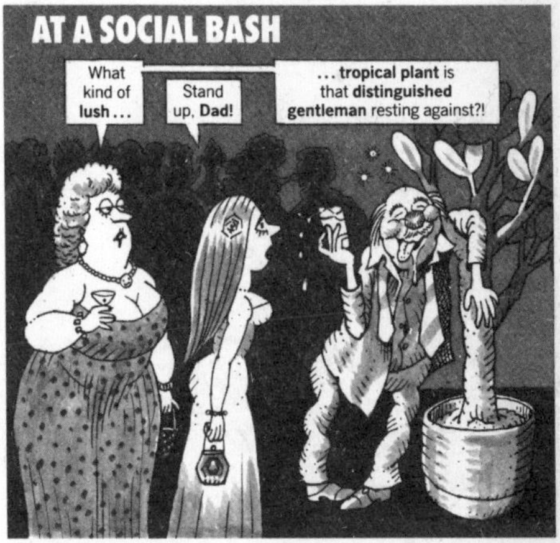
AT A SOCIAL BASH
What kind of **lush . . .**
Stand up, **Dad!**
. . . tropical plant is that **distinguished gentleman** resting against?!

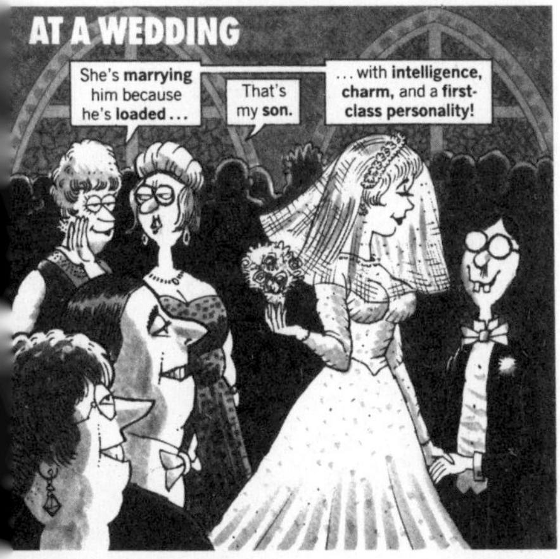
AT A WEDDING
She's **marrying** him because he's **loaded . . .**
That's my **son.**
. . . with **intelligence, charm,** and a **first-class personality!**

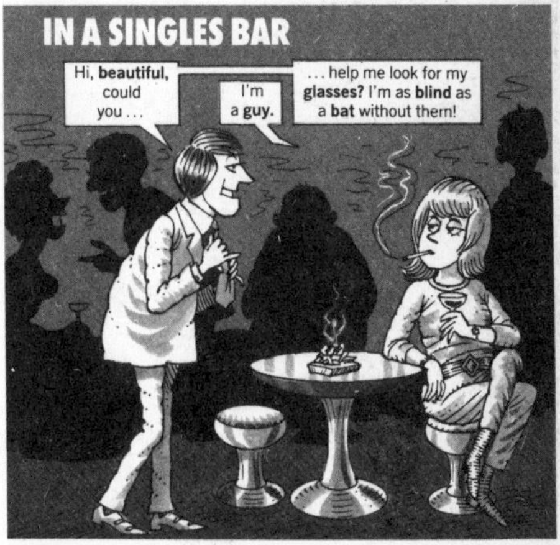
IN A SINGLES BAR
Hi, **beautiful,** could you . . .
I'm a **guy.**
. . . help me look for my **glasses?** I'm as **blind** as a **bat** without them!

THE LATEST FASTEN TREND DEPT.

DRAMA ON PAGE 218

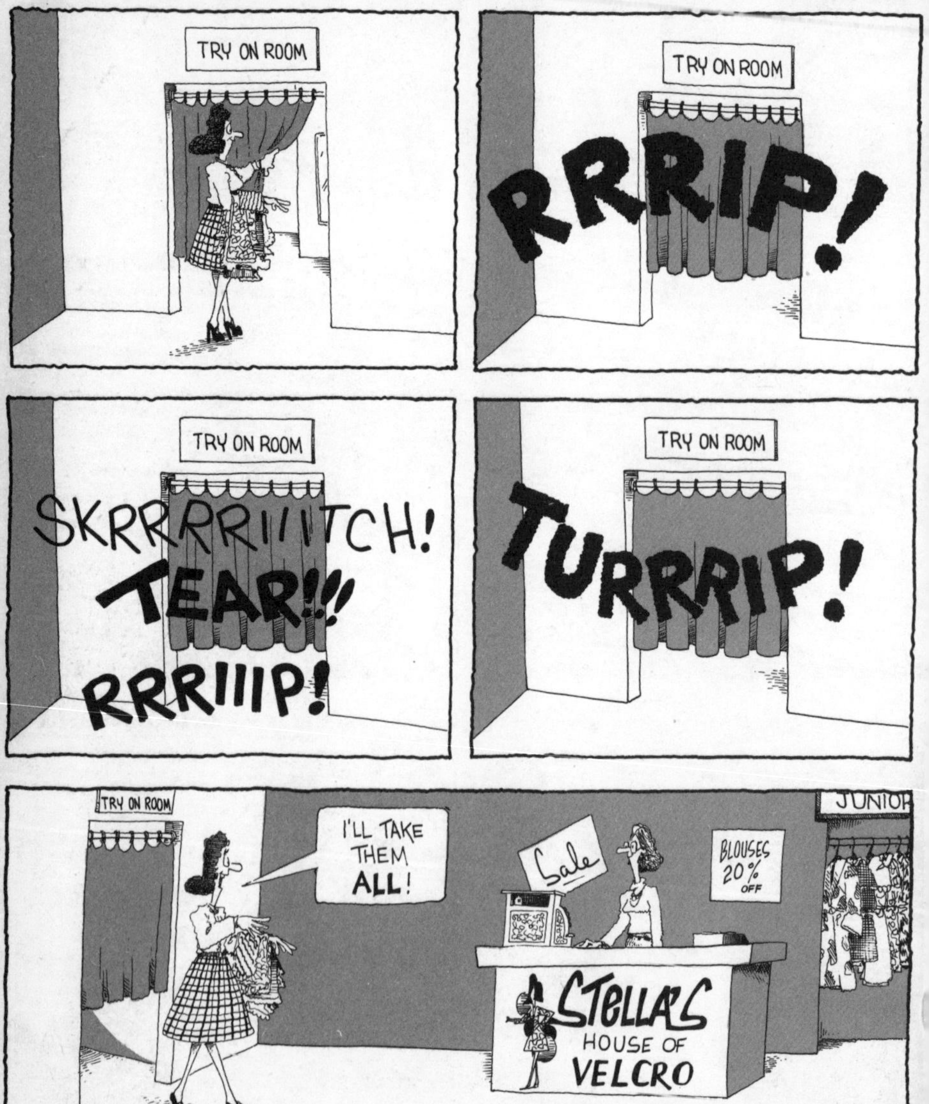
TRY ON ROOM
TRY ON ROOM
RRRIP!
TRY ON ROOM
SKRRRRIIITCH!
TEAR!!!
RRRIIIP!
TRY ON ROOM
TURRRIP!
TRY ON ROOM
I'LL TAKE THEM ALL!
JUNIOR
Sale
BLOUSES 20% OFF
STELLA'S HOUSE OF VELCRO
CALDWELL

ARTIST AND WRITER: JOHN CALDWELL

TOOTH IN ADVERTISING DEPT.

An Important Message for Unsuccessful People Everywhere From Sheldon Vinegar, D.D.S., President of the

2 HOUR SCHOOL OF DENTISTRY

ARTIST: TOM BUNK WRITERS: JOE RAIOLA AND CHARLIE KADAU

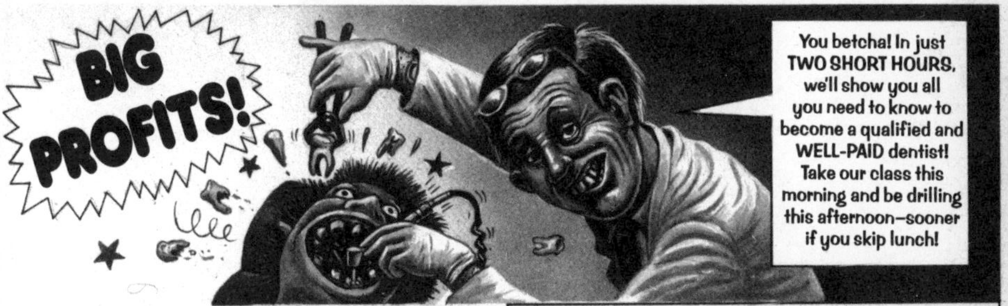
BIG PROFITS!
You betcha! In just TWO SHORT HOURS, we'll show you all you need to know to become a qualified and WELL-PAID dentist! Take our class this morning and be drilling this afternoon—sooner if you skip lunch!

HOW do we do it? We don't waste time on unimportant things like X-rays and Novocain. You learn by doing! In just 120 minutes we'll teach you EVERYTHING you need to be familiar with as a graduate of the 2 HOUR SCHOOL OF DENTISTRY, including:

DRILLING AND FILLING	OUT OF COURT SETTLEMENTS
ROOT CANAL	TOOTH CAPPING
MALPRACTICE SUITS	PLEA BARGAINING
GUM REBUILDING	CHANGING YOUR IDENTITY

Take this short quiz to see if you qualify:

This man's problem is

A) Pyorrhea

B) Plaque buildup

C) Agreeing to pose for this photo

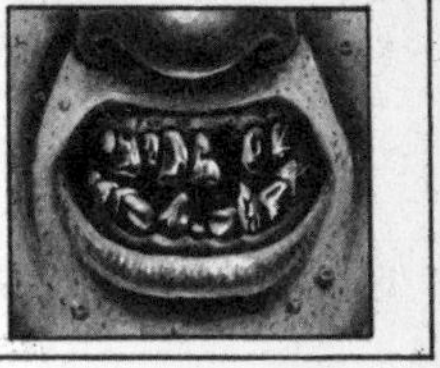

ANSWER: It doesn't matter! If you took the time to take this quiz, you're qualified!

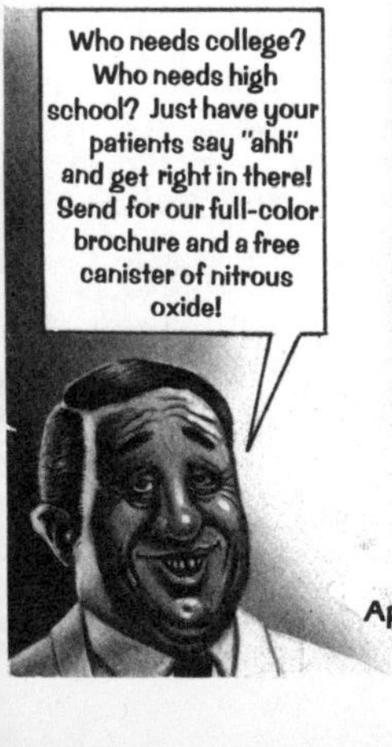
Who needs college? Who needs high school? Just have your patients say "ahh" and get right in there! Send for our full-color brochure and a free canister of nitrous oxide!

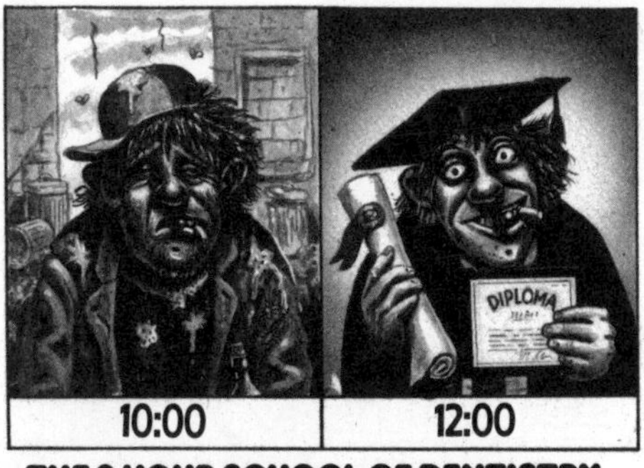
DIPLOMA
10:00
12:00

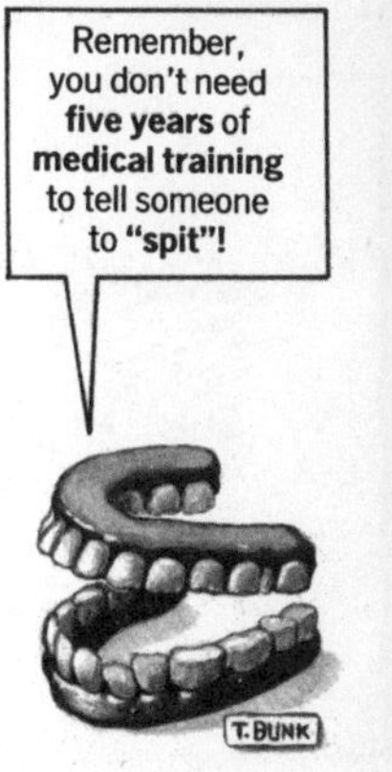
Remember, you don't need five years of medical training to tell someone to "spit"!
T. BUNK

THE 2 HOUR SCHOOL OF DENTISTRY

P.O. Box 181, New York, NY 10108

Approved and recommended by the same people who run The Six Minute School of Eye Surgery

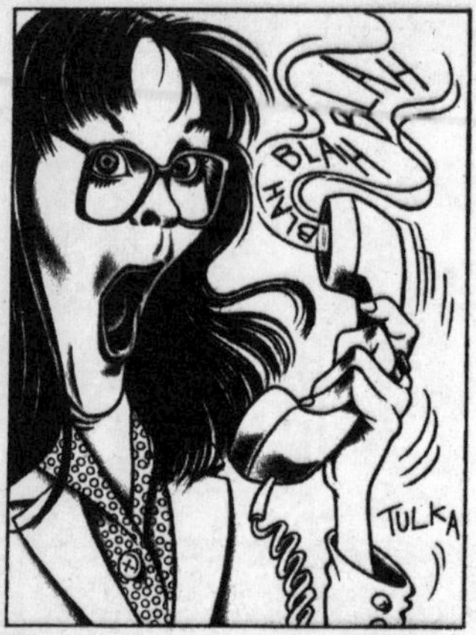
BLAH
BLAH
BLAH
TULKA

The guy from your class who used to be a flaming liberal calls and says he's now selling tax-free municipal bonds.

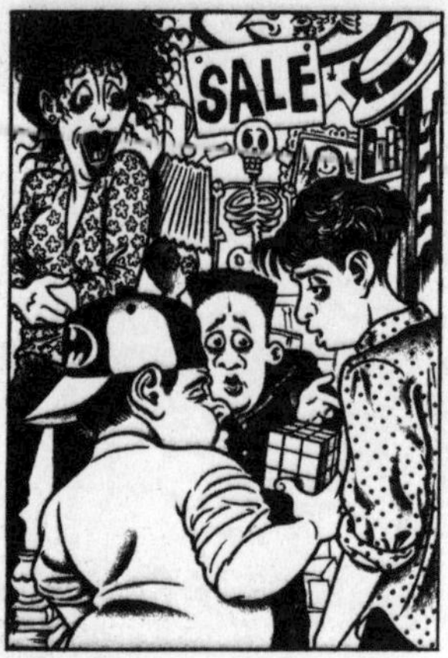
SALE

You offer your old Rubik's Cube at a garage sale, and the neighbor kids don't know what it is.

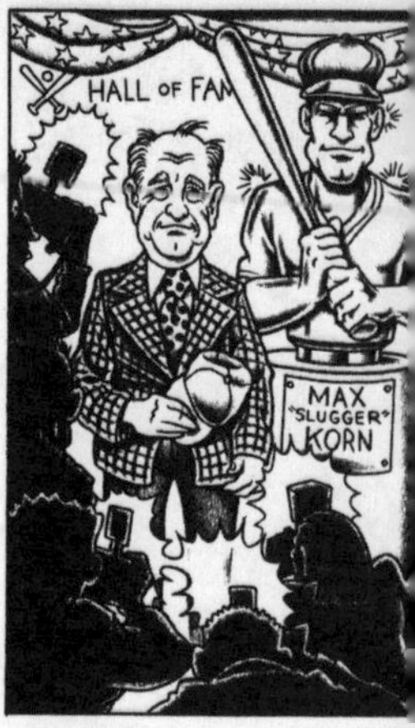
HALL OF FAM
MAX
"SLUGGER"
KORN

Your childhood baseball idol gets elected to the Hall of Fame.

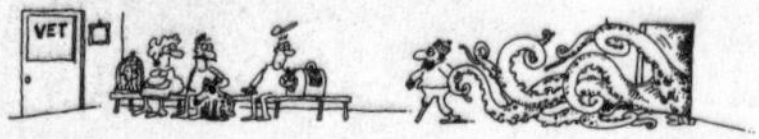
VET

GROWING UP ALL OVER THE PLACE DEPT.

12 SURE SIGNS THAT YOU'VE

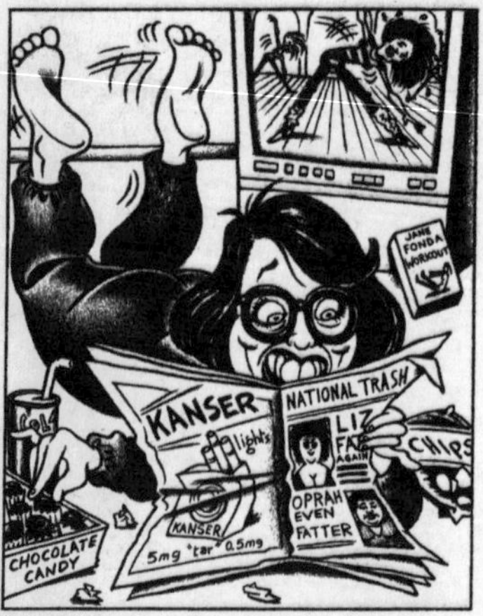
JANE FONDA WORKOUT
KANSER
lights
NATIONAL TRASH
OPRAH EVEN FATTER
KANSER
5mg 'tar' 0.5mg
CHOCOLATE CANDY
CHIPS

You read in the paper that Jane Fonda has a daughter who is only about five years younger than you assumed Jane Fonda to be.

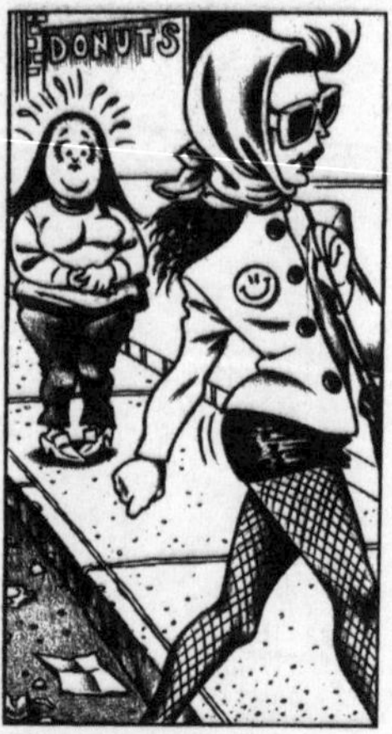
DONUTS

You can recall when this season's new fashions were popular the first time.

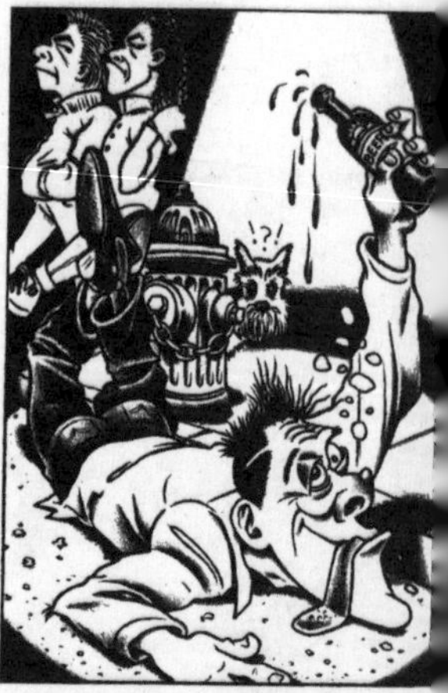
!?!

Your friends stop regarding you as macho when you drink a lot, and start regarding you as a slobbering idiot

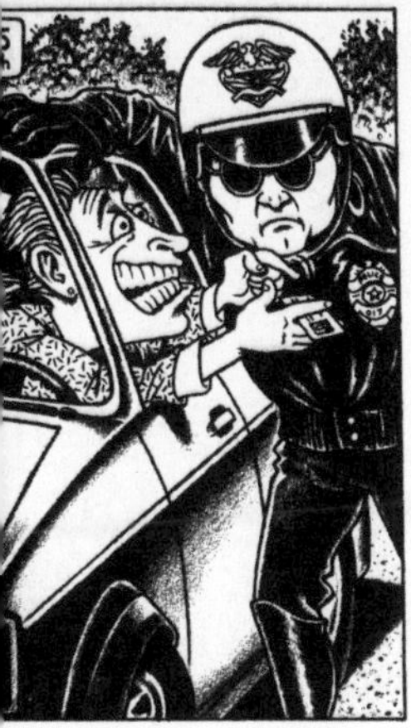

cop who pulls you over is a
you went to grade school with.

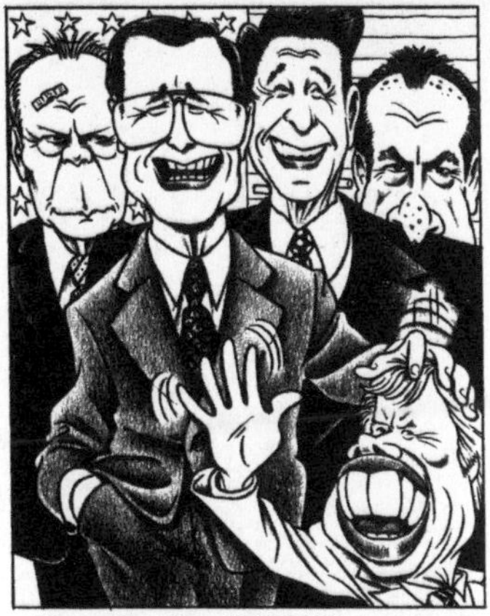

You realize that 50,000,000 Americans are too young to recall a time when we had a President who wasn't a Republican.

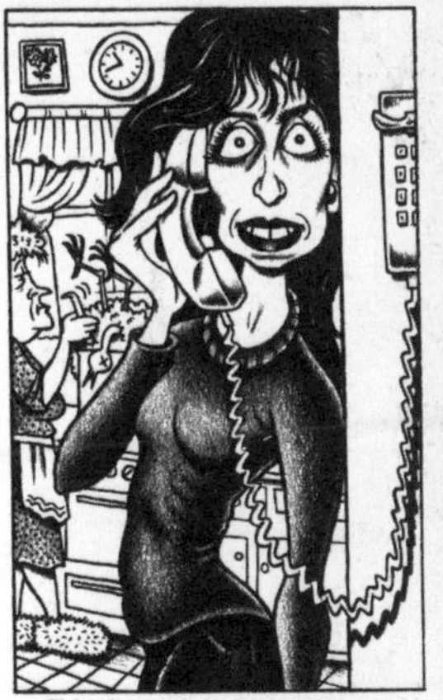

Telephone solicitors give you their sales pitch instead of asking to talk to your mother.

REACHED ADULTHOOD

ARTIST: RICK TULKA WRITER: TOM KOCH

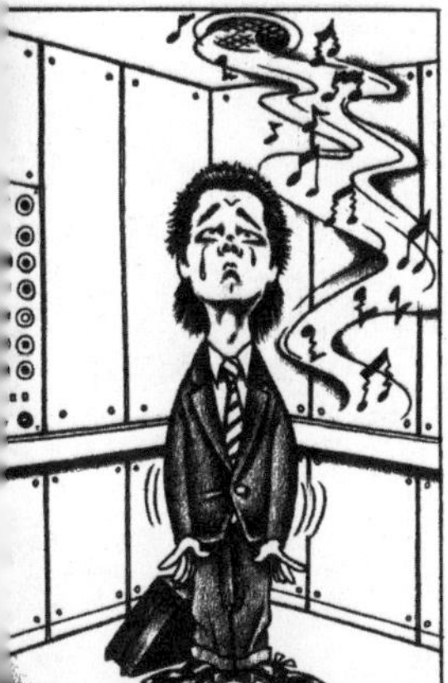

he rock group you worshipped as
kid is now heard only as Muzak
medical building elevators.

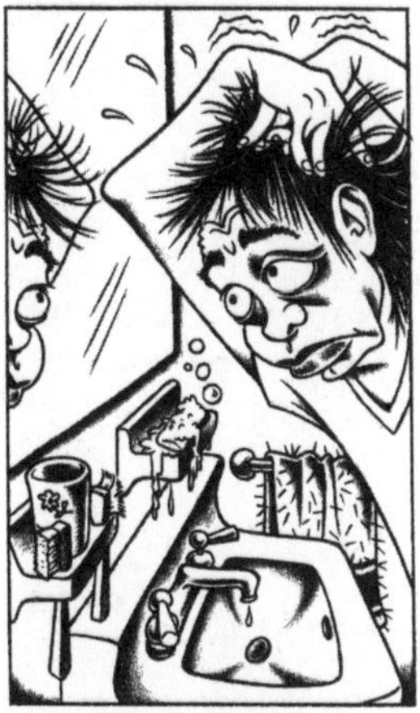

You begin looking for telltale signs that you've inherited your father's baldness.

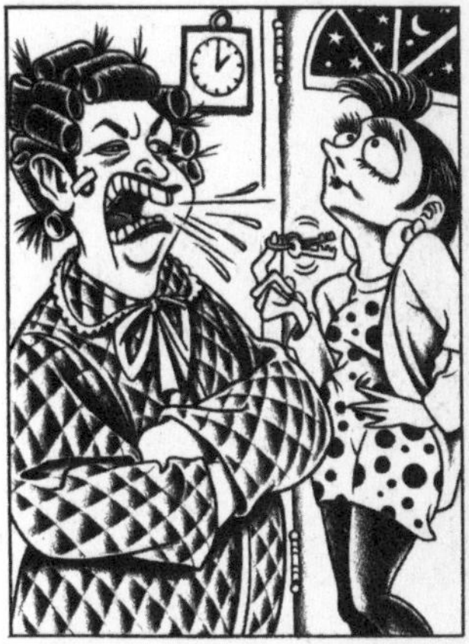

Your mother stops complaining that you're too young to go steady, and starts complaining that you still haven't made a commitment to anyone.

IT'S A NO DARWIN SITUATION DEPT.

Darwin's theory of evolution holds that human beings, with the exception of a few Republican
progressed from monkeys and are forever moving forward in a constant state of change. But w

A MAD GUIDE T

COMEDY GROUP

The Three Marx Brothers

The Three Stooges

The Three Amigos

TOP NATIONAL ISSUE

Civil Rights

Watergate

Flag Burning

TV DOCTOR

James Kildare

Hawkeye Pierce

Doogie Howser

ARCHITECTURE

The Pyramids

The Great Wall of China

Trump Tower

t MAD challenge this naive assumption! The truth is that society is rapidly deteriorating and hings are getting progressively worse! You'll know just what we mean when you take a look at...

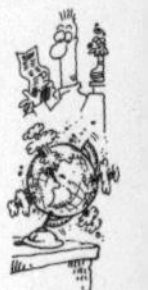

D DEVOLUTION

WRITER: HY BENDER

OG ROLE MODEL

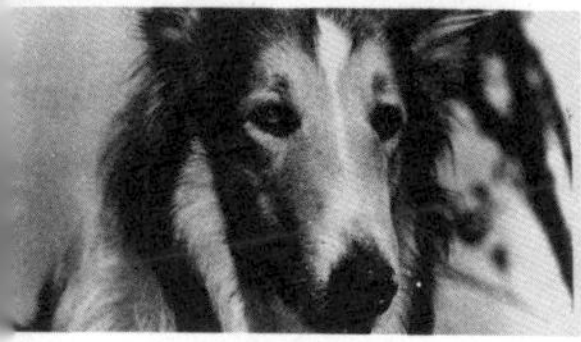

Lassie

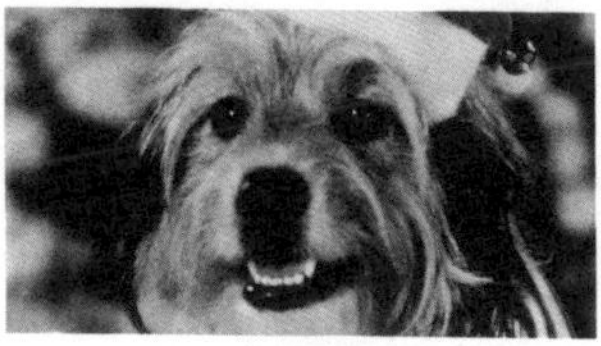

Benji

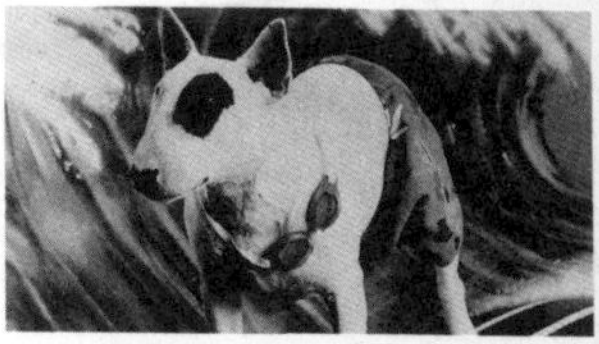

Spuds MacKenzie

AMOUS SHIPS

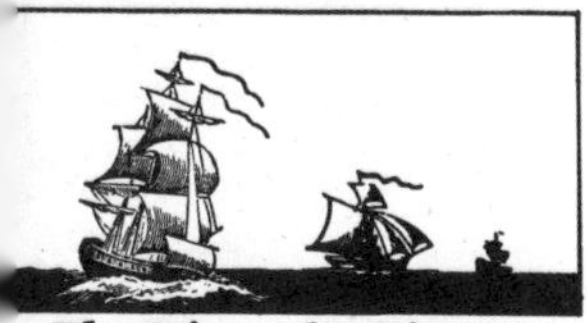

The Nina, the Pinta, and the Santa Maria

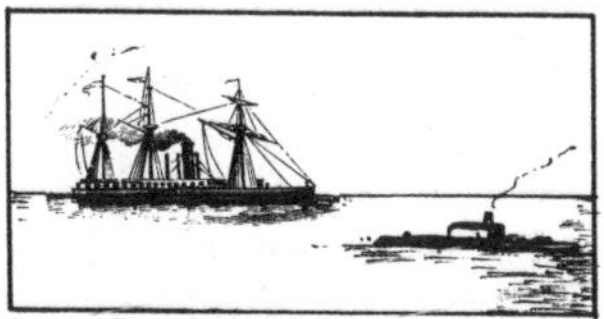

The Monitor and the Merrimack

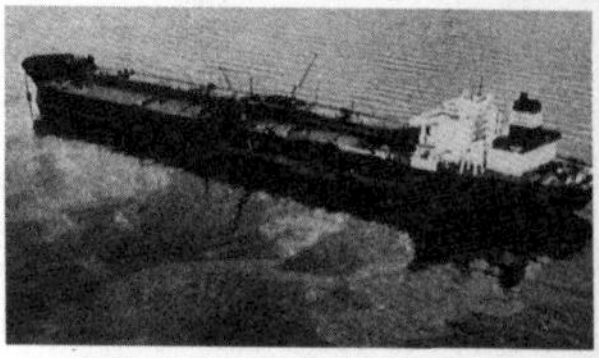

The Exxon Valdez

RUSADING JOURNALIST

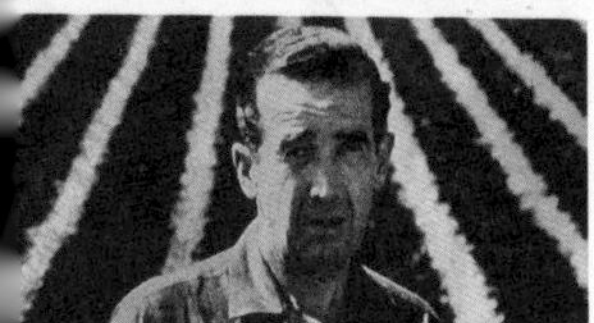

Edward R. Murrow

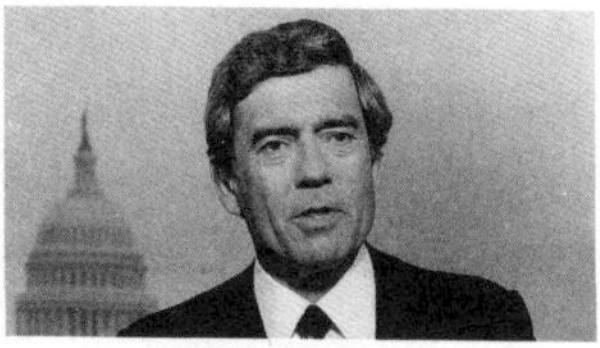

Dan Rather

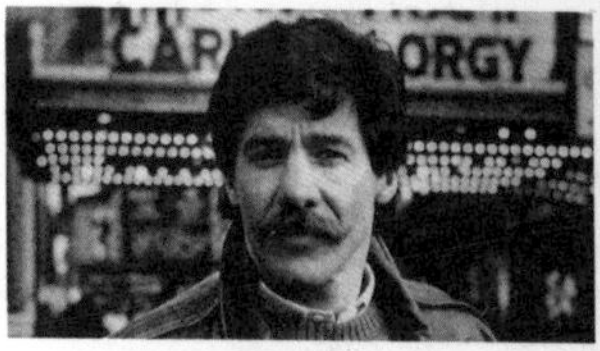

Geraldo Rivera

NURTURING TV MOM

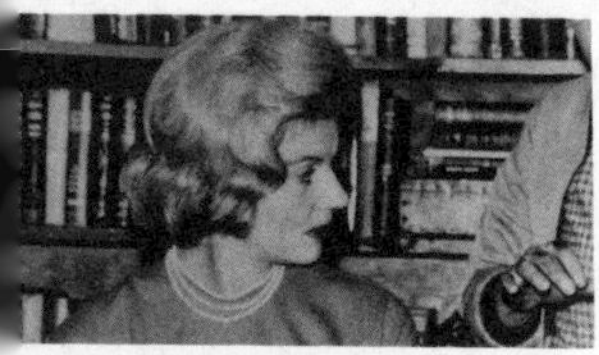

June Cleaver

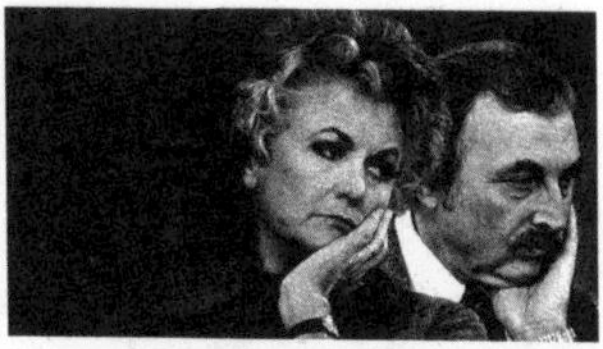

Maude Findlay

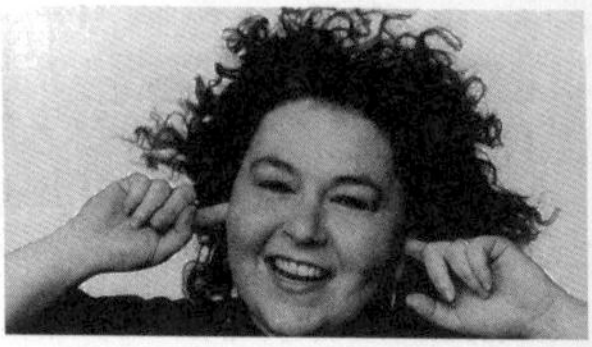

Roseanne Conner

TALES FROM THE DUCK SIDE DEPT.

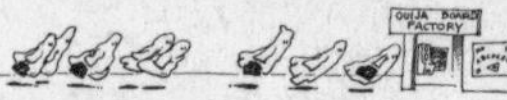

THE LUSTY LEDGE LEGEND

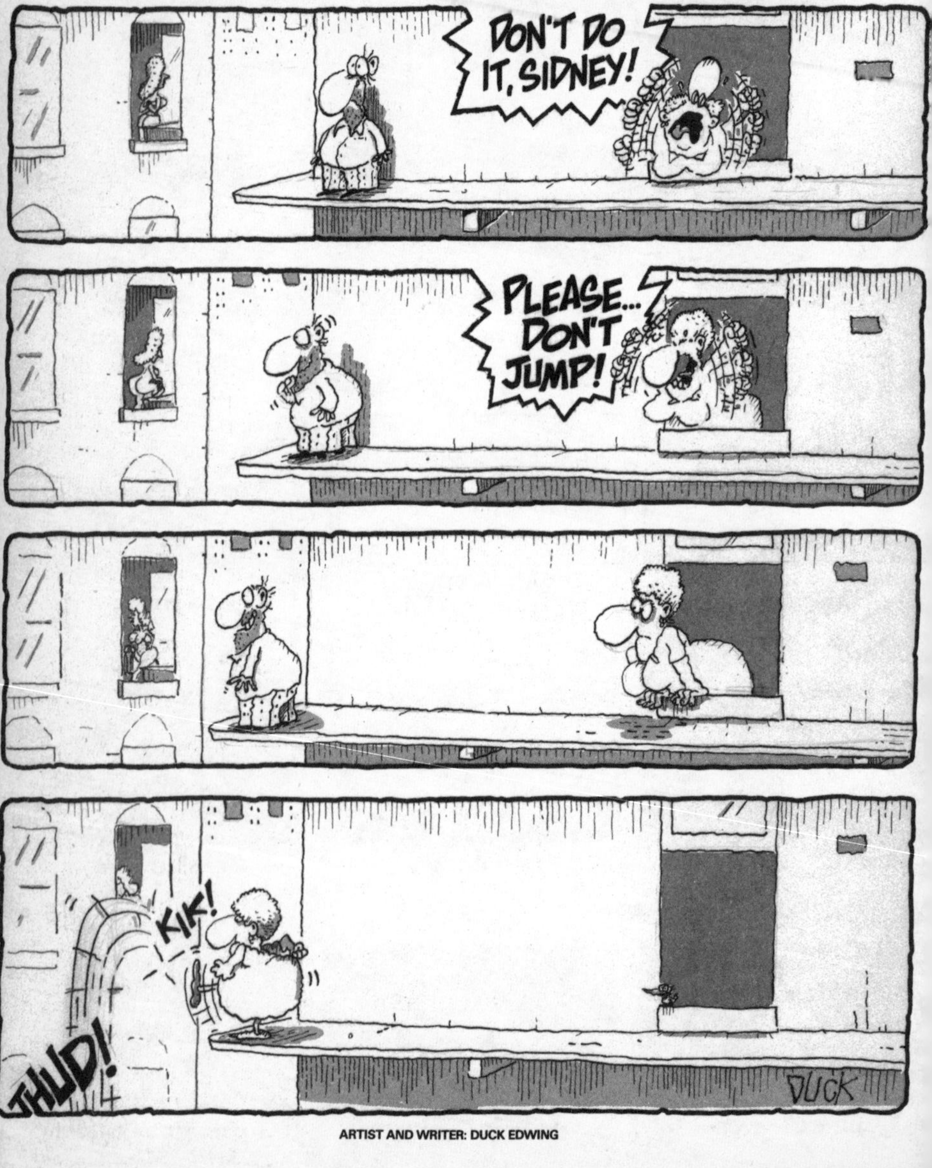
DON'T DO IT, SIDNEY!
PLEASE... DON'T JUMP!
KIK!
THUD!
DUCK

ARTIST AND WRITER: DUCK EDWING

SERGE-IN GENERAL DEPT.

A MAD LOOK AT BOXING

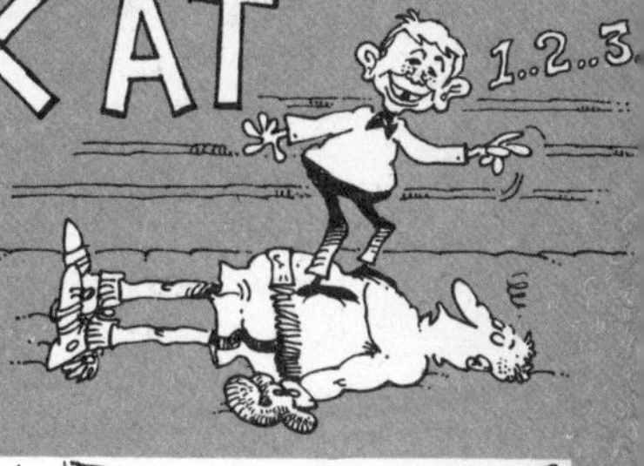
1..2..3

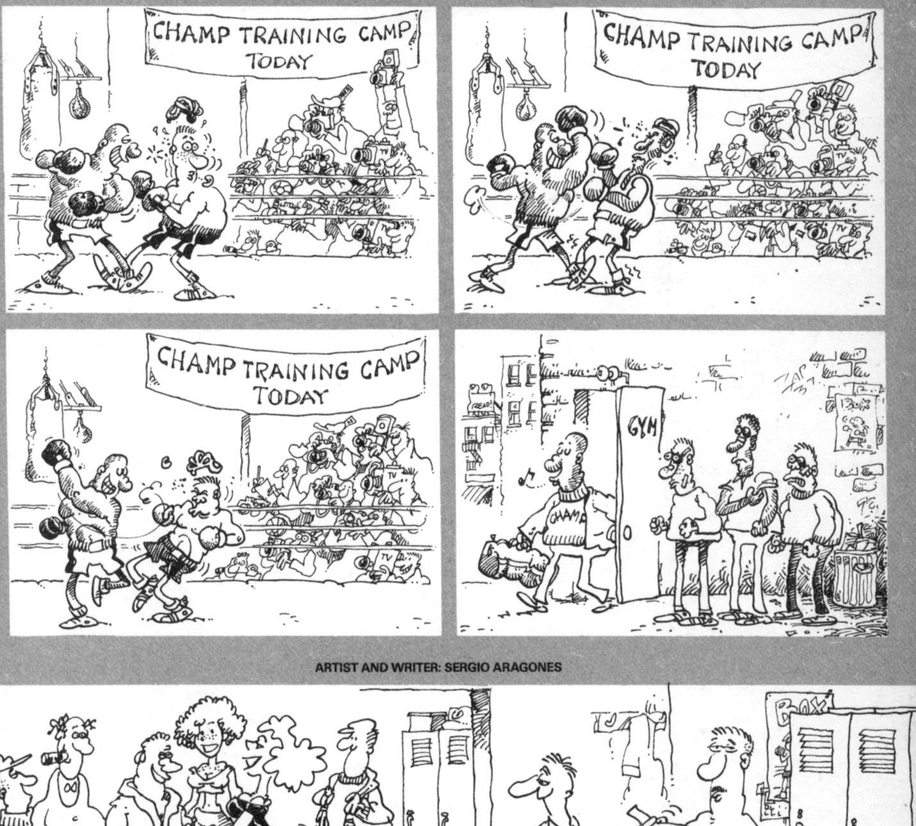
CHAMP TRAINING CAMP
TODAY
CHAMP TRAINING CAMP
TODAY
CHAMP TRAINING CAMP
TODAY
GYM
CHAMP

ARTIST AND WRITER: SERGIO ARAGONES

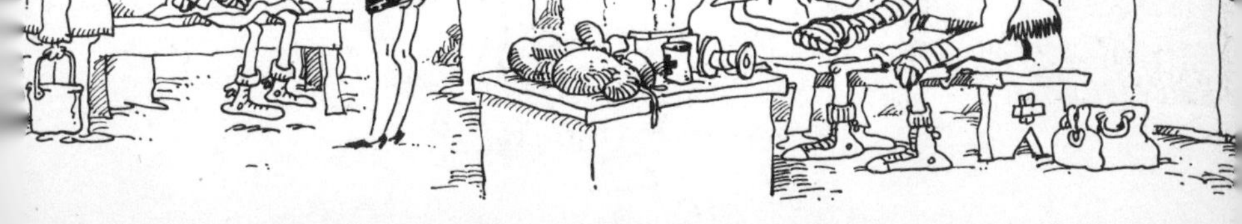

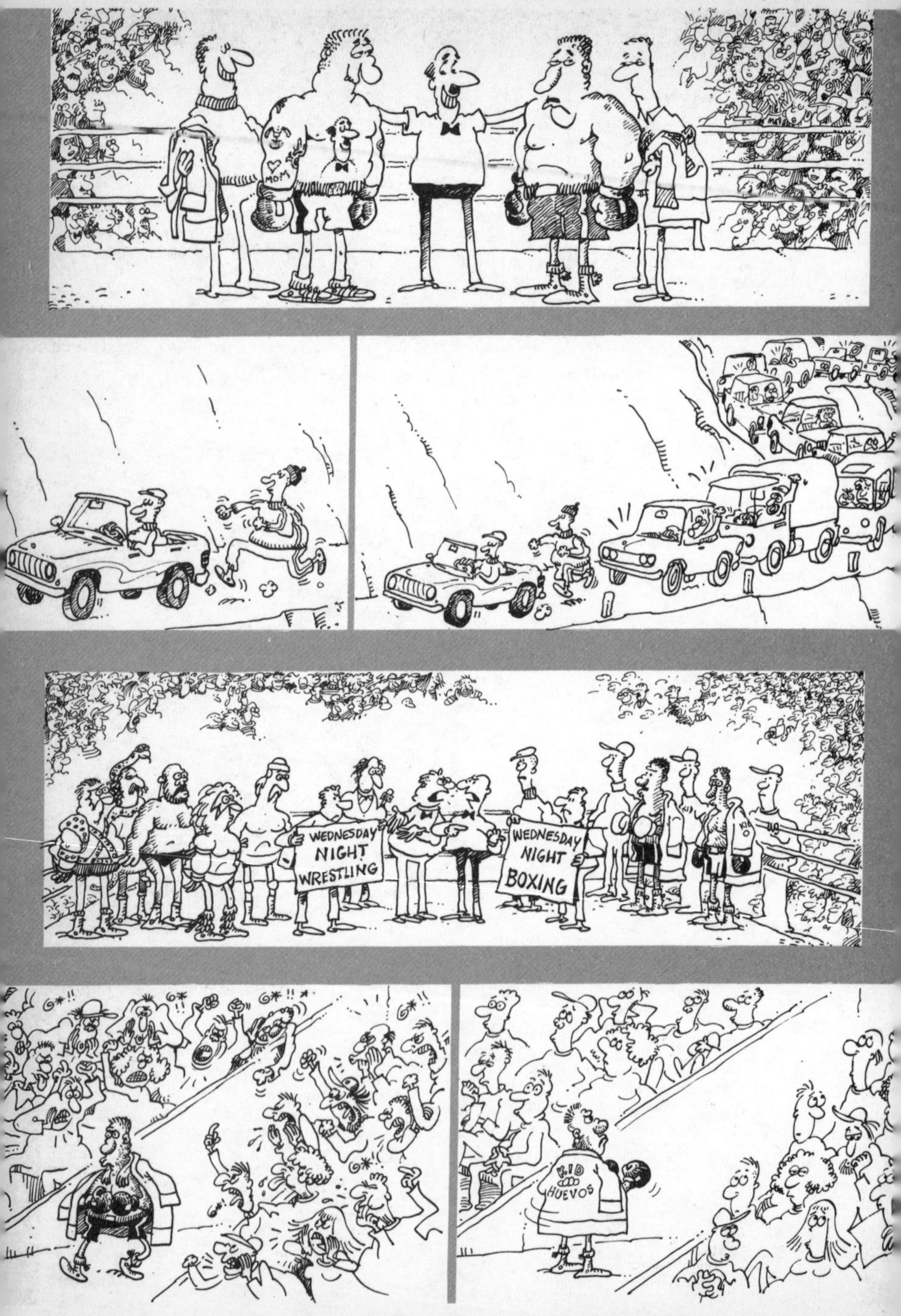
MOM
WEDNESDAY NIGHT WRESTLING
WEDNESDAY NIGHT BOXING
KID HUEVOS

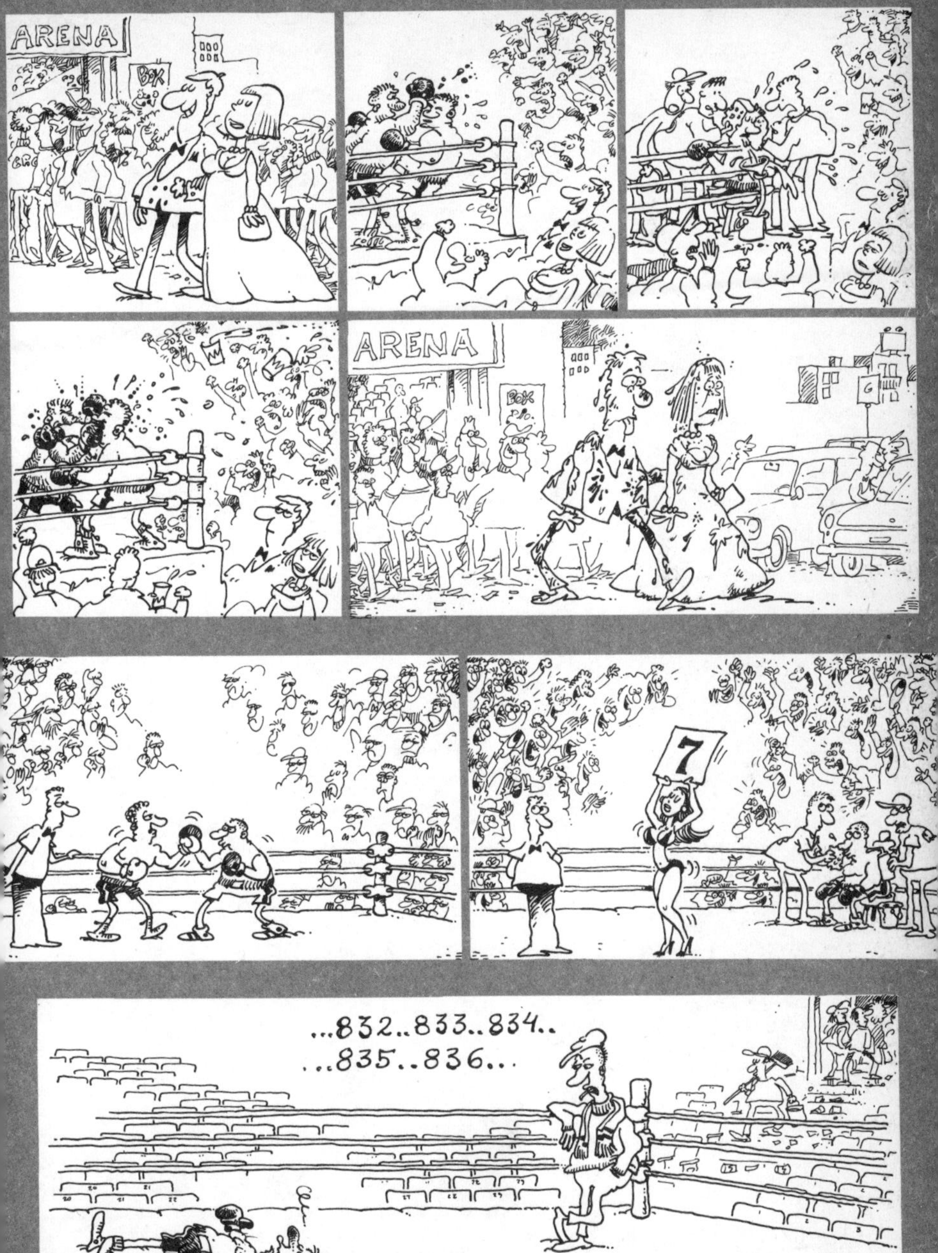

ARENA
BOX
ARENA
BOX
7
...832..833..834..
..835..836...
ARAGONÉS

HARD ATTACK DEPT.

Real Di

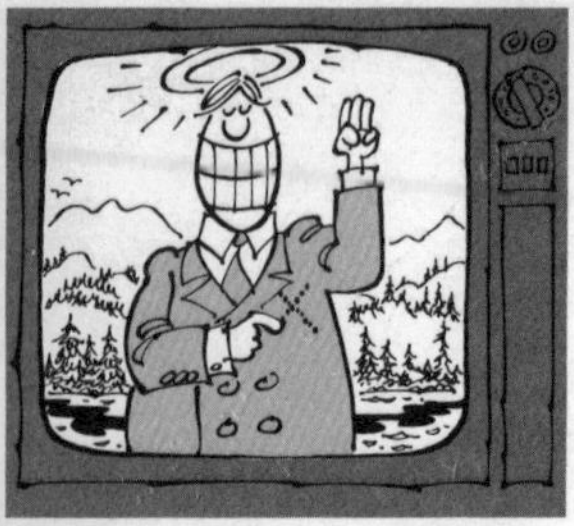

Believing anything Exxon says.

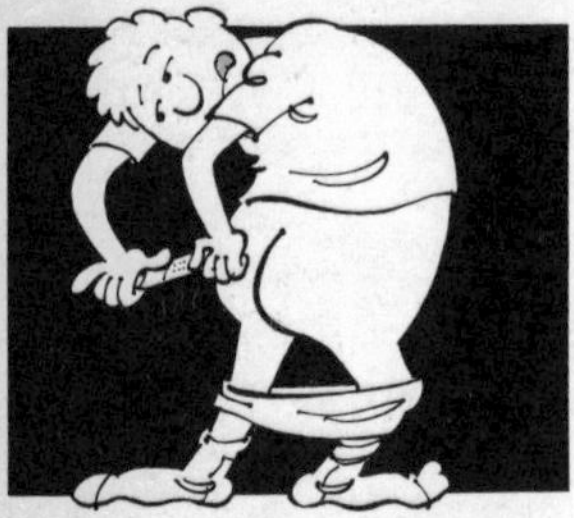

Centering a Band-Aid on certain body parts on the first try.

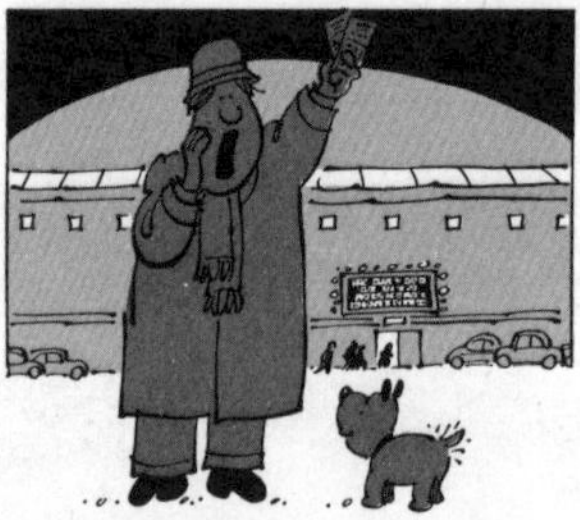

Scalping tickets for a New Jersey Nets/Miami Heat basketball game.

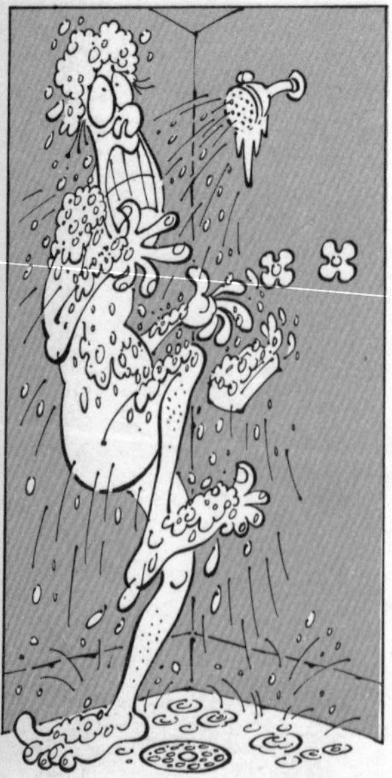

Removing the soap from your body after the water turns cold in the middle of a shower.

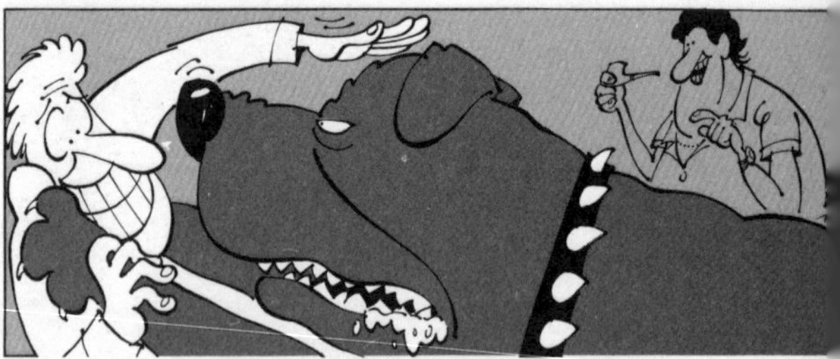

Maintaining a friendly expression after a friend tells you that his rottweiler can "smell fear."

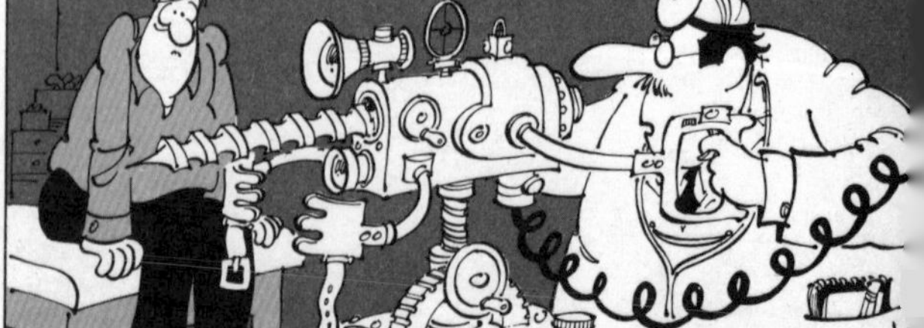

Looking calm during a physical exam when your doctor suddenly brings out some weird instrument and tells you to take off your clothes.

...y ...ficult Is...

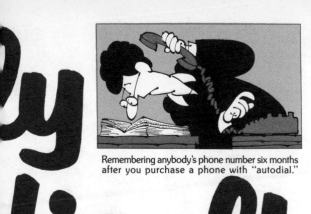

Remembering anybody's phone number six months after you purchase a phone with "autodial."

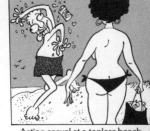

Acting casual at a topless beach.

SALE
½ OFF

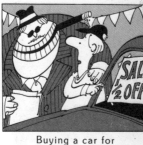

Buying a car for the advertised price.

FRESH CEMENT

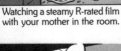

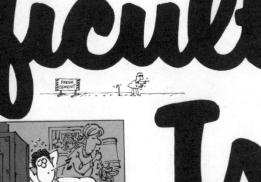

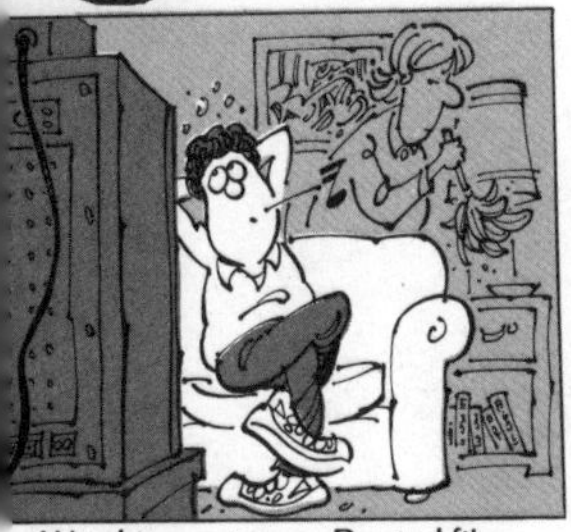

Watching a steamy R-rated film with your mother in the room.

DOWN WITH COPS

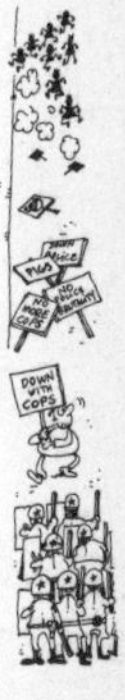

ARTIST: PAUL COKER   WRITER: FRANK JACOBS

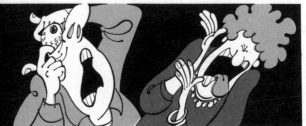

Retrieving a contact lens that's traveled up to the back of your eye —or watching someone else do it.

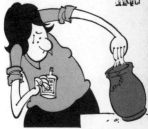

Mending something with Super Glue and not winding up with your fingers stuck together.

Really Difficult Is...

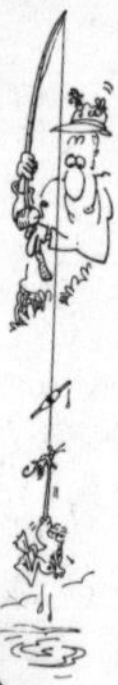

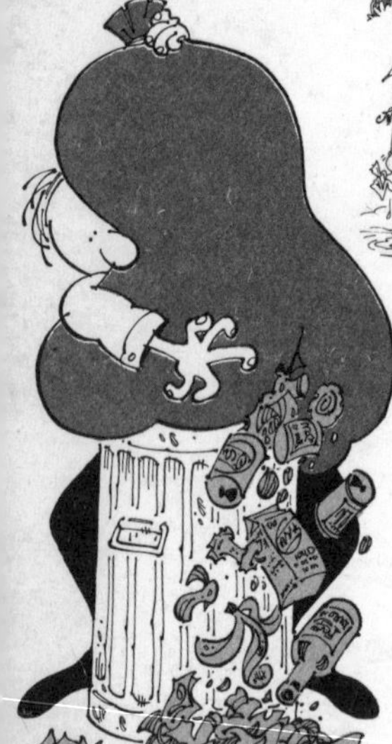

Getting a giant plastic bag of trash into the can once it splits.

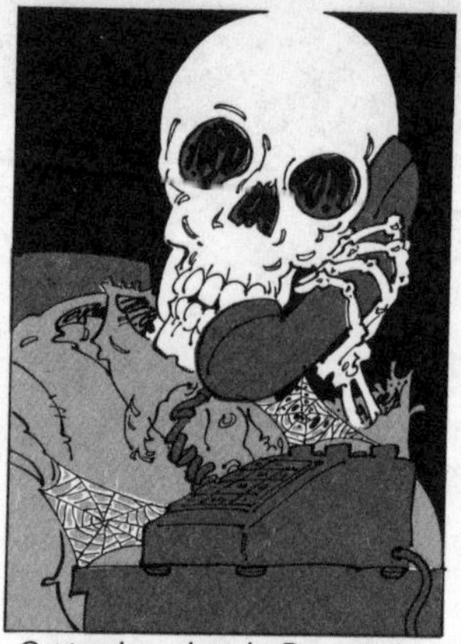

Getting through to the Department of Motor Vehicles by telephone.

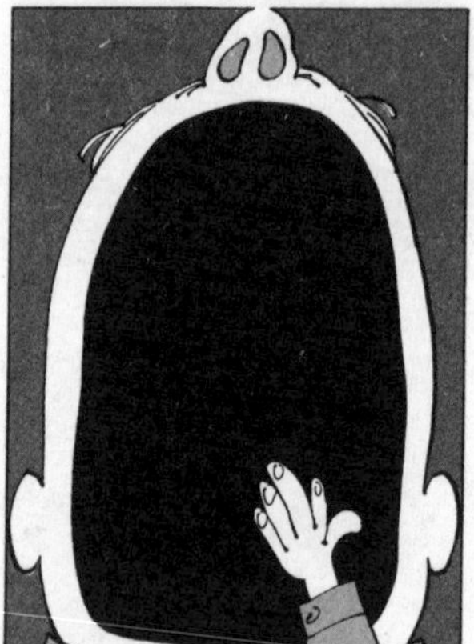

Getting excited about the annual Bud Bowl.

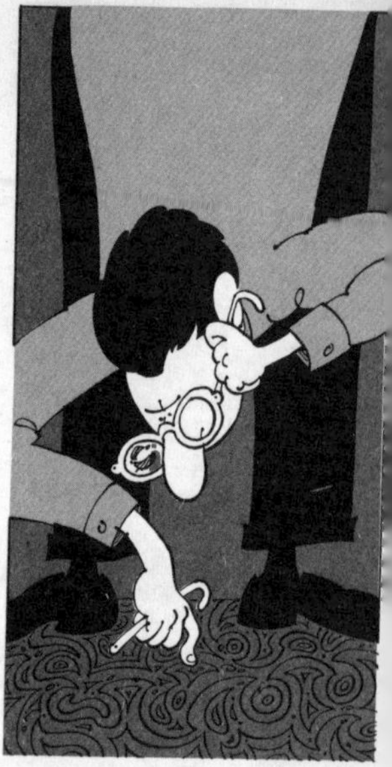

Finding the little screw that just popped out of your glasses.

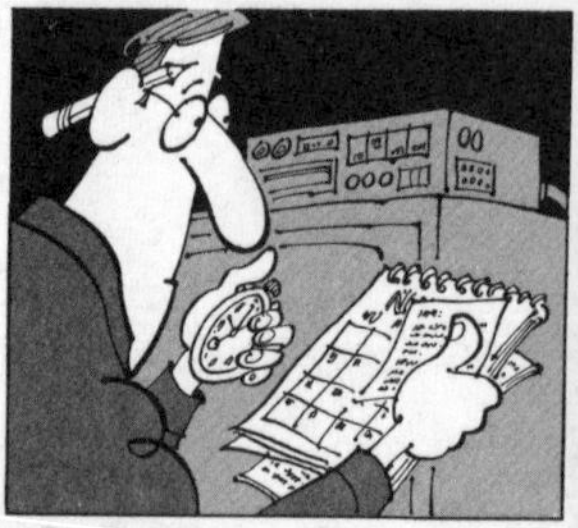

Programming a VCR for a show airing two weeks from Sunday.

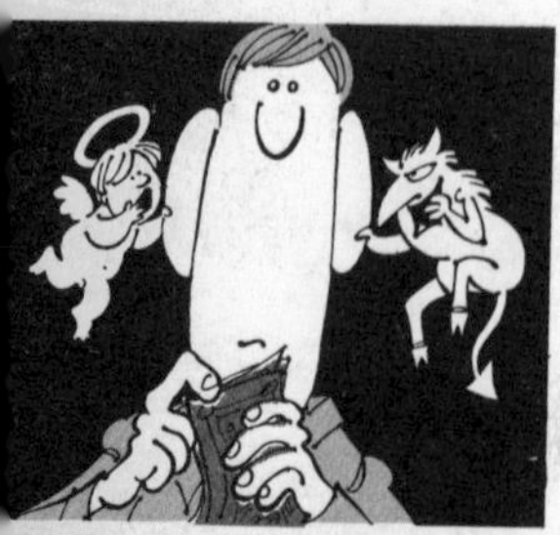

Telling the saleslady that she gave you change for ten dollars, when you only gave her five.

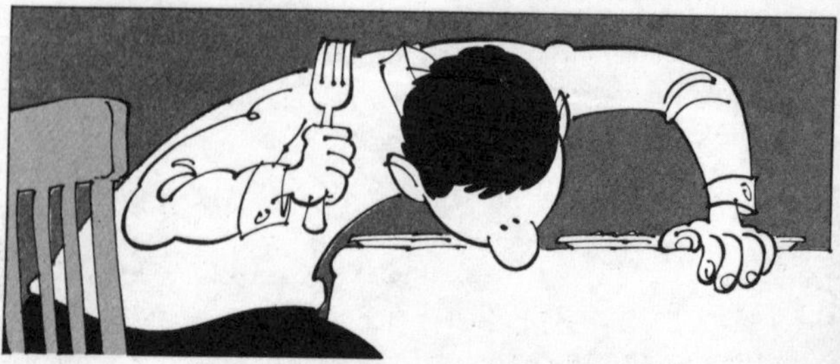

Resisting the temptation to pick up that last piece of incredibly delicious chocolate cake that just fell on the floor, and eat it.

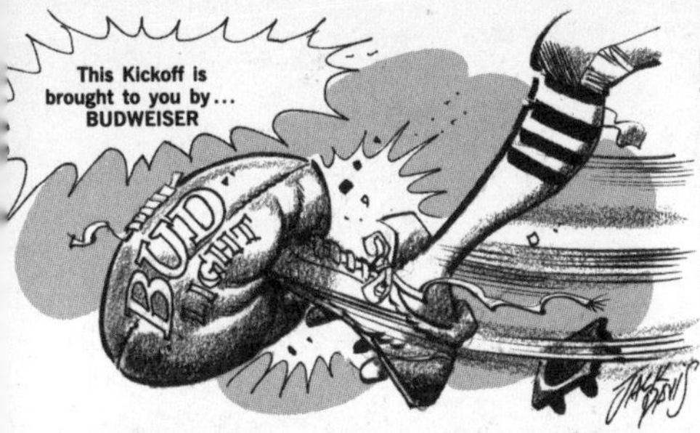
This Kickoff is brought to you by... BUDWEISER
BUD LIGHT

ENDORSE OF A DIFFERENT COLOR DEPT.

This nauseating travesty is no doubt familiar to anyone who watches sports on TV: Convinced that 90 minutes of commercials in a 3-hour sportscast isn't enough, networks and advertisers are now "encroaching" on the games themselves! So far, these annoying mini-ads have been limited to kickoffs, home runs and the like, but you can bet your Miller-Lite Beer mug that there will come a day pretty soon...

WHEN TV SPORTS ADVERTISERS decide to "SPONSOR" MORE than just KICKOFFS & HOME RUNS

ARTIST: JACK DAVIS WRITER: MIKE SNIDER

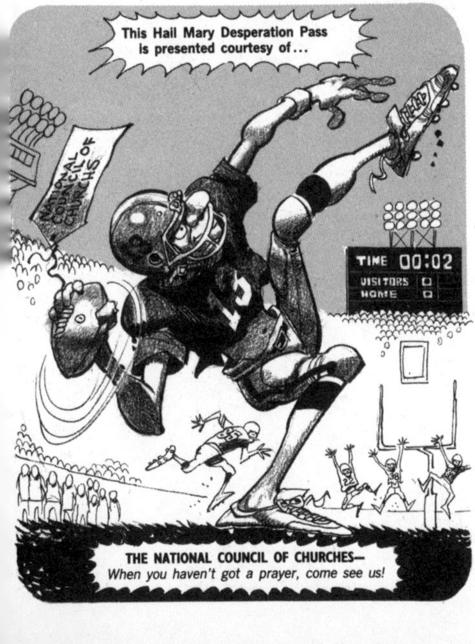
This Hail Mary Desperation Pass is presented courtesy of...
NATIONAL COUNCIL OF CHURCHS
TIME 00:02
VISITORS 0
HOME 0
THE NATIONAL COUNCIL OF CHURCHES—
When you haven't got a prayer, come see us!

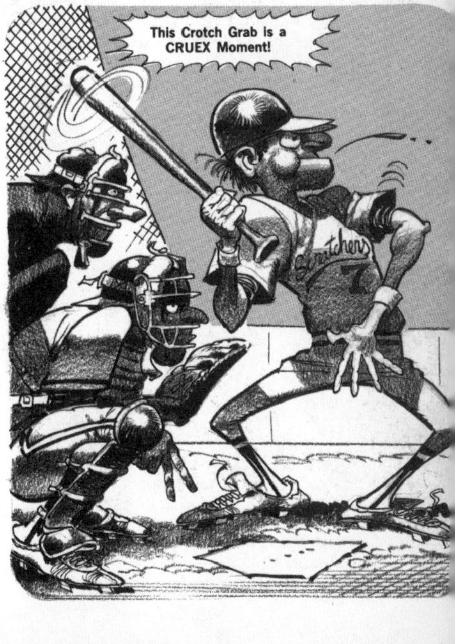
This Crotch Grab is a CRUEX Moment!
Scratchers
7

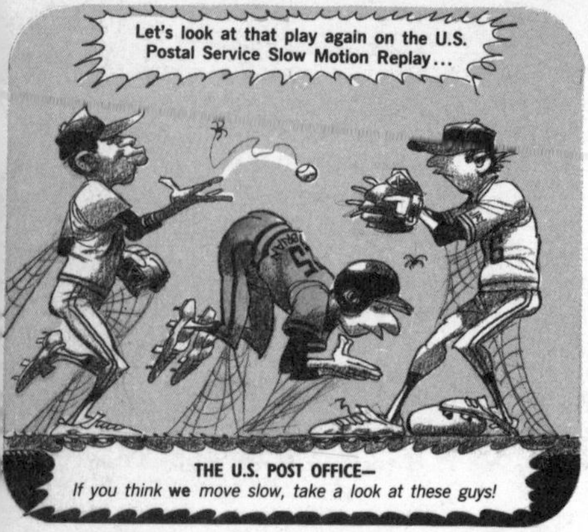
Let's look at that play again on the U.S. Postal Service Slow Motion Replay...
THE U.S. POST OFFICE—
If you think we move slow, take a look at these guys!

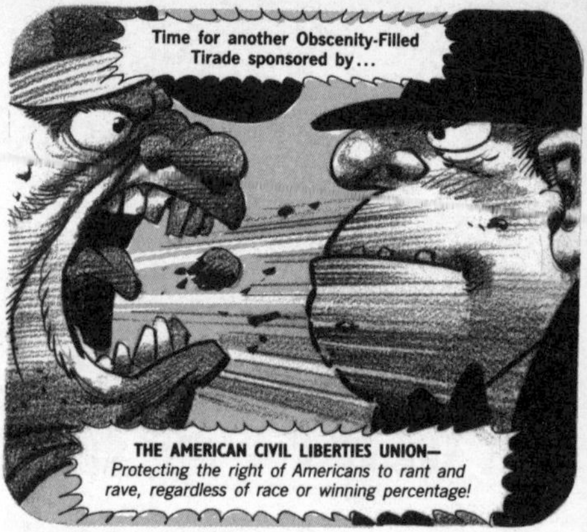
Time for another Obscenity-Filled Tirade sponsored by...
THE AMERICAN CIVIL LIBERTIES UNION—
Protecting the right of Americans to rant and rave, regardless of race or winning percentage!

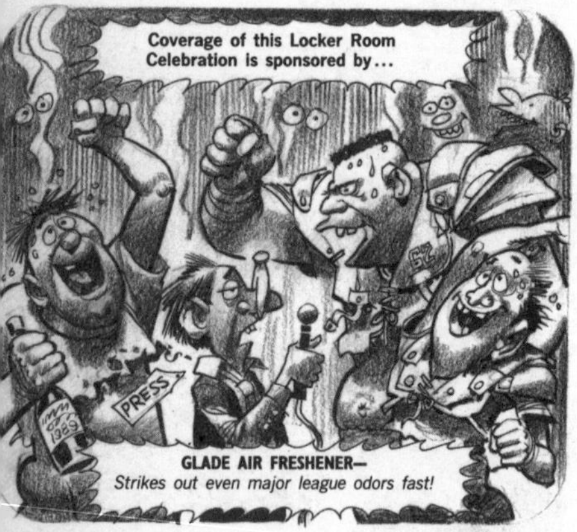
Coverage of this Locker Room Celebration is sponsored by...
PRESS
GLADE AIR FRESHENER—
Strikes out even major league odors fast!

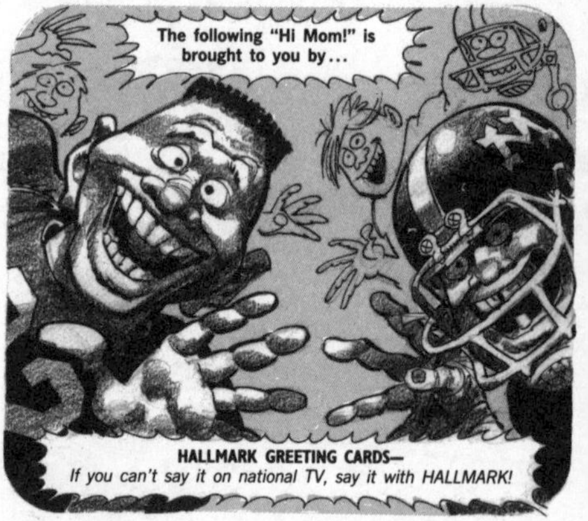
The following "Hi Mom!" is brought to you by...
HALLMARK GREETING CARDS—
If you can't say it on national TV, say it with HALLMARK!

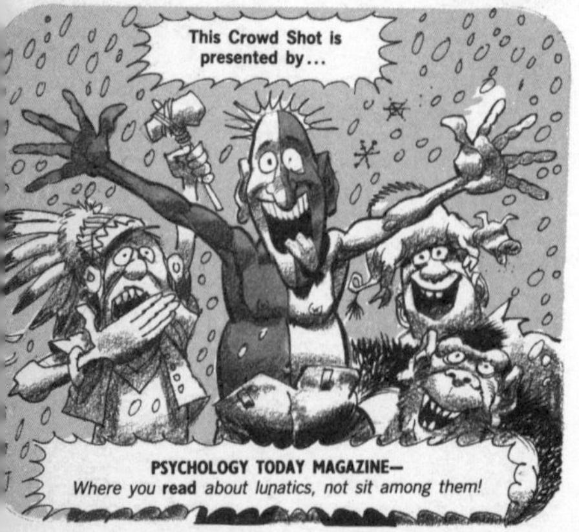
This Crowd Shot is presented by...
PSYCHOLOGY TODAY MAGAZINE—
Where you read about lunatics, not sit among them!

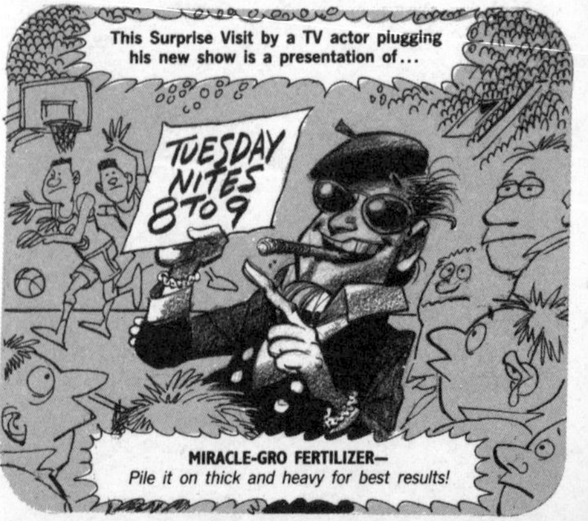
This Surprise Visit by a TV actor plugging his new show is a presentation of...
TUESDAY NITES 8 TO 9
MIRACLE-GRO FERTILIZER—
Pile it on thick and heavy for best results!

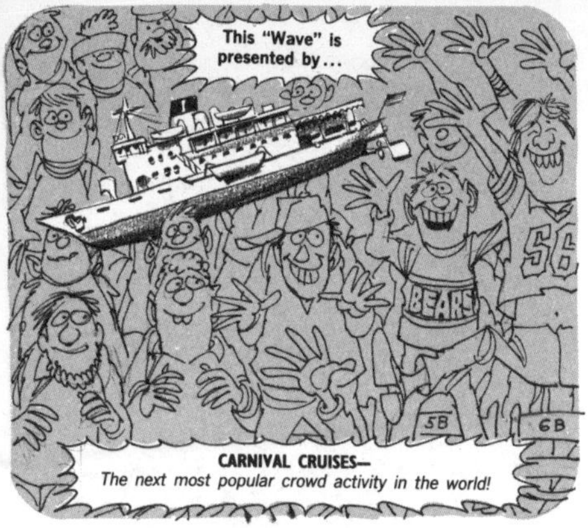
This "Wave" is presented by...
BEARS
CARNIVAL CRUISES—
The next most popular crowd activity in the world!

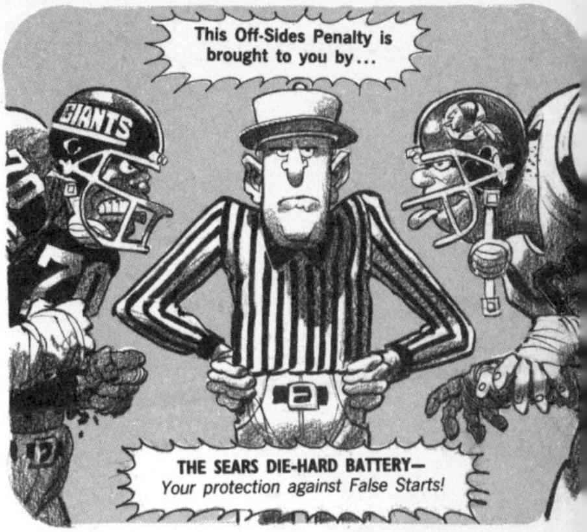
This Off-Sides Penalty is brought to you by...
GIANTS
THE SEARS DIE-HARD BATTERY—
Your protection against False Starts!

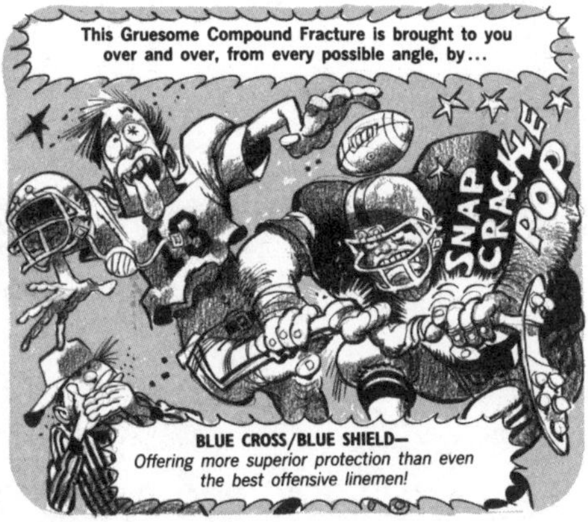
This Gruesome Compound Fracture is brought to you over and over, from every possible angle, by...
SNAP
CRACKLE
POP
BLUE CROSS/BLUE SHIELD—
Offering more superior protection than even the best offensive linemen!

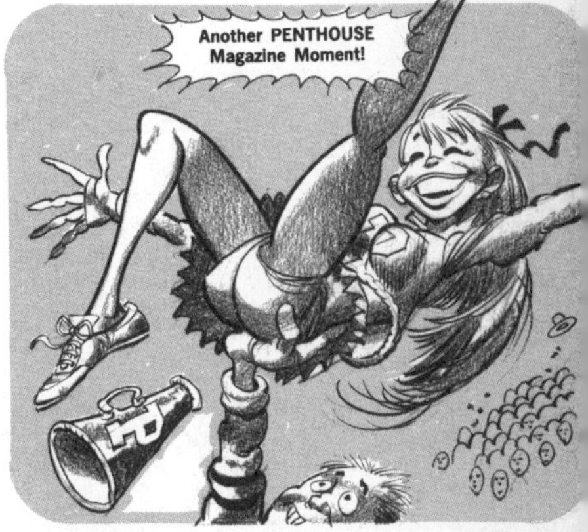
Another PENTHOUSE Magazine Moment!

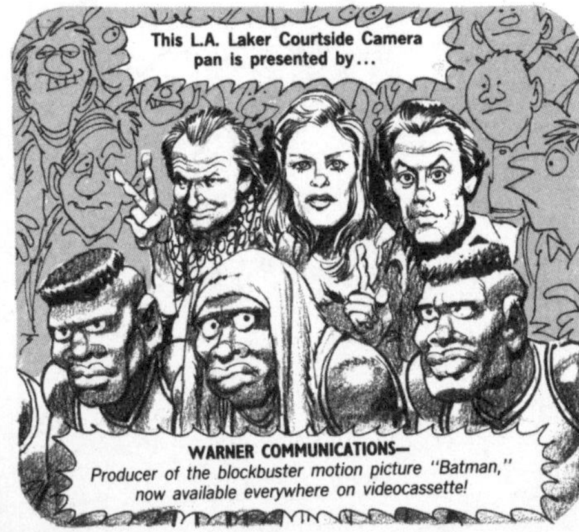
This L.A. Laker Courtside Camera pan is presented by...
WARNER COMMUNICATIONS—
Producer of the blockbuster motion picture "Batman," now available everywhere on videocassette!

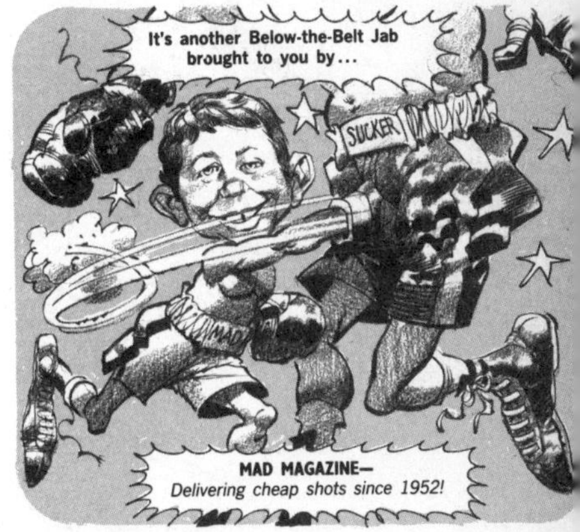
It's another Below-the-Belt Jab brought to you by...
SUCKER
MAD MAGAZINE—
Delivering cheap shots since 1952!

DECIBILL OF GOODS DEPT.

Here's a word you've probably missed: *onomatopoeia*. Since we're a humor magazine, you may think we made it up, like we did those other silly words, *nerfecsterpoc* and *vog*. YOU FOOL!! An onomatopoeia is a word that sounds like the thing it denotes. For example, "buzz" is an onomatopoeia. Get it?? Probably not, which is why we're scrapping our plans to call this article "A MAD Look at Brand Name Onomatopoeias," and simply calling it

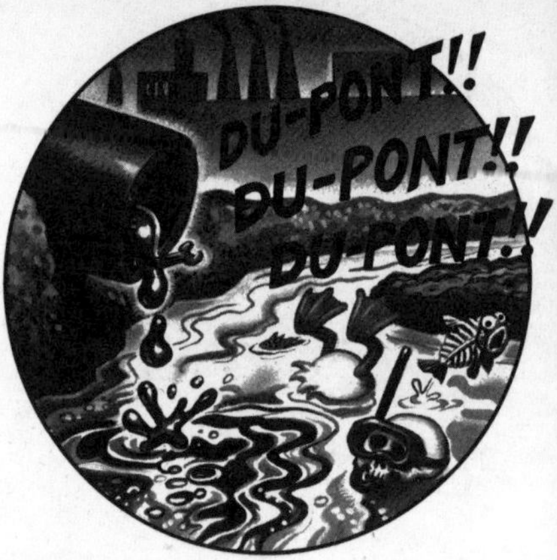

DU-PONT!!
DU-PONT!!
DU-PONT!!

REALLY APPROPRIATE BRAND NAME

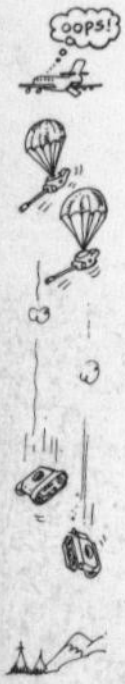

OOPS!

ARTIST: JOHN POUND WRITER: RUSS COOPER

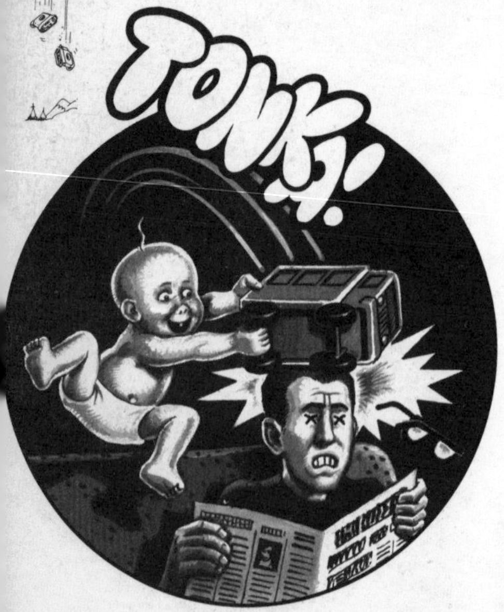

TONKA!

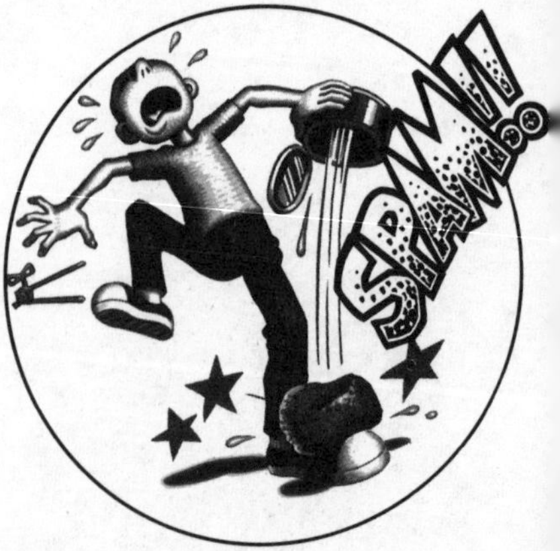

SPAM!®

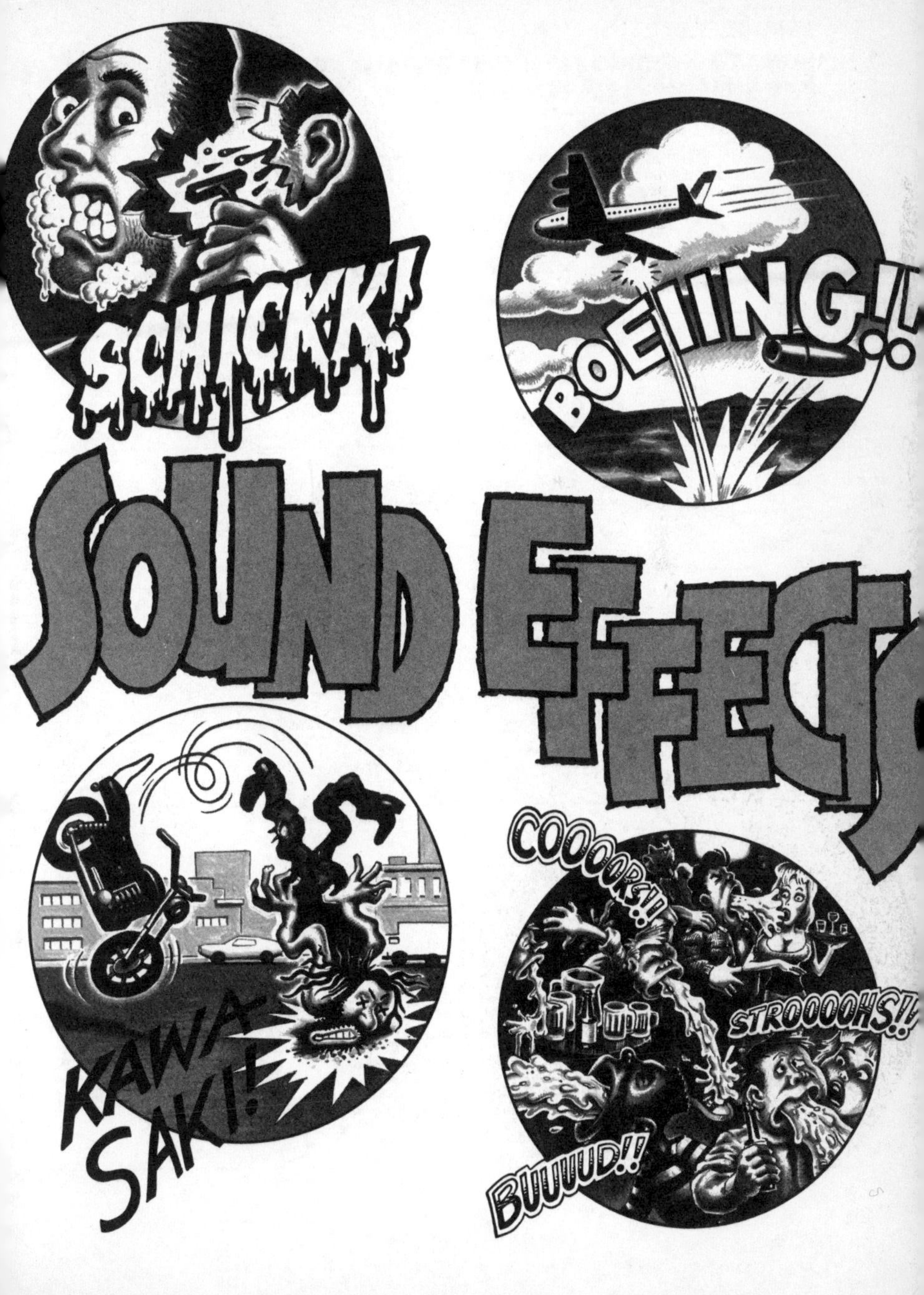
SCHICKK!
BOEIIING!!
SOUND EFFECTS
KAWASAKI!
COOOOORS!!
STROOOOOHS!!
BUUUUD!!

TALES FROM THE DUCK SIDE DEPT.

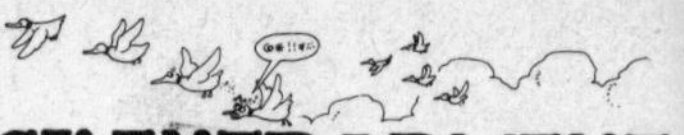

THE EXTRAORDINARY EULOGY ENTRAPMENT

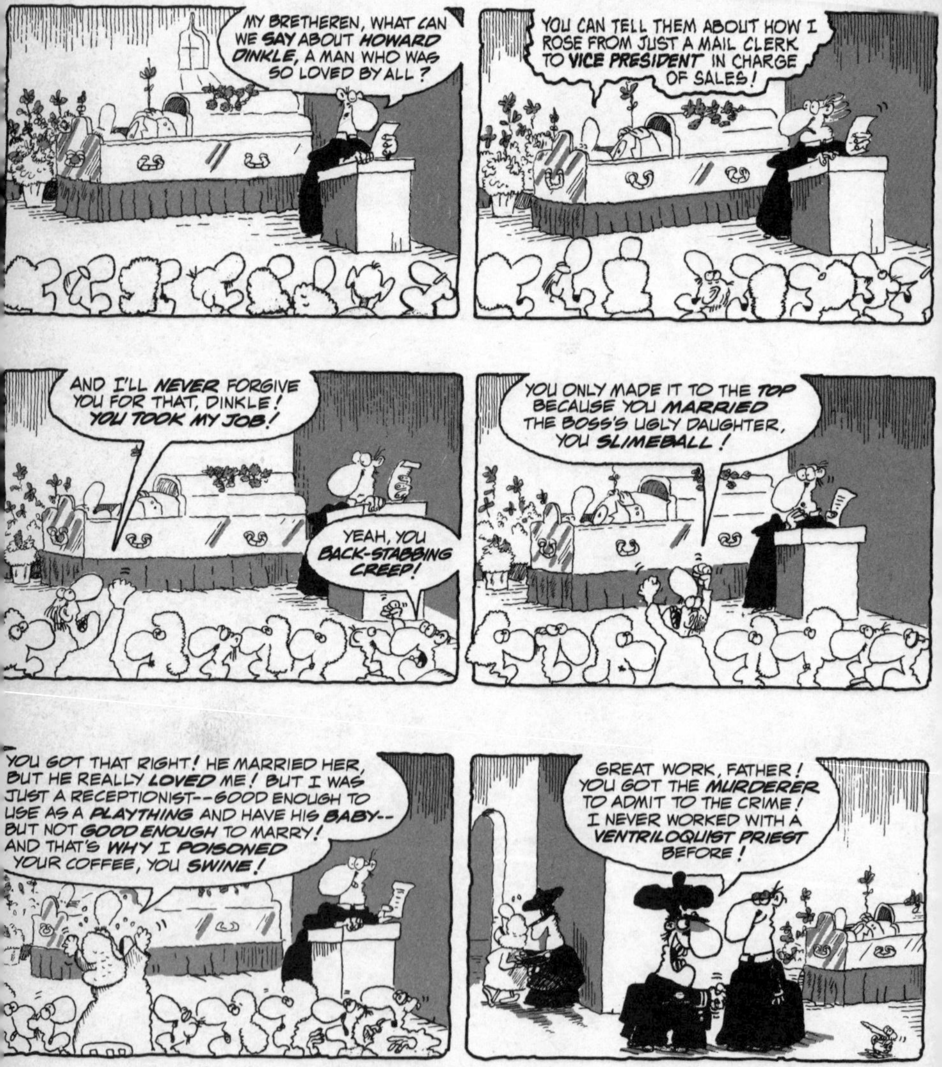
MY BRETHEREN, WHAT CAN WE SAY ABOUT HOWARD DINKLE, A MAN WHO WAS SO LOVED BY ALL?
YOU CAN TELL THEM ABOUT HOW I ROSE FROM JUST A MAIL CLERK TO VICE PRESIDENT IN CHARGE OF SALES!
AND I'LL NEVER FORGIVE YOU FOR THAT, DINKLE! YOU TOOK MY JOB!
YEAH, YOU BACK-STABBING CREEP!
YOU ONLY MADE IT TO THE TOP BECAUSE YOU MARRIED THE BOSS'S UGLY DAUGHTER, YOU SLIMEBALL!
YOU GOT THAT RIGHT! HE MARRIED HER, BUT HE REALLY LOVED ME! BUT I WAS JUST A RECEPTIONIST--GOOD ENOUGH TO USE AS A PLAYTHING AND HAVE HIS BABY--BUT NOT GOOD ENOUGH TO MARRY! AND THAT'S WHY I POISONED YOUR COFFEE, YOU SWINE!
GREAT WORK, FATHER! YOU GOT THE MURDERER TO ADMIT TO THE CRIME! I NEVER WORKED WITH A VENTRILOQUIST PRIEST BEFORE!

ARTIST & WRITER: DUCK EDWING

TAKING THEM TO TUSK DEPT.

Tens of thousands of kiddies have grown up reading about Babar, the king of the land of the elephants. Babar lives in a kinder, gentler world where everything turns out for the best for the elephants and their friends. Yet who knows? Maybe one day they'll have to deal with the not-so-kind, not-so-gentle real world, and we'll have to read

BABAR'S FINAL ADVENTURE

ARTIST: BOB CLARKE WRITER: FRANK JACOBS

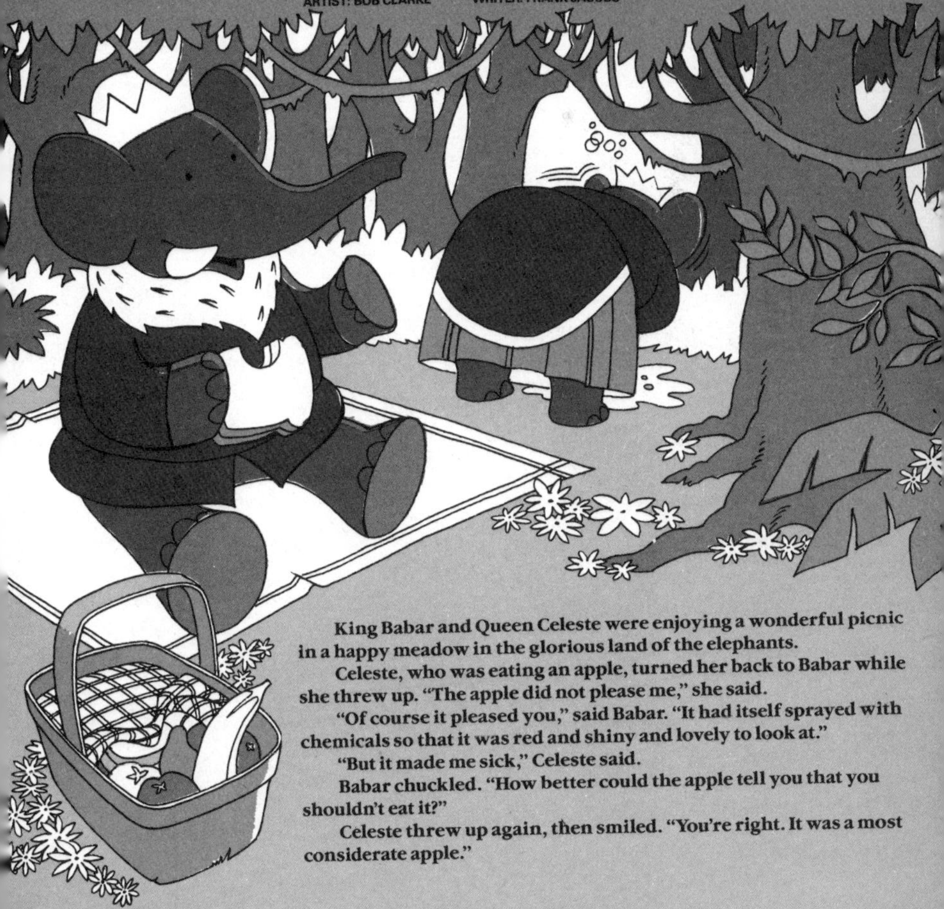

King Babar and Queen Celeste were enjoying a wonderful picnic in a happy meadow in the glorious land of the elephants.

Celeste, who was eating an apple, turned her back to Babar while she threw up. "The apple did not please me," she said.

"Of course it pleased you," said Babar. "It had itself sprayed with chemicals so that it was red and shiny and lovely to look at."

"But it made me sick," Celeste said.

Babar chuckled. "How better could the apple tell you that you shouldn't eat it?"

Celeste threw up again, then smiled. "You're right. It was a most considerate apple."

"Oh, look," Celeste exclaimed. "A truck is taking away Zephir the monkey. I am sad to see him go."

"You shouldn't be," Babar said. "He is being given a chance to help humanity."

"I thought he liked it here," said Celeste.

"He did, but now he will serve medical research by being injected with viruses and implanted with electrodes."

"How nice for him," said Celeste, waving her trunk. "Bye-bye, Zephir. Be sure and write."

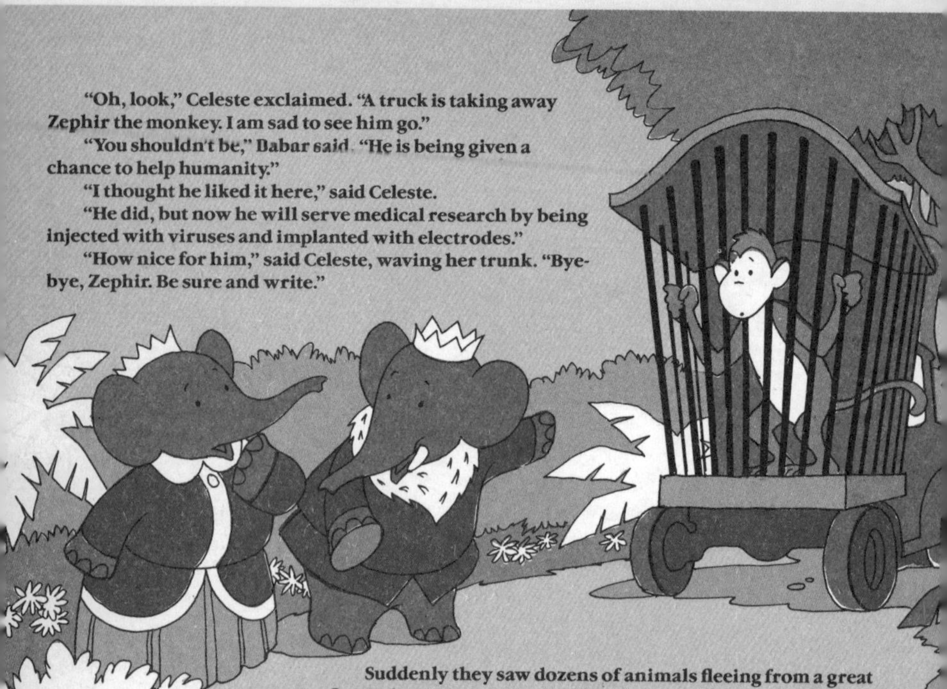

Suddenly they saw dozens of animals fleeing from a great fire. Babar recognized his old friend, Duane the giraffe.

"The rain forest is burning!" Duane gasped. "It's a disaster!"

"No, silly," Babar said reassuringly. "It's progress. The timber companies cut down the trees, providing space for the gold miners and cocoa plant growers. What they haven't cut, they burn. Everyone profits!"

"But what about the animals who lose their homes?" asked Celeste.

"They are given the opportunity to relocate and discover if they have the ability to survive," Babar explained.

"In other words, they're being given a *fresh start!*" Celeste exclaimed.

"Exactly," said Babar.

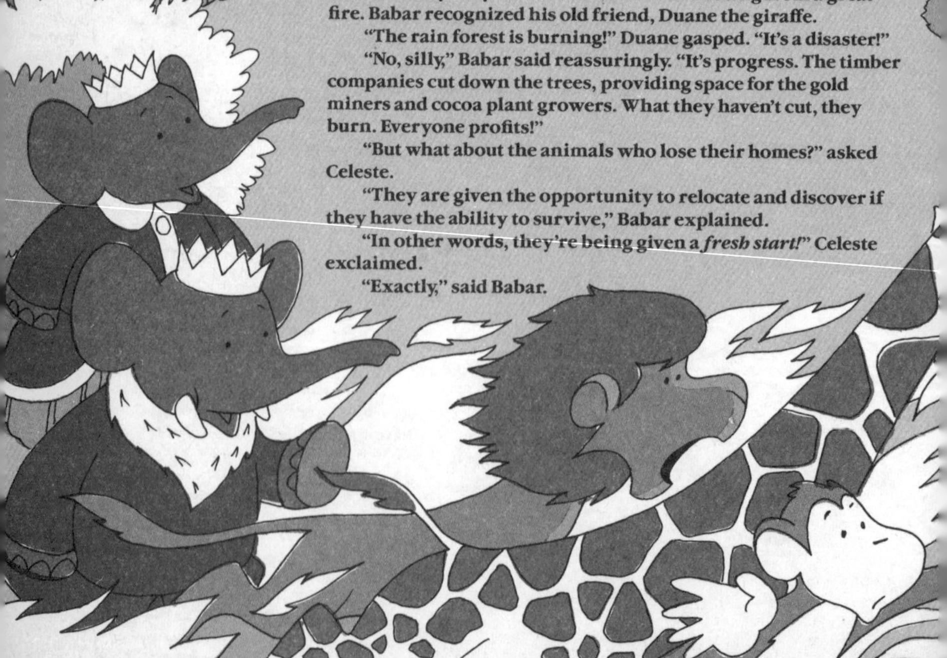

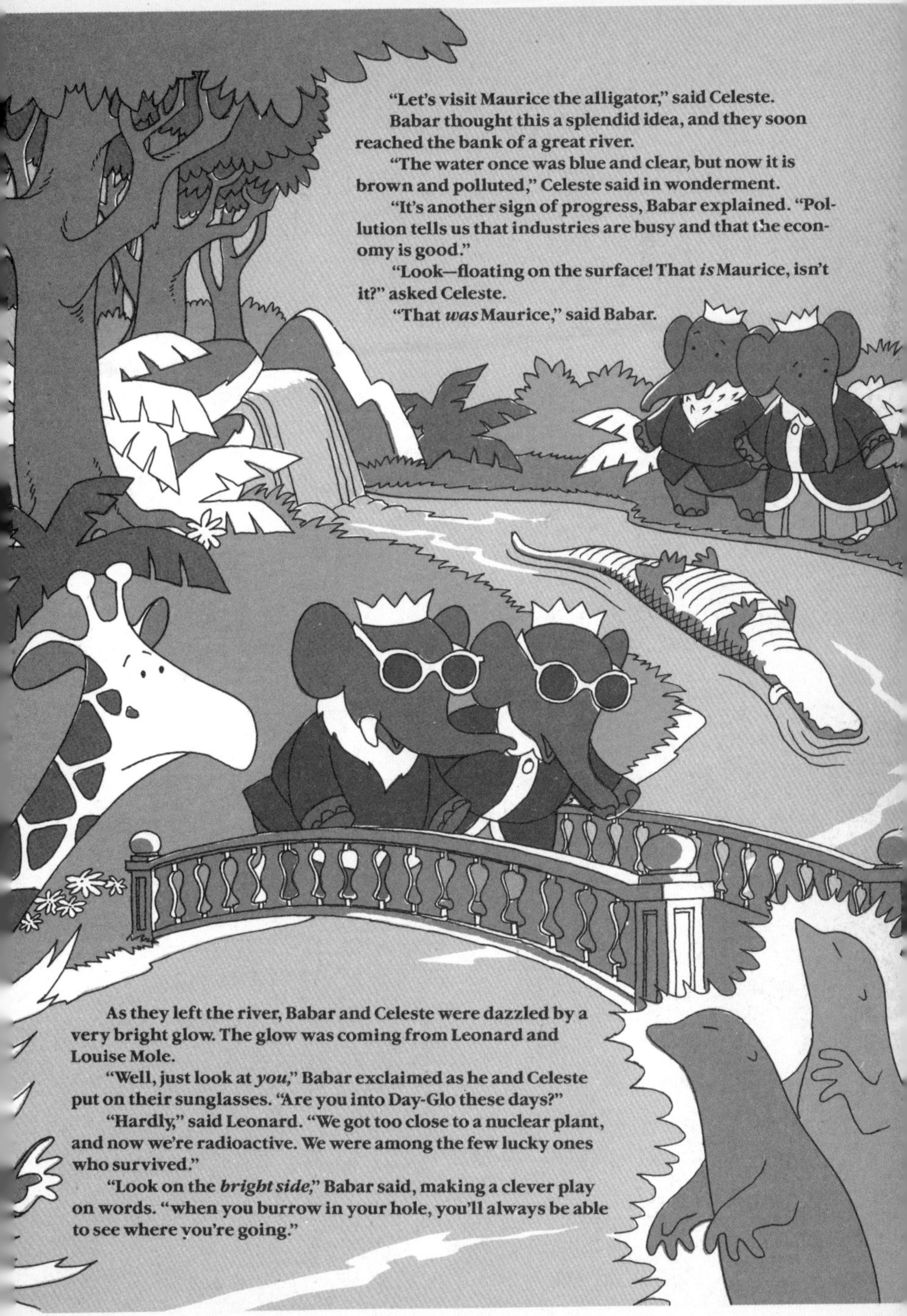

"Let's visit Maurice the alligator," said Celeste.

Babar thought this a splendid idea, and they soon reached the bank of a great river.

"The water once was blue and clear, but now it is brown and polluted," Celeste said in wonderment.

"It's another sign of progress, Babar explained. "Pollution tells us that industries are busy and that the economy is good."

"Look—floating on the surface! That *is* Maurice, isn't it?" asked Celeste.

"That *was* Maurice," said Babar.

As they left the river, Babar and Celeste were dazzled by a very bright glow. The glow was coming from Leonard and Louise Mole.

"Well, just look at *you,*" Babar exclaimed as he and Celeste put on their sunglasses. "Are you into Day-Glo these days?"

"Hardly," said Leonard. "We got too close to a nuclear plant, and now we're radioactive. We were among the few lucky ones who survived."

"Look on the *bright side,*" Babar said, making a clever play on words. "when you burrow in your hole, you'll always be able to see where you're going."

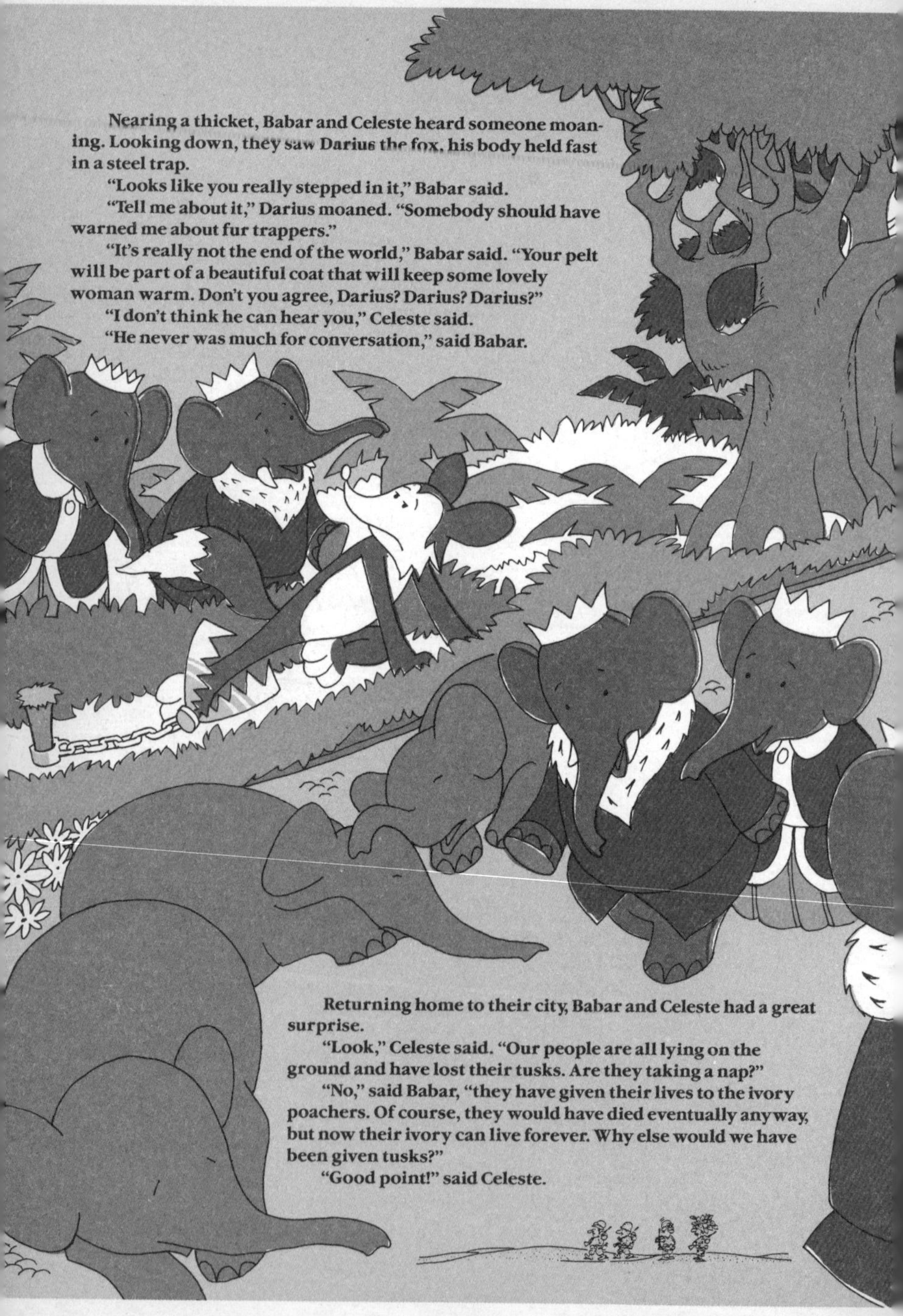

Nearing a thicket, Babar and Celeste heard someone moaning. Looking down, they saw Darius the fox, his body held fast in a steel trap.

"Looks like you really stepped in it," Babar said.

"Tell me about it," Darius moaned. "Somebody should have warned me about fur trappers."

"It's really not the end of the world," Babar said. "Your pelt will be part of a beautiful coat that will keep some lovely woman warm. Don't you agree, Darius? Darius? Darius?"

"I don't think he can hear you," Celeste said.

"He never was much for conversation," said Babar.

Returning home to their city, Babar and Celeste had a great surprise.

"Look," Celeste said. "Our people are all lying on the ground and have lost their tusks. Are they taking a nap?"

"No," said Babar, "they have given their lives to the ivory poachers. Of course, they would have died eventually anyway, but now their ivory can live forever. Why else would we have been given tusks?"

"Good point!" said Celeste.

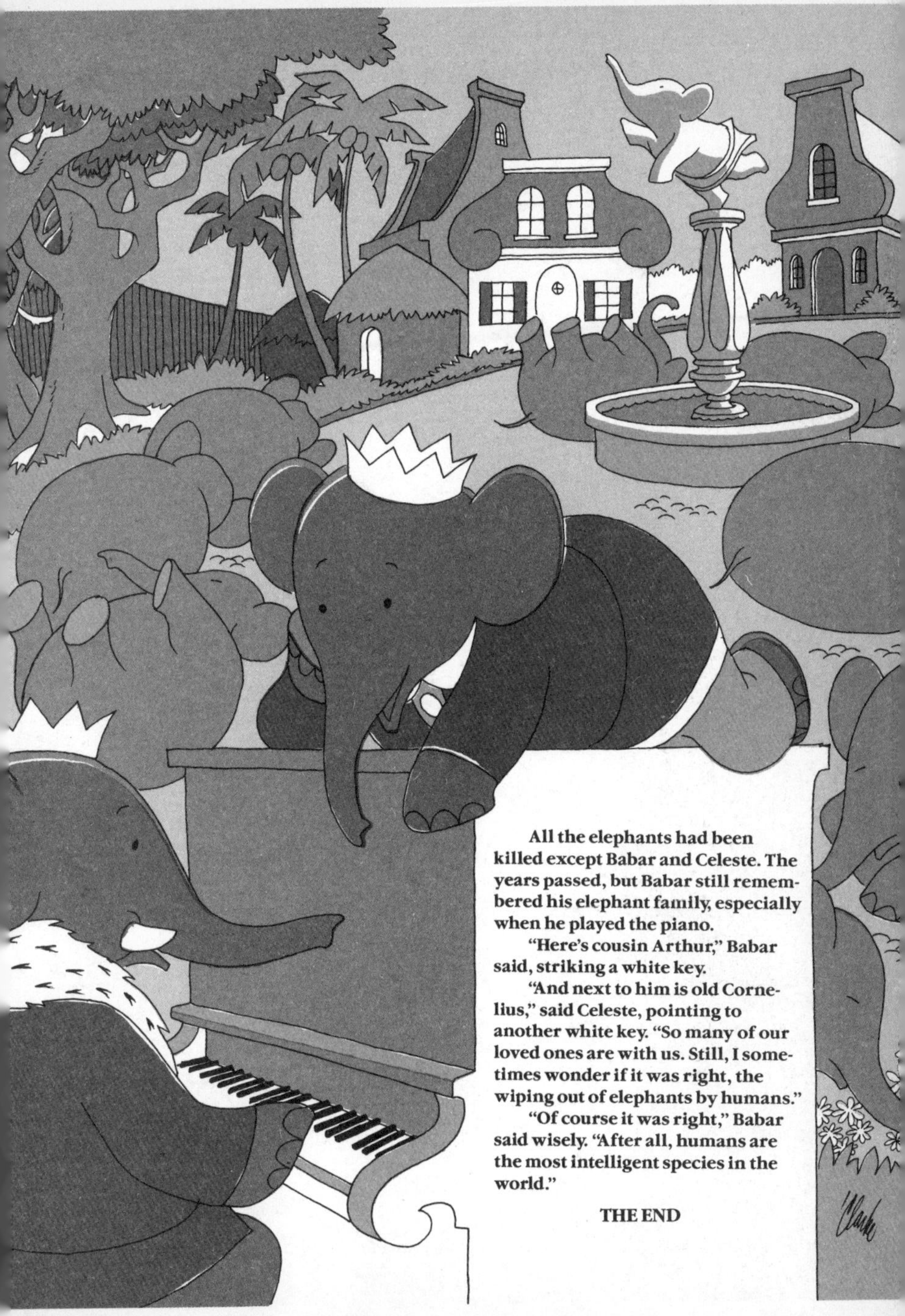
Clarke

All the elephants had been killed except Babar and Celeste. The years passed, but Babar still remembered his elephant family, especially when he played the piano.

"Here's cousin Arthur," Babar said, striking a white key.

"And next to him is old Cornelius," said Celeste, pointing to another white key. "So many of our loved ones are with us. Still, I sometimes wonder if it was right, the wiping out of elephants by humans."

"Of course it was right," Babar said wisely. "After all, humans are the most intelligent species in the world."

THE END

BANG THE DUMB SLOWLY DEPT.

MAD's Handy Clues, Hints And Tipoffs That You're Really, Unquestionably, Without A Doubt...

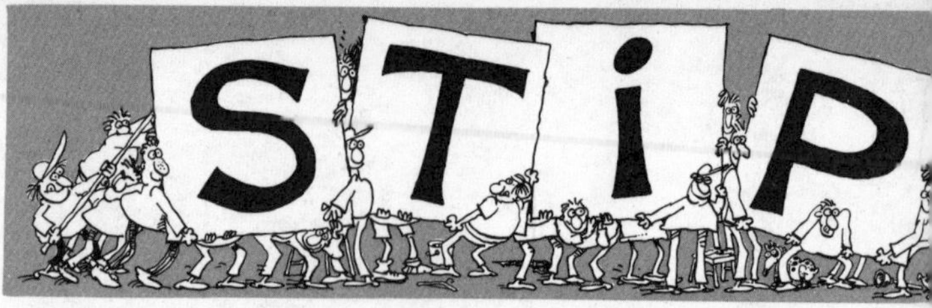

STiP

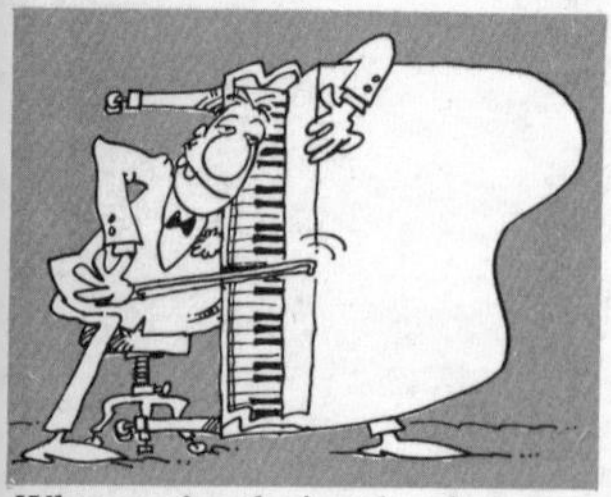

When you're playing the piano you frequently lose your grip on the bow.

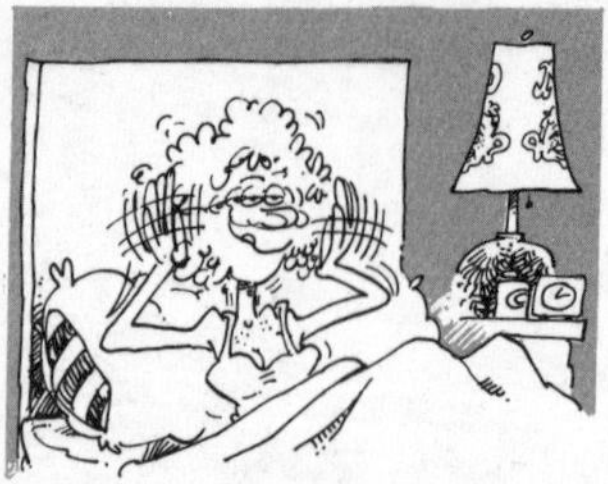

You go to bed and accidentally fluff up your head.

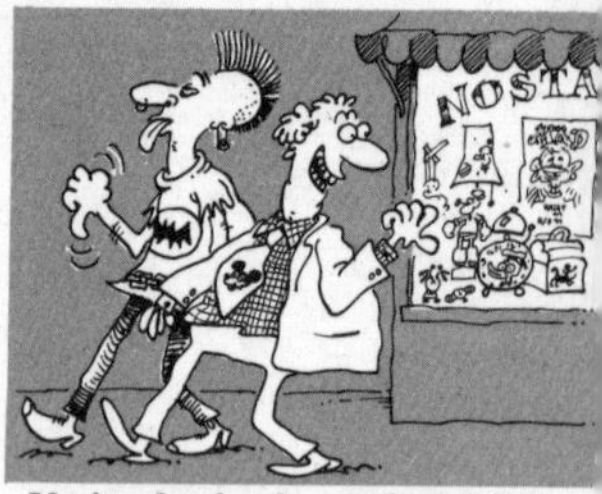

NOSTA

You're absolutely convinced that nostalgia is a thing of the past.

ARTIST: SERGIO ARAGONES

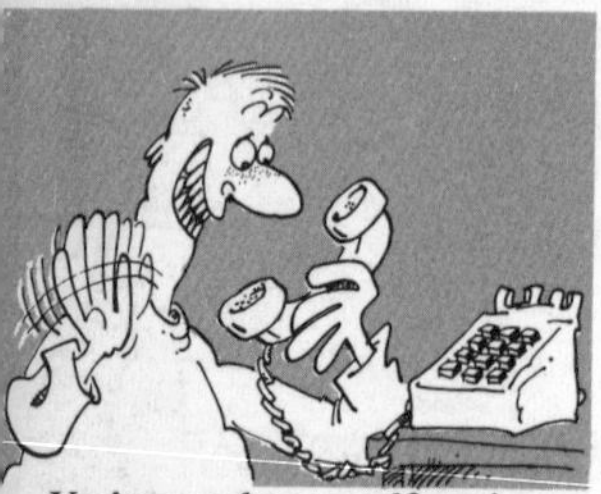

You've caught yourself waving "Goodbye" instead of "Hello" when answering the telephone.

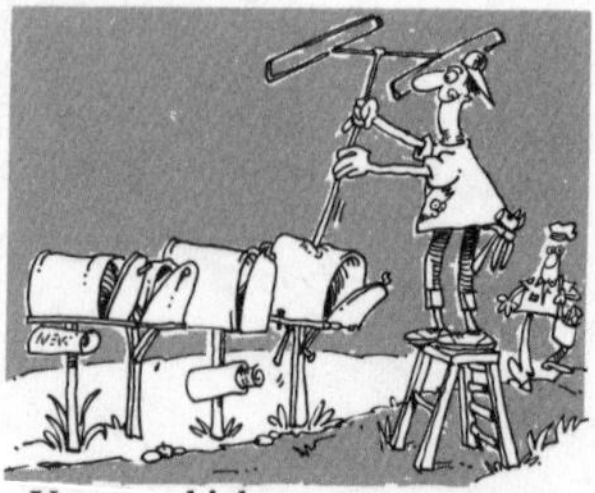

You put a higher antenna on your mailbox in an attempt to receive mail from people farther away.

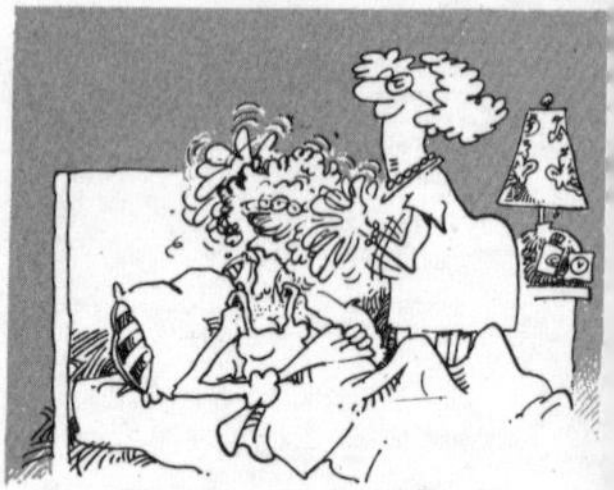

You go to bed and family members attempt to fluff up your head.

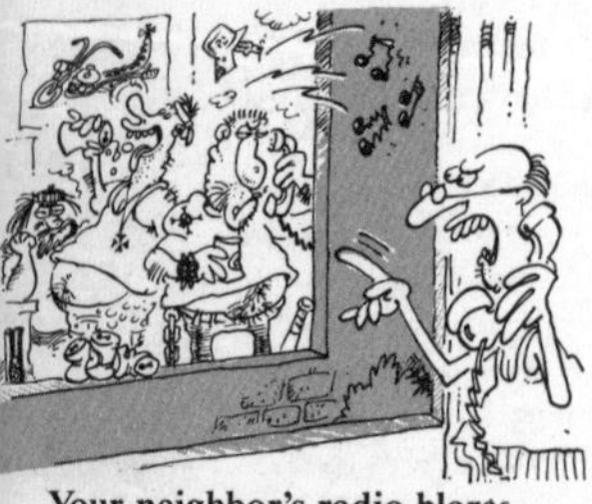

Your neighbor's radio blares at three A.M. and you angrily call him up to demand that he change the station at once.

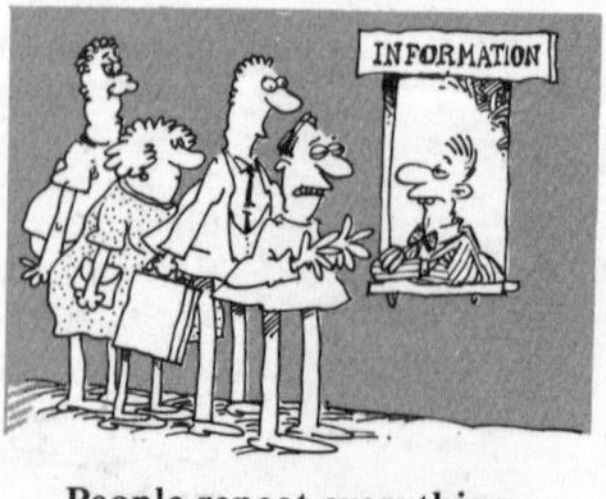

INFORMATION

People repeat everything they say to you because you look way too stupid to grasp things the first time around.

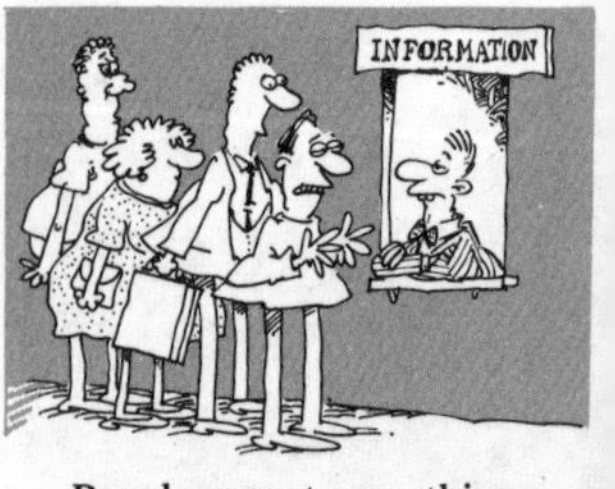

INFORMATION

People repeat everything they say to you because you look way too stupid to grasp things the first time around.

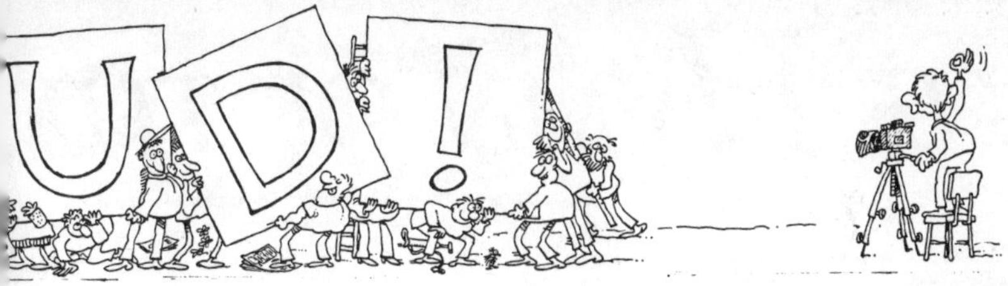
UD!

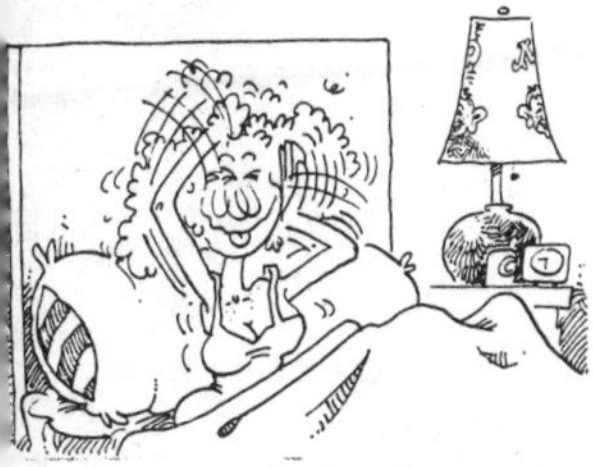

You go to bed and purposely fluff up your head.

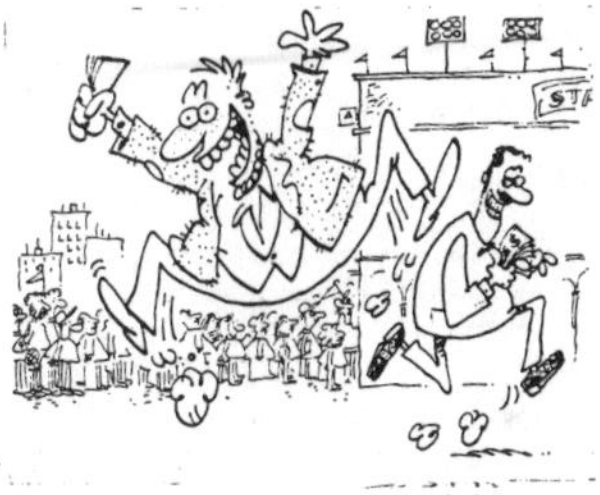

You purchase season tickets to the Super Bowl.

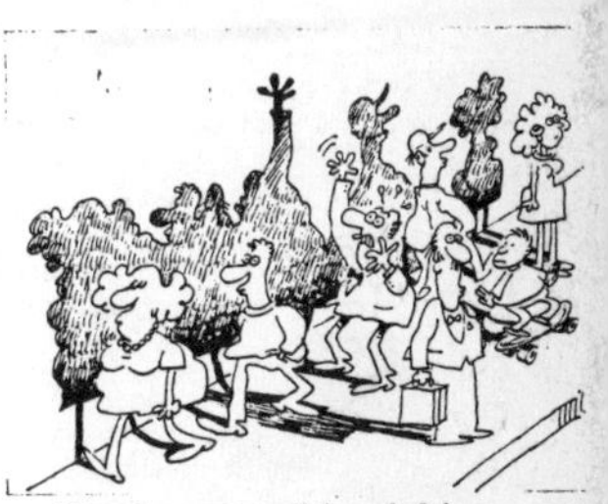

You have trouble picking your shadow out of a crowd.

WRITER: DAN BIRTCHER

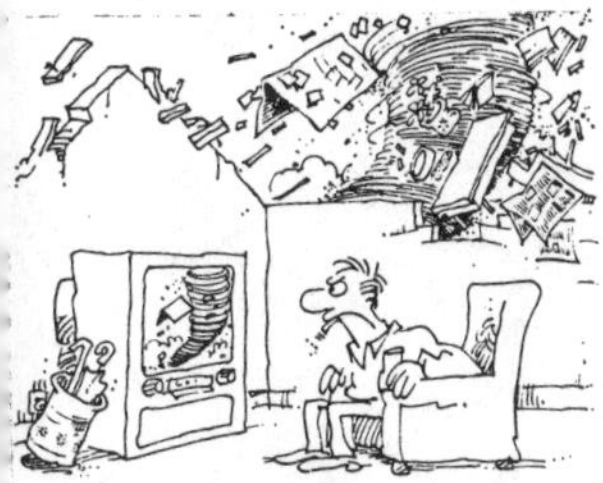

You fret over the fact that they never mention what a hurricane's last name is.

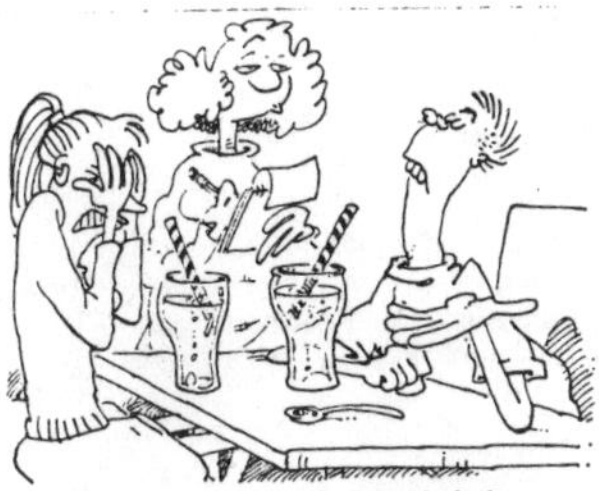

You find yourself complaining to a waitress that the straw in your glass is upside down.

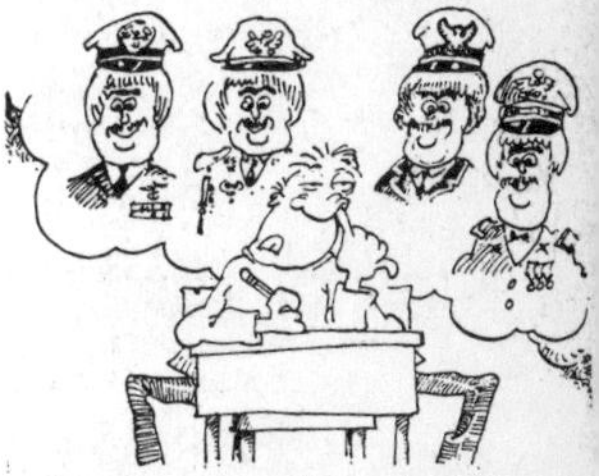

You find yourself wondering what branch of the military Captain Kangaroo was in.

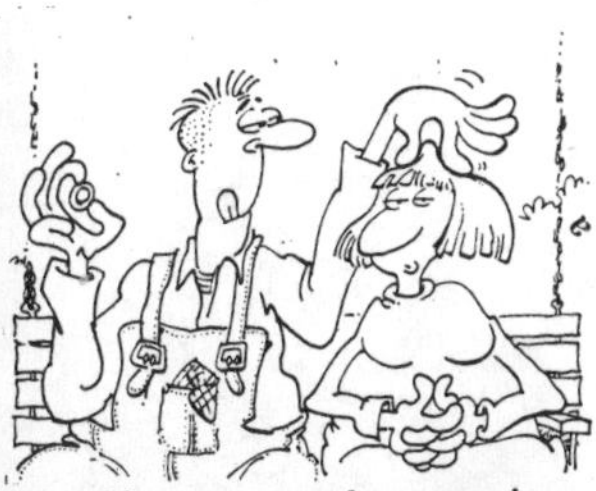

Your biggest worry about marriage is getting that little ring over your loved one's head, down their arm and onto their second finger.

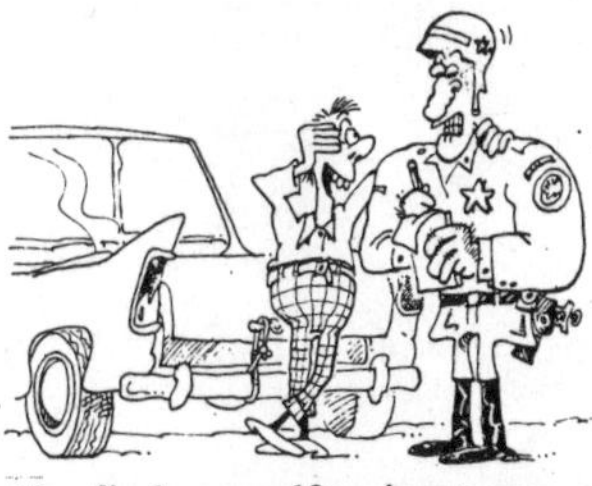

You find yourself trying to convince a policeman who's pulled you over for a burned-out headlight that he merely has one eye closed.

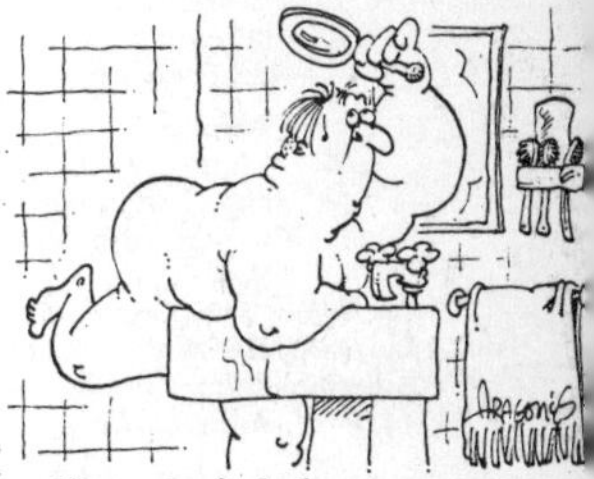

You worried about a sore that wouldn't heal, only to find out later that it was a natural body opening.

FRANK ON A ROLL DEPT.

THE HYMN OF THE

ARTIST: GEORGE WOODBRIDGE WRITER: FRANK JACOBS

Our eyes have seen the sorrow of a nation gone to pot,
Where the loonies carry handguns and the passersby get shot,
Where the farms are going under and the cities burn and rot—
The Glory Days are gone!

Lordy, Lordy, how'd we do..it?
Now..we have to suffer through..it!
Had..our chance but really blew..it!
The Glory Days are gone!

We've a budget we can't balance, though we once were in the chips;
We've been overspending billions for outmoded planes and ships;
If you haven't figured out who'll foot the bill, just read our lips—
The debt keeps piling on!

Kindly, gently, how they stroke..us
With..their fiscal hocus-pocus!
All..the time they're out to soak..us!
The debt keeps piling on!

We have seen the big polluters fill our waterways with swill;
We have smelled the fishes dying from the latest tanker spill;
If the oil doesn't kill them, then the garbage surely will—
The crud keeps flowing on!

Pity, pity, our poor na-tion!
Who..can stop the devasta-tion?
May-be Bo knows conserva-tion!
The crud keeps flowing on!

We get smacked by soaring prices when we gas up at the pumps;
We have seen the reckless loggers turn our forests into stumps;
Now we're bailing out the S&Ls who've played us all for chumps—
The greed goes marching on!

Surely, surely, trouble's brew-ing
From..the damage that they're do-ing!
We're..the ones who get the screw-ing!
The greed goes marching on!

We have heard those scuzzy rappers spouting sleaze for easy cash;
We're turned off by TV sitcoms spewing out their mindless trash;
All which makes us very thankful for old episodes of "M*A*S*H"—
The drek keeps coming on!

Cowabunga! how we're hat-ing
What..they'll do to get a rat-ing!
Like..a whale regurgitat-ing!
The dreck keeps coming on!

In the alleys of our cities where the poor and homeless dwell,
You can see the victims dying from the crack that pushers sell,
While the bankers launder money for the Medellín cartel—
The crime keeps marching on!

Spurting, gushing, blood is flow-ing,
While..the murder rate is grow-ing!
Down..the tubes we're surely go-ing!
The Glory Days are gone!

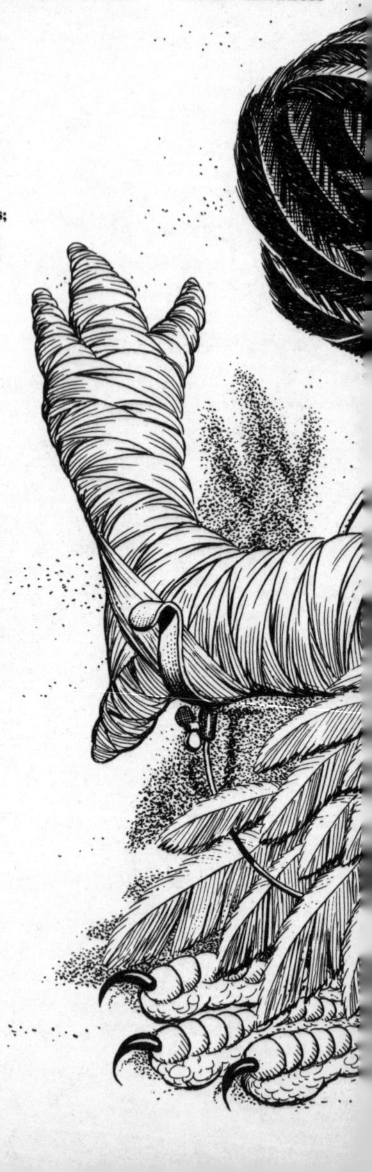

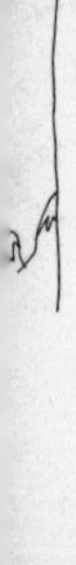

BATTERED REPUBLIC

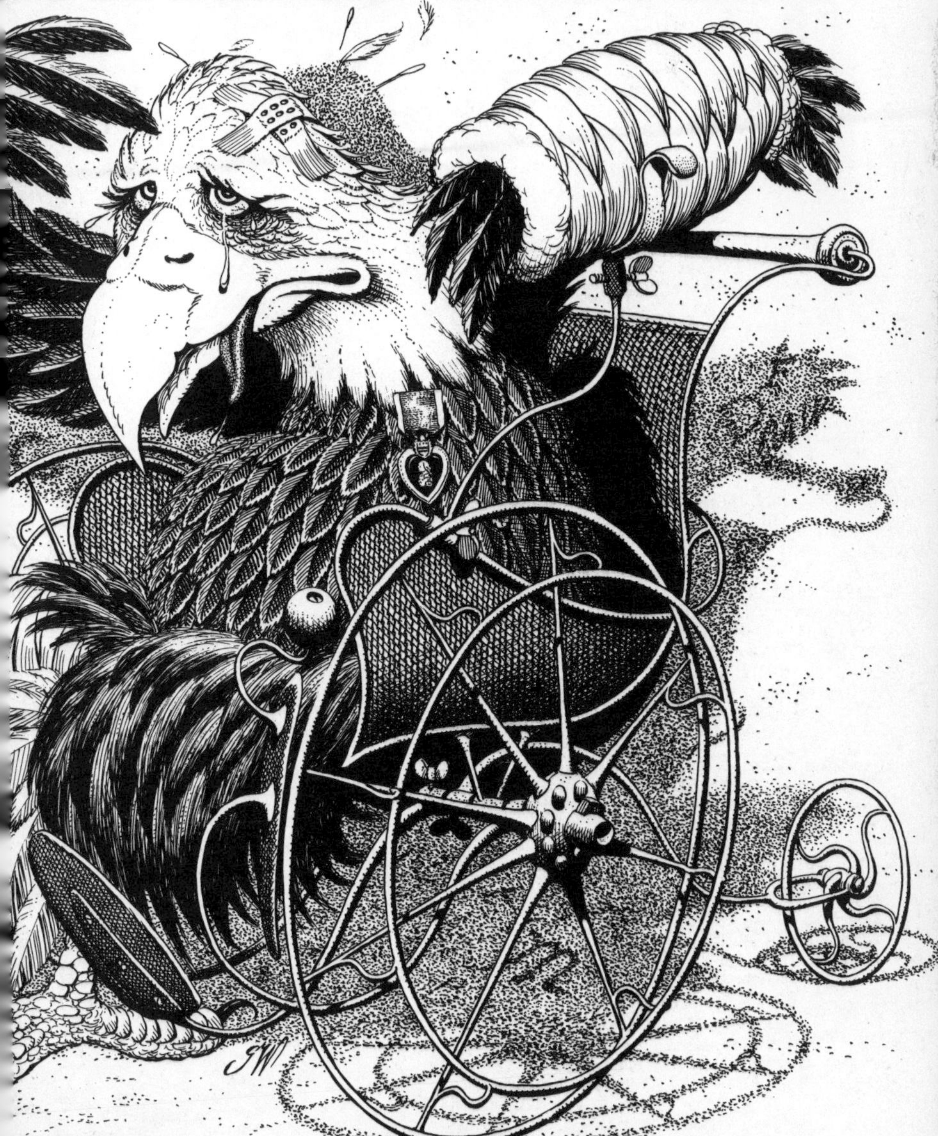

THE MORE THINGS CHANGE, THE MORE THEY STAY THE LAME DEPT.

Why do we study history? Because they make us! And because they're right—those who do
remember the past are doomed to relive it! But things never happen quite the same w

SMALL SCALE EX

HISTORY REP

50,000 B.C. Through sheer will power, man makes it through the Ice Age.

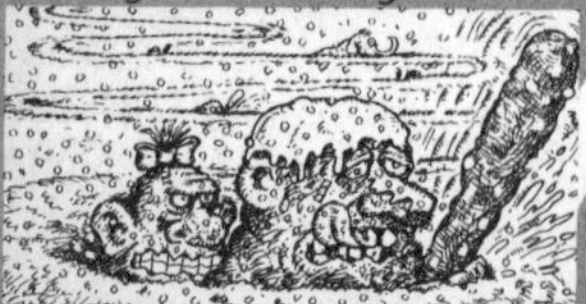

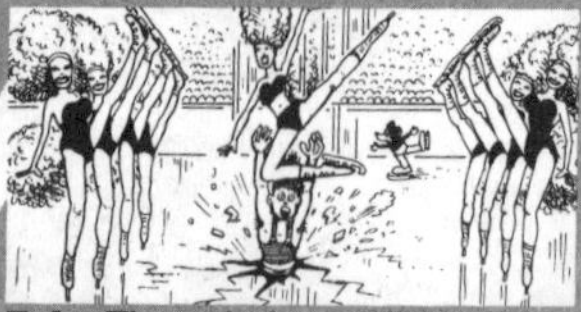

Today Through sheer will power, man makes it through the Ice Capades.

1787 The Founding Fathers creat a new nation at the Constitution al Convention in Philadelphia

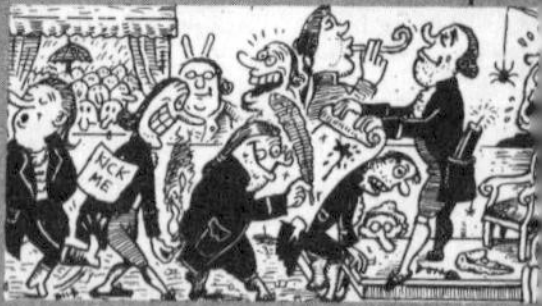
KICK ME

1860 The Pony Express begins, with riders taking care of the horses at every opportunity.

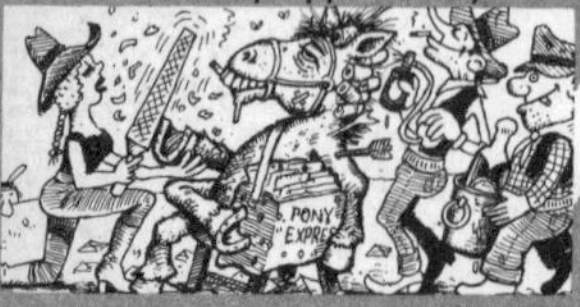

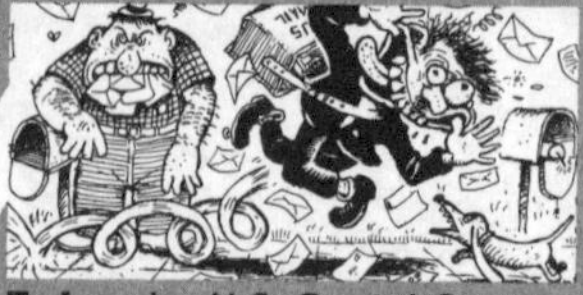

Today the U.S. Postal Service continues, with employees taking every opportunity to horse around.

2 Billion B.C. Life forms in a swamp's ancient, soupy goo.

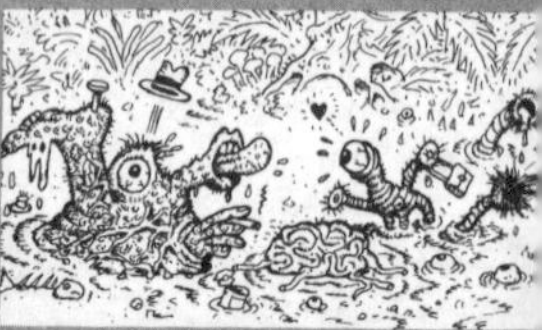

2200 B.C. Lust for immortality spurs the Egyptians to wrap themselves in precious linens.

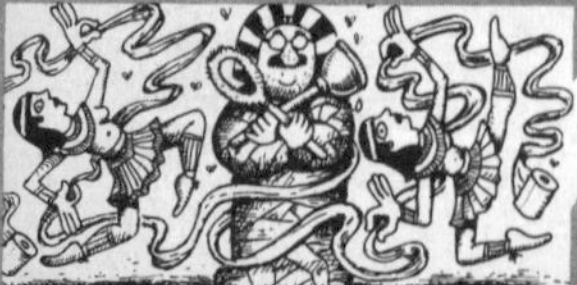

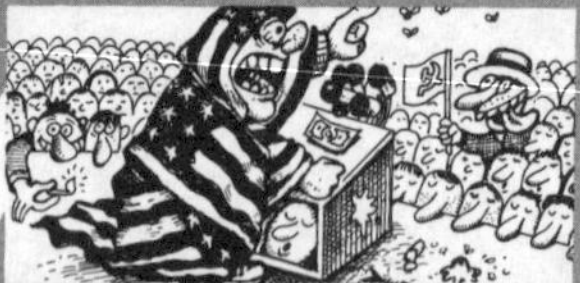

Today Lust for high office spurs politicians to wrap themselves in precious linens.

1839 Samuel Morse sees his telegraph is built and taps out "What hath God wrought?"

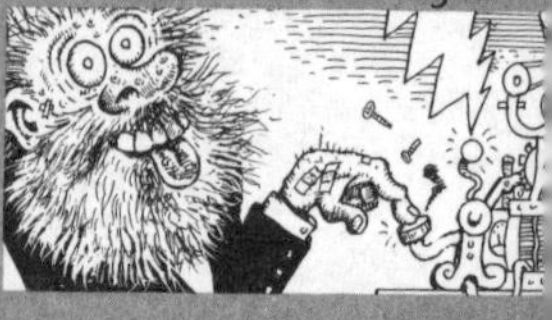

1778 Love of country prompts George Washington to spend cruel winter at Valley Forge.

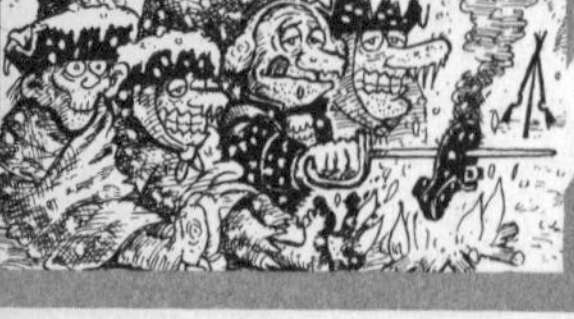

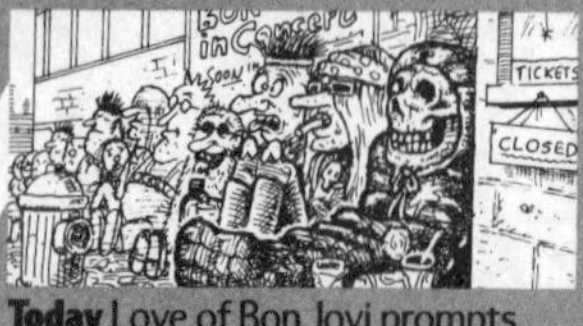
BON
in Concert
TICKETS
CLOSED

Today Love of Bon Jovi prompts Sally Greps to spend cruel night in line at arena ticket office.

1804 Curiosity spurs Lewis and Clark to go explore the Louisiana Territory.

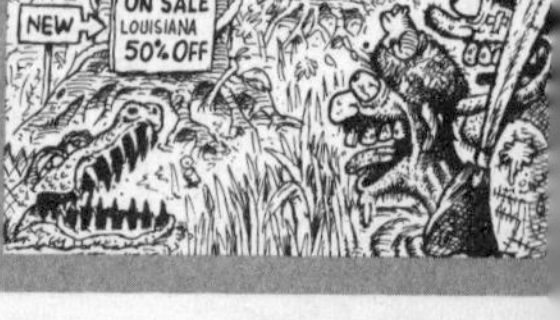
NEW
ON SALE
LOUISIANA
50% OFF

twice! Sometimes you have to look pretty closely to spot the repetition...or let us look for you! So, without further ado (and just in time for that big test!), we proudly present some

AMPLES OF HOW
EATS ITSELF!

ARTIST: TOM BUNK WRITER: DAN BIRTCHER

Today Fred's father creates a sensation at the Confectioners' Convention in Atlantic City.

Today Life forms in a diner's old, gooey soup.

BILL PART 2

Today Mr. Fiksman sees his telephone bill and shrieks out, "Who in God's name can afford this?!"

Today Curiosity spurs Louis and Claire to consider going to a different bowling alley.

30 million B.C. Apes leave the trees and regroup on the ground in order to achieve a better life.

1810 Napoleon is painted with his hand in his coat because that is the style in France.

1620 Desire to be free of England drives pilgrims to the New World.

HOW TO BUILD A NEW HOME

1066 The Normans invade England and make it their home.

Today The Monkees leave retirement and regroup on the stage in order to recapture the good life.

Today Congressmen are videotaped with their hands in the cookie jar because that is the style in D.C.

Today Desire to be free of wife drives Mr. Hanrahan to his basement workshop.

TOM BUNK

Today Norman's uncle invades his apartment and makes it his home.

COMPANY TRADEMOCKS DEPT.

The Jolly Green Giant. The Pillsbury Doughboy. Spuds MacKenzie. The California Raisins. Th
list is endless! All of them the products of an ad executive's limited imagination, and a
of them rammed down our throats until they become the beloved symbols of the goods they we

ADVERTISING CHARACTE

THAT BETTER REFLECT THE MISER

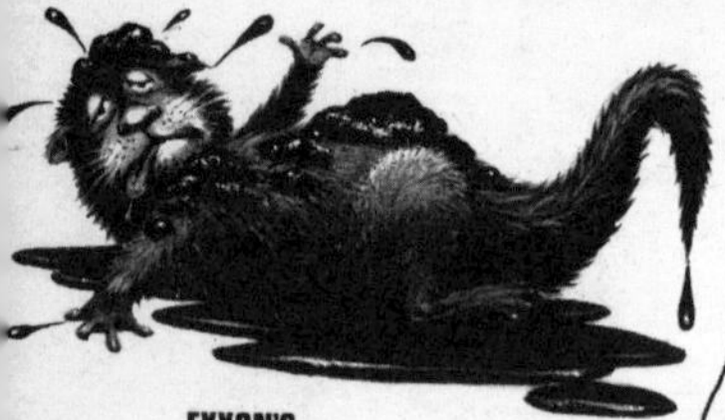

EXXON'S
Oscar, the Oily Otter

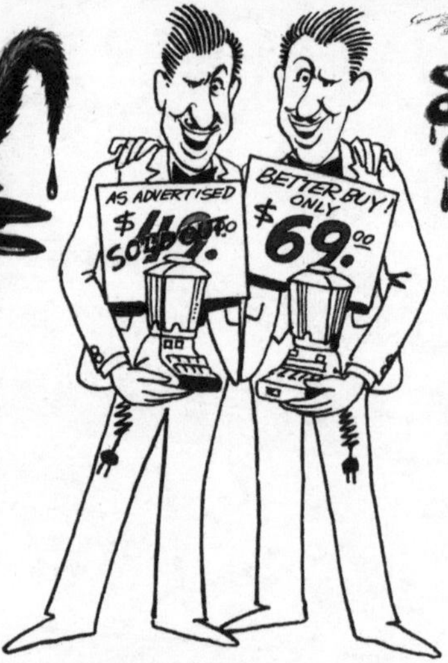
AS ADVERTISED
BETTER BUY! ONLY
$69.00

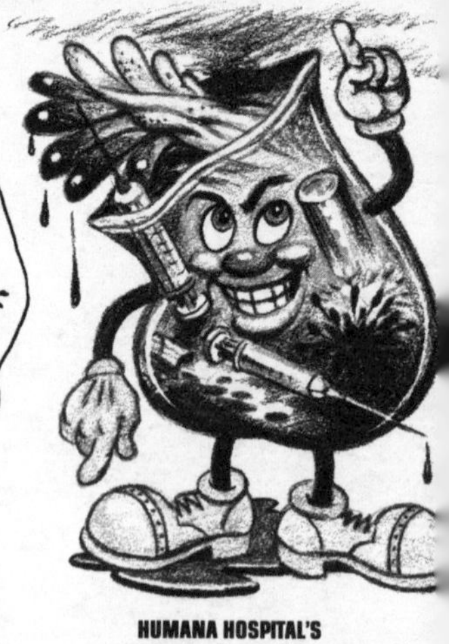

HUMANA HOSPITAL'S
Hank, the Talking Bag of Infectious Medical Waste

KENMORE'S
Bait & Switch, the Shady Sears Appliance Salesmen

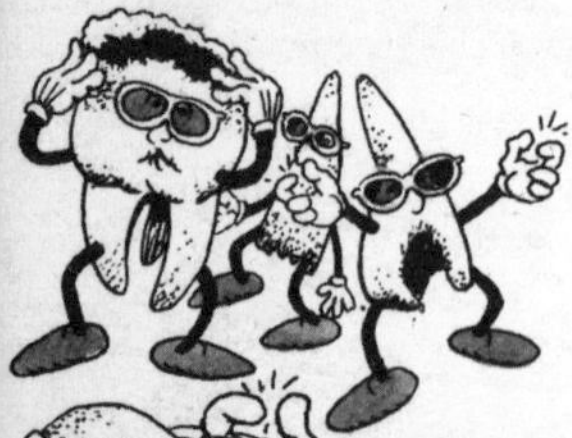

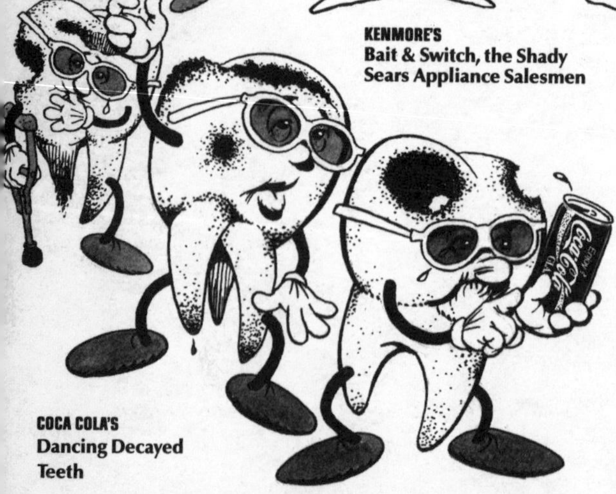
Coca-Cola

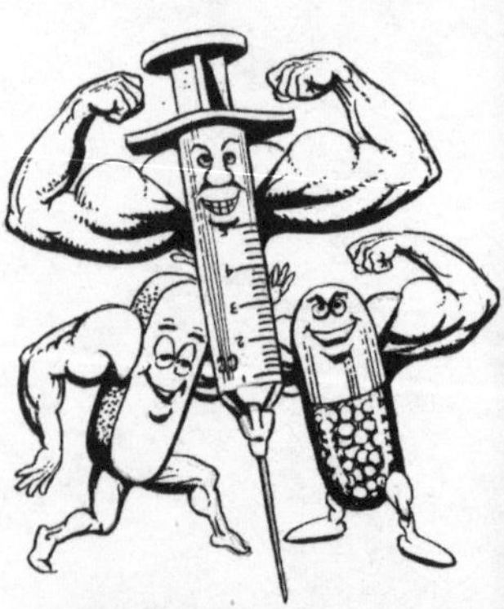

COCA COLA'S
Dancing Decayed Teeth

THE NATIONAL FOOTBALL LEAGUE'S
Anabolic Steroid Family

ARTIST: GEORGE WOODBRIDGE WRITER: CHARLIE KADAU

eated to huckster for! We've always found something phony about these characters, though. e just don't think they truly represent what their respective companies are like! Besides ıth in advertising, we'd like to see some truth in advertising *characters!* We'd like some...

S & CORPORATE MASCOTS

LE COMPANIES THEY WORK FOR

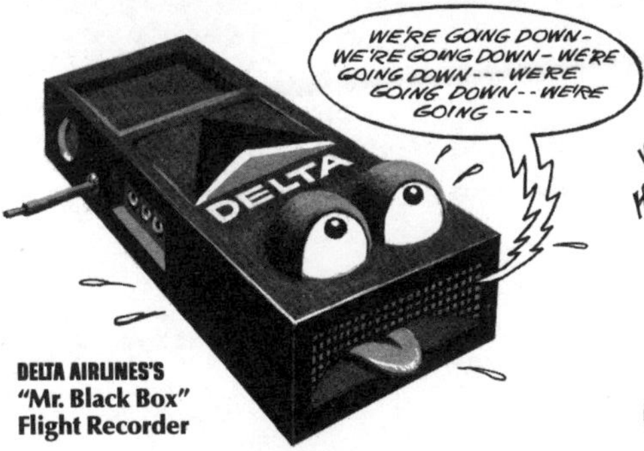
WE'RE GOING DOWN- WE'RE GOING DOWN- WE'RE GOING DOWN--- WE'RE GOING DOWN-- WE'RE GOING ---
DELTA

DELTA AIRLINES'S
"Mr. Black Box" Flight Recorder

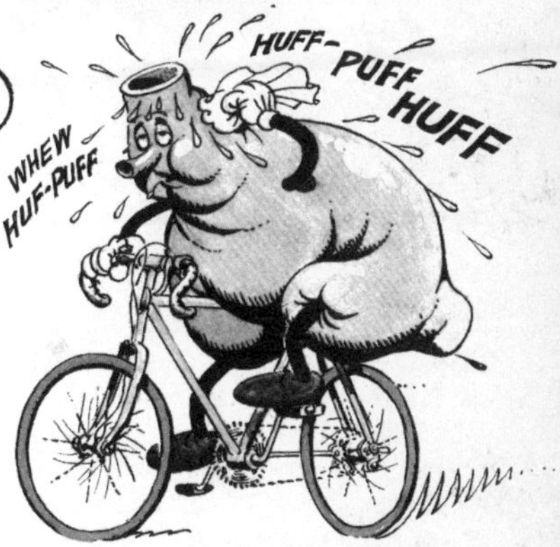
HUFF- PUFF HUFF
WHEW HUF-PUFF

THE NATIONAL BEEF COUNCIL'S
Clogged Artery Boy

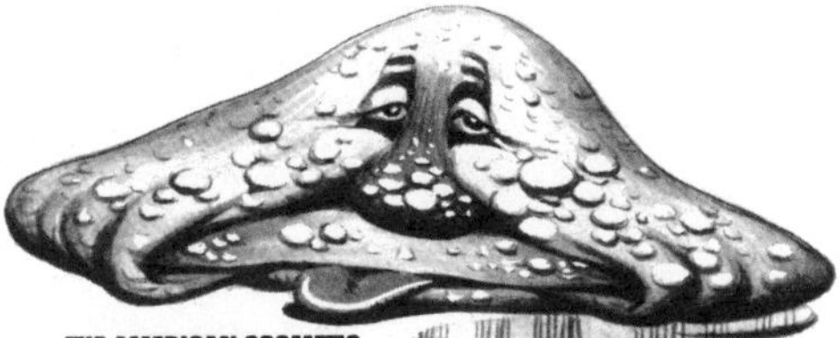

THE AMERICAN COSMETIC SURGEONS ASSOCIATION'S
Liposuctioned Fat Blob

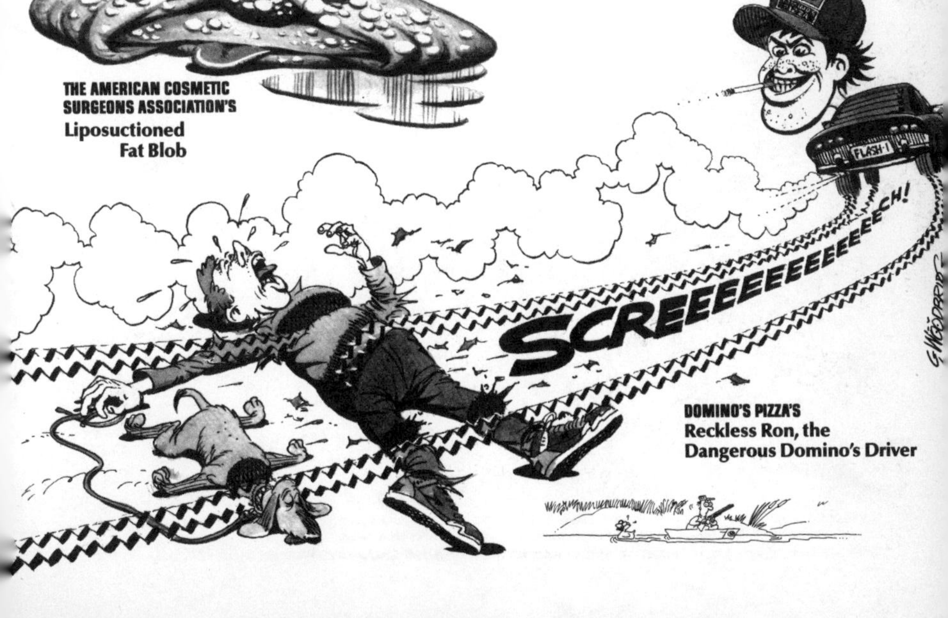
FLASH-1
SCREEEEEEEEEEEEEEECH!

DOMINO'S PIZZA'S
Reckless Ron, the Dangerous Domino's Driver

The latest VCRs can be set to record a program two weeks from now, by which time any show worth watching will probably have been cancelled.

Many new cigarette brands have been developed to attract very specific economic and ethnic groups, which means that all Americans now have an equal opportunity to get lung cancer.

THERE'S ALWAYS GLOOM FOR IMPROVEMENT DEPT.

Most Americans know Murphy's Law—"Whatever can go wrong will go wrong!" And you probably know the Peter Principle ("Individuals rise to their levels of incompetence.") and Parkinson's Law ("Work expands to fill the time left for its completion."). But do you know the theory that really explains what's wrong with modern life? Find out! Follow us into the informational void as we take...

THE MAD MAXIM:
"EXPERTS NEVER STOP MAKING 'IMPROVEMENTS' UNTIL EVERYTHING BECOMES IMPRACTICAL!"

A MAD LO

HOW

WE'VE

ARTIST PAUL COKER

By spending hundreds of billions of dollars, the Pentagon has developed a new and sophisticated military establishment that can allegedly win a full scale nuclear war in outer space—but not in Central America.

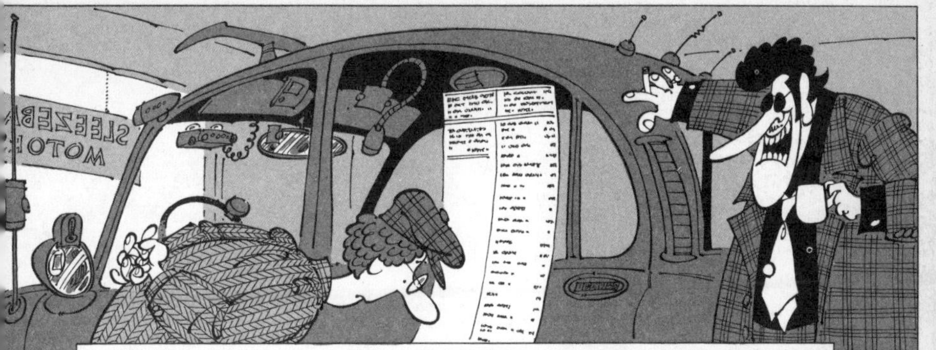

So many glitzy accessories have been added to new cars that buyers who only want an AM radio and a heater are warned that they're now going to have to pay substantially more for such a unique "customized" model.

K AT

FAR

COME

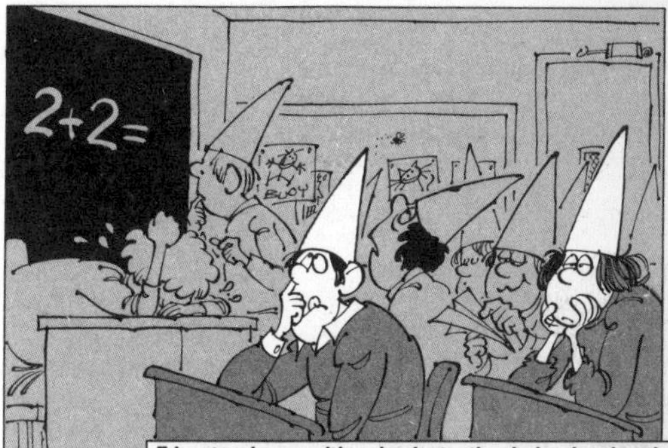
2+2=

Educators keep writing simpler textbooks hoping that they will encourage underachievers, with the result that bright kids now don't learn anything except how to underachieve.

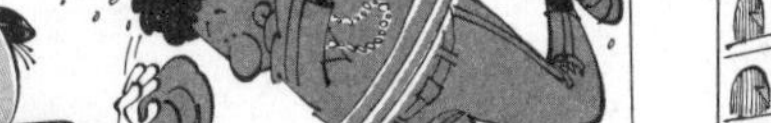

ITER: TOM KOCH

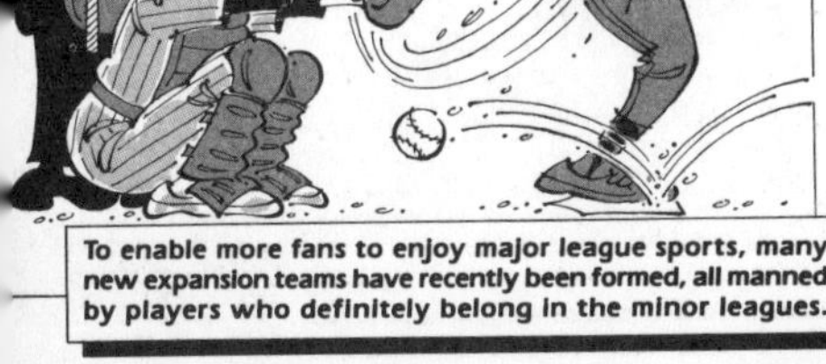

To enable more fans to enjoy major league sports, many new expansion teams have recently been formed, all manned by players who definitely belong in the minor leagues.

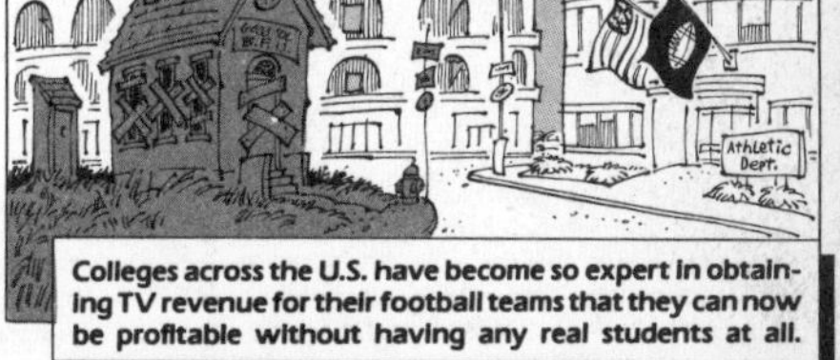
Athletic Dept.

Colleges across the U.S. have become so expert in obtaining TV revenue for their football teams that they can now be profitable without having any real students at all.

THE MAD MAXIM: "EXPERTS NEVER STOP MAKING 'IMPROVEMENTS' UNTIL EVERYTHING BECOMES IMPRACTICAL!"

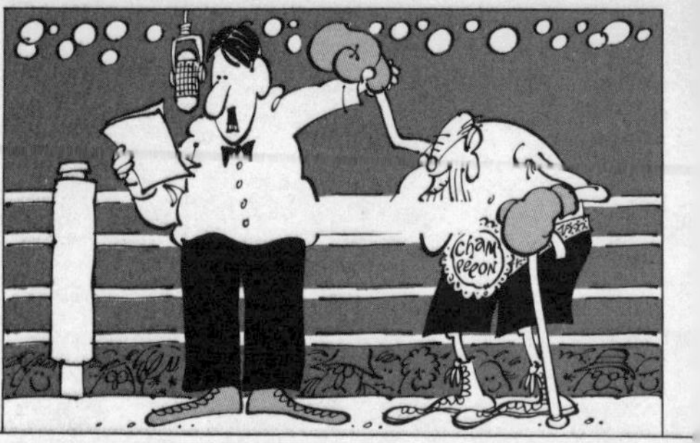

CHAM
PEEON

Organizational skill within professional boxing can be thanked for giving us so many different weight divisions and so many different Federations that every fighter in the world is now the champion of something.

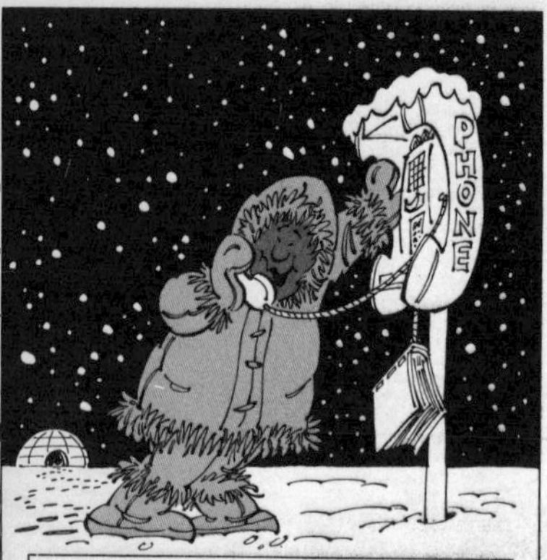

PHONE

The miracle of direct long distance dialing has become so widespread that it is now possible for almost any drunk anywhere in the world to wake you at three in the morning.

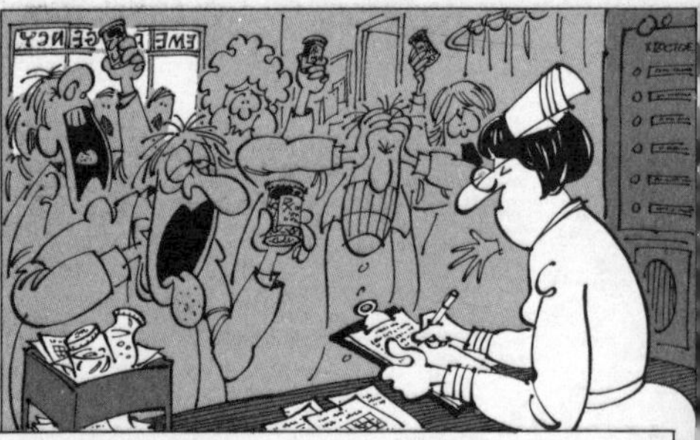

Pharmaceutical companies have introduced so many new life-saving drugs that hospital emergency rooms have become filled with scores of people suffering from the harmful side effects of taking them.

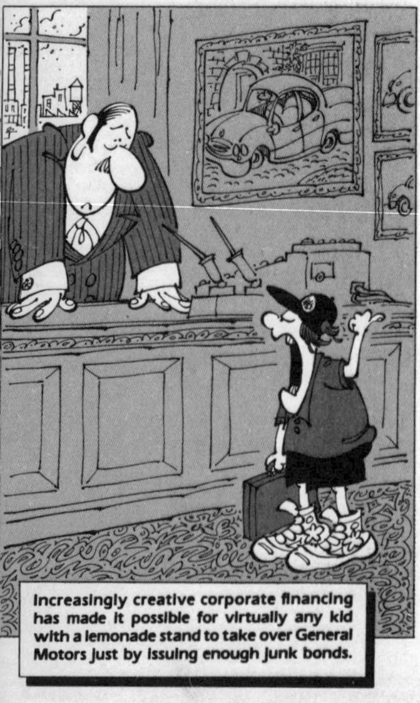

Increasingly creative corporate financing has made it possible for virtually any kid with a lemonade stand to take over General Motors just by issuing enough junk bonds.

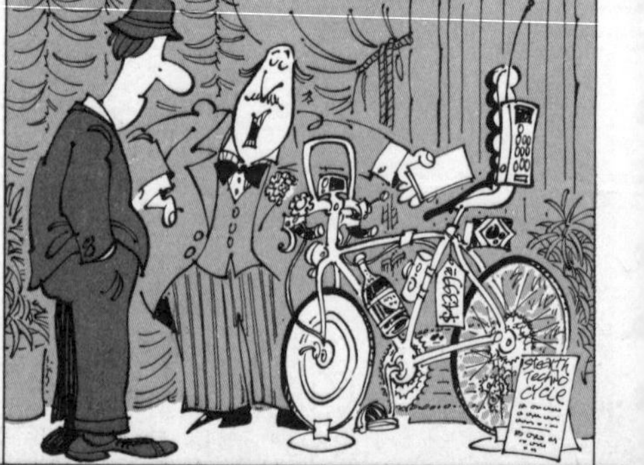

Stealth
Techno
Cycle

Bicycles, which became popular as inexpensive alternatives to the automobile, have been so upgraded that the same people who could not afford to buy a car now also cannot afford to buy a bicycle.

ALL JAFFEE DEPT.

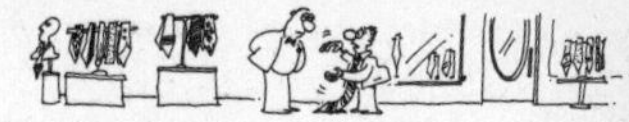

In our complicated, modern world, there are tons of books around which explain how complex and sophisticated contraptions such as the Stronifium Zertometer and the Digital Shovel operate. But here at MAD, we are bold enough to ask: "Of what use is it to know the innermost workings of an Autoflab HamChip, if you have no appreciation for life's simple pleasures??" Wise words indeed. Well, Here at MAD, no one is as simple-minded as Al Jaffee, who concocted this handy guide explaining how simple things work! Coincidentally, the name of this article is...

A MAD GUIDE TO HOW SIMPLE THINGS WORK PART II

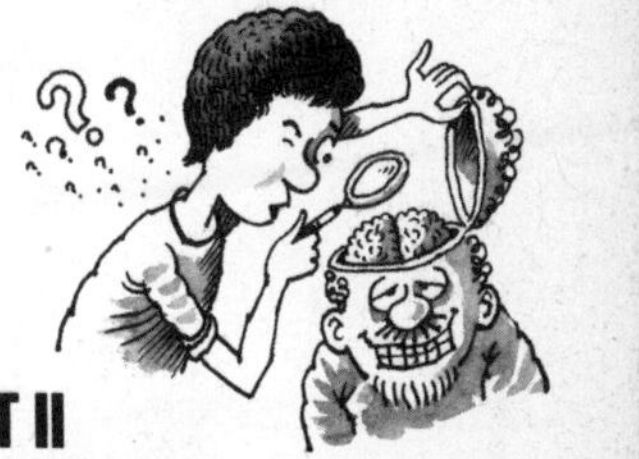

THE COTTON SWAB

The cotton swab (or "Q" tip, as it's commonly referred to) is a soft plastic stick with little pieces of cotton wrapped on each end.

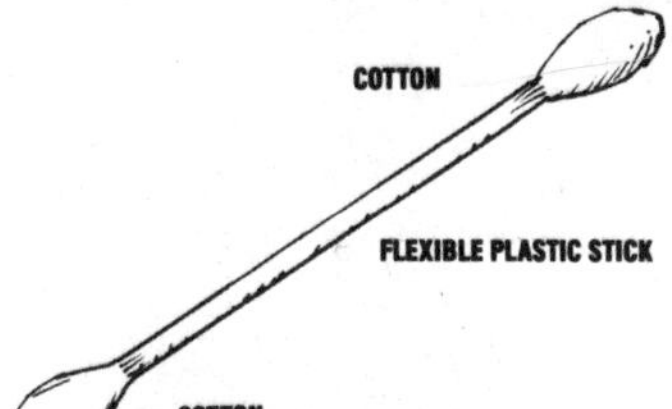
COTTON
FLEXIBLE PLASTIC STICK
COTTON

ARTIST AND WRITER: AL JAFFEE

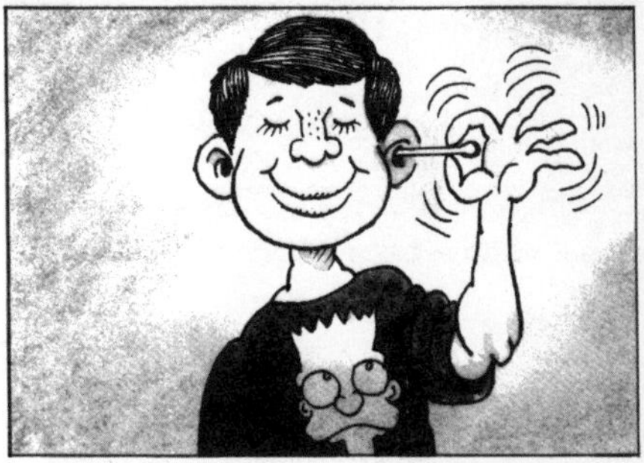

The cotton swab has no equal when it comes to cleaning out any orifice in the human body. However, since this is a family magazine, we will only discuss cleaning wax out of the ears.

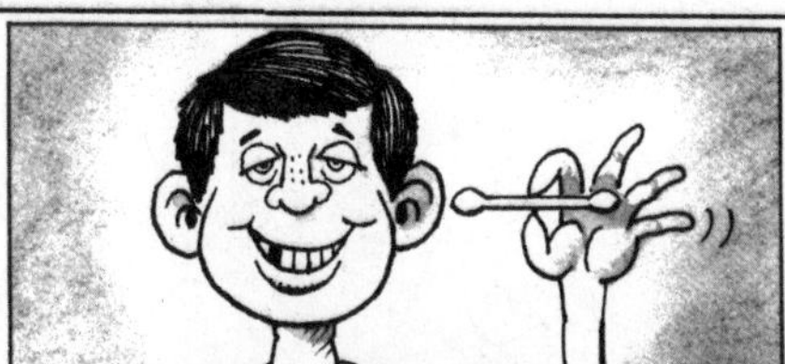

As with any product that is inserted into part of the anatomy, special care must be taken to avoid injuring delicate tissue.

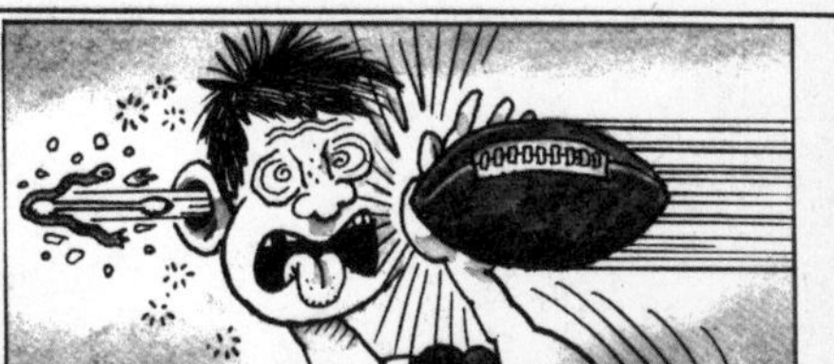

If for some unexpected reason the cotton swab has been inserted too far, you may want to consult an ear doctor. If it has been inserted way too far, you may want to consult a brain surgeon!

THE DOG LEASH

The dog leash is a leather or cloth strap with a clasp at one end and a loop at the other end.

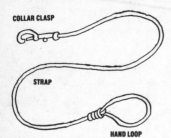

COLLAR CLASP

STRAP

HAND LOOP

To use, you simply open the clasp to the desired width and gently clip it to the dog's collar ring.

THE KEY CHAIN

The key chain is simply a length of chain with a metal or plastic clasp on one end and a key ring on the other end.

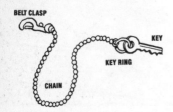

BELT CLASP

KEY

KEY RING

CHAIN

The clasp easily attaches to a belt or belt loop while the keys at the other end are safely tucked into a pocket.

THE NUTCRACKER

The basic nutcracker consists of two steel handles joined by a hinge. Each handle has teeth with which to hold the nut in place.

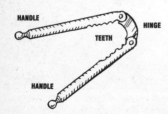

HANDLE

HINGE

TEETH

HANDLE

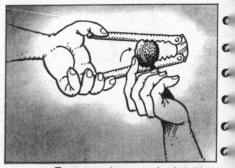

To operate, the nutcracker is held in one hand while the nut is placed between its teeth with the other hand.

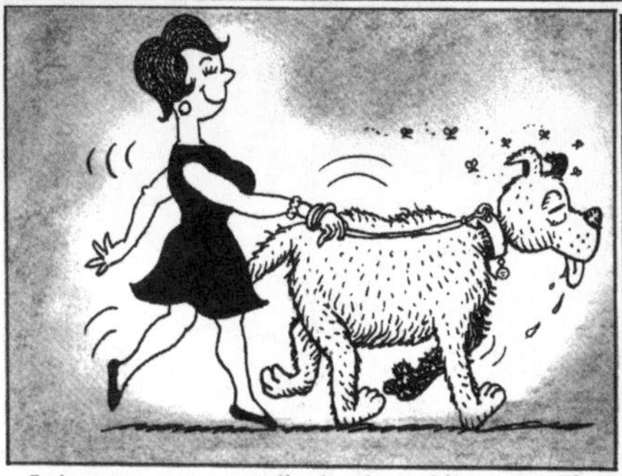

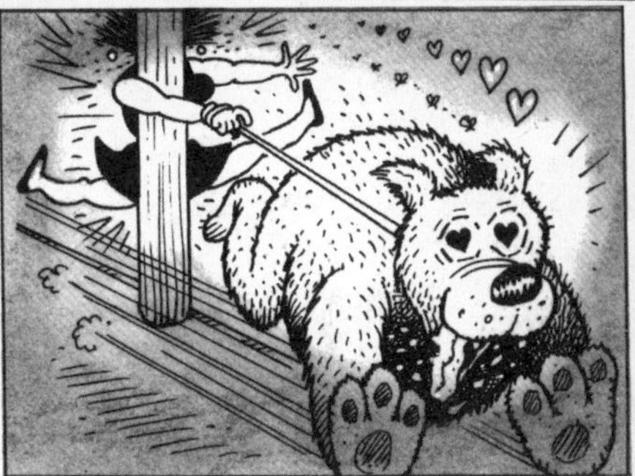

It is now easy to walk the dog while controlling its movement. If the dog is large, you may want to make a few turns of the loop end around your hand.

This, however, is not always advisable, especially if your dog happens to be a male in heat with amorous designs on the poodle down the street!

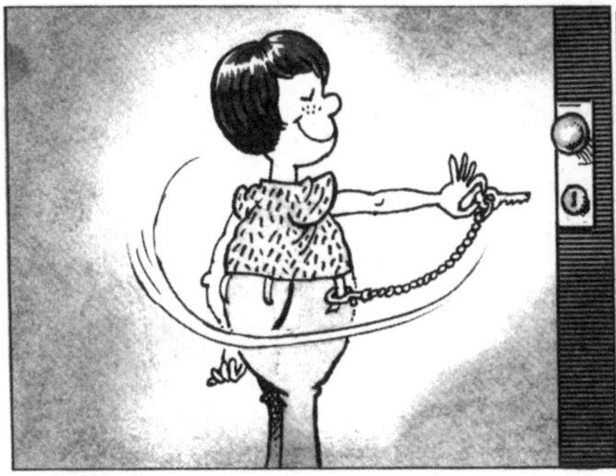

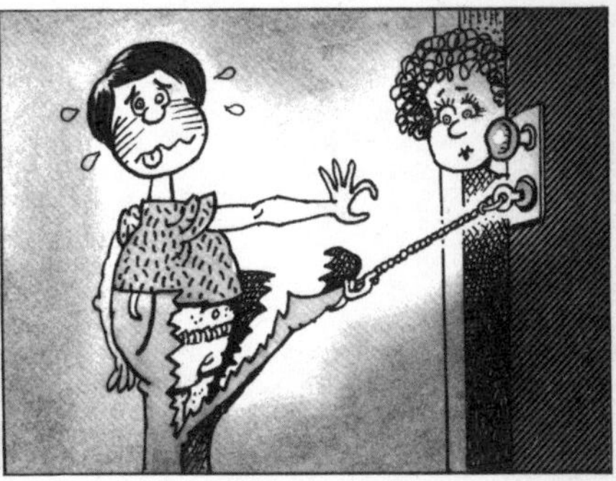

A quick tug on the chain produces the key you require for easy insertion into the keyhole.

It is advisable to make sure no one is home to suddenly open the door with embarrassing results!

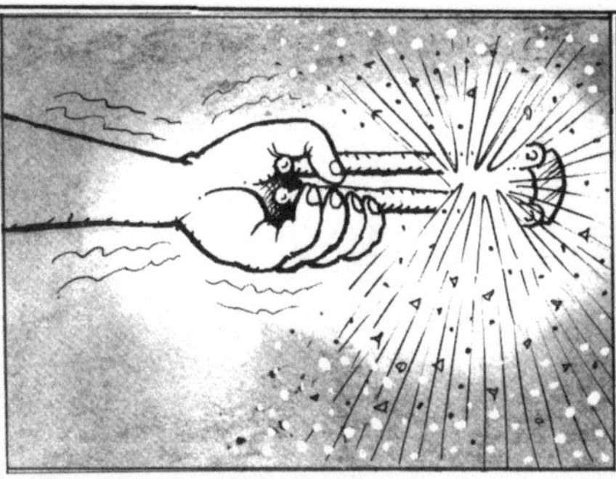

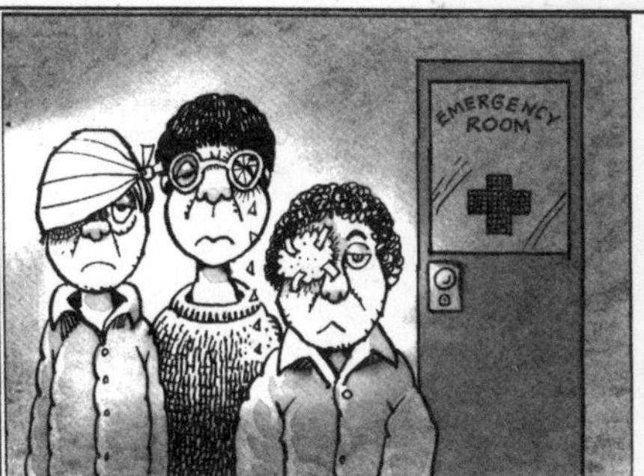
EMERGENCY ROOM

To crack the nut, the handles are carefully and slowly brought together. For most nuts a modest amount of pressure will suffice.

Every now and then, certain nuts (notably Brazil nuts) resist being cracked. If both hands must be employed, be sure no one is nearby, since the sudden explosion is like flying shrapnel!

THE SAFETY MATCH

The safety match is a small wooden stick with flame producing chemicals at the tip.

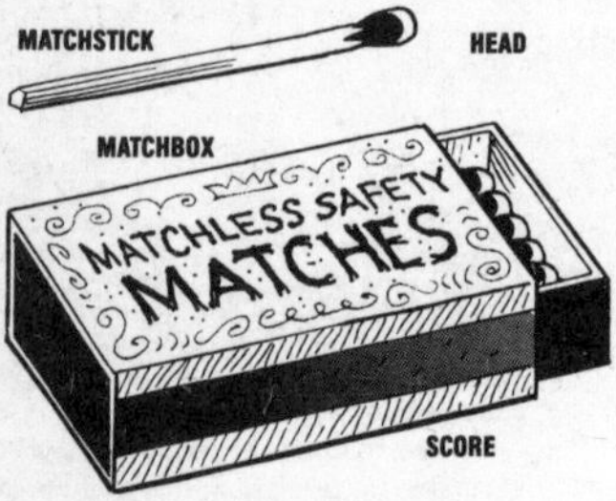
MATCHSTICK
HEAD
MATCHBOX
MATCHLESS SAFETY
MATCHES
SCORE

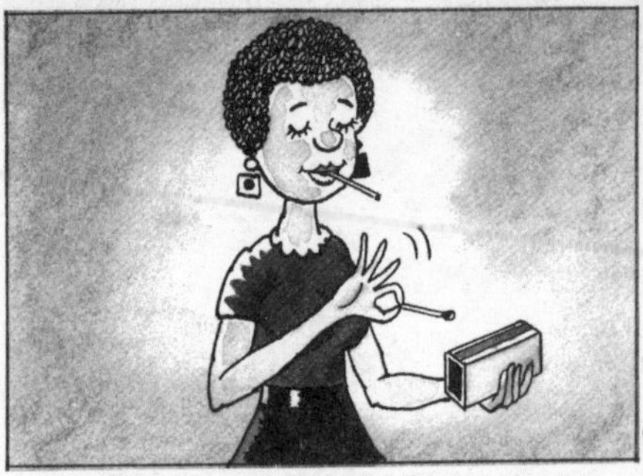

What makes it a "safety" match is that it will only light when rubbed against the specially treated "score" on the match box.

THE DESKTOP TAPE DISPENSER

The dispenser is a heavy molded metal or plastic container into which a roll of tape is inserted. It is heavily weighted so that it will stay firmly in place allowing for convenient one-handed use.

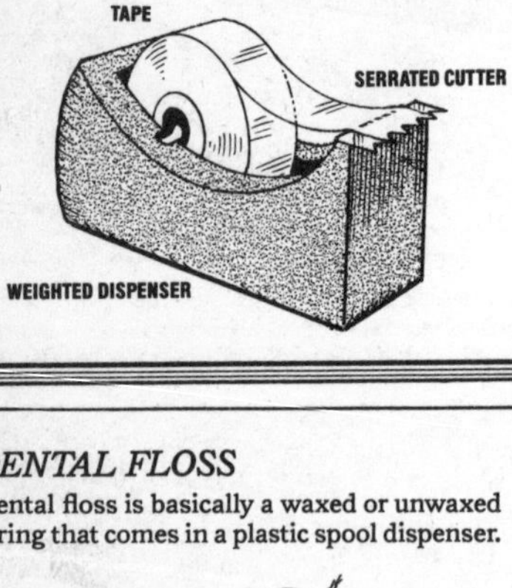
TAPE
SERRATED CUTTER
WEIGHTED DISPENSER

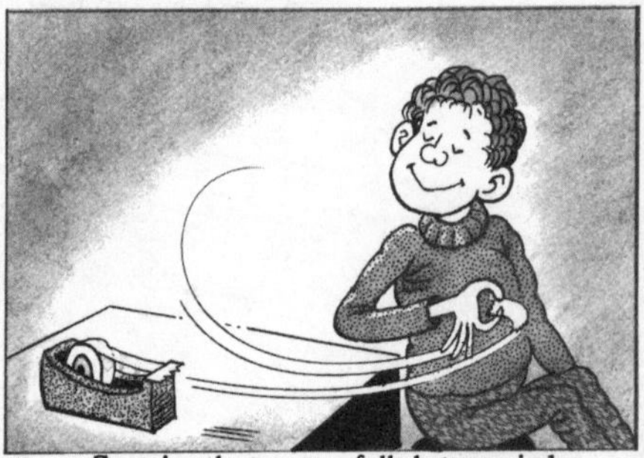

Grasping the tape carefully between index finger and thumb, it is pulled across the sharp serrated cutter. A swift downward pull cuts off a piece of the desired length.

DENTAL FLOSS

Dental floss is basically a waxed or unwaxed string that comes in a plastic spool dispenser.

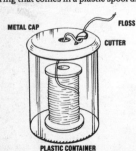

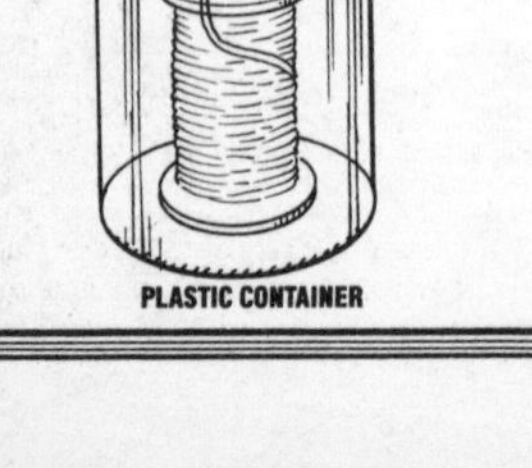
METAL CAP
FLOSS
CUTTER
PLASTIC CONTAINER

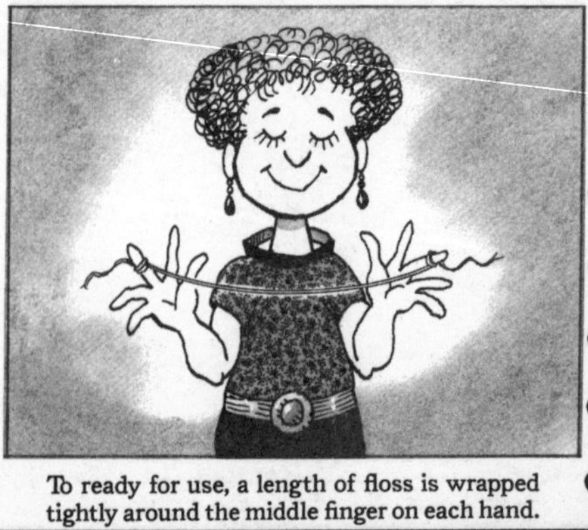

To ready for use, a length of floss is wrapped tightly around the middle finger on each hand.

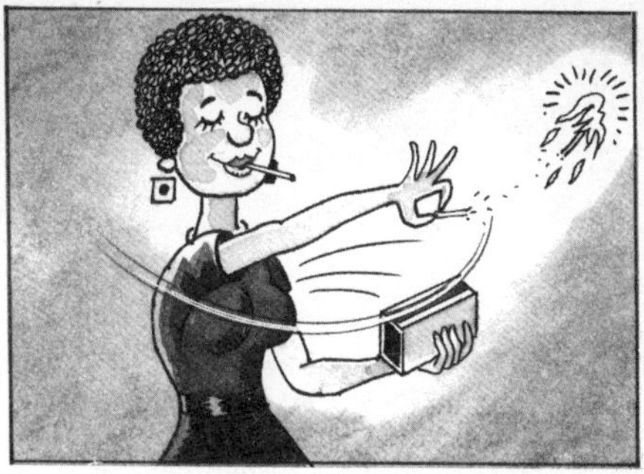

To use, one merely has to firmly strike the match head against the matchbox strip. (Not too firmly! There are often weak spots in the match stick!)

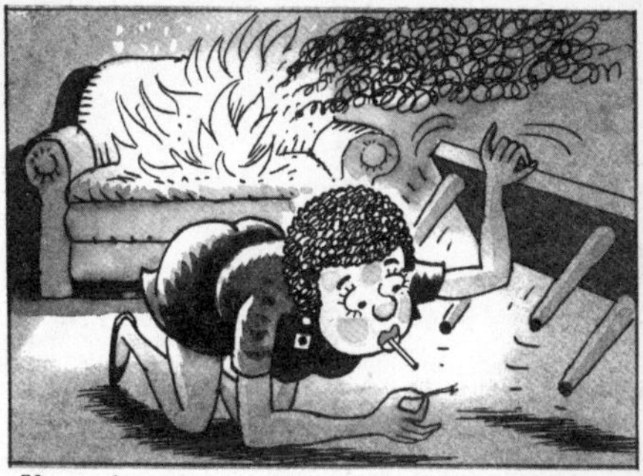

If a weak spot causes the match stick to break and fly off, make sure you follow its flight path. A lost safety match can lose its safeness mighty fast!

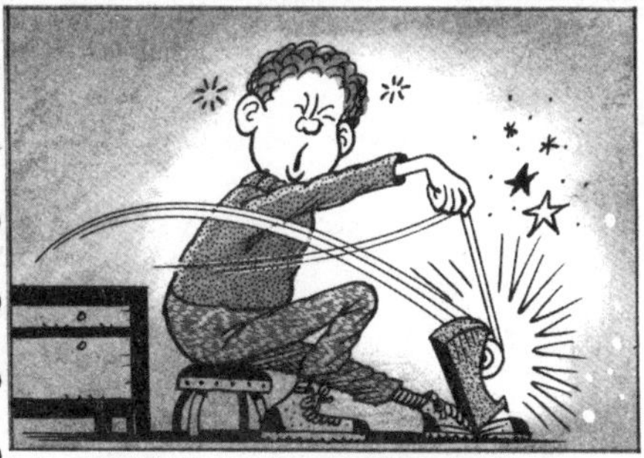

CAUTION

Serrated Cutter Problem #1: Cutter too dull. Tape won't cut, resulting in the heavy dispenser falling off desk!

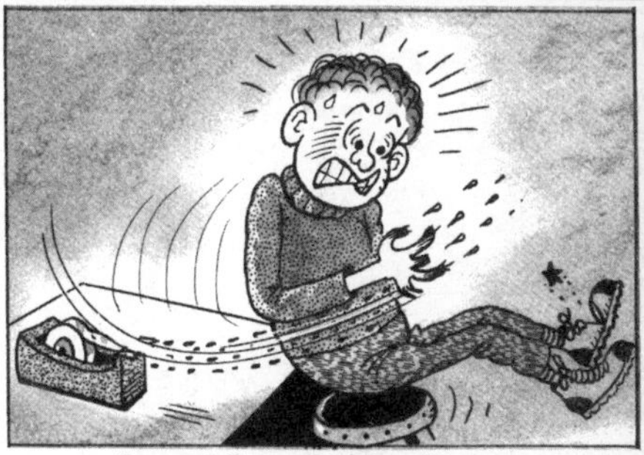

Serrated Cutter Problem #2: Cutter too sharp. Tape cuts easily, but so do your fingers, resulting in blood and agony!

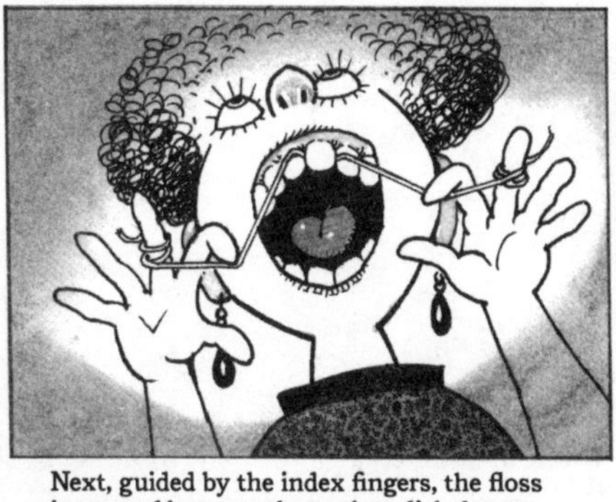

Next, guided by the index fingers, the floss is pressed between the teeth to dislodge any rotting, decayed food particles stuck there.

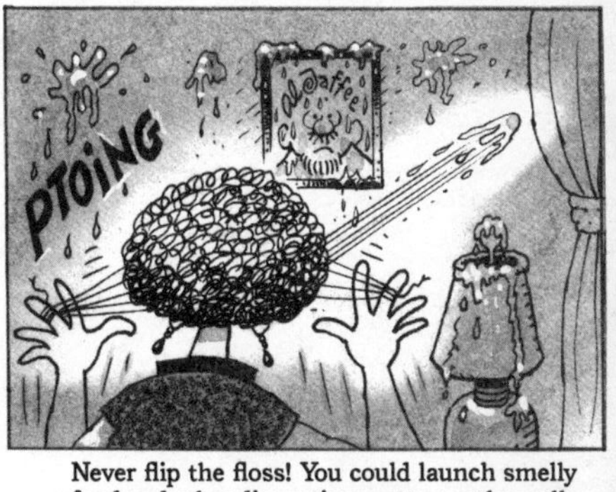
PTOING

Never flip the floss! You could launch smelly food and other disgusting matter on the walls and furnishings creating an unpleasant mess!

ASSUMING THE FUTILE POSITION DEPT.

IF YOU'RE TIRED OF READING INANE INTRODUCTIO

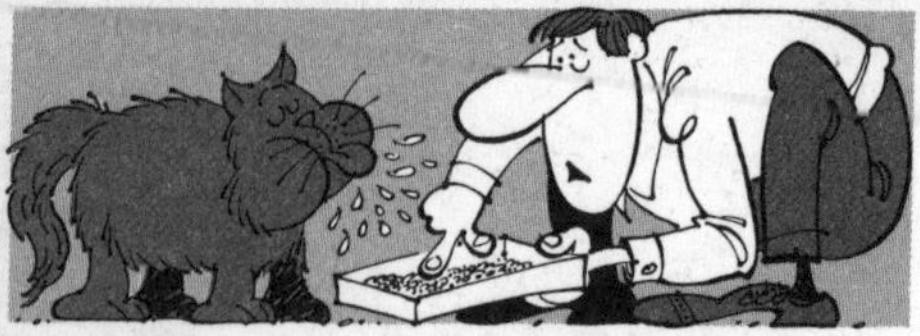

IF you've been training your cat to go in its box for the last 14 years and the little flea-bag still takes a wizz wherever it feels like . . .

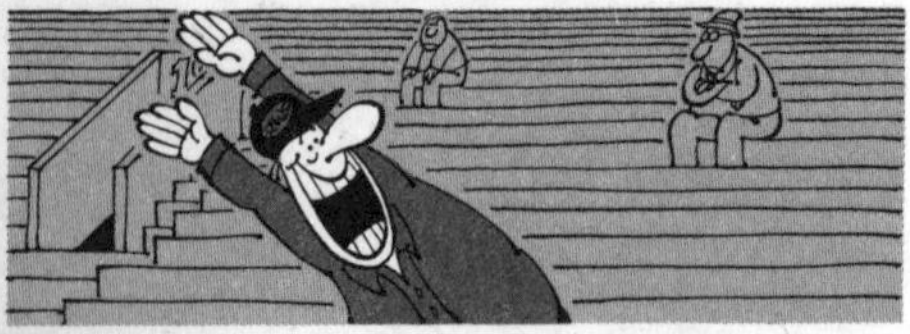

IF your team is down by 40 in the fourth quarter and you're frantically trying to get a Wave started in the crowd . . .

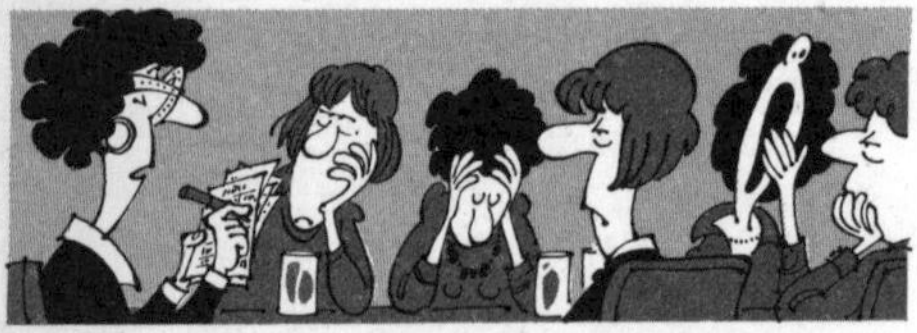

IF you're into your second hour of trying to figure out who had what instead of just splitting the restaurant check evenly among the ten of you . . .

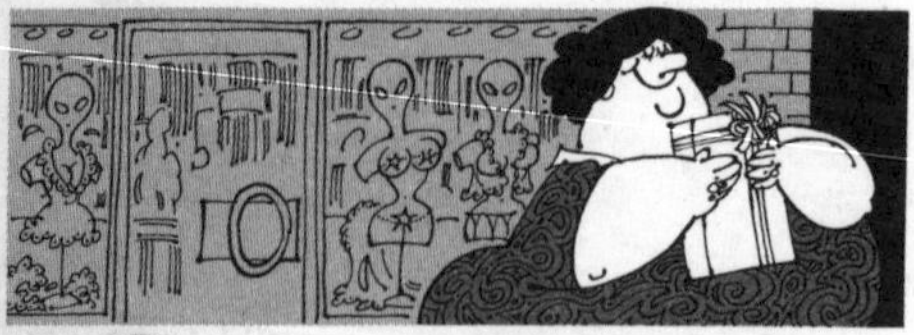

IF you weigh 196 pounds or more and still buy negligees from Frederick's of Hollywood . . .

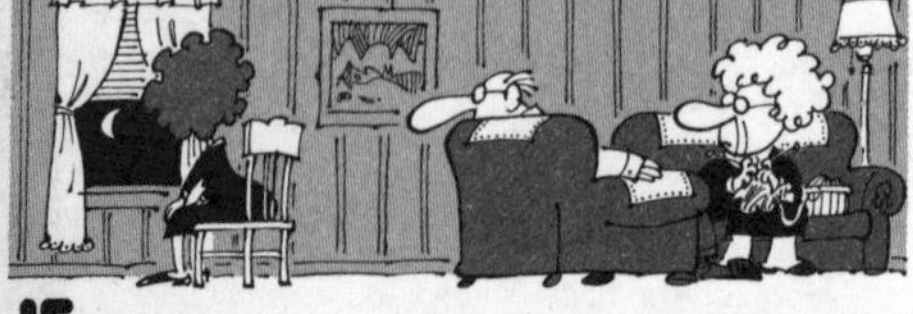

IF you're 46 years old, still live at home with your parents and are determined to save yourself for the right man . . .

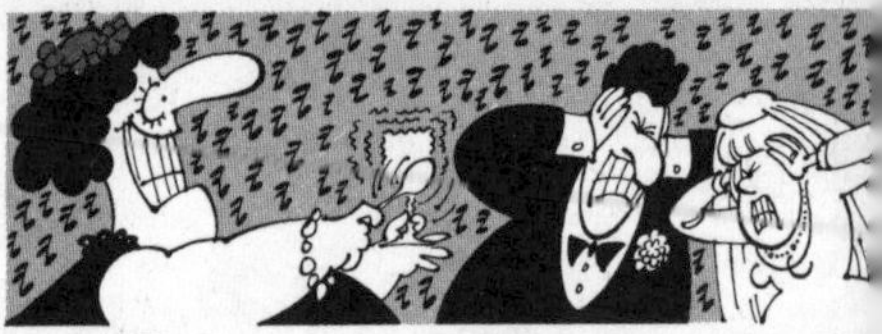

IF you spend most of your time at a wedding reception trying to get the bride and groom to kiss by continuously clinking your glass . . .

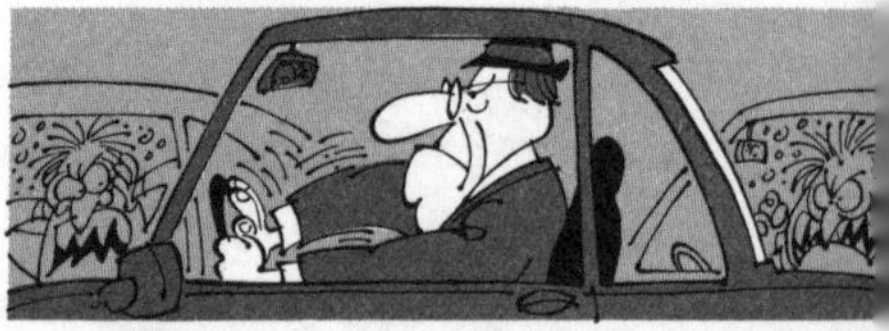

IF you've been blaring your car's horn for five straight minutes and traffic still hasn't moved . . .

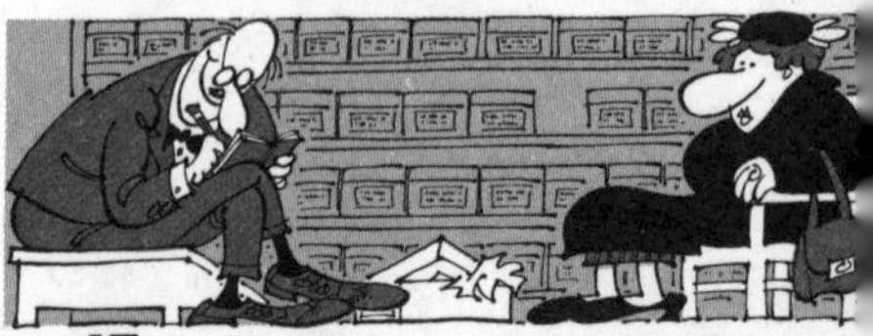

IF you religiously keep a diary of everything that happens to you at your job at the shoe store because you're convinced it will someday make a great movie . . .

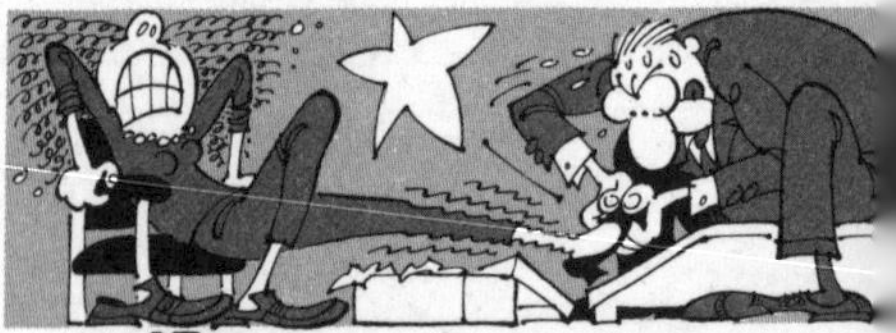

IF it's your lifelong quest to find a pair of good-looking shoes that are comfortable too . . .

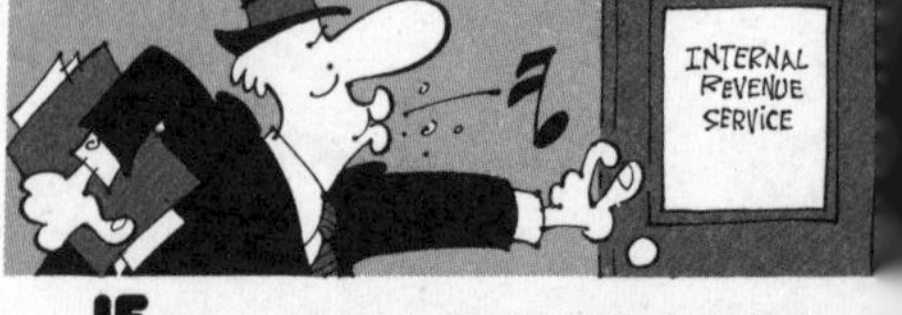
INTERNAL
REVENUE
SERVICE

IF you're desperately clinging to the hope that the IRS is summoning you down to their offices to compliment you on the neatness of your tax return . . .

O INANE MAD ARTICLES...

GIVE IT UP!

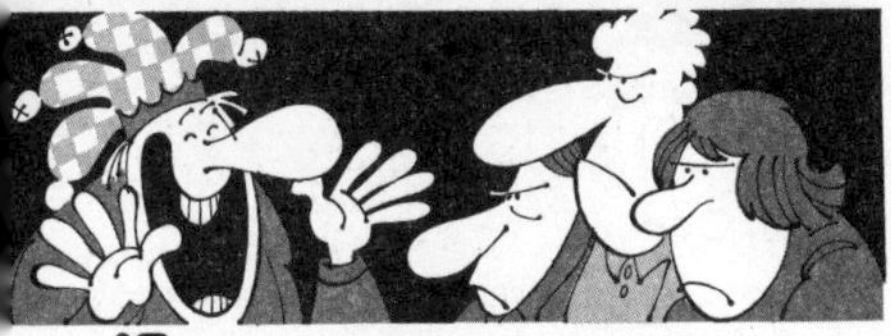

IF you're still trying to make people laugh with phrases like "Where's the Beef?", "You Look Marvelous!" and "Read My Lips!"...

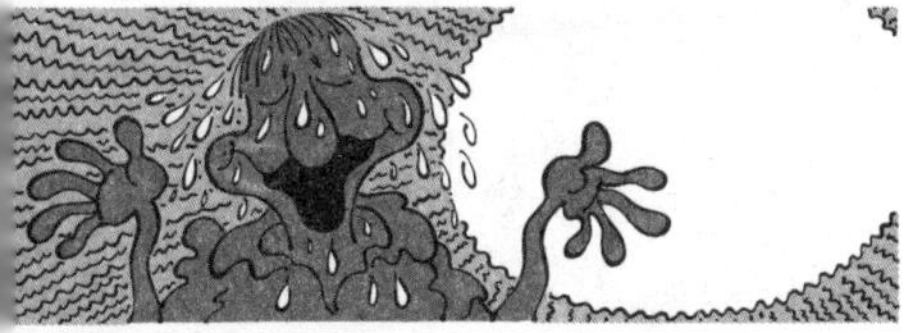

IF you continue to insist that 110 degrees isn't hot where you live because there's "no humidity"...

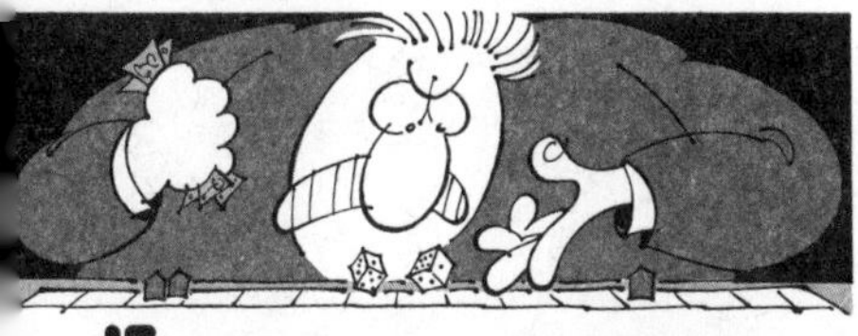

IF your long-term plan for winning Monopoly is to wrestle control of Mediterranean Avenue and Baltic Avenue, regardless of the cost...

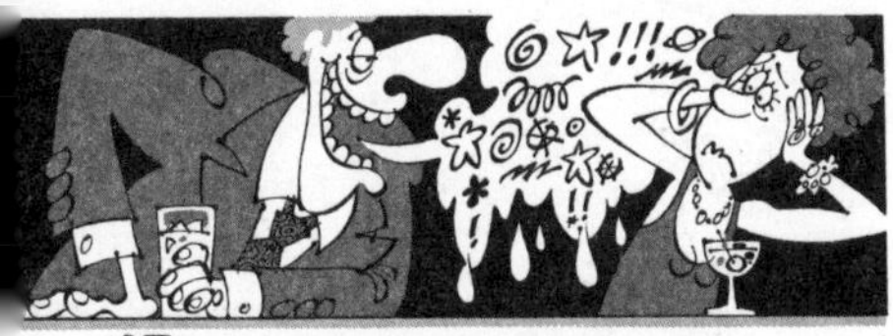

IF your new strategy for picking up women is to quote "love lyrics" from 2 Live Crew...

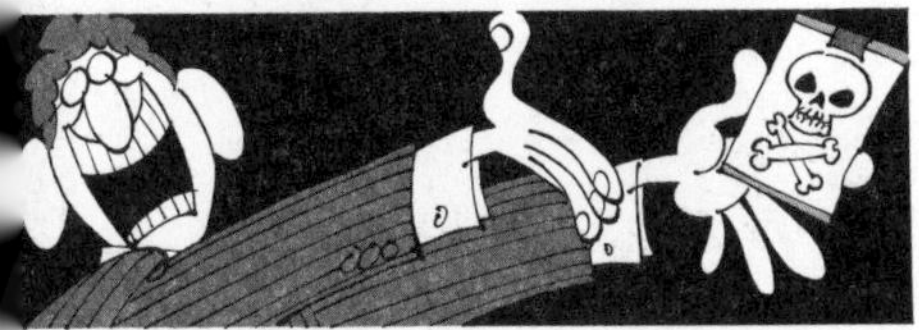

IF it's your job to be the press person for the cigarette industry's American Tobacco Institute...

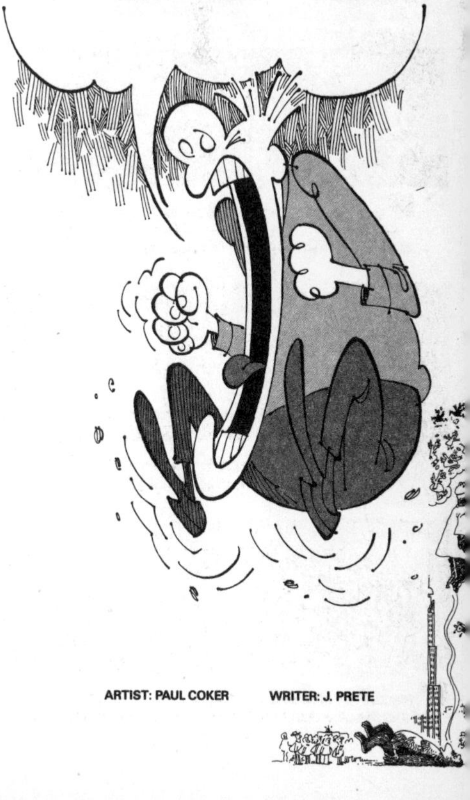

ARTIST: PAUL COKER WRITER: J. PRETE

SUMS DOWN DEPT.

MAD'S BY-THE-N
PREDICTING TV TABLOID A

ARTIST: RICK TULK

1 CHILD ACTOR

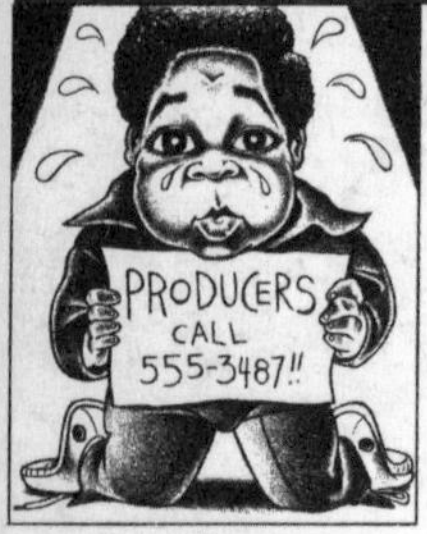
PRODUCERS CALL 555-3487!!

is
Gary Coleman begging for work

2 CHILD ACTORS

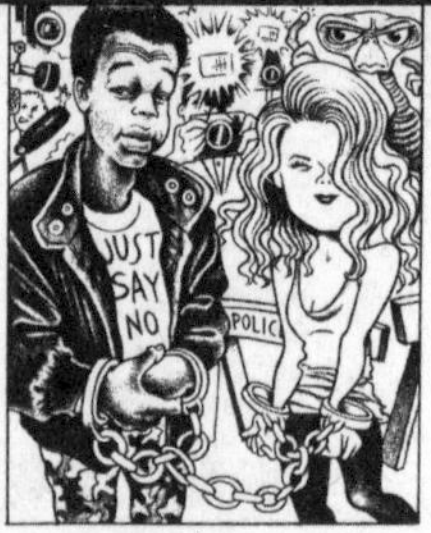
JUST SAY NO
POLIC

is a
Beverly Hills drug bust

3 CHILD ACTORS

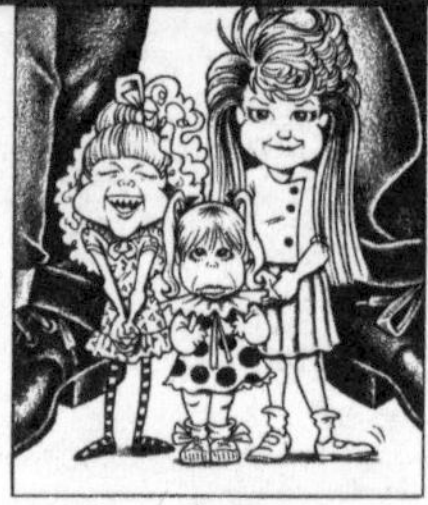

is a
new ABC sitcom with too many—or too few—Dads

4 CHILD ACTORS

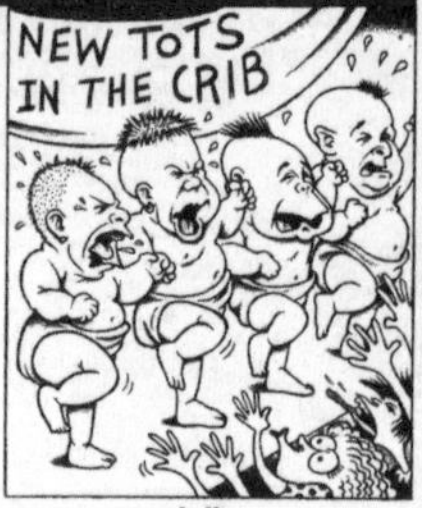
NEW TOTS IN THE CRIB

is the
next "made-to-order" pop-music sensation

1 ACTRESS

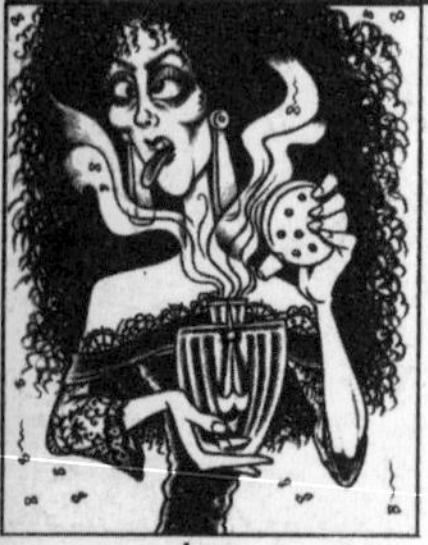

is a
new perfume campaign

2 ACTRESSES

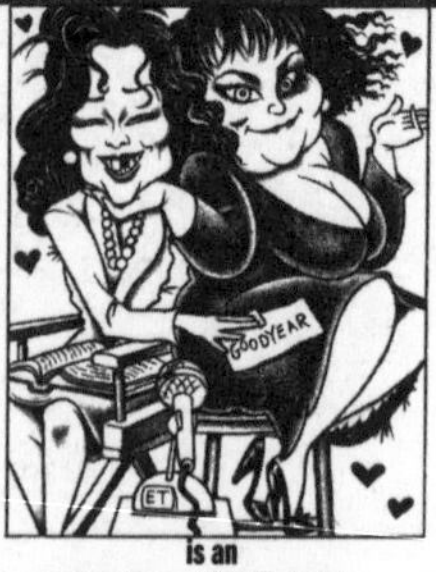
GOODYEAR
ET

is an
"on-the-set feud" denial

3 ACTRESSES

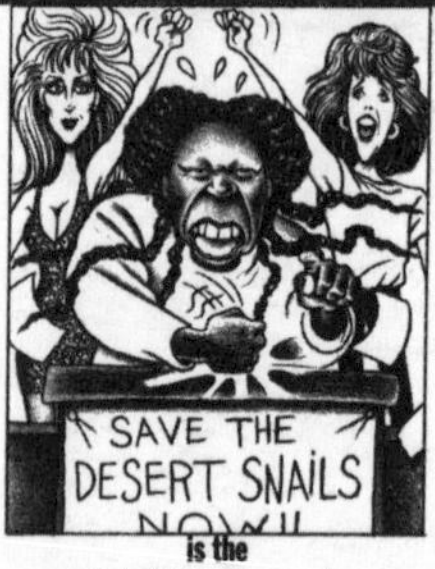
SAVE THE DESERT SNAILS

is the
latest "trendy cause"

4 ACTRESSES

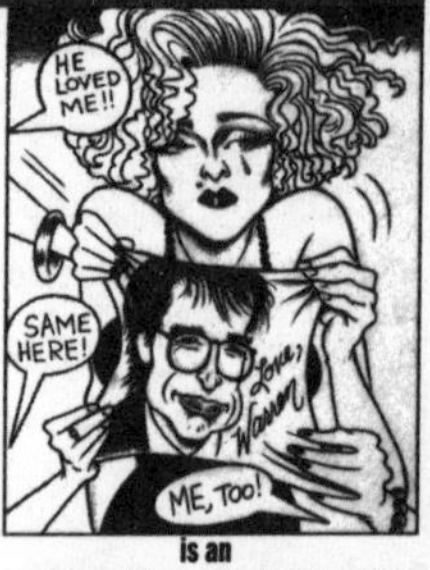
HE LOVED ME!!
SAME HERE!
Love, Warren
ME, TOO!

is an
expose on Warren Beatty's love life

1 SOUTHERN REDNECK

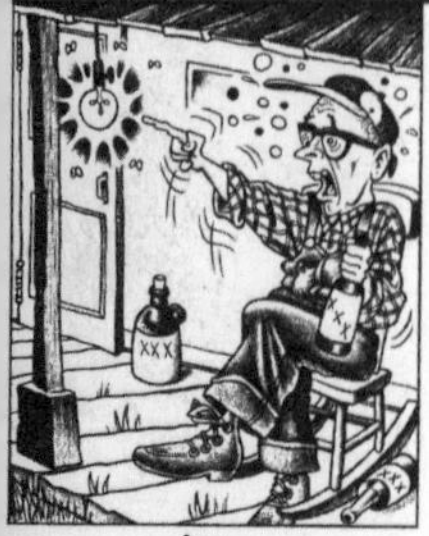
XXX

is a
UFO sighting

2 SOUTHERN REDNECKS

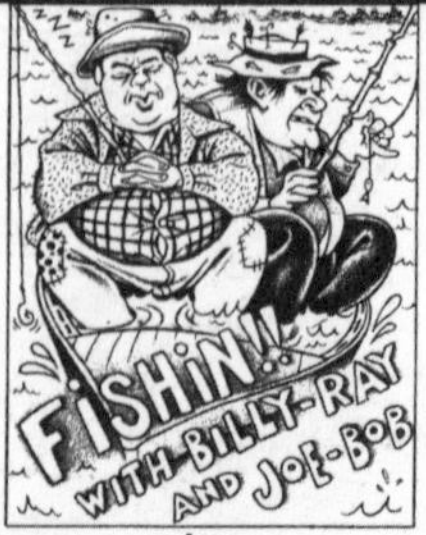
FISHIN' WITH BILLY-RAY AND JOE-BOB

is a
promo for a fishing show on ESPN

3 SOUTHERN REDNECKS

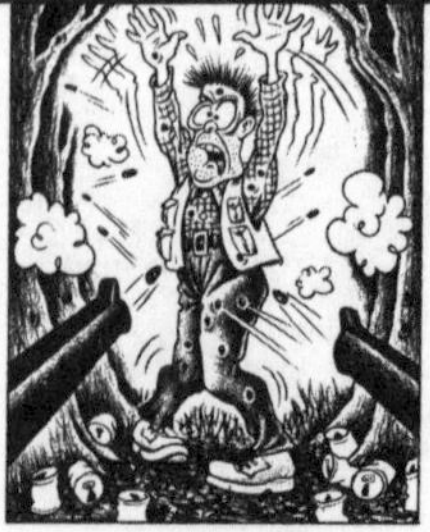

is a
fatal hunting accident

4 SOUTHERN REDNECKS

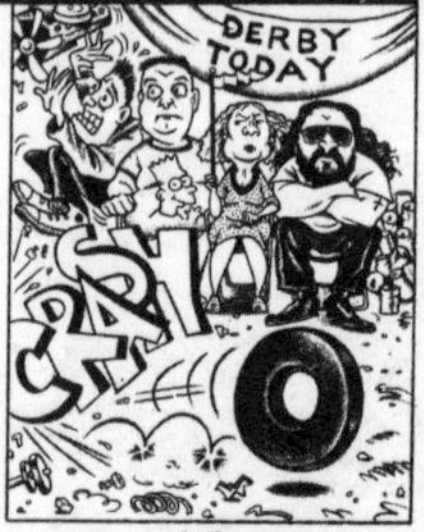
DERBY TODAY

is the
front row at a demolition derby

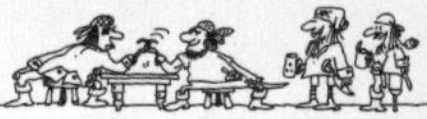

MBERS GUIDE TO
"INFO-TAINMENT" STORIES

WRITER: MIKE SNIDER

1 FUNDAMENTALIST

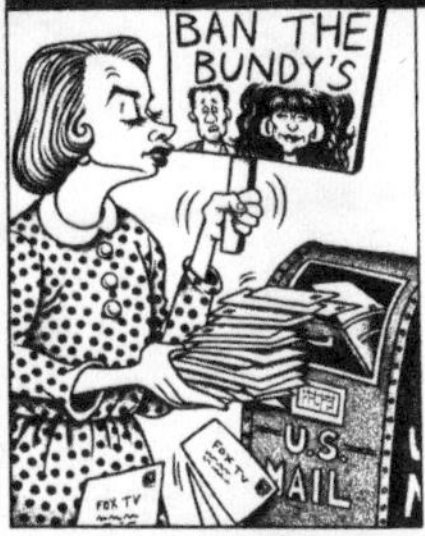

BAN THE BUNDY'S
U.S. MAIL
FOX TV

is a letter-writing campaign against "Married . . . with Children"

2 FUNDAMENTALISTS

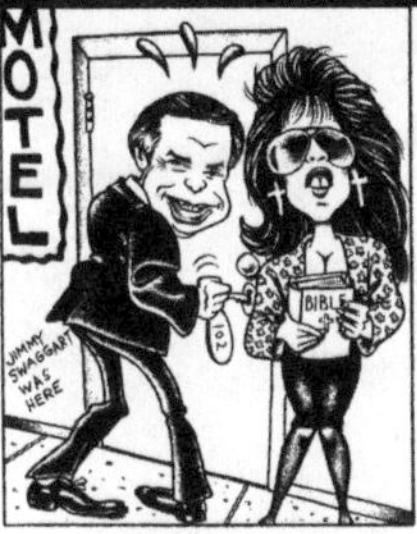

MOTEL
JIMMY SWAGGART WAS HERE
BIBLE

is a sex scandal

3 FUNDAMENTALISTS

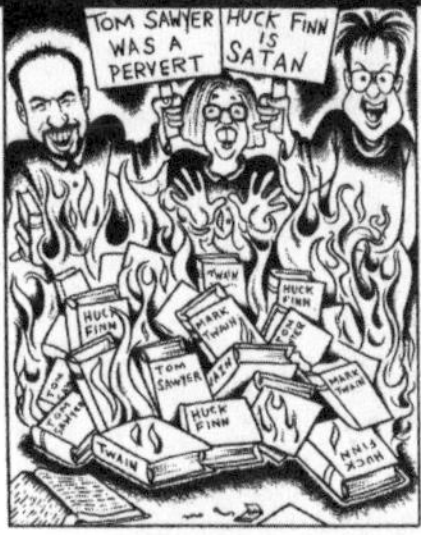

TOM SAWYER WAS A PERVERT
HUCK FINN IS SATAN
HUCK FINN
MARK TWAIN
TOM SAWYER

is a Mark Twain book-burning

4 FUNDAMENTALISTS

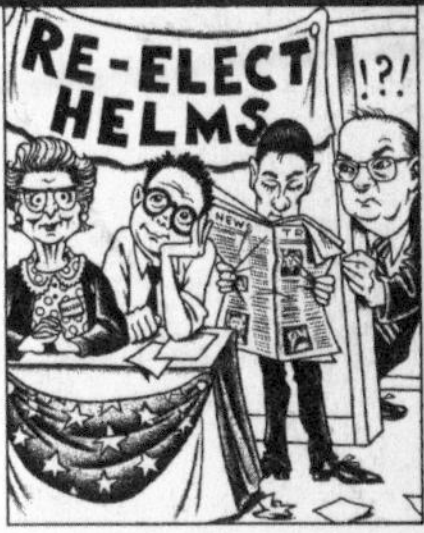

RE-ELECT HELMS
!?!

is Jesse Helms' re-election campaign

1 COLLEGE ATHLETE

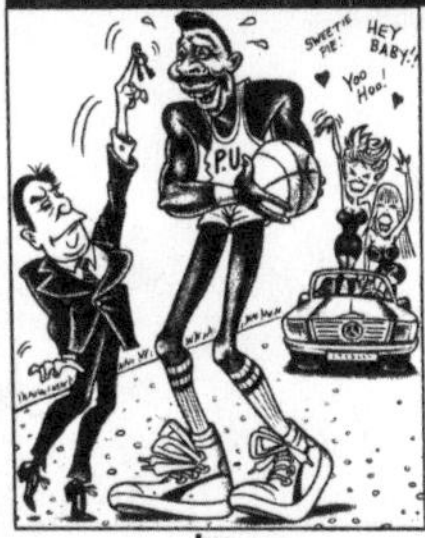

SWEETIE PIE!
HEY BABY!!
Yoo! Hoo!

is a recruiting scandal

2 COLLEGE ATHLETES

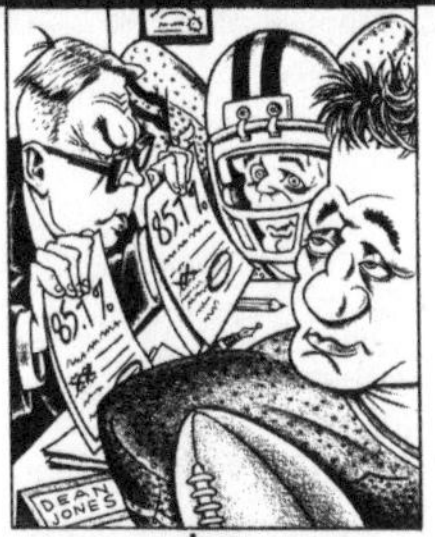

85.1%
DEAN JONES

is an academic-cheating suspension

3 COLLEGE ATHLETES

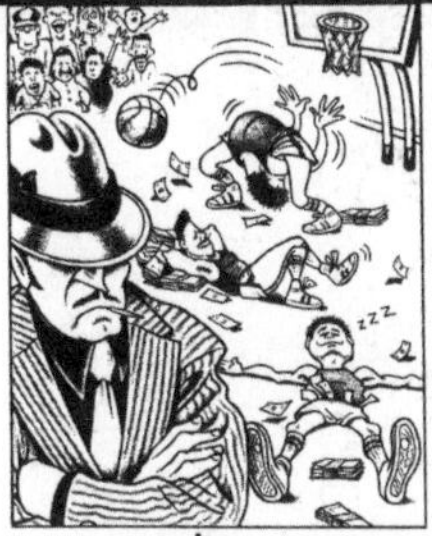

is a "point-shaving" conspiracy

4 COLLEGE ATHLETES

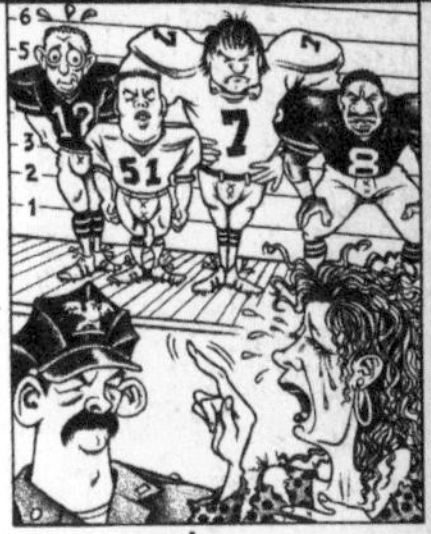

is a police line-up

1 PSYCHIC/ASTROLOGER

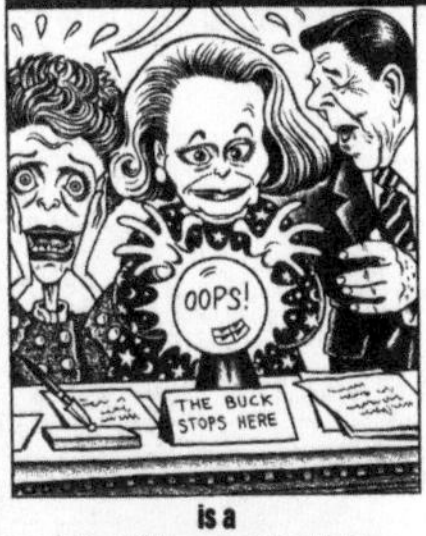

OOPS!
THE BUCK STOPS HERE

is a look at "The powers inside the Reagan White House"

2 PSYCHIC/ASTROLOGERS

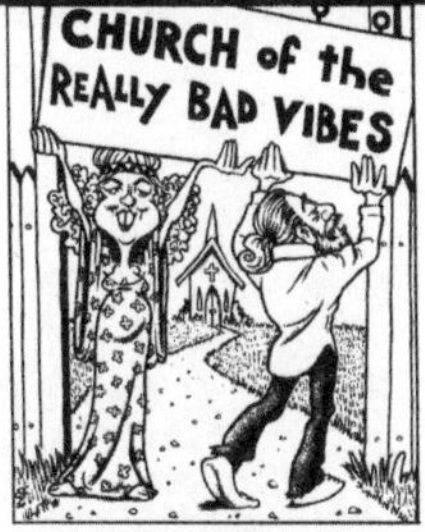

CHURCH of the REALLY BAD VIBES

is another "New Age" California cult

3 PSYCHIC/ASTROLOGERS

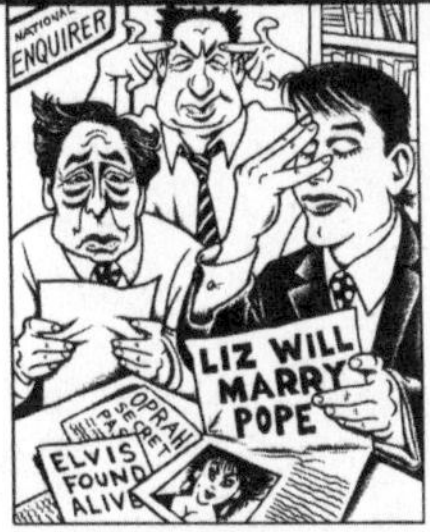

NATIONAL ENQUIRER
LIZ WILL MARRY POPE
OPRAH
ELVIS FOUND ALIVE

is the National Enquirer editorial board

4 PSYCHIC/ASTROLOGERS

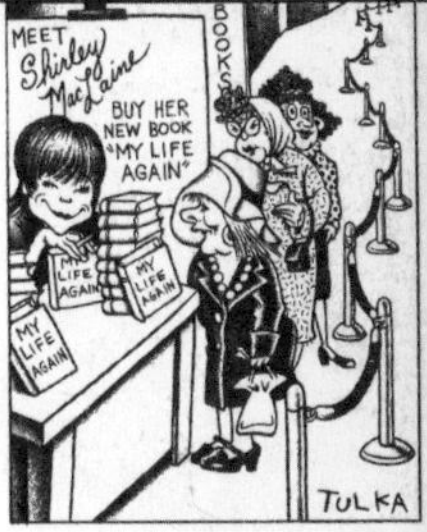

MEET Shirley MacLaine
BUY HER NEW BOOK "MY LIFE AGAIN"
MY LIFE AGAIN
BOOKS
TULKA

is a Shirley MacLaine book-signing

SCARS AND GRIPES DEPT.

AMERICA

LAND OF OPPORTUNITY

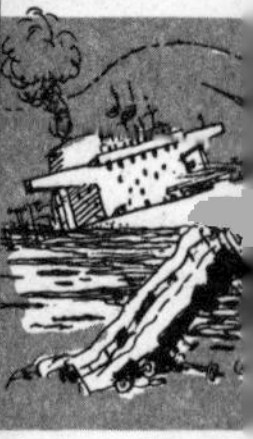

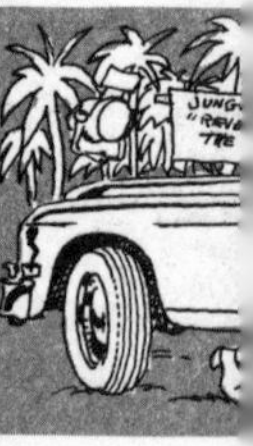

ARTIST: GEORGE WOODBRIDGE WRITER: MIKE SNIDER

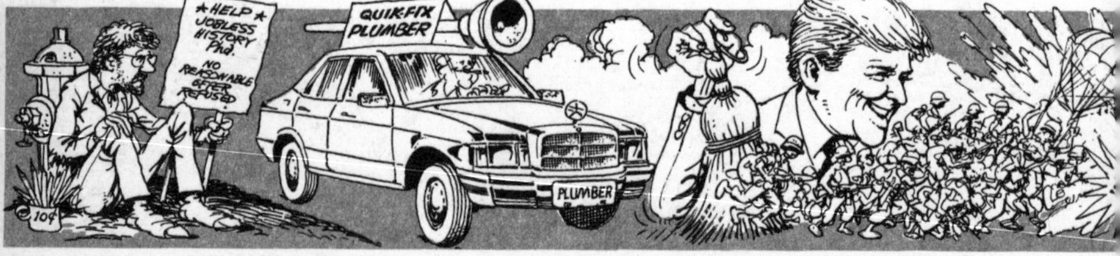

HELP JOBLESS HISTORY Phd. NO REASONABLE OFFER REFUSED
QUIK-FIX PLUMBER
PLUMBER
10¢

...where those who excelled in school can earn half as much as plumbers who didn't!

...where a former Draft Dodger can rise almost to the position of power to send brave volunteers into war!

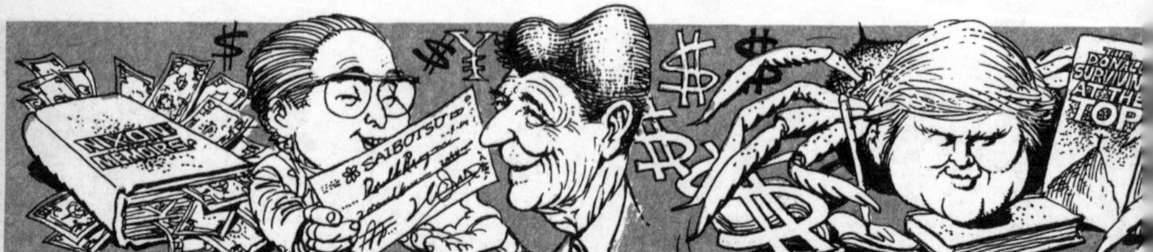

SAIBOTSU
TOP

...where the Presidency is just an entry-level position to a really big-money career!

...where a tycoon undergoing total financial meltdown can sell thousands of copies of his book, "Surviving at the Top!"

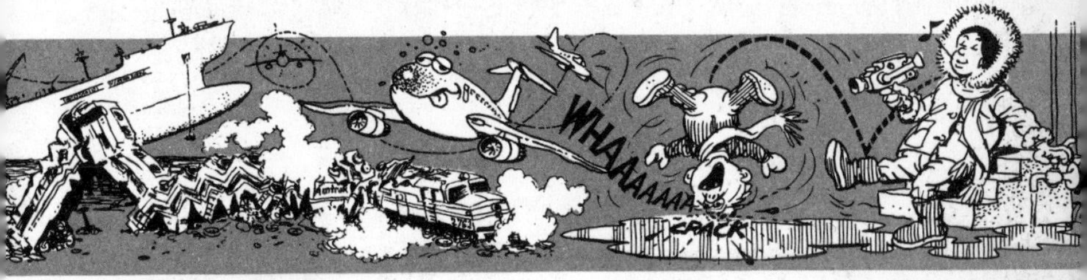
WHAAAAAAAA
CRACK

...where crucial jobs in transportation are open to all—regardless of criminal record or level of intoxication!

...where a video camera and an expendable loved-one are your ticket to a chance at $100,000!

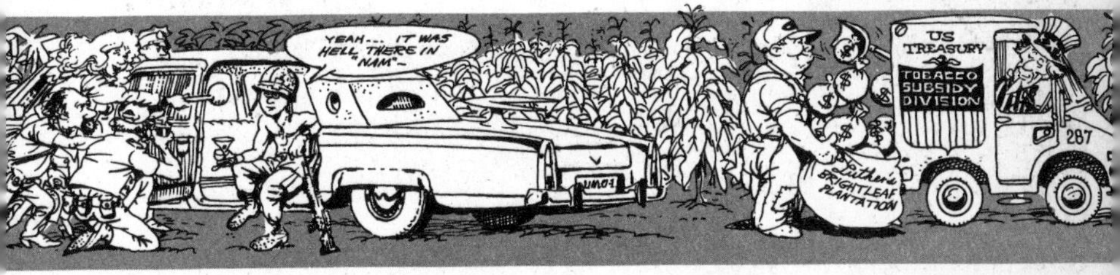
YEAH... IT WAS HELL THERE IN "NAM"~
US TREASURY
TOBACCO SUBSIDY DIVISION
287
Luther's BRIGHTLEAF PLANTATION

...where merely acting in a film about something makes you more of an "expert" than people who lived through it!

...where the government will actually pay people to grow a deadly substance it's trying to eradicate!

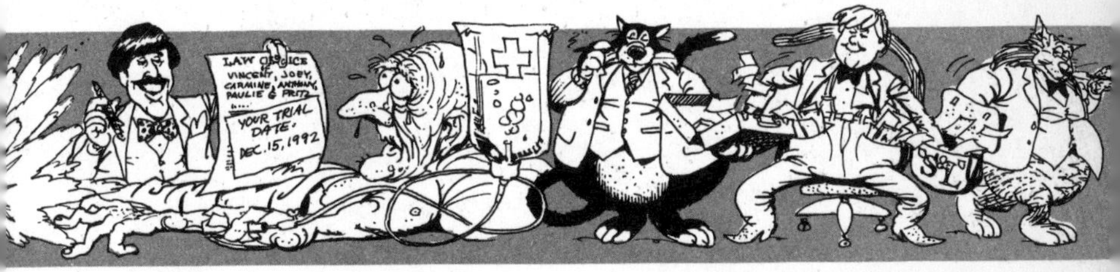
YOUR TRIAL DATE: DEC. 15, 1992

...where any citizen with a bottomless bank account and five years to spare can have his "day in court"!

...where Congressmen from every state—no matter how small or poor—can line their pockets equally!

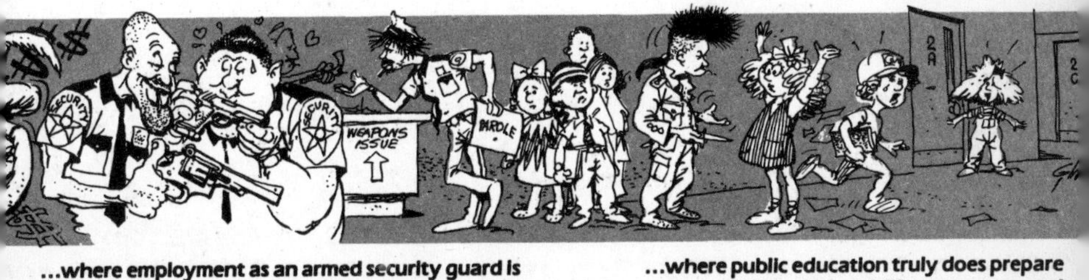
SECURITY
SECURITY
WEAPONS ISSUE
PAROLE
2A
2C

...where employment as an armed security guard is open to all—regardless of prior criminal record!

...where public education truly does prepare young children for real life as grown-ups!

JUST A PHRASE WE'RE GOING THROUGH DEPT.

Several issues back, we astutely pointed out to you the true UNimportance of words in everyday life. It is not the words that are significant, we explained, so much as the particular context in which the words are used. Judging by the letters we received after publishing this

MORE SAME WORDS... *DIFF*

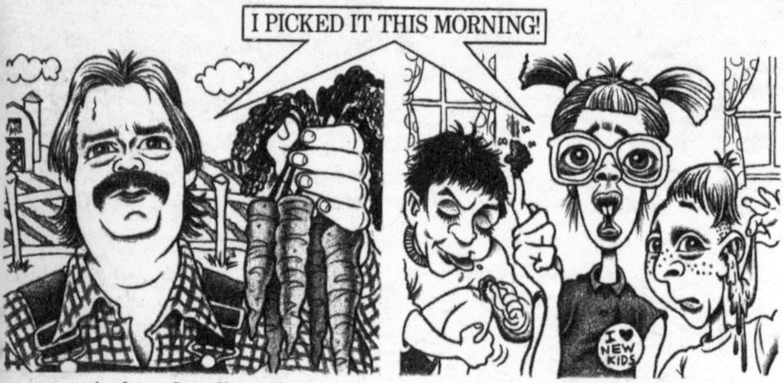

I PICKED IT THIS MORNING!
I ♥ NEW KIDS

...is okay when discussing fruits and vegetables.

...not okay for just about anything else!

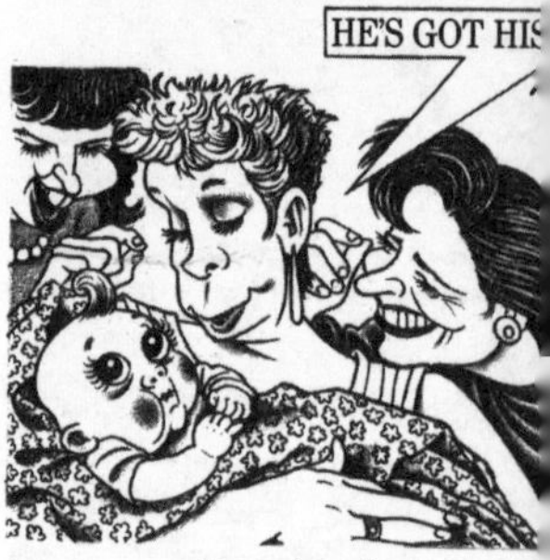

HE'S GOT HIS

...is cute when cuddling a newborn.

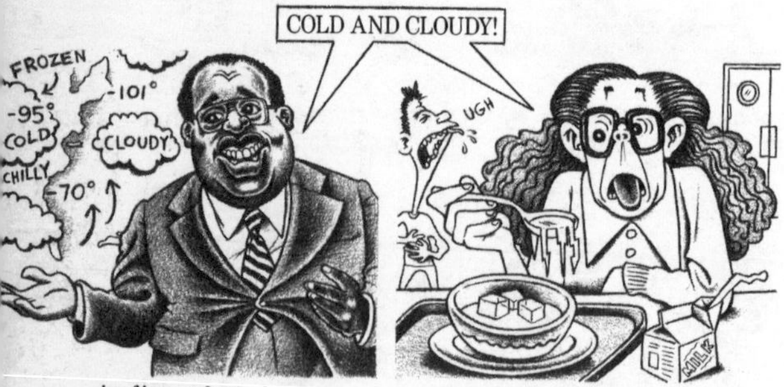

COLD AND CLOUDY!
FROZEN
-101°
-95°
COLD
CLOUDY
CHILLY
70°
UGH
MILK

...is fine when describing today's weather.

...revolting when describing your school cafeteria's soup du jour!

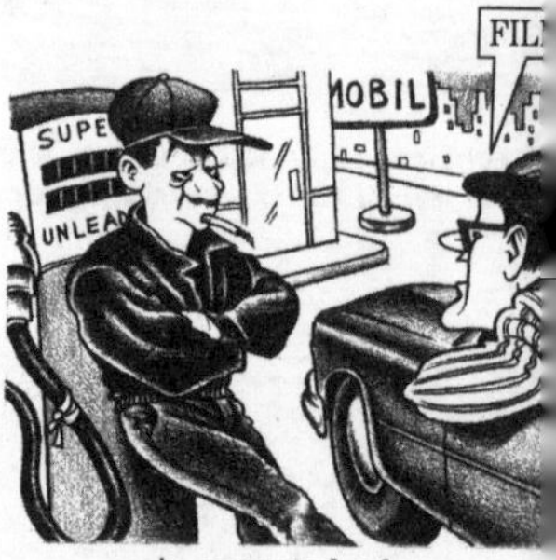

FIL
MOBIL
SUPE
UNLEA

...is expected when pumping gas is your job.

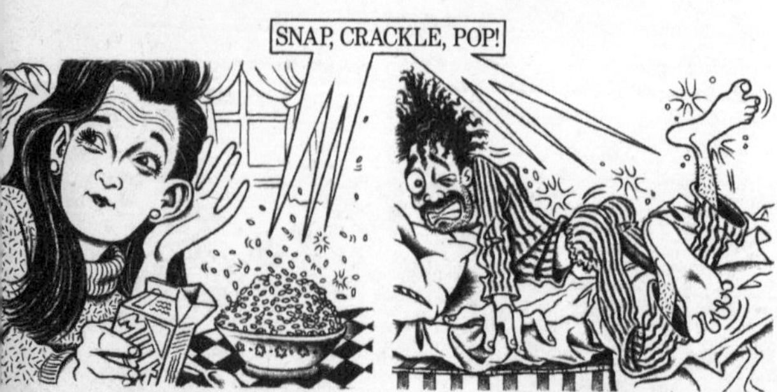

SNAP, CRACKLE, POP!

...is pleasant when it's the sound made by your cereal every morning.

...unpleasant when it's the sound made by your body every morning!

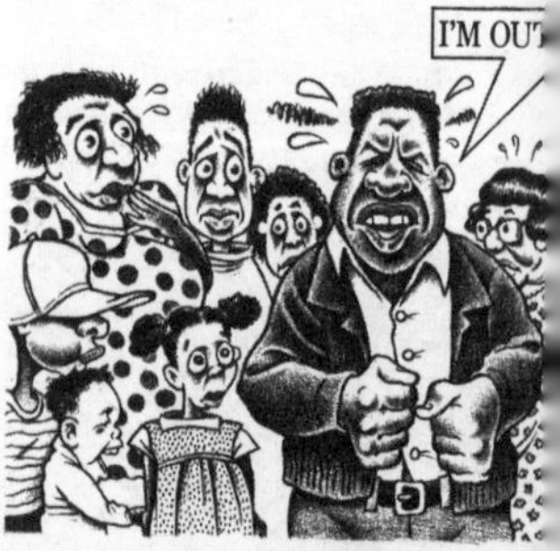

I'M OUT

...is bad news when it's your father or mother.

article, we came to the conclusion that you applauded this amazingly clever and bold observation (although our conclusion could change once we actually get around to reading those three letters)! In any event, using *different* words and *different* circumstances, we now present...

RENT CIRCUMSTANCES!

ARTIST: RICK TULKA WRITER: J. PRETE

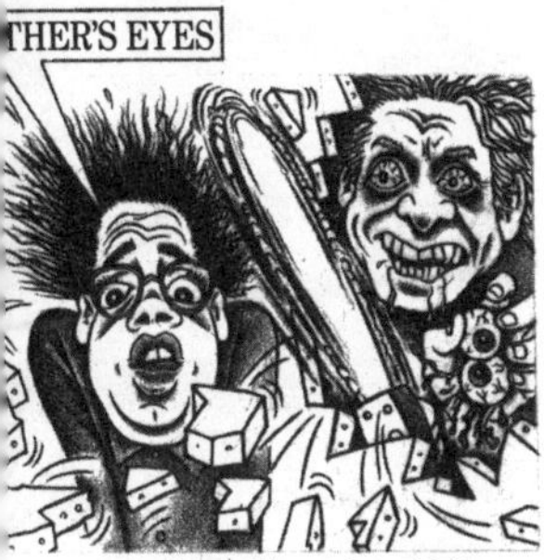
THER'S EYES

...a tad disturbing when hiding from a psychotic homicidal maniac!

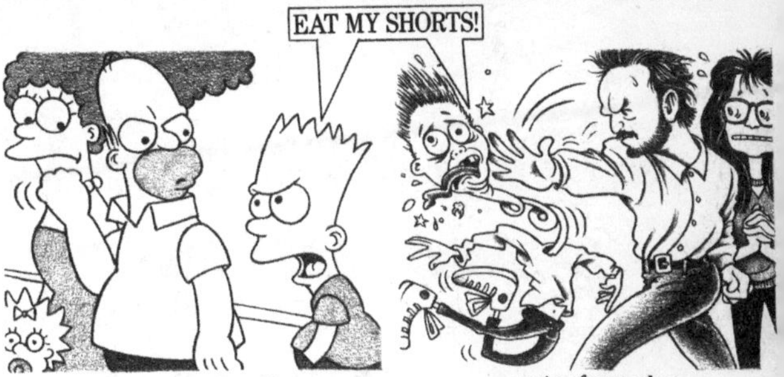
EAT MY SHORTS!

...is funny when Bart Simpson yells it at his Mom and Dad.

...not so funny when you yell it at yours!

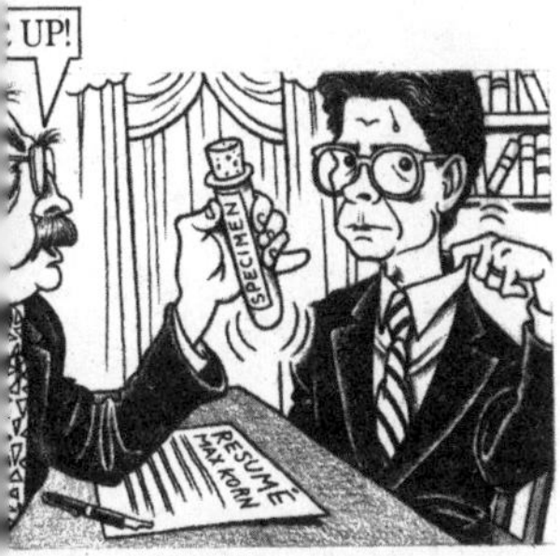
UP!
SPECIMEN
RESUME
MAX KORN

...insulting when you are applying for a job!

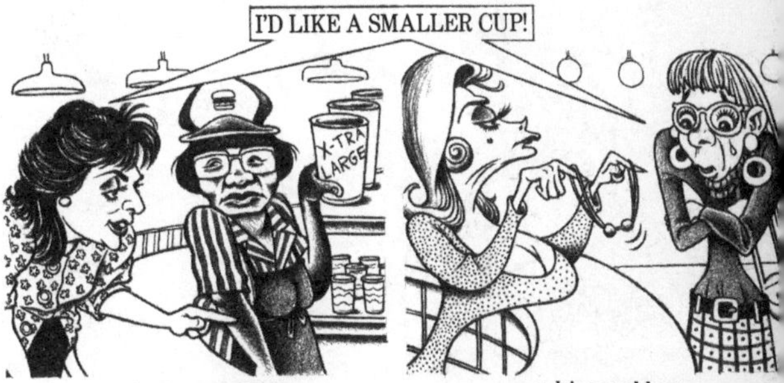
I'D LIKE A SMALLER CUP!
X-TRA LARGE

...is no problem when buying a soda.

...a big problem when buying a bra!

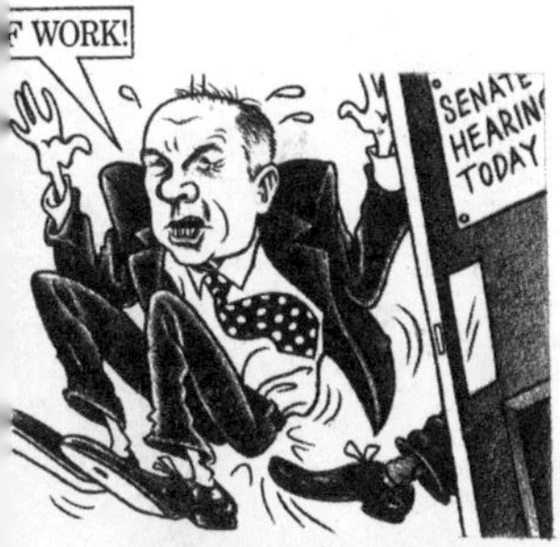
WORK!
SENATE HEARING TODAY

...great news when it's one of the Senators involved in the Savings and Loan Scandal!

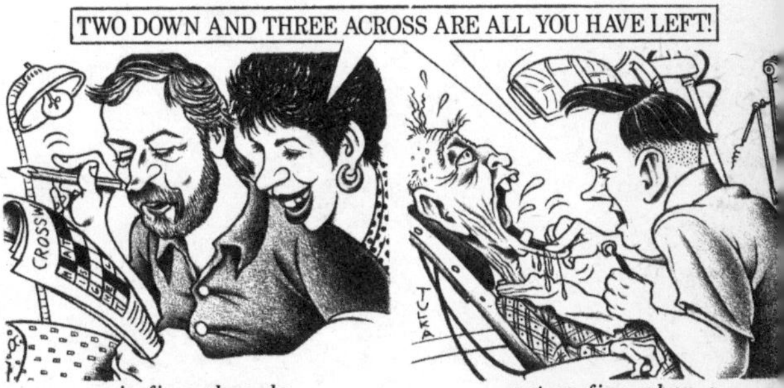
TWO DOWN AND THREE ACROSS ARE ALL YOU HAVE LEFT!
CROSSW
TULKA

...is fine when describing the last clues to a crossword puzzle.

...not so fine when a dentist is describing your last remaining teeth!

JARGON IN PLACE DEPT.

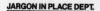

A MAD
SPORTS
On and Off th

The "PICK AND ROLL"
...on the Court

The "PICK AND ROLL"
...in the Stands!

The "BLITZ"
...on the Field

"PILING-ON"
...on the Field

"PILING-ON"
...in the Stands!

GIANTS

The "SUICIDE SQUEEZE PLAY"
...on the Field

Guide to PHRASES Playing Field

ARTIST: JACK DAVIS   WRITER: MIKE SNIDER

The "BLITZ"
...in the Stands!

"BODY CHECK"
...on the Rink

"BODY CHECK"
...in the Stands!

The "SUICIDE SQUEEZE PLAY"
...in the Stands!

"BANK SHOT"
...on the Court

"BANK SHOT"
...in the Stands!

A **"LEFT-RIGHT COMBINATION"**
... in the Ring

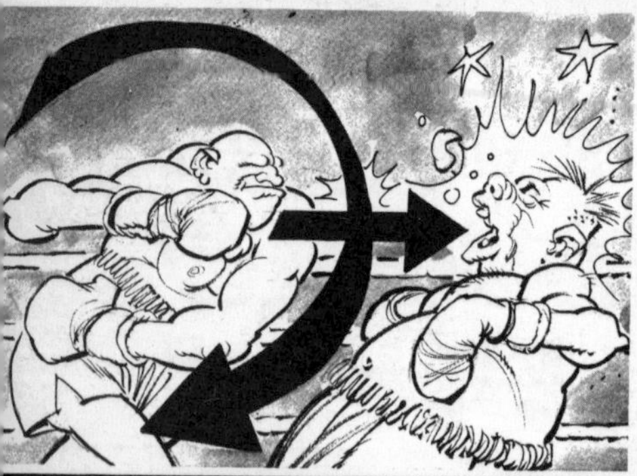

A **"LEFT-RIGHT COMBINATION"**
... in the Stands!

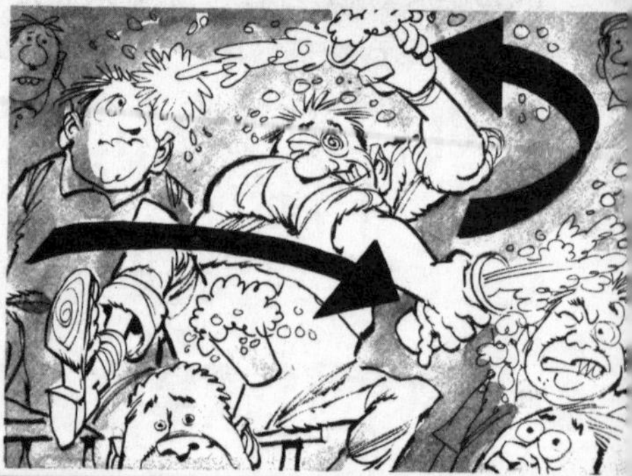

"HOLDING"
... on the Field

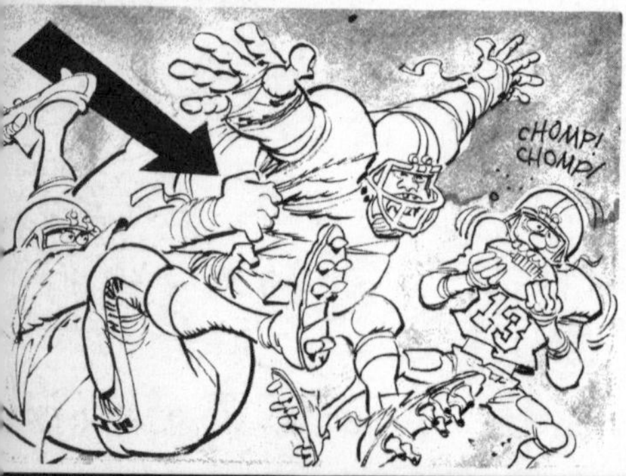
CHOMP! CHOMP!

"HOLDING"
... in the Stands!

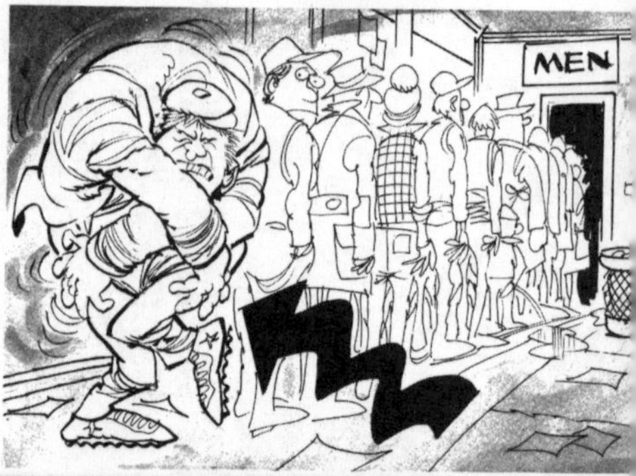
MEN

"FAST BREAK"
... on the Court

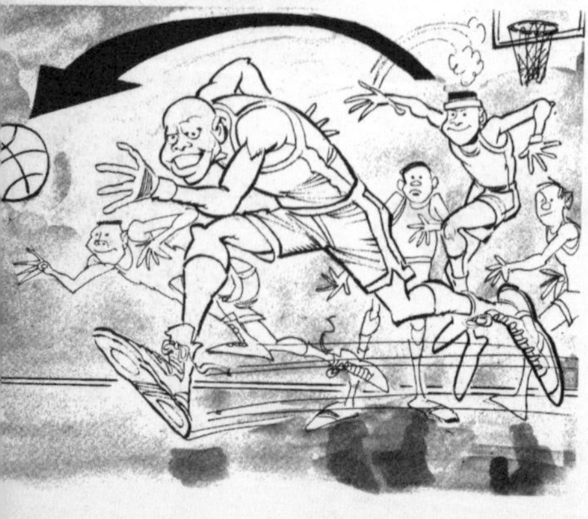

"FAST BREAK"
... in the Stands!

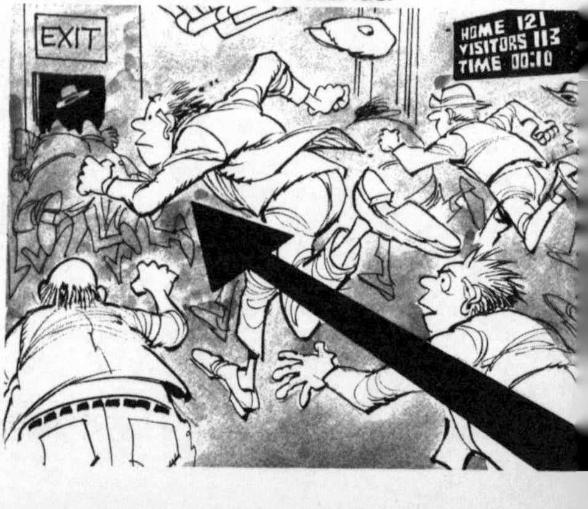
EXIT
HOME 121
VISITORS 113
TIME 00:10

STRING FEVER DEPT.

When you need to know about Yo-Yo tricks, you should come to the Yo-Yos here at MAD! We are the official keeper of the list of...

UNOFFICIAL YO-YO TRICKS EVERY KID KNOWS

ARTIST: PAUL COKER WRITER: DAN BIRTCHER

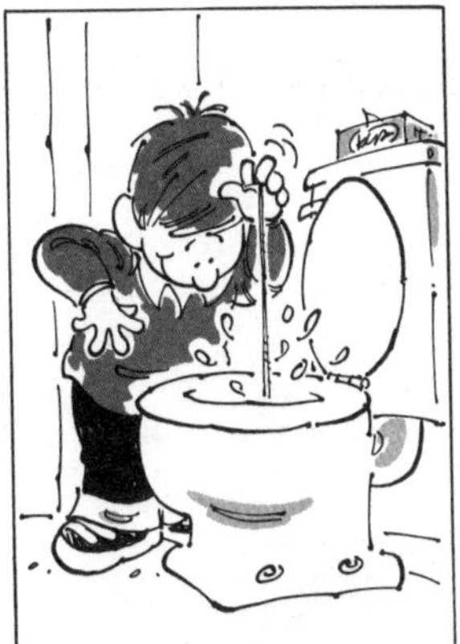

PLUMBING THE DEPTHS

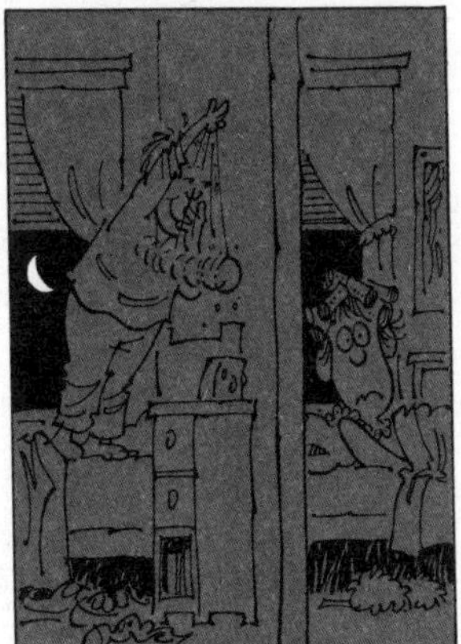

BUMPS IN THE NIGHT

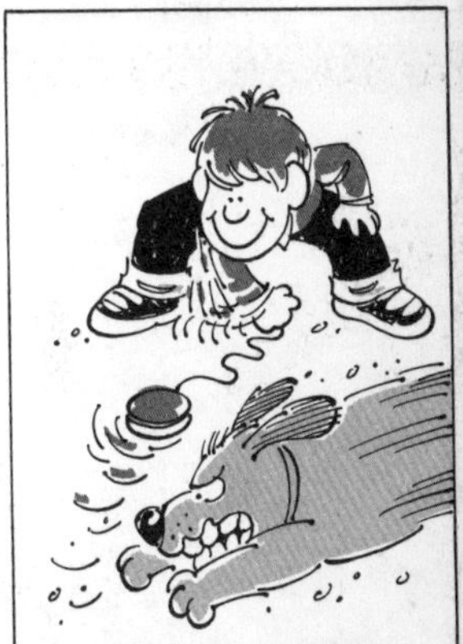

TEASING THE BEAST-THING

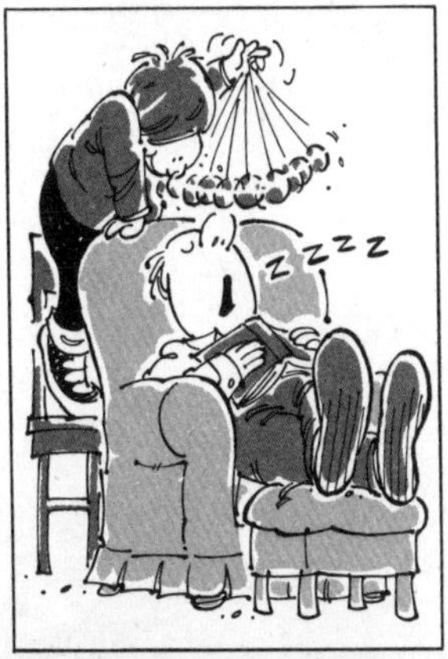
Z Z Z Z

FLIRTING WITH DEATH

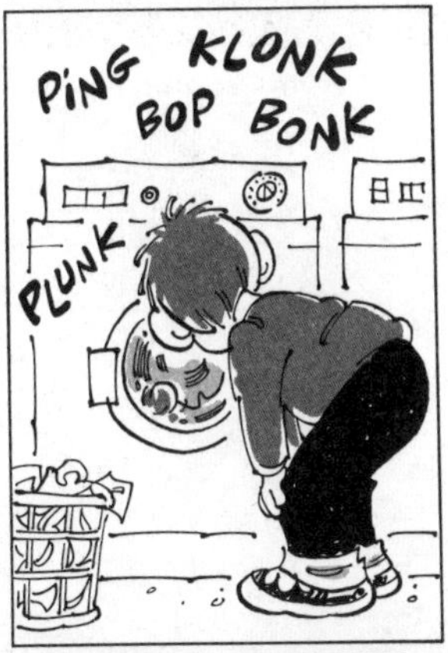
PING
KLONK
BOP
BONK
PLUNK

SYMPHONY FOR DRYER

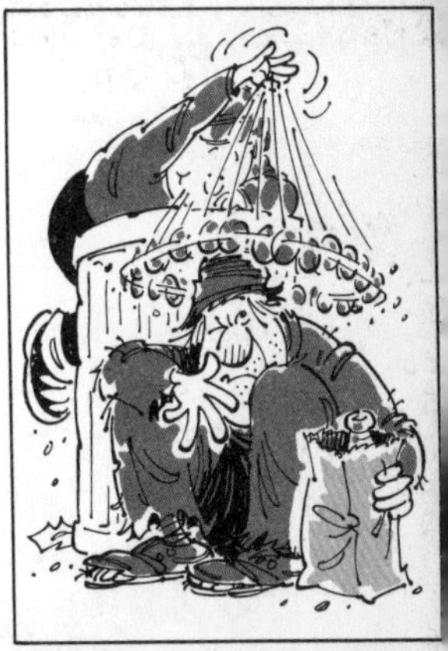

CONFUSING THE DRUNK

MAIM THAT TUNE DEPT.

Each year, millions of tiny kids are herded into day care centers and Sunday schools where they are commanded to join in the singing of traditional songs and carols before they are old enough to read and understand the lyrics. The result is tragically predictable. They sing the words they think they hear, and form a pattern that often lasts a lifetime. Many preoccupied grownups keep right on singing the same muddled words to the same songs in the same way. This, of course, makes us sound like a nation of idiots as we stand reverently at such somber events as patriotic rallies, church services and even baseball games to fill the air with ...

AMERICA'S T

AS THEY SOUN

My Uncle, Liz And Me

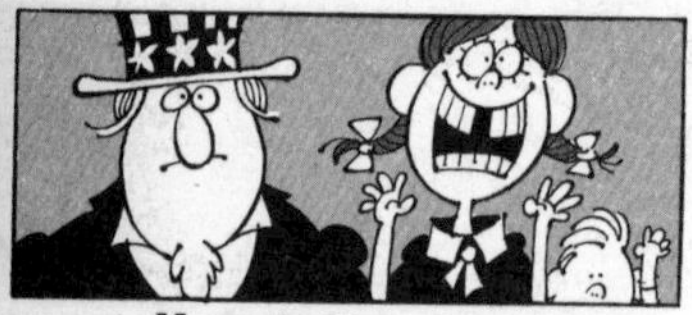

My uncle, Liz and me

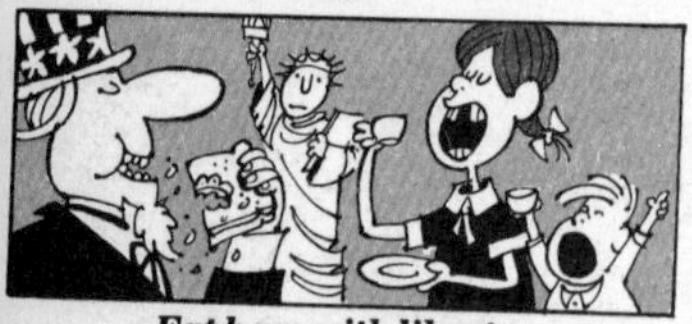

Eat ham with liberty.
Of tea, we sing.

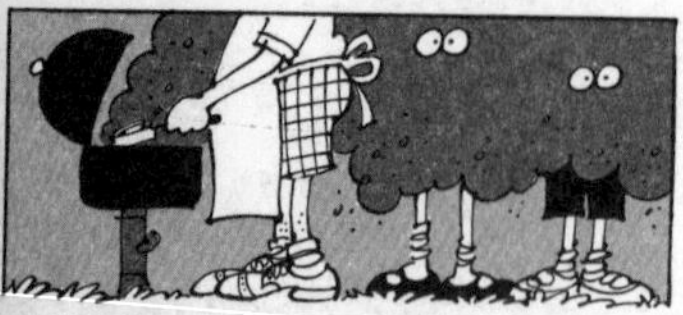

Ham that my father fried;
Ham when the children cried.

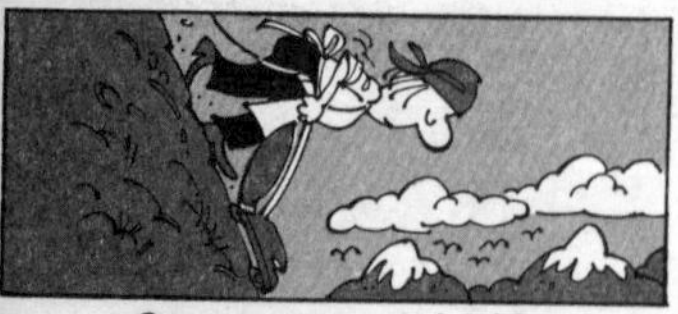

On every mountainside,
Let's clean 'til Spring.

The Star Strangled Grandma

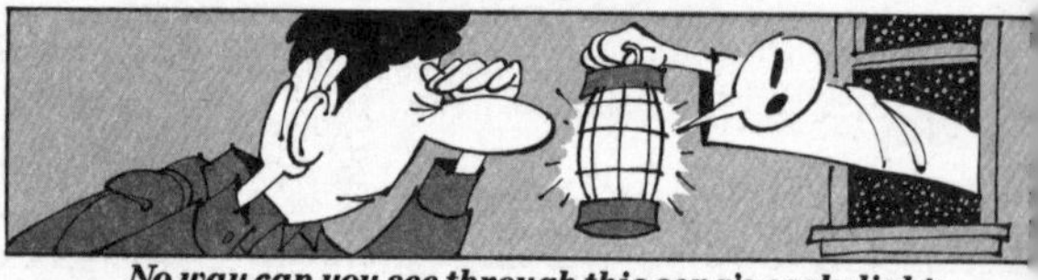
!

No way can you see through this song's early light
What had sounded like hail at the night light's loud screaming

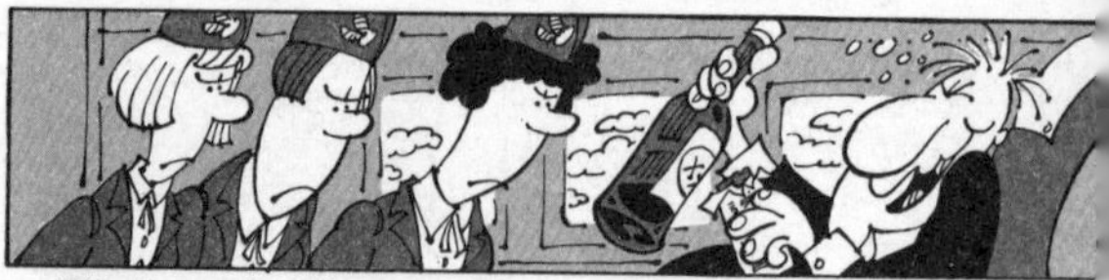

Who brought tripe and Mars bars to the last Eastern flight
On the rampage with scotch while the gals were all steaming.

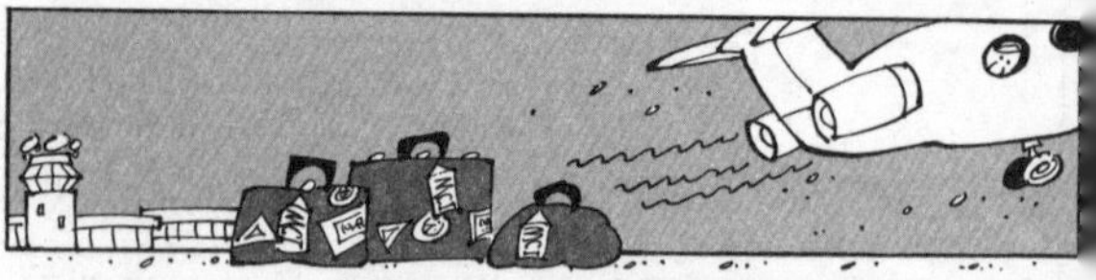

And our pockets were bare
When they first hit the air
As they proved we were right and our bags were still there.

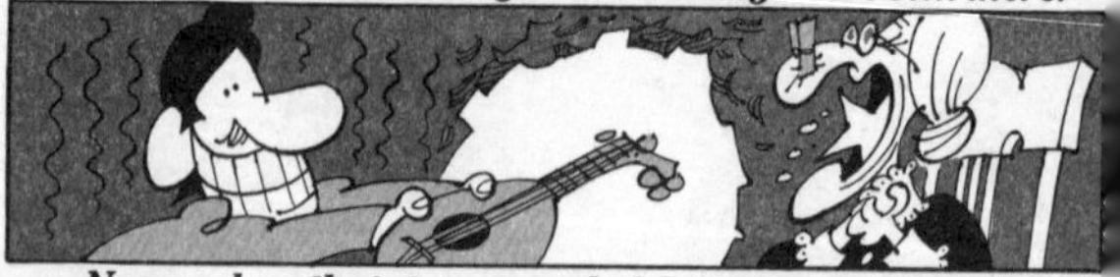

No way does that star strangled Grandma smell Dave,
For the mandolin is free,
And our home is a cave.

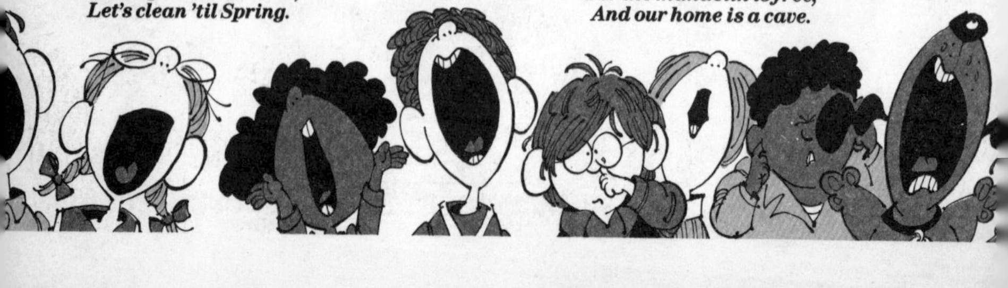

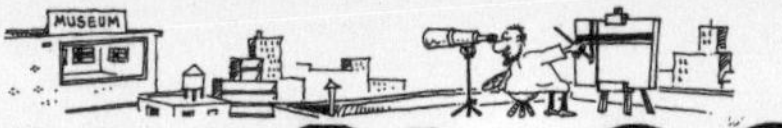

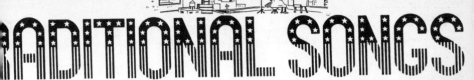

MUSEUM

RADITIONAL SONGS

ARTIST: PAUL COKER WRITER: TOM KOCH

TO FIVE-YEAR-OLDS

That Marine! Him!

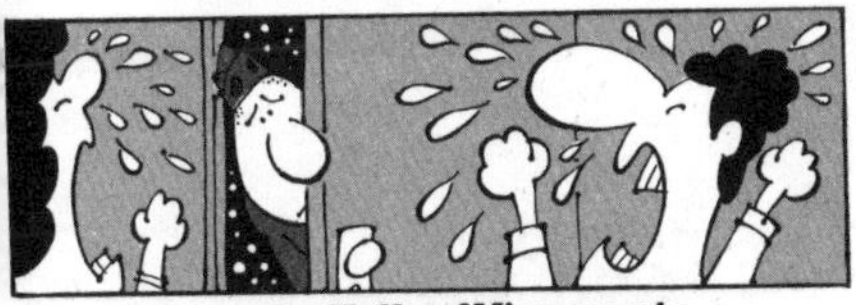

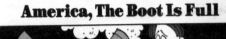

From the Halls of Minneso-ota
To the doors of misery,

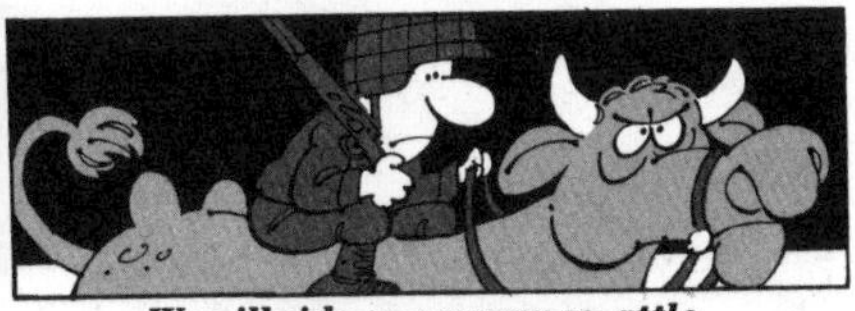

We will ride on grumpy ca-attle
In Iran and Italy.

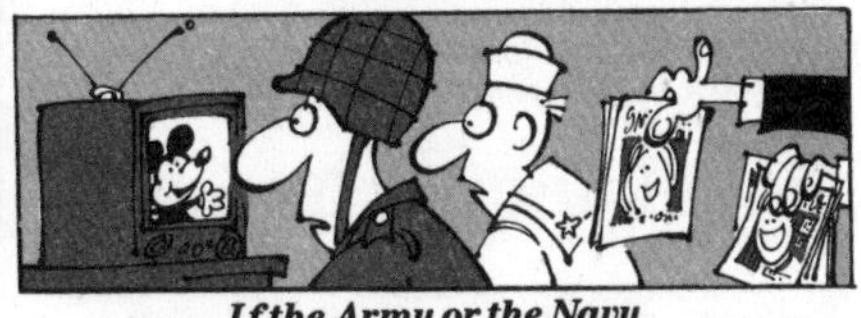

If the Army or the Navy
Ever look at magazines,

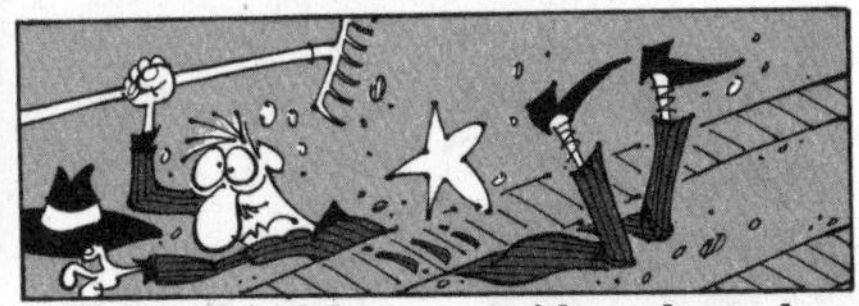

They will find the creeps with garden tools
Have been smashed to smithereens.

America, The Boot Is Full

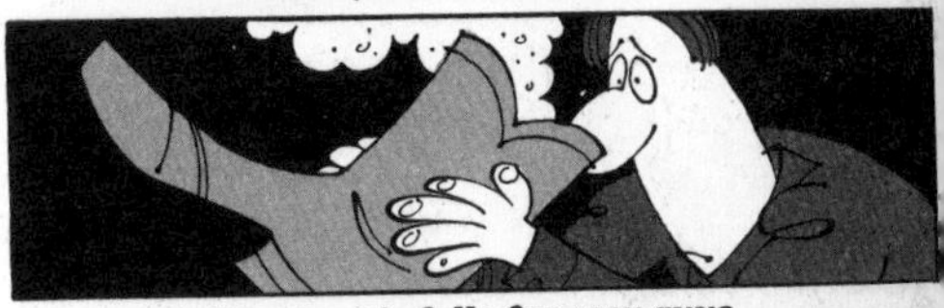

Your boot is full of spacey guys,
And candles made by Jane,

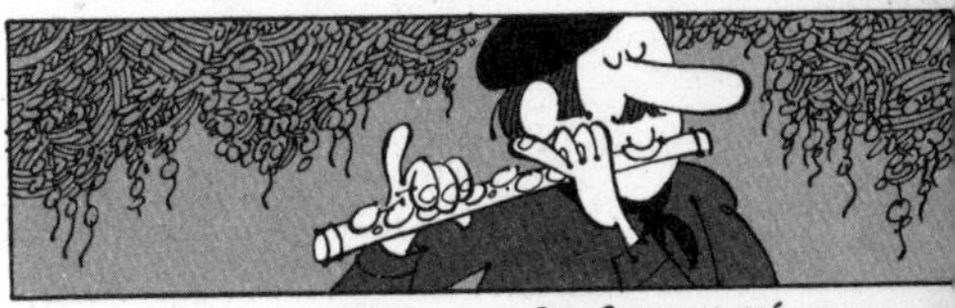

From curdled mounds of macramé
Above the flutes in Spain.

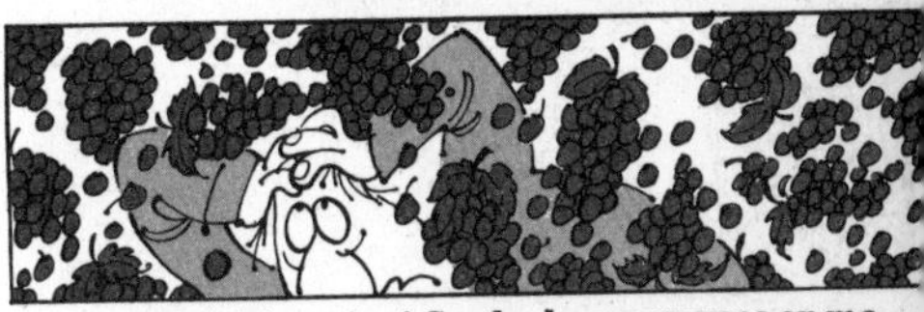

America! America! Go shed your grapes on me.

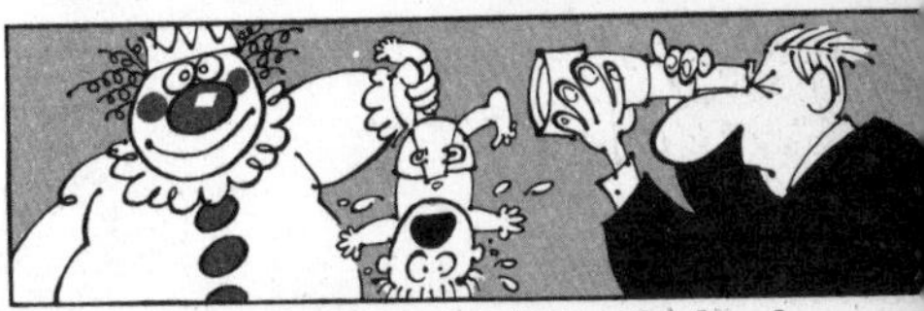

Your clown's no good at motherhood.
We'll see what we shall see.

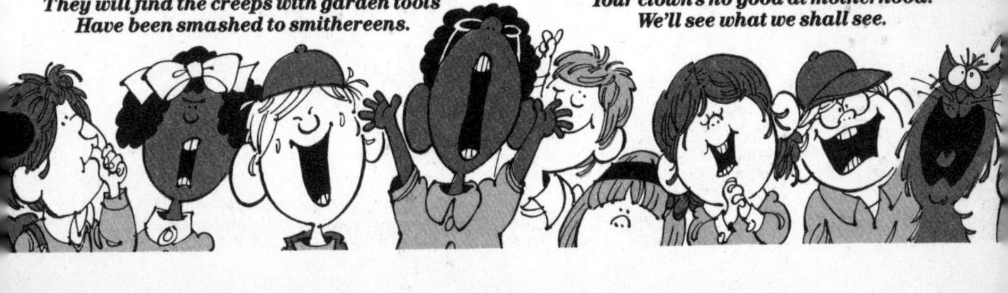

A MANIC FOR ALL SEASONS DEPT.

Every year around Christmas, magazines are filled with articles about how millions of people suffer from Christmas depression (brought on, no doubt, by those very same articles!). Unlike

WHY WE GET THE

ARTIST: GEORGE WOODBRIDGE

Valentine's Day

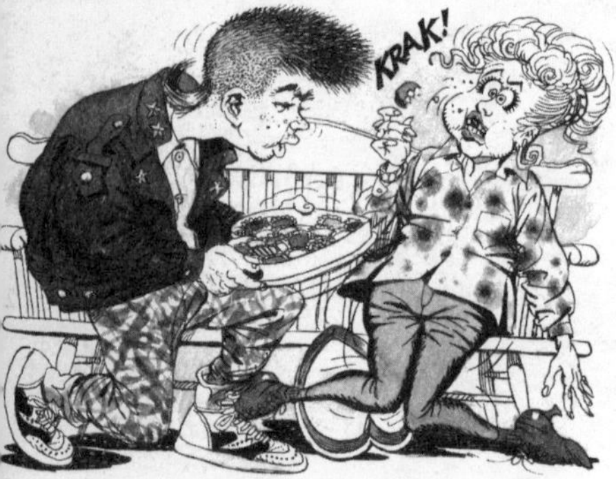
KRAK!

...is the time of the year when our loved ones show their affection towards us by giving us a 20 lb. box of chocolate that's been sitting in a warehouse all year long.

President's Day

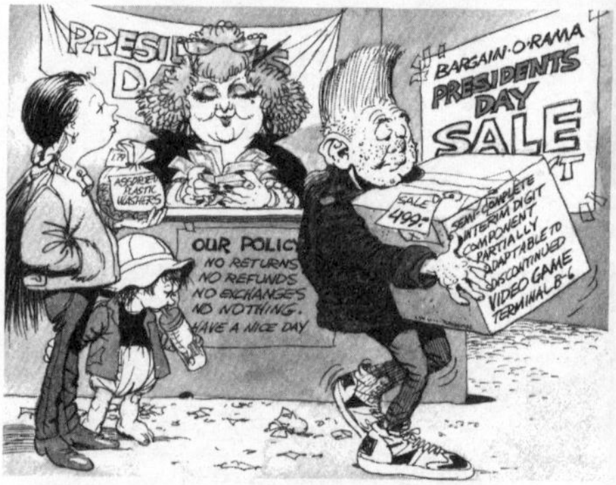
BARGAIN-O-RAMA
PRESIDENTS DAY SALE
ASSORTED PLASTIC WASHERS
OUR POLICY
NO RETURNS
NO REFUNDS
NO EXCHANGES
NO NOTHING.
HAVE A NICE DAY
SALE 499.
SEMI-COMPLETE INTERIM DIGIT COMPONENT PARTIALLY ADAPTABLE TO DISCONTINUED VIDEO GAME TERMINAL B-6

...is the time of the year when greedy store owners honor a President who never told a lie by running deceptive ads, and a President who freed the slaves by keeping American consumers in continual debt.

Arbor Day

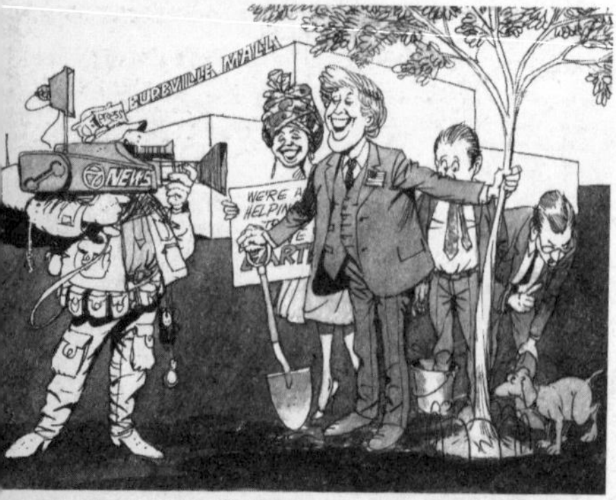
BUREVILLE MALL
NEWS

...is the time of the year when politicians who have passed legislation that's destroyed rivers and forests show their concern for ecology by planting a tree at a shopping mall.

Memorial Day

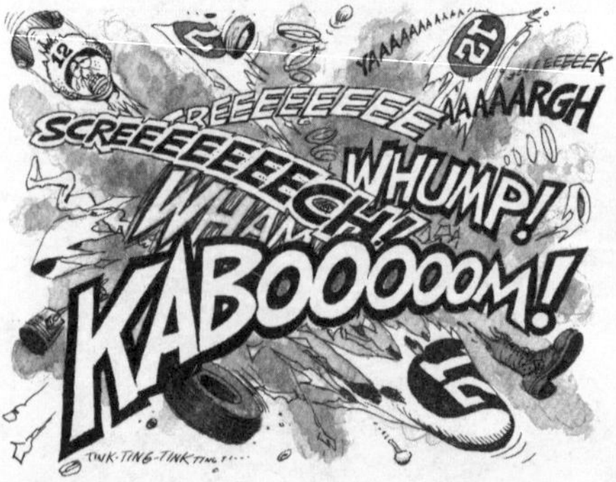
YAAAAAAAA
EEEEEK
AAAAARGH
SCREEEEEEEEEECH!
WHUMP!
KABOOOOOM!
TINK-TING-TINK

...is the time of the year when television announcers tell us to drive carefully so that we can watch race-car drivers kill themselves during the Indianapolis 500.

other magazines, though, MAD would *never* print depressing articles about Christmas. No, we'd rather run a depressing article about *every* holiday! So get ready as we give you a rundown of…

HOLIDAY BLAHS

WRITER: BARRY LIEBMAN

St. Patrick's Day

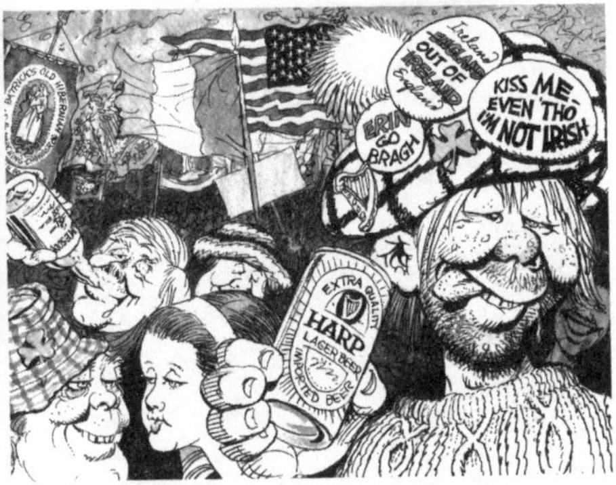
Ireland OUT OF England
ENGLAND OUT OF IRELAND
ERIN GO BRAGH
KISS ME EVEN THO' I'M NOT IRISH
EXTRA QUALITY HARP LAGER BEER IMPORTED BEER

…is the time of the year when we show our respect for Irish-Americans by getting stinking drunk in their honor and throwing up our guts at their parade.

Mother's and Father's Day

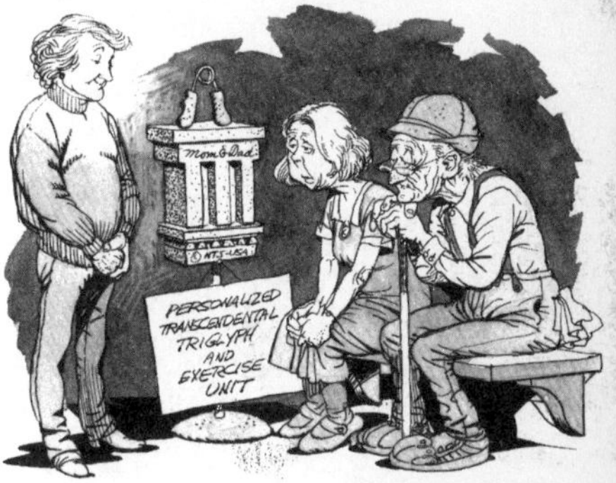
Mom & Dad
PERSONALIZED TRANSCENDENTAL TRIGLYPH AND EXERCISE UNIT

…are the times of the year when every piece of junk that can't be unloaded on anybody at any other time is advertised as being "perfect for both Mom and Dad."

Labor Day

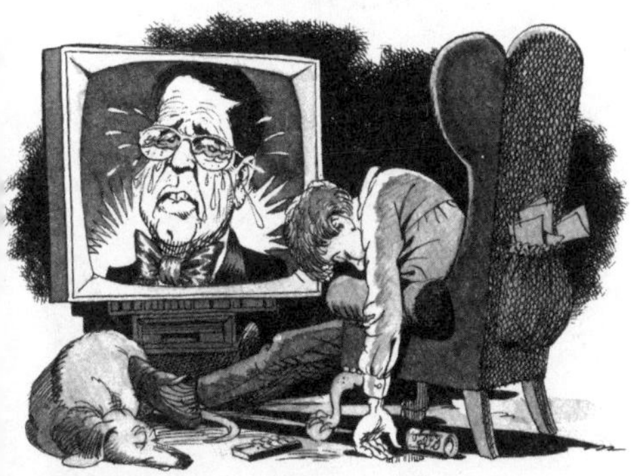

…is the time of the year when we celebrate our last remaining days of vacation by going out and enduring endless traffic jams, or staying in and enduring twenty hours of Jerry Lewis.

Columbus Day

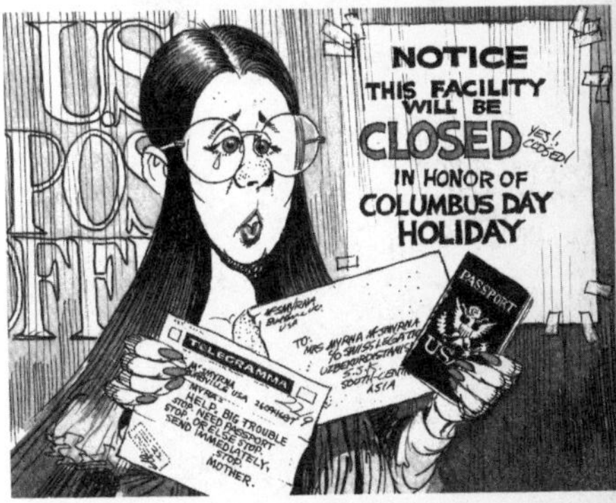
NOTICE
THIS FACILITY WILL BE
CLOSED
YES!, CLOSED!
IN HONOR OF
COLUMBUS DAY
HOLIDAY
TELEGRAMMA
HELP. BIG TROUBLE STOP. NEED PASSPORT STOP. OR ELSE STOP. SEND IMMEDIATELY. STOP. MOTHER.
PASSPORT
USA

…is the time of the year when we commemorate a man who lost two boats and ended up totally off-course by keeping the post office closed.

Halloween

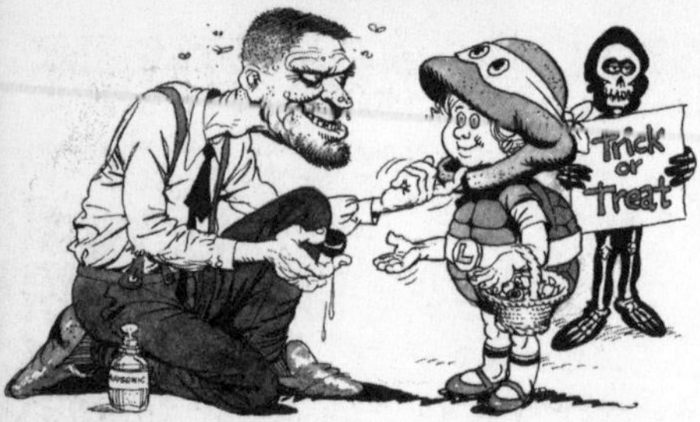
Trick or Treat

... is the time of the year when stories of ghosts, goblins, and things that go bump in the night pale next to stories about psychos poisoning Trick or Treat candy.

Election Day

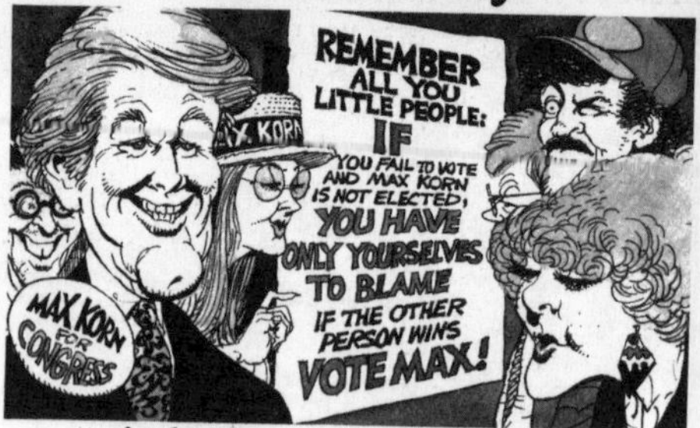
REMEMBER ALL YOU LITTLE PEOPLE:
IF YOU FAIL TO VOTE AND MAX KORN IS NOT ELECTED, YOU HAVE ONLY YOURSELVES TO BLAME IF THE OTHER PERSON WINS
VOTE MAX!
MAX KORN FOR CONGRESS

... is the time of the year when we officially give someone who has spent $20 million to get a $100,000 job the chance to manage our money.

Veteran's Day

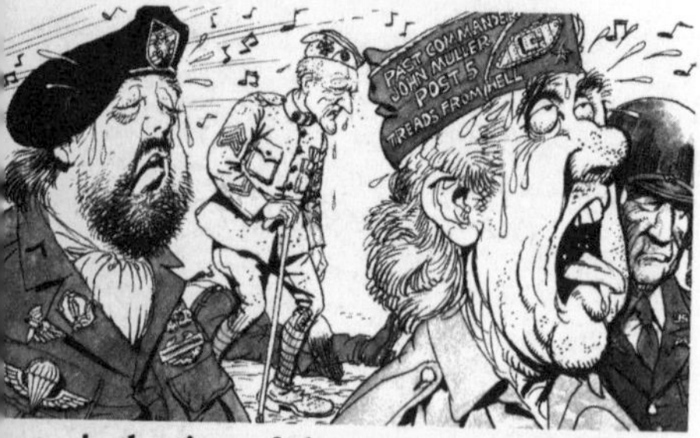
PAST COMMANDER JOHN MULLER POST 5 TREADS FROM HELL

... is the time of the year when we show our appreciation to all the old soldiers who hated marching in 10-mile hikes by allowing them to march in 10-mile parades.

Thanksgiving

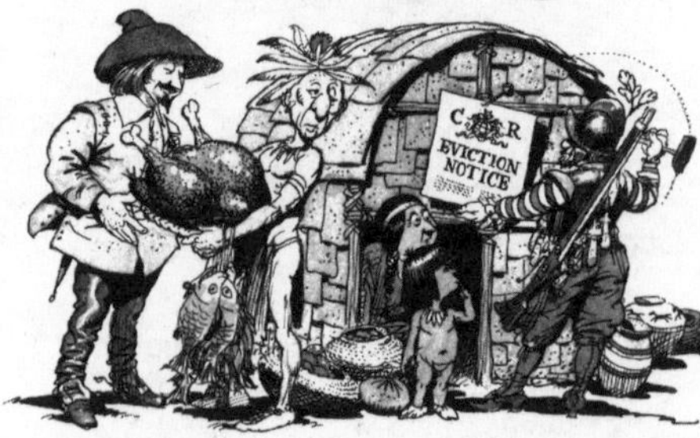
EVICTION NOTICE

... is the time of the year when we honor the notion of sharing by recounting how the Indians fed the same people who would eventually steal their land away from them.

Christmas

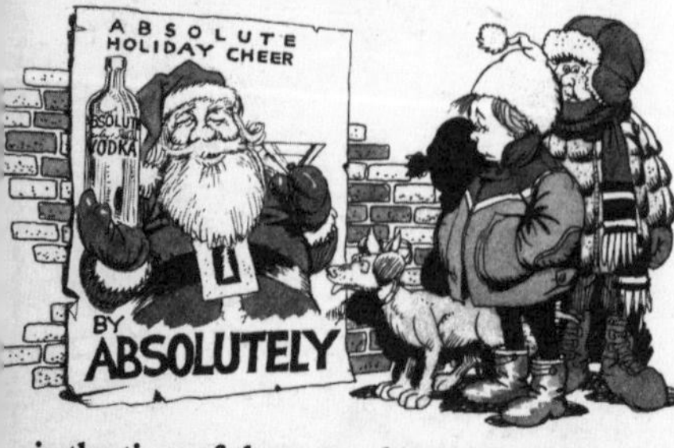
ABSOLUTE HOLIDAY CHEER
BY ABSOLUTELY

.. is the time of the year when parents have to xplain why the same Santa who's so worried bout kids being naughty or nice is urging them o smoke and drink in cigarette and liquor ads.

New Year's Eve

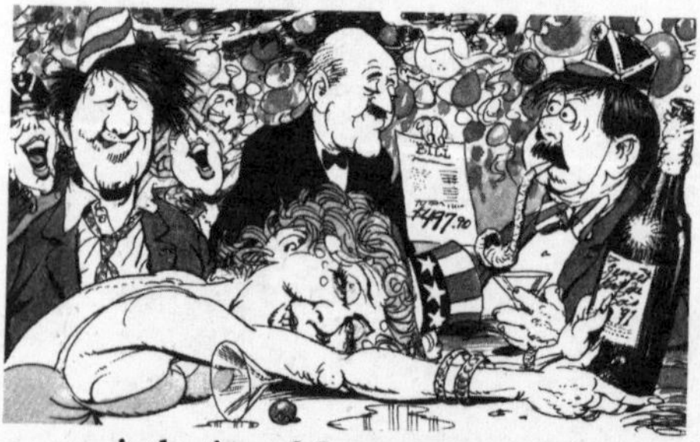

... is the time of the year when all the restaurants and night clubs show their holiday spirit by handing out noise-makers and raising their prices 400%.

TALES FROM THE DUCK SIDE DEPT.

THE ASTOUNDING AERONAUTIC ADVENTURE

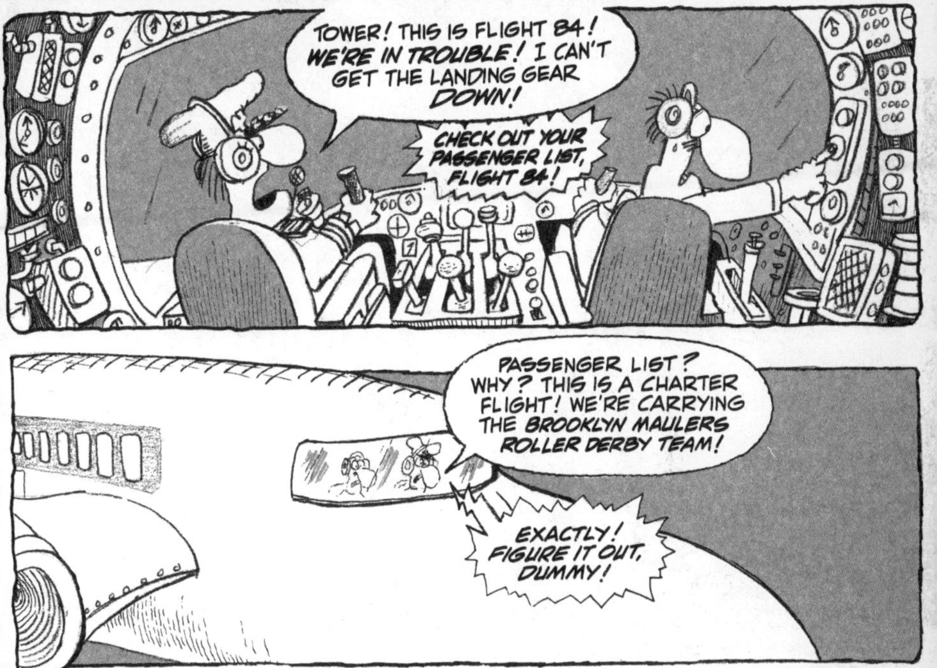
TOWER! THIS IS FLIGHT 84! WE'RE IN TROUBLE! I CAN'T GET THE LANDING GEAR DOWN!
CHECK OUT YOUR PASSENGER LIST, FLIGHT 84!
PASSENGER LIST? WHY? THIS IS A CHARTER FLIGHT! WE'RE CARRYING THE BROOKLYN MAULERS ROLLER DERBY TEAM!
EXACTLY! FIGURE IT OUT, DUMMY!

ARTIST & WRITER: DUCK EDWING

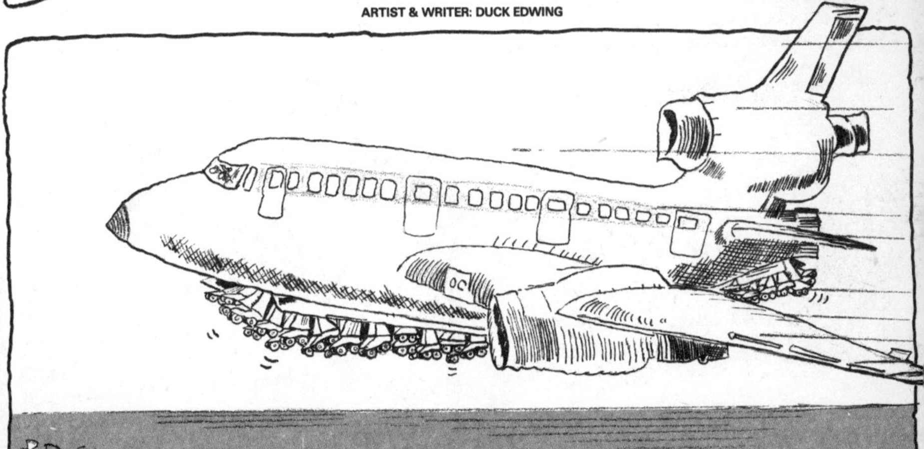
DUCK

FATAL DISTRACTIONS DEPT.

With violence in sports
attracting such a wide
audience, it won't be

MAKING
M
DANC

ARTIST AND WR

GRENADE HOCKEY

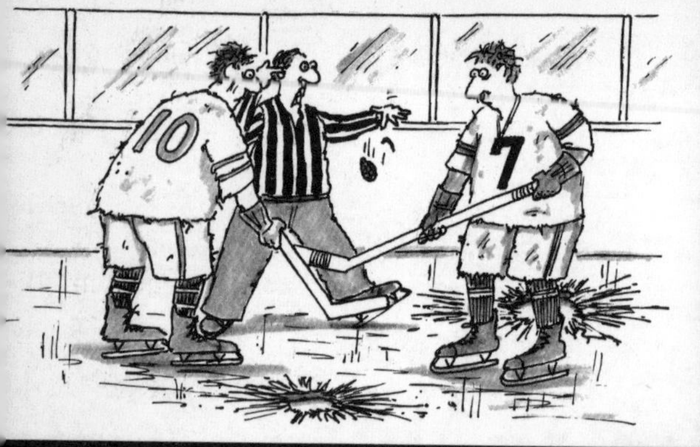

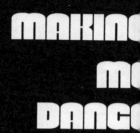

TAG TEAM BRIDGE

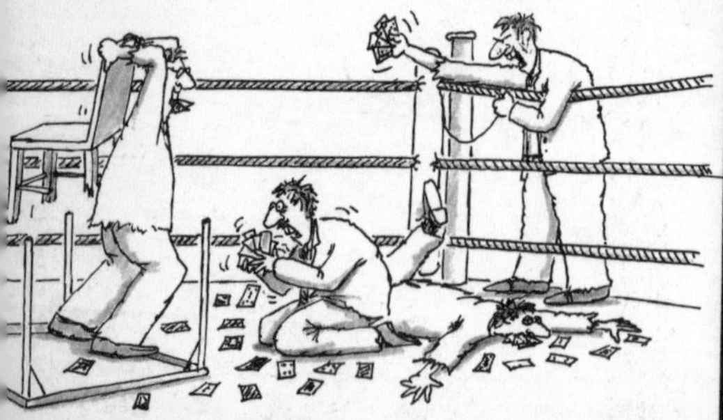

BOBBING FOR PIRANHA

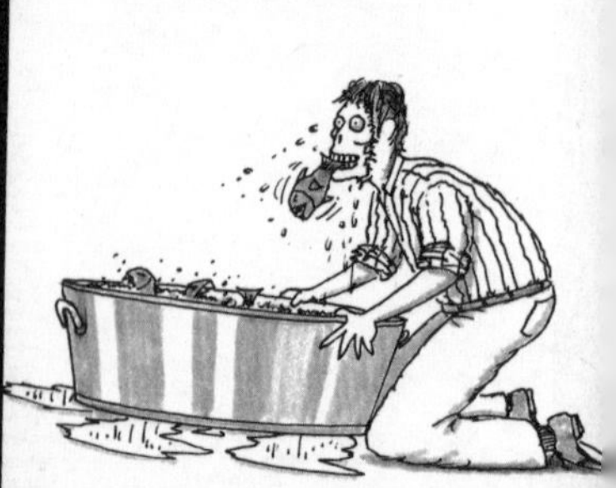

.12 GAUGE PING PONG

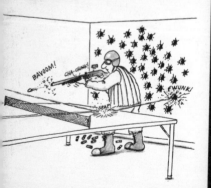

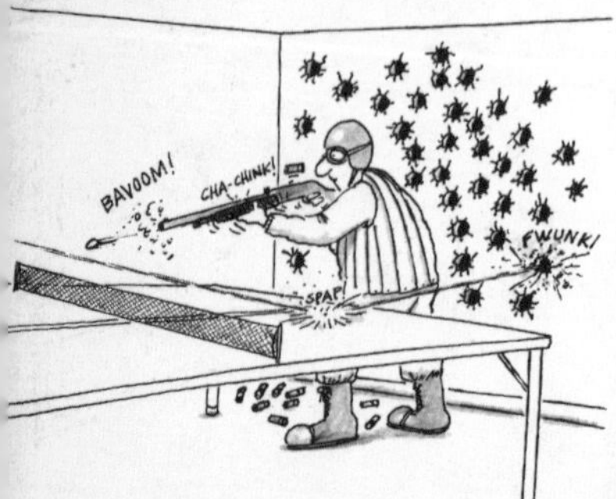
BAVOOM!
CHA-CHINK!
FWUNK!
SPAP!

PHONE BOOTH CROQUET

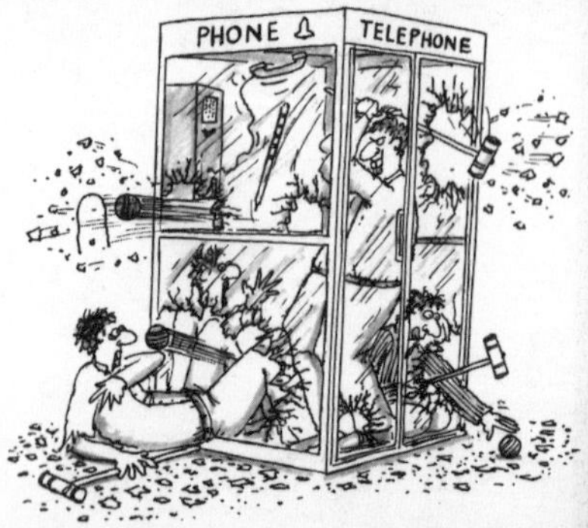
PHONE
TELEPHONE

too long before other activities join the new trend towards...

GAMES
RE
ROUS

M CHENEY

BLINDMAN'S BLENDER

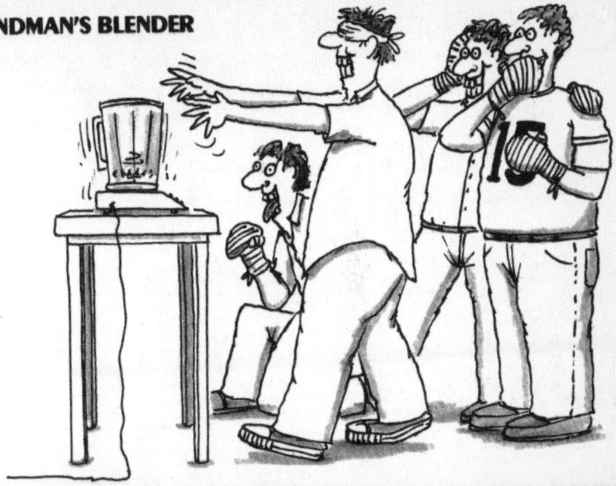
15

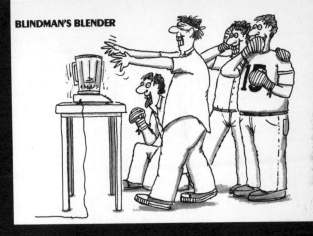

BOULEVARD BADMINTON

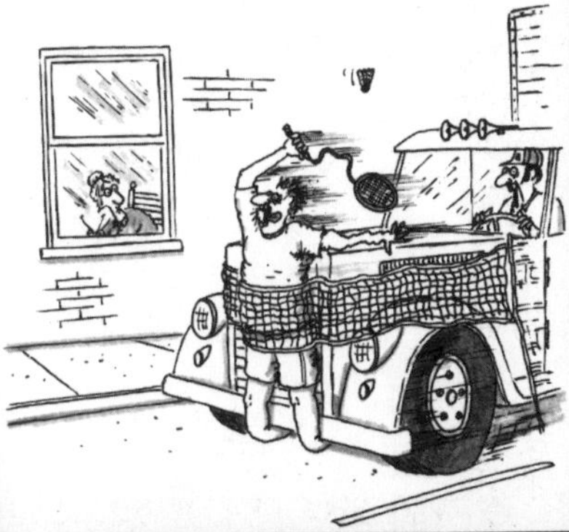

VERTICAL SKATEBOARDING

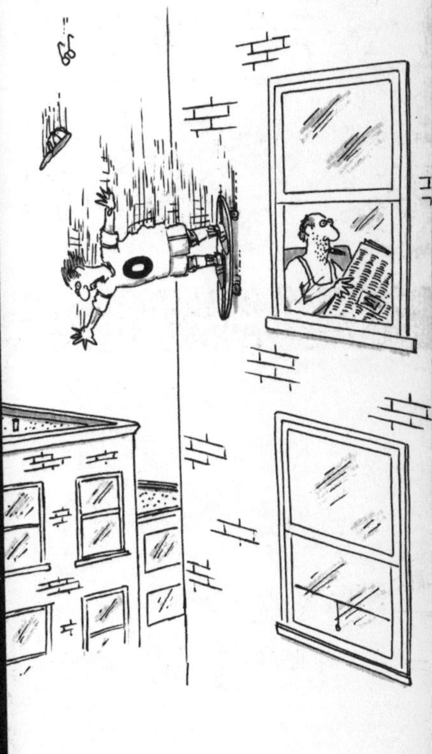
0

DEMOLITION CHESS

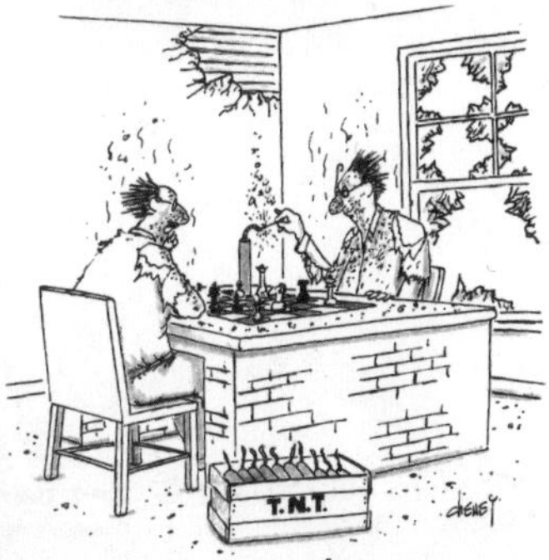
T.N.T.
cheney

OUT OF SIGHT, OUT OF LINE DEPT.

Everyone does something they take pride in, something they love to do while the whole wo

ONLY WHEN

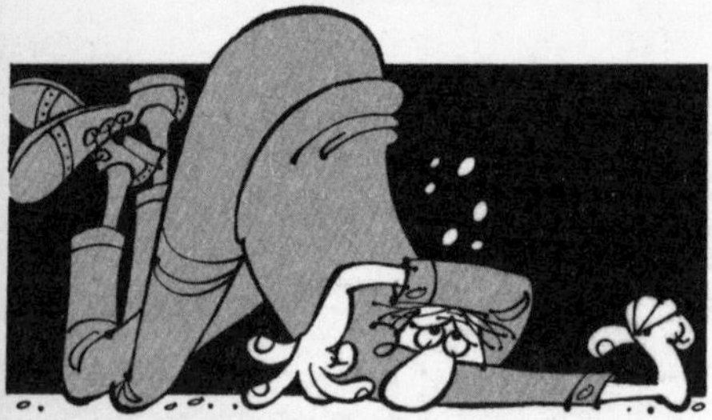

...can you trip over your own big feet and not look back for some imaginary obstacle!

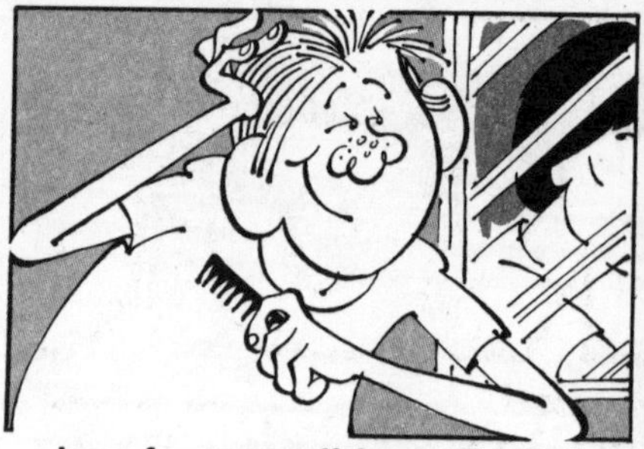

...do you fancy yourself the next Tom Cruise!

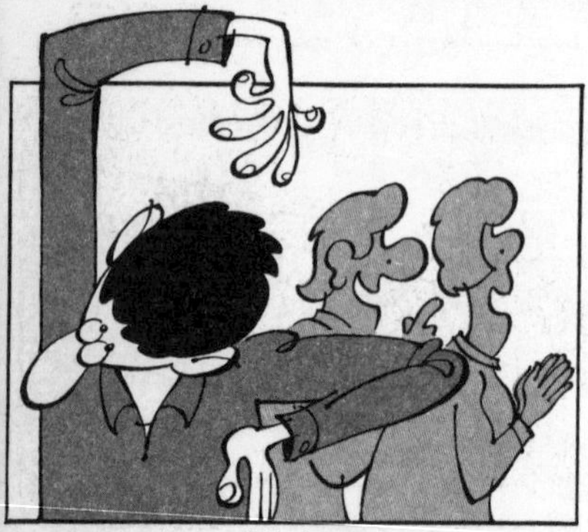

...can you do a quick deodorant check!

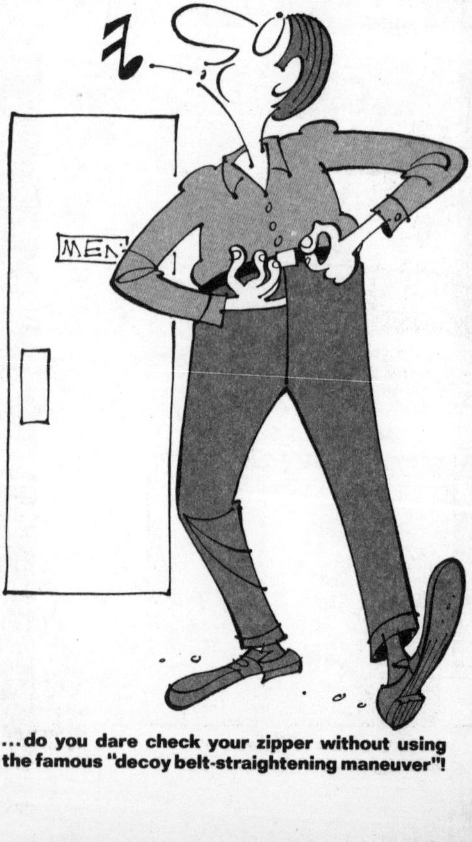
MEN

...do you dare check your zipper without using the famous "decoy belt-straightening maneuver"!

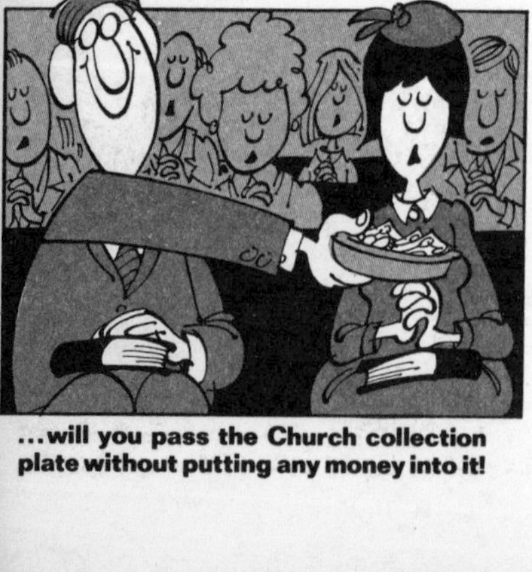

...will you pass the Church collection plate without putting any money into it!

oks on. But there are other things people are not so proud of—vile things best performed...

OU'RE SURE

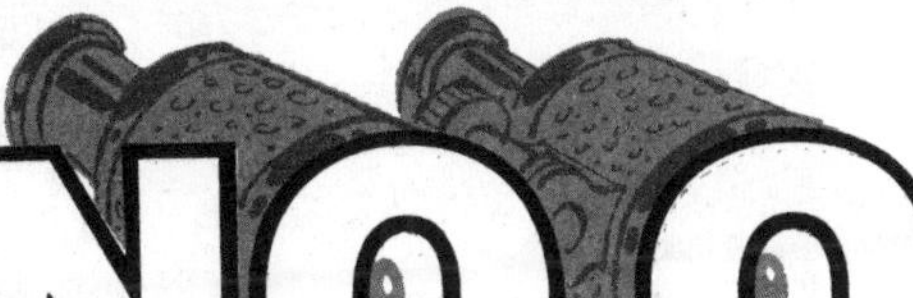

NO ONE IS WATCHING...

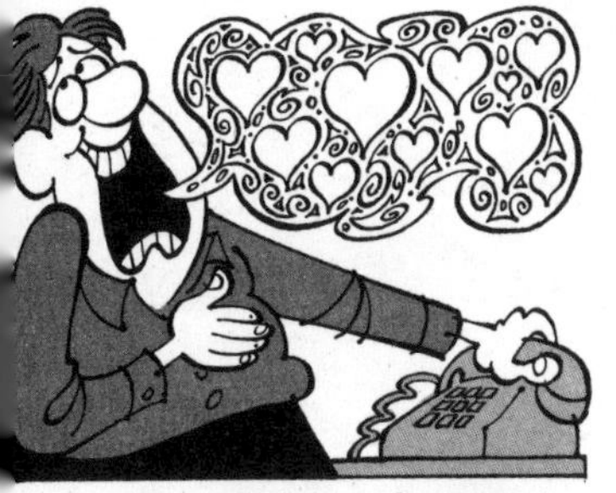

...do you rehearse important phone conversations out loud!

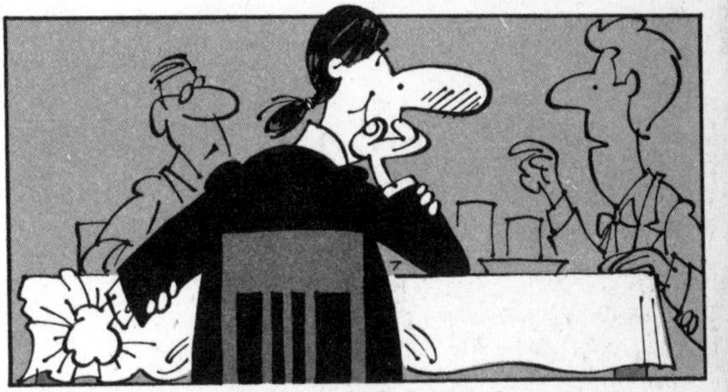

...can you do anything with the hand you sneeze on because you didn't have a handkerchief!

ARTIST: PAUL COKER WRITER: MIKE SNIDER

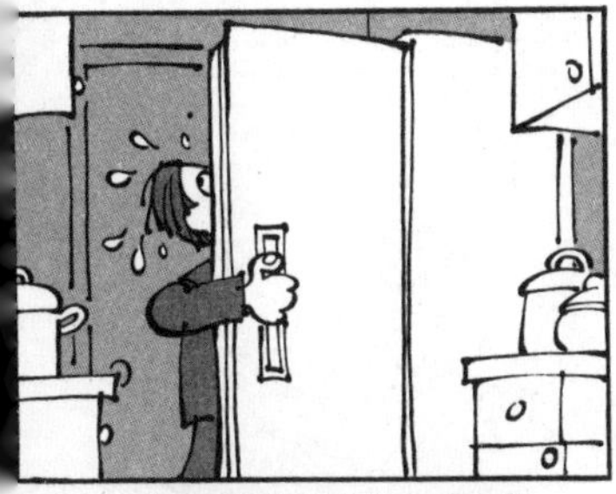

...do you take a big swig of milk right out of the carton!

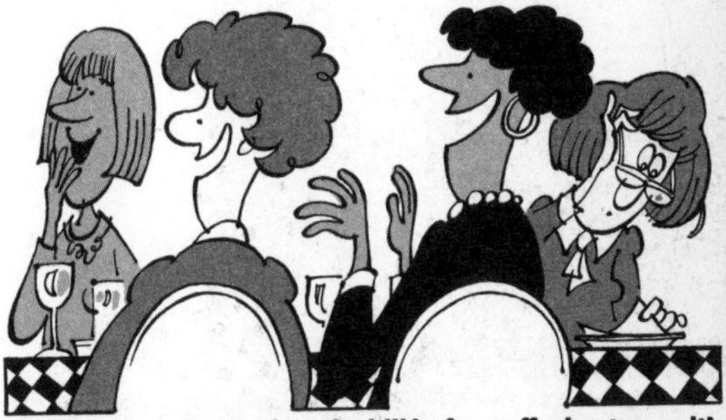

...do you sneak a peek at the bill before offering to pay it!

AN EMBARRASSMENT OF RICHARD'S DEPT.

When you're shopping, there are certain things a salesman might say to you that should tip you off that he's about to give you the proverbial 1-2 shaftaroony! For example, "I'm about to give you the proverbial 1-2 shaftaroony!", although most salesmen are more clever and use subtler techniques. In any case, whatever he's recommending you buy, the thing to do is select another model—or better yet, another salesman! But really, pal, take it from us, if you want a really great deal on an unbeatable MAD article, then you must check out...

SALESMEN
THA

When Buying a Microwave Oven

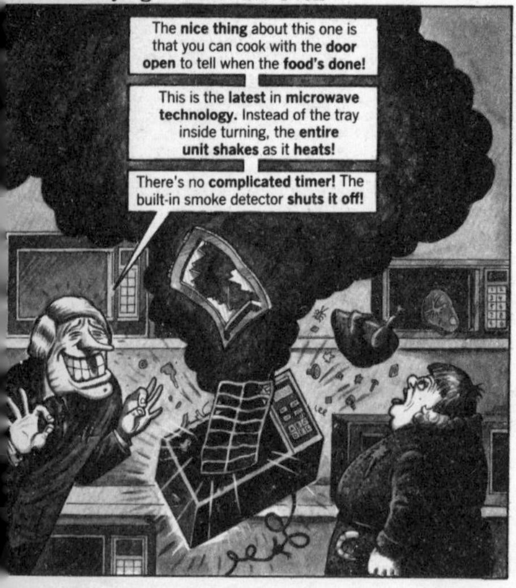
The nice thing about this one is that you can cook with the door open to tell when the food's done!
This is the latest in microwave technology. Instead of the tray inside turning, the entire unit shakes as it heats!
There's no complicated timer! The built-in smoke detector shuts it off!

When Buying a Watch

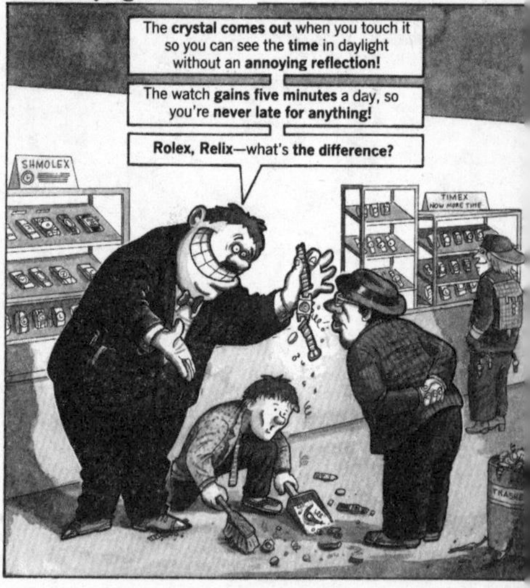
The crystal comes out when you touch it so you can see the time in daylight without an annoying reflection!
The watch gains five minutes a day, so you're never late for anything!
Rolex, Relix—what's the difference?
SHMOLEX
TIMEX

ARTIST: TOM BUN

When Buying a Computer

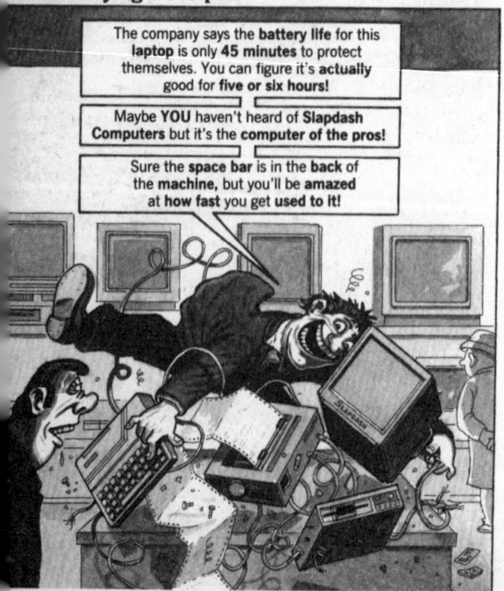
The company says the battery life for this laptop is only 45 minutes to protect themselves. You can figure it's actually good for five or six hours!
Maybe YOU haven't heard of Slapdash Computers but it's the computer of the pros!
Sure the space bar is in the back of the machine, but you'll be amazed at how fast you get used to it!
SLAPDASH

When Buying a Camera

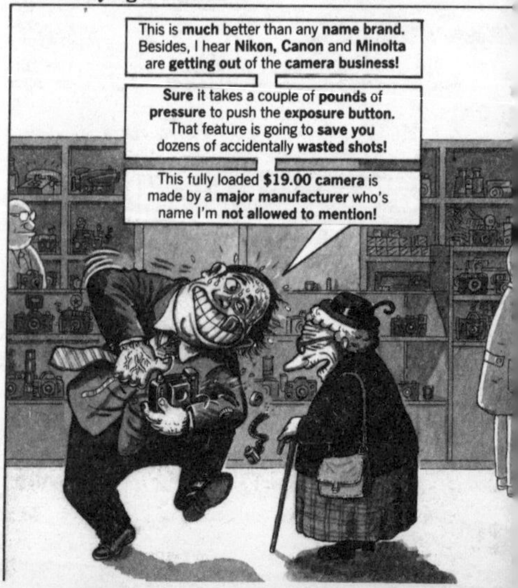
This is much better than any name brand. Besides, I hear Nikon, Canon and Minolta are getting out of the camera business!
Sure it takes a couple of pounds of pressure to push the exposure button. That feature is going to save you dozens of accidentally wasted shots!
This fully loaded $19.00 camera is made by a major manufacturer who's name I'm not allowed to mention!

CLAIMS AND COME-ONS
HOULD SET YOU RUNNING

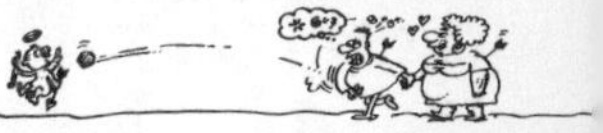

When Buying a Backpack

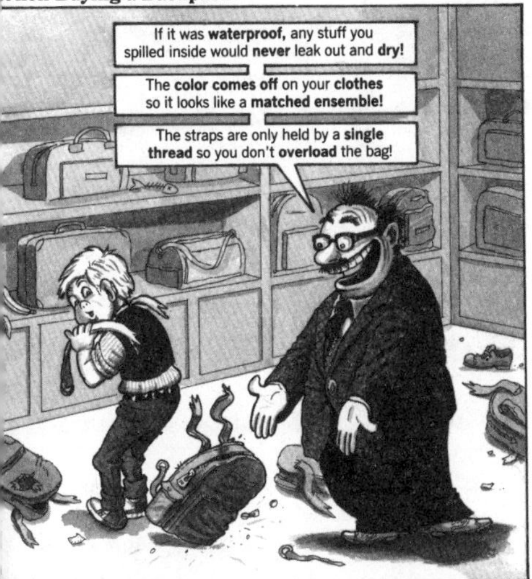
If it was **waterproof,** any stuff you spilled inside would **never** leak out and **dry!**
The **color comes off** on your **clothes** so it looks like a **matched ensemble!**
The straps are only held by a **single thread** so you don't **overload** the bag!

When Buying an Air Conditioner

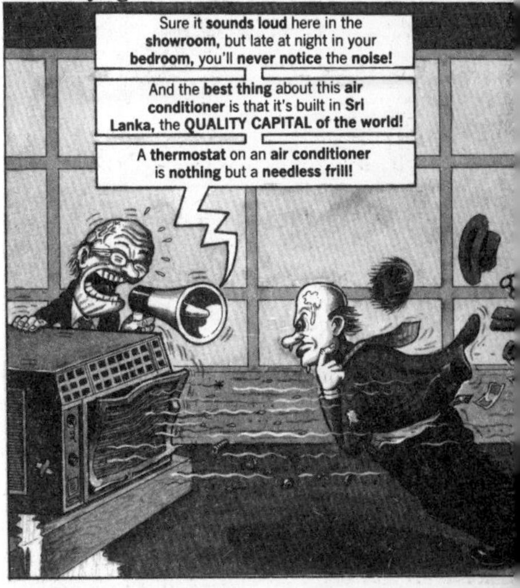
Sure it **sounds loud** here in the **showroom,** but late at night in your **bedroom,** you'll **never notice** the **noise!**
And the **best thing** about this **air conditioner** is that it's built in **Sri Lanka,** the **QUALITY CAPITAL of the world!**
A **thermostat** on an **air conditioner** is **nothing** but a **needless frill!**

WRITER: DICK DEBARTOLO

When Buying a VCR

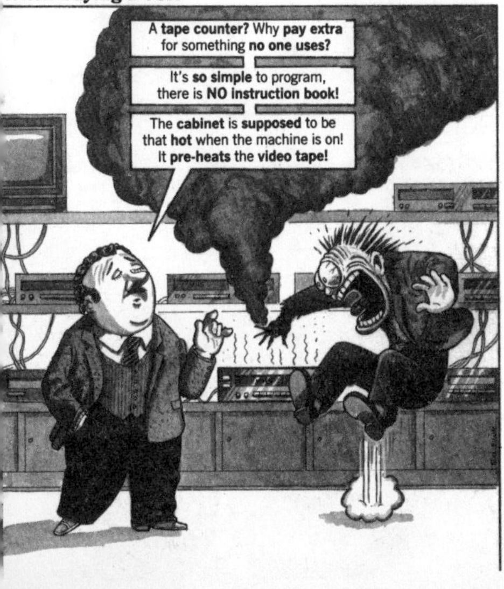
A **tape counter?** Why **pay extra** for something **no one uses?**
It's **so simple** to program, there is **NO instruction book!**
The **cabinet** is **supposed** to be that **hot** when the machine is on! It **pre-heats** the **video tape!**

When Buying a Color TV

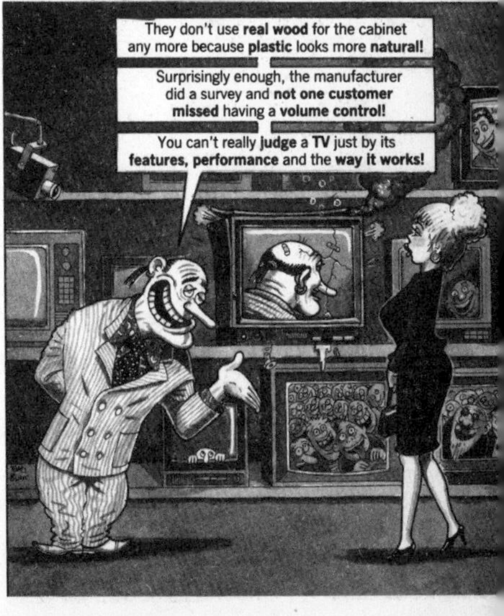
They don't use **real wood** for the cabinet any more because **plastic** looks more **natural!**
Surprisingly enough, the manufacturer did a survey and **not one customer missed** having a **volume control!**
You can't really **judge** a **TV** just by its **features, performance** and the **way it works!**

A MASSIVE CHART ATTACK DEPT.

Ever wonder about the correlation between seemingly unrelated events– between say, the number of crimes per 1000 households and the number o

CAUSE OR CO

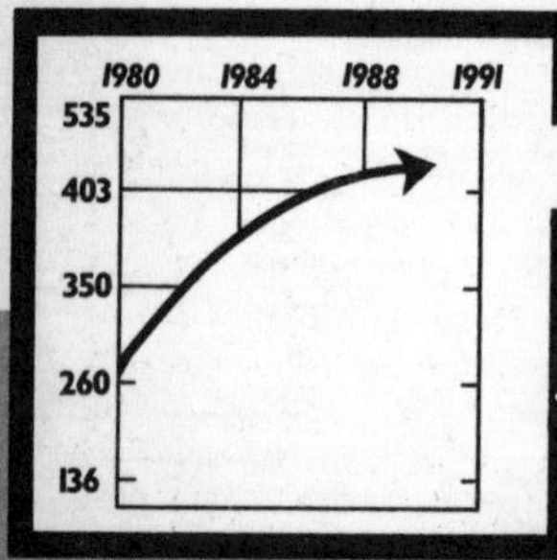

1980
1984
1988
1991
535
403
350
260
136

POLITICIANS RE-ELECTED TO CONGRESS

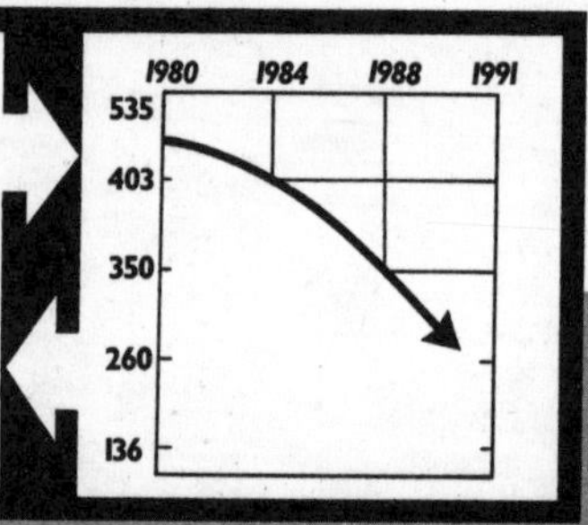

1980
1984
1988
1991
535
403
350
260
136

VOTER S.A.T. SCORES

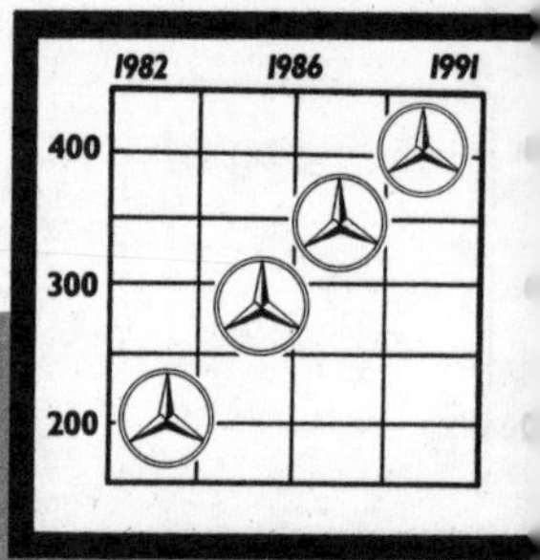

1982
1986
1991
400
300
200

CAR CHASES ON T.V.

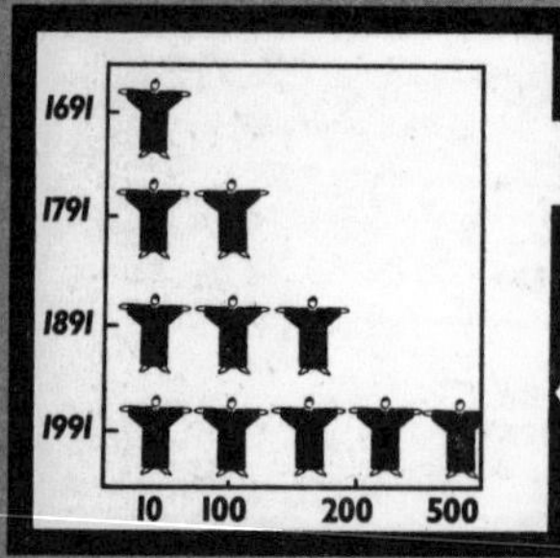

1691
1791
1891
1991
10
100
200
500

SELF-PROCLAIMED EVANGELISTS

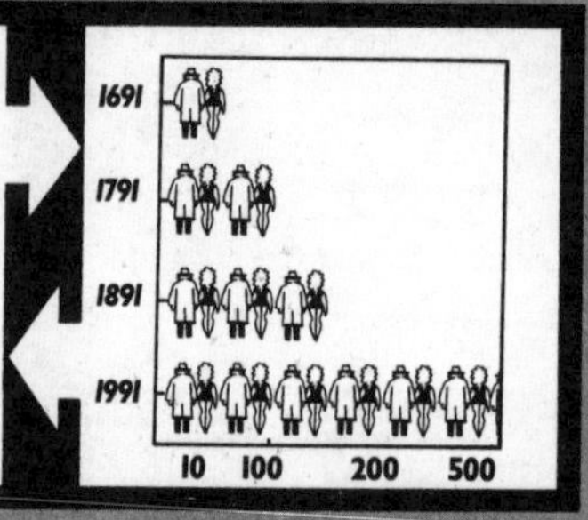

1691
1791
1891
1991
10
100
200
500

HOTEL RESERVATIONS UNDER THE NAME "JOHN SMITH"

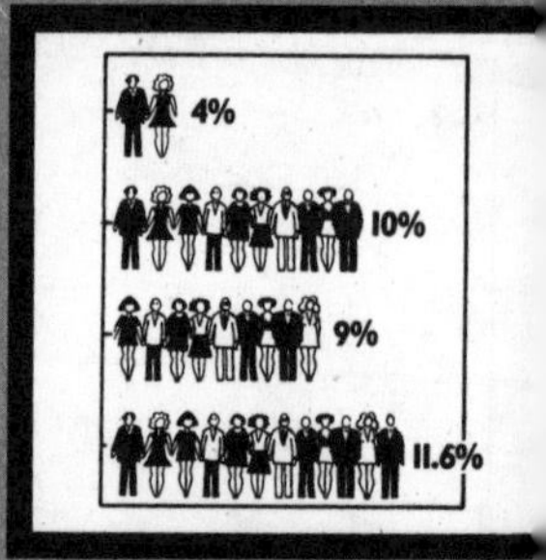

4%
10%
9%
11.6%

CLEVELANDERS LEAVING CLEVELAND FOREVER

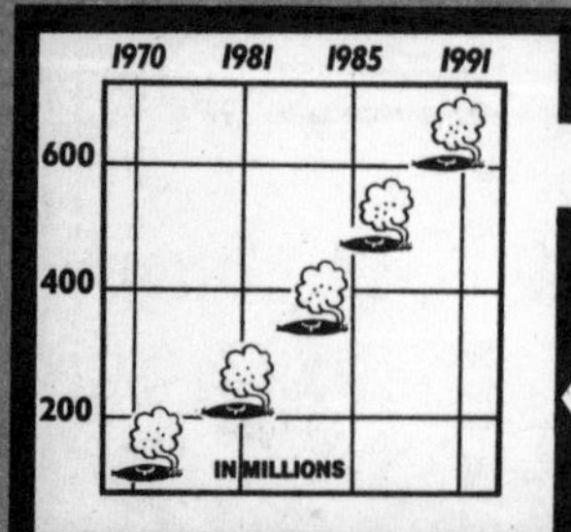

1970
1981
1985
1991
600
400
200
IN MILLIONS

CIGAR SALES

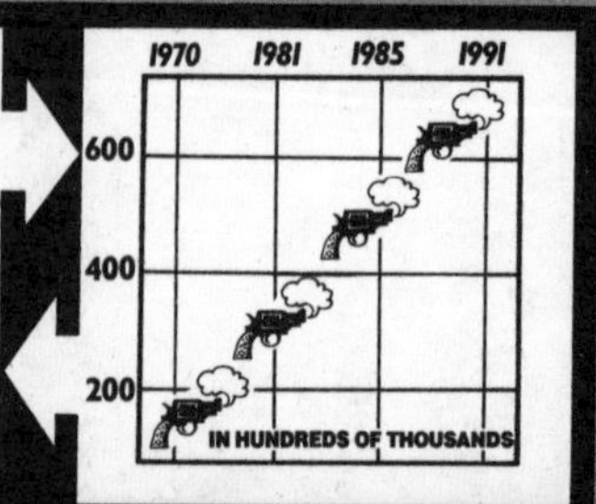

1970
1981
1985
1991
600
400
200
IN HUNDREDS OF THOUSANDS

WOMEN WHO OWN GUNS

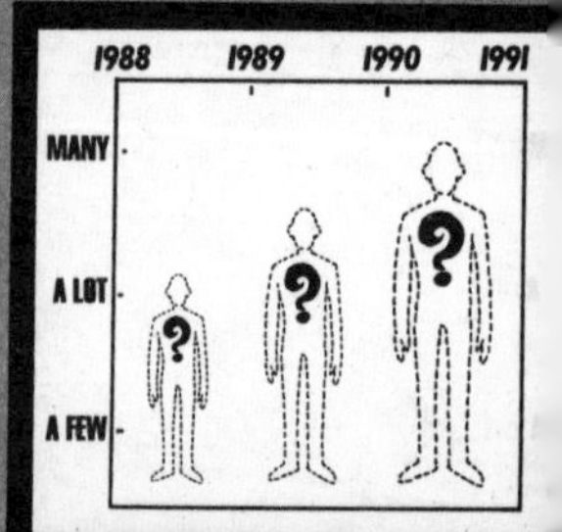

1988
1989
1990
1991
MANY
A LOT
A FEW

MISSING PERSONS

iomes that display plastic snowmen? Is there a connection?? *Ummm*...no.
3ut other statistical pairs *do* suggest definite links. You decide! Are they...

INCIDENCE??

ARTIST: GEORGE WOODBRIDGE WRITER: DAN BIRTCHER

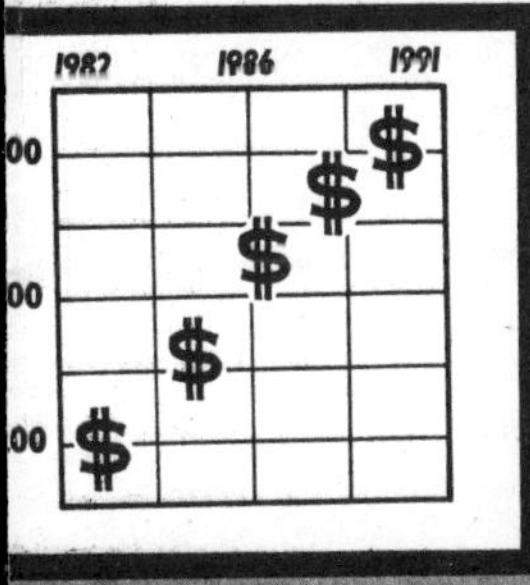
1982
1986
1991
00
00
00
CAR INSURANCE PREMIUMS

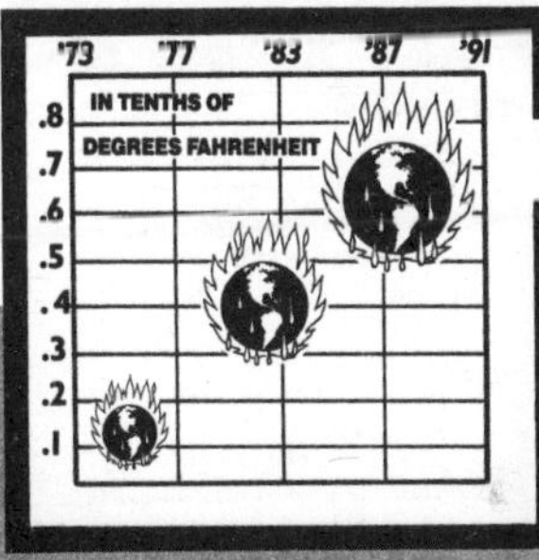
'73
'77
'83
'87
'91
IN TENTHS OF
DEGREES FAHRENHEIT
.8
.7
.6
.5
.4
.3
.2
.1
GLOBAL WARMING

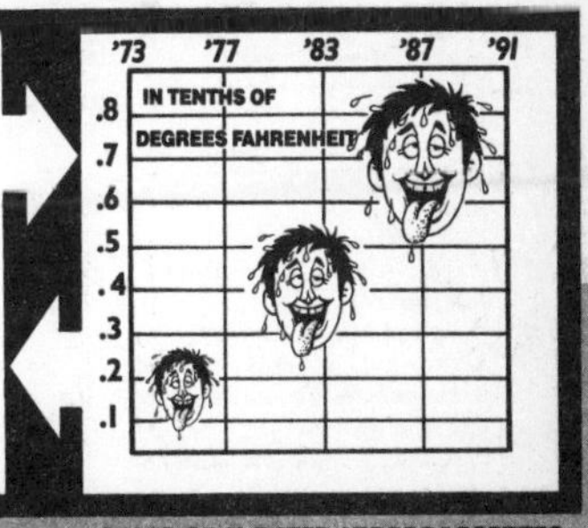
'73
'77
'83
'87
'91
IN TENTHS OF
DEGREES FAHRENHEIT
.8
.7
.6
.5
.4
.3
.2
.1
SALES OF X-RATED VIDEOCASSETTES

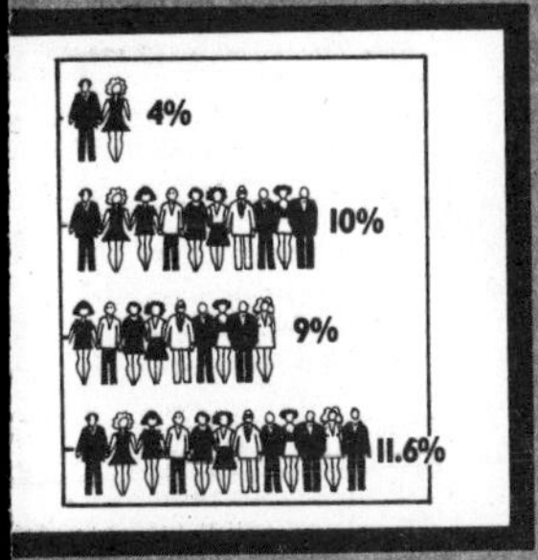
4%
10%
9%
11.6%
CLEVELANDERS WHO REALIZE THEY'RE IN CLEVELAND

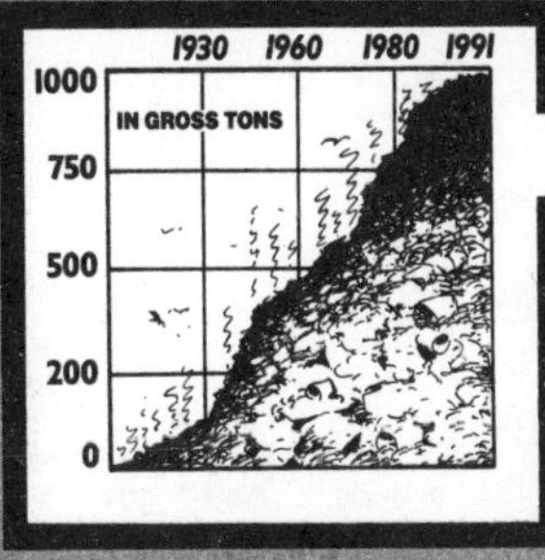
1930
1960
1980
1991
1000
IN GROSS TONS
750
500
200
0
LANDFILL INCREASE

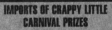

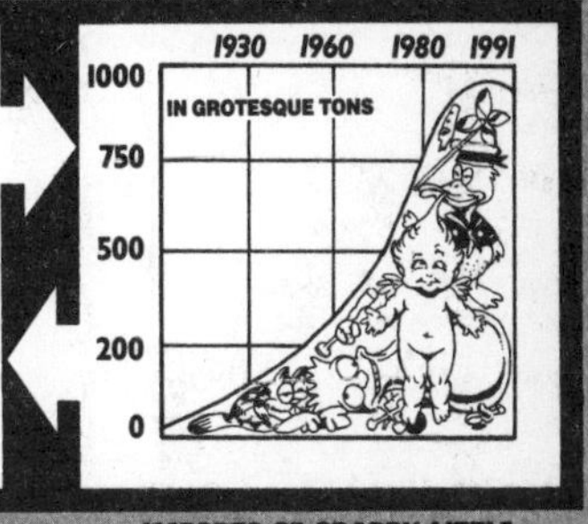
1930
1960
1980
1991
1000
IN GROTESQUE TONS
750
500
200
0
IMPORTS OF CRAPPY LITTLE CARNIVAL PRIZES

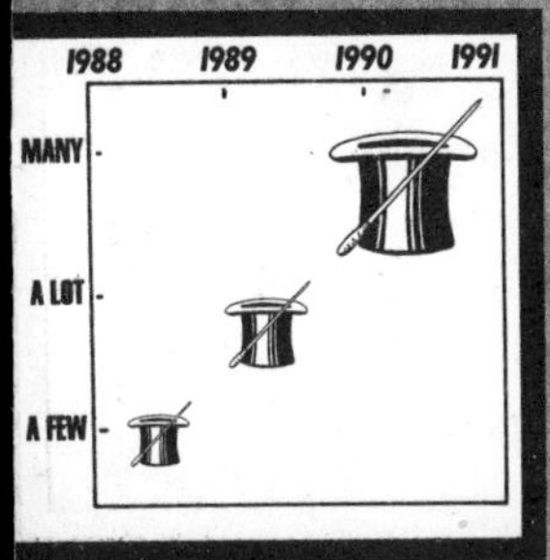
1988
1989
1990
1991
MANY
A LOT
A FEW
AVID COPPERFIELD PERFORMANCES

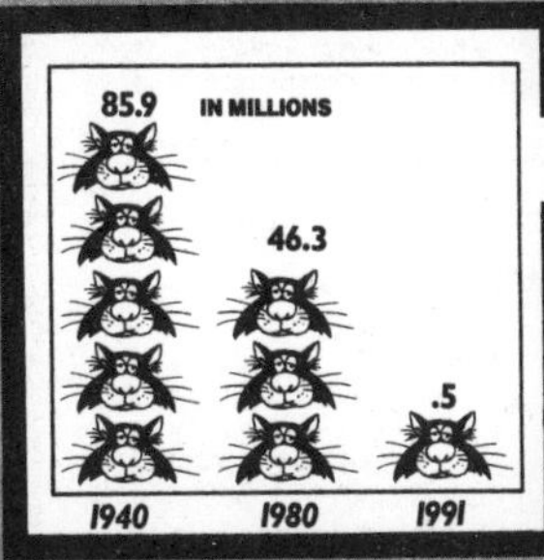
85.9
IN MILLIONS
46.3
.5
1940
1980
1991
CAT POPULATION

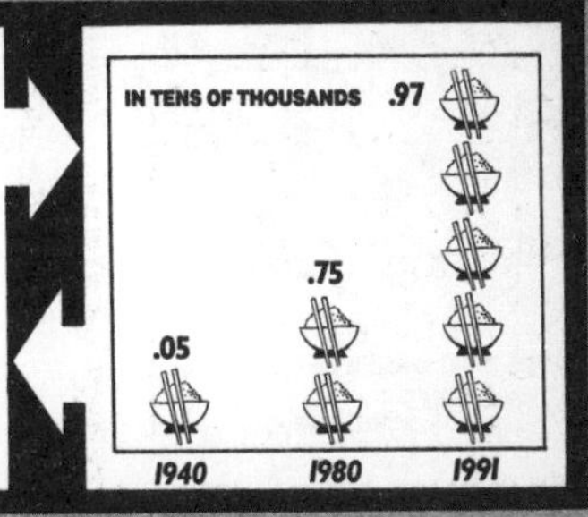
IN TENS OF THOUSANDS
.97
.75
.05
1940
1980
1991
NUMBER OF CHINESE RESTAURANTS

B-S.A.T. DEPT.

Thinking about what career to get into? Wondering whether or not you'll fit in? Well, here's the seventh in a series of tests designed to help you choose your future line of work. Mainly, discover your true abilities by taking...

MAD'S APTITUDE TEST NUMBER SEVEN

WILL YOU MAKE A GOOD FLIGHT ATTENDANT?

ARTIST: GEORGE WOODBRIDGE WRITER: FRANK JACOBS

1. You have a burning desire to become a Flight Attendant. This indicates that:
   A. You're turned on by visiting exotic places like Altoona, Fresno and Wheeling.
   B. You enjoy exercising total power over several hundred strapped-in, uncomfortable, nervous people.
   C. You have a high tolerance for monotony and tedium.
   D. Any of the above.

2. You see a passenger struggling to fit a bulky suitcase into an overhead compartment. Your clear-cut duty is to:
   A. Tell him he's blocking the aisle.
   B. Inform him that the suitcase is too large for carry-on luggage, and that he must remove it from the plane, go back to the ticket counter and check it through as luggage.
   C. Attend to more urgent duties, such as getting it on with the wealthy-looking dude you spotted sitting in First Class.
   D. Any of the above.

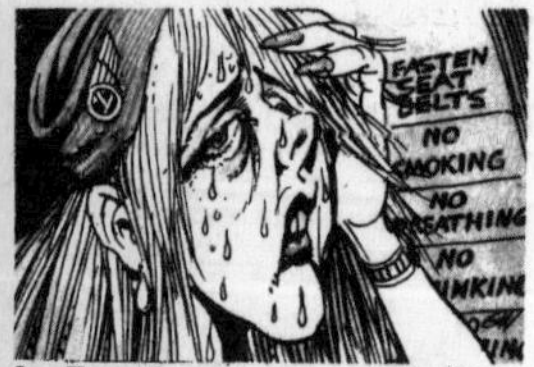
FASTEN SEAT BELTS
NO
NO
NO

3. From the appearance of this Flight Attendant, you should be able to tell that she:
   A. Has just taken a look at the meal being served to the coach passengers.
   B. Has just taken a look at a toilet after it's been used by over 100 people on a 9-hour flight.
   C. Has just taken a look in the mirror at *herself* after a 9-hour flight.
   D. Any of the above.

4. If you are married, being a Flight Attendant can be advantageous because:
   A. The complaints and arguments you get at home prepare you for the abuse you get from passengers.
   B. You can carry on affairs in a dozen different cities without your mate getting wise.
   C. Returning to your mate, you can blame your lack of interest in sex on jet lag.
   D. All of the above.

5. Complete this sentence: A Flight Attendant must be trim and agile so that she ____________.
   A. Can dodge elbows in the groin while hurrying up the narrow aisles.
   B. Can make a fast get-away after bringing a passenger an air-sickness bag.
   C. Can elude the groping for her body by the Captain or other members of the Flight Crew.
   D. All of the above.

6. During the In-Flight Movie, you spy two passengers making passionate love. What should you do?
   A. Turn on the "Fasten Seatbelts" sign, figuring why should they be having more fun than you.
   B. Stand there and watch, figuring you may learn what you've been doing wrong.
   C. Bring the Captain or other members of the Flight Crew back so that they can learn what *they've* been doing wrong.
   D. Any of the above.

7. Although most flights are routine, a good Flight Attendant must always be prepared for the unexpected. Which of these offers the greatest challenge to your self-composure and ability to adjust to the extraordinary?
   A. A coach passenger at mealtime asking for seconds.
   B. An entire cabin paying close attention to your "What To Do In Case Of Forced Landing" demonstration.
   C. A passenger finding an article of interest in the monthly airline magazine.
   D. Any of the above.

8. Towards the end of the flight, you suddenly hear angry cursing followed by a piercing scream. From experience, you know that it is
   A. A passenger attempting to cross his legs while sitting in coach.
   B. A passenger attempting to get an audible sound from his rented headset.
   C. Another Flight Attendant exhibiting the first tell-tale sign of "In-Flight Burn-Out."
   D. Any of the above.

9. You overhear a passenger refer to you as "nothing more than a Flying Waitress!" What should be your immediate comment?
   A. "It's nice to hear something complimentary for a change!"
   B. "Waitresses get tips and respect. I should be so lucky!"
   C. "Is that better or worse than a 'bleeping gofer'?"
   D. Any of the above.

10. After eight or ten years, you will finally gain Seniority. This is desirable because:
   A. You will now have first choice of flights, meaning you can pick Altoona, Fresno *OR* Wheeling.
   B. You can now palm off arduous jobs like drink-cart pulling on the newcomers.
   C. You no longer have to concern yourself with things like "ambition" and "career potential" because for you they are no longer relevant.
   D. All of the above.

SCORING

If you answered "D" to all questions, you have the ability to make a good Flight Attendant.

THE PAST, PRESENT AND FUTILE DEPT.

The average five-year-old thinks he's made a brilliant discovery when he smugly announces that any story beginning "Once upon a time..." is a fairy tale that didn't happen. Well, the average five-year-old is wrong! Many things dismissed as fantasy were very real in years gone by. Let MAD give you the straight poop on the way it was...

Once Upon A Time...

ARTIST: SERGIO ARAGONES WRITER: TOM KOCH

...THERE WAS ONLY ONE TYPE OF COCA-COLA, AND IT ONLY CAME IN ONE SIZE BOTTLE

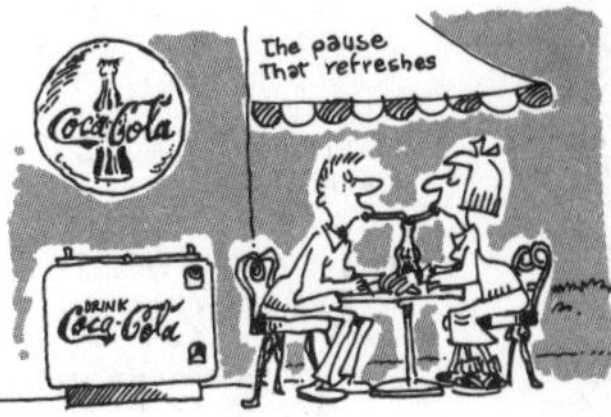
Coca-Cola
The pause That refreshes
DRINK Coca-Cola

—AND EVERYBODY SEEMED SATISFIED ...AND KIDS LEARNED

ALL ABOUT KINKY SEX FROM THEIR FRIENDS ON THE STREETS—NOT FROM GERALDO

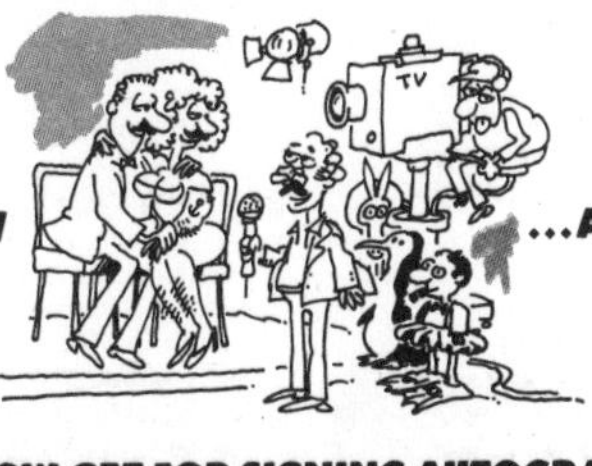
TV

RIVERA ON TV ...AND BASEBALL PLAYERS PLAYED FOR LESS MONEY

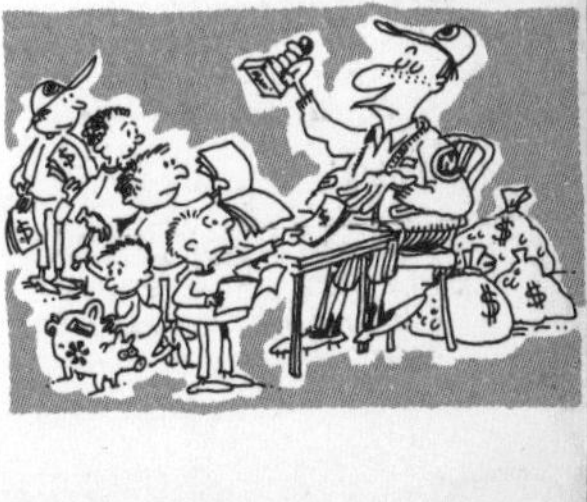

THAN THEY NOW GET FOR SIGNING AUTOGRAPHS AT CARD SHOWS

...AND RADIO STATIONS KEPT THE SAME CALL LETTERS FOREVER, EVEN IF THEY DIDN'T SP

A TIME...THERE WASN'T ONE TENNIS TOURNAMENT IN THE WHOLE WORLD NA

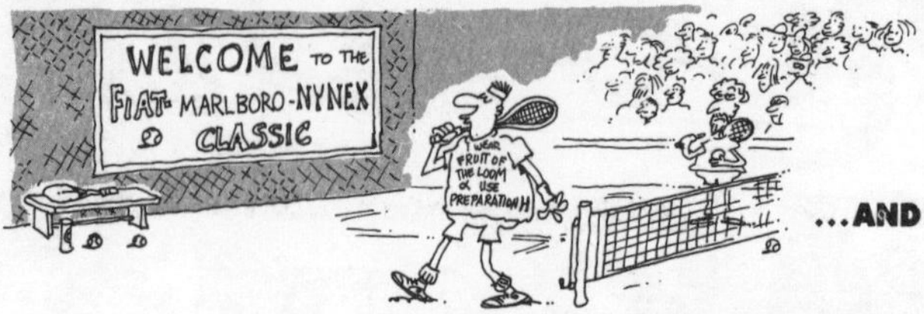
WELCOME TO THE
FIAT-MARLBORO-NYNEX
CLASSIC
WEAR FRUIT OF THE LOOM & USE PREPARATION H

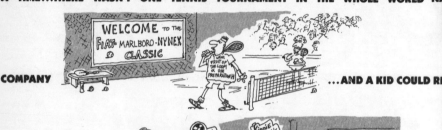

COMPANY **...AND A KID COULD R**

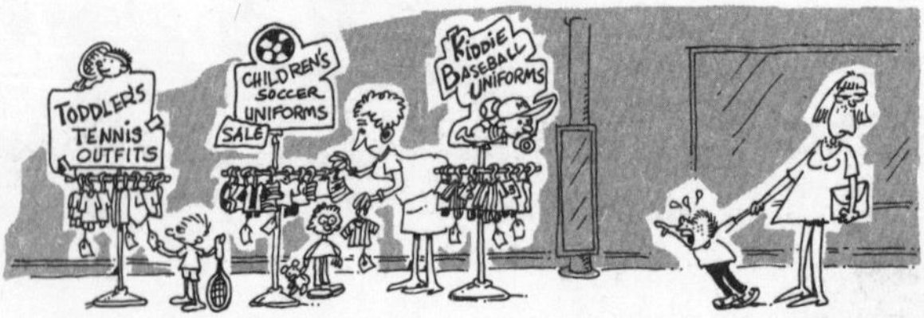
TODDLER'S TENNIS OUTFITS
CHILDREN'S SOCCER UNIFORMS
SALE
KIDDIE BASEBALL UNIFORMS

FOR EACH ACTIVITY **...AND**

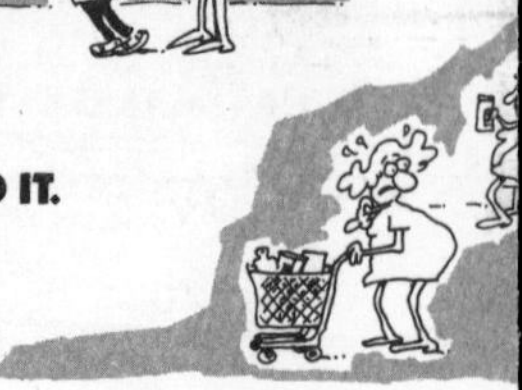

ITEM BEFORE YOU KNEW WHETHER OR NOT YOU COULD AFFORD IT.

TO SELL $8.95 WALL CALENDARS BECAUSE MOST OTHER BUSINESSES IN TOWN GAVE THEM

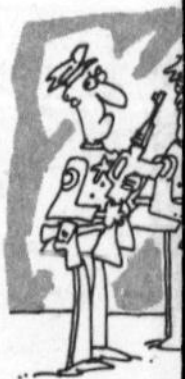

PRIZED BASEBALL CARDS IN AN OLD CIGAR BOX—NOT A SAFETY DEPOSIT BOX

ANYWHERE ABOUT WHETHER OAT BRAN WAS GOOD OR BAD FOR YOU. IT WAS JUST FED TO

YTHING CUTE.

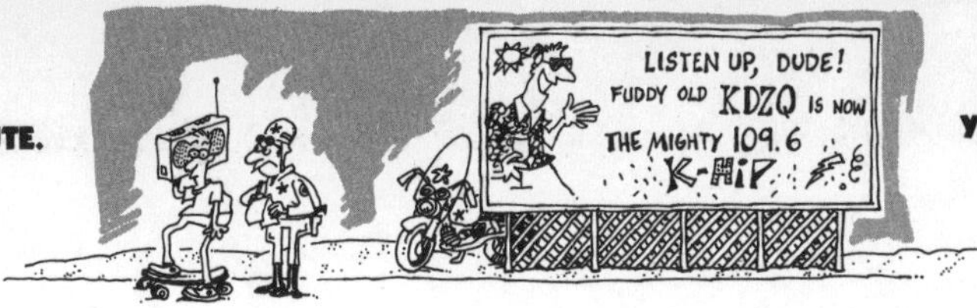
LISTEN UP, DUDE!
FUDDY OLD KDZQ IS NOW
THE MIGHTY 109.6
K-HIP

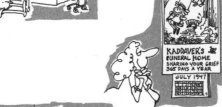

YES, ONCE UPON

AFTER A CIGARETTE MANUFACTURER OR A FOREIGN CAR MAKER OR A PHONE

BIKE OR PLAY TENNIS OR EVEN KICK A BALL WITHOUT HAVING TO WEAR A SEPARATE OUTFIT

DIDN'T HAVE TO WAIT FOR THE CASHIER'S SCANNER TO READ THE BAR CODE ON A GROCERY

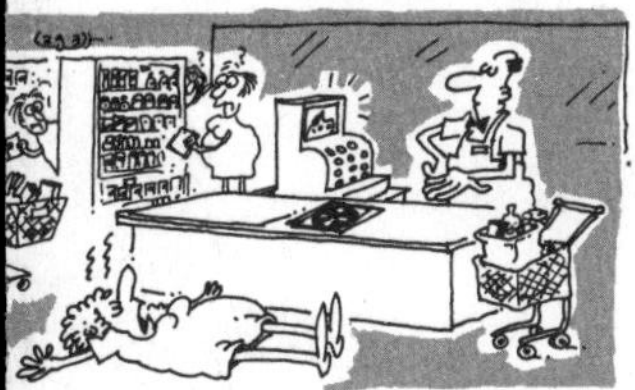

...ONCE UPON A TIME...GIFT SHOPS DIDN'T EVEN TRY

V FOR FREE

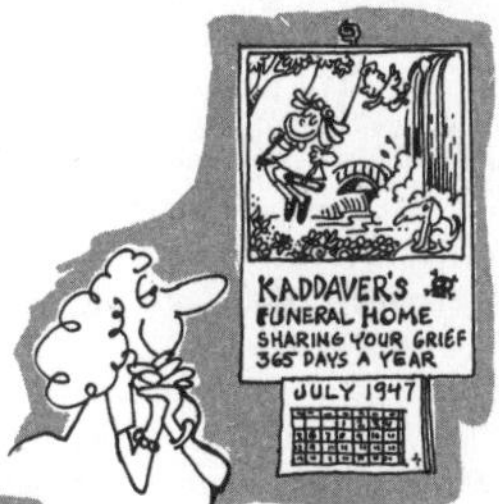
KADDAVER'S
FUNERAL HOME
SHARING YOUR GRIEF
365 DAYS A YEAR
JULY 1947

...AND KIDS KEPT THEIR MOST

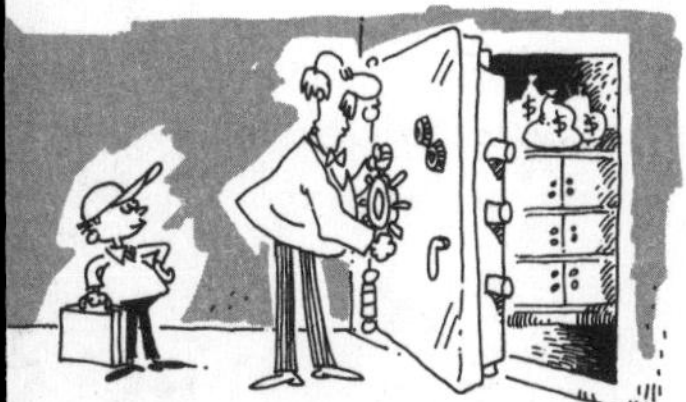

...AND THERE WASN'T A SINGLE ARGUMENT

ESTOCK AND FORGOTTEN.

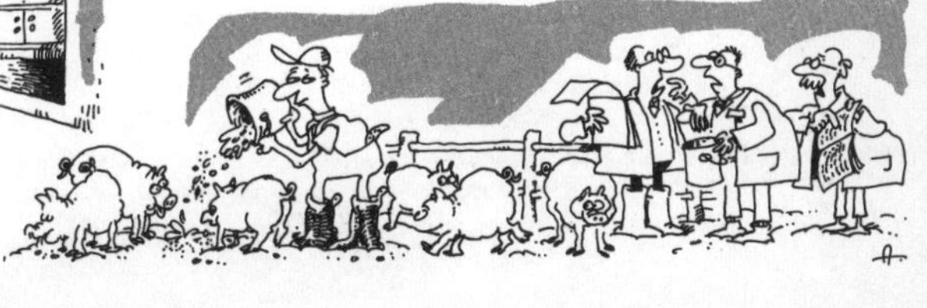

FRANK ON A ROLL DEPT.

I SENT A LETTER THROUGH THE MAIL . . .

(With Post Apologies to Henry Wadsworth Longfellow)

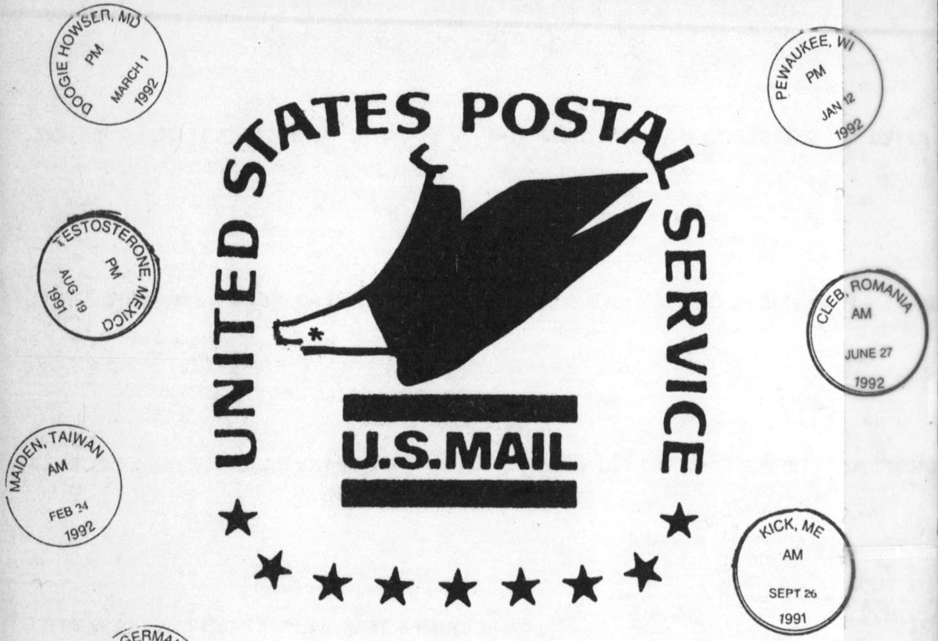
DOOGIE HOWSER, MD
PM
MARCH 1
1992
PEWAUKEE, WI
PM
JAN 12
1992
UNITED STATES POSTAL SERVICE
U.S.MAIL
TESTOSTERONE, MEXICO
PM
AUG 19
1991
CLEB, ROMANIA
AM
JUNE 27
1992
MAIDEN, TAIWAN
AM
FEB 24
1992
KICK, ME
AM
SEPT 26
1991

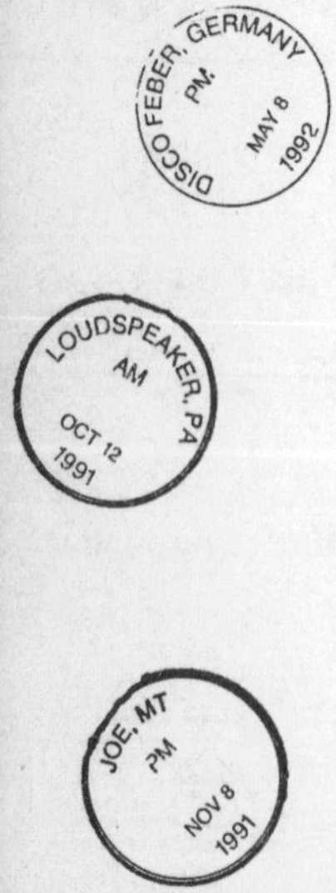
DISCO FEBER, GERMANY
PM.
MAY 8
1992
LOUDSPEAKER, PA
AM
OCT 12
1991
JOE, MT
PM
NOV 8
1991

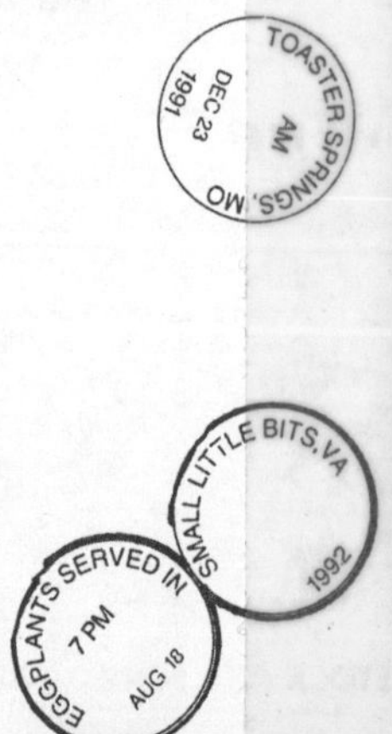
TOASTER SPRINGS, MO
AM
DEC 23
1991
EGGPLANTS SERVED IN SMALL LITTLE BITS, VA
7 PM
AUG 18
1992

I sent a letter through the mail;
It wound up ... well, that's quite a tale;
I dropped it in a box, you see,
On Saturday, 'round half past three;
Through Sunday in that box it lay
(and Monday was a holiday),
Till late on Tuesday, by some luck,
Arrived a Postal Service truck,
Which hauled the mail and dumped it in
A postal worker's sorting bin.

My letter now was on its way—
To Little Rock through San Jose,
Then on to Boise, Idaho,
By way of downtown Buffalo,
Proceeding then to Bangor, Maine,
And, somehow, Barcelona, Spain,
Until, at last, it came to earth
In Texas, somewhere near Fort Worth;
Small wonder that it's got me down—
I mailed it to a friend cross-town.

WRITER: FRANK JACOBS